P9-CPV-094

Consumer Behavior

Consumer Behavior

Leon G. Schiffman
J. Donald Kennedy Chair in E-Commerce
Peter J. Tobin College of Business
St. John's University, New York City

Leslie Lazar Kanuk
Emeritus Professor of Marketing
Graduate School and University Center
City University of New York

PEARSON
Prentice
Hall

Upper Saddle River, New Jersey 07458

Library of Congress Cataloging-in-Publication Data

Schiffman, Leon G.

   Consumer behavior / Leon G. Schiffman and Leslie Lazar Kanuk.—9th ed.

     p. cm.

   Includes bibliographical references and index.

   ISBN 0-13-186960-4 (alk. paper)

   1. Consumer behavior.   2. Motivation research (Marketing)   I. Kanuk, Leslie
Lazar. II. Title.

   HF5415.32.S35 2007

   658.8'342—dc22

                                                 2005029392

Acquisitions Editor: Katie Stevens
VP/Editorial Director: Jeff Shelstad
Product Development Manager: Ashley Santora
Editorial Assistant: Christine Ietto
Media Project Manager: Peter Snell
Marketing Manager: Ashaki Charles
Marketing Assistant: Joanna Sabella
Associate Director Production Editorial: Judy Leale
Managing Editor (Production): Renata Butera
Senior Production Editor: Theresa Festa
Permissions Supervisor: Charles Morris
Permission Researcher: Kathy Weisbrod
Production Manager: Arnold Vila
Design Manager: Christy Mahon
Designer: Steve Frim
Interior Design: David Levy/Black Diamond Graphics
Cover Design: Steve Frim
Cover Illustration/Photo: Argosy
Composition/Full-Service Project Management: Integra/Carlisle Publishing Services
Printer/Binder: Courier-Kendallville/Phoenix
Typeface: 9/11 Times

Credits and acknowledgments borrowed from other sources and reproduced, with permission, in this textbook appear on appropriate page within text.

**Copyright © 2007, 2004, 2000, 1997, 1991 by Pearson Education, Inc., Upper
Saddle River, New Jersey, 07458.** Pearson Prentice Hall. All rights reserved. Printed in
the United States of America. This publication is protected by Copyright and permission
should be obtained from the publisher prior to any prohibited reproduction, storage in a
retrieval system, or transmission in any form or by any means, electronic, mechanical,
photocopying, recording, or likewise. For information regarding permission(s), write to:
Rights and Permissions Department.

Pearson Prentice Hall™ is a trademark of Pearson Education, Inc.
Pearson® is a registered trademark of Pearson plc
Prentice Hall® is a registered trademark of Pearson Education, Inc.

Pearson Education LTD.
Pearson Education Singapore, Pte. Ltd
Pearson Education, Canada, Ltd
Pearson Education—Japan

Pearson Education Australia PTY, Limited
Pearson Education North Asia Ltd
Pearson Educación de Mexico, S.A. de C.V.
Pearson Education Malaysia, Pte. Ltd

10 9 8 7 6 5 4 3 2 1
ISBN: 0-13-186960-4

To Randi and Van Dauler;
Jack, Jaqui, and Alan Kanuk;
and Max and Sarah

To Elaine, Janet, and David Schiffman;
Dana and Bradley; Alan;
Melissa and Rob;
and Allison, Noah, Reid, Jordyn and Emily

Brief Contents

Contents

PART TWO   The Consumer as an Individual   80

chapter**four**

> **Consumer Motivation   80**

chapter**five**

> **Personality and Consumer Behavior   114**

chapter**six**

> **Consumer Perception   150**

chapterseven

chaptereight

chapternine

chapter**thirteen**

chapter**fourteen**

PART FOUR   The Consumer's Decision-Making
Process   480

chapter**fifteen**

chaptersixteen

Preface

S ince the very first edition of this text, we have focused on the examination and application of consumer behavior principles to the development and implemention of marketing strategies. We continue this managerial emphasis in the ninth edition of *Consumer Behavior*. Our thinking and writing has been greatly influenced by the impact that the "new media" (e.g., the expansive Internet, enhanced cellphones, specialized search engines, E-commerce-oriented web sites, and Tivo-like devices) have had on the marketer's ability to more precisely track and understand consumer behavior, and to use this knowledge to compete more effectively in the marketplace.

To enhance our examination of consumer behavior, we focus on the impact of the new media on consumer information seeking, purchasing options, and decision making, recognizing that consumers now have fast and convenient access to information about virtually any product or service they may wish to purchase. In particular, we give substantial attention to consumers' online behavior, and the importance and power of the Internet and other digital technologies in facilitating consumers' communications with their peers and with marketers, as well as their ability to purchase products online.

In this new edition, we have intensified our emphasis on marketing strategy, using both a theoretical and applications-oriented approach. Always true believers in the marketing concept, we have tried our best to meet the needs of our own consumers—students, professors of consumer behavior, and marketing practitioners—by providing a text that is highly readable and that clearly explains the relevant and timely concepts on which the discipline of consumer behavior is based. We have supplemented this material with a great many real-world examples in order to demonstrate how consumer behavioral concepts are used by marketing practitioners to solve marketing problems and to develop and implement effective marketing strategies.

We have sought to maintain an even balance of basic behavioral concepts, research findings, and applied marketing examples. We remain convinced that effective market segmentation provides the structure and direction for successful market practice; to this end, we have paid particular attention to revising and refining the discussion of market segmentation.

overview of major changes

The text has been thoroughly updated and revised, yet substantially shortened to focus attention on critical consumer behavior concepts and to highlight the linkages between interrelated principles and processes. Some of the major changes include:

- A major emphasis on marketing ethics and social responsibility throughout the book.
- The replacement of 32 short cases (two per chapter) introduced in the last edition, with entirely new cases. As before, our goal is to help students learn by applying behavioral concepts to real-world business problems.

■   An enhanced global outlook that fosters a richer understanding of the dynamics of cultural differences and enhances students' appreciation of the universality of consumer behavior.

■   A comprehensive model of consumer decision making, built on the simple model presented in the first chapter of the text, highlights the interrelationships between and among the concepts examined throughout the book, and both simplifies and facilitates retention of the material covered.

organization of the text

This ninth edition of *Consumer Behavior* is divided into four parts, consisting of 16 chapters.

Part I provides the background and tools for a strong and comprehensive understanding of the consumer behavior principles examined throughout the rest of the book. Chapter 1, *Consumer Behavior: Its Origins and Strategic Applications*, sets the tone for the book. It introduces the reader to the study of consumer behavior, its diversity, its development, the latest evolution of the marketing concept and discusses marketing ethics and consumer responsibility. It examines how companies use past consumption behavior as the foundation for creating and keeping satisfied and profitable lifetime customers. The chapter also introduces a simple model of consumer decision making that provides a structural framework for understanding the interrelationships among the consumer behavior principles examined throughout the book. Chapter 2, *Consumer Research*, provides readers with a detailed overview of the critical consumer research process and the techniques associated with consumer behavior research. Chapter 3 presents a comprehensive examination of the newest insights into effective market segmentation.

Part II discusses the consumer as an individual. Chapter 4 presents an in-depth discussion of consumer needs and motivations, exploring both the rational and emotional bases of consumer actions. Chapter 5 discusses the impact of the full range of personality theories on consumer behavior and explores consumer materialism, fixated consumption, and compulsive consumption behavior. The chapter considers the related concepts of self and self-image and includes an expanded discussion of virtual personality and self. Chapter 6 provides a comprehensive examination of the impact of consumer perception on marketing strategy and the importance of product positioning and repositioning. Chapter 7 examines how consumers learn, and discusses behavioral and cognitive learning theories, limited and extensive information processing, and the applications of consumer involvement theory to marketing practice. Chapter 8 offers an in-depth examination of consumer attitudes. Chapter 9, *Communication and Consumer Behavior*, demonstrates that communication is the bridge between individuals and the world and people around them, and includes a timely discussion of advertising, traditional and new media, and the effective use of persuasion.

Part III is concerned with the social and cultural dimensions of consumer behavior. Chapter 10 begins with a discussion of consumer reference groups (including virtual groups and virtual communities), family role orientations, and changing family lifestyles. Chapters 11 and 12 present consumers in terms of their socioeconomic and social class standing, as well as their social and cultural milieus; and discusses the emergence of the "techno class." Chapter 13 investigates the impact of societal and subcultural values, beliefs, and customs on consumer behavior. Chapter 14 concludes this part with an extensive discussion of cross-cultural marketing within an increasingly global marketplace.

Part IV explores various aspects of consumer decision making. Chapter 15 offers a comprehensive discussion of personal influence, opinion leadership, and the diffusion of innovations. Chapter 16 describes how consumers make product decisions, and expands on the increasingly important practice of relationship marketing. This section concludes with a deeper and more comprehensive examination of a model of consumer decision making (building on the overview model briefly introduced in Chapter 1), and ties together the psychological, social, and cultural concepts discussed throughout the book. It includes an in depth examination of consumer gifting behavior and a discussion of the expanding research focus on individual consumption behavior and the symbolic meanings of consumer possessions.

supplements for instructors

The following supplements are available to adopting instructors. For detailed descriptions, please visit: **www.prenhall.com/schiffman**

Instructor's Resource Center (IRC) online: Login at **www.prenhall.com/irc**

Instructor's Resource Center (IRC) on CD-ROM—ISBN: 0-13-186965-5

Printed Instructor's Manual—ISBN: 0-13-186964-7

Printed Test Item File—ISBN: 0-13-186961-2

TestGen test generating software—Visit the IRC (both online and on CD-ROM)

PowerPoint slides—Visit the IRC (both online and on CD-ROM)

Classroom Response System (CRS) Slides—Visit the IRC (both online and on CD-ROM)

Image Library—Visit the IRC on CD-ROM

Custom Videos on DVD—ISBN: 0-13-186968-X

Custom Videos on VHS—ISBN: 0-13-186967-1

Instructor's resource center

Register. Redeem. Login.

www.prenhall.com/irc is where instructors can access a variety of print, media, and presentation resources available with this text in downloadable, digital format.

It gets better. Once you register, you will not have additional forms to fill out, or multiple usernames and passwords to remember to access new titles and/or editions. As a registered faculty member, you can login directly to download resource files, and receive immediate access and instructions for installing Course Management content to your campus server.

Need help? Our dedicated Technical Support team is ready to assist instructors with questions about the media supplements that accompany this text. Visit: **http://247.prenhall.com/** for answers to frequently asked questions and toll-free user support phone numbers.

For students

■   **www.prenhall.com/schiffman** contains valuable resources for both students and professors, including free access to an interactive student study guide.

Feedback

The author and product team would appreciate hearing from you! Let us know what you think about this textbook by writing to **college_marketing@prenhall.com**. Please include "Feedback about Schiffman/Kanuk 9e" in the subject line.

If you have questions related to this text, please contact our customer service department online at **www.247.prenhall.com**

acknowledgments

Of the many people who have been enormously helpful in the preparation of this ninth edition of *Consumer Behavior*, we are especially grateful to our own consumers, the graduate and undergraduate students of consumer behavior and their professors, who have provided us with invaluable experiential feedback to our earlier editions.

We would also like to thank colleagues and friends at the Tobin College of Business at St. John's University, in particular: Dean Richard A. Highfield and Associate Dean Susan McTiernan; Dr. John Dobbins and the St. John's Department of Marketing for providing a warm and friendly environment in which to write. Our thanks go, too, to our many friends and colleagues in the Department of Marketing at Baruch's Zicklin School of Business, Pace's Lubin School of Business, and the Zarb School of Business at Hofstra University.

We especially would like to thank the following people who reviewed the ninth edition and offered many thoughtful comments and suggestions: Peter Bloch, University of Missouri; Stephen P. Ramocki, Rhode Island College; Kay Palas, Iowa State University; and Ronald J. Adams, The University of North Florida.

Over the years, we have received many thoughtful suggestions, insights, and highly constructive comments from the following professors: Benny Barak and Elaine Sherman of Hofstra University; Martin Topol, Pace University; Harold Kassarjian, UCLA; David Brinberg, Virginia Polytechnic Institute; Steve Gould, Baruch College; John Holmes, Simmons College; Joel Saegert, The University of Texas at San Antonio; Lewis Hershey, Eastern Missouri State College; William R. Dillon, Southern Methodist University; Havva J. Meric, East Carolina University; Ron Goldsmith, Florida State University; Richard Yalch, University of Washington; Mark Young, Winona State University; Michael Taylor, Marietta College; Daniel Johnson, Bradford University; Bob Settle, San Diego State University; Gerald Cavallo, Fairfield University; Kristina Cannon-Bonventre, Northeastern University; Kathy Petit, University of Idaho; Douglas W. Mellott, Jr., Radford University; Darvin R. Hoffman, Texas A&I; David Sheperd, University of Tennessee at Chattanooga; John T. Shaw, Providence College; Janet G. Hibbard, Eastern Kentucky University; Ron Lennon, Barry University; Jeanne Mueller, Cornell University; Charles Gulas, Wright State University; James W. Cagley, University of Tulsa; Kenneth R. Lord, Niagara University; Paul Chao, University of Northern Iowa; John H. Holmes, Skidmore College; Sheri Zeigler, University of Hawaii; Christina Goulding, Wolverhampton

University, United Kingdom; U. B. Bradley, London Guildhall University, United Kingdom; Adrienne Czerwin-Abbott, Dublin Institute of Technology, Ireland; and Bernard A. Delagneau, The University of Wales, Aberystwyth, United Kingdom.

A very special thanks to Lisa A. Harap of St. John's University for her dedication and assistance in the preparation of this ninth edition. Many other professors, students, and colleagues have made contributions to our thinking; among these are Amit Srivastav, Shawn Fitzgerald, and Martha Cook of Baruch College; Mary Kay of Montclair State University; Mary Long of Pace University; and Charles McMellon of Hofstra University. Deborah Y. Cohn of Yeshiva University provided some original thinking and an interesting perspective on consumer gifting. Joyce Jenkins and Evie Reisman have provided us with unique insights into individual consumer behavior. Norma Bakke has given us important, on-site perspectives on global consumer behavior.

We would like to warmly acknowledge Alan Pollack, who has provided us with invaluable insights into legal issues on intellectual property and the marketing process. We also acknowledge Horace Phillimore of Gardmat Electronics; Ken Weinstein of Honeywell International, Inc.; Hank Edelman of Patek Philippe; Don Siebert, an independent marketing consultant; Ross Copper of Gold 'n Fish Marketing Group; Lancy Herman of Mediamark Research; and Walter McCullough and Moya Amateau of Monroe Mendelsohn Research. We are grateful to the executives and staff of the following research firms for their continuous flow of interesting illustrative materials: Claritas Corporation, Simmons Marketing Research Bureau, Donnelley Marketing Information Services, and SRI International.

Our sincerest thanks go to the many people at Prentice Hall who aided and supported us in the editorial, design, and production processes of this ninth edition, specifically our editor, Katie Stevens who has provided us with invaluable direction and encouragement; Theresa Festa, our ever-diligent and supportive production editor; Ashley Santora, Product Development Manager; Ashaki Charles, Marketing Manager; Christine Ietto, Editorial Assistant; Steve Frim, Designer; Kathy Weisbrod, Permission Researcher; and Lynn Steines, Project Editor, Carlisle Publishing Services.

Finally, we would like to give very special recognition to Professor Stanley Garfunkel of CUNY and to Professor Joseph Wisenblit, Chairman of the Marketing Department at Seton Hall University, for their untiring support, assistance, advice, encouragement, and, most of all, friendship.

Consumer Behavior

PART 1 PROVIDES THE BACKGROUND AND THE TOOLS FOR A STRONG AND COMPREHENSIVE UNDERSTANDING OF CONSUMER BEHAVIOR

Chapter 1 introduces the reader to the study of consumer behavior, its diversity, its development, and the role of consumer research. It concludes with a detailed discussion of ethical considerations in marketing and consumer practices and introduces a simple model of consumer decision making. Chapter 2 provides a detailed overview of the critical research process and the techniques associated with consumer behavior research, including a discussion of positivist and interpretivist research methods. Chapter 3 presents a comprehensive examination of market segmentation and demonstrates how consumer behavior variables provide both the conceptual framework and the strategic direction for the practical segmentation of markets.

chapter**one**

Consumer Behavior: Its Origins and Strategic Applications

Consumer behavior has changed dramatically in the past decade. Today, consumers can order online many customized products ranging from sneakers to computers. Many have replaced their daily newspapers with customized, online editions of these media and are increasingly receiving information from online sources. Students choosing a university no longer rely on information from mailed catalogs; instead, they have online access to all the pertinent information about the university's courses and professors and, in some cases, can visit, virtually, actual classes. People wanting to sell their old computers or grandma's antique credenza no longer need to advertise in the local newspaper or rely on a pricy auction house; instead, they can sell these items via ebay.com. Consumers who want out-of-print books no longer have to visit out-of-the-way stores with hundreds of poorly organized dusty shelves, and those who wish to purchase a book published in another country no longer have to call foreign publishers or deal with the bureaucratic nuances of overseas shipping; instead, they visit amazon.com where they can easily locate and place orders for the books they seek. TV viewers can now avoid advertising commercials by using the "skip" features of their digital video recorders and order on-demand previously shown TV programs as well as

The new, more responsive 3. Advanced, lightweight suspension and 50-50 weight distribution combine for unrivaled agility. Innovative, 6-cylinder Valvetronic engine packs even more power, with increased fuel efficiency. To experience all that's gone into the new BMW 3 Series is to experience perfection, quite possibly, perfected.

©2005 BMW of North America, LLC. The BMW name and logo are registered trademarks. *MSRP for 325i includes destination and handling charges. Price excludes license, registration, taxes and options. Actual price determined by your BMW center. As shown: 325i with Sport Package and metallic paint, $33,070.

The All-New BMW
3 Series
from $30,995*

bmwusa.com
1-800-334-4BMW

The Ultimate
Driving Machine®

movies. All of these new ways of selling products and services became available to consumers during the past fifteen years and are the result of digital technologies. And they also have another thing in common: They exist today because they reflect an understanding of consumer needs and consumer behavior.

The term *consumer behavior* is defined as the behavior that consumers display in *searching for, purchasing, using, evaluating, and disposing of products and services that they expect will satisfy their needs.* Consumer behavior focuses on how individuals make decisions to spend their available resources (time, money, effort) on consumption-related items. That includes what they buy, why they buy it, when they buy it, where they buy it, how often they buy it, how often they use it, how they evaluate it after the purchase, the impact of such evaluations on future purchases, and how they dispose of it.

Clearly, as individuals, we are all unique. However, one of the most important constants among all of us, despite our differences, is that, above all, we are consumers. We use or consume on a regular basis food, clothing, shelter, transportation, education, equipment, vacations, necessities, luxuries, services, and even ideas. As consumers, we play a vital role in the health of the economy—local, national, and international. The purchase decisions we make affect the demand for basic raw materials, for transportation, for production, for banking; they affect the employment of workers and the deployment of resources, the success of some industries and the failure of others. In order to succeed in any business, and especially in today's dynamic and rapidly evolving marketplace, marketers need to know everything they can about consumers—what they want, what they think, how they work, how they spend their leisure time. They need to understand the personal and group influences that affect consumer decisions and how these decisions are made. And, in these days of ever-widening media choices, they need to not only identify their target audiences, but they need to know where and how to reach them.

The term *consumer behavior* describes two different kinds of consuming entities: the personal consumer and the organizational consumer. The **personal consumer** buys goods and services for his or her own use, for the use of the household, or as a gift for a friend. In each of these contexts, the products are bought for final use by individuals, who are referred to as *end users* or ultimate consumers. The second category of consumer—the **organizational consumer**—includes profit and not-for-profit businesses, government agencies (local, state, and national), and institutions (e.g., schools, hospitals, and prisons), all of which must buy products, equipment, and services in order to run their organizations. Despite the importance of both categories of consumers—individuals and organizations—this book will focus on the individual consumer, who purchases for his or her own personal use or for household use. End-use consumption is perhaps the most pervasive of all types of consumer behavior, for it involves every individual, of every age and background, in the role of either buyer or user, or both.

development of the marketing concept

The field of consumer behavior is rooted in the **marketing concept**, a business orientation that evolved in the 1950s through several alternative approaches toward doing business: the *production concept*, the *product concept*, and the *selling concept.*

No single product has impacted Americans more than the personal automobile. And the business leader who gave us the affordable car and the business approach called the **production concept** was Henry Ford. Before the early 1900s, only wealthy consumers could afford automobiles because cars were assembled individually and it took considerable time and expense to produce each car. In the early 1900s, Henry Ford became consumed with the idea of producing cars that average Americans could afford. In 1908, Ford began selling the sturdy and reliable Model T for $850—an inexpensive price for that day. Soon he found out that he could not meet the overwhelming consumer demand for his cars and, in 1913, he introduced the assembly line. The new production method enabled Ford to produce good-quality cars more quickly and much less expensively. In 1916, Ford sold Model Ts for $360 and sold more than 100 times as many cars as he did in 1908.[1] In only eight years, Americans got the product that led to our nation's extensive system of highways and the emergence of suburbs with their adjacent shopping malls—two key features of our lives and consumption patterns even today.

The production concept assumes that consumers are mostly interested in product availability at low prices; its implicit marketing objectives are cheap, efficient production and intensive distribution. This orientation makes sense when consumers are more interested in obtaining the product than they are in specific features, and will buy what's available rather than wait for what they really want. Today, using this orientation makes sense in developing countries or in other situations in which the main objective is to expand the market.

The **product concept** assumes that consumers will buy the product that offers them the highest quality, the best performance, and the most features. A product orientation leads the company to strive constantly to improve the quality of its product and to add new features that are technically feasible, without finding out first whether or not consumers really want these features. A product orientation often leads to "marketing myopia," that is, a focus on the product rather than on the consumer needs it presumes to satisfy. Marketing myopia may cause a company to ignore crucial changes in the marketplace because it causes marketers to look in the mirror rather than through the window. Thus, American railroads today are a far less significant economic force than they were some 50 years ago because their management was convinced that travelers wanted trains and overlooked the competition for transportation from personal cars, airlines, buses, and trucks. These railroad executives focused on the product (i.e., trains) rather than the need that it satisfies (transportation).[2] Similarly, designers and engineers working on a new model of a personal digital assistant (PDA) must always remember that people do not buy PDAs—they buy ways to organize and retrieve data in a manner that will save them time and effort. If PDA designers and engineers forget this simple fact, they may improve the product in ways that makes sense to them but that do not correspond with consumer needs.

A natural evolution from both the production concept and the product concept is the **selling concept**, in which a marketer's primary focus is selling the product(s) that it has unilaterally decided to produce. The assumption of the selling concept is that consumers are unlikely to buy the product unless they are aggressively persuaded to do so— mostly through the "hard sell" approach. The problem with this approach is that it fails to consider customer satisfaction. When consumers are induced to buy products they do not want or need, they will not buy them again. Also, they are likely to communicate any dissatisfaction with the product through negative word-of-mouth that serves to dissuade potential consumers from making similar purchases. Today the selling concept is typically utilized by marketers of unsought goods (such as life insurance), by political parties "selling" their candidates aggressively to apathetic voters, and by firms that have excess inventory.

The marketing concept

The field of consumer behavior is rooted in a marketing strategy that evolved in the late 1950s, when some marketers began to realize that they could sell more goods, more easily, if they produced only those goods they had already determined that consumers would buy. Instead of trying to persuade customers to buy what the firm had already produced, marketing-oriented firms found that it was a lot easier to produce only products they had first confirmed, through research, that consumers wanted. Consumer needs and wants became the firm's primary focus. This consumer-oriented marketing philosophy came to be known as the **marketing concept**. Although the idea of producing and selling only those goods that match consumer needs took hold during the 1950s, it was articulated much earlier and, ironically, by a competitor of Henry Ford. In 1923, as the automobile market was growing rapidly thanks to Ford's mass production, *Alfred P. Sloan* became president and chairman of General Motors. He inherited a company that was built through takeovers of small car companies, and therefore produced many ill-sorted models unguided by clear business objectives. Sloan reorganized the company and in 1924 articulated the company's product strategy as "a car for every purse and purpose." While Ford continued to produce the

Model T until 1927, GM offered a variety of affordable mass-produced models—from the aristocratic Cadillac to the proletarian Chevrolet—and took over a large portion of Ford's market share.[3] About 30 years before the birth of the marketing concept, Alfred Sloan realized that all consumers are not alike and the importance of segmenting the market—now known as **market segmentation**—a concept that is the cornerstone of modern marketing today.

The key assumption underlying the marketing concept is that, to be successful, a company must determine the needs and wants of specific target markets and deliver the desired satisfactions better than the competition. The marketing concept is based on the premise that a marketer should make what it can sell, instead of trying to sell what it has made. Whereas the selling concept focuses on the needs of the *sellers* and on existing products, the marketing concept focuses on the needs of the *buyer*. The selling concept focuses on profits through sales volume; the marketing concept focuses on profits based on customer satisfaction.

It is interesting to note that even before the evolution of the marketing concept, an intuitive understanding of consumer behavior was the key to the growth of companies that have remained highly successful, even today. For example, in the 1930s, *Colonel Sanders* opened a roadside restaurant where he developed the recipes and cooking methods that were the key to KFC's successes. As the restaurant grew in popularity, Sanders enlarged it and also opened a roadside motel. At that time, motels had a bad reputation and "nice" people driving long distances generally stayed at downtown hotels. Sanders decided to try and overcome this image by putting a sample room of his clean and comfortable motel in the middle of his successful restaurant, and even put the entrance to the restaurant's ladies' room in that room. Sanders understood the importance of image and of turning an offering into a success by *repositioning*, long before this idea was articulated as a business objective. Later on, Sanders came up with the idea of franchising his cooking methods and chicken recipe, while keeping the ingredients of the recipe a secret, and founded KFC and a business model that has since been adopted by many other fast-food chains.[4] In the early 1950s, *Ray Kroc*, who purchased the idea of fast food from the McDonald brothers and established the McDonald's Corporation, selected locations for new outlets by flying over towns and looking for church steeples. He believed that where there were churches there were good American families—the kind of people he wanted as customers. Intuitively, Kroc understood and practiced *market targeting*.[5] Apparently, companies focused on understanding their customers are the ones that continue to grow, and remain leaders in their industries in spite of increased competition and changing business environments.

Implementing the marketing concept

The widespread adoption of the marketing concept by American business provided the impetus for the study of consumer behavior. To identify unsatisfied consumer needs, companies had to engage in extensive marketing research. In so doing, they discovered that consumers were highly complex individuals, subject to a variety of psychological and social needs quite apart from their survival needs. They discovered that the needs and priorities of different consumer segments differed dramatically, and in order to design new products and marketing strategies that would fulfill consumer needs, they had to study consumers and their consumption behavior in depth. The term **consumer research** represents the process and tools used to study consumer behavior. The adoption of the marketing concept underscores the importance of consumer research and provides the groundwork for the application of consumer behavior principles to marketing strategy. The tools and processes of consumer research are discussed in detail in Chapter 2.

Segmentation, targeting, and positioning

The focus of the marketing concept is consumer needs. At the same time, recognizing the high degree of diversity among us, consumer researchers seek to identify the many similarities—or constants—that exist among the peoples of the world. For example, we all have the same kinds of biological needs, no matter where we are born—the needs for food, for nourishment, for water, for air, and for shelter from the elements. We also acquire needs after we are born. These needs are shaped by the environment and the culture in which we live, by our education, and by our experiences. The interesting thing about acquired needs is that there are usually many people who develop the same needs. This commonality of need or interest constitutes a market segment, which enables the marketer to target consumers with specifically designed products and/or promotional appeals that satisfy the needs of that segment. The marketer must also adapt the image of its product (i.e., *position* it), so that each market segment perceives the product as better fulfilling its specific needs than competitive products. The three elements of this strategic framework are *market segmentation*, *targeting*, and *positioning*.

Market segmentation is the process of dividing a market into subsets of consumers with common needs or characteristics. The variables and methods used to form such subsets are discussed in Chapter 3. Because most companies have limited resources, few companies can pursue all of the market segments identified. **Market targeting** is the selection of one or more of the segments identified for the company to pursue. The criteria for selecting target markets are detailed in Chapter 3.

Positioning refers to the development of a distinct image for the product or service in the mind of the consumer, an image that will differentiate the offering from competing ones and squarely communicate to the target audience that the particular product or service will fulfill their needs better than competing brands. Successful positioning centers around two key principles: first, communicating the *benefits* that the product will provide rather than the product's features. As one marketing sage pointed out: ". . . consumers do not buy drill bits—they buy ways to make holes." Second, because there are many similar products in almost any marketplace, an effective positioning strategy must develop and communicate a *unique selling proposition*—a distinct benefit or point of difference—for the product or service. In fact, most of the new products introduced by marketers (including new forms of existing products such as new flavors, sizes, etc.) fail to capture a significant market share and are discontinued because they are perceived by consumers as "me too" products lacking a unique image or benefit. The concepts and tools of positioning are explored in Chapter 6.

The marketing mix

The **marketing mix** consists of a company's service and/or product offerings to consumers and the methods and tools it selects to accomplish the exchange. The marketing mix consists of four elements (known as the **four Ps**): (1) the *product* or *service* (i.e., the features, designs, brands, and packaging offered, along with postpurchase benefits such as warranties and return policies); (2) the *price* (the list price, including discounts, allowances, and payment methods); (3) the *place* (the distribution of the product or service through specific store and nonstore outlets); (4) *promotion* (the advertising, sales promotion, public relations, and sales efforts designed to build awareness of and demand for the product or service). Table 1.1 depicts the implementation of the elements of the marketing concept by Rollerblade.

customer value, satisfaction, and retention

Since its emergence in the 1950s, many companies have very successfully adopted the marketing concept. The result has been more products, in more sizes, models, versions, and packages, offered to more precisely targeted (and often smaller) target markets. This has resulted in an increasingly competitive marketplace. And, during the last decade, the digital revolution enabled many marketers to offer even more products and services and distribute them more widely, while reducing the costs and barriers of entering many

| **TABLE 1.1** | **Rollerblade: Effective Implementation of the Marketing Concept** |

Less than two decades ago, in-line skates were an off-season training tool for hockey players. In the mid-1980s, Rollerblade developed marketing strategies that positioned in-line skating as a new sport. The company sold in-line skates to bicycle and conventional skate rental stores in two trend-setting places: Miami Beach, Florida, and Venice Beach, California, and a new form of recreational sport that appeals to many age groups and social classes was born. Backed by aggressive marketing and public relations, the popularity of the new sport soared. As competition appeared, Rollerblade continued to lead the market with such innovations as breathable shoe liners, buckle closure systems, and female-specific skates; today the company holds several hundred patented innovations.

The company's product line illustrates the utilization of segmentation, targeting, and positioning strategies. The company targets four segments and offers models that provide different benefits to the members of each segment: (1) experienced skaters; (2) men and women seeking *fitness and recreation*; (3) the *Street/Vert* line, which combines performance and increased structural support; and (4) several models for *kids*. Some of the models offered include brakes.

Rollerblade's entire marketing mix stems from its core product. In addition to the skates, the company sells protective gear, accessories, and replacement parts. The skates are priced along a range varying from very expensive models offered to aggressive skaters looking for maximum performance, to value-oriented skaters, to recreational skaters. The products are distributed in a variety of outlets—both domestic and overseas—in a way that reflects the market segments targeted and the skate models' prices. The company advertises its products in the mass media, issues frequent press releases as part of its public relations, and promotes its products through athletic and event sponsorships, as well as its "Skate School."

The company's Web site includes features on skating, maintaining the skates, using rollerblading for fitness, tips on skating safety, and a dealer locator. These features show that Rollerblade has a thorough understanding of customer retention as well as social responsibility, concepts that are discussed later in this chapter.

Source: Developed from material available at **www.rollerblade.com**.

industries. It has accelerated the rate at which new competitors enter markets and also speeded up the rate at which successful segmentation, targeting, and positioning approaches must be updated or changed, as they are imitated or made obsolete by the offerings of new business rivals.

Savvy marketers today realize that in order to outperform competitors they must achieve the full profit potential from each and every customer. They must make the customer the core of the company's organizational culture, across all departments and functions, and ensure that each and every employee views any exchange with a customer as part of a *customer relationship*, not as a *transaction*. The three drivers of successful relationships between marketers and customers are *customer value*, high levels of *customer satisfaction,* and building a structure that ensures *customer retention*.

Providing customer value

Customer value is defined as the *ratio between the customer's perceived benefits* (economic, functional and psychological) and the *resources* (monetary, time, effort, psychological) *used to obtain those benefits*. Perceived value is relative and subjective. For example, diners at an exclusive French restaurant in Washington, D.C., where a meal with beverages may cost up to $300 per person, may expect unique and delicious food, immaculate service, and beautiful decor. Some diners may receive even more than they had expected and will leave the restaurant feeling that the experience was worth the money and other resources expended (such as a month-long wait for a reservation). Other diners may go with expectations so high that they leave the restaurant disappointed. On the other hand, many millions of customers each year visit thousands of McDonald's restaurants, in scores of countries around the globe, where they purchase standard, inexpensive meals from franchise owners and employees systematically trained by the McDonald's Corporation to deliver the company's four core standards: *quality, service, cleanliness, and value*. Customers flock to McDonald's outlets repeatedly because the restaurants are uniform, customers know what to expect, and they feel that they are getting value for the resources they expend.

Developing a *value proposition* (a term rapidly replacing the popular business phrase "unique selling proposition") is the core of successful positioning. For example, Lexus claims to deliver to its buyers *quality, zero defects in manufacturing*, and *superior, personal postpurchase service*. Dell's value proposition for personal computer users consists of *customized* PC systems *assembled speedily* and sold at *economical prices*. Apple's iPod is *the best digital jukebox*, and it provides users with many options to purchase, share, personalize, and listen to their favorite music. The value propositions stated above create customer expectations that these companies must continuously fulfill and even exceed as competitors try to win over their markets. Measures of customers' expectations and evaluations of products and services are discussed in Chapter 2, and the strategic applications of perceived customer value are explored in Chapter 6.

Customer satisfaction

Customer satisfaction is the individual's perception of the performance of the product or service in relation to his or her expectations. As noted earlier, customers will have drastically different expectations of an expensive French restaurant and a McDonald's, although both are part of the restaurant industry. The concept of customer satisfaction is a function of customer expectations. A customer whose experience falls below expectations (e.g., a limited wine list at an expensive restaurant or cold fries served at a McDonald's) will be dissatisfied. Diners whose experiences match expectations will be satisfied. And customers whose expectations are exceeded (e.g., by small samples of delicious food "from the Chef" served between courses at the expensive restaurant, or a well-designed play area for children at a McDonald's outlet) will be very satisfied or delighted.

A widely quoted study that linked levels of customer satisfaction with customer behavior identified several types of customers: completely satisfied customers who are either *loyalists* who keep purchasing, or *apostles* whose experiences exceed their expectations and who provide very positive word-of-mouth about the company to others; "*defectors*" who feel neutral or merely satisfied and are just as likely to stop doing business with the company; consumer "*terrorists*" who have had negative experiences with the company and who spread negative word-of-mouth. "*Hostages*" are unhappy customers who stay with the company because of a monopolistic environment or low prices and who are difficult and costly to deal with because of their frequent complaints; *mercenaries* are very satisfied customers who have no real loyalty to the company and may defect because of a lower price elsewhere or on impulse, defying the satisfaction–loyalty rationale. The researchers propose that companies should strive to create *apostles*, raise the satisfaction of *defectors* and turn them into *loyalists*, avoid having *terrorists* or *hostages*, and reduce the number of *mercenaries*.[6] Customer satisfaction measurement tools and techniques are discussed in Chapter 2.

Customer retention

The overall objective of providing value to customers continuously and more effectively than the competition is to have and to retain highly satisfied customers; this strategy of **customer retention** makes it in the best interests of customers to stay with the company rather than switch to another firm. In almost all business situations, it is more expensive to win new customers than to keep existing ones. Studies have shown that small reductions in customer defections produce significant increases in profits because (1) loyal customers buy more products; (2) loyal customers are less price sensitive and pay less attention to competitors' advertising; (3) servicing existing customers, who are familiar with the firm's offerings and processes, is cheaper; and (4) loyal customers spread positive word-of-mouth and refer other customers. Furthermore, marketing efforts aimed at attracting new customers are expensive; indeed, in saturated markets, it may be impossible to find new customers.[7] Today the Internet and electronic marketer–consumer interactions are ideal tools for tailoring products and services to the specific needs of consumers (often termed *one-to-one marketing*), offering them more value through increased *customer intimacy* and keeping the customers returning to the company.

Marketers who designate increasing customer retention rates as a strategic corporate goal must also recognize that all customers are not equal. Sophisticated marketers build *selective relationships* with customers, based on where customers rank in terms of profitability, rather than merely strive "to retain customers." A customer retention–savvy company closely monitors its customers' consumption volume and patterns, establishes tiers of customers according to their profitability levels, and develops distinct strategies toward each group of customers. For example, some stockbrokers program their phones to recognize the phone numbers of high-volume traders to ensure that their calls receive priority. Customers who have purchased and registered several of a company's products should receive extensive and expedited customer support. On the other hand, a bank's less profitable customers who, say, make little use of their credit cards or maintain the minimum balance needed to receive free checking should not have penalties waived for bounced checks or late payments. Some companies also identify customer groups that are unlikely to purchase more even if pursued aggressively; such customers are often discouraged from staying with the company, or even "fired" as customers.

Classifying customers according to profitability levels goes beyond traditional segmentation methods that subdivide consumers on the basis of demographic, sociocultural, or behavioral characteristics. *Customer profitability-focused marketing* tracks costs and revenues of individual customers and then categorizes them into tiers based on consumption behaviors that are specific to the company's offerings. Such a strategy is a very effective way to utilize the knowledge of consumer behavior. For example, a recent study advocates using a "customer pyramid" where customers are grouped into four tiers: (1) The *platinum tier* includes heavy users who are not price sensitive and who are willing to try new offerings; (2) the *gold tier* consists of customers who are heavy users but not as profitable because they are more price sensitive than those in the higher tier, ask for more discounts, and are likely to buy from several providers; (3) the *iron tier* consists of customers whose spending volume and profitability do not merit special treatment from the company; and (4) the *lead tier* includes customers who actually cost the company money because they claim more attention than is merited by their spending, tie up company resources, and spread negative word-of-mouth. The authors of the study urge companies to develop distinct marketing responses for each group.[8] Methods for collecting the customer data needed to develop the kind of retention systems discussed here are described in Chapter 2.

A corporate philosophy centered on customer value, satisfaction, and retention evolves from the marketing concept and unfolds new dimensions of marketing. Table 1.2 compares traditional marketing with perceived value and retention marketing. Applications of consumer behavior concepts to value and retention-focused marketing are discussed throughout the book.

TABLE 1.2	The Traditional Marketing Concept Versus Value- and Retention-Focused Marketing

THE TRADITIONAL MARKETING CONCEPT	VALUE- AND RETENTION-FOCUSED MARKETING
Make only what you can sell instead of trying to sell what you make.	Use technology that enables customers to customize what you make.
Do not focus on the product; focus on the need that it satisfies.	Focus on the product's perceived value, as well as the need that it satisfies.
Market products and services that match customers' needs better than competitors' offerings.	Utilize an understanding of customer needs to develop offerings that customers perceive as more valuable than competitors' offerings.
Research consumer needs and characteristics.	Research the levels of profit associated with various consumer needs and characteristics.
Understand the purchase behavior process and the influences on consumer behavior.	Understand consumer behavior in relation to the company's product.
Realize that each customer transaction is a discrete sale.	Make each customer transaction part of an ongoing relationship with the customer.
Segment the market based on customers' geographic, demographic, psychological, sociocultural, lifestyle, and product-usage related characteristics.	Use hybrid segmentation that combines the traditional segmentation bases with data on the customer's purchase levels and patterns of use of the company's products.
Target large groups of customers that share common characteristics with messages transmitted through mass media.	Invest in technologies that enable you to send one-to-one promotional messages via digital channels.
Use one-way promotions whose effectiveness is measured through sales data or marketing surveys.	Use interactive communications in which messages to customers are tailored according to their responses to previous communications.
Create loyalty programs based on the volume purchased.	Create customer tiers based on both volume and consumption patterns.
Encourage customers to stay with the company and buy more.	Make it very unattractive for your customers to switch to a competitor and encourage them to purchase "better"—in a manner that will raise the company's profitability levels.
Determine marketing budgets on the basis of the numbers of customers you are trying to reach.	Base your marketing budget on the "lifetime value" of typical customers in each of the targeted segments compared with the resources needed to acquire them as customers.
Conduct customer satisfaction surveys and present the results to management.	Conduct customer satisfaction surveys that include a component that studies the customer's word-of-mouth about the company, and use the results immediately to enhance customer relationships.
Create customer trust and loyalty to the company and high levels of customer satisfaction.	Create customer intimacy and bonds with completely satisfied, "delighted" customers.

Source: Joseph Wisenblit, "Beyond the Marketing Concept: From 'Make Only What You Can Sell' to 'Let Customers Customize What You Make'," The Stillman School of Business, Seton Hall University, South Orange, NJ.

the impact of digital technologies on marketing strategies

Digital technologies allow much greater customization of products, services, and promotional messages than older marketing tools. They enable marketers to adapt the elements of the marketing mix to consumers' needs more quickly and efficiently, and to build and maintain relationships with customers on a much greater scale. By using new technologies, marketers can collect and analyze increasingly complex data on consumers' buying patterns and personal characteristics, and quickly analyze and use this information for targeting increasingly smaller and focused groups of consumers. On the other hand, the same technologies enable consumers to find more information about products and services (including prices) more easily, efficiently, and, for the most part, from the comfort of their own homes. Therefore, more than ever before, marketers must ensure that their products and services provide the right benefits and value and are positioned effectively to reach them.

Online communication and emerging digital technologies have introduced several dramatic changes into the business environment:

Consumers have more power than ever before. They can use "intelligent agents" to locate the best prices for products or services, bid on various marketing offerings, bypass distribution outlets and middlemen, and shop for goods around the globe and around the clock from the convenience of their homes. Therefore, marketers must offer more competitively priced products and more options.

Consumers have access to more information than ever before. They can easily find reviews for products they are considering buying that have been posted by previous buyers, click a button to compare the features of different product models at the sites of online retailers, and subscribe to "virtual communities" of persons who share the same interests they do. In turn, marketers must be aware of the limits of their promotional messages and assume that consumers know all of their buying options.

Marketers can and must offer more services and products than ever before. The digitization of information enables sellers to *customize* the products and services they are selling and still sell them at reasonable prices. It also allows marketers to customize the promotional messages directed at many customers. For example, Amazon.com sends personalized e-mails to previous book purchasers announcing newly published books; these suggestions are based on a determination of the interests of the targeted consumers derived from their past purchases. Similarly, an online drugstore may vary the initial display returning buyers see when they revisit its Web site. Buyers whose past purchases indicate that they tend to buy national brands will see a display arranged by brand. Past purchasers who bought mostly products that were on sale or generic brands will see a display categorized by price and discounted products.

The exchange between marketers and customers is increasingly interactive and instantaneous. Traditional advertising is a one-way street where the marketer pays a large sum of money to reach a large number of potential buyers via a mass medium, and then assesses (usually after the fact) whether or not the message was effective on the basis of future sales or market studies. On the other hand, digital communication enables a two-way interactive exchange in which consumers can instantly react to the marketer's message by, say, clicking on links within a given Web site or even by leaving the site. Thus, marketers can quickly gauge the effectiveness of their promotional messages rather than rely on delayed feedback through sales information that is collected after the fact.

Marketers can gather more information about consumers more quickly and easily. Marketers can track consumers' online behavior and also gather information by requiring visitors to Web sites to register and provide some information about themselves before they get access to the site's features. Thus, marketers can construct and update their consumer databases efficiently and inexpensively. As a result, many marketers now employ **narrowcasting**—a method that enables them to develop and deliver more customized messages to increasingly smaller markets on an ongoing basis.

Impact reaches beyond the PC-based connection to the Web. Presently, most of the digital communications between consumers and marketers takes place via a PC connected to the Web through a phone line, a cable modem or other high-speed connection, or wirelessly. However, the digital revolution also gave us PDAs (personal digital assistants) that are rapidly becoming connected to the Web, also wirelessly. And it is likely that very soon our cell phones and PDAs will be combined into one product. In some European countries, consumers can already purchase products via their mobile phones. Cell phones with built-in GPS systems are likely to become a medium that will deliver customized promotional messages to consumers everywhere. In addition, many U.S. homes now have TV cable boxes that enable two-way communications with broadcasters; as we switch to high-definition TV, all cable subscribers will have such boxes. Also, as we receive more and more TV programming on PCs, some companies are merging the TV and the PC into a single device that provides households with hundreds of cable channels, interactive capabilities with broadcasters, and high-speed, wireless access to the Web. Supermarket scanners that keep track of households' purchases and instantly provide personalized coupons at the checkout counter, and telephone devices that enable us to identify callers without picking up the phone, are two of the many additional products made possible by recently developed technologies.

Challenges marketers face

The digital revolution in the marketplace, and its impact on consumer behavior, presents many challenges for today's marketers. For example, the TiVo digital recorder allows viewers to control what they watch on TV, when they watch it, and whether or not to view the commercials for which marketers spend billions of dollars per year. The TiVo recorder downloads programming information and allows users to record many hours of TV programming onto a hard drive without the hassle of videocassettes. Users can program the recorder by topic or keyword, easily play back selected segments, and, to the delight of many viewers, hit a single button for preprogrammed quick skips of strings of TV commercials. Since TiVo and other similar devices are shifting the power over viewing behavior from the broadcaster to the viewer, broadcasters are facing a new set of challenges: Should they develop their own TiVo-like systems? Should they try to block the sales of such devices legally on the grounds that they contribute to copyright infringement? Or should they develop business models centered on viewers paying for content? These questions are no longer hypothetical and will have to be addressed relatively soon.

As consumers spend more time online and have more technological tools that enable them to avoid exposure to TV ads, some marketers have begun reducing their advertising expenditures on the major networks and investing their advertising dollars in the newer media, such as the Web or even e-mail. Unilever has recently developed a series of amusing "Webisodes" targeted to women over 35 to view on the Web, and hopefully, to e-mail to their friends and family, thus encouraging word-of-mouth about their non-butter spray.[9]

Marketers have begun to insist that broadcasters develop new measurement systems to more accurately estimate the number and demographics of their viewers. Some marketers are considering investing in technologies that embed electronic tags of ads visible only to digital video recorder users, as some advertisers are already doing.

At Nike's Web site, buyers can now choose among many models of sneakers in different price ranges, customize the selected shoe using several colors and features (e.g., some models even allow buyers to choose the colors of the Nike Swoosh and the laces), put a personal ID on each shoe, pay for the product, and have it shipped directly to them. Should Nike and other companies that produce nondurable consumer goods begin shifting resources away from building consumer demand by advertising products carried by independently owned retailers, and into direct distribution systems based on customized offerings?

Some suggest that because virtual competition eliminates distance and location-based benefits (such as a desirable store location), online sellers will compete almost exclusively on the basis of price for branded merchandise. Does this mean that competitive differentiation—a key feature of modern marketing—will become meaningless in the virtual marketplace? These are only some of the many challenges marketers face as our technologies continue to evolve and change our daily lives and consumption patterns.

marketing ethics and social responsibility

The marketing concept as we know it—fulfilling the needs of target audiences—is sometimes inappropriate. This is particularly true in situations in which the means for need satisfaction, the product or service provided to satisfy customer "needs," can be harmful to the individual or to society (e.g., drugs, tobacco) or cause environmental deterioration. Given the fact that all companies prosper when society prospers, many people believe that all of us, companies as well as individuals, would be better off if social responsibility were an integral component of every marketing decision. A reassessment of the traditional marketing concept suggests that a more appropriate conceptualization for the times in which we live would balance the needs of society with the needs of the individual and the organization. The **societal marketing concept** requires that all marketers adhere to principles of social responsibility in the marketing of their goods and services; that is, they should endeavor to satisfy the needs and wants of their target markets in ways that preserve and enhance the well-being of consumers and society as a whole. Thus, a restructured definition of the marketing concept calls on marketers to *fulfill the needs of the target audience in ways that improve society as a whole, while fulfilling the objectives of the organization.* According to the societal marketing concept, fast-food restaurants should develop foods that contain less fat and starch and more nutrients, and marketers should not advertise foods to young people in ways that encourage overeating, or use professional athletes in liquor or tobacco advertisements, because celebrities so often serve as role models for the young.

A serious deterrent to widespread implementation of the societal marketing concept is the *short-term orientation* embraced by most business executives in their drive for increased market share and quick profits. This short-term orientation derives from the fact that managerial performance usually is evaluated on the basis of short-term results. Thus, a young and ambitious advertising executive may create a striking advertising campaign using unreasonably slim females with pale faces and withdrawn expressions in order to dramatically increase the sales of the advertised product, without considering the negative impact of the campaign, such as an increase in eating disorders among young women or the implicit approval of drug-taking reflected in the models' appearances. The societal marketing concept advocates a *long-term perspective.* It recognizes that all companies would be better off in a stronger, healthier society, and that companies that incorporate ethical behavior and social responsibility in all of their business dealings attract and maintain loyal consumer support over the long term.

The primary purpose for studying consumer behavior as part of a marketing curriculum is to understand why and how consumers make their purchase decisions. These insights enable marketers to design more effective marketing strategies, especially today when advanced technologies enable marketers to collect more data about consumers and target them more precisely. Some critics are concerned that an in-depth understanding of consumer behavior makes it possible for unethical marketers to exploit human vulnerabilities in the marketplace and engage in other unethical marketing practices in order to achieve individual business objectives.

As a result, many trade associations have developed industry-wide *codes of ethics*, because they recognize that industry-wide self-regulation is in every member's best interests in that it deters government from imposing its own regulations on the industry. A number of companies have incorporated specific social goals into their mission statements and include programs in support of these goals as integral components of their strategic planning. They believe that **marketing ethics** and **social responsibility** are important components of organizational effectiveness. Most companies recognize that socially responsible activities improve their image among consumers, stockholders, the financial community, and other relevant publics. They have found that ethical and socially responsible practices are simply good business, resulting not only in a favorable image, but ultimately in increased sales. The converse is also true: Perceptions of a company's lack of social responsibility or unethical marketing strategies negatively affect consumer purchase decisions. Applicable marketing ethics and social responsibility issues are discussed throughout the book.

consumer behavior and decision making are interdisciplinary

Consumer behavior was a relatively new field of study in the mid- to late-1960s. Because it had no history or body of research of its own, marketing theorists borrowed heavily from concepts developed in other scientific disciplines, such as *psychology* (the study of the individual), *sociology* (the study of groups), *social psychology* (the study of how an individual operates in groups), *anthropology* (the influence of society on the individual), and *economics* to form the basis of this new marketing discipline. Many early theories concerning consumer behavior were based on economic theory, on the notion that individuals act rationally to maximize their benefits (satisfactions) in the purchase of goods and services. Later research discovered that consumers are just as likely to purchase impulsively and to be influenced not only by family and friends, by advertisers and role models, but also by mood, situation, and emotion. All of these factors combine to form a comprehensive model of consumer behavior that reflects both the cognitive and emotional aspects of consumer decision making.

A simplified model of consumer decision making

The process of **consumer decision making** can be viewed as three distinct but interlocking stages: the **input** stage, the **process** stage, and the **output** stage. These stages are depicted in the simplified model of consumer decision making in Figure 1.1.

The *input* stage influences the consumer's recognition of a product need and consists of two major sources of information: the firm's marketing efforts (the product itself, its price, its promotion, and where it is sold) and the external sociological influences on the consumer (family, friends, neighbors, other informal and noncommercial sources, social class, and cultural and subcultural memberships). The cumulative impact of each firm's marketing efforts, the influence of family, friends, and neighbors, and society's existing code of behavior are all inputs that are likely to affect what consumers purchase and how they use what they buy.

The *process* stage of the model focuses on how consumers make decisions. The psychological factors inherent in each individual (motivation, perception, learning, personality, and attitudes) affect how the external inputs from the input stage influence the consumer's recognition of a need, prepurchase search for information, and evaluation of alternatives. The experience gained through evaluation of alternatives, in turn, affects the consumer's existing psychological attributes.

The *output* stage of the consumer decision-making model consists of two closely related postdecision activities: purchase behavior and postpurchase evaluation. Purchase behavior for a low-cost, nondurable product (e.g., a new shampoo) may be influenced by a manufacturer's coupon and may actually be a trial purchase; if the consumer is satisfied, he or she may repeat the purchase. The trial is the exploratory phase of purchase behavior in which the consumer evaluates the product through direct use. A repeat purchase usually signifies product adoption. For a relatively durable product such as a laptop ("relatively" durable because of the rapid rate of obsolescence), the purchase is more likely to signify adoption.

The consumer decision-making model is examined in greater depth in Chapter 16, where it ties together in great detail the psychological and sociocultural concepts explored throughout the book.

FIGURE 1.1

A Simple Model of Consumer Decision Making

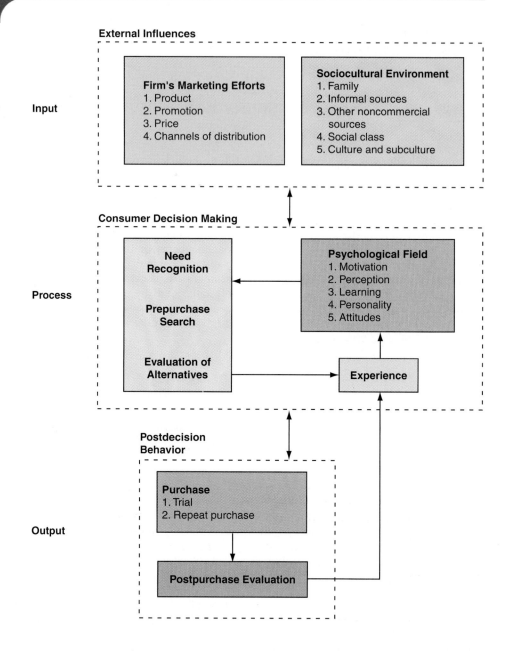

the plan of this book

In an effort to build a useful conceptual framework that both enhances understanding and permits practical application of consumer behavior principles to marketing strategy, this book is divided into four parts: Part 1 gives an introduction to the study of consumer behavior, Part 2 discusses the consumer as an individual, Part 3 examines consumers in their social and cultural settings, and Part 4 synthesizes all of the variables discussed earlier into the consumer decision-making process.

Chapter 1 introduced the reader to the study of consumer behavior as an interdisciplinary science that investigates the consumption-related activities of individuals. It described the reasons for the development of consumer behavior as an academic discipline and as an applied science, and introduced a simplified model of consumer decision making that links together all of the personal and group influences that affect consumption decisions. Chapter 2 examines the methodology of consumer research, including the assumptions underlying qualitative and quantitative research approaches. Chapter 3 discusses the process of market segmentation, including the demographic, sociocultural, and psychographic bases for segmenting markets.

Part 2 focuses on the psychological characteristics of the consumer. Chapter 4 discusses how individuals are motivated, Chapter 5 examines the impact of individual personality characteristics on consumer behavior, Chapter 6 explores consumer perception, Chapter 7 examines how consumers learn, Chapter 8 discusses consumer attitudes, and Chapter 9 concludes Part 2 with an examination of the communications process that links consumers to the world around them.

Part 3 focuses on consumers as members of society, subject to varying external influences on their buying behavior, such as their group and family memberships (see Chapter 10), social class (Chapter 11), and the broad cultural and specific subcultural groups to which they belong (Chapters 12 and 13). The importance of cross-cultural consumer research to international marketing is explored in Chapter 14.

Part 4 examines the consumer decision-making process. Chapter 15 discusses the consumer's reactions to innovation and change and describes the process by which new products are adopted and diffused throughout society. The book concludes with Chapter 16, an in-depth discussion of consumer decision making that shows how all the psychological and sociocultural variables discussed in Parts 2 and 3 influence the consumer's decision-making process.

SUMMARY

The study of consumer behavior enables marketers to understand and predict consumer behavior in the marketplace; it is concerned not only with what consumers buy but also with why, when, where, how, and how often they buy it. Consumer research is the methodology used to study consumer behavior and takes place at every phase of the consumption process: before, during, and after the purchase.

The field of consumer behavior is rooted in the **marketing concept**, a business orientation that evolved in the 1950s through several alternative approaches, referred to, respectively, as the *production concept*, the *product concept*, and the *selling concept*. The three major strategic tools of marketing are *market segmentation, targeting*, and *positioning*. The **marketing mix** consists of a company's service and/or product offerings to consumers and the pricing, promotion, and distribution methods needed to accomplish the exchange.

Skilled marketers make the customer the core of the company's organizational culture and ensure that all employees view any exchange with a customer as part of a *customer relationship*, not as a *transaction*. The three drivers of successful relationships between marketers and customers are *customer value*, high levels of *customer satisfaction*, and building a structure for *customer retention*.

Digital technologies allow much greater customization of products, services, and promotional messages than do older marketing tools. They enable marketers to adapt the elements of the marketing mix to consumers' needs more quickly and efficiently, and to build and maintain relationships with customers on a much greater scale. However, these technologies also represent significant challenges to marketers and to business models that have been used for decades.

Consumer behavior is interdisciplinary; that is, it is based on concepts and theories about people that have been developed by scientists in such diverse disciplines as psychology, sociology, social psychology, cultural anthropology, and economics.

Consumer behavior has become an integral part of strategic market planning. The belief that ethics and social responsibility should also be integral components of every marketing decision is embodied in a revised marketing concept—**the societal marketing concept**—that calls on marketers to fulfill the needs of their target markets in ways that improve society as a whole.

1. Describe the interrelationship between consumer behavior as an academic discipline and the marketing concept.

2. Describe the interrelationships between consumer research, market segmentation and targeting, and the development of the marketing mix for a manufacturer of high-definition TV sets.

3. Define the societal marketing concept and discuss the importance of integrating marketing ethics into the company's philosophy and operations.

4. Discuss the interrelationships among customer expectations and satisfaction, perceived value, and customer retention. Why is customer retention essential?

5. Discuss the role of the social and behavioral sciences in developing the consumer decision-making model.

6. Apply each of the two models depicted in Table 1.2 (i.e., traditional marketing and value and retention marketing) to the marketing of cellular phone services. You may want to incorporate into your answer your own and your peers' experiences in selecting cellular communications providers.

1. You are the marketing manager of Citibank's Online Banking Division. How would you apply the concepts of providing value, customer satisfaction, and customer retention to designing and marketing effective online banking?

2. Locate two examples (e.g., advertisements, articles, etc.) depicting practices that are consistent with the societal marketing concept and two examples of business practices that contradict this concept. Explain your choices.

3. Apply each of the concepts featured in the section describing the development of the marketing concept to manufacturing and marketing high-definition TVs.

- **consumer behavior**
- **consumer decision making**
- **consumer research**
- **customer expectations vs. customer satisfaction**
- **customer retention**
- **customer satisfaction**
- **customer value**
- **digital technologies**

- **marketing concept**
- **marketing ethics**
- **marketing mix**
- **marketing myopia**
- **market segmentation**
- **market targeting**
- **narrowcasting vs. broadcasting**
- **organizational consumer vs. personal consumer**

- **positioning**
- **production concept vs. the product concept**
- **selling concept**
- **social responsibility**
- **societal marketing concept**
- **targeting**

1. Davis Hounshell, *From the American System to Mass Production 1800–1932* (Baltimore/London: John Hopkins University Press, 1984), 224.

2. Theodore Levitt, "Marketing Myopia," *Harvard Business Review* (July–August 1960): 45–56.

3. **www.gm.com/company/corp_info/history**

4. *Colonel Sanders, America's Chicken King*, VHS Tape, A&E Television Networks, 1998

5. *Ray Kroc, Fast Food McMillionaire*, VHS Tape, A&E Television Networks, 1998

6. Thomas O. Jones and W. Earl Sasser, Jr., "Why Satisfied Customers Defect," *Harvard Business Review* (November–December 1995): 88–99.

7. Frederick F. Reichheld and W. Earl Sasser, Jr., "Zero Defections: Quality Comes to Services," *Harvard Business Review* (September–October 1990): 105–111; Michael Treacy and Fred Wiersema, "Customer Intimacy and Other Value Disciplines," *Harvard Business Review* (January–February 1993): 84–93.

8. Valerie A. Zeithaml, Roland T. Rust, and Katherine N. Lemon, "The Customer Pyramid: Creating and Serving Profitable Customers," *California Management Review* (Summer 2001): 118–142.

9. Stuart Elliott, "I Can't Believe It's Not a TV AD!" *The New York Times*, July 26, 2005, C4.

chaptertwo

> # Consumer Research

The *marketing concept* states that, to be successful, a company must understand the needs of specific groups of consumers (i.e., target markets) and then satisfy these needs more effectively than the competition. The satisfaction of consumer needs is delivered in the form of the *marketing mix,* which consists of the so-called "4 Ps": product, price, place, and promotion. Marketers who have a thorough understanding of the consumer decision-making process are likely to design products, establish prices, select distribution outlets, and design promotional messages that will favorably influence consumer purchase decisions.

The field of consumer research developed as an extension of the field of marketing research. Just as the findings of marketing research are used to improve managerial decision making, so too are the findings of consumer research. Studying consumer behavior, in all its ramifications, enables marketers to predict how consumers will react to promotional messages and to understand why they make the purchase decisions they do. Marketers realize that the more they know about their target consumers'

GODIVA
Chocolatier

EVERY WOMAN IS
ONE PART
GODIVA
MUCH TO THE
DISMAY
OF EVERY MAN.

The 2004 Limited Edition
Truffle Collection
by Godiva
793 Madison Avenue
GODIVA.COM

decision-making process, the more likely they are to design marketing strategies and pro-motional messages that will favorably influence these consumers. Savvy marketers recognize that consumer research is a unique subset of marketing research, which merits the use of specialized research methods to collect customer data. *Consumer research* enables marketers to study and understand consumers' needs and wants, and how they make consumption decisions.

consumer research paradigms

The early consumer researchers gave little thought to the impact of mood, emotion, or situation on consumer decisions. They believed that marketing was simply applied economics, and that consumers were rational decision makers who objectively evaluated the goods and services available to them and selected those that gave them the highest utility (satisfaction) at the lowest cost. Later on, researchers realized that consumers were not always consciously aware of why they made the decisions they did. Even when they were aware of their basic motivations, consumers were not always willing to reveal those reasons. In 1939, a Viennese psychoanalyst named Ernest Dichter began to use Freudian psychoanalytic techniques to uncover the hidden motivations of consumers. By the late 1950s, his research methodology (called **motivational research**), which was essentially qualitative in approach, was widely adopted by consumer researchers. As a result of Dichter's work and subsequent research designed to search deep within the consumer's psyche, consumer researchers today use two different types of research methodology to study consumer behavior: **quantitative research** and **qualitative research**.

Quantitative research

Quantitative research is descriptive in nature and is used by researchers to understand the effects of various promotional inputs on the consumer, thus enabling marketers to "predict" consumer behavior. This research approach is known as **positivism**. The research methods used in quantitative research consist of experiments, survey techniques, and observation. The findings are descriptive, empirical, and, if collected randomly (i.e., using a probability sample), can be generalized to larger populations. Because the data collected are quantitative, they lend themselves to sophisticated statistical analysis.

Qualitative research

Qualitative research methods include depth interviews, focus groups, metaphor analysis, collage research, and projective techniques. These techniques are administered by highly trained interviewer–analysts who also analyze the findings; thus, the findings tend to be somewhat subjective. Because sample sizes are necessarily small, findings cannot be generalized to larger populations. They are primarily used to obtain new ideas for promotional campaigns and products that can be tested more thoroughly in larger, more comprehensive studies.

Qualitative methods are also used by consumer behavior researchers who are interested in the act of *consumption* rather than in the act of *buying* (i.e., decision making). They view consumer behavior as a subset of human behavior, and increased understanding as a key to reducing negative aspects of consumer behavior—the so-called "dark side" of consumer behavior—such as drug addiction, shoplifting, alcoholism, and compulsive buying. Research focused on understanding consumer *experiences* is called **interpretivism**. Table 2.1 compares the quantitative and qualitative research designs.

Combining qualitative and quantitative research findings

Marketers often use a combination of quantitative and qualitative research to help make strategic marketing decisions. For example, they use qualitative research findings to discover new ideas and to develop promotional strategy, and quantitative research findings to predict consumer reactions to various promotional inputs. Frequently, ideas stemming from qualitative research are tested empirically through quantitative studies. The predictions made possible by quantitative research and the understanding provided by qualitative research together produce a richer and more robust profile of consumer behavior than either research approach used alone. The combined findings enable marketers to design more meaningful and effective marketing strategies.

TABLE 2.1	Comparisons Between Quantitative and Qualitative Research Designs	
	QUALITATIVE RESEARCH	**QUANTITATIVE RESEARCH**
Study Purpose	Studies designed to provide insights about new product ideas and positioning strategies. Ideas uncovered should be tested via quantitative studies. Often used in exploratory research to refine the objectives of quantitative studies.	Studies aimed at describing a target market—its characteristics and possible reactions of various segments to the elements of the marketing mix. Results are used for making strategic marketing decisions.
Types of Questions and Data Collection Methods	Open-ended, unstructured questions and further probing by the interviewer. Projective techniques include disguised questions where the respondents do not know the true purpose of the questions and are asked to freely respond to stimuli such as words or pictures. Depth interviews and focus groups are used.	Closed-ended questions with predefined possible responses and open-ended questions that have to be coded numerically. Most questionnaires include attitude scales and, generally, the questions are not disguised. Questionnaires are used in surveys conducted in person, by phone or mail, or online. Observation of respondents is also used. Experimentation is used to test cause-and-effect relationships.
Sampling Methods	Small, nonprobability samples; the findings are generally not representative of the universe under study.	Large, probability samples. Providing that the data collection instruments are valid and reliable, the results can be viewed as representative of the universe.
Data Analysis	Data collected are analyzed by the researchers who have collected it and who have expertise in the behavioral sciences. The analysis consists of looking for "key words" and establishing categories for the respondents' answers; it is subjective because it reflects the researchers' judgments.	The data is collected by a field force retained by the researcher, and then coded, tabulated, and entered into the database. The researcher analyzes the data by using objective, standardized statistical methods consisting mainly of comparisons of averages among the predefined variables and significance tests that estimate the extent to which the results represent the universe.

the consumer research process

The major steps in the consumer research process include (1) defining the objectives of the research, (2) collecting and evaluating secondary data, (3) designing a primary research study, (4) collecting primary data, (5) analyzing the data, and (6) preparing a report on the findings. Figure 2.1 depicts a model of the consumer research process.

Developing research objectives

The first and most difficult step in the consumer research process is to carefully define the objectives of the study. Is it to segment the market for plasma television sets? To find out consumer attitudes about and experiences with online shopping? To determine what percentage of households do their food shopping online? It is important for the marketing manager and the research manager (either in-house or retained for the specific study) to agree at the outset on the purposes and objectives of the study to ensure that

FIGURE 2.1

**The Consumer
Research Process**

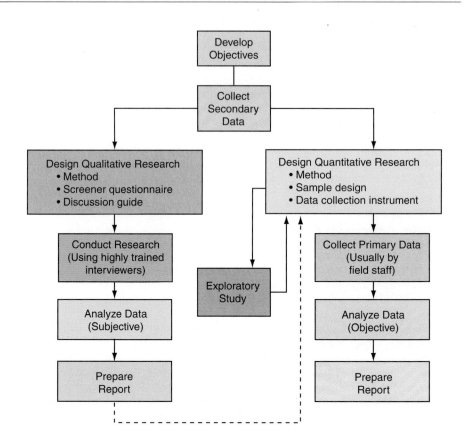

the research design is appropriate. A carefully thought-out statement of objectives helps to define the type and level of information needed.

For example, if the purpose of the study is to come up with new ideas for products or promotional campaigns, then a qualitative study is usually undertaken, in which respondents spend a significant amount of time face-to-face with a highly trained professional interviewer-analyst who also does the analysis. Because of the high costs of each interview, a fairly small sample of respondents is studied; thus, the findings are not projectable to the marketplace. If the purpose of the study is to find out how many people in the population (i.e., what percentage) use certain products and how frequently they use them, then a quantitative study that can be computer analyzed is undertaken. Sometimes, in designing a quantitative study, the researcher may not know what questions to ask. In such cases, before undertaking a full-scale study, the researcher is likely to conduct a small-scale *exploratory study* to identify the critical issues needed to develop narrow and more precise research objectives.

Collecting secondary data

A search for **secondary data** generally follows the statement of objectives. Secondary information is any data originally generated for some purpose other than the present research objectives. (Original data performed by individual researchers or organizations to meet specific objectives is called **primary data**.) Secondary data includes both **internal** and **external data**.

Internal secondary data consists of such information as data generated in-house for earlier studies as well as analysis of customer files, such as past customer transactions, letters from customers, sales-call reports, and data collected via warranty cards. Increasingly, companies use internal secondary data to compute **customer lifetime value profiles** for various customer segments. These profiles include customer acquisition costs (the resources needed to establish a relationship with the customer), the profits generated from individual sales to each customer, the costs of handling customers and their orders (some customers may place more complex and variable orders that cost more to handle), and the expected duration of the relationship.

External secondary data consists of any data collected by an outside organization. The major source of these data is the federal government, which publishes information collected by scores of government agencies about the economy, business, and virtually all demographics of the U.S. population. An excellent way to access selected parts of these data is FedStats (**www.fedstats.gov**). The U.S. Census Bureau (**www.census.gov**) collects data on the age, education, occupation, and income of U.S. residents by state and region and also provides projections on the future growth or decline of various demographic segments. Any firm operating globally may find key statistics about any country in the world in the CIA's electronic *The World Factbook* (**www.cia.gov/cia/publications/factbook**). Business-relevant secondary data from periodicals, newspapers, and books is readily accessible via two search engines—*ProQuest* and *Lexis-Nexis*. These engines access major newspapers such as *The Wall Street Journal* and *The New York Times*; business magazines such as *Business Week, Forbes, Fortune*, and *Harvard Business Review*; and journals focused specifically on marketing, such as *Advertising Age, Brandweek Magazine, Marketing News, Journal of Marketing, Journal of Marketing Research*, and *Journal of Consumer Research*.

Commercial data is available from marketing research companies that routinely monitor specific aspects of consumer behavior and sell the data to marketers. For example, *Claritas* provides demographic and lifestyle profiles of the consumers residing in each U.S. zip code (**http://www.clusterbigip1.claritas.com/MyBestSegments/Default.jsp? ID=0&SubID= &pageName=Home**). *Yankelovich* monitors consumers' lifestyles and consumption patterns, as well as more targeted studies focused on the consumer behavior of specific ethnic groups (**http://www.yankelovich.com/y-monitor.asp**). *Mediamark Research Inc.* conducts segmentation studies of consumers' leisure activities and buying styles, and also studies focused specifically on consumer innovators (**http://www.mediamark.com**).

Secondary data is also provided by companies that routinely monitor a particular consumption-related behavior. For example, one of the primary challenges marketers face is placing their advertisements in media that are most likely to reach their target customers. For decades, Nielsen Media Research has monitored the characteristics and size of audiences of TV programs. Nielsen did so through studying a presumably representative sample of U.S. households who agreed to install computerized boxes with modems connected to each set in their homes; many of these households also used *people meters*, on which each family member watching a particular program "logged on" for the duration of their viewing. A company called *Arbitron* has provided similar data about the audiences of radio programs. Marketers use this data to decide where to place their promotional messages, and the managers of the TV and radio stations use this data to determine how much to charge the marketers. This figure is usually based on the size of the audience and is expressed as the *cpm*, or cost to reach 1000 people. Obviously, the larger the audience of a particular program, the more money is charged for the commercial time within it. Although marketers understand that, by using the Nielsen and Arbitron data, they are also reaching many consumers who are not within their target markets (and unfortunately paying for this "wasted" advertising), they have no other options since the Nielsen and Arbitron data are used universally.

Recognizing that new technologies provide opportunities for far more sophisticated monitoring techniques, Nielsen and Arbitron are now testing *portable people meters*. These meters are small devices that consumers clip to their belts or to other clothing and wear during their waking hours. This device monitors all the radio and TV programming a person is exposed to during the day. Eventually, the device will monitor the person's exposure to all media programming and advertising, such as Web streaming, supermarket Muzak, and, when GPS systems are integrated into the new meter, exposure to outdoor advertising. At night, the meter is plugged into a cradle that transmits this data for analysis. But perhaps the real future of researching consumers' exposure to media will not entail monitoring the behavior of several thousand consumers wearing portable meters, but monitoring the media exposure of almost all consumers via digital cable set-top boxes that are now present in many homes and are likely to be placed in the majority of American homes, as digital TV replaces analog broadcasts. Presently, digital cable boxes are primarily used to send signals to consumers' TVs in order to enable them to watch movies-on-demand. However, the digital boxes can easily record all the programs that consumers are tuned into, including, of course, channel surfing, attempts at avoiding commercial breaks, and recordings for later viewing, using devices such as TiVo or digital video recorders that cable companies increasingly offer to subscribers. So far, cable companies have been reluctant to use this data due to privacy concerns. However, some innovative companies are now developing methods that will transform data from digital cable boxes into information that can be used for precise targeting of consumers while still protecting privacy.[1] The portable people meters and the two-way digital cable boxes demonstrate the profound and dynamic changes that technology is bringing to consumer research. The numerous new technologies that are being developed will enable marketers to study consumers' media exposure much more precisely and collect data that will enable them to customize or *narrowcast* their promotional messages, and thus expend their advertising dollars more effectively.

For decades, marketers have purchased data from secondary data providers who collected data from **consumer panels**. The members of these panels were consumers who were paid for recording their purchases or media viewing habits in diaries that were then summarized and analyzed by the data providers. Today, online technologies enable companies to collect increasingly sophisticated data from respondents. For example, a manufacturer of customized snowboards had discovered that 10,000 snowboarding fans used its site to discuss their hobbies and buying habits, and also to rate different designs of snowboards. The snowboards marketer then started *selling* the data it collected from this online panel to other marketers interested in targeting the young, mostly male respondents who so enthusiastically revealed so much about themselves while discussing snowboards online. Similarly, GM is collecting data from 30,000 car buyers a month via an online site. One of the most important issues GM investigated was the point at which rising fuel prices significantly impact car buyers' priorities—data that can be used to alter production schedules as gas prices fluctuate and also in the design of future models.[2]

Obtaining secondary data before engaging in primary research offers several advantages. First, secondary data may provide a solution to the research problem and eliminate the need for primary research altogether. But even if this is not the case, secondary data, used in exploratory research, may help to clarify and redefine the objectives of the primary study and provide ideas for the methods to be used and the difficulties that are likely to occur during the full-scale study.

Although secondary information can be obtained more cheaply and quickly than primary data, it has some limitations. First, information may be categorized in units that are different from those that the researcher seeks (e.g., clustering consumers into the 15–20 and 21–25 age groups renders it useless to a researcher interested in consumers 17–24 years old). Some secondary data may not be accurate because of errors in gathering or analyzing the data for the original study or because the data had been collected in a biased fashion in order to support a particular point of view. Also, care must be taken not to use secondary data that may be outdated.

Designing primary research

The design of a research study is based on the purposes of the study. If descriptive information is needed, then a quantitative study is likely to be undertaken; if the purpose is to get new ideas (e.g., for positioning or repositioning a product), then a qualitative study is undertaken. Because the approach for each type of research differs in terms of method of data collection, sample design, and type of data collection instrument used, each research approach is discussed separately below.

Quantitative research designs

A quantitative research study consists of a research design, the data collection methods and instruments to be used, and the sample design. Three basic designs are used in quantitative research: observation, experimentation (in a laboratory or in the field, such as in a retail store), or survey (i.e., by questioning people).

Observational Research   **Observational research** is an important method of consumer research because marketers recognize that the best way to gain an in-depth understanding of the relationship between people and products is by watching them in the process of buying and/or using the products. Doing so enables observational researchers to comprehend what the product symbolizes to a consumer and provides greater insight into the bond between people and products that is the essence of brand loyalty. Many large corporations and advertising agencies use trained researchers/observers to watch, note, and sometimes videotape consumers in stores, malls, or their own homes. For example, in studying responses to a new mint-flavored Listerine, the Warner Lambert Company hired a research firm that paid 37 New York City families to let it install cameras in their bathrooms to videotape mouthwash usage. The study found that consumers who used Scope gave the product a swish and spit it out. On the other hand, users of the new Listerine kept the mouthwash in their mouths for much longer (one subject even held the mouthwash in his mouth as he left home and got into the car, and only spit it out after driving a couple of blocks).[3] Procter & Gamble (P&G) sent video crews to scores of households around the world, which enabled P&G executives in Cincinnati to watch a mother in Thailand feed her baby. They discovered that the mother was multitasking while feeding her baby and even glanced at her TV from time to time. Understanding such behavior can lead to the development of products and packages that will give P&G a strong competitive advantage in the marketplace.[4]

   Mechanical observation uses a mechanical or electronic device to record customer behavior or response to a particular marketing stimulus. For example, when Duane Reade—a large chain of drugstores in New York City—considers a location for a new store, the company uses electronic beams or hand counters to count the numbers of passersby at different times and under different weather conditions.[5] Government planners use data collected from electronic EZ Pass devices in passenger cars to decide which roads should be expanded, and banks use security cameras to observe problems customers may have in using ATMs.

   Increasingly, consumers use automated systems in their purchases because these instruments make purchases easier and often provide rewards for using them. For example, consumers who use supermarket frequency shopping cards often receive offers for promotional discounts tailored specifically for them at checkout counters. Moviegoers who order tickets online can pick them up at ATM-like devices at movie theaters and avoid waiting in line at the box office. As consumers use more and more highly convenient technologies, such as credit and ATM cards, EZ Passes, frequency cards, automated phone systems, and online shopping, there are more and more electronic records of their consumption patterns. As a consequence, observation of consumer behavior via electronic means has grown significantly and, as illustrated in the earlier discussion of portable people meters and two-way digital cable boxes, electronic observation of consumption behavior will become increasingly sophisticated.

   Gambling casinos have been in the forefront of developing systems that track individual customer data collected during the various stages of a customer's visit, and cross-matching them with data collected on previous visits by that customer (including spending usage). They use this data to classify visitors into categories based on their "loyalty levels," and implement corresponding rewards that are delivered almost immediately. For example, normally about 50,000 people a day visit the Foxwood Casino in Connecticut. Most of them use magnetic cards called "frequent player cards." Sophisticated electronic network systems monitor the gaming patterns, eating habits, and room preferences of all visitors. When a player sits at a table, within seconds, the casino's manager can read the guest's history on the screen, including alcoholic beverages preferred and gaming habits. Because there are electronic tags in the chips issued to each player, when a player leaves the table, his or her record is updated instantly and made available at any contact point for that customer throughout the entire casino complex. Thus, the casino can instantly reward customers who are good for business by giving free meals and room upgrades and inviting them to gamble in designated VIP lounges. The customers love the frequency cards because they enable them to keep track of their spending, and the casinos benefit from each swipe of the card because it provides more information about customers. The casino

FIGURE 2.2   *Source:* Courtesy of Kim S. Nash, "Casinos Hit Jackpot with Customer Data," *Computer World,* July 2, 2001, 17.

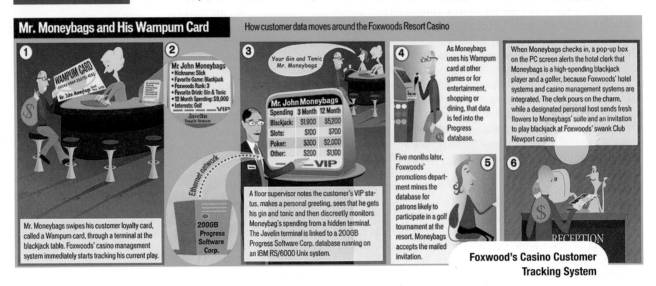

has two identical computer systems and, if needed, can switch to a backup immediately and thus avoid the many thousands of dollars that may be lost during an even brief period of operating without computers.[6] Figure 2.2 depicts Foxwood's customer tracking system. More casinos are employing increasingly sophisticated software to create real-time and personal rewards to day-trippers who bet relatively small amounts of money—$50 to $100 per visit—but who visit the casinos frequently. Casinos have recognized that although these consumers wage little money per trip, they view gaming as their primary entertainment, and observing their behavior and immediately using the data to encourage them to spend more money is likely to increase profits greatly over time.[7]

An audit is another type of mechanical observation that entails monitoring the sales of products. A key component of Wal-Mart's competitive advantage is the retailing giant's use of technology in its product audits. At any given moment, the company knows what is selling, how fast, and how much of the product remains in its inventory. Maintaining small inventories and moving products quickly enables the company to lower its prices and attract more customers. Wal-Mart's record profits are derived from low per-item profits multiplied by selling billions of products quickly, and also moving products rapidly to where consumers are likely to buy them. For example, after observing that the sales of strawberry Pop-Tarts increased dramatically before a hurricane and that the top pre-seller before a hurricane was beer, the company quickly transports large quantities of these items to areas expected to be hit by an approaching storm.[8]

Marketers also use **physiological observation** devices that monitor respondents' patterns of information processing. For example, an electronic eye camera may be used to monitor the *eye movements* of subjects looking at a series of advertisements for various products, and electronic sensors placed on the subjects' heads can monitor the *brain activity* and attentiveness levels involved in viewing each ad. Neuroscientists monitoring cognitive functions in twelve different regions of the brain while consumers watched commercials for different products claimed that the data collected shows the respondents' levels of attention and the decoding and recall of the promotional messages.[9]

Experimentation   It is possible to test the relative sales appeal of many types of variables, such as package designs, prices, promotional offers, or copy themes through experiments designed to identify cause and effect. In such experiments (called *causal research*), only some variables are manipulated (the *independent variables*), while all other elements are kept constant. A **controlled experiment** of this type ensures that any difference in the outcome (the *dependent variable*) is due to different treatments of the variable under study and not to extraneous factors. For example, one study tested the effectiveness of using an attractive versus unattractive endorser in promoting two types of products: products that are used to enhance one's attractiveness (e.g., a men's cologne) and products that are not (e.g., a pen). The endorser used was a fictitious character named Phil Johnson who was described as a member of the U.S. Olympic water polo team. The photograph depicting the attractive endorser was a scanned image of an attractive athletic man, whereas the picture depicting the unattractive endorser was the same image graphically modified to reduce attractiveness. The subjects viewed each endorser-product combination for 15 seconds (simulating the viewing of an actual print ad) and then filled out a questionnaire that measured their attitudes and purchase intentions toward the products advertised. In this study, the combinations of the product (i.e., used/not used to enhance one's attractiveness) and the endorser's attractiveness (i.e., attractive/non-attractive endorser) were the *manipulated treatments* (i.e., the independent variables) and the combination of the attitudes and purchase intentions toward the product was the *dependent variable*. The study discovered that the attractive endorser was more effective in promoting both types of products.[10]

A major application of causal research is **test marketing**, in which, prior to launching a new product, elements such as package, price, and promotion are manipulated in a controlled setting in order to predict sales or gauge the possible responses to the product. Today some researchers employ *virtual reality methods*. For example, in a market test, respondents can view, on a computer screen, supermarket shelves that are stocked with many products, including different versions of the same product; they can "pick up" an item by touching the image, examine it by rotating the image with a track ball, and place it in a shopping cart if they decide to buy it. The researchers observe how long the respondents spend in looking at the product, the time spent in examining each side of the package, the products purchased, and the order of the purchases.

Surveys   If researchers wish to ask consumers about their purchase preferences and consumption experiences, they can do so in person, by mail, by telephone, or online. Each of these survey methods has certain advantages and certain disadvantages that the researcher must weigh when selecting the method of contact (see Table 2.2).

Personal interview surveys most often take place in the home or in retail shopping areas. The latter, referred to as *mall intercepts*, are used more frequently than home interviews because of the high incidence of not-at-home working women and the reluctance of many people today to allow a stranger into their home.

Telephone surveys are also used to collect consumer data; however, evenings and weekends are often the only times to reach telephone respondents, who tend to be less responsive—even hostile—to calls that interrupt dinner, television viewing, or general relaxation. The difficulties of reaching people with unlisted telephone numbers have been

TABLE 2.2   Comparative Advantages and Disadvantages of Mail, Telephone, Personal Interview, and Online Surveys

	MAIL	TELEPHONE	PERSONAL INTERVIEW	ONLINE
Cost	Low	Moderate	High	Low
Speed	Slow	Immediate	Slow	Fast
Response Rate	Low	Moderate	High	Self-selected
Geographic Flexibility	Excellent	Good	Difficult	Excellent
Interviewer Bias	N/A	Moderate	Problematic	N/A
Interviewer Supervision	N/A	Easy	Difficult	N/A
Quality of Response	Limited	Limited	Excellent	Excellent

solved through random-digit dialing, and the costs of a widespread telephone survey are often minimized by using toll-free telephone lines. Other problems arise, however, from the increased use of answering machines and caller ID to screen calls. Some market research companies have tried to automate telephone surveys, but many respondents are even less willing to interact with an electronic voice than with a live interviewer.

Mail surveys are conducted by sending questionnaires directly to individuals at their homes. One of the major problems of mail questionnaires is a low response rate, but researchers have developed a number of techniques to increase returns, such as enclosing a stamped, self-addressed envelope, using a provocative questionnaire, and sending prenotification letters as well as follow-up letters. A number of commercial research firms that specialize in consumer surveys have set up panels of consumers who, for a token fee, agree to complete the research company's mail questionnaires on a regular basis. Sometimes panel members are also asked to keep diaries of their purchases.

Online surveys are sometimes conducted on the Internet. Respondents are directed to the marketer's (or researcher's) Web site by computer ads or home pages. Because the sample's respondents are self-selected, the results cannot be projected to the larger population. Most computer polls ask respondents to complete a profile consisting of demographic questions that enable the researchers to classify the responses to the substantive product or service questions.

Researchers who conduct computer polling believe that the anonymity of the Internet encourages respondents to be more forthright and honest than they would be if asked the same questions in person or by mail; others believe that the data collected may be suspect because some respondents may create new online personalities that do not reflect their own beliefs or behavior. Some survey organizations cite the inherent advantages of wide reach and affordability in online polling.

Quantitative research data collection instruments

Data collection instruments are developed as part of a study's total research design to systematize the collection of data and to ensure that all respondents are asked the same questions in the same order. Data collection instruments include questionnaires, personal inventories, and attitude scales. Data collection instruments are usually pretested and "debugged" to assure the validity and reliability of the research study. A study is said to have **validity** if it does, in fact, collect the appropriate data needed to answer the questions or objectives stated in the first (objectives) stage of the research process. A study is said to have **reliability** if the same questions, asked of a similar sample, produce the same findings. Often a sample is systematically divided in two, and each half is given the same questionnaire to complete. If the results from each half are similar, the questionnaire is said to have *split-half reliability*.

Questionnaires   For quantitative research, the primary data collection instrument is the questionnaire, which can be sent through the mail to selected respondents for self-administration or can be administered by field interviewers in person or by telephone. In order to motivate respondents to take the time to respond to surveys, researchers have found that questionnaires must be interesting, objective, unambiguous, easy to complete, and generally not burdensome. To enhance the analysis and facilitate the classification of responses into meaningful categories, questionnaires include both substantive questions that are relevant to the purposes of the study and pertinent demographic questions.

The questionnaire itself can be *disguised* or *undisguised* as to its true purpose; a disguised questionnaire sometimes yields more truthful answers and avoids responses that respondents may think are expected or sought. Questions can be *open-ended* (requiring answers in the respondent's own words) or *closed-ended* (the respondent merely checks the appropriate answer from a list of options). Open-ended questions yield more insightful information but are more difficult to code and to analyze; closed-ended questions are relatively simple to tabulate and analyze, but the answers are limited to the alternative responses provided (i.e., to the existing insights of the questionnaire designer). For example, a survey of U.S. merchant mariners in the late 1970s included both open-ended and

TABLE 2.3	Guidelines for Wording Questions

1. *Avoid leading questions.* For example, a question such as "Do you often shop at such cost-saving stores as Staples?" or "Weren't you satisfied with the service you received at Staples today?" introduce bias into the survey

2. *Avoid two questions in one.* For example, "In your view, did you save money and receive good service when you last visited Staples?" is really two questions combined and they should be stated separately.

3. *Questions must be clear.* For example, "Where do you usually shop for your home-office supplies?" is unclear because the term "usually" is vague.

4. *Use words that consumers routinely use.* For example, do not use the verb "to rectify"; use the verb "to correct."

5. *Respondents must be able to answer the question.* For example, it is unlikely that any respondent can accurately answer a question such as "how many newspaper or TV ads for Staples did you read or see during the past month?"

6. *Respondents must be willing to answer the question.* Questions about money, health issues, personal hygiene, or sexual preferences can embarrass respondents and cause them not to answer. Sometimes, asking the question in a less personal fashion might help generate more responses. For example, rather than asking older consumers whether they experience incontinence, the researcher should ask "millions of Americans experience some level of incontinence. Do you or anyone you know experience this difficulty?"

closed-ended questions asking why the respondent first joined the merchant marine. The closed-ended question, which appeared toward the beginning of the 45-page questionnaire, resulted in a majority response that they were intrigued with the excitement and romance of the high seas. The open-ended question, which appeared toward the end of this very lengthy questionnaire, resulted in a preponderance of responses "to avoid the draft in World War II." This was an option the questionnaire designers never even contemplated.

Wording the questions represents the biggest challenge in constructing questionnaires; Table 2.3 includes guidelines for writing clear and effective questions. The sequence of questions is also important: The opening questions must be interesting enough to "draw" the respondent into participating, they must proceed in a logical order, and demographic (classification) questions should be placed at the end, where they are more likely to be answered. The format of the questionnaire and the wording and sequence of the questions affect the validity of the responses and, in the case of mail questionnaires, the number (rate) of responses received. Questionnaires usually offer respondents confidentiality or anonymity to dispel any reluctance about self-disclosure.

Attitude Scales   Researchers often present respondents with a list of products or product attributes for which they are asked to indicate their relative feelings or evaluations. The instruments most frequently used to capture this evaluative data are called **attitude scales**. The most frequently used attitude scales are Likert scales, semantic differential scales, behavior intention scales, and rank-order scales.

The ***Likert scale*** is the most popular form of attitude scale because it is easy for researchers to prepare and to interpret, and simple for consumers to answer. They check or write the number corresponding to their level of "agreement" or "disagreement" with each of a series of statements that describes the attitude object under investigation. The scale consists of an equal number of agreement/disagreement choices on either side of a neutral choice. A principal benefit of the Likert scale is that it gives the researcher the option of considering the responses to each statement separately or of combining the responses to produce an overall score.

The *semantic differential scale*, like the Likert scale, is relatively easy to construct and administer. The scale typically consists of a series of bipolar adjectives (such as good/bad, hot/cold, like/dislike, or expensive/inexpensive) anchored at the ends of an odd-numbered (e.g., five- or seven-point) continuum. Respondents are asked to evaluate a concept (or a product or company) on the basis of each attribute by checking the point on the continuum that best reflects their feelings or beliefs. Care must be taken to vary the location of positive and negative terms from the left side of the continuum to the right side to avoid consumer response bias. Sometimes an even-numbered scale is used to eliminate the option of a neutral answer. An important feature of the semantic differential scale is that it can be used to develop graphic consumer profiles of the concept under study. Semantic differential profiles are also used to compare consumer perceptions of competitive products and to indicate areas for product improvement when perceptions of the existing product are measured against perceptions of the "ideal" product.

The *behavior intention scale* measures the likelihood that consumers will act in a certain way in the future, such as buying the product again or recommending it to a friend. These scales are easy to construct, and consumers are asked to make subjective judgments regarding their future behavior.

With *rank-order scales*, subjects are asked to rank items such as products (or retail stores or Web sites) in order of preference in terms of some criterion, such as overall quality or value for the money. Rank-order scaling procedures provide important competitive information and enable marketers to identify needed areas of improvement in product design and product positioning. Figure 2.3 provides examples of the attitude scales that are frequently utilized in consumer research.

Qualitative research designs and data collection methods

In selecting the appropriate research format for a qualitative study, the researcher has to take into consideration the purpose of the study and the types of data needed. Although the research methods used may differ in composition, they all have roots in psychoanalytic and clinical aspects of psychology, and they stress open-ended and free-response types of questions to stimulate respondents to reveal their innermost thoughts and beliefs.

The key data collection techniques for qualitative studies are depth interviews, focus groups, discussion guides, projective techniques, and metaphor analysis. These techniques are regularly used in the early stages of attitude research to pinpoint relevant product-related beliefs or attributes and to develop an initial picture of consumer attitudes (especially the beliefs and attributes they associate with particular products and services).

Depth Interviews   A **depth interview** is a lengthy (generally 30 minutes to an hour), nonstructured interview between a respondent and a highly trained interviewer, who minimizes his or her own participation in the discussion after establishing the general subject to be discussed. (However, as noted earlier, interpretative researchers often take a more active role in the discussion.) Respondents are encouraged to talk freely about their activities, attitudes, and interests in addition to the product category or brand under study. Transcripts, videotapes, or audiotape recordings of interviews are then carefully studied, together with reports of respondents' moods and any gestures or "body language" they may have used to convey attitudes or motives. Such studies provide marketers with valuable ideas about product design or redesign and provide insights for positioning or repositioning the product. Sometimes, as part of depth interviews, researchers show respondents photos, videos, and audiotapes of their own shopping behavior and ask them to explicitly comment on their consumption actions.

Focus Groups   A **focus group** consists of 8 to 10 respondents who meet with a moderator-analyst for a group discussion "focused" on a particular product or product category (or any other subject of research interest). Respondents are encouraged to discuss their interests, attitudes, reactions, motives, lifestyles, feelings about the product or product category, usage experience, and so forth.

LIKERT SCALE

For each of the following statements, please record the number that best describes the extent to which you agree or disagree with each statement.

| 1. Strongly Agree | 2. Somewhat Agree | 3. Neither Agree nor Disagree | 4. Somewhat Disagree | 5. Strongly Disagree |

_____ It's fun to shop online.
_____ I am afraid to give my credit card number online.

Two widely used applications of the Likert Scale to measure consumer attitudes are:

SATISFACTION MEASURES

Over all, how satisfied are you with Bank X's online banking? _____

| 1. Very Satisfied | 2. Somewhat Satisfied | 3. Neither Satisfied nor Dissatisfied | 4. Somewhat Dissatisfied | 5. Very Dissatisfied |

IMPORTANCE SCALES

The following list of features are associated with shopping on the Internet. For each feature, please record the one alternative that best expresses how important or unimportant that feature is to you.

| 1. Extremely Important | 2. Somewhat Important | 3. Neither Important nor Unimportant | 4. Somewhat Unimportant | 5. Not at all Important |

_____ Speed of downloading the order form
_____ Being able to register with the site

SEMANTIC DIFFERENTIAL SCALE

For each of the following features, please check one alternative that best expresses your impression of how that feature applies to **online banking:**

Competitive rates ├──┼──┼──┼──┼──┼──┤ Noncompetitive rates
Reliable ├──┼──┼──┼──┼──┼──┤ Unreliable

Note: The same semantic differential scale can be applied to two competitive offerings, such as online banking and regular banking, and a graphic representation of the profiles of the two alternatives, along with the bipolar adjectives included in the scale, can be easily constructed.

BEHAVIOR INTENTION SCALES

How likely are you to continue using Bank X's online banking for the next six months? _____

| 1. Definitely Will Continue | 2. Probably Will Continue | 3. Might or Might Not Continue | 4. Probably Will Not Continue | 5. Definitely Will Not Continue |

How likely are you to recommend Bank X's online banking to a friend? _____

| 1. Definitely Will Recommend | 2. Probably Will Recommend | 3. Might or Might Not Recommend | 4. Probably Will Not Recommend | 5. Definitely Will Not Recommend |

RANK ORDER SCALE

We would like to find out about your preferences regarding banking methods. Please rank the following banking methods by placing a "1" in front of the method that you prefer most, a "2" next to your second preference, and continuing until you have ranked all of the methods.

_____ Inside the bank   _____ Online banking   _____ Banking by telephone
_____ ATM   _____ Banking by mail

FIGURE 2.4

**Selected Portions
of a Discussion Guide**

1. Why did you decide to use your current cellular company? (Probe)

2. How long have you used your current cellular company? (Probe)

3. Have you ever switched services? When? What caused the change? (Probe)

4. What do you think of the overall quality of your current service? (Probe)

5. What are the important criteria in selecting a cellular service? (Probe)

Examples of Probe questions:

a. Tell me more about that . . .

b. Share your thinking on this . . .

c. Does anyone see it differently . . .

Because a focus group takes about 2 hours to complete, a researcher can easily conduct two or three focus groups (with a total of 30 respondents) in one day, while it might take that same researcher five or six days to conduct 30 individual depth interviews. Analysis of responses in both depth interviews and focus groups requires a great deal of skill on the part of the researcher. Focus group sessions are invariably taped, and sometimes videotaped, to assist in the analysis. Interviews are usually held in specially designed conference rooms with one-way mirrors that enable marketers and advertising agency staff to observe the sessions without disrupting or inhibiting the responses.

Respondents are recruited on the basis of a carefully drawn consumer profile (called a **screener questionnaire**) based on specifications defined by marketing management, and usually are paid a fee for their participation. Sometimes users of the company's brands are clustered in one or more groups, and their responses are compared to those of nonusers interviewed in other groups.

Some marketers prefer focus groups to individual depth interviews because it takes less time overall to complete the study, and they feel that the freewheeling group discussions and group dynamics tend to yield a greater number of new ideas and insights than depth interviews. Other marketers prefer individual depth interviews because they feel that respondents are free of group pressure and thus are less likely to give socially acceptable (and not necessarily truthful) responses, are more likely to remain attentive during the entire interview, and—because of the greater personal attention received—are more likely to reveal private thoughts. Figure 2.4 presents a portion of a discussion guide that might be used in a focus-group session to gain insights into the attitudes of consumers toward various cellular service providers. The findings would be equally relevant to the positioning of a new cellular service provider or the repositioning of an existing provider.

Projective Techniques   **Projective techniques** are designed to tap the underlying motives of individuals despite their unconscious rationalizations or efforts at conscious concealment. They consist of a variety of disguised "tests" that contain ambiguous stimuli, such as incomplete sentences, untitled pictures or cartoons, ink blots, word-association tests, and other-person characterizations. Projective techniques are sometimes administered as part of a focus group but more often are used during depth interviews. Because projective methods are closely associated with researching consumer needs and motivations they are more fully discussed in Chapter 4.

Metaphor Analysis   In the 1990s, a stream of consumer research emerged suggesting that most communication is nonverbal and that people do not think in words but in images. If consumers' thought processes consist of series of images, or pictures in their minds, then it is likely that many respondents cannot adequately convey their feelings and attitudes about the research subject (such as a product or brand) through the use of words alone. Therefore, it is important to enable consumers to represent their images in an alternate, nonverbal form—through the use, say, of sounds, music, drawings, or pictures. The use of one form of expression to describe or represent feelings about another is called a *metaphor*. A number of consumer theorists have come to believe that people use metaphors as the most basic method of thought and communication.

The **Zaltman Metaphor Elicitation Technique** (ZMET)—the first patented marketing research tool in the United States—relies on visual images to assess consumers' deep and subconscious thoughts about products, services, and marketing strategies. In one study about consumer perceptions of advertising, prescreened respondents were asked to bring into a depth interview pictures that illustrated their perceptions of the value of advertising. They were asked to bring pictures from magazines, newspapers, artwork, photos they took especially for the study or from existing collections, but not actual print advertisements. Each respondent participated in a two-hour videotaped interview (on average, each respondent brought in 13 images representing his or her impressions of the value of advertising). The interview used several methods that are part of the ZMET technique to elicit key metaphors and the interrelationships among them from the respondents. The interviews were then analyzed by qualified researchers according to the ZMET criteria. The findings revealed that the *ambivalent* respondents had both favorable (e.g., information and entertainment values) and unfavorable (e.g., misrepresentation of reality) impressions of advertising; *skeptics* had mostly negative, but some positive impressions of advertising; and *hostile* respondents viewed advertising as an all-negative force.[11]

Customer satisfaction measurement

Gauging the level of customer satisfaction and its determinants is critical for every company. Marketers can use such data to retain customers, sell more products and services, improve the quality and value of their offerings, and operate more effectively and efficiently. **Customer satisfaction measurement** includes quantitative and qualitative measures, as well as a variety of contact methods with customers.

Customer satisfaction surveys measure how satisfied the customers are with relevant attributes of the product or service, and the relative importance of these attributes (using an importance scale). Generally, these surveys use 5-point semantic differential scales ranging from "very dissatisfied" to "very satisfied." Research shows that customers who indicate they are "very satisfied" (typically a score of 5 on the satisfaction scale) are much more profitable and loyal than customers who indicate that they are "satisfied" (a score of 4). Therefore, companies that merely strive to have "satisfied" customers are making a crucial error.[12] Some marketers maintain that customers' satisfaction or dissatisfaction is a function of the difference between what they had *expected* to get from the product or service purchased and their perceptions of what they *received*. A group of researchers developed a scale that measures the performance of the service received against two expectation levels: *adequate* service and *desired* service, and also measures the customers' future intentions regarding purchasing the service.[13] This approach is more sophisticated than standard customer satisfaction surveys and more likely to yield results that can be used to develop corrective measures for products and services that fall short of customers' expectations.

Mystery shoppers are professional observers who pose as customers in order to interact with and provide unbiased evaluations of the company's service personnel in order to identify opportunities for improving productivity and efficiency. For example, one bank used mystery shoppers who, while dealing with a bank employee on another matter, dropped hints about buying a house or seeking to borrow college funds. Employees were scored on how quickly and effectively they provided information about the bank's pertinent products or services. A company that requires sales clerks to check youthful customers' IDs when they seek to buy video games with violent content may employ mystery shoppers to see whether their employees are actually doing so.

Analyzing customer complaints is crucial for improving products and customer service. Research indicates that only a few unsatisfied customers actually complain. Most unsatisfied customers say nothing but switch to competitors. A good **complaint analysis** system should encourage customers to (1) complain about an unsatisfactory product or service and (2) provide suggestions for improvements by completing forms asking specific questions beyond the routine "how was everything?" and (3) establish "listening posts" such as hotlines where specially designated employees either listen to customers' comments or actively solicit input from them (e.g., in a hotel lobby or on checkout lines). Since each complaint, by itself, provides little information, the company must have a system in which complaints are categorized and analyzed so that the results may be used to improve its operations.

Analyzing customer defections consists of finding out *why* customers leave the company. Customer loyalty rates are important because it is generally much cheaper to retain customers than to get new ones. Therefore, finding out why customers defect, and also *intervening* when customers' behaviors show that they may be considering leaving is crucial. For example, one bank that was losing about 20% of its customers every year discovered that segmenting defecting customers along demographic and family life-cycle characteristics was ineffective in reducing defection rates. The bank then compared 500 transaction records of loyal customers with 500 transaction records of defectors, using such dimensions as number of transactions, frequency of transactions, and fluctuations in average balances. The bank then identified transaction patterns that may indicate future defection and started targeting potential defectors and encouraging them to stay.[14]

Sampling and data collection

Since it is almost always impossible to obtain information from *every* member of the *population* or *universe* being studied, researchers use samples. A **sample** is a subset of the population that is used to estimate the characteristics of the entire population. Therefore, the sample must be *representative* of the universe under study. As the well-established Nielsen Media Research company recently found out, suspicions that a sample may not be representative of its universe endanger the credibility of all the data collected, and therefore must be addressed promptly. Although Nielsen's TV ratings have been used to estimate TV audiences and calculate advertising rates for many decades, its clients recently charged that the Nielsen sample was no longer representative of the U.S. population because it did not reflect accurately America's changing demographics and the large numbers of consumers who use devices such as TiVo to "time shift" and to avoid commercials during both live and recorded programs. In response to these criticisms, Nielsen has redesigned its sample to include significantly more ethnic groupings and to reflect the changes in TV viewing habits.[15]

An integral component of a research design is the sampling plan. Specifically, the sampling plan addresses three questions: whom to survey (the sampling unit), how many to survey (the sample size), and how to select them (the sampling procedure). Deciding whom to survey requires explicit definition of the *universe* or boundaries of the market from which data are sought so that an appropriate sample can be selected (such as working mothers). The size of the sample is dependent both on the size of the budget and on the degree of confidence that the marketer wants to place in the findings. The larger the sample, the more likely the responses will reflect the total universe under study. It is interesting to note, however, that a small sample can often provide highly reliable findings, depending on the sampling procedure adopted. (The exact number needed to achieve a specific level of confidence in the accuracy of the findings can be computed with a mathematical formula that is beyond the scope of this discussion.)

There are two types of samples: in a **probability sample**, respondents are selected in such a way that every member of the population studied has a known, non-zero chance of being selected. In a **nonprobability sample**, specific elements from the population under study have been predetermined in a nonrandom fashion on the basis of the researcher's judgment or decision to select a given number of respondents from a particular group. Table 2.4 summarizes the features of various types of probability and nonprobability designs.

As indicated earlier, qualitative studies usually require highly trained social scientists to collect data. A quantitative study generally uses a field staff that is either recruited and trained directly by the researcher or contracted from a company that specializes in conducting field interviews. In either case, it is often necessary to verify whether the interviews have,

TABLE 2.4	**Sampling**
PROBABILITY SAMPLE	
Simple Random Sample	Every member of the population has a known and equal chance of being selected.
Systematic Random Sample	A member of the population is selected at random and then every "*n*th" person is selected.
Stratified Random Sample	The population is divided into mutually exclusive groups (such as age groups), and random samples are drawn from each group.
Cluster (area) Sample	The population is divided into mutually exclusive groups (such as blocks), and the researcher draws a sample of the groups to interview.
NONPROBABILITY SAMPLE	
Convenience Sample	The researcher selects the most accessible population members from whom to obtain information (e.g., students in a classroom).
Judgment Sample	The researcher uses his or her judgment to select population members who are good sources for accurate information (e.g., experts in the relevant field of study).
Quota Sample	The researcher interviews a prescribed number of people in each of several categories (e.g., 50 men and 50 women).

in fact, taken place. This is sometimes done by a postcard mailing to respondents asking them to verify that they participated in an interview on the date recorded on the questionnaire form. Completed questionnaires are reviewed on a regular basis as the research study progresses to ensure that the recorded responses are clear, complete, and legible.

Data analysis and reporting research findings

In qualitative research, the moderator or test administrator usually analyzes the responses received. In quantitative research, the researcher supervises the analysis: Open-ended responses are first coded and quantified (i.e., converted into numerical scores); then all of the responses are tabulated and analyzed using sophisticated analytical programs that correlate the data by selected variables and cluster the data by selected demographic characteristics.

In both qualitative and quantitative research, the research report includes a brief executive summary of the findings. Depending on the assignment from marketing management, the research report may or may not include recommendations for marketing action. The body of the report includes a full description of the methodology used and, for quantitative research, also includes tables and graphics to support the findings. A sample of the questionnaire is usually included in the appendix to enable management to evaluate the objectivity of the findings.

Conducting a research study

In designing a research study, researchers adapt the research processes described in the previous sections to the special needs of the study. For example, if a researcher is told that the purpose of the study is to develop a segmentation strategy for a new online dating service, he or she would first collect secondary data, such as population statistics (e.g., the number of men and women online in selected metropolitan areas within a certain age range, their marital status, and occupations). Then, together with the marketing manager, the researcher would specify the parameters (i.e., define the sampling unit) of the population to be studied (e.g., single, college-educated men and women between the ages of 18 and 45 who live or work within the Boston metropolitan area). A qualitative study (e.g., focus groups) might be undertaken first to gather information about the target population's attitudes and concerns about meeting people online, their special interests, and the specific services and precautions they would like an online dating service to provide. This phase of the research should result in tentative generalizations about the specific age group(s) to target and the services to offer.

The marketing manager then might instruct the researcher to conduct a quantitative study to confirm and attach "hard" numbers (percentages) to the findings that emerged from the focus groups. The first-phase study should have provided sufficient insights to develop a research design and to launch directly into a large-scale survey. If, however, there is still doubt about any element of the research design, such as question wording or format, they might decide first to do a small-scale exploratory study. Then, after refining the questionnaire and any other needed elements of the research design, they would launch a full-scale quantitative survey, using a probability sample that would allow them to project the findings to the total population of singles (as originally defined). The analysis should cluster prospective consumers of the online dating service into segments based on relevant sociocultural or lifestyle characteristics and on media habits, attitudes, perceptions, and geodemographic characteristics.

ethics in consumer research

Consumer researchers must ensure that studies are objective and free of bias. Some studies are commissioned by organizations seeking to justify a particular position. For example, an organization opposed to the president of the United States may retain a research firm that will generate a national sample and ask respondents "do you believe that the president should be doing a better job in running the country?" Such a study may discover that, say, 65% of Americans believe that the president should be doing a better job. At the same time, another study using a national sample may ask respondents "do you approve or disapprove of the way the president is doing her job?" may also discover that 65% of Americans approve of the way the president is doing her job. The second study is more objective because the question was not stated in a biased fashion.

Researchers seeking to support a predetermined conclusion often do so by using biased samples and biased questions, manipulating statistical analyses, or ignoring relevant information. For example, a company offering a program for quitting smoking should not use only the successful graduates of its program in a study to be cited as evidence of the program's effectiveness.

Mistreating respondents is another ethical problem. Consumer researchers should avoid unnecessarily long interviews stemming from the logic that "as long as we are interviewing the person we may also try to find out. . . ." Lengthy interviews where consumers are held on the phone for 30 minutes (and often lied to when they ask how much longer the call is going to take) or mall-intercept surveys where respondents are asked "can we have a few minutes of your time" and later subjected to a 40-minute questioning must be avoided. Such methods severely hurt the credibility of consumer research because they cause more and more people to refuse to participate in studies. Another unethical approach is sales pitches from telemarketers disguised as research studies.

At the start of all surveys, interviewers must clearly identify themselves and the company for which they are working, explain what the survey entails, and state the true expected duration of the interview. They should reassure respondents that there are no right or wrong answers to the questions. If the respondents are being paid, they should be so notified at the start of the interview. Perhaps most importantly, the privacy of respondents must be protected and guaranteed. Regrettably, although interviewers routinely promise research subjects the confidentiality of responses and anonymity (i.e., not identifying respondents by name in data analysis or reports), some unethical consumer researchers have sold data about consumers to marketers seeking persons with specific characteristics that will be targeted as prospective buyers.

SUMMARY

The field of consumer research developed as an extension of the field of marketing research to enable marketers to predict how consumers would react in the marketplace and to understand the reasons they made the purchase decisions they did. Consumer research undertaken from a managerial perspective to improve strategic marketing decisions is known as positivism. Positivist research is quantitative and empirical and tries to identify cause-and-effect relationships in buying situations. It is often supplemented with qualitative research.

Qualitative research is concerned with probing deep within the consumer's psyche to understand the motivations, feelings, and emotions that drive consumer behavior. Qualitative research findings cannot be projected to larger populations but are used primarily to provide new ideas and insights for the development of positioning strategies. Interpretivism, a qualitative research perspective, is generally more concerned with understanding the act of consuming rather than the act of buying (consumer decision making). Interpretivists view consumer behaviour as a subset of human behavior, and increased understanding as a key to eliminating some of the ills associated with destructive consumer behavior.

Each theoretical research perspective is based on its own specific assumptions and uses its own research techniques. Positivists typically use probability studies that can be generalized to larger populations. Interpretivists tend to view consumption experiences as unique situations that occur at specific moments in time; therefore, they cannot be generalized to larger populations. The two theoretical research orientations are highly complementary and, when used together, provide a deeper and more insightful understanding of consumer behavior than either approach used alone.

The consumer research process—whether quantitative or qualitative in approach—consists of six steps: defining objectives, collecting secondary data, developing a research design, collecting primary data, analyzing the data, and preparing a report of the findings. The research objectives should be formulated jointly by the marketer and the person or company that will conduct the actual research. Findings from secondary data and exploratory research are used to refine the research objectives. The collection of secondary data includes both internal and external sources. Quantitative research designs consist of observation, experimentation or surveys, and, for the most part, questionnaires (that often include attitude scales) are used to collect the data.

Qualitative designs and data collection methods include depth interviews, focus groups, projective techniques, and metaphor analysis. Customer satisfaction measurement is an integral part of consumer research. In large, quantitative studies, the researcher must make every effort to ensure that the research findings are reliable (that a replication of the study would provide the same results) and valid (that they answer the specific questions for which the study was originally undertaken). The selection and design of the sample is crucial since the type of sample used determines the degree to which the results of the study are representative of the population. Following the data collection, the results are analyzed and specific analytic techniques applied respectively to qualitative or quantitative data. Consumer researchers must also observe specific ethical guidelines to ensure the integrity of their studies and the privacy of respondents.

DISCUSSION QUESTIONS

1. Have you ever been selected as a respondent in a marketing research survey? If yes, how were you contacted and where were you interviewed? Why do you think you, in particular, were selected? Did you know or could you guess the purpose of the survey? Do you know the name of the company or brand involved in the survey?

2. A consumer who rarely listens to music played on a portable device (e.g., an iPod) has purchased, on impulse and for $500, a pair of sunglasses with built-in earphones and the capability of playing MP3 files. Would the positivist or interpretivist research paradigm be a more appropriate way to study this consumption behavior? Explain your answer.

3. What is the difference between primary and secondary research? Under what circumstances might the availability of secondary data make primary research unnecessary? What are some major sources of secondary data?

4. What are the advantages and limitations of secondary data?

5. A manufacturer of a new product for whitening teeth would like to investigate the effects of package design and label information on consumers' perceptions of the product and their intentions to buy it. Would you advise the manufacturer to use observational research, experimentation, or a survey? Explain your choice.

6. Why might a researcher prefer to use focus groups rather than depth interviews? When might depth interviews be preferable?

7. Compare the advantages and disadvantages of mail, telephone, personal, and online surveys.

8. How would the interpretation of survey results change if the researcher used a probability sample rather than a nonprobability sample? Explain your answer.

9. Why is observation becoming a more important component of consumer research? Describe two new technologies that can be used to observe consumption behavior and explain why they are better to use than questioning consumers about the behavior being observed.

EXERCISES

1. Neutrogena is a manufacturer of personal care products for young adults. The company would like to extend its facial cleansers product line. Design (1) a qualitative and (2) a quantitative research design for the company focused on this objective.

2. A real-life customer tracking model is featured in Figure 2.2. Develop a similar model for tracking customers' visits to one of Disney's theme parks.

3. Using one of the customer satisfaction measures, construct an instrument to assess your fellow students' satisfaction with the technological support services provided by your university.

4. Using the scales in Figure 2.3, develop a questionnaire to measure students' attitudes toward the instructor in this course.

   a. Prepare five statements measuring students' attitudes via a Likert scale.

   b. Prepare five semantic differential scales to measure student attitudes. Can the same dimensions be measured by using either scaling technique? Explain your answer.

KEY TERMS

- **attitude scales**
- **complaint analysis**
- **consumer panel**
- **controlled experiment**
- **customer lifetime value profiles**
- **customer satisfaction measurement**
- **depth interview**
- **experimentation**
- **exploratory study**
- **focus group**

- **interpretivism**
- **mail surveys**
- **mechanical observation**
- **motivational research**
- **mystery shoppers**
- **nonprobability sample**
- **observational research**
- **online surveys**
- **personal interview survey**
- **physiological observation**
- **positivism**

- **primary data**
- **probability sample**
- **projective techniques**
- **qualitative research**
- **quantitative research**
- **reliability**
- **research objectives**
- **secondary data (internal and external)**
- **test marketing**
- **validity**

NOTES

1. Jon Gertner, "Our Rating, Ourselves," **www.nytimes.com**, April 10, 2005.

2. Melanie Wells, "Have It Your Way," *Forbes*, February 14, 2005, 78.

3. Leslie Kaufman, "Enough Talk," *Newsweek*, August 19, 1997, 48–49.

4. Emily Nelson, "P&G Checks Out Real Life," *Wall Street Journal* (Eastern Edition), May 17, 2001, B1.

5. Ian Mount, "The Mystery of Duane Reade," *New York Magazine*, June 6, 2005, 28–31.

6. Kim S. Nash, "Casinos Hit Jackpot with Customer Data," *Computer World*, July 2, 2001, 16–17; *Modern Marvels: Casino Technology*, VHS Tape, 1999, A&E Television Networks.

7. Alex Salkever, "The Technology of Personalized Pitches," *Business Week Online*, June 22, 2004.

8. Constance L. Hays, "What Wal-Mart Knows About Customers' Habits," **www.nytimes.com**, November 14, 2004.

9. Melanie Wells, "In Search of the Buy Button," *Forbes*, September 1, 2003, 62.

10. Brian D. Till and Michael Busler, "The Match-Up Hypothesis: Physical Attractiveness, Expertise, and the Role of Fit on Brand Attitude, Purchase Intent and Brand Beliefs," *Journal of Advertising* (Fall 2000): 1–13.

11. Robin A. Coutler, Gerald Zaltman, and Keith S. Coutler, "Interpreting Consumer Perceptions of Advertising: An Application of the Zaltman Metaphor Elicitation Technique," *Journal of Advertising* (Winter 2001): 1–21.

12. Thomas O. Jones and W. Earl Sasser, Jr., "Why Satisfied Customers Defect," *Harvard Business Review* (November–December 1995): 88–99.

13. A. Parasuraman, Valarie A. Zeithaml, and Leonard L. Berry, "Moving Forward in Service Quality Research: Measuring Different Customer-Expectation Levels, Comparing Alternative Scales, and Examining the Performance-Behavioral Intentions Link," Report No. 94-114, Marketing Science Institute, 1994.

14. Michael M. Pearson and Guy H. Gessner, "Transactional Segmentation to Slow Customer Defections," *Marketing Management* (Summer 1999): 16–23.

15. Stuart Elliott, "Nielsen Presents a Research Plan to Quell Concerns About Accuracy," **www.nytimes.com**, February 22, 2005; Stuart Elliott, "Nielsen Will Address Potential Undercounting of Minority TV Viewers," **www.nytimes.com**, March 24, 2005.

chapter**three**

> ## Market Segmentation

Market segmentation and diversity are complementary concepts. Without a diverse marketplace composed of many different peoples with different backgrounds, countries of origin, interests, needs and wants, and perceptions, there would be little reason to segment markets. Diversity in the global marketplace makes market segmentation an attractive, viable, and potentially highly profitable strategy. The necessary conditions for successful segmentation of any market are a large enough population with sufficient money to spend (general affluence) and sufficient diversity to lend itself to partitioning the market into sizable segments on the basis of demographic, psychological, or other strategic variables. The presence of these conditions in the United States, Canada, Western Europe, Japan, Australia, and other industrialized nations makes these marketplaces extremely attractive to global marketers.

When marketers provide a range of product or service choices to meet diverse consumer interests, consumers are better satisfied, and their overall happiness, satisfaction, and quality of life are ultimately enhanced. Thus, market segmentation is a positive force for both consumers and marketers alike.

Speed.
Selection.
Savings.

The Hertz #1 Club.®
That's renting wisely.

Sign up free at hertz.com. There are three ways The Hertz #1 Club can get your vacation off to a great start. **Speed.** The improved Hertz #1 Club lets you make reservations faster. And a special #1 Club Express® counter speeds you on your way. **Selection.** Now you can get the specific brand and model car you want, like the Ford Mustang, when you book a weekly or weekend rental. So the car you want is the one you get. Just go to hertz.com or call 1-800-654-3131. **Savings.** When you're a member of The Hertz #1 Club, you're also entitled to special deals. Like email offers for discounts, upgrades and more. And you can take advantage of all these benefits free. Just go to **hertz.com** to enroll. We'll take it from there. It's just another advantage of renting wisely.

Rent Wisely.™

what is market segmentation?

Market segmentation can be defined as the process of dividing a market into distinct subsets of consumers with common needs or characteristics and selecting one or more segments to target with a distinct marketing mix. Before the widespread acceptance of market segmentation, the prevailing way of doing business with consumers was through **mass marketing**—that is, offering the same product and marketing mix to all consumers. The essence of this strategy was summed up by the entrepreneur Henry Ford, who offered the Model T automobile to the public "in any color they wanted, as long as it was black."

If all consumers were alike—if they all had the same needs, wants, and desires, and the same background, education, and experience—mass (undifferentiated) marketing would be a logical strategy. Its primary advantage is that it costs less: Only one advertising campaign is needed, only one marketing strategy is developed, and usually only one standardized product is offered. Some companies, primarily those that deal in agricultural products or very basic manufactured goods, successfully follow a mass-marketing strategy. Other marketers, however, see major drawbacks in an undifferentiated marketing approach. When trying to sell the same product to every prospective customer with a single advertising campaign, the marketer must portray its product as a means for satisfying a common or generic need and, therefore, often ends up appealing to no one. A refrigerator may fulfill a widespread need to provide the home with a place to store perishable food that needs to be kept either cold or frozen (so that it does not spoil), but a standard-size refrigerator may be too big for a grandmother who lives alone and too small for a family of six. Without market differentiation, both the grandmother and the family of six would have to make do with the very same model, and, as we all know, "making do" is a far cry from being satisfied.

The strategy of segmentation allows producers to avoid head-on competition in the marketplace by differentiating their offerings, not only on the basis of price but also through styling, packaging, promotional appeal, method of distribution, and superior service. Marketers have found that the costs of consumer segmentation research, shorter production runs, and differentiated promotional campaigns are usually more than offset by increased sales. In most cases, consumers readily accept the passed-through cost increases for products that more closely satisfy their specific needs.

Market segmentation is just the first step in a three-phase marketing strategy. After segmenting the market into homogeneous clusters, the marketer then must select one or more segments to target. To accomplish this, the marketer must decide on a specific marketing mix—that is, a specific product, price, channel, and/or promotional appeal for each distinct segment. The third step is **positioning** the product so that it is perceived by the consumers in each target segment as satisfying their needs better than other competitive offerings.

Who uses market segmentation?

Because the strategy of market segmentation benefits both the consumer *and* the marketer, marketers of consumer goods are eager practitioners. For example, Chevrolet (**www.chevrolet.com**) targets its new Cobalt automobile with its sporty styling, minimal rear seat, and small trunk to young singles; it targets its Impala, a much larger vehicle, at the family car buyer needing a roomier vehicle. Another example is the market segmentation of marketers of wristwatches. To illustrate, Fossil (**www.fossil.com**), a manufacturer of popular priced fashion-conscious wristwatches, makes wristwatches to appeal to the demographics and functional-lifestyle need of consumers. More specifically, Fossil's watches (and those of many other wristwatch manufacturers) can be segmented in terms of four segments: (1) *gender of the wearer* (e.g., adult male versus adult female users), (2) *age of users* (e.g., first or starter watches, children's watches, or adult watches); (3) *function or lifestyle* (business dress, runners' watches, swimmers or divers watches, cell phone watches, etc.), and (4) *price* (e.g., watches costing less than $100, $100–$200, more than $200). Some limited edition and highly collectable wristwatches (e.g., some of those manufactured by firms like Carter, Rolex, and Patek Philippe) can cost $50,000 and up!

Hotels also segment their markets and target different chains to different market segments. For example, the Hilton Hotels family of brands (**www.hilton.com**) includes nine different hotel chains. A few examples of its lodging options and the prime target segments that Hilton is aiming at include *Embassy Suites Hotels* (for those desiring a two-room suite, cooked-to-order breakfast, and a nightly manager's reception), *Doubletree Hotels* (for those seeking contemporary, upscale accommodations), *Hampton Inns* (for price conscious travelers), *Homewood Suites* (for those seeking apartment-like accommodations for extended stays), and *Hilton Hotels* (stylish and sophisticated hotels for business and vacation travelers).

Industrial firms also segment their markets, as do not-for-profit organizations. For example, Peterbilt Motors Company (**www.peterbilt.com**) produces different models of trucks to meet the needs of long-haul truckers, construction projects, refuse collection companies, logging firms, and so on. The company's Web site offers a listing of its various vehicles by segment type. Charities such as the American Cancer Society (**www.cancer.org**) and UNICEF (**www.unicef.org**) frequently focus their fund-raising efforts on "heavy givers." Some performing arts centers segment their subscribers on the basis of *benefits sought* and have succeeded in increasing attendance through specialized promotional appeals.

How market segmentation operates

Segmentation studies are designed to discover the needs and wants of specific groups of consumers, so that specialized goods and services can be developed and promoted to satisfy each group's needs. Many new products have been developed to fill gaps in the marketplace revealed by segmentation research. For instance, Bayer Aspirin (**www.bayeraspirin.com**) has developed a variety of products that are designed to appeal directly to individuals with specific health issues (e.g., Bayer Rapid Headache Relief Formula, Bayer Back and Body Pain Formula, and Bayer Night Time Relief Formula).

In addition to filling product gaps, segmentation research is regularly used by marketers to identify the most appropriate media in which to place advertisements. Almost all media vehicles—from TV and radio stations to newspapers and magazines—use segmentation research to determine the characteristics of their audience and to publicize their findings in order to attract advertisers seeking a similar audience.

In some cases, if segments of customers are large enough and can attract enough advertising, the media will spin off separate programs or publications targeted to the specific segments. For example, *People* (**www.people.com**) has created a separate magazine for teenagers titled *Teen People* (**www.teenpeople.com**). In a somewhat similar fashion, *TIME* (**www.time.com**) targets different segments with special editions of its magazine. Not only does an advertiser have the choice of placing an ad in geographically based editions (e.g., international, U.S., regional, state, and spot market versions of each issue), but also some of the other editions offered by the magazine include a "Gold" edition for upscale mature adults, an "Inside Business" edition for top, middle, and technical management, and a "Women's" edition for affluent professional women. The magazine's Web site indicates that "there are more than 400 ways to buy advertising in *TIME*." New magazines, TV stations, and radio stations are constantly being created to meet the unfulfilled needs of specific market segments.

bases for segmentation

The first step in developing a segmentation strategy is to select the most appropriate base(s) on which to segment the market. Nine major categories of consumer characteristics provide the most popular bases for market segmentation. They include geographic factors, demographic factors, psychological factors, psychographic (lifestyle) characteristics, sociocultural variables, use-related characteristics, use-situation factors, benefits sought, and forms of **hybrid segmentation**—such as demographic-psychographic profiles, geodemographic factors, and values and lifestyles. Hybrid segmentation formats each use a combination of several segmentation bases to create rich and comprehensive profiles of particular consumer segments (e.g., a combination of a specific age range, income range, lifestyle, and profession). For example, the Bump Fighter Shaving System, manufactured by the American Safety Razor Company (**www.asrco.com**), is a replaceable-blade razor designed specifically for African American males. The product line has been expanded to now include shaving gel, skin conditioner, a disposable version of the razor, and a treatment mask (to be applied prior to sleeping). Table 3.1 lists the nine segmentation bases, divided into specific variables with examples of each. The following section discusses each of the nine segmentation bases. (Various psychological and sociocultural segmentation variables are examined in greater depth in later chapters.)

TABLE 3.1	Market Segmentation Categories and Selected Variables
SEGMENTATION BASE	**SELECTED SEGMENTATION VARIABLES**
GEOGRAPHIC SEGMENTATION	
Region	Southwest, Mountain states, Alaska, Hawaii
City size	Major metropolitan areas, small cities, towns
Density of area	Urban, suburban, exurban, rural
Climate	Temperate, hot, humid, rainy
DEMOGRAPHIC SEGMENTATION	
Age	Under 12, 12–17, 18–34, 35–49, 50–64, 65–74, 75–99, 100+
Sex	Male, female
Marital status	Single, married, divorced, living together, widowed
Income	Under $25,000, $25,000–$34,999, $35,000–$49,999, $50,000–$74,999, $75,000–$99,999, $100,000–$149,000, $150,000 and over
Education	Some high school, high school graduate, some college, college graduate, postgraduate
Occupation	Professional, blue-collar, white-collar, agricultural, military
PSYCHOLOGICAL SEGMENTATION	
Needs-motivation	Shelter, safety, security, affection, sense of self-worth
Personality	Extroverts, novelty seekers, aggressives, innovators
Perception	Low-risk, moderate-risk, high-risk
Learning-involvement	Low-involvement, high-involvement
Attitudes	Positive attitude, negative attitude
PSYCHOGRAPHIC	
(Lifestyle) Segmentation	Economy-minded, couch potatoes, outdoors enthusiasts, status seekers
SOCIOCULTURAL SEGMENTATION	
Cultures	American, Greek, Chinese, German, Mexican, French, Pakistani
Religion	Catholic, Protestant, Moslem, Jewish, other

(Continued)

TABLE 3.1	Continued

Subcultures (race/ethnic)	African American, Caucasian, Asian, Hispanic
Social class	Lower, middle, upper
Family life cycle	Bachelors, young marrieds, full nesters, empty nesters

USE-RELATED SEGMENTATION

Usage rate	Super heavy users, heavy users, medium users, light users, nonusers
Awareness status	Unaware, aware, interested, enthusiastic
Brand loyalty	None, some, strong

USE-SITUATION SEGMENTATION

Time	Leisure, work, rush, morning, night
Objective	Personal, gift, snack, fun, achievement
Location	Home, work, friend's home, in-store
Person	Self, family members, friends, boss, peer

BENEFIT SEGMENTATION

| | Convenience, social acceptance, long lasting, economy, value-for-the-money |

HYBRID SEGMENTATION

Demographic/psychographic	Combination of demographic and psychographic profiles of consumer segments profiles
PRIZM NE (Geodemographics)	"Movers & Shakers," "New Empty Nests," "Boomtown Singles," "Bedrock America"
SRI VALS™	Innovators, Thinkers, Believer, Achievers, Strivers, Experiencer, Makers, Survivors

PRIZM NE is an example of a geodemographic profile. VALS™ is an example of a demographic/psychographic profile.

Geographic segmentation

In **geographic segmentation**, the market is divided by location. The theory behind this strategy is that people who live in the same area share some similar needs and wants and that these needs and wants differ from those of people living in other areas. To illustrate, certain supermarket and specialty related products sell better in one market, or a particular region, than in others. For example, whereas coffee-bean grinders are a "must have" in kitchens of people living in the Northwest, they are much less common anywhere else in the United States; and, similarly, Starbucks Coffee (**www.starbucks.com**) sells plenty of full-body coffees on the West Coast, but needed to introduce a line of Milder Dimensions® coffees to better satisfy its East Coast consumers (who tend to prefer a milder coffee than their West Coast counterparts).[1]

Some marketing scholars have argued that direct-mail merchandise catalogs, national toll-free telephone numbers, satellite television transmission, global communication networks, and especially the Internet have erased all regional boundaries and that geographic segmentation should be replaced by a single global marketing strategy. Clearly, any company that decides to put its catalog on the Internet makes it easy for individuals all over the world to browse and become customers. For example, vintage wristwatch dealers in New York, Boston, or Dallas (primarily selling 1940s–1970s high-end wristwatches to collectors) have posted their catalogs on the Web, advertise their Web addresses in *International Wristwatch* and other similar magazines, and gladly accept orders from both U.S. and overseas customers. For the consumers who shop on the Internet, it often makes little difference if online retailers are around the corner or halfway around the world—the only factor that differs is the shipping charge.

Other marketers have, for a number of years, been moving in the opposite direction and developing highly regionalized marketing strategies. For example, Campbell's Soup (**www.campbellsoup.com**) segments its domestic market into more than 20 regions, each with its own advertising and promotion budget. Within each region, Campbell's sales managers have the authority to develop specific advertising and promotional campaigns geared to local market needs and conditions, using local media ranging from newspapers to church bulletins. They work closely with local retailers on displays and promotions and report that their **micromarketing** strategies have won strong consumer support.

Marketers have observed divergent consumer purchasing patterns among urban, suburban, and rural areas. Throughout the United States, more furs and expensive jewelry are sold in cities than in small towns. Even within a large metropolitan area, different types of household furnishings and leisure products are sold in the central city than in the suburbs. Convertible sofas and small appliances are more likely to be bought by city apartment dwellers; suburban homeowners are better prospects for lawn mowers and barbecue grills. Probably the best example of successful segmentation based on geographic density is the giant Wal-Mart operation (**www.walmart.com**). Historically, Wal-Mart's basic marketing strategy was to locate discount stores in small towns (often in rural areas) that other major retail chain operations were ignoring at the time. Now that Wal-Mart has become the largest retailer in the world with 3,600 stores in the United States and 1,500 stores outside the United States, the firm has opened new stores in more populated locales, such as San Diego, California, and the Long Island, New York suburban towns of Westbury and East Meadow (both suburbs of New York City).

In summary, geographic segmentation is a useful strategy for many marketers. It is relatively easy to find geographically based differences for many products. In addition, geographic segments can be easily reached through the local media, including newspapers, TV and radio, and regional editions of magazines.

Demographic segmentation

Demography refers to the vital and measurable statistics of a population. **Demographic characteristics**, such as age, sex, marital status, income, occupation, and education, are most often used as the basis for market segmentation. Demographics help to *locate* a target market, whereas psychological and sociocultural characteristics help to *describe* how its members *think* and how they *feel*. Demographic information is often the most accessible and cost-effective way to identify a target market. Indeed, most secondary data, including census data, are expressed in demographic terms. Demographics are easier to measure than other segmentation variables; they are invariably included in psychographic and sociocultural studies because they add meaning to the findings.

Demographic variables reveal ongoing trends that signal business opportunities, such as shifts in age, gender, and income distribution. For example, demographic studies consistently show that the "mature-adult market" (the 50+ market) has a much greater proportion of disposable income than its younger counterparts. This factor alone makes consumers over age 50 a critical market segment for products and services that they buy for themselves, for their adult children, and for their grandchildren.

Age

Product needs and interests often vary with consumers' age. For instance, younger investors (those in their 30s to late 40s) as might be expected, tend to seek long-term gains when they invest, whereas those over 55 years of age tend to be more cautious and place more importance on the intermediate gain and current income of a potential investment. Because of such age-motivated differences, marketers have found age to be a particularly useful demographic variable for market segmentation.

The largest demographic segment in the U.S. population consists of baby boomers, the 78 million consumers born between 1946 and 1964. They spend over $1 trillion annually,

TABLE 3.2	Segmenting Baby Boomers			
SEGMENT NAME	**LOOKING FOR BALANCE**	**CONFIDENT AND LIVING WELL**	**AT EASE**	**OVERWHELMED**
Percent of Boomers	27%	23%	31%	19%
Characteristics	Very active and busy lifestyle. Money is important, but so is saving time.	Have highest incomes, are first to buy a new product or service. Technologically oriented, stylish, and trendy.	At peace with themselves and do not worry about the future. Lowest interest in luxury goods, and do not travel much. Most home-centric and family-oriented group.	Lowest income segment, worried about the future and financial security. Least active group— health is a big concern. Least social group. Do not use high-tech products.
Marketing Implications	Want great experiences— a market for travel-related businesses and food service businesses.	Travel is a favorite interest. Want luxury goods and services.	A good market for traditional household products and services. Like trusted brand names. Low interest in new products.	Opportunity for marketers of certain financial service and healthcare products/ services.

Source: Dick Chay, "New Segments of Boomers Reveal New Mktg. Implications," *Marketing News,* March 15, 2005, 24.

and control 70 percent of the nation's wealth. While sometimes thought of as being "old" and "sickly," the reality is that 40 percent of all boomers believe that they are currently living the best years of their lives, and another 40 percent feel that the best years of their lives are still ahead of them. They are wealthy, optimistic, and have moved from a materialistic to a more experiential phase of their lives. Findings from a recent study, presented in Table 3.2 has segmented baby boomers into four subsegments—those "looking for balance," those "confident and living well," those "at ease," and those "overwhelmed."[2]

Many marketers have carved themselves a niche in the marketplace by concentrating on a specific age segment. For example, Heinz introduced EZ Squirt ketchup (which includes one version that is green in color) to better appeal to tweens,[3] and Aqua Velva, a 50-year-old brand of men's aftershave, is now targeting younger adult males with a new product, Ice Balm, which it advertises on both network and cable TV stations like Spike, ESPN, and the Speed Channel. Indeed, the men's grooming products category, which generates over $1 billion annually in sales, is experiencing a rapid expansion in terms of the number of new products being introduced each year. For instance, one firm, Sharps, positions itself as an outcast and tells users to "contemplate the goat" that appears on the product's package as part of the product usage instructions. It targets its products to young men who do not fit into a Hugo Boss or Calvin Klein category, and who view themselves as risk takers and marginally countercultural.[4] Still further, while four years ago McDonald's (**www.mcdonalds.com**) spent 80 percent of its advertising budget on prime-time television, today it spends less than half its budget on prime-time TV and has increased its spending on Internet portals in an effort to reach young customers online. Similarly, Coke is spending more than $3 million on interactive media in an attempt to better connect with 12- to 24-year-old consumers.[5]

Age, especially chronological age, implies a number of underlying forces. In particular, demographers have drawn an important distinction between *age effects* (occurrences due to chronological age) and *cohort effects* (occurrences due to growing up during a specific time period). Examples of the *age effect* are the heightened interest in leisure travel that often occurs for people (single and married) during middle age (particularly in their late

TABLE 3.3	Examples of Country-Specific or Region-Specific Cohort Defining Moments	
EVENT*	**DATE**	**COUNTRY AFFECTED**
John Profumo scandal	1963	UK
Nelson Mandela's imprisonment and release	1964 and 1990	South Africa
Cultural Revolution	1966–1976	China
Six Days War	1967	Jordan, Israel, and Egypt
Khmer Rouge Rule	1975–1979	Cambodia and South East Asia
Assassination of Anwar Sadat	1981	Egypt
Falklands War	1982	UK and Argentina
Assassination of Olof Palme	1986	Sweden
Tiananmen Square massacre	1989	China
Manuel Noriega's arrest and extradition to USA	1989	Panama
Japanese Economic 'bubble' bursts	1991	Japan
Irish legalisation of divorce	1995	Ireland

* These events are not ranked in order of importance, but by date.

Source: Charles D. Schewe and Geoffrey Meredith, "Segmenting Global Markets by Generational Cohorts: Determining Motivations by Age," *Journal of Consumer Behavior*, 4, October 2004, 56.

fifties or early sixties) and the interest in learning to play golf. Although people of all ages learn to play golf, it is particularly prevalent among people in their fifties. These two trends are examples of age effects because they especially seem to happen as people reach a particular age category.[6]

In contrast, the nature of *cohort effects* is captured by the idea that people hold onto the interests they grew up to appreciate. If 10 years from today it is determined that many rock-and-roll fans are over 55, it would not be because older people have suddenly altered their musical tastes but because the baby boomers who grew up with rock and roll have become older. As Bill Whitehead, CEO of the advertising agency Bates North America, noted: "When baby boomers are 70, they'll still eat pizza and still listen to the [Rolling] Stones."[7] It is important for marketers to be aware of the distinction between age effects and cohort effects: One stresses the impact of aging, whereas the second stresses the influence of the period when a person is born and the shared experiences with others of the same age. Table 3.3 presents a sample of "defining moments" that shaped particular age cohorts in specific countries or regions. We must remember that cohort effects are ongoing and lifelong. To illustrate this point, Table 3.4 identifies and distinguishes among seven different American age cohort groupings.[8]

The selected age segments will receive more attention in our discussion of age as a subculture in Chapter 13.

Sex

Like age, gender is quite frequently a distinguishing segmentation variable. Some products and services are quite naturally associated more or less with males or females. For instance, women have traditionally been the main users of such products as hair coloring and cosmetics, and men have been the main users of tools and shaving preparations. However, sex roles have blurred, and gender is no longer an accurate way to distinguish consumers in some product categories. For example, women are buying household repair tools, and men have become significant users of skin care and hair products. It is becoming increasingly common to see magazine ads and TV commercials that depict men and women in roles traditionally occupied by the opposite sex. For example, many ads reflect the expanded child-nurturing roles of young fathers in today's society.

TABLE 3.4	Four Selected American Cohorts
Leading-edge baby boomer cohort (born from 1946–1954; came of age during the turmoil of the 1960s; aged 50–58 in 2004)	This group remembers the assassinations of John and Robert Kennedy and Martin Luther King, Jr. It was the loss of JFK that largely shaped this cohort's values. They became adults during the Vietnam War and watched as the first man walked on the moon. Leading-edge boomers were dichotomous: they championed causes (Greenpeace, civil rights, women's rights), yet were simultaneously hedonistic and self-indulgent (pot, 'free love,' sensuality).
Trailing-edge baby boomer cohort (born from 1955–1965; came of age during the first sustained economic downturn since the Depression; aged 39–49 in 2004)	This group witnessed the fall of Vietnam, Watergate Nixon's resignation. The oil embargo, the raging inflation rate, and the more than 30 percent decline in the S&P Index led these individuals, to be less optimistic about their financial future than the leading-edge boomers.
Generation X cohort (born from 1965–1976; came of age during a time of instability and uncertainty; aged 28–38 in 2004)	These are the latchkey children of divorce who have received the most negative publicity. This cohort has delayed marriage and children, and they do not take these commitments lightly. More than other groups, this cohort accepts cultural diversity and puts quality of personal life ahead of work life. They are 'free agents' not 'team players.' Despite a rocky start into adulthood, this group shows a spirit of entrepreneurship unmatched by any other cohort.
N Generation cohort (born from 1977–?; came of age during the 'Information Revolution'; aged 27 and under in 2004)	The youngest cohort is called the 'N Generation' or 'N-Gen' because the advent of the Internet is a defining event for them, and because they will be the 'engine' of growth over the next two decades. While still a work in progress, their core value structure seems to be quite different from that of Gen-X. They are more idealistic and social-cause oriented, without the cynical, 'What's in it for me?' free-agent mindset of many Gen-Xers.

Source: Charles D. Schewe and Geoffrey Meredith, "Segmenting Global Markets by Generational Cohorts: Determining Motivations by Age," *Journal of Consumer Behavior,* 4, October 2004, 54.

Much of the change in sex roles has occurred because of the continued impact of dual-income households. One consequence for marketers is that women are not as readily accessible through traditional media as they once were. Because working women do not have much time to watch TV or listen to the radio, many advertisers now emphasize magazines in their media schedules, especially those specifically aimed at working women (e.g., *Working Mother*). Direct marketers also have been targeting time-pressured working women who use merchandise catalogs, convenient 800 numbers, and Internet sites as ways of shopping for personal clothing and accessories, as well as many household and family needs. Recent research has shown that men and women differ in terms of the way they look at their Internet usage. Specifically, men tend to "click on" a Web site because they are "information hungry," whereas women click because "they expect communications media to entertain and educate."[9] Interestingly, analysis undertaken by Wal-Mart has revealed that more women than men shop their Web site, and that their typical online customer is a working mom who uses the Internet to satisfy a portion of her shopping needs.[10] Still further, the research indicates that 92 percent of Wal-Mart's online shoppers visit a Wal-Mart store at least once a month, and these online customers have higher income and education levels than their only in-store shopper counterparts. Table 3.5 presents additional male and female differences when it comes to using the Internet and compares some key usage situations and favorite Internet materials for men versus women.

Furthermore, when it comes to being "hungry," research shows that young men are "more likely than average to go to a quick service restaurant for breakfast." Burger King, which controls only 10 percent of this breakfast market (compared to McDonald's 40 percent), has come to the conclusion that young men want tasty food, and are

TABLE 3.5	Male and Female Segments of Internet Users	
	KEY USAGE SITUATION	**FAVORITE INTERNET MATERIALS**
FEMALE SEGMENTS		
Social Sally	Making friends	Chat and personal Web page
New Age Crusader	Fighting for causes	Books and government information
Cautious Mom	Nurturing children	Cooking and medical facts
Playful Pretender	Role-playing	Chat and games
Master Producer	Job productivity	White pages and government information
MALE SEGMENTS		
Bits and Bytes	Computers and hobbies	Investments, discovery, software
Practical Pete	Personal productivity	Investments, company listings
Viking Gamer	Competing and winning	Games, chat, software
Sensitive Sam	Helping family and friends	Investments, government information
World Citizen	Connecting with world	Discovery, software, investments

Source: Scott Smith and David Whitlark, "Men and Women Online: What Makes Them Click," *Marketing Research*, Summer 2001, 22.

unconcerned about calories and fat content. Consequently, Burger King is now offering the *Enormous Omelet*, complete with 730 calories, 47 grams of fat, 415 mg of cholesterol, and 1,860 mg of sodium.[11] In contrast to both McDonalds and Burger King, Wendy's has tended to feature menu options like its *Fresh Fruit Bowl* that appeal to women.

Marital status

Traditionally, the family has been the focus of most marketing efforts, and for many products and services, the household continues to be the relevant consuming unit. Marketers are interested in the number and kinds of households that buy and/or own certain products. They also are interested in determining the demographic and media profiles of household decision makers (the persons involved in the actual selection of the product) to develop appropriate marketing strategies.

Marketers have discovered the benefits of targeting specific marital status groupings, such as singles, divorced individuals, single parents, and dual-income married couples. For instance, singles, especially one-person households with incomes greater than $50,000, comprise a market segment that tends to be above average in the usage of products not traditionally associated with supermarkets (e.g., cognac, books, loose tea) and below average in their consumption of traditional supermarket products (e.g., catsup, peanut butter, mayonnaise). Such insights can be particularly useful to a supermarket manager operating in a neighborhood of one-person households when deciding on the merchandise mix for the store. Some marketers target one-person households with single-serving foods (e.g., Bumble Bee tuna's 3 oz. easy-open cans, Pringles single serving-size cans, Orville Redenbacher's popcorn mini-bags, Campbell's Soup To Go!) and others with mini-appliances such as small microwave ovens and two-cup coffee makers. (The family as a consuming unit is discussed in greater detail in Chapter 10.)

Income, education, and occupation

Income has long been an important variable for distinguishing between market segments. Marketers commonly segment markets on the basis of income because they feel that it is a strong indicator of the ability (or inability) to pay for a product or a specific model of the product. For instance, consider *Panache*, the lifestyle magazine of the Fort Worth (TX) *Star-Telegram*. It struggled for six years at 16 pages per issue, and was basically going nowhere. But then, using the PRIZM geodemographic segmentation scheme from Claritas (which will be discussed later in this chapter), *Panache*'s distribution was changed so that it was only delivered to the homes of subscribers with $100,000+ annual incomes. Advertisers become enthusiastic about the magazine, and within a few months it grew to a 40 page per issue publication.[12]

Income is often combined with other demographic variables to more accurately define target markets. To illustrate, high income has been combined with age to identify the important *affluent elderly* segment. It also has been combined with both age and occupational status to produce the so-called *yuppie* segment, a sought-after subgroup of the baby boomer market.

Education, occupation, and income tend to be closely correlated in almost a cause-and-effect relationship. High-level occupations that produce high incomes usually require advanced educational training. Individuals with little education rarely qualify for high-level jobs. Insights on Internet usage preferences tend to support the close relationship among income, occupation, and education. Research reveals that consumers with lower incomes, lower education, as well as those with blue-collar occupations, tend to spend more time online at home than those with higher income, higher education, and white-collar occupations.[13] One possible reason for this difference is that those in blue-collar jobs often do not have access to the Internet during the course of the workday.

Psychological segmentation

Psychological characteristics refer to the inner or intrinsic qualities of the individual consumer. Consumer segmentation strategies are often based on specific psychological variables. For instance, consumers may be segmented in terms of their *motivations, personality, perceptions, learning,* and *attitudes.* (Part 2 examines in detail the wide range of psychological variables that influence consumer decision-making and consumption behavior.)

Psychographic segmentation

Marketing practitioners have heartily embraced psychographic research, which is closely aligned with psychological research, especially personality and attitude measurement. This form of applied consumer research (commonly referred to as lifestyle analysis) has proven to be a valuable marketing tool that helps identify promising consumer segments that are likely to be responsive to specific marketing messages.

The psychographic profile of a consumer segment can be thought of as a composite of consumers' measured **activities, interests, and opinions (AIOs)**. As an approach to constructing consumer psychographic profiles, AIO research seeks consumers' responses to a large number of statements that measure activities (how the consumer or family spends time, e.g., camping, volunteering at a local hospital, going to baseball games), interests (the consumer's or family's preferences and priorities, e.g., home, fashion, food), and opinions (how the consumer feels about a wide variety of events and political issues, social issues, the state of the economy, ecology). In their most common form, AIO-psychographic studies use a battery of statements (a **psychographic inventory**) designed to identify relevant aspects of a consumer's personality, buying motives, interests, attitudes, beliefs, and values. Table 3.6 presents a portion of a psychographic inventory designed to gauge "techno-road-warriors," businesspeople who spend a high percentage of their workweek on the road, equipped with laptops, pagers, cellular telephones, and electronic organizers. Table 3.7 presents a likely psychographic profile of a techno-road-warrior. The appeal of psychographic research lies in the frequently vivid and practical profiles of consumer segments that it can produce (which will be illustrated later in this chapter).

TABLE 3.6	A Portion of an AIO Inventory Used to Identify Techno-Road-Warriors

Instructions: *Please read each statement and place an "x" in the box that **best** indicates how strongly you **"agree"** or **"disagree"** with the statement.*

	AGREE COMPLETELY						DISAGREE COMPLETELY
I feel that my life is moving faster and faster, sometimes just too fast.	[1]	[2]	[3]	[4]	[5]	[6]	[7]
If I could consider the "pluses" and "minuses," technology has been good for me.	[1]	[2]	[3]	[4]	[5]	[6]	[7]
I find that I have to pull myself away from e-mail.	[1]	[2]	[3]	[4]	[5]	[6]	[7]
Given my lifestyle, I have more of a shortage of time than money.	[1]	[2]	[3]	[4]	[5]	[6]	[7]
I like the benefits of the Internet, but I often don't have the time to take advantage of them.	[1]	[2]	[3]	[4]	[5]	[6]	[7]
I am generally open to considering new practices and new technology.	[1]	[2]	[3]	[4]	[5]	[6]	[7]

AIO research has even been employed to explore pet ownership as a segmentation base. One study has found that people who do **not** have pets are more conservative in nature, more brand loyal, and more likely to agree with statements such as "I am very good at managing money" and "It is important for me to look well dressed." Such findings can be used by marketers when developing promotional messages for their products and services.[14]

The results of psychographic segmentation efforts are frequently reflected in firms' marketing messages. For instance, Asics running shoes (see Figure 3.1) are targeted to individuals (in this case, women) who thrive on the challenge of running (**www.asics.com**). Psychographic segmentation is further discussed later in the chapter, where we consider hybrid segmentation strategies that combine psychographic and demographic variables to create rich descriptive profiles of consumer segments.

Sociocultural segmentation

Sociological (group) and *anthropological* (cultural) variables—that is, **sociocultural variables**—provide further bases for market segmentation. For example, consumer markets have been successfully subdivided into segments on the basis of stage in the

TABLE 3.7	A Hypothetical Psychographic Profile of the Techno-Road-Warrior

- *Goes on the Internet more than six times a week*
- *Sends and/or receives 15 or more e-mail messages a week*
- *Regularly visits Web sites to gather information and/or to comparison shop*
- *Often buys personal items via 800 numbers and/or over the Internet*
- *May trade stocks and/or make travel reservations over the Internet*
- *Earns $100,000 or more a year*
- *Belongs to several rewards programs (e.g., frequent flyer programs, hotel programs, rent-a-car programs)*

FIGURE 3.1

Source: © asics

Asics Targets a "Runner's" Lifestyle

family life cycle, social class, core cultural values, subcultural memberships, and cross-cultural affiliation.

Family life cycle

Family life-cycle segmentation is based on the premise that many families pass through similar phases in their formation, growth, and final dissolution. At each phase, the family unit needs different products and services. Young single people, for example, need basic furniture for their first apartment, whereas their parents, finally free of child rearing, often refurnish their homes with more elaborate pieces. Family life cycle is a composite variable based explicitly on *marital* and *family status* but implicitly reflects *relative age, income,* and *employment status.* Each of the stages in the traditional family life cycle (*bachelorhood, honeymooners, parenthood, postparenthood,* and *dissolution*) represents an important target segment to a variety of marketers. For example, the financial services industry frequently segments customers in terms of family life-cycle stages because families' financial needs tend to shift as they progress through the various stages of life. (Chapter 10 discusses the family life cycle in greater depth and shows how marketers cater to the needs and wishes of consumers in each stage of the life cycle.)

Social class

Social class (or relative status in the community) can be used as a base for market segmentation and is usually measured by a weighted index of several demographic variables, such as education, occupation, and income. The concept of *social class* implies a hierarchy in which individuals in the same class generally have the same degree of status, whereas members of other classes have either higher or lower status. Studies have shown that consumers in different social classes vary in terms of values, product preferences, and buying habits. Many major banks and investment companies, for example, offer a variety of different levels of service to people of different social classes (e.g., private banking services to the upper classes). For example, some investment companies appeal to upper-class customers with offering them options that correspond to their wealthy status. In contrast, a financial program targeted to a lower social class might talk instead about savings accounts or certificates of deposit. Chapter 11 discusses in depth the use of social class as a segmentation variable.

Culture and subculture

Some marketers have found it useful to segment their markets on the basis of cultural heritage because members of the same culture tend to share the same values, beliefs, and customs. Marketers who use cultural segmentation stress specific, widely held cultural values with which they hope consumers will identify (e.g., for American consumers, *youthfulness* and *fitness and health*). Cultural segmentation is particularly successful in international marketing, but it is important for the marketer to understand fully the target country's beliefs, values, and customs (the cross-cultural context).

Within the larger culture, distinct subgroups (subcultures) often are united by certain experiences, values, or beliefs that make effective market segments. These groupings could be based on a specific demographic characteristic (such as race, religion, ethnicity, or age) or lifestyle characteristic (teachers, joggers). In the United States, African Americans, Hispanic Americans, Asian Americans, and the elderly are important subcultural market segments. Research on subcultural differences, which will be discussed more fully in Chapter 13, tends to reveal that consumers are more responsive to promotional messages that they perceive relate to their own ethnicity (e.g., African American consumers tend to respond favorably to marketers who recognize and respond positively to their specific interests and background).[15]

Culturally distinct segments can be prospects for the same product but often are targeted more efficiently with different promotional appeals. For example, a bicycle might be promoted as an efficient means of transportation in parts of Asia and as a health-and-fitness product in the United States. Moreover, a recent study that divided China's urban consumers into four segments ("working poor," "salary class," "little rich," and "yuppies") found that for all four groups, television was the most popular medium of entertainment and information. However, the working poor spend the most time listening to radio, while yuppies and the little rich spend the most time reading newspapers and magazines.[16] (Chapters 12, 13, and 14 examine cultural, subcultural, and cross-cultural bases of market segmentation in greater detail.)

Cross-cultural or global marketing segmentation

As the world has gotten smaller and smaller, a true global marketplace has developed. For example, as you read this you may be sitting on an IKEA chair or sofa (Sweden), drinking Earl Grey tea (England), wearing a Swatch watch (Switzerland), Nike sneakers (China), a Polo golf shirt (Mexico), and Dockers pants (Dominican Republic). Some global market segments, such as teenagers, appear to want the same types of products, regardless of which nation they call home—products that are trendy, entertaining, and image oriented. This global "sameness" allowed Reebok, for example, to launch its Instapump line of sneakers using the same global advertising campaign in approximately 140 countries.[17] (The issue of global or international marketing segmentation will be more fully discussed in Chapter 14.)

Use-related segmentation

An extremely popular and effective form of segmentation categorizes consumers in terms of product, service, or brand usage characteristics, such as level of usage, level of awareness, and degree of brand loyalty.

Rate of usage segmentation differentiates among heavy users, medium users, light users, and nonusers of a specific product, service, or brand. For example, research has consistently indicated that between 25 and 35 percent of beer drinkers account for more than 70 percent of all beer consumed. For this reason, most marketers prefer to target their advertising campaigns to heavy users rather than spend considerably more money trying to attract light users. This also explains the successful targeting of light beer to heavy drinkers on the basis that it is less filling (and, thus, can be consumed in greater quantities) than regular beer. Recent studies have found that heavy soup users were more socially active, creative, optimistic, witty, and less stubborn than light users and nonusers, and they were also less likely to read entertainment and sports magazines and more likely to read family and home magazines. Likewise, heavy users of travel agents in Singapore were more involved with and more enthusiastic about vacation travel, more innovative with regard to their selection of vacation travel products, more likely to travel for pleasure, and more widely exposed to travel information from the mass media.[18]

Marketers of a host of other products have also found that a relatively small group of heavy users accounts for a disproportionately large percentage of product usage; targeting these heavy users has become the basis of their marketing strategies. Other marketers take note of the gaps in market coverage for light and medium users and profitably target those segments. Table 3.8 presents an overview of a segmentation strategy especially suitable for marketers seeking to organize their database of customers into an action-oriented framework. The framework proposes a way to identify a firm's best customers by dividing the database into the following segments: (1) *LoLows* (low current share, low-consumption customers), (2) *HiLows* (high current share, low-consumption customers), (3) *LowHighs* (low current share, high-consumption customers), and (4) *HiHighs* (high current share, high-consumption customers). Moreover, the framework suggests the following specific strategies for each of the four segments: "starve" the *LoLows*, "tickle" the *HiLows*, "chase" the *LowHighs*, and "stroke" the *HiHighs*.[19]

In addition to segmenting customers in terms of rate of usage or other usage patterns, consumers can also be segmented in terms of their *awareness status*. In particular,

---

TABLE 3.8	A Framework for Segmenting a Firm's Database of Customers	
SEGMENT NAME	**SEGMENT CHARACTERISTIC**	**COMPANY ACTION**
LoLows	Low current share, low-consumption customers	Starve
HiLows	High current share, low-consumption customers	Tickle
LowHighs	Low current share, high-consumption customers	Chase
HiHighs	High current share, high-consumption customers	Stroke

Source: Richard G. Barlow, "How to Court Various Target Markets," *Marketing News*, October 9, 2000, 22.

FIGURE 3.2

Source: © Veterinary Pet Insurance Company.

VPI Pet Insurance Seeks to Create Awareness and Interest

You love your pet. You want her to get the best care when she gets sick or hurt. With VPI Pet Insurance, you can be sure of it. As the nation's largest and oldest provider of health insurance for pets, VPI offers affordable coverage for emergency and major medical care, plus routine procedures like spaying/neutering and vaccinations. We even help cover prescriptions and lab fees. What's more, you can go to the veterinarian of your choice. Which leads us to the biggest benefit of all: peace of mind. For an instant quote, visit petinsurance.com or call 800-USA-PETS (800-872-7387)

Enroll Today
it's *Easy* and *Affordable*
petinsurance.com
800-USA-PETS

The health insurance is
FOR HER
Many of the benefits are
FOR YOU

All applications are subject to underwriting approval/Underwritten by Veterinary Pet Insurance Co. (CA), Brea, CA/National Casuality Co. (Nat), Macison, WI, an A+ 15 rated company/©2005 Veterinary Pet Insurance Co.

the notion of consumer awareness of the product, interest level in the product, readiness to buy the product, or whether consumers need to be informed about the product are all aspects of awareness. Figure 3.2 presents an ad for VPI Pet Insurance™ (**www.petinsurance.com**) that is designed to create both awareness and interest, among pet owners, for their pet insurance.

Sometimes *brand loyalty* is used as the basis for segmentation. Marketers often try to identify the characteristics of their brand-loyal consumers so that they can direct their promotional efforts to people with similar characteristics in the larger population. Other marketers target consumers who show no brand loyalty ("brand switchers") in the belief that such people represent greater market potential than consumers who are loyal to competing brands. Also, almost by definition, consumer innovators—often a prime

FIGURE 3.3

Source: © 2005 Hertz System, Inc. Hertz is a registered service mark and trademark of Hertz System, Inc.

Speed.
Selection.
Savings.

The Hertz #1 Club.®
That's renting wisely.

Hertz—"Speed. Selection. Savings."

Sign up free at hertz.com. There are three ways The Hertz #1 Club can get your vacation off to a great start. **Speed.** The improved Hertz #1 Club lets you make reservations faster. And a special #1 Club Express® counter speeds you on your way. **Selection.** Now you can get the specific brand and model car you want, like the Ford Mustang, when you book a weekly or weekend rental. So the car you want is the one you get. Just go to hertz.com or call 1-800-654-3131. **Savings.** When you're a member of The Hertz #1 Club, you're also entitled to special deals. Like email offers for discounts, upgrades and more. And you can take advantage of all these benefits free. Just go to **hertz.com** to enroll. We'll take it from there. It's just another advantage of renting wisely.

Rent Wisely.™

target for new products—tend *not* to be brand loyal. (Chapter 15 discusses the characteristics of consumer innovators.)

Increasingly, marketers stimulate and reward brand loyalty by offering special benefits to consistent or frequent customers. Such frequent usage or relationship programs often take the form of a membership club (e.g., Continental Airline's OnePass Platinum Elite Status, Hilton HHonors Diamond VIP Membership, Avis' Wizard Preferred Service Program). Relationship programs, such as The Hertz #1 Club® as in Figure 3.3, tend to provide special accommodations and services, as well as free extras, to keep these frequent customers loyal and happy.

Usage-situation segmentation

Marketers recognize that the occasion or situation often determines what consumers will purchase or consume. For this reason, they sometimes focus on the **usage situation** as a segmentation variable.

The following three statements reveal the potential of situation segmentation: "Whenever our son Eric gets a raise or a promotion, we always take him out to dinner"; "When I'm away on business for a week or more, I try to stay at a Suites hotel"; "I always buy my wife candy on Valentine's Day." Under other circumstances, in other situations, and on other occasions, the same consumer might make other choices. Some situational factors that might influence a purchase or consumption choice includes whether it is a weekday or weekend (e.g., going to a movie); whether there is sufficient time (e.g., use of regular mail or express mail); whether it is a gift for a girlfriend, a parent, or a self-gift (a reward to one's self).

Many products are promoted for special usage occasions. The greeting card industry, for example, stresses special cards for a variety of occasions that seem to be increasing almost daily (Grandparents' Day, Secretaries' Day, etc.). The florist and candy industries promote their products for Valentine's Day and Mother's Day, the diamond industry promotes diamond rings as an engagement symbol, and the wristwatch industry promotes its products as graduation gifts. The Russell Stover® ad in Figure 3.4 (**www.russellstover.com**) is an example of situational, special usage segmentation. It appeared in magazines several weeks prior to holidays such as Christmas and Valentine's Day. The particular ad is making the point that they have been around for the holiday—since 1923.

A recent study found that individuals who purchase their magazines at newsstands are more active consumers and are more receptive to advertising than consumers who subscribe to the very same magazines. As the research noted, "this is the holy grail for advertisers."[20] Table 3.9 presents a comparison of newsstand magazine buyers versus magazine subscribers.

Situational factors as a base for segmentation have also been studied in relation to retailing. For example, in situations where the shopper has ample time, shopping atmosphere, stocking the right brands, and general familiarity with the retailer are important. Conversely, a shopper with less time wants to shop where a large selection of merchandise is immediately available, with no transaction hassles (i.e., for clothing, the ability to touch and try on merchandise).[21]

Benefit segmentation

Marketing and advertising executives constantly attempt to identify the one most important benefit of their product or service that will be most meaningful to consumers. Examples of benefits that are commonly used include *cleaner teeth* (Oral-B), *financial security* (Transamerica), *protection of data* (Norton Antivirus), *soft skin* (Olay), *allergy relief* (Allegra), and *peace of mind* (Liberty Mutual Insurance Company).

In targeting Indian consumers in terms of benefits sought, research revealed that an important segment of Indian consumers of Dettol soap were hygiene-conscious and seeking protection from germs and contamination, rather than more common benefits of beauty, fragrance, freshness, or economy.[22] Still further, a segmentation study examining what drives consumer preferences for micro or craft beer, identified the following five strategic brand benefits: (1) functional (i.e., quality), (2) value for the money, (3) social benefit, (4) positive emotional benefits, and 5) negative emotional benefits.[23]

FIGURE 3.4

Source: © Russell Stover
Candies. Inc. Used with
permission. All rights reserved.

**An Example of One Russell
Stover Candy's Special Holiday
Promotion**

Changing lifestyles also play a major role in determining the product benefits that are important to consumers and provide marketers with opportunities for new products and services. For example, the microwave oven was the perfect solution to the needs of dual-income households, where neither the husband nor the wife has the time for lengthy meal preparation. Food marketers offer busy families the *benefit* of breakfast products that require only seconds to prepare.

Benefit segmentation can be used to position various brands within the same product category.[24] The classic case of successful benefit segmentation is the market for toothpaste, and a recent article suggested that if consumers are socially active, they want a toothpaste that can deliver white teeth and fresh breath; if they smoke, they want a

TABLE 3.9	**Newsstand Magazine Buyers versus Magazine Subscribers**

Consumers who buy magazines on the newsstand are:

- Two times as likely to enjoy reading ads in magazines
- 63 percent more likely to remember products advertised in magazines when they are shopping
- 48 percent more likely to shop frequently
- 50 percent more likely to buy things on the spur of the moment
- Twice as likely to spend more money on cosmetics than subscribers
- 58 percent more likely to buy leading cosmetic brands
- Nearly twice as likely to enjoy shopping for clothes
- 50 percent more likely to try new alcoholic drinks than subscribers
- 58 percent more likely to drink super-premium vodka
- Four times more likely to download music than subscribers
- More than twice as likely to purchase video games in the last 12 months
- Twice as likely to purchase designer jeans

Source: "New Study Reveals Newsstand Magazine Buyers to be More Active Consumers and More Receptive to Advertising," *Business Wire*, September 8, 2004, 1.

toothpaste to fight stains; if disease prevention is their major focus, then they want a toothpaste that will fight germs; and if they have children, they want to lower their dental bills[25] (see Figure 3.5).

Hybrid segmentation approaches

Marketers commonly segment markets by combining several segmentation variables rather than relying on a single segmentation base. This section examines three hybrid segmentation approaches that provide marketers with richer and more accurately defined consumer segments than can be derived from using a single segmentation variable. These include psychographic-demographic profiles, geodemographics, VALS, and Yankelovich's Mindbase Segmentation.

Psychographic, lifestyle, and demographic profiles

Psychographic (including lifestyles) and demographic profiles are highly complementary approaches that work best when used together. By combining the knowledge gained from including both demographic and psychographic factors, marketers are provided with powerful information about their target markets.

Demographic-psychographic profiling has been widely used in the development of advertising campaigns to answer three questions: "Whom should we target?" "What should we say?" "Where should we say it?" To help advertisers answer the third question, many advertising media vehicles sponsor demographic-lifestyle research on which they base very detailed *audience profiles*. Tables 3.10 and 3.11 present a portion of the demographic and psychographic-lifestyle profiles of *USA Today* (i.e., its newspaper, its Web site, and both) that is independently prepared by MMI (i.e., an audience research firm that prepares profiles of many magazine and newspaper readers). In the case of *USA Today*, such information is made available in the form of advertising information kits or alternatively is available on their Web sites (**www.usatoday.com**). *USA Today*, as well as many other newspapers and magazines, provide potential and current advertisers with such profiles to assist advertisers in making decisions as to where they are going to

FIGURE 3.5

Source: Courtesy of Procter &
Gamble Co.

Introducing a toothpaste that's
sensitive to apple pie à la
mode lovers

spend their advertising budgets. By offering media advertisers such carefully defined profiles of their audiences, mass media publishers and broadcasters make it possible for advertisers to select media whose audiences most closely resemble their target markets.

Finally, advertisers are increasingly designing ads that depict in words and/or pictures the essence of a particular target-market lifestyle or segment that they want to reach. In this spirit, Dream Catcher is seeking to inform its target audiences—about its cost effective destination club (see Figure 3.6).

TABLE 3.10	Selected Demographic Profile of USA Today		
	USA TODAY	**USATODAY.COM**	**USA TODAY NETWORK***
Total Readers	5,227,000	1,870,000	6,219,000
Gender			
Men	66%	70%	66%
Women	34%	30%	34%
Age			
Age 18–49	62%	73%	64%
Age 25–54	65%	78%	67%
Age 55+	27%	18%	25%
Average Age	45	43	45
Education			
Attended college or beyond	77%	83%	77%
College graduate or beyond	55%	65%	56%
Occupation			
Professional/Managerial	34%	52%	36%
Top/Middle Manager	33%	36%	32%
Employed	80%	85%	81%
Income			
HHI $50,000 or more	75%	79%	75%
HHI $60,000 or more	66%	68%	65%
HHI $75,000 or more	50%	56%	50%
HHI $100,000 or more	31%	30%	30%
Average HHI	$91,210	$90,861	$89,572
Median HHI	$74,715	$80,628	$74,838

* Unduplicated combined daily audience for USA TODAY and USATODAY.com.

Source: Fall 2004 MRI

Geodemographic segmentation

This type of hybrid segmentation scheme is based on the notion that people who live close to one another are likely to have similar financial means, tastes, preferences, lifestyles, and consumption habits (similar to the old adage, "Birds of a feather flock together"). This segmentation approach uses computers to generate geodemographic market clusters of like consumers. Specifically, computer software clusters the nation's 250,000+ neighborhoods into lifestyle groupings based on postal zip codes. Clusters are created based on consumer lifestyles, and a specific cluster includes zip codes that are composed of people with similar lifestyles widely scattered throughout the country. Marketers use the cluster data for direct-mail campaigns, to select retail sites and appropriate merchandise mixes, to locate banks and restaurants, and to design marketing strategies for specific market segments. For example, Eddie Bauer (**www.eddiebauer.com**) has employed Claritas demographics (**www.claritas.com**) to evaluate new retail store locations and is PRIZM coding current customers, and Duke Energy Corporation (**www.duke-energy.com**) has profiled its residential and small business customers with Claritas's databases as part of its customer retention program.[26] Table 3.12 presents four examples of geodemographic clusters.

TABLE 3.11	Selected Lifestyle Profile of USA Today		
		% COMP	**INDEX**
Tech Savvy Readers			
Use Internet more than once a day		32%	174
Internet access at home		79%	128
Online purchase for business or personal use in past 30 days		40%	182
Household owns a PC		84%	119
Own a digital camera		22%	130
Leisure Activities			
Attended movies in last 6 months		73%	120
Bought music CDs/tapes in last 12 months		46%	126
Attended live music performance in last 12 months		29%	123
Book reading		45%	120
Entertain friends or relatives at home in last 12 months		48%	123
Household subscribes to cable		69%	112
Sports Enthusiasts			
Golf—personally participated last 12 months		21%	185
Walking for exercise		30%	107
Engage in regular exercise program (2+ times a week)		50%	126
Personally participate in any sports in past 12 months		77%	120
Attend any sports events		48%	152
Watch any sports events on TV		79%	120
Financially Aware			
Tracked investments or traded securities online in past 30 days		26%	246
Banked via PC/Internet in last 12 months		26%	159
Own securities		30%	133
Own mutual funds		25%	143
Have retirement savings plan (401K, IRA, Keogh)		31%	139
Domestic and Foreign Travelers			
Any foreign travel in last 3 years		27%	118
Any domestic travel in past year		63%	117
Member of frequent flyer program		30%	173
Own a valid passport		31%	120

Source: Spring 2004 MRI

Over the past 25 years, as the firm that started the clustering phenomenon, Claritas has increased the number of segments in American society from the 40 segments used in the 1970s and 1980s to the 66 segments it uses today. The Claritas search engine will pick the top five lifestyle clusters for each zip code; you can find out about your zip code by visiting **www.yawyl.claritas.com**.

While cross-cultural or global marketing segmentation was discussed earlier in the chapter, it is of interest to note that Claritas recently extended its geodemographic segmentation tool, PRIZM, to the Canadian marketplace. Prism CE (CE = Canadian Edition) lists 66 different consumer "clusters," including 28 urban groups, 11 ethnic groups, and 15 francophone categories.[27]

FIGURE 3.6

Source: © Dream Catcher. Used
with permission. All rights
reserved (www.dcr.com/dp).

Dream Catcher—"Unique
vacation homes, superior
service, limited membership."

Introducing DREAM CATCHER℠
Unique Vacation Homes, Superior Service, Limited Membership.

THE EVOLUTION OF THE DESTINATION CLUB
Over the past few years, the destination club has emerged as a cost-effective
alternative to vacation home ownership. But as with any good idea, it can be improved.

At Dream Catcher,™ we believe that the vacations you remember require more than
outsized homes and infinity pools. So we focus on the total experience, and go to
extraordinary lengths to provide those special places where memories are made.

→ UNIQUE VACATION HOMES Our buyers know the luxury home market, and we pay a
   premium for distinctive homes and those hidden gems with style and local character.
→ SUPERIOR SERVICE We built Dream Catcher around the elusive elements of
   exceptional service. We know our members, anticipate their needs, and consistently
   focus on the details that ensure a memorable, carefree vacation experience.
→ LIMITED MEMBERSHIP Dream Catcher was created to be all things to a few people.
   We limit membership in order to deliver the superior service and assured access
   our members expect.

THE PURSUIT OF HAPPINESS™
To learn more about Dream Catcher and our introductory membership offer, please
visit our website at www.dcr.com/dp or call 1·800·690·7820.

By its very nature, Dream Catcher is not for everyone. In order to assure our high
level of personal service, a significant deposit is required to secure membership.

DREAM CATCHER
A DESTINATION CLUB

Geodemographic segmentation is most useful when an advertiser's or marketer's best prospects (in terms of consumer personalities, goals, and interests) can be isolated in terms of where they live. However, for products and services used by a broad cross section of the American public, other segmentation schemes may be more productive.

SRI consulting business intelligence's (SRIC–BI's) and VALS™ system

Drawing on Maslow's need hierarchy (see Chapter 4) and the concept of social character (see Chapter 5), in the late 1970s researchers at SRI International (**www.sric-bi.com**) developed a generalized segmentation scheme of the American population known as the values and lifestyle (**VALS**™) system. This original system was designed to explain the dynamics of societal change, was based on social values, and was quickly adapted as a marketing tool.

In 1989 the VALS system was revised to focus more explicitly on explaining consumer purchasing behavior. The VALS typology classifies the American adult population into eight distinctive subgroups (segments) based on consumer responses to both

| TABLE 3.12 | Four PRISM NE Geodemographic Segments |

MOVERS & SHAKERS

- 1.59% of U.S. households
- Median household income: $95,372
- Predominant employment: Professional
- Social group: Elite suburbs
- Lifestage group: Midlife success
- Key education level: College grad+
- Adult age range: 35–64

CHARACTERISTICS: Movers & Shakers is home to America's up-and-coming business class: a wealthy suburban world of dual-income couples who are highly educated, typically between the ages of 35 and 54 and often with children. Given its high percentage of executives and white-collar professionals, there's a decided business bent to this segment: Movers & Shakers rank number-one for owning a small business and having a home office.

LIFESTYLE TRAITS:

- Go scuba diving/snorkeling
- Plan travel on the Internet
- Read *PC Magazine*
- Listen to adult contemporary radio
- Drive a Porsche

NEW EMPTY NESTS

- 1.05% of U.S. households
- Median household income: $65,832
- Predominant employment: Professional, white-collar
- Social group: The Affluentials
- Lifestage group: Conservative classics
- Key education level: College Grad+
- Adult age range: 65+

CHARACTERISTICS: With their grown-up children recently out of the house, New Empty Nests is composed of upscale older Americans who pursue active — and activist — lifestyles. Nearly three-quarters of residents are over 65 years old, but they show no interest in a rest-home retirement. This is the top-ranked segment for all-inclusive travel packages; the favorite destination is Italy.

LIFESTYLE TRAITS:

- Choose all-inclusive travel pkg.
- Belong to a fraternal order
- Read *Smithsonian*
- Watch *Meet the Press*
- Drive a Buick Park Avenue

BOOMTOWN SINGLES

- 1.22% of U.S. households
- Median household income: $37,407
- Predominant employment: White-collar, service
- Social group: City Centers
- Lifestage group: Young Achievers

(Continued)

TABLE 3.12 Continued

- Key education level: H.S./College
- Adult age range: Under 35

CHARACTERISTICS: Affordable housing, abundant entry-level jobs and a thriving singles scene—all have given rise to the Boomtown Singles segment in fast-growing satellite cities. Young, single and working-class, these residents pursue active lifestyles amid sprawling apartment complexes, bars, convenience stores, and laundromats.

LIFESTYLE TRAITS:

- Buy alternative music
- Play soccer
- Read *Muscle & Fitness*
- Watch MTV
- Drive a Daewoo

BEDROCK AMERICA

- 1.79% of U.S. households
- Median household income: $26,037
- Predominant employment: Service, BC, Farm
- Social group: Rustic living
- Lifestage group: Sustaining families
- Key education level: Elementary/H.S.
- Adult age range: Under 35

CHARACTERISTICS: Bedrock America consists of young, economically challenged families in small, isolated towns located throughout the nation's heartland. With modest educations, sprawling families, and blue-collar jobs, many of these residents struggle to make ends meet. One quarter live in mobile homes. One in three haven't finished high school. Rich in scenery, Bedrock America is a haven for fishing, hunting, hiking, and camping.

LIFESTYLE TRAITS:

- Go freshwater fishing
- Buy kids' bicycles
- Read baby magazines
- Watch *Days of Our Lives*
- Drive a Chevy S10 pickup

Source: Courtesy of Claritas Inc.

attitudinal and demographic questions. Figure 3.7 depicts the current VALS classification scheme. Examining the scheme, from left to right (Figure 3.7), the diagram identifies three *primary motivations*: the *ideals motivated* (these consumer segments are guided by knowledge and principles), the *achievement motivated* (these consumer segments are looking for products and services that demonstrate success to their peers), and the *self-expression motivated* (these consumer segments desire social or physical activity, variety, and risk).[28] Furthermore, each of these three major self-motivations represents distinct attitudes, lifestyles, and decision-making styles. Refocusing and examining Figure 3.7, from top to bottom, the diagram reveals a kind of continuum in terms of resources and innovation—that is, *high resources-high innovation* (on the top) to *low resources-low innovation* (on the bottom). This range of resources/innovation (again, from most to

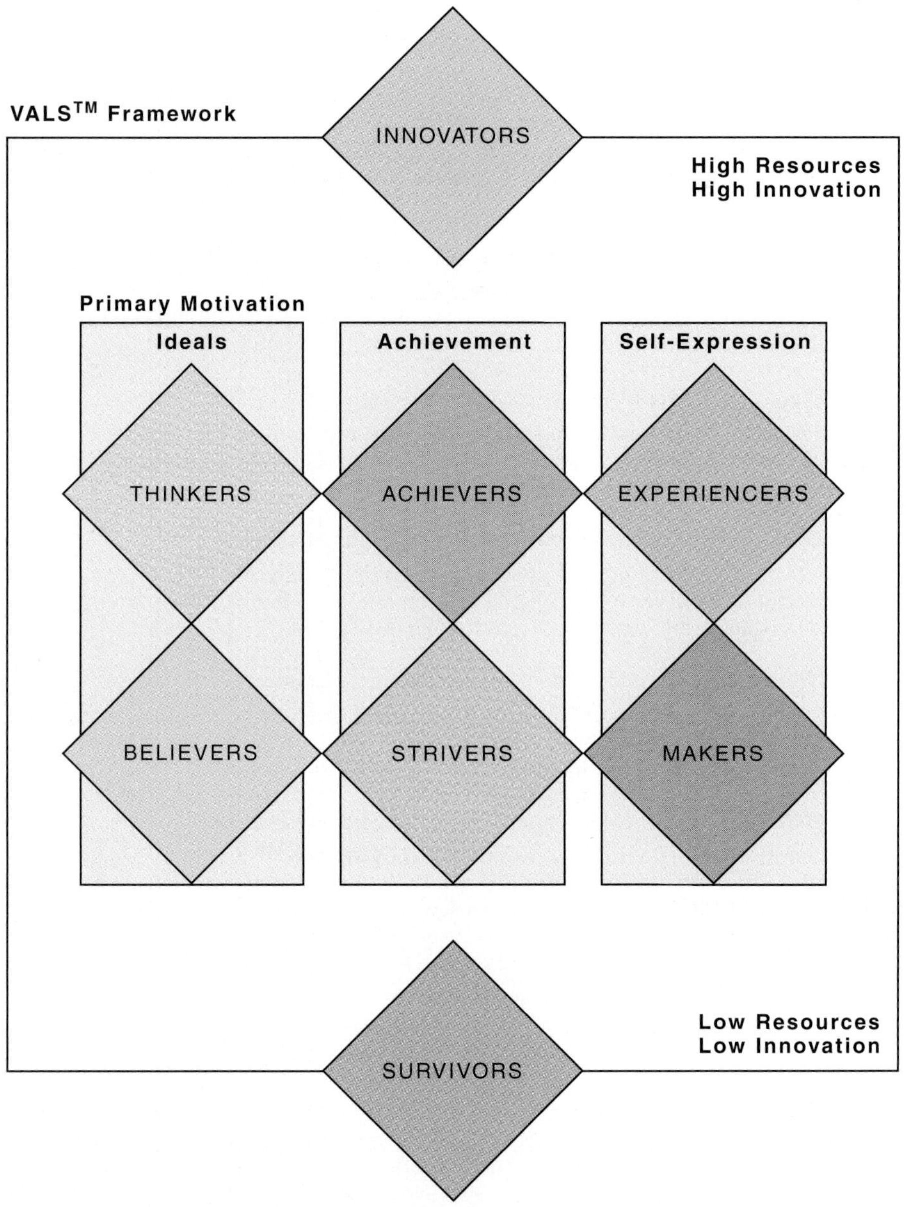

FIGURE 3.7

Summary Diagram of SRI VALS™ Segments

Source: Reprinted with permission of SRI Consulting Business Intelligence.

VALS™ Framework

INNOVATORS

High Resources High Innovation

Primary Motivation

| Ideals | Achievement | Self-Expression |

THINKERS   ACHIEVERS   EXPERIENCERS

BELIEVERS   STRIVERS   MAKERS

Low Resources Low Innovation

SURVIVORS

least) include the range of psychological, physical, demographic, and material means and capacities consumers have to draw upon, including education, income, self-confidence, health, eagerness to buy, and energy level, as well as the consumer's propensity to try new products.

All eight VALS segments (defined in Table 3.13) contain between 10 and 17 percent of the U.S. adult population, with Believers, at 17 percent, being the largest VALS group. In terms of consumer characteristics, the eight VALS segments differ in some important ways. For instance, *Believers* tend to buy American-made products and are slow to alter their consumption-related habits, whereas *Innovators* are drawn to top-of-the-line and new products, especially innovative technologies. Therefore, it is not surprising that

TABLE 3.13	A Brief Description of the Eight VALS™ New Edition Segments

INNOVATORS

Innovators are successful, sophisticated, take-charge people with high self-esteem. Because they have such abundant resources, they exhibit all three primary motivations in varying degrees. They are change leaders and are the most receptive to new ideas and technologies. Their purchases reflect cultivated tastes for upscale, niche products and services.

THINKERS*   Motivated by ideals; high resources

Thinkers are mature, satisfied, comfortable, and reflective. They tend to be well educated and actively seek out information in the decision-making process. They favor durability, functionality, and value in products.

BELIEVERS   Motivated by ideals; low resources

Believers are strongly traditional and respect rules and authority. Because they are fundamentally conservative, they are slow to change and technology averse. They choose familiar products and established brands.

ACHIEVERS   Motivated by achievement; high resources

Achievers have goal-oriented lifestyles that center on family and career. They avoid situations that encourage a high degree of stimulation or change. They prefer premium products that demonstrate success to their peers.

STRIVERS   Motivated by achievement; low resources

Strivers are trendy and fun loving. They have little discretionary income and tend to have narrow interests. They favor stylish products that emulate the purchases of people with greater material wealth.

EXPERIENCERS   Motivated by self-expression; high resources

Experiencers appreciate the unconventional. They are active and impulsive, seeking stimulation from the new, offbeat, and risky. They spend a comparatively high proportion of their income on fashion, socializing, and entertainment.

MAKERS   Motivated by self-expression; low resources

Makers value practicality and self-sufficiency. They choose hands-on constructive activities and spend leisure time with family and close friends. Because they prefer value to luxury, they buy basic products.

SURVIVORS

Survivors lead narrowly focused lives. Because they have the fewest resources, they do not exhibit a primary motivation and often feel powerless. They are primarily concerned about safety and security, so they tend to be brand loyal and buy discounted merchandise.

*VALS™ segments the U.S. English-speaking population age 18 or older into eight consumer groups. Their primary motivation and ability to express themselves in the marketplace distinguish the groups.

Source: Reprinted with permission of SRI Consulting Business Intelligence.

marketers of intelligent in-vehicle technologies (e.g., global positioning devices) must first target *Innovators*, because they are early adopters of new products.

In addition to the U.S. VALS system, there is a Japan VALS system and a U.K. VALS system. GeoVALS™ estimates the proportion of the eight U.S. VALS types by U.S. zip code and by black group.

TABLE 3.14	Representative VALS™ Projects

COMMERCIALIZATION

- A European luxury automobile manufacturer used VALS to identify online, mobile applications that would appeal to affluent, early-adopter consumers within the next five years. VALS research identified early-adopter groups and explored their reactions to a variety of mobile services for use in automobiles. The VALS analysis enabled the company to prioritize applications for development and determine the best strategic alliances to pursue.

- A major telecommunications-product company used VALS to select an early-adopter target for a new telecommunications concept. VALS enabled the company to develop the product prototype and prioritize features and benefits, with a focus on the early-adopter target. The company used VALS to select the best name and logo, choose an overall positioning strategy, and set an initial price point.

POSITIONING

- A major stockbrokerage firm focused on providing excellent service to a select group of affluent consumers used VALS to redefine its image and develop a new corporate slogan. Within 18 months, advertising recall scores increased dramatically from 8% to 55%.

- A Minnesota medical center planned to offer a new line of service: cosmetic surgery. It used VALS to identify target consumers (those most interested and able to afford the service). By understanding the underlying motivations of the target, the center and its ad agency were able to develop a compelling selling proposition. The resulting advertising was so successful that just a few weeks into the campaign, the center exceeded its scheduling capabilities.

COMMUNICATIONS

- U.S. long-distance carrier used VALS to select its spokesperson in a major television campaign to increase its customer base. By understanding consumers who are heavy users of long-distance service, the company was able to select a spokesperson to whom the target could relate.

- An electric utility used VALS to increase participation in its energy-conservation program by developing a targeted direct mail campaign. Two distinctly different VALS segments were key targets. By developing unique strategies for each audience and identifying ZIP codes with high percentages of each target, the utility reported a 25% increase in participation.

Source: Reprinted with permission of SRI Consulting Business Intelligence.

To conclude our discussion of VALS, Table 3.14 presents a brief description of a number of different strategic applications of VALS.

Yankelovich mindbase® segmentation

Starting with their Monitor Survey of American Values and Attitudes, Yankelovich researchers have over the years created a number of different market segmentation methodologies that focus on household consumers (**see www.yankelovich.com**). A relatively recent effort has been the revision of the Yankelovich Mindbase,® which consists of eight consumer segments (see Table 3.15), and additional three smaller subsegments for each of the eight segments (for a total of 24 segments). A particularly attractive direct marketing feature of this segmentation framework is that it has been employed to categories the members of selected consumer databases (which contain the names and addresses of consumers who have been categories in terms of their Mindbase segmentation membership).

TABLE 3.15	An Overview Profile of the Eight Yankelovich Mindbase® Segments

SEGMENT 1—EXPRESSIVE CONSUMERS (11.1% OF THE U.S. POPULATION)

Personal Motto "Carpe Diem"

Profile:

Members of this segment see themselves as stylish, daring, and intense. They make an effort to live life to the fullest. They strive to reveal who they are to those they come in contact with—"It's who I am and I'm not afraid to express myself."

As shoppers they are open to the opinions of their friends; however, they personally look for brands that show their friends that they are "in the know." The interest in identifying "hot styles," and search magazines and online, and specialty stores and catalogs for what is new and in-style.

They are open to marketers who will entertain them, offer them "Stuff" that's new and that fits their personal definition of style.

Traits that sum them up:

-Bold

-Fun over work

-Active imagination

-Seek novelty

Their Demographics:

-Median age is 22

-Median income is $56,000

-Not married—68%

-Have children—37%

SEGMENT 2—DRIVEN CONSUMERS (14.9% OF THE U.S. POPULATION)

Personal Motto "Nothing ventured, nothing gained"

Profile:

Members of this segment are ambitious and working towards achieving their personal dreams and goals. They have an entrepreneurial spirit and seek to be the best in what they do at home and at work. They are well organized and self motivated to accomplish what they set out to do. They have a "life plan" and they are always working towards reaching it.

As consumers they especially like tools that help them achieve and accomplish. They like electronic gadgets because they are fun and because they are also useful.

They are open to marketers who will help them reach their dreams and goals.

Traits that sum them up:

-Looking for ways to excel

-Value education and personal growth

-See themselves as "workaholics"

-Wants to be seen as "unconventional"

Their Demographics:

-Median age is 22

-Median income is $56,000

-Married—57%

-Have children—58%

(Continued)

TABLE 3.15	Continued

SEGMENT 3—AT CAPACITY (12.0% OF THE U.S. POPULATION)

Personal Motto "Time is of the essence"

Profile:

This third segment consists of individuals who see their lives as busy and hectic and wish to simplify and take control of things. Besides reducing their obligations, a high priority is to invest in themselves and be more available to their families.

When shopping, online or in stores, convenience is especially important. They also demand excellent service, variety or choices, and even bargain.

Traits that sum them up:

-Seek control

-Crave to simplify and eliminate the nonessential

-Ambitious in their careers and desiring a more flexible work schedule

-Wish to be involved in their communities

Their Demographics:

-Median age is 32

-Median income is $50,000

-Married—67%

-Have children—75%

SEGMENT 4—ROCK STEADY CONSUMERS (11.3% OF THE U.S. POPULATION)

Personal Motto "Do the Right Thing"

Profile:

Members of this segment see themselves living a "contented life." They are content with themselves and their families. They see themselves as "dependable" and "generous" people, who are dedicated to enhancing their homes (by decorating and do-it-yourself projects).

As shoppers they do not like to be pressured nor do they pay much attention to "marketing tactics," rather they select retailers that give them a sense of providing quality products and good value.

Traits that sum them up:

-Happily married and spend their time at home

-Easygoing people

-They follow the rules

-They trust their instincts

Their Demographics:

-Median age is 45

-Median income is $67,000

-Married—80%

-Have children—85%

SEGMENT 5—DOWN TO EARTH CONSUMERS (12.8% OF THE U.S. POPULATION)

Personal Motto "Easy on down the road"

Profile:

Members of this fifth segment seek to define their own path (their future) and want to maintain control over their own destiny. They are respectful of an individual having

(Continued)

TABLE 3.15	**Continued**

the right to have their own point of view. They are satisfied with their own lives and take every day as it comes. They are venturesome and interested in exploring other viewpoints, as well as new experiences.

In terms of consuming, members of this segment seek to "treat" themselves by buying "little things" (e.g., buying a piece of jewelry) or relaxing at home, possibly listening to music.

Traits that sum them up:

-Seek to "stretch" themselves

-Enjoy people with different viewpoints

-Don't do things just because they are "mainstream"

-Relax and take it easy on the weekends

Their Demographics:

-Median age is 44

-Median income is $55,000

-Married—64%

-Have children—76%

SEGMENT 6—SOPHISTICATED CONSUMERS (11.8% OF THE U.S. POPULATION)

Personal Motto "Sense and sensibility"

Profile:

This segment perceives themselves as being "intelligent," "confident," "sensitive," and as creative and expressive. Their work consumes most of their time and they define much of who they are through their work. Outside of work they seek to rejuvenate themselves by traveling, cooking, and spending time with their pets. For them new experiences tend to be more important than acquiring more "things."

They see themselves as being demanding consumers—they research what to buy and they expect the best in terms of quality, convenience, and service. They are also very vocal if a shopping experience falls short of what they were expecting.

Traits that sum them up:

-Value integrity

-Work to reduce personal stress

-Want to be a role model for others

-Are open-minded and seek new experiences

Their Demographics:

-Median age is 48

-Median income is $56,000

-Married—59%

-Have children—70%

SEGMENT 7—MEASURE TWICE (11.9% OF THE U.S. POPULATION)

Personal Motto "An ounce of prevention"

Profile:

Segment 7 people are careful planners. They plan when it comes to their health, their financial well-being, and their future security. They remain open to new ideas as to ways to improve their lives, even to start a new career when they retire. They like to

(Continued)

TABLE 3.15	**Continued**

be up-to-date in terms of current events, and are active with regard to their hobbies and leisure-time pursuits.

They favor department stores and catalog shopping.

Traits that sum them up:

-On top of taking care of their health and financial security

-They have found a balanced life

-They are open to a new career when they retire

-They see themselves as "good citizens"

Their Demographics:

-Median age is 65

-Median income is $52,000

-Married—65%

-Have children—85%

SEGMENT 8—DEVOTED CONSUMERS (14.2% OF THE U.S. POPULATION)

Personal Motto "Home is where the heart is"

Profile:

The eighth and final segment is made up of individuals who see themselves as being "traditional" people. They are content with their lives, and do not feel that they are really missing anything. Their lives appear to be what they expected their lives to be. They are quite spiritual and have a great deal of faith in their religion. They hesitate to try something different, especially new technology; rather they are comfortable with what is familiar, especially their homes.

When shopping they favor familiar establishments with low prices.

Traits that sum them up:

-Share religious values with others

-Prefer things that are already proven trustworthy

-Feel closer to people with the same background

-Seen as feeling "complete"

Their Demographics:

-Median age is 67

-Median income is $32,000

-Married—60%

-Have children—85%

Source: "Yankelovich Mindbase® Segment Profiles, Introductory Information," PDF files supplied by Yankelovich, January 2005.

criteria for effective targeting of market segments

The previous sections have described various bases on which consumers can be clustered into homogeneous market segments. The next challenge for the marketer is to select one or more segments to target with an appropriate marketing mix. To be an effective target, a market segment should be (1) identifiable, (2) sufficient (in terms of size), (3) stable or growing, and (4) accessible (reachable) in terms of both media and cost.

Identification

To divide the market into separate segments on the basis of a series of *common* or *shared* needs or characteristics that are relevant to the product or service, a marketer must be able to identify these relevant characteristics. Some segmentation variables, such as *geography* (location) or *demographics* (age, gender, occupation, race), are relatively easy to identify or are even observable. Others, such as *education, income,* or *marital status,* can be determined through questionnaires. However, other characteristics, such as *benefits sought* or *lifestyle,* are more difficult to identify. A knowledge of consumer behavior is especially useful to marketers who use such intangible consumer characteristics as the basis for market segmentation.

Sufficiency

For a market segment to be a worthwhile target, it must consist of a sufficient number of people to warrant tailoring a product or promotional campaign to its specific needs or interests. To estimate the size of each segment under consideration, marketers often use secondary demographic data, such as that provided by the United States Census Bureau (available at many libraries and online via the Internet), or they undertake a probability survey whose findings can be projected to the total market. (Consumer research methodology was described in Chapter 2.)

Stability

Most marketers prefer to target consumer segments that are relatively stable in terms of demographic and psychological factors and are likely to grow larger over time. They prefer to avoid "fickle" segments that are unpredictable in embracing fads. For example, teens are a sizable and easily identifiable market segment, eager to buy, able to spend, and easily reached. Yet, by the time a marketer produces merchandise for a popular teenage fad, interest in it may have waned.

Accessibility

A fourth requirement for effective targeting is accessibility, which means that marketers must be able to reach the market segments they want to target in an economical way. Despite the wide availability of special-interest magazines and cable TV programs, marketers are constantly looking for new media that will enable them to reach their target markets with minimum waste of circulation and competition. One way this can be accomplished is via the Internet. Upon the request of the consumer, a growing number of Web sites periodically send e-mail messages concerning a subject of special interest to the computer user. For example, a resident of Houston, Texas, who likes to take short vacation trips, might have Continental Airlines e-mail her the coming weekend's special airfare, hotel, and rent-a-car deals.

implementing segmentation strategies

Firms that use market segmentation can pursue a *concentrated* marketing strategy or a *differentiated* marketing strategy. In certain instances, they might use a **countersegmentation** strategy.

Concentrated versus differentiated marketing

Once an organization has identified its most promising market segments, it must decide whether to target one segment or several segments. The premise behind market segmentation is that each targeted segment receives a specially designed marketing mix, that is, a specially tailored product, price, distribution network, and/or promotional campaign. Targeting several segments using individual marketing mixes is called **differentiated marketing**; targeting just one segment with a unique marketing mix is called **concentrated marketing**.

Differentiated marketing is a highly appropriate segmentation strategy for financially strong companies that are well established in a product category and competitive with other firms that also are strong in the category (e.g., soft drinks, automobiles, or detergents). However, if a company is small or new to the field, concentrated marketing is probably a better bet. A company can survive and prosper by filling a niche not occupied by stronger companies. For example, Viadent toothpaste has become a leader in the small but increasingly important submarket of the overall tooth care market that focuses on products that fight gingivitis and other gum diseases.

Countersegmentation

Sometimes companies find that they must reconsider the extent to which they are segmenting their markets. They might find that some segments have contracted over time to the point that they do not warrant an individually designed marketing program. In such cases, the company seeks to discover a more generic need or consumer characteristic that would apply to the members of two or more segments and recombine those segments into a larger single segment that could be targeted with an individually tailored product or promotional campaign. This is called a *countersegmentation* strategy. Some business schools with wide course offerings in each department were forced to adopt a countersegmentation strategy when they discovered that students simply did not have enough available credits to take a full spectrum of in-depth courses in their major area of study. As a result, some courses had to be canceled each semester because of inadequate registration. For some schools, a countersegmentation strategy effectively solved the problem (e.g., by combining *advertising, publicity, sales promotion*, and *personal selling* courses into a single course called Promotion).

SUMMARY

Market segmentation and diversity are complementary concepts. Without a diverse marketplace, composed of many different peoples with different backgrounds, countries of origin, interests, needs, and wants, there really would be little reason to segment markets.

Before the widespread adoption of the marketing concept, mass marketing (offering the same product or marketing mix to everyone) was the marketing strategy most widely used. Market segmentation followed as a more logical way to meet consumer needs. Segmentation is defined as the process of dividing a potential market into distinct subsets of consumers with a common need or characteristic and selecting one or more segments to target with a specially designed marketing mix. Besides aiding in the development of new products, segmentation studies assist in the redesign and repositioning of existing products, in the creation of promotional appeals, and the selection of advertising media.

Because segmentation strategies benefit both marketers and consumers, they have received wide support from both sides of the marketplace. Market segmentation is now widely used by manufacturers, retailers, and the nonprofit sector.

Nine major classes of consumer characteristics serve as the most common bases for market segmentation. These include geographic factors, demographic factors, psychological factors, psychographic characteristics, sociocultural variables, use-related characteristics, use-situation factors, benefits sought, and hybrid forms of segmentation (e.g., psychographic-demographic profiles, such as VALS™, and geodemographic factors, such as PRIZM™). Important criteria for segmenting markets include identification, sufficiency, stability, and accessibility. Once an organization has identified promising target markets, it must decide whether to target several segments (differentiated marketing) or just one segment (concentrated marketing). It then develops a positioning strategy for each targeted segment. In certain instances, a company might decide to follow a countersegmentation strategy and recombine two or more segments into one larger segment.

DISCUSSION QUESTIONS

1. What is market segmentation? How is the practice of market segmentation related to the marketing concept?

2. How are market segmentation, targeting, and positioning interrelated? Illustrate how these three concepts can be used to develop a marketing strategy for a product of your choice.

3. Discuss the advantages and disadvantages of using demographics as a basis for segmentation. Can demographics and psychographics be used together to segment markets? Illustrate your answer with a specific example.

4. Many marketers have found that a relatively small group of heavy users accounts for a disproportionately large amount of the total products consumed. What are the advantages and disadvantages of targeting these heavy users?

5. Under which circumstances and for what types of products should a marketer segment the market on the basis of (a) awareness status, (b) brand loyalty, and (c) usage situation?

6. Some marketers consider benefit segmentation as the segmentation approach most consistent with the marketing concept. Do you agree or disagree with this view? Why?

7. Club Med is a prominent company in the vacation and travel industry. Describe how the company can use demographics and psychographics to identify TV shows and magazines in which to place its advertisements.

8. How can a marketer for a chain of health clubs use the VALS™ segmentation profiles to develop an advertising campaign? Which segments should be targeted? How should the health club be positioned to each of these segments?

9. For each of the following products, identify the segmentation base that you consider best for targeting consumers: (a) coffee, (b) soups, (c) home exercise equipment, (d) portable telephones, and (e) nonfat frozen yogurt. Explain your choices.

10. Apply the criteria for effective segmentation to marketing a product of your choice to college students.

EXERCISES

1. Select a product and brand that you use frequently and list the benefits you receive from using it. Without disclosing your list, ask a fellow student who uses a different brand in this product category (preferably, a friend of the opposite sex) to make a similar list for his or her brand. Compare the two lists and identify the implications for using benefit segmentation to market the two brands.

2. Does your lifestyle differ significantly from your parents' lifestyle? If so, how are the two lifestyles different? What factors cause these differences?

3. Do you anticipate any major changes in your lifestyle in the next five years? If so, into which VALS segment are you likely to belong five years from now? Explain.

4. The owners of a local health-food restaurant have asked you to prepare a psychographic profile of families living in the community surrounding the restaurant's location. Construct a 10-question psychographic inventory appropriate for segmenting families on the basis of their dining-out preferences.

5. Find three print advertisements that you believe are targeted at a particular psychographic segment. How effective do you think each ad is in terms of achieving its objective? Why?

KEY TERMS

- **AIOs (activities, interests, opinions)**
- **benefit segmentation**
- **concentrated marketing**
- **countersegmentation**
- **demographic characteristics**
- **demographic segmentation**
- **differentiated marketing**
- **geographic segmentation**
- **hybrid segmentation**
- **mass marketing**
- **market segmentation**
- **micromarketing**
- **positioning**
- **psychographic inventory**
- **psychographic segmentation**
- **psychological segmentation**
- **repositioning**
- **sociocultural variables**
- **use-related segmentation**
- **usage situation**
- **VALS**

NOTES

1. "Parallel Universe," *American Demographics* (October 1999): 58–63.

2. FNA Dick Chay, "New Segments of Boomers Reveal New Mktg. Implications," *Marketing News*, March 15, 2005, 24.

3. "Superstars of Spending," *Advertising Age*, February 12, 2001, S1, S10.

4. Rob Walker, "Grooming for Guys," *The New York Times Sunday Magazine*, July 25, 2004, 22; and Sandra O'Loughlin, " 'Not-Your-Dad's' Aqua Velva Refreshes Its Appearance," *Brandweek*, April 11, 2005, 17.

5. Roger Grover, "Mad Ave Is Starry-Eyed Over Net Video," *Business Week*, May 23, 2005, 36–39; and Kris Oser and Kate MacArthur, "Coke Pours More Online, Chases Next Generation," *Advertising Age*, April 4, 2005, 4.

6. Linda Morton, "Segmenting Publics by Life Development Stages," *Public Relations Quarterly* (Spring 1999): 46.

7. Geoffrey Meredith and Charles Schewe, "The Power of Cohorts," *American Demographics* (December 1994): 22–31; and Michael M. Phillips, "Selling by Evoking What Defines a Generation," *Wall Street Journal*, August 13, 1996, B1.

8. Charles D. Schewe and Geoffrey Meredith, "Segmenting Global Markets by Generational Cohorts: Determining Motivations by Age," *Journal of Consumer Behavior*, 4 (October 2004): 51–63.

9. Scott Smith and David Whitlark, "Men and Women Online: What Makes Them Click?" *Marketing Research* (Summer 2001): 20–25.

10. Sandra O'Loughlin, "New CMO Says Wal-Mart Will Reach More Customers," *Brandweek*, May 2, 2005, 5.

11. Kate MacArthur, "BK Offers Fat to the Land," *Advertising Age*, April 4, 2005, 1 & 60.

12. John McManus, "Street Wiser," *American Demographics* (2004): D30–D32.

13. "Less Well-To-Do Web Surfers Spend More Time Online Than More Affluent People, According to Nielsen//NetRatings," *Business Wire*, September 21, 2000, 1.

14. William James, Charles A. McMellon, and Gladys Torres-Baumgarten, "Dogs and Cats Rule: A New Insight into Segmentation," *Journal of Targeting, Measurement and Analysis for Marketing*, 13 (October 2004): 70–77.

15. Mark R. Forehand and Rohit Deshpandè, "What We See Makes Us Who We Are: Priming Ethnic Self-Awareness and Advertising Response," *Journal of Marketing Research*, 38 (August 2001): 336–348.

16. Geng Cui and Quiming Liu, "Emerging Market Segments in a Transitional Economy: A Study of Urban Consumers in China," *Journal of International Marketing*, 9, no. 1 (2001): 84–106.

17. V. Kumar and Anish Nagpal, "Segmenting Global Markets: Look Before You Leap," *Marketing Research* (Spring 2001): 8–13.

18. Brian Wansink and Sea Bum Park, "Methods and Measures That Profile Heavy Users," *Journal of Advertising Research* (July–August 2000): 61–72; Ronald E. Goldsmith and Stephen W. Litvin, "Heavy Users of Travel Agents: A Segmentation Analysis of Vacation Travelers," *Journal of Travel Research* (November 1999): 127–133.

19. Richard G. Barlow, "How to Court Various Target Markets," *Marketing News*, October 9, 2000, 22.

20. "New Study Reveals Newsstand Magazine Buyers to be More Active Consumers and More Receptive to Advertising," *Business Wire*, September 8, 2004, 1.

21. Kenneth C. Gehrt and Ruoh-Nan Yan, "Situational, Consumer, and Retailer Factors Affecting Internet, Catalog, and Store Shopping," *International Journal of Retail & Distribution Management*, 32, no. 1 (2004): 5–18.

22. "India: Mantras to Work Brand Magic," *Businessline*, April 26, 2001, 1–4.

23. Ulrich R. Orth, Mina McDaniel, Tom Shellhammer, and Kannapon Lopetcharat, "Promoting Brand Benefits: The Role of Consumer Psychographics and Lifestyle," *The Journal of Consumer Marketing*, 21, no. 2/3 (2004): 97–108.

24. Russell Haley, "Benefit Segmentation: A Decision-Oriented Research Tool," *Marketing Management*, 4 (Summer 1995): 59–62; Dianne Cermak, Karen Maru File, and Russ Alan Prince, "A Benefit Segmentation of the Major Donor Market," *Journal of Business Research* (February 1994): 121–130; and Elisabeth Kastenholz, Duane Davis, and Gordon Paul, "Segmenting Tourism in Rural Areas: The Case of North and Central Portugal," *Journal of Travel Research*, 37 (May 1999): 353–363.

25. William Trombetta, "A Strategic Overview," *Pharmaceutical Executive Supplement* (May 2001): 8–16.

26. **www. claritas. com**; Patricia Lloyd Williams, "Energy Marketing: What Do Customers Want?" *Fortnightly's Energy Customer Management* (Fall 2000): 36–41.

27. Dana Flavelle, "Pollster Pegs Our Social Values; Finds 66 Different 'Consumer Types' Formal Based on Income, Age," *Toronto Star*, September 10, 2004, A1.

28. **www.scri-bi.com/VALS/types.shtml**.

PART 2 DISCUSSES THE CONSUMER AS AN INDIVIDUAL

Chapters 4 through 8 provide the reader with a comprehensive picture of consumer psychology. These chapters explain the basic psychological concepts that account for individual behavior and demonstrate how these concepts influence the individual's consumption-related behavior. Chapter 9 shows how communication links consumers as individuals to the world and people around them.

chapter**four**

Consumer Motivation

Human needs—consumer needs—are the basis of all modern marketing. Needs are the essence of the marketing concept. The key to a company's survival, profitability, and growth in a highly competitive marketplace is its ability to identify and satisfy unfulfilled consumer needs better and sooner than the competition.

Marketers do not create needs, though in some instances they may make consumers more keenly aware of unfelt needs. Successful marketers define their markets in terms of the needs they presume to satisfy, not in terms of the products they sell. This is a market-oriented, rather than a production-oriented, approach to marketing. A marketing orientation focuses on the needs of the buyer; a production orientation focuses on the needs of the seller. The marketing concept implies that the manufacturer will make only what it knows people will buy; a production orientation implies that the manufacturer will try to sell whatever it decides to make.

The philosophy and marketing strategy of Charles Revson, the builder of the Revlon cosmetics empire, depict an insightful understanding of consumer needs. Charles Revson started by manufacturing nail polish, but he defined nail polish as a fashion accessory and not merely a nail covering. His strategy was designed to induce women to use different shades of nail polish to match different

There's a place
where a rock is a mountain.
The sky reaches down to your boots.
Museums are outdoors,
stories are painted, not spoken,
and dreamtime follows you home.
A different culture.
A different yesterday.

A different light.

Australia. An island of open arms that reach out across a continent of natural wonders. Explore the incredible range of Aussie experiences beginning with the urban elegance of the Sydney Opera House to the raw beauty of Uluru (Ayers Rock). Take the first step toward an unforgettable vacation that's just right for you. The entire country is literally at your fingertips when you visit Australia.com.

Australia
australia.com

outfits, moods, and occasions. This approach vastly broadened the market for the product, because it persuaded women to buy and use many different colors of nail polish in the same season rather than wait to finish one bottle before buying another one. And Revson ensured that women would buy more and more bottles of nail polish by introducing new nail color fashions every season. Emulating GM's strategy of planned obsolescence (i.e., introducing new automobile models every year), Revlon would introduce new nail colors every fall and spring and, through heavy and effective advertising, would persuade women that buying the new colors would satisfy their needs to appear fashionable and attractive.[1]

TABLE 4.1	**Companies Can Define Themselves as Product-Oriented versus Need-Oriented**	
	PRODUCT-ORIENTED	**NEED-ORIENTED**
Pfizer	We make pharmaceuticals.	"We dedicate ourselves to humanity's quest for longer, healthier, happier lives through innovation in pharmaceutical, consumer, and animal health products." (**www.pfizer.com**)
Logitech	We make cameras and PC tracking devices.	"Logitech designs, manufactures and markets personal peripherals that enable people to effectively work, play, and communicate in the digital world. The company's products combine essential core technologies, continuing innovation, award-winning industrial design and excellent price performance." (**www.logitech.com**)
Ritz-Carlton	We rent rooms and provide facilities for meetings and events.	The company's credo stresses the genuine care and comfort of the guests, the finest personal service and facilities, a warm yet refined ambience, and an experience that fulfills even the unexpressed needs and wishes of the guests. (**www.ritzcarlton.com**)

Similar to GM's segmentation strategy, Revson developed separate cosmetic lines targeting different consumer segments, such as the popularly priced *Revlon* (which Revson equated with the positioning of the Pontiac), *Natural Wonder* (targeting the youth market), and *Marcella Borghese* (positioned as the high-class line with international "flavor"). Most importantly, Revson understood that he was not selling women the physical product (e.g., nail lacquer to cover their nails) but the fantasy that the nail polish would attract attention and bestow class and glamour on the user. Thus, Revson did not sell deep red polish; he sold *Fire and Ice.* He did not sell dark red polish; he sold *Berry Bon Bon.* Charles Revson summed up his philosophy by saying "In the factory, we make cosmetics; in the store, we sell hope." And selling hope, rather than the physical product known as cosmetics, allowed Revson to charge much more for his products. Rather than compete with other manufacturers on the basis of price, Revson competed on the basis of perceived quality and greater satisfaction of women's needs for fantasy and attention.[2]

Savvy companies define their missions in terms of the consumer needs they satisfy rather than the products they produce and sell. Because consumers' basic needs do not change but the products that satisfy them do, a corporate focus on developing products that will satisfy consumers' needs ensures that the company stays in the forefront of the search for new and effective solutions. By doing so, such companies are likely to survive and grow despite strong competition or adverse economic conditions. On the other hand, companies that define themselves in terms of the products they make may suffer or even go out of business when their products are replaced by competitive offerings that better satisfy the same need. Table 4.1 includes examples of companies that define themselves as need-oriented rather than product-oriented.

This chapter discusses basic needs that operate in most people to motivate behavior. It explores the influence that such needs have on consumption behavior. Later chapters in Part 2 explain why and how these basic human needs, or motives, are expressed in so many diverse ways.

motivation as a psychological force

Motivation is the *driving force within individuals that impels them to action.* This driving force is produced by a state of tension, which exists as the result of an unfulfilled need. Individuals strive both consciously and subconsciously to reduce this tension through behavior that they anticipate will fulfill their needs and thus relieve them of the stress they feel. The specific goals they select and the patterns of action they undertake to achieve their goals are the results of individual thinking and learning. Figure 4.1 presents a model of the motivational process. It portrays motivation as a state of need-induced tension that "drives" the individual to engage in behavior that he or she believes will satisfy the need and thus reduce the tension. Whether gratification is actually achieved depends on the course of action pursued. The specific goals that consumers wish to achieve and the courses of action they take to attain these goals are selected on the basis of their thinking processes (cognition) and previous learning (e.g., experience). Therefore, marketers must view motivation as the force that induces consumption and, through consumption experiences, the process of consumer learning (discussed in Chapter 7).

Needs

Every individual has needs: some are innate, others are acquired. **Innate needs** are physiological (i.e., *biogenic*); they include the needs for food, water, air, clothing, shelter, and sex. Because they are needed to sustain biological life, the biogenic needs are considered **primary needs** or motives.

Acquired needs are needs that we learn in response to our culture or environment. These may include needs for self-esteem, prestige, affection, power, and learning. Because acquired needs are generally psychological (i.e., *psychogenic*), they are considered **secondary needs** or motives. They result from the individual's subjective psychological state and from relationships with others. For example, all individuals need shelter from the elements; thus, finding a place to live fulfills an important primary need for a newly transferred executive. However, the kind of home she rents or buys may be the result of secondary needs. She may seek a place in which she and her husband can entertain large

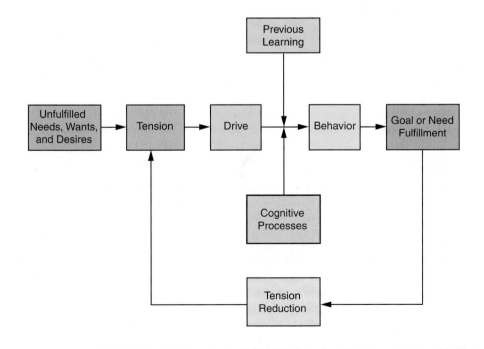

Model of the Motivation Process

Source: From Jeffrey F. Dugree et al., "Observations: Translating Values into Product Wants," *Journal of Advertising Research,* 36, 6 (November 1996). Reprinted by permission of the *Journal of the American Marketing Association.*

FIGURE 4.1

groups of people (and fulfill social needs); she may want to live in an exclusive community to impress her friends and family (and fulfill ego needs). The place where an individual ultimately chooses to live thus may serve to fulfill both primary and secondary needs.

Goals

Goals are the sought-after results of motivated behavior. As Figure 4.1 indicated, all behavior is goal oriented. Our discussion of motivation in this chapter is in part concerned with **generic goals**, that is, the general classes or categories of goals that consumers see as a means to fulfill their needs. If a student tells his parents that he wants to become a medical doctor, he has stated a generic goal. If he says he wants to get an M.D. degree from UCLA, he has expressed a **product-specific goal**. Marketers are particularly concerned with product-specific goals, that is, the specifically branded products and services that consumers select for goal fulfillment.

Individuals set goals on the basis of their personal values, and they select means (or behaviors) that they believe will help them achieve their desired goals. Figures 4.2 A, B, and C depict a framework of the goal structure behind losing weight and maintaining weight loss and the results of a study based on this model. Figure 4.2A depicts an overall framework for pursuing consumption-related goals. Figure 4.2B depicts the inter-relationship among the needs driving the goal of losing weight (e.g., increased self-confidence, looking and feeling better, and living longer) and the behaviors required to achieve the goal (i.e., exercising and/or dieting). Figure 4.2C depicts the complex nature of goal setting based on subjects' responses to questions regarding their reasons for selecting weight loss as a goal, providing justification for each reason, and explaining each justification.[3] The three diagrams together depict the complexity of goal setting and the difficulties in understanding this process through a set theoretical model. Figure 4.3 depicts an ad that portrays subscribing to a health magazine as a means to achieve several physical appearance-related goals.

The selection of goals

For any given need, there are many different and appropriate goals. The goals selected by individuals depend on their personal experiences, physical capacity, prevailing cultural norms and values, and the goal's accessibility in the physical and social environment. For example, a young woman may wish to get a deep, even tan and may envision spending time in the sun as a way to achieve her goal. However, if her dermatologist advises her to avoid direct exposure to the sun, she may settle for a self-tanning cosmetic product instead. The goal object has to be both socially acceptable and physically accessible. If cosmetic companies did not offer effective alternatives to tanning in the sun, our young woman would have to either ignore the advice of her dermatologist or select a substitute goal, such as untanned (but undamaged) youthful-looking skin.

An individual's personal characteristics and own perception of self also influence the specific goals selected. Research on personal goal orientation distinguished two types of people: (1) persons with *promotion focus* are interested in their growth and development, have more hopes and aspirations and favor the presence of positive outcomes; (2) persons with a *prevention focus* are interested in safety and security, are more concerned with duties and obligations and favor the absence of negative outcomes. One study found that, in forming consumption-related goals, consumers with a prevention focus favored the status quo and inaction over action.[4] Another study distinguished between two types of goals: (1) **ideals**, which represent hopes, wishes, and aspirations; and (2) **oughts**, which represent duties, obligations, and responsibilities. The study showed that people concerned with *ideals* relied more on feelings and affects in evaluating advertisements, while people more concerned with *oughts* relied more heavily on the substantive and factual contents of ads.[5] In yet another study, some consumers were led to believe that they obtained a discount in the purchase price of a PC because of their good negotiating skills and were encouraged to feel proud, while others were led to believe that they received the discount because the computer was on sale and were not encouraged to feel proud. In addition, the goals

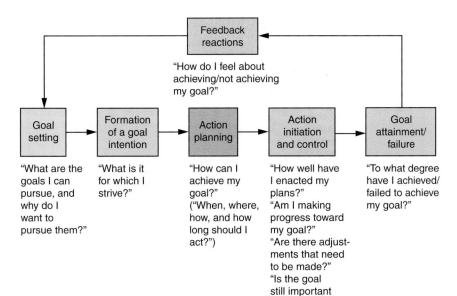

FIGURE 4.2

The Needs and Goals Behind Losing or Maintaining Body Weight

Source: From "Goal Setting and Goal Pursuit in the Regulation of Body Weight," by Richard Bagozzi and Elizabeth Edwards originally published in *Psychology and Health, 13,* 1998. Reprinted by permission of Taylor & Francis Ltd., www.tandf.co.uk/journals.

(A)

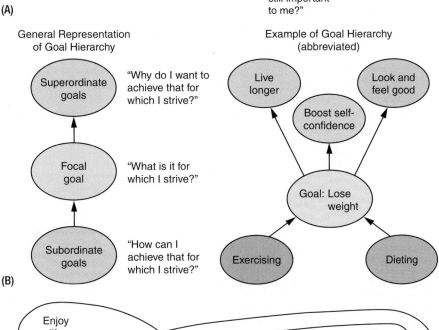

(B)

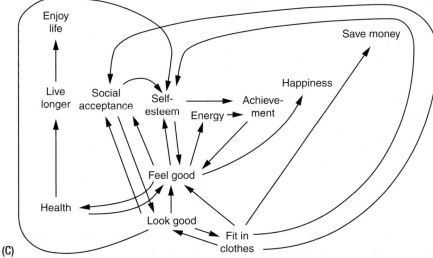

(C)

FIGURE 4.3

Source: Courtesy of Weider Publications, Inc.

Achieving Goals by Subscribing to a Magazine

that the consumers were encouraged to believe they had obtained were stated as either gains (i.e., promotion goals) or the avoidance of losses (i.e., prevention goals). The study showed that people who felt proud of their negotiating skills and also believed that they avoided losses were less likely to repurchase the product than persons who felt proud and also believed that they had achieved gains. For the people who did not feel proud, the type of goals they believed they had accomplished had no impact on intentions to repurchase the product.[6]

Goals are also related to negative forms of consumption behavior. One study found that personal goals that focus on extrinsic benefits (such as financial success, social status, and being attractive to others) are associated with higher degrees of

Source: Courtesy of Illuminating Experiences. Agency is BrandStreet Advertising LLC. Copy by Ed Shankman, art by Dave Frank, and design by Joe Gwgliuzza. **FIGURE 4.4**

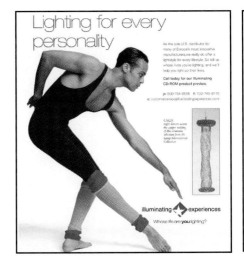  

Different Appeals for Same Goal Object

compulsive buying than goals that stress intrinsic benefits (such as self-acceptance, affiliation, and connection with community).[7] These studies illustrate the complexity of the ways consumers conceptualize goals and the impact of set or achieved goals on consumption behavior.

Figure 4.4 shows appeals to three different target audiences for the same goal object—lighting. Figure 4.5 presents a series of advertisements for American Airlines illustrating that individuals have different reasons and seek to accomplish different goals when flying the airline. The statement that the airline knows what these goals are conveys the company's focus on its customers' needs.

Interdependence of needs and goals

Needs and goals are interdependent; neither exists without the other. However, people are often not as aware of their needs as they are of their goals. For example, a teenager may not consciously be aware of his social needs but may join a number of chat groups online to meet new friends. A person may not consciously be aware of a power need but may choose to run for public office when an elective position becomes available. A college student may not consciously recognize her need for achievement but may strive to attain a straight A grade point average.

Individuals are usually somewhat more aware of their *physiological* needs than they are of their *psychological* needs. Most people know when they are hungry, thirsty, or cold, and they take appropriate steps to satisfy these needs. The same people may not consciously be aware of their needs for acceptance, self-esteem, or status. They may, however, subconsciously engage in behavior that satisfies their psychological (acquired) needs.

Positive and negative motivation

Motivation can be **positive** or **negative** in direction. We may feel a driving force *toward* some object or condition or a driving force *away* from some object or condition. For example, a person may be impelled toward a restaurant to fulfill a hunger need, and away from motorcycle transportation to fulfill a safety need.

Some psychologists refer to positive drives as needs, wants, or desires and to negative drives as fears or aversions. However, although positive and negative motivational

Source: © American Airlines, Inc. Used with permission. All rights reserved. (www.aa.com)

FIGURE 4.5

Different Appeals for Same Goal Object American Airlines

forces seem to differ dramatically in terms of physical (and sometimes emotional) activity, they are basically similar in that both serve to initiate and sustain human behavior. For this reason, researchers often refer to both kinds of drives or motives as *needs, wants*, and *desires*. Some theorists distinguish *wants* from *needs* by defining wants as product-specific needs. Others differentiate between desires, on the one hand, and needs and wants on the other. Thus, there is no uniformly accepted distinction among the terms needs, wants, and desires.

Needs, wants, or desires may lead to goals that can be positive or negative. A positive goal is one toward which behavior is directed; thus, it is often referred to as an **approach object**. A negative goal is one from which behavior is directed away and is referred to as an **avoidance object**. Because both approach and avoidance goals are the results of motivated behavior, most researchers refer to both simply as *goals*. Consider this example: A middle-aged woman with a positive goal of fitness may join a health club to work out regularly. Her husband, who views getting fat as a negative goal, joins a health club to guide his exercise. In the former case, the wife's actions are designed to achieve the *positive* goal of health and fitness; in the latter case, her husband's actions are designed to avoid a *negative* goal—a flabby physique. Figure 4.6 shows two ads for Neutrogena sun lotion—one stressing *positive motivation* and the other *negative motivation*.

Rational versus emotional motives

Some consumer behaviorists distinguish between so-called **rational motives** and **emotional motives**. They use the term *rationality* in the traditional economic sense, which assumes that consumers behave rationally by carefully considering all alternatives and choosing those that give them the greatest utility. In a marketing context, the term *rationality* implies that consumers select goals based on totally objective criteria, such as size, weight, price, or miles per gallon. Emotional motives imply the selection of goals according to personal or subjective criteria (e.g., pride, fear, affection, or status).

The assumption underlying this distinction is that subjective or emotional criteria do not maximize utility or satisfaction. However, it is reasonable to assume that consumers always attempt to select alternatives that, in their view, serve to best satisfy

FIGURE 4.6

Source: © Neutrogena
Corporation.

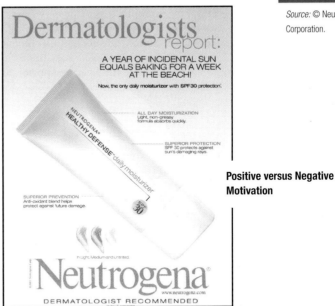

**Positive versus Negative
Motivation**

their needs. Obviously, the assessment of satisfaction is a very personal process, based on the individual's own need structure, as well as on past behavioral and social (or learned) experiences. What may appear irrational to an outside observer may be perfectly rational in the context of the consumer's own psychological field. For example, a person who pursues extensive facial cosmetic surgery in order to appear younger uses significant economic resources (e.g., hefty surgical fees, time lost in recovery, inconvenience, and the risk that something may go wrong) to achieve her goal. To that person, undergoing the surgery, and expending the considerable financial and physical costs required, are perfectly rational decisions to achieve her goal. However, to many other persons within the same culture who are less concerned with aging, and to persons from other cultures that are not so preoccupied with personal appearance, these decisions appear completely irrational.

the dynamics of motivation

Motivation is a highly dynamic construct that is constantly changing in reaction to life experiences. Needs and goals change and grow in response to an individual's physical condition, environment, interactions with others, and experiences. As individuals attain their goals, they develop new ones. If they do not attain their goals, they continue to strive for old goals or they develop substitute goals. Some of the reasons why need-driven human activity never ceases include the following: (1) Many needs are never fully satisfied; they continually impel actions designed to attain or maintain satisfaction. (2) As needs become satisfied, new and higher-order needs emerge that cause tension and induce activity. (3) People who achieve their goals set new and higher goals for themselves.

Needs are never fully satisfied

Most human needs are never fully or permanently satisfied. For example, at fairly regular intervals throughout each day individuals experience hunger needs that must be satisfied. Most people regularly seek companionship and approval from others to satisfy their social needs. Even more complex psychological needs are rarely fully satisfied. For example, a person may partially satisfy a need for power by working as administrative assistant to a local politician, but this vicarious taste of power may not sufficiently satisfy her need; thus, she may strive to work for a state legislator or even to run for political office herself. In this instance, temporary goal achievement does not adequately satisfy the need for power, and the individual strives ever harder to more fully satisfy that need.

New needs emerge as old needs are satisfied

Some motivational theorists believe that a hierarchy of needs exists and that new, higher-order needs emerge as lower-order needs are fulfilled.[8] For example, a man whose basic physiological needs (e.g., food, housing, etc.) are fairly well satisfied may turn his efforts to achieving acceptance among his neighbors by joining their political clubs and supporting their candidates. Once he is confident that he has achieved acceptance, he then may seek recognition by giving lavish parties or building a larger house.

Marketers must be attuned to changing needs. For example, the Mercedes-Benz ad shown in Figure 4.7 portrays three different car models corresponding to an individual's needs as he or she matures.

Success and failure influence goals

A number of researchers have explored the nature of the goals that individuals set for themselves. Broadly speaking, they have concluded that individuals who successfully achieve their goals usually set new and higher goals for themselves; that is, they raise their **levels of aspiration**. This may be due to the fact that their success in reaching lower goals makes them more confident of their ability to reach higher goals. Conversely, those who do not reach their goals sometimes lower their levels of aspiration.[9] Thus, goal selection is often a function of success and failure. For example, a college senior who is not accepted into medical school may try instead to become a dentist or a podiatrist.

The nature and persistence of an individual's behavior are often influenced by expectations of success or failure in reaching certain goals. Those expectations, in turn, are often based on past experience. A person who takes good snapshots with an inexpensive camera may be motivated to buy a more sophisticated camera in the belief that it will enable him to take even better photographs, and eventually he may upgrade his camera by several hundred dollars. On the other hand, a person who has not been able to take good photographs is just as likely to keep the same camera or even to lose all interest in photography.

These effects of success and failure on goal selection have strategy implications for marketers. Goals should be reasonably attainable. Advertisements should not promise more than the product will deliver. Products and services are often evaluated by the size and direction of the gap between consumer expectations and objective performance. Thus, even a good product will not be repurchased if it fails to live up to unrealistic expectations created by ads that "overpromise." Similarly, a consumer is likely to regard a mediocre product with greater satisfaction than it warrants if its performance exceeds her expectations.

Substitute goals

When an individual cannot attain a specific goal or type of goal that he or she anticipates will satisfy certain needs, behavior may be directed to a **substitute goal**. Although the substitute goal may not be as satisfactory as the primary goal, it may be sufficient to dispel uncomfortable tension. Continued deprivation of a primary goal may result in the substitute goal assuming primary-goal status. For example, a woman who has

FIGURE 4.7

Source: Courtesy of Mercedes-Benz. Image © Jake Chessum.

Product Alternatives for Changing Consumer Needs

stopped drinking whole milk because she is dieting may actually begin to prefer skim milk. A man who cannot afford a BMW may convince himself that a new sporty Chrysler Sebring has an image he clearly prefers.

Frustration

Failure to achieve a goal often results in feelings of frustration. At one time or another, everyone has experienced the frustration that comes from the inability to attain a goal.

The barrier that prevents attainment of a goal may be personal to the individual (e.g., limited physical or financial resources) or an obstacle in the physical or social environment (e.g., a storm that causes the postponement of a long-awaited vacation). Regardless of the cause, individuals react differently to frustrating situations. Some people manage to cope by finding their way around the obstacle or, if that fails, by selecting a substitute goal. Others are less adaptive and may regard their inability to achieve a goal as a personal failure. Such people are likely to adopt a defense mechanism to protect their egos from feelings of inadequacy. The creation of a new type of children's board game represents a creative response to the concept of frustration. Unlike most board games, where a child who has lost may be frustrated and subject to the ridicule of other children, the new game is centered on skill-building activities and provides every child with a chance to shine. While the game is built on a "nobody loses" concept, the designers have carefully built in an element of competition because a complete lack of competition may make a game seem boring.[10]

Defense mechanisms

People who cannot cope with frustration often mentally redefine their frustrating situations in order to protect their self-images and self-esteem. For example, a young woman may yearn for a European vacation she cannot afford. The coping individual may select a less expensive vacation trip to Disneyland or to a national park. The person who cannot cope may react with anger toward her boss for not paying her enough money to afford the vacation she prefers, or she may persuade herself that Europe is unseasonably warm this year. These last two possibilities are examples, respectively, of *aggression* and *rationalization*, **defense mechanisms** that people sometimes adopt to protect their egos from feelings of failure when they do not attain their goals. Other defense mechanisms include *regression, withdrawal, projection, daydreaming, identification*, and *repression*. These defense mechanisms are described in Table 4.2. This listing of defense mechanisms is far from exhaustive, because individuals tend to develop their own ways of redefining frustrating situations to protect their self-esteem from the anxieties that result from experiencing failure. Marketers often consider this fact in their selection of advertising appeals and construct advertisements that portray a person resolving a particular frustration through the use of the advertised product.

Multiplicity of needs and variation of goals

A consumer's behavior often fulfills more than one need. In fact, it is likely that specific goals are selected because they fulfill several needs. We buy clothing for protection and for a certain degree of modesty; in addition, our clothing fulfills a wide range of personal and social needs, such as acceptance or ego needs.

One cannot accurately infer motives from behavior. People with different needs may seek fulfillment through selection of the same goal; people with the same needs may seek fulfillment through different goals. Consider the following examples. Five people who are active in a neighborhood association may each belong for a different reason. The first may be genuinely concerned with protecting the interests of the neighborhood's residents; the second may be concerned about the possibility of increased crime in the area; the third may seek social contacts from organizational meetings; the fourth may enjoy the power of directing a large group; and the fifth may enjoy the status provided by membership in an attention-getting organization.

Similarly, five people may be driven by the same need (e.g., an ego need) to seek fulfillment in different ways. The first may seek advancement and recognition through a professional career; the second may become active in a political organization; the third may run in regional marathons; the fourth may take professional dance lessons; and the fifth may seek attention by monopolizing classroom discussions.

Realizing that many people have a need to make new friends as well as have a place to live, new apartment buildings in New York City now include such facilities as private parks, entertainment rooms, card rooms, exercise rooms, billiard rooms adjacent

TABLE 4.2	Defense Mechanisms
DEFENSE MECHANISM	**DESCRIPTION AND ILLUSTRATIONS**
Aggression	In response to frustration, individuals may resort to aggressive behavior in attempting to protect their self-esteem. The tennis pro who slams his tennis racket to the ground when disappointed with his game or the baseball player who physically intimidates an empire for his call are examples of such conduct. So are consumer boycotts of companies or stores.
Rationalization	People sometimes resolve frustration by inventing plausible reasons for being unable to attain their goals (e.g., not having enough time to practice) or deciding that the goal is not really worth pursuing (e.g., how important is it to achieve a high bowling score?).
Regression	An individual may react to a frustrating situation with childish or immature behavior. A shopper attending a bargain sale, for example, may fight over merchandise and even rip a garment that another shopper will not relinquish rather than allow the other person to have it.
Withdrawal	Frustration may be resolved by simply withdrawing from the situation. For instance, a person who has difficulty achieving officer status in an organization may decide he can use his time more constructively in other activities and simply quit that organization.
Projection	An individual may redefine a frustrating situation by projecting blame for his or her own failures and inabilities on other objects or persons. Thus, the golfer who misses a stroke may blame his golf clubs or his caddy.
Daydreaming	Daydreaming, or fantasizing, enables the individual to attain imaginary gratification of unfulfilled needs. A person who is shy and lonely, for example, may daydream about a romantic love affair.
Identification	People resolve feelings of frustration by subconsciously identifying with other persons or situations that they consider relevant. For example, slice-of-life commercials often portray a stereotypical situation in which an individual experiences a frustration and then overcomes the problem by using the advertised product. If the viewer can identify with the frustrating situation, he or she may very likely adopt the proposed solution and buy the product advertised.
Repression	Another way that individuals avoid the tension arising from frustration is by repressing the unsatisfied need. Thus, individuals may "force" the need out of their conscious awareness. Sometimes repressed needs manifest themselves indirectly. The wife who is unable to bear children may teach school or work in a library; her husband may do volunteer work in a boys' club. The manifestation of repressed needs in a socially acceptable form is called *sublimation*, another type of defense mechanism.

to laundry rooms, and other types of common areas that convey a sense of community and facilitate meetings with neighbors.[11]

Arousal of motives

Most of an individual's specific needs are dormant much of the time. The arousal of any particular set of needs at a specific moment in time may be caused by internal stimuli found in the individual's physiological condition, by emotional or cognitive processes, or by stimuli in the outside environment.

Physiological arousal

Bodily needs at any one specific moment in time are based on the individual's physiological condition at that moment. A drop in blood sugar level or stomach contractions will trigger awareness of a hunger need. Secretion of sex hormones will awaken the sex need. A decrease in body temperature will induce shivering, which makes the individual aware of the need for warmth. Most of these physiological cues are involuntary; however, they arouse related needs that cause uncomfortable tensions until they are satisfied. For example, a person who is cold may turn up the heat in his bedroom and also make a mental note to buy a warm cardigan sweater to wear around the house. Figure 4.8 demonstrates arousal of a physiological need.

Emotional arousal

Sometimes daydreaming results in the arousal or stimulation of latent needs. People who are bored or who are frustrated in trying to achieve their goals often engage in daydreaming (autistic thinking), in which they imagine themselves in all sorts of desirable situations. These thoughts tend to arouse dormant needs, which may produce uncomfortable tensions that drive them into goal-oriented behavior. A young woman who daydreams of a torrid romance may spend her free time in Internet single chat rooms; a young man who dreams of being a famous novelist may enroll in a writing workshop.

Cognitive arousal

Sometimes random thoughts can lead to a cognitive awareness of needs. An advertisement that provides reminders of home might trigger instant yearning to speak with one's parents. This is the basis for many long-distance telephone company campaigns that stress the low cost of international long-distance rates.

Environmental (or situational) arousal

The set of needs an individual experiences at a particular time are often activated by specific cues in the environment. Without these cues, the needs might remain dormant. For example, the 6 o'clock news, the sight or smell of bakery goods, fast-food commercials on television, the end of the school day—all of these may arouse the "need" for food. In such cases, modification of the environment may be necessary to reduce the arousal of hunger.

A most potent form of situational cue is the goal object itself. A woman may experience an overwhelming desire to visit Australia when she is drawn to the scene depicted in Figure 4.9; a man may suddenly experience a "need" for a new car when passing a dealer's display window. Sometimes an advertisement or other environmental cue produces a psychological imbalance in the viewer's mind. For example, a young college student who constantly uses his cell phone may see a new, slick-looking cell phone model with more features displayed in a store window. The exposure may make him unhappy with his old cell phone and cause him to experience tension that will be reduced only when he buys himself the new cell phone model.

FIGURE 4.8

Source: © The Procter &
Gamble Company. Used by
permission.

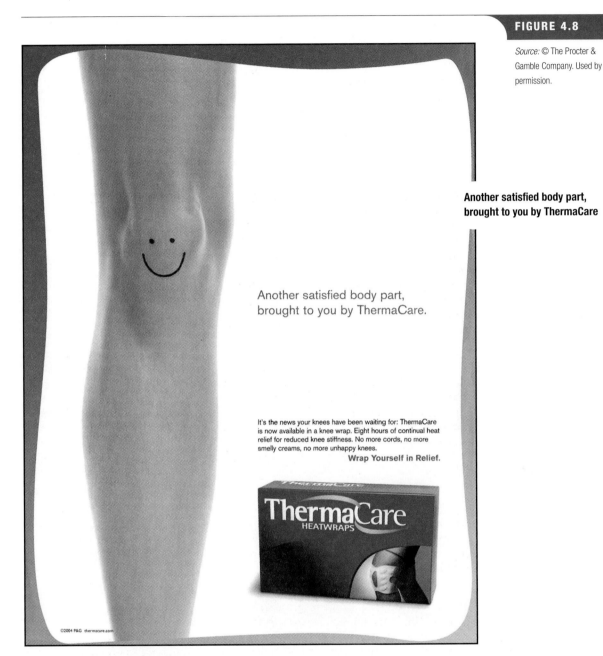

**Another satisfied body part,
brought to you by ThermaCare**

Another satisfied body part,
brought to you by ThermaCare.

It's the news your knees have been waiting for: ThermaCare
is now available in a knee wrap. Eight hours of continual heat
relief for reduced knee stiffness. No more cords, no more
smelly creams, no more unhappy knees.

Wrap Yourself in Relief.

When people live in a complex and highly varied environment, they experience
many opportunities for need arousal. Conversely, when their environment is poor or
deprived, fewer needs are activated. This explains why television has had such a mixed
effect on the lives of people in underdeveloped countries. It exposes them to various
lifestyles and expensive products that they would not otherwise see, and it awakens
wants and desires that they have little opportunity or even hope of satisfying. Thus,
while television enriches many lives, it also serves to frustrate people with little money
or education or hope, and may result in the adoption of such aggressive defense mechanisms as robbery, boycotts, or even revolts.

Source: © Tourism Australia. Used with permission. All rights reserved. (www.australia.com)

FIGURE 4.9

Environmental Arousal

There are two opposing philosophies concerned with the arousal of human motives. The **behaviorist school** considers motivation to be a mechanical process; behavior is seen as the response to a stimulus, and elements of conscious thought are ignored. An extreme example of the *stimulus–response* theory of motivation is the impulse buyer who reacts largely to external stimuli in the buying situation. According to this theory, the consumer's cognitive control is limited; he or she does not act but reacts to stimuli in the marketplace (e.g., an ice cream truck on the corner). The **cognitive school** believes that all behavior is directed at goal achievement.

Needs and past experiences are reasoned, categorized, and transformed into attitudes and beliefs that act as predispositions focused on helping the individual satisfy needs, and they determine the actions that he or she takes to achieve this satisfaction.

types and systems of needs

For many years, psychologists and others interested in human behavior have attempted to develop exhaustive lists of human needs. Most lists of human needs tend to be diverse in content as well as in length. Although there is little disagreement about specific physiological needs, there is considerable disagreement about specific psychological (i.e., psychogenic) needs.

In 1938, the psychologist Henry Murray prepared a detailed list of 28 psychogenic needs. This research was probably the first systematic approach to the understanding of nonbiological human needs. Murray believed that everyone has the same basic set of needs but that individuals differ in their priority ranking of these needs. Murray's basic needs include many motives that are assumed to play an important role in consumer behavior, such as acquisition, achievement, recognition, and exhibition (see Table 4.3).

Hierarchy of needs

Dr. Abraham Maslow, a clinical psychologist, formulated a widely accepted theory of human motivation based on the notion of a universal hierarchy of human needs.[12] Maslow's theory identifies five basic levels of human needs, which rank in order of importance from lower-level (biogenic) needs to higher-level (psychogenic) needs. The theory postulates that individuals seek to satisfy lower-level needs before higher-level needs emerge. The lowest level of chronically unsatisfied need that an individual experiences serves to motivate his or her behavior. When that need is "fairly well" satisfied, a new (and higher) need emerges that the individual is motivated to fulfill. When this need is satisfied, a new (and still higher) need emerges, and so on. Of course, if a lower-level need experiences some renewed deprivation (e.g., thirst), it may temporarily become dominant again.

Figure 4.10 presents a diagram of **Maslow's hierarchy of needs**. For clarity, each level is depicted as mutually exclusive. According to the theory, however, there is some overlap between each level, as no need is ever completely satisfied. For this reason, although all levels of need below the level that is currently dominant continue to motivate behavior to some extent, the prime motivator—the major driving force within the individual—is the lowest level of need that remains largely unsatisfied.

Physiological needs

In the hierarchy-of-needs theory, physiological needs are the first and most basic level of human needs. These needs, which are required to sustain biological life, include food, water, air, shelter, clothing, sex—all the biogenic needs, in fact, that were listed as primary needs earlier.

According to Maslow, physiological needs are dominant when they are chronically unsatisfied: "For the man who is extremely and dangerously hungry, no other interest exists but food. He dreams food, he remembers food, he thinks about food, he emotes only about food, he perceives only food, and he wants only food."[13] For many people in this country, the biogenic needs tend to be satisfied, and higher-level needs are dominant. Unfortunately, however, the lives of the many homeless people in major cities and in physically devastated areas are focused almost entirely on satisfying their biogenic needs, such as the needs for food, clothing, and shelter.

TABLE 4.3	Murray's List of Psychogenic Needs

NEEDS ASSOCIATED WITH INANIMATE OBJECTS

Acquisition

Conservancy

Order

Retention

Construction

NEEDS THAT REFLECT AMBITION, POWER, ACCOMPLISHMENT, AND PRESTIGE

Superiority

Achievement

Recognition

Exhibition

Inviolacy (inviolate attitude)

Infavoidance (to avoid shame, failure, humiliation, ridicule)

Defendance (defensive attitude)

Counteraction (counteractive attitude)

NEEDS CONCERNED WITH HUMAN POWER

Dominance

Deferrence

Similance (suggestible attitude)

Autonomy

Contrariance (to act differently from others)

SADOMASOCHISTIC NEEDS

Aggression

Abasement

NEEDS CONCERNED WITH AFFECTION BETWEEN PEOPLE

Affiliation

Rejection

Nurturance (to nourish, aid, or protect the helpless)

Succorance (to seek aid, protection, or sympathy)

Play

NEEDS CONCERNED WITH SOCIAL INTERCOURSE (THE NEEDS TO ASK AND TELL)

Cognizance (inquiring attitude)

Exposition (expositive attitude)

Source: Adapted from Henry A. Murray, "Types of Human Needs," in David C. McClelland, *Studies in Motivation* (New York: Appleton-Century-Crofts, 1955), 63–66. Reprinted by permission of Irvington Publishers, Inc.

Safety needs

After the first level of need is satisfied, safety and security needs become the driving force behind an individual's behavior. These needs are concerned not only with physical safety but also include order, stability, routine, familiarity, and control over one's life and environment. Health and the availability of health care are important safety concerns. Savings accounts, insurance policies, education,

FIGURE 4.10

Maslow's Hierarchy of Needs

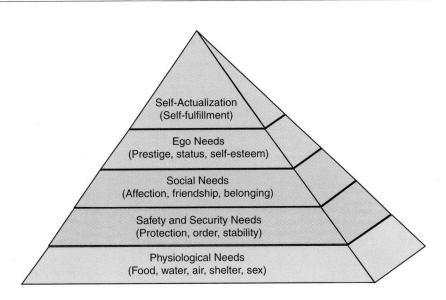

and vocational training are all means by which individuals satisfy the need for security.

Social needs

The third level of Maslow's hierarchy includes such needs as love, affection, belonging, and acceptance. People seek warm and satisfying human relationships with other people and are motivated by love for their families. Because of the importance of social motives in our society, advertisers of many product categories emphasize this appeal in their advertisements.

Egoistic needs

When social needs are more or less satisfied, the fourth level of Maslow's hierarchy becomes operative. This level is concerned with egoistic needs. These needs can take either an inward or an outward orientation, or both. Inwardly directed ego needs reflect an individual's need for self-acceptance, self-esteem, success, independence, and personal satisfaction with a job well done. Outwardly directed ego needs include the needs for prestige, reputation, status, and recognition from others. Figure 4.11 presents an ad designed to fulfill both an inward and outward orientation.

Need for self-actualization

According to Maslow, most people do not satisfy their ego needs sufficiently to ever move to the fifth level—the need for self-actualization (self-fulfillment). This need refers to an individual's desire to fulfill his or her potential—to become everything he or she is capable of becoming. In Maslow's words, "What a man can be, he must be."[14] This need is expressed in different ways by different people. A young man may desire to be an Olympic star and work single-mindedly for years to become the best in his sport. An artist may need to express herself on canvas; a research scientist may strive to find a new drug that eradicates cancer. Maslow noted that the self-actualization need is not necessarily a creative urge but that it is likely to take that form in people with some capacity for creativity. Some of our largest corporations encourage their highly paid employees to look beyond their paychecks to find gratification and self-fulfillment in the workplace—to view their jobs

FIGURE 4.11

Source: © The Marketing
Directors Inc. Used with
permission. All rights reserved.

Appeal to Egoistic Needs

as the way to become "all they can be." Figure 4.12 shows an ad for athletic shoes based on a self-actualization appeal (note that the shoes themselves are not featured in the ad).

An evaluation of the need hierarchy and marketing applications

Maslow's hierarchy-of-needs theory postulates a five-level hierarchy of prepotent human needs. Higher-order needs become the driving force behind human behavior as

FIGURE 4.12

Source: Courtesy of Converse.

Appeal to Self-Actualization

lower-level needs are satisfied. The theory says, in effect, that dissatisfaction, not satisfaction, motivates behavior.

The need hierarchy has received wide acceptance in many social disciplines because it appears to reflect the assumed or inferred motivations of many people in our society. The five levels of need are sufficiently generic to encompass most lists of individual needs. The major problem with the theory is that it cannot be tested empirically; there is no way to measure precisely how satisfied one level of need must be before the next higher need becomes operative. The need hierarchy also appears to be very closely bound to our contemporary American culture (i.e., it appears to be both culture- and time-bound).

Despite these limitations, the hierarchy offers a highly useful framework for marketers trying to develop appropriate advertising appeals for their products. It is adaptable in two ways: First, it enables marketers to focus their advertising appeals on a need level that is likely to be shared by a large segment of the target audience; second, it facilitates product positioning or repositioning.

Segmentation and promotional applications

Maslow's need hierarchy is readily adaptable to market segmentation and the development of advertising appeals because there are consumer goods designed to satisfy each of the need levels and because most needs are shared by large segments of consumers. For example, individuals buy health foods, medicines, and low-fat products to satisfy physiological needs. They buy insurance, preventive medical services, and home security systems to satisfy safety and security needs. Almost all personal care and grooming products (e.g., cosmetics, mouthwash, shaving cream), as well as most clothes, are bought to satisfy social needs. High-tech products such as elaborate sound systems and luxury products (e.g., furs, big cars, or expensive furniture) are often bought to fulfill ego and esteem needs. Postgraduate college education, hobby-related products, exotic and physically challenging adventure trips are sold as ways of achieving self-fulfillment.

The need hierarchy is often used as the basis for market segmentation, with specific advertising appeals directed to one or more need-segment levels. For example, the BMW ad presented in Figure 4.13 stresses power, an egoistic need. An ad for a very expensive sports car may use a self-actualization appeal such as "you deserve the very best."

Advertisers may use the need hierarchy for **positioning** products—that is, deciding how the product should be perceived by prospective consumers. The key to positioning is to find a niche—an unsatisfied need—that is not occupied by a competing product or brand. The need hierarchy is a very versatile tool for developing positioning strategies because different appeals for the same product can be based on different needs included in this framework. For example, many ads for soft drinks stress social appeal by showing a group of young people enjoying themselves and the advertised product; others stress refreshment (a physiological need); still others may focus on low caloric content (thus indirectly appealing to the ego need).

A trio of needs

Some psychologists believe in the existence of a trio of basic needs: the needs for power, for affiliation, and for achievement. These needs can each be subsumed within Maslow's need hierarchy; considered individually, however, each has a unique relevance to consumer motivation.

Power

The power need relates to an individual's desire to control his or her environment. It includes the need to control other persons and various objects. This need appears to be closely related to the ego need, in that many individuals experience increased self-esteem when they exercise power over objects or people.

Affiliation

Affiliation is a well-known and well-researched social motive that has far-reaching influence on consumer behavior. The affiliation need suggests that behavior is strongly influenced by the desire for friendship, for acceptance, for belonging. People with high affiliation needs tend to be socially dependent on others. They often select goods they feel will meet with the approval of friends. Teenagers who hang out at

FIGURE 4.13

Source: Courtesy of BMW.

Appeal to the Power Need

malls or techies who congregate at computer shows often do so more for the satisfaction of being with others than for making a purchase. An appeal to the affiliation needs of young adults is shown in Figure 4.14. The affiliation need is very similar to Maslow's social need.

Achievement

A considerable number of research studies have focused on the achievement need.[15] Individuals with a strong need for achievement often regard personal accomplishment as an end in itself. The achievement need is closely related to both the egoistic need and the self-actualization need. People with a high need for achievement tend to be more self-confident, enjoy taking calculated risks, actively research their environments, and value feedback. Monetary rewards provide an important type of

FIGURE 4.14

Source: Photograph by James
Mollison. Courtesy of United
Colors of Benetton.

Appeal to the Affiliation Need

feedback as to how they are doing. People with high achievement needs prefer situations in which they can take personal responsibility for finding solutions. High achievement is a useful promotional strategy for many products and services targeted to educated and affluent consumers. Figure 4.15 demonstrates an appeal to the achievement need.

In summary, individuals with specific psychological needs tend to be receptive to advertising appeals directed at those needs. They also tend to be receptive to certain kinds of products. Thus, a knowledge of motivational theory provides marketers with key bases for segmenting markets and developing promotional strategies.

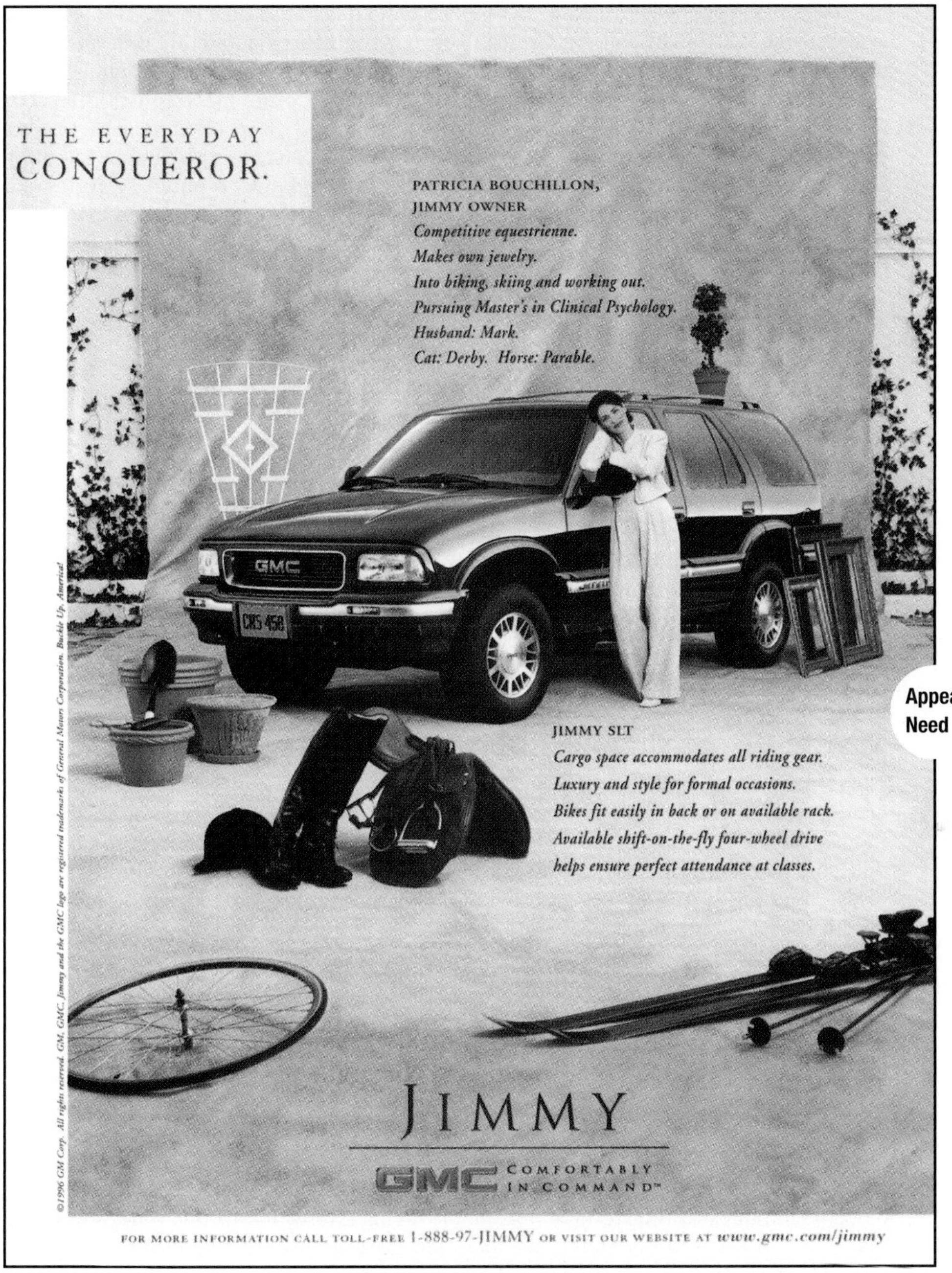
THE EVERYDAY
CONQUEROR.
PATRICIA BOUCHILLON,
JIMMY OWNER
Competitive equestrienne.
Makes own jewelry.
Into biking, skiing and working out.
Pursuing Master's in Clinical Psychology.
Husband: Mark.
Cat: Derby. Horse: Parable.
GMC
JIMMY SLT
Cargo space accommodates all riding gear.
Luxury and style for formal occasions.
Bikes fit easily in back or on available rack.
Available shift-on-the-fly four-wheel drive
helps ensure perfect attendance at classes.
JIMMY
GMC COMFORTABLY IN COMMAND™
FOR MORE INFORMATION CALL TOLL-FREE 1-888-97-JIMMY OR VISIT OUR WEBSITE AT www.gmc.com/jimmy
©1996 GM Corp. All rights reserved. GM, GMC, Jimmy and the GMC logo are registered trademarks of General Motors Corporation. Buckle Up, America!

FIGURE 4.15

Source: Courtesy of General Motors Corporation.

Appeal to the Achievement Need

the measurement of motives

How are motives identified? How are they measured? How do researchers know which motives are responsible for certain kinds of behavior? These are difficult questions to answer because motives are hypothetical constructs—that is, they cannot be seen or touched, handled, smelled, or otherwise tangibly observed. For this reason, no single measurement method can be considered a reliable index. Instead, researchers usually rely on a combination of various research techniques to try to establish the presence and/or the strength of various motives. By using a combination of assessments based on behavioral data (observation), subjective data (self-reports), and qualitative data (projective tests, collage research, etc.), many consumer researchers feel confident that they are achieving more valid insights into consumer motivations than they would by using any one technique alone.

Constructing a scale that measures a specific need, while meeting the criteria of reliability and validity, can be complex. For example, a recent research project employed six different studies to develop and validate a seemingly simple five-item scale to measure status consumption (defined as the tendency to purchase goods and services for the prestige that owning them bestows). Respondents are asked to indicate their level of agreement or disagreement (i.e., using a Likert scale) on the following five items:[16]

1. I would buy a product just because it has status.
2. I am interested in new products with status.
3. I would pay more for a product if it had status.
4. The status of the product is irrelevant to me.
5. A product is more valuable to me if it has some snob appeal.

As discussed in Chapter 2, the findings of qualitative research methods are highly dependent on the analyst; they focus not only on the data themselves but also on what the analyst thinks they imply. Though some marketers are concerned that qualitative research does not produce hard numbers that objectively "prove" the point under investigation, others are convinced that qualitative studies are more revealing than quantitative studies. However, there is a clear need for improved methodological procedures for measuring human motives.

Motivational research

The term **motivational research**, which should logically include all types of research into human motives, has become a "term of art" used to refer to qualitative research designed to uncover the consumer's subconscious or hidden motivations. Based on the premise that consumers are not always aware of the reasons for their actions, motivational research attempts to discover underlying feelings, attitudes, and emotions concerning product, service, or brand use.

The development of motivational research

Sigmund Freud's psychoanalytic theory of personality (discussed in Chapter 5) provided the foundation for the development of motivational research. This theory was built on the premise that unconscious needs or drives—especially biological and sexual drives—are at the heart of human motivation and personality. Freud constructed his theory from patients' recollections of early childhood experiences, analysis of their dreams, and the specific nature of their mental and physical adjustment problems.

Dr. Ernest Dichter, formerly a psychoanalyst in Vienna, adapted Freud's psychoanalytical techniques to the study of consumer buying habits. Up to this time, marketing research had focused on what consumers did (i.e., quantitative, descriptive studies). Dichter used qualitative research methods to find out *why* they did it. Marketers were quickly fascinated by the glib, entertaining, and usually surprising explanations offered for consumer behavior, especially since many of these explanations were grounded in sex. For example, marketers were told that cigarettes and Lifesaver candies were bought because of their sexual symbolism, that men regarded convertible cars as surrogate mistresses, and that women baked cakes to fulfill their reproductive yearnings. Before long, almost every major advertising agency in the country had a psychologist on staff to conduct motivational research studies. Four product profiles developed by Dichter and their applications to contemporary products are presented in Table 4.4.

By the early 1960s, however, marketers realized that motivational research had a number of drawbacks. Because of the intensive nature of qualitative research, samples

TABLE 4.4	Dichter's Research: Selected Product Personality Profiles and Current Applications

BAKING

Dichter described *baking* as an expression of femininity and motherhood, evoking nostalgic memories of delicious odors pervading the house when the mother was baking. He said that when baking a cake, a woman is subconsciously and symbolically going through the act of giving birth, and the most fertile moment occurs when the baked product is pulled from the oven. Dichter also maintained that when a woman bakes a cake for a man, she is offering him a symbol of fertility.[a] The Betty Crocker image was based on this profile.

AUTOMOBILES

According to Dichter, the car allows consumers to convert their subconscious urges to destroy and their fear of death—two key forces in the human psyche—into reality. For example, the expression "step on it" stems from the desire to feel power, and the phrase "I just missed that car by inches" reflects the desire to play with danger. Based on this view, Dichter advised Esso (now Exxon) to tap into consumers' aggressive motives for driving cars in promoting the superiority of its gasoline product. The slogan "Put a tiger in your tank" was developed as a result of his advice.[b]

Dichter also maintained that cars have personalities, and that people become attached to their cars and view them as companions rather than objects. This notion stands behind his views that a man views a convertible as a mistress and a sedan as his wife.

DOLLS

Dolls play an important part in the socialization of children and are universally accepted as an essential toy for girls. Parents choose dolls that have the kind of characteristics they want their children to have, and the doll is an object for both the parents and the children to enjoy. When Mattel introduced *Barbie* in 1959, the company hired Dichter as a consultant. His research indicated that while girls liked the doll, their mothers detested the doll's perfect bodily proportions and Teutonic appearance. Dichter advised Mattel to market the doll as a teenage fashion model, reflecting the mother's desire for a daughter's proper and fashionable appearance. The advertising themes used subtly told mothers that it is better for their daughters to appear attractive to men rather than nondescript.[c]

ICE CREAM

Dichter described ice cream as an effortless food that does not have to be chewed and that melts in your mouth, a sign of abundance, an almost orgiastic kind of food that people eat as if they want it to run down their chins. Accordingly, he recommended that ice cream packaging should be round, with illustrations that run around the box panel, suggesting unlimited quantity.

Sources: [a]Ernest Dichter, *Handbook of Consumer Motivations* (New York: McGraw-Hill Book Company, 1964); Jack Hitt, "Does the Smell of Coffee Brewing Remind You of Your Mother?" *New York Times Magazine*, May 7, 2000, 6, 71. [b]Phil Patton, "Car Shrinks," *Fortune*, March 18, 2002, 6. [c]Barbara Lippert, "B-Ball Barbie," *Adweek*, November 9, 1998, 39.

necessarily were small; thus, there was concern about generalizing findings to the total market. Also, marketers soon realized that the analysis of projective tests and depth interviews was highly subjective. The same data given to three different analysts could produce three different reports, each offering its own explanation of the consumer behavior examined. Critics noted that many of the projective tests that were used had originally been developed for clinical purposes rather than for studies of marketing or consumer behavior. (One of the basic criteria for test development is that the test be developed and validated for the specific purpose and on the specific audience profile from which information is desired.)

Other consumer theorists noted additional inconsistencies in applying Freudian theory to the study of consumer behavior. First, psychoanalytic theory was structured specifically for use with disturbed people, whereas consumer behaviorists were interested in explaining the behavior of "typical" consumers. Second, Freudian theory was developed in an entirely different social context (nineteenth-century Vienna), whereas motivational research was introduced in the 1950s in postwar America. Finally, too many motivational researchers imputed highly exotic (usually sexual) reasons to rather prosaic consumer purchases. Marketers began to question their recommendations (e.g., Is it better to sell a man a pair of suspenders as a means of holding up his pants or as a "reaction to castration anxiety"? Is it easier to persuade a woman to buy a garden hose to water her lawn or as a symbol of "genital competition with males"?).

Qualitative research techniques used in motivational research
There are a number of qualitative research techniques that are used to delve into the consumer's unconscious or hidden motivations, such as *metaphor analysis, storytelling, word association, sentence completion, thematic apperception tests, drawing pictures*, and *photo sorts*.

Metaphor Analysis   This method, including the tool termed *ZMET*, was discussed in detail in Chapter 2. When DuPont used metaphor analysis to study women's emotions regarding pantyhose, women revealed that they evoked feelings of sensuality and being sexy and attractive to men. The implication of these findings is that pantyhose ads must appeal less to women's executive personas and more to their sensual feelings.[17]

Storytelling   This method consists of having customers tell real-life stories regarding their use of the product under study. By using this method to study parents' perceptions of diapers, Kimberly-Clark discovered that parents viewed diapers as clothing related to a particular stage in the child's development. Thus, if their children wore diapers too long, parents became distressed and embarrassed because they viewed it as their failure to toilet train their children. Using these data, the company introduced its highly successful Huggies Pull-Ups training pants—a product that established a new category in the U.S. diaper industry.[18] One application of the storytelling method requires subjects to tell a story about *someone else*. For example, persons who are afraid to fly may feel embarrassed to elaborate on the reasons for that fear when asked directly. However, if asked to describe the reasons why an individual would be afraid to fly, subjects are likely to ascribe their own fears to another person. In doing so, they "project" their own apprehensions and anxieties regarding flying onto this third person.

Word Association and Sentence Completion   In the word association method, respondents are presented with words, one at a time, and asked to say the first word that comes to mind. This method is highly useful in determining consumers' associations with existing brand names and those under development. In sentence completion, respondents are asked to complete a sentence upon hearing the opening phrase (e.g., "People who drive convertibles . . .").

Thematic Apperception Test   Developed by Henry A. Murray, this test consists of showing pictures to individual respondents and asking them to tell a story about each picture. For example, research conducted for Clearasil employed an image of a female looking into a mirror under the caption "Here is a teenager looking into the mirror and seeing pimples." The researchers discovered that teenagers view their lives as fast-paced and socially active and that the discovery of a pimple abruptly disturbs the swiftness of their lives. The resulting advertising depicted a teenage male walking briskly down the street and spotting a pimple on his face in a store window. All motion around him stops. He applies Clearasil, the pimple disappears, and life resumes its pace.[19]

Drawing Pictures and Photo Sorts   Visual images are often used to study consumers' perceptions of various brands and to develop new advertising strategies. For example, when respondents were asked to draw pictures of the typical Pillsbury cake-mix user, their drawings depicted old-fashioned, chubby females wearing frilly aprons. When asked to draw pictures of the Duncan Hines cake-mix user, their drawings showed slim, "with it" women wearing heels and miniskirts. These findings provided important input to Pillsbury concerning the need to reposition its product.[20]

In a study using photo sorts conducted by the advertising agency for Playtex (a manufacturer of bras), respondents received stacks of photos depicting different types of women and asked to select pictures portraying their own self-images. Although many of the respondents were overweight, full-breasted, and old-fashioned in appearance, they selected photos showing physically fit, well-dressed, and independent women. The advertising agency advised Playtex to stop stressing the comfort of its bras in its ads and designed a new campaign showing sexy, thin, and big-bosomed women under the slogan "The fit that makes the fashion."[21]

Evaluation of motivational research

Despite its criticisms, motivational research is still regarded as an important tool by marketers who want to gain deeper insights into the *whys* of consumer behavior than conventional marketing research techniques can yield. Since motivational research often reveals unsuspected consumer motivations concerning product or brand usage, its principal use today is in the development of new ideas for promotional campaigns, ideas that can penetrate the consumer's conscious awareness by appealing to unrecognized needs.

Motivational research also provides marketers with a basic orientation for new product categories and enables them to explore consumer reactions to ideas and advertising copy at an early stage to avoid costly errors. Furthermore, as with all qualitative research techniques, motivational research findings provide consumer researchers with basic insights that enable them to design structured, quantitative marketing research studies to be conducted on larger, more representative samples of consumers.

ethics and consumer motivation

While some critics accuse marketers of "creating" needs and of manipulating consumers into buying goods they do not need, most people agree that marketers cannot create needs; however, they can awaken latent needs and encourage consumers to engage in unwholesome behaviors. For example, the pleasurable and social aspects of smoking, drinking, and gambling are often promoted as enticing and socially acceptable, while the addictive and health aspects are downplayed. Marketers sometimes target vulnerable consumers such as children, teenagers, and the elderly, who may not have the knowledge or experience to evaluate the products or services being promoted. These marketing practices may be legal, but many groups consider them unethical, and are pushing for new regulations and legislation to restrict their use. Many national advertisers voluntarily restrict these questionable marketing practices in order to maintain and enhance their images with their target publics.

Although marketers may not be able to sell consumers things they do not truly need, advertising often motivates consumers to buy and consume *larger amounts* of certain products. For example, in 2004, the food industry spent $10 billion on marketing to children, significantly contributing to the number of obese or overweight children, a population that has doubled in the past 20 years (no pun intended). As a result, some law makers have called for legislation regulating food advertising to children.[22] In response to these criticisms, Kraft Foods stopped TV advertising of certain products to children, and increased their advertising of sugar-free drinks and smaller packages of cookies.[23] McDonald's, a company frequently accused of selling junk foods with too much fat and poor nutritional quality, has eliminated some of its "super-sized" offerings and begun selling more salads. They even offer apples as a desert alternative to calorie-laden pies.[24]

Children are not the only vulnerable population. Teenagers and college students are often provided with too much easy credit, which puts them into financial difficulties for years. For example, as a result of very aggressive marketing of credit cards to college students, college loan debt has been rising, and the average graduate leaves college with over $18,000 in credit card debt, often coupled with a low credit rating, which can bring about a financial crisis for years to come.[25] One study showed that, on average, students received their first credit card at age 18 (some did so when they were as young as 15), more than 10 percent owned more than five cards, and most of these young people did not keep credit card receipts, did not check their monthly statements against their purchases, were unaware of the interest rates they were charged, and about 10 percent paid only the minimum required payment every month.[26] Recognizing that the marketing of credit cards to college students has become far too aggressive and against society's best interests, many states have passed, or are in the process of passing, strict rules limiting the marketing of banks and credit card companies on college campuses.[27]

Some insurance companies have been accused of using retired military officers to aggressively market life insurance, high-cost loans, and other financial products to young recruits and junior officers on American military bases. Because of legislative pressures and very negative publicity, several military insurance providers have begun offering full cash refunds to military personnel.

Direct-to-consumer pharmaceutical advertising, permitted since 1997, has increased the consumption of numerous categories of medications. Consumers confirm that they obtain most of the information about these medications from TV commercials rather than from their physicians.[28] Recognizing that direct-to-consumer advertising has become too aggressive, the pharmaceuticals industry has developed voluntary restrictions regarding this marketing method. The Senate majority leader has called for a two-year moratorium on advertising new drugs to consumers; one major pharmaceutical company has volunteered not to advertise new drugs to consumers during their first year on the market.[29]

We live in a complex, technologically advanced and competitive society where some offerings that are available, such as alcohol, tobacco and gambling, hurt consumers and ruin lives. Some researchers are studying the personal and situational attributes that contribute to dysfunctional consumption behavior.[30] Others have suggested that too many consumption choices make consumers confused, unsatisfied, less happy, psychologically drained, and more likely to experience negative emotions.[31] Some consumers confess to feeling "paralyzed" by the vast array of choices in retail aisles, and tend to defensively cling to their old brands, or to buy nothing at all.

The examples cited above clearly indicate that aggressive advertising can increase the level of demand for some products, sometimes in a manner that is detrimental to the well-being of the consumers targeted and to society. Societal forces are effective in curtailing seemingly unethical behavior by marketers. Marketers do respond (or are forced by legislation to respond) when their advertising efforts are viewed as socially undesirable.

SUMMARY

Motivation is the driving force within individuals that impels them to action. This driving force is produced by a state of uncomfortable tension, which exists as the result of an unsatisfied need. All individuals have needs, wants, and desires. The individual's subconscious drive to reduce need-induced tensions results in behavior that he or she anticipates will satisfy needs and thus bring about a more comfortable internal state.

All behavior is goal oriented. Goals are the sought-after results of motivated behavior. The form or direction that behavior takes—the goal that is selected—is a result of thinking processes (cognition) and previous learning (e.g., experience). There are two types of goals: generic goals and product-specific goals. A generic goal is a general category of goal that may fulfill a certain need; a product-specific goal is a specifically branded or labeled product that the individual sees as a way to fulfill a need. Product-specific needs are sometimes referred to as wants.

Innate needs—those an individual is born with—are physiological (biogenic) in nature; they include all the factors required to sustain physical life (e.g., food, water, clothing, shelter, sex, and physical safety). Acquired needs—those an individual develops after birth—are primarily psychological (psychogenic); they include love, acceptance, esteem, and self-fulfillment. For any given need, there are many different and appropriate goals. The specific goal selected depends on the individual's experiences, physical capacity, prevailing cultural norms and values, and the goal's accessibility in the physical and social environment.

Needs and goals are interdependent and change in response to the individual's physical condition, environment, interaction with other people, and experiences. As needs become satisfied, new, higher-order needs emerge that must be fulfilled.

Failure to achieve a goal often results in feelings of frustration. Individuals react to frustration in two ways: "fight" or "flight." They may cope by finding a way around the obstacle that prohibits goal attainment or by adopting a substitute goal (fight); or they may adopt a defense mechanism that enables them to protect their self-esteem (flight). Defense mechanisms include aggression, regression, rationalization, withdrawal, projection, daydreaming, identification, and repression.

Motives cannot easily be inferred from consumer behavior. People with different needs may seek fulfillment through selection of the same goals; people with the same needs may seek fulfillment through different goals. Although some psychologists have suggested that individuals have different need priorities, others believe that most human beings experience the same basic needs, to which they assign a similar priority ranking. Maslow's hierarchy-of-needs theory proposes five levels of human needs: physiological needs, safety needs, social needs, egoistic needs, and self-actualization needs. Other needs widely integrated into consumer advertising include the needs for power, affiliation, and achievement.

There are three commonly used methods for identifying and "measuring" human motives: observation and inference, subjective reports, and qualitative research (including projective techniques). None of these methods is completely reliable by itself. Therefore, researchers often use a combination of two or three techniques in tandem to assess the presence or strength of consumer motives. Motivational research is qualitative research designed to delve below the consumer's level of conscious awareness. Despite some shortcomings, motivational research has proved to be of great value to marketers concerned with developing new ideas and new copy appeals.

The ethical issues regarding motivation and consumption behavior are focused on the promotion by some marketers of undesirable behaviors (e.g., smoking, drinking, gambling, compulsive buying), and the targeting of vulnerable populations. However, when undesirable consequences affect large numbers of consumers, societal forces put pressure on the marketers responsible and persuade them (or require them) to curtail or eliminate these unethical marketing practices.

DISCUSSION QUESTIONS

1. Discuss the ethical issues related to the statement "marketers don't create needs; needs preexist marketers." Can marketing efforts *change* consumers' needs? Why or why not?

2. Consumers have both innate and acquired needs. Give examples of each kind of need and show how the same purchase can serve to fulfill either or both kinds of needs.

3. Specify both innate and acquired needs that would be useful bases for developing promotional strategies for
   a. global positioning systems
   b. sunglasses with built-in earphones and an MP3 player
   c. recruiting high school seniors to join the armed forces
   d. a new super-compact and powerful digital camera

4. Why are consumers' needs and goals constantly changing? What factors influence the formation of new goals?

5. How can marketers use consumers' failures at achieving goals in developing promotional appeals for specific products and services? Give examples.

6. For each of the situations listed in question 3, select one level from Maslow's hierarchy of human needs that can be used to segment the market and position the product (or the organization). Explain your choices. What are the advantages and disadvantages of using Maslow's need hierarchy for segmentation and positioning applications?

7. a. How do researchers identify and measure human motives? Give examples.
   b. Does motivational research differ from qualitative research? Discuss.
   c. What are the strengths and weaknesses of motivational research?

EXERCISES

1. Find two advertisements that depict two different defense mechanisms and discuss their effectiveness.
2. Find three advertisements that appeal to the needs for power, affiliation, and achievement and discuss their effectiveness.
3. Most human needs are dormant much of the time. What factors cause their arousal? Find two examples

of ads that are designed to arouse latent consumer needs and discuss their effectiveness.

4. Find an ad or a recent article related to one of the ethical issues explored in this chapter and discuss it.

KEY TERMS

- **acquired needs**
- **approach object**
- **avoidance object**
- **defense mechanisms**
- **emotional motives**
- **generic goals**
- **innate needs**

- **levels of aspiration**
- **maslow's hierarchy of needs**
- **motivation**
- **motivational research**
- **motivational research techniques**
- **positioning**

- **positive versus negative motivation**
- **primary needs**
- **product-specific goals**
- **rational motives**
- **secondary needs**
- **substitute goal**

NOTES

1. Andrew Tobias, *Fire and Ice* (New York: William Morrow and Company, 1976), Chapter 8.

2. Ibid.

3. Richard P. Bagozzi and Utpal Dholakia, "Goal Setting and Goal Striving in Consumer Behavior," *Journal of Marketing* (1999): 19–32.

4. Alexander Chernev, "Goal Orientation and Consumer Preference for the Status Quo," *Journal of Consumer Research* (December 2004): 557–565.

5. Michel Tuan Pham and Tamar Avnet, "Ideals and Oughts and the Reliance of Affect versus Substance in Persuasion," *Journal of Consumer Research* (March 2004): 503–519.

6. Maria J. Louro, Rik Pieters, and Marcel Zeelenberg, "Negative Returns on Positive Emotions: The Influence of Pride and Self-Regulatory Goals on Repurchase Decisions," *Journal of Consumer Research* (March 2005): 833–841.

7. James A. Roberts and Stephen F. Pirog, III, "Personal Goals and Their Role in Consumer Behavior: The Case of Compulsive Buying," *Journal of Marketing Theory and Practice* (Summer 2004): 61–73.

8. See Abraham H. Maslow, "A Theory of Human Motivation," *Psychological Review* 50 (1943): 370–396; Abraham H. Maslow, *Motivation and Personality* (New York: Harper & Row, 1954); and Abraham H. Maslow, *Toward a Psychology of Being* (New York: Van Nostrand Reinhold, 1968), 189–215.

9. A number of studies have focused on human levels of aspiration. See, for example, Kurt Lewin et al., "Level of Aspiration," in *Personality and Behavior Disorders*, ed. J. McV. Hunt (New York: Ronald Press, 1944); Howard Garland, "Goal Levels and Task Performance, a Compelling Replication of Some Compelling Results," *Journal of Applied Psychology* 67 (1982): 245–248; Edwin A. Locke, Elizabeth Frederick, Cynthia Lee, and Philip Bobko, "Effect of Self Efficacy, Goals and Task Strategies on Task Performance," *Journal of Applied Psychology* 69, no. 2 (1984): 241–251; Edwin A. Locke, Elizabeth Frederick, Elizabeth Buckner, and Philip Bobko, "Effect of Previously Assigned Goals on Self Set Goals and Performance," *Journal of Applied Psychology* 72, no. 2 (1987): 204–211; and John R. Hollenbeck and Howard J. Klein, "Goal Commitment and the Goal Setting Process: Problems, Prospects and Proposals for Future Research," *Journal of Applied Psychology* 2 (1987): 212–220.

10. Clive Thompson, "The Play's the Thing," *New York Times Magazine*, November 11, 2004, 49+.

11. Jhonna Robledo, "They'll Be There for You," *New York Magazine*, June 6, 2005, 58.

12. Maslow, "A Theory of Human Motivation," 380.

13. Ibid.

14. Ibid.

15. See, for example, David C. McClelland, *Studies in Motivation* (New York: Appleton Century Crofts, 1955); David C. McClelland, "Business Drive and National Achievement," *Harvard Business Review* (July–August 1962); "Achievement Motivation Can Be Developed," *Harvard Business Review* 5, no. 24 (November–December 1965); and Abraham K. Korman, *The Psychology of Motivation* (Upper Saddle River, NJ: Prentice Hall, 1974).

16. Jacqueline K. Eastman, Ronald E. Goldsmith, and Lisa Reinecke Flynn, "Status Consumption in Consumer Behavior: Scale Development and Validation," *Journal of Marketing Theory and Practice* (Summer 1999): 41–52.

17. Emily Eakin, "Penetrating the Mind by Metaphor," *The New York Times*, February 23, 2002, B9, B11.

18. Ronald B. Leiber, "Storytelling: A New Way to Get Close to Your Customer," *Fortune*, February 3, 1997.

19. Bernice Kramer, "Mind Games," *New York*, May 8, 1989, 33–40.

20. Ibid.

21. Ibid.

22. Melanie Warner, "Guidelines Are Urged in Food Ads for Children," **www.nytimes.com**, March 17, 2005.

23. Ibid.

24. Melanie Warner, "You Want Any Fruit With That Big Mac?" **www.nytimes.com**, February 20, 2005.

25. "Credit Scores Plummet as Student Debt Rises," *Business Wire*, New York, April 8, 2005.

26. So-hyun Joo, John E. Grable, and Dorothy C. Bagwell, "Credit Card Attitudes and Behaviors of College Students," *College Student Journal* (September 2003): 405–416.

27. "New York Law Targets Credit Card Ads at Universities," *Bank Marketing International*, December 2004, 1.

28. R. Stephen Parker and Charles E. Pettijohn, "Ethical Considerations in the Use of Direct-To-Consumer Advertising and Pharmaceutical Promotions: The Impact on Pharmaceutical Sales and Physicians," *Journal of Business Ethics* (December 2003): 279–287; Nat Ives, "Consumers Are Looking Past Commercials to Study Prescription Drugs," **www.nytimes.com**, March 25, 2005.

29. Stephanie Saul, "A Self-Imposed Ban on Drug Ads," **www.nytimes.com**, June 15, 2005.

30. For example, Aviv Shoham and Maja Makovec Brencic, "Compulsive Buying Behavior," *Journal of Consumer Marketing*, 20, no. 2/3 (2003): 127–139; Matthew J Bernthal, David Crockett, and Randall L Rose, "Credit Cards as Lifestyle Facilitators," *Journal of Consumer Research* (June 2005): 130–146.

31. For example, Barry Schwartz, "The Tyranny of Choice," *Scientific American* (April 2004): 71–75; David Glen Mick, Susan M. Broniarczyk, and Jonathan Haidt, "Choose, Choose, Choose, Choose, Choose, Choose, Choose: Emerging and Prospective Research on the Deleterious Effects of Living in Consumer Hyperchoice," *Journal of Business Ethics* (June 2004): 207–212.

chapter**five**

> # Personality and Consumer Behavior

Marketers have long tried to appeal to consumers in terms of their personality characteristics. They have intuitively felt that what consumers purchase, and when and how they consume, are likely to be influenced by personality factors. For this reason, marketing and advertising people have frequently depicted (or incorporated) specific personality traits or characteristics in their marketing and advertising messages. Some recent examples are an appeal to *individuality* for the Harley-Davidson motorcycle (headline: "We're all created equal. But after that, it's up to you"—**www.harley-davidson.com**), an appeal to *status and/or innovativeness* for Audi (headline: "Never Follow"—**www.audiusa.com**), an appeal to *nonconformity* in introducing the new Saab 97X SUV (headline: "For those who consider conformity a serious road hazard"—**www.saabusa.com**), and an appeal by Aflac to investors' *sense of self-assurance* (headline: "Invest wisely. Relax happily"—**www.aflac.com**).

This chapter is designed to provide the reader with an understanding of how *personality* and *self-concept* are related to various aspects of consumer behavior. It examines what personality is, reviews several major personality theories, and describes how

Ditched the do.

Lost the leg warmers.

Kept the Quaker Rice Snacks.

Fads come and go, but true goodness lasts forever.
With 70 calories, it's the classic crunch.
Quaker® Rice Snacks. Classic.

©2002 QOC

these theories have stimulated marketing interest in the study of consumer personality. The chapter considers the important topics of *brand personality,* how the related concepts of *self* and *self-image* influence consumer attitudes and behavior, and concludes with an exploration of *virtual personality* or *self.*

what is personality?

The study of **personality** has been approached by theorists in a variety of ways. Some have emphasized the dual influence of heredity and early childhood experiences on personality development; others have stressed broader social and environmental influences and the fact that personalities develop continuously over time. Some theorists prefer to view personality as a unified whole; others focus on specific traits. The wide variation in viewpoints makes it difficult to arrive at a single definition. However, we propose that personality can be defined as *those inner psychological characteristics that both determine and reflect how a person responds to his or her environment.*

The emphasis in this definition is on *inner characteristics*—those specific qualities, attributes, traits, factors, and mannerisms that distinguish one individual from other individuals. As discussed later in the chapter, the deeply ingrained characteristics that we call personality are likely to influence the individual's product choices: They affect the way consumers respond to marketers' promotional efforts, and when, where, and how they consume particular products or services. Therefore, the identification of specific personality characteristics associated with consumer behavior has proven to be highly useful in the development of a firm's market segmentation strategies.

The nature of personality

In the study of personality, three distinct properties are of central importance: (1) *personality reflects individual differences*; (2) *personality is consistent and enduring*; and (3) *personality can change.*

Personality reflects individual differences

Because the inner characteristics that constitute an individual's personality are a unique combination of factors, no two individuals are exactly alike. Nevertheless, many individuals may be similar in terms of a single personality characteristic but not in terms of others. For instance, some people can be described as "high" in *venturesomeness* (e.g., willing to accept the risk of doing something new or different, such as skydiving or mountain climbing), whereas others can be described as "low" in *venturesomeness* (e.g., afraid to buy a recently introduced product). Personality is a useful concept because it enables us to categorize consumers into different groups on the basis of one or even several traits. If each person were different in terms of all personality traits, it would be impossible to group consumers into segments, and there would be little reason for marketers to develop products and promotional campaigns targeted to particular segments.

Personality is consistent and enduring

An individual's personality tends to be both consistent and enduring. Indeed, the sibling who comments that his brother "has always wanted to be different from the day he was born" is supporting the contention that personality has both consistency and endurance. Both qualities are essential if marketers are to explain or predict consumer behavior in terms of personality.

Although marketers cannot change consumers' personalities to conform to their products, if they know which personality characteristics influence specific consumer responses, they can attempt to appeal to the relevant traits inherent in their target group of consumers.

Even though consumers' personalities may be consistent, their consumption behavior often varies considerably because of the various psychological, sociocultural, environmental, and situational factors that affect behavior. For instance, although an individual's personality may be relatively stable, specific needs or motives, attitudes, reactions to group pressures, and even responses to newly available brands may cause a change in the person's behavior. Personality is only one of a combination of factors that influence how a consumer behaves.

Personality can change

Under certain circumstances personalities change. For instance, an individual's personality may be altered by major life events, such as marriage, the birth of a child, the death of a parent, or a change of job and/or profession. An individual's personality changes not only in response to abrupt events but also as part of a gradual maturing process—"She's growing up, she is much calmer," says an uncle after not seeing his niece for five years.

There is also evidence that personality stereotypes may change over time. More specifically, although it is felt that men's personality has generally remained relatively constant over the past 50 years, women's personality has seemed to become increasingly more masculine and should continue to do so over the next 50 years. This prediction indicates a *convergence* in the personality characteristics of men and women.[1] The reason for this shift is that women have been moving more and more into occupations that have traditionally been dominated by men and, therefore, have increasingly been associated with masculine personality attributes.

theories of personality

This section briefly reviews three major theories of personality: (1) **Freudian theory**, (2) **neo-Freudian theory**, and (3) **trait theory**. These theories have been chosen for discussion from among many theories of personality because each has played a prominent role in the study of the relationship between consumer behavior and personality.

Freudian theory

Sigmund Freud's **psychoanalytic theory of personality** is a cornerstone of modern psychology. This theory was built on the premise that *unconscious needs* or *drives*, especially sexual and other biological drives, are at the heart of human motivation and personality. Freud constructed his theory on the basis of patients' recollections of early childhood experiences, analysis of their dreams, and the specific nature of their mental and physical adjustment problems.

Id, superego, and ego

Based on his analyses, Freud proposed that the human personality consists of three interacting systems: the *id*, the *superego*, and the *ego*. The id was conceptualized as a "warehouse" of primitive and impulsive drives—basic physiological needs such as thirst, hunger, and sex—for which the individual seeks immediate satisfaction without concern for the specific means of satisfaction. The ad for Godiva Chocolatier (see Figure 5.1) captures some of the mystery and the excitement associated with the "forces" of primitive drives.

In contrast to the id, the *superego* is conceptualized as the individual's internal expression of society's moral and ethical codes of conduct. The superego's role is to see that the individual satisfies needs in a socially acceptable fashion. Thus, the superego is a kind of "brake" that restrains or inhibits the impulsive forces of the id.

Finally, the *ego* is the individual's conscious control. It functions as an internal monitor that attempts to balance the impulsive demands of the id and the sociocultural constraints of the superego. Figure 5.2 represents the interrelationships among the three interacting systems. In addition to specifying a structure for personality, Freud emphasized that an individual's personality is formed as he or she passes through a number of distinct stages of infant and childhood development. These are the *oral, anal, phallic, latent*, and *genital* stages. Freud labeled four of these stages of development to conform to the area of the body on which he believed the child's sexual instincts are focused at the time.

According to Freudian theory, an adult's personality is determined by how well he or she deals with the crises that are experienced while passing through each of these

Source: © Godiva Chocolatier, Inc. Used with permission. All rights reserved. Photography by CLANG.

FIGURE 5.1

"Every woman is one part Godiva, much to the dismay of every man."

stages (particularly the first three). For instance, if a child's oral needs are not adequately satisfied at the first stage of development, the person may become fixated at this stage and as an adult display a personality that includes such traits as dependence and excessive oral activity (e.g., gum chewing and smoking). When an individual is fixated at the anal stage, the adult personality may display other traits, such as an excessive need for neatness.

FIGURE 5.2

A Representation of the Interrelationships Among the Id, Ego, and Superego

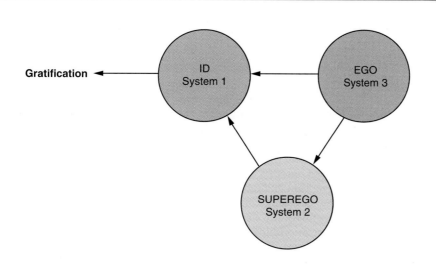

Freudian theory and "product personality"

Researchers who apply Freud's psychoanalytic theory to the study of consumer personality believe that human drives are largely *unconscious* and that consumers are primarily unaware of their true reasons for buying what they buy. These researchers tend to see consumer purchases and/or consumption situations as a reflection and an extension of the consumer's own personality. In other words, they consider the consumer's appearance and possessions—grooming, clothing, jewelry, and so forth—as reflections of the individual's personality. Table 5.1 presents the results of a study of 19,000 consumers that examines the link between snack food perceptions and selected personality traits.[2] The findings of the research, for example, reveal that potato chips are associated with being ambitious, successful, and a high achiever and impatient with less than the best, whereas

TABLE 5.1	Snack Foods and Personality Traits
SNACK FOODS	**PERSONALITY TRAITS**
Potato chips	Ambitious, successful, high achiever, impatient with less than the best.
Tortilla chips	Perfectionist, high expectations, punctual, conservative, responsible.
Pretzels	Lively, easily bored with same old routine, flirtatious, intuitive, may overcommit to projects.
Snack crackers	Rational, logical, contemplative, shy, prefers time alone.
Cheese curls	Conscientious, principled, proper, fair, may appear rigid but has great integrity, plans ahead, loves order.
Nuts	Easygoing, empathetic, understanding, calm, even-tempered.
Popcorn	Takes charge, pitches in often, modest, self-confident but not a show-off.
Meat snacks	Gregarious, generous, trustworthy, tends to be overly trusting.

Source: From *What Flavor is Your Personality? Discover Who You Are by Looking at What You Eat,* by Alan Hirsch, MD (Naperville, IL: Sourcebooks, 2001).

popcorn seems to be related to a personality that takes charge, pitches in often, is modest and self-confident but not a show-off. (The related topics of *brand personality*, and the self and *self-images* are considered later in the chapter.)

Neo-Freudian personality theory

Several of Freud's colleagues disagreed with his contention that personality is primarily instinctual and sexual in nature. Instead, these neo-Freudians believed that *social relationships* are fundamental to the formation and development of personality. For instance, Alfred Adler viewed human beings as seeking to attain various rational goals, which he called *style of life*. He also placed much emphasis on the individual's efforts to overcome *feelings of inferiority* (i.e., by striving for superiority).

Harry Stack Sullivan, another neo-Freudian, stressed that people continuously attempt to establish significant and rewarding relationships with others. He was particularly concerned with the individual's efforts to reduce tensions, such as anxiety.

Like Sullivan, Karen Horney was also interested in *anxiety*. She focused on the impact of child–parent relationships and the individual's desire to conquer feelings of anxiety. Horney proposed that individuals be classified into three personality groups: *compliant, aggressive*, and *detached*.[3]

1. Compliant individuals are those who move toward others (they desire to be loved, wanted, and appreciated).
2. Aggressive individuals are those who move against others (they desire to excel and win admiration).
3. Detached individuals are those who move away from others (they desire independence, self-reliance, self-sufficiency, and individualism or freedom from obligations).

A personality test based on Horney's theory (the CAD) has been developed and tested within the context of consumer behavior.[4] The initial CAD research uncovered a number of tentative relationships between college students' scores and their product and brand usage patterns. For example, highly *compliant* students were found to prefer name-brand products such as Bayer aspirin (**www.bayer.com**); students classified as *aggressive* showed a preference for Old Spice deodorant (**www.oldspice.com**) over other brands (seemingly because of its masculine appeal); and highly *detached* students proved to be heavy tea drinkers (possibly reflecting their desire not to conform). More recent research has found that children who scored high in self-reliance—who preferred to do things independently of others (i.e., *detached* personalities)—were *less* likely to be brand loyal and were *more* likely to try different brands.[5]

Many marketers use some of these neo-Freudian theories intuitively. For example, marketers who position their products or services as providing an opportunity to belong or to be appreciated by others in a group or social setting would seem to be guided by Horney's characterization of the *detached* individual. Figure 5.3 shows an ad for the Suzuki Reno that captures a positive image of the detached (or individualistic or nonconformist) person. Its headline declares: "180° from those other squares." This clever ad is referring to competitors' vehicles that are "square" and their "square" owners.

Trait theory

Trait theory constitutes a major departure from the *qualitative* measures that typify the Freudian and neo-Freudian movements (e.g., personal observation, self-reported experiences, dream analysis, projective techniques).

The orientation of trait theory is primarily quantitative or empirical; it focuses on the measurement of personality in terms of specific psychological characteristics, called traits. A *trait* is defined as "any distinguishing, relatively enduring way in which one individual differs from another."[6] Trait theorists are concerned with the construction of personality tests (or inventories) that enable them to pinpoint individual differences in terms of specific traits.

Selected *single-trait personality* tests (which measure just one trait, such as self-confidence) are often developed specifically for use in consumer behavior studies.

FIGURE 5.3

Source: © American Suzuki
Motors Corporation 2005.
Reprinted with permission.

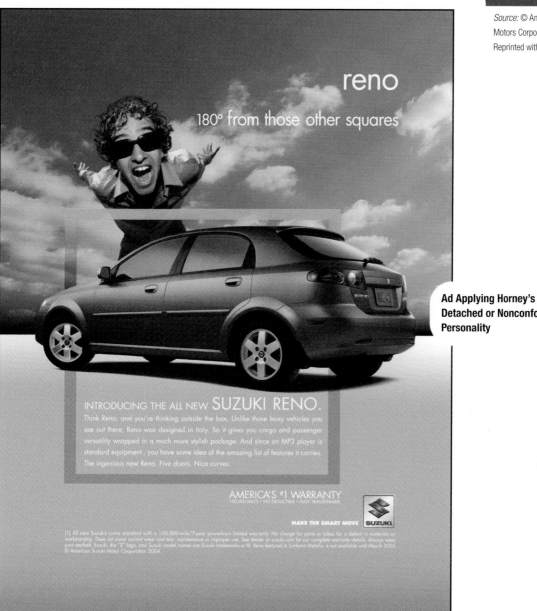

**Ad Applying Horney's
Detached or Nonconformist
Personality**

These tailor-made personality tests measure such traits as **consumer innovativeness** (how receptive a person is to new experiences), **consumer materialism** (the degree of the consumer's attachment to "worldly possessions"), and **consumer ethnocentrism** (the consumer's likelihood to accept or reject foreign-made products).

Trait researchers have found that it is generally more realistic to expect personality to be linked to how consumers *make their choices* and to the purchase or consumption of *a broad product category* rather than a specific brand. For example, there is more likely to be a relationship between a personality trait and whether or not an individual owns an SUV than between a personality trait and the brand of SUV purchased. It is of interest to note that a study of over 1,000 U.S. adults found very different traits among soup-lovers having preferences for different types of soups (e.g., chicken noodle versus

TABLE 5.2	Soup and Soup-Lovers' Traits

CHICKEN NOODLE SOUP LOVERS
- Watch a lot of TV
- Are family oriented
- Have a great sense of humor
- Are outgoing and loyal
- Like daytime talk shows
- Most likely to go to church

TOMATO SOUP LOVERS
- Passionate about reading
- Love pets
- Like meeting people for coffee
- Aren't usually the life of the party

VEGETABLE/MINESTRONE SOUP LOVERS
- Enjoy the outdoors
- Usually game for trying new things
- Spend more money than any other group dining in fancy restaurants
- Likely to be physically fit
- Gardening is often a favorite hobby

CHILI-BEEF SOUP LOVERS
- Generally preferred by males
- Its enthusiasts are the most social of all soup-lovers
- They are the life of the party
- They love telling jokes
- They watch sporting events
- They watch sitcoms on TV

NEW ENGLAND CLAM CHOWDER LOVERS
- Most conservative of all soup-lovers
- Pride themselves on being realistic and down-to-earth
- Can occasionally be cynical

Source: Gwen Carden, "Your Favorite Soup Reveals Your Personality," *Sioux City Journal*, January 2, 2001, p. 5.

New England clam chowder).[7] Table 5.2 presents the traits associated with six different types of soups.

The next section shows how measures of personality traits are used to expand our understanding of consumer behavior.

personality and understanding consumer diversity

Marketers are interested in understanding how personality influences consumption behavior because such knowledge enables them to better understand consumers and to segment and target those consumers who are likely to respond positively to their product or service communications. Several specific personality traits that provide insights about consumer behavior are examined next.

Consumer innovativeness and related personality traits

Marketing practitioners try to learn all they can about **consumer innovators**—those who are *open* to new ideas and to be among the first to try new products, services, or practices—for the market response of such innovators is often a critical indication of the eventual success or failure of a new product or service.

Personality traits that have been useful in differentiating between consumer innovators and noninnovators include *consumer innovativeness, dogmatism, social character, need for uniqueness, optimum stimulation level, sensation seeking,* and *variety-novelty seeking.* (Chapter 15 examines nonpersonality characteristics that distinguish between consumer innovators and noninnovators.)

Consumer innovativeness

Consumer researchers have endeavored to develop measurement instruments to gauge the level of consumer innovativeness, because such measures of personality traits provide important insights into the nature and boundaries of a consumer's willingness to innovate.[8] Over the years, the trait of consumer innovativeness has been linked to the need for stimulation, novelty seeking, and the need for uniqueness—three other traits that will be discussed later in this chapter.[9] Table 5.3 presents two alternative scales for measuring consumer innovativeness, the first scale measuring general innovativeness and the second measuring domain specific (i.e., product-specific) innovativeness.

Available consumer research indicates a positive relationship between innovative use of the Internet and buying online.[10] Other research exploring the association between personality traits and innovative Internet behavior has reported that Internet shoppers tend to see themselves as being able to control their own future, using the Internet to seek out information, enjoying change, and ***not*** being afraid of uncertainty.[11]

Dogmatism

Consumer responses to distinctively unfamiliar products or product features (i.e., level of dogmatism—a personality-linked behavior) is of keen interest to many marketers,

---

TABLE 5.3	Two Consumer Innovativeness Measurement Scales

A "GENERAL" CONSUMER INNOVATIVENESS SCALE

1. I would rather stick to a brand I usually buy than try something I am not very sure of.
2. When I go to a restaurant, I feel it is safer to order dishes I am familiar with.
3. If I like a brand, I rarely switch from it just to try something different.
4. I enjoy taking chances in buying unfamiliar brands just to get some variety in my purchase.
5. When I see a new brand on the shelf, I'm not afraid of giving it a try.

A DOMAIN SPECIFIC CONSUMER INNOVATIVENESS SCALE

1. Compared to my friends, I own few rock albums.
2. In general, I am the last in my circle of friends to know the titles of the latest rock albums.
3. In general, I am among the first in my circle of friends to buy a new rock album when it appears.
4. If I heard that a new rock album was available in the store, I would be interested enough to buy it.
5. I will buy a new rock album, even if I haven't heard it yet.
6. I know the names of new rock acts before other people do.

Source: Gilles Roehrich, "Consumer Innovativeness: Concepts and Measurements," *Journal of Business Research,* 57 (June 2004): 674.

especially marketers of technologically rich products. **Dogmatism** is a personality trait that measures the degree of rigidity (versus openness) that individuals display toward the unfamiliar and toward information that is contrary to their own established beliefs.[12] A person who is *highly dogmatic* approaches the unfamiliar defensively and with considerable discomfort and uncertainty. At the other end of the spectrum, a person who is *low dogmatic* will readily consider unfamiliar or opposing beliefs.

Consumers who are low in dogmatism (*open-minded*) are more likely to prefer innovative products to established or traditional alternatives. In contrast, highly dogmatic (*closed-minded*) consumers are more likely to choose established, rather than innovative, product alternatives.

Highly dogmatic consumers tend to be more receptive to ads for new products or services that contain an appeal from an authoritative figure. To this end, marketers have used celebrities and experts in their new-product advertising to make it easier for potentially reluctant consumers (noninnovators) to accept the innovation. In contrast, low-dogmatic consumers (who are frequently high in innovativeness) seem to be more receptive to messages that stress factual differences, product benefits, and other forms of product-usage information.

Social character

The personality trait known as *social character* has its origins in sociological research, which focuses on the identification and classification of individuals into distinct sociocultural types. As used in consumer psychology, social character is a personality trait that ranges on a continuum from **inner-directedness** to **other-directedness**. Inner-directed consumers tend to rely on their own inner values or standards in evaluating new products and are likely to be consumer innovators. Conversely, other-directed consumers tend to look to others for guidance as to what is appropriate or inappropriate; thus, they are *less* likely to be consumer innovators.

Inner- and other-directed consumers are attracted to different types of promotional messages. Inner-directed people seem to prefer ads that stress product features and personal benefits (enabling them to use their own values and standards in evaluating products), whereas other-directed people prefer ads that feature an approving social environment or social acceptance (this in keeping with their tendency to look to others or to act as part of a group). Thus, other-directed individuals may be more responsive to appeals that are based on social or group affiliations, rather than the informational content of an ad.

Need for uniqueness

We all know people who seek to be unique. For these people, conformity to others' expectations or standards, either in appearance or in their possessions, is something to be avoided. Moreover, we would expect that it is easier to express or act uniquely if one does not have to pay a price in the form of others' criticism. Supporting this perspective, a recent study of consumers' need for uniqueness (NFU) explored the circumstances under which high NFU individuals do (and do not) make unconventional (i.e., unique) choices. The research revealed that when consumers are asked to explain their choices, but are not concerned about being criticized by others, they are more receptive to making unique choices.[13] Seeing the importance of NFU, other consumer researchers have developed an inventory to measure the trait within the context of consumer behavior. Table 5.4 presents a sample of items drawn from the inventory.

Optimum stimulation level

Some people seem to prefer a simple, uncluttered, and calm existence, whereas others prefer an environment crammed with novel, complex, and unusual experiences. Consumer research has examined how such variations in individual needs for stimulation may be related to consumer behavior. Research has found that high **optimum stimulation levels** (OSLs) are linked with greater willingness to take risks, to try new products, to be innovative, to seek purchase-related information, and to accept new retail facilities than low OSLs. One recent study investigated college students' willingness to select *mass customization* of fashion items (e.g., a pair of jeans that are especially measured, cut, and sewn so they offer

TABLE 5.4	Sample Items from a Consumers' Need for Uniqueness Scale[a]

I collect unusual products as a way of telling people I'm different.

When dressing, I have sometimes dared to be different in ways that others are likely to disapprove.

When products or brands I like become extremely popular, I lose interest in them.

As far as I'm concerned, when it comes to the products I buy and the situations in which I use them, customs and rules are made to be broken.

I have sometimes purchased unusual products or brands as a way to create a more distinctive personal image.

I sometimes look for one-of-a-kind products or brands so that I create a style that is all my own.

I avoid products or brands that have already been accepted and purchased by the average consumer.

[a]This inventory is measured on a 5-point Likert scale ranging from "strongly agree" to "strongly disagree."

Source: Kelly Tepper Tian, William O. Bearden, and Gary L. Hunter, "Consumers' Need for Uniqueness: Scale Development and Validation," *Journal of Consumer Research*, 28 (June 2001): 50–66. Reprinted by permission of the publisher.

a better fit or appearance), found that OSL predicted two factors—students' openness to *experimentation with appearance* (e.g., "I try on some of the newest clothes each season to see how I look in the styles") and *enhancement of individuality* (e.g., "I try to buy clothes that are very unusual").[14]

OSL scores also seem to reflect a person's desired level of lifestyle stimulation.[15] For instance, consumers whose actual lifestyles are equivalent to their OSL scores appear to be *quite satisfied,* whereas those whose lifestyles are understimulated (i.e., their OSL scores are greater than the lifestyle they are currently living) are likely to be *bored.* Those whose lifestyles are overstimulated (i.e., their OSLs are lower than current reality) are likely to seek *rest* or *relief.* This suggests that the relationship between consumers' lifestyles and their OSLs is likely to influence their choices of products or services and how they manage and spend their time. For instance, a person who feels bored (an understimulated consumer) is likely to be attracted to a vacation that offers a great deal of activity and excitement. In contrast, a person who feels overwhelmed (an overstimulated consumer) is likely to seek a quiet, isolated, relaxing, and rejuvenating vacation.

Sensation seeking

Closely related to the OSL concept is **sensation seeking** (SS), which has been defined as "a trait characterized by the need for varied, novel, and complex sensations and experience, and the willingness to take physical and social risks for the sake of such experience." Research evidence shows that teenage males with higher SS scores are more likely than other teenagers to prefer listening to heavy metal music and to engage in reckless or even dangerous behavior.[16]

Variety-novelty seeking

Still another personality-driven trait quite similar to and related to OSL is **variety** or **novelty seeking**. There appear to be many different types of consumer variety seeking: *exploratory purchase behavior* (e.g., switching brands to experience new, different, and possibly better alternatives), *vicarious exploration* (e.g., securing information about a new or different alternative and then contemplating or even daydreaming about the option), and *use innovativeness* (using an already adopted product in a new or novel way).[17] The use innovativeness trait is particularly relevant to technological products (such as home electronics products), in which some models offer an abundance of features and functions, whereas others contain just a few essential features or functions. For example, a consumer with a high variety-seeking score might purchase a digital video recorder with more features than a consumer with a lower variety-seeking score. Consumers with high variety-seeking scores are also more likely to be attracted to brands that claim to have novel features or multiple uses or applications. Still further, there appears to be a relationship between variety seeking and time of day, with greater variety-seeking behavior occurring when the consumer is experiencing arousal lows (as opposed to arousal peaks). And during the time of day when arousal seeking is relatively minimal, leader brands fare better, while follower brands do better during periods of the day when variety seeking is heightened.[18]

Marketers, up to a point, benefit by offering additional options to consumers seeking more product variety because consumers with a high need for variety tend to search for marketers that provide a diverse product line (offering much choice).[19] However, a point may be reached where a marketer might offer too many products with too many features. In such a case, the consumer may be turned off and avoid a product line with too much variety. Ultimately, in searching for the "just right," marketers must walk the fine line between offering consumers too little and too much choice. Additionally, research has shown that variety seekers often use price promotions as a low-cost way to try different brands over time—high-variety seekers tend to pay lower prices for the same item than do low-variety seekers.[20]

The stream of research examined here indicates that the consumer innovator differs from the noninnovator in terms of personality orientation. A knowledge of such personality differences should help marketers select target segments for new products and then to design distinctive promotional strategies for specific segments.

Cognitive personality factors

Consumer researchers have been increasingly interested in how **cognitive personality** factors influence various aspects of consumer behavior. In particular, two cognitive personality traits—**need for cognition** and **visualizers versus verbalizers**—have been useful in understanding selected aspects of consumer behavior.

Need for cognition

A promising cognitive personality characteristic is need for cognition (NC). It measures a person's craving for or enjoyment of *thinking*. Available research indicates that consumers who are *high* in NC are more likely to be responsive to the part of an ad that is rich in product-related information or description; consumers who are relatively *low* in NC are more likely to be attracted to the background or peripheral aspects of an ad, such as an attractive model or well-known celebrity.[21] In this realm, research among adolescents compared the effectiveness of a cartoon message and a written message. As expected, for those low in NC, the cartoon message was more effective in changing attitudes and subjective norms, whereas the written message was more effective for those high in NC.[22] In still another study, it was found that message framing (e.g., positively emphasizing a brand's advantages) has more impact on individuals low in NC than it has on individuals high in NC.[23] Furthermore, research suggests that consumers who are high in NC are likely to spend more time processing print advertisements, which results in superior brand and ad claim recall.[24]

Need for cognition also seems to play a role in an individual's use of the Internet. More precisely, NC has been positively related to using the Internet to seek product information, current events and news, and learning and education—all activities that incorporate a cognitive element.[25] A recent study examined both need for cognition and sensation seeking (discussed earlier in this chapter) with regard to Web site complexity. The research discovered that the subjects preferred Web sites with a medium level of complexity (rather than high or low complexity). Still further, those with a high need for cognition tended to evaluate Web sites with low visual complexity and high verbal complexity more favorably. In contrast, those who were high sensation seekers tended to prefer complex visual designs, whereas those who were low sensation seekers preferred simple visual designs.[26] Such research insights provide advertisers with

FIGURE 5.4

Source: Courtesy of General Motors Corporation.

Pontiac Targeting the Visualizer

valuable guidelines for creating advertising messages (including supporting art) that appeal to a particular target audience grouping's *need for cognition*.

Visualizers versus verbalizers

It is fairly well established that some people seem to be more open to and prefer the written word as a way of securing information, whereas others are more likely to respond to and prefer visual images or messages as sources of information. Consistent with such individual differences, cognitive personality research classifies consumers into two groups: *visualizers* (consumers who prefer visual information and products that stress the visual, such as membership in a videotape club) or *verbalizers* (consumers who prefer written or verbal information and products, such as membership in book clubs or audiotape clubs). Some marketers stress strong visual dimensions in order to attract visualizers (see Figure 5.4); others raise a question and provide the answer, or feature a detailed description or point-by-point explanation to attract verbalizers (see Figure 5.5).

Source: © Rosetta Stone. Used with permission. All rights reserved.

FIGURE 5.5

From consumer materialism to compulsive consumption

Consumer researchers have become increasingly interested in exploring various consumption and possession traits. These traits range from *consumer materialism* to *fixated consumption behavior* to *consumer compulsive behavior.*

Consumer materialism

Materialism (the extent to which a person is considered materialistic) is a topic frequently discussed in newspapers, in magazines, and on TV (e.g., "Americans are very materialistic") and in everyday conversations between friends ("He's so materialistic!"). Materialism, as a personality-like trait, distinguishes between individuals who regard possessions as essential to their identities and their lives and those for whom possessions

TABLE 5.5	Sample Items from a Materialism Scale

SUCCESS

- I admire people who own expensive homes, cars, and clothes.
- I like to own things that impress people.
- I don't place much emphasis on the amount of material objects people own as a sign of success. (R)

CENTRALITY

- I usually buy only the things I need. (R)
- I try to keep my life simple, as far as possessions are concerned. (R)
- I like a lot of luxury in my life.

HAPPINESS

- I have all the things I really need to enjoy life. (R)
- My life would be better if I owned certain things I don't have.
- It sometimes bothers me quite a bit that I can't afford to buy all the things I'd like.

Note: Measured on a 5 point "agreement" scale. Items with a (R) are scored inversely.

Source: Marsha L. Richins, "The Material Values Scale: Measurement Properties and Development of a Short Form," *Journal of Consumer Research*, 31 (June 2004): 217–218.

are secondary.[27] Researchers have found some general support for the following characteristics of materialistic people: (1) They especially value acquiring and showing off possessions; (2) they are particularly self-centered and selfish; (3) they seek lifestyles full of possessions (e.g., they desire to have lots of "things," rather than a simple, uncluttered lifestyle); and (4) their many possessions do not give them greater personal satisfaction (i.e., their possessions do not lead to greater happiness).[28] Table 5.5 presents sample items from a materialism scale.

Materialism has often been linked to advertising, and researchers have suggested that in the United States there has been an increasing emphasis on materialism in the print media. It is important to remember, though, that the extent of consumer materialism can vary from country to country (e.g., consumer materialism is less developed in Mexico than in the United States) and, therefore, marketers must be careful when trying to export a successful U.S. marketing mix to another country.[29]

Fixated consumption behavior

Somewhere between materialism and compulsion, with respect to buying or possessing objects, is the notion of being *fixated* with regard to consuming or possessing. Like materialism, *fixated consumption behavior* is in the realm of normal and socially acceptable behavior. Fixated consumers do not keep their objects or purchases of interest a secret; rather, they frequently display them, and their involvement is openly shared with others who have a similar interest. In the world of serious collectors (Barbie dolls, Carnival glass, rare antique teddy bears, or almost anything else that has drawn collectors), there are countless millions of *fixated consumers* pursuing their interests and trying to add to their collections.

Fixated consumers typically possess the following characteristics: (1) a deep (possibly passionate) interest in a particular object or product category, (2) a willingness to go to considerable lengths to secure additional examples of the object or product category of interest, and (3) the dedication of a considerable amount of discretionary time and money to searching out the object or product.[30] This profile of the fixated consumer describes many collectors or hobbyists (e.g., collectors of coins, stamps, antiques, vintage wristwatches, or fountain pens). Research exploring the dynamics of the fixated consumer (in this case, coin collectors) revealed that, for fixated consumers, there is not only

TABLE 5.6	Sample Items from Scales to Measure Compulsive Buying

VALENCE, D'ASTOUS, AND FORTIER COMPULSIVE BUYING SCALE

1. When I have money, I cannot help but spend part or the whole of it.
2. I am often impulsive in my buying behavior.
3. As soon as I enter a shopping center, I have an irresistible urge to go into a shop to buy something.
4. I am one of those people who often responds to direct-mail offers (e.g., books or compact discs).
5. I have often bought a product that I did not need, while knowing I had very little money left.

FABER AND O'GUINN COMPULSIVE BUYING SCALE

1. If I have any money left at the end of the pay period, I just have to spend it.
2. I felt others would be horrified if they knew my spending habits.
3. I have bought things even though I couldn't afford them.
4. I wrote a check when I knew I didn't have enough money in the bank to cover it.
5. I bought something in order to make myself feel better.

Source: Gilles Valence, Alain d'Astous, and Louis Fortier, "Compulsive Buying: Concept and Measurement," *Journal of Consumer Policy,* 11 (1988): 419–433; Ronald J. Faber and Thomas C. O'Guinn, "A Clinical Screener for Compulsive Buying," *Journal of Consumer Research,* 19 (December 1992): 459–469; and Leslie Cole and Dan Sherrell, "Comparing Scales to Measure Compulsive Buying: An Exploration of Their Dimensionality," in *Advances in Consumer Research,* 22, ed. Frank R. Kardes and Mita Sujan (Provo, UT: Association for Consumer Research, 1995), 419–427.

an enduring involvement in the object category itself but also a considerable amount of involvement in the process of acquiring the object (sometimes referred to as the "hunt").

Compulsive consumption behavior

Unlike materialism and fixated consumption, **compulsive consumption** is in the realm of abnormal behavior—an example of the dark side of consumption. Consumers who are compulsive have an *addiction;* in some respects they are out of control, and their actions may have damaging consequences to them and to those around them. Examples of compulsive consumption problems are uncontrollable shopping, gambling, drug addiction, alcoholism, and various food and eating disorders.[31] For instance, there are many women and a small number of men who are *chocoholics*—they have an intense craving (also termed an addiction) for chocolate.[32] From a marketing and consumer behavior perspective, *compulsive buying* can also be included in any list of compulsive activities. To control or possibly eliminate such compulsive problems generally requires some type of therapy or clinical treatment.

There have been some research efforts to develop a screener inventory to pinpoint compulsive buying behavior. Table 5.6 presents sample questions from several of these scales. Evidence suggests that some consumers use self-gifting, impulse buying, and compulsive buying as a way to influence or manage their moods; that is, the act of purchasing may convert a negative mood to a more positive one ("I'm depressed, I'll go out shopping and I'll feel better").[33]

Consumer ethnocentrism: responses to foreign-made products

In an effort to distinguish between consumer segments that are likely to be receptive to foreign-made products and those that are not, researchers have developed and tested the *consumer ethnocentrism* scale, called CETSCALE (see Table 5.7).[34] The CETSCALE has

TABLE 5.7	**The Consumer Ethnocentrism Scale—CETSCALE**

1. American people should always buy American-made products instead of imports.

2. Only those products that are unavailable in the United States should be imported.

3. Buy American-made products. Keep America working.

4. American products, first, last, and foremost.

5. Purchasing foreign-made products is un-American.

6. It is not right to purchase foreign products, because it puts Americans out of jobs.

7. A real American should always buy American-made products.

8. We should purchase products manufactured in America instead of letting other countries get rich off us.

9. It is always best to purchase American products.

10. There should be very little trading or purchasing of goods from other countries unless out of necessity.

11. Americans should not buy foreign products, because this hurts American business and causes unemployment.

12. Curbs should be put on all imports.

13. It may cost me in the long run but I prefer to support American products.

14. Foreigners should not be allowed to put their products on our markets.

15. Foreign products should be taxed heavily to reduce their entry into the United States.

16. We should buy from foreign countries only those products that we cannot obtain within our own country.

17. American consumers who purchase products made in other countries are responsible for putting their fellow Americans out of work.

Notes: Response format is a 7-point Likert-type scale (strongly agree = 7, strongly disagree = 1). Range of scores is from 17 to 119. Calculated from confirmatory factor analysis of data from 4-area study.

Source: Terence A. Shimp and Subhash Sharma, "Consumer Ethnocentrism: Construction and Validation of the CETSCALE," *Journal of Marketing Research*, 24 (August 1987): 282. Reprinted by permission.

been successful in identifying consumers with a predisposition to accept (or reject) foreign-made products. Consumers who are highly ethnocentric are likely to feel that it is inappropriate or wrong to purchase foreign-made products because of the resulting economic impact on the domestic economy, whereas nonethnocentric consumers tend to evaluate foreign-made products—ostensibly more objectively—for their extrinsic characteristics (e.g., "how good are they?"). A portion of the consumers who would score low on an ethnocentric scale are actually likely to be quite receptive to products made in foreign countries.

Ethnocentrism has been found to vary by country and product. Mexican consumers, for example, are more ethnocentric than their French and American counterparts; and Malaysian consumers, while preferring to purchase slacks, shirts, undergarments, and belts that are locally manufactured, want to buy imported sunglasses and watches.[35] Other evidence suggests that some older American consumers, in remembrance of World War II, still refuse to purchase German- and/or Japanese-made products, whereas some German and Japanese consumers may feel similarly about American-made products.[36]

Marketers successfully target ethnocentric consumers in any national market by stressing a nationalistic theme in their promotional appeals (e.g., "Made in America" or "Made in France") because this segment is predisposed to buy products made in their native land. Honda, the Japanese automaker, in an indirect appeal to ethnocentric Americans, had advertised that its Accord wagon is "Exported from America" to other markets (reinforcing that some of its automobiles are made in the United States).

TABLE 5.8	Strategies for Managing Country-of-Origin Effects	
	COUNTRY IMAGE	
MARKETING MIX	**POSITIVE**	**NEGATIVE**
Product	Emphasize "Made In"	Emphasize Brand Name
Price	Premium Price	Low Price to Attract Value Conscious
Place (Channel of Distribution)	Exclusive Locations	Establish Supply Chain Partners
Promotion	Country Image	Brand Image
	Nation Sponsored	Manufacturer Sponsored

Source: Osman Mohamad, Zafar U. Ahmed, Earl D. Honeycutt, Jr., and Taizoon Hyder Tyebkhan, "Does 'Made In. . .' Matter to Consumers? A Malaysian Study of Country of Origin Effect," *Multinational Business Review* (Fall 2000): 73. Reprinted with permission.

However, a study examining the preferences of U.K. consumers across eight product categories found that domestic country bias (i.e., a preference for products manufactured in a consumer's country of residence) varied among product categories. This means that a domestic manufacturer cannot expect that local consumers will automatically prefer their offerings over imported ones.[37] Still further, one research study found that low-knowledge consumers' product attitude (i.e., the consumer has little knowledge about the product) is more strongly influenced by country-of-origin perceptions than high-knowledge consumers' product attitude.[38] Table 5.8 presents a marketing mix strategy that can be used to manage country-of-origin effects. Specifically, if marketers determine that the potential customers in a particular country possess a *positive* image of products made in the country in which their products originate, the marketers may be able to create a marketing mix strategy that follows options in the *Positive* column. In contrast, if marketers assess that the potential customers in a particular country possess a *negative* image of products made in the country in which their products originate, the marketers might be wise to elect a marketing mix strategy that follows options in the *Negative* column of Table 5.8.

In this era of multinational marketing, it may be unclear to many consumers as to whether a particular product is domestic or imported. Consider Toyota, for example. Some of the models it sells in the United States are manufactured in Japan, some are manufactured in the United States, and some are manufactured in both nations (and end up being sold in the United States). One study conducted among business school students in New York City has examined eight different products, from green tea to jazz music, to determine if they differ in terms of "degree of globilization." As presented in Figure 5.6,

Object Degree of Globalization

Source: Jufei Kao, "Is It a Foreign Product? A Scale to Classify Products in an Era of Globalization," *Advances in Consumer Research*, 31 (2004): 680.

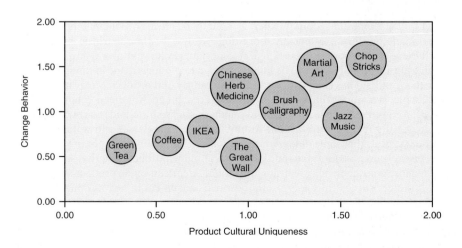

FIGURE 5.6

FIGURE 5.7

Causal Relationship Among Foreign Product Competence, Product Expertise, Involvement, Attitude, and Cross-Cultural Adoption Intention

Source: Jufei Kao, "Is It a Foreign Product? A Scale to Classify Products in an Era of Globalization," *Advances in Consumer Research,* 31 (2004): 681.

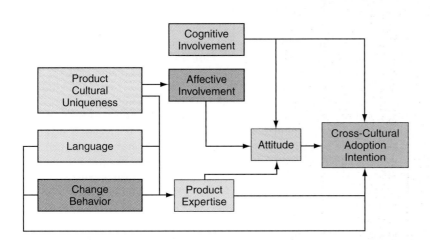

products in the lower-left corner have a higher degree of globalization, meaning that consumers view them to be low in product cultural uniqueness (i.e., they are viewed as nonforeign), while those in the upper right-hand corner are thought of as being "foreign."[39] Still further, Figure 5.7 illustrates the factors, including product cultural uniqueness, that lead to cross-cultural product adoption intention.

brand personality

Early in this chapter, as part of our discussion of Freudian theory, we introduced the notion of *product personality.* Consumers also subscribe to the notion of *brand personality;* that is, they attribute various descriptive personality-like traits or characteristics to different brands in a wide variety of product categories. For instance, with some help from frequent advertising, consumers tend to see Perdue (chickens) as representing freshness (**www.perdue.com**), Nike as the athlete in all of us (**www.nike.com**), and BMW as performance driven (**www.bmw.com**).[40] In a similar fashion, the brand personality for Levi's 501 jeans (**www.levi.com**) is "dependable and rugged," "real and authentic," and "American and Western." Such personality-like images of brands reflect consumers' visions of the inner core of many strong brands of consumer products. As these examples reveal, a brand's personality can either be functional ("dependable and rugged") or symbolic ("the athlete in all of us").[41] There is common sense and research evidence to conclude that any brand personality, as long as it is *strong* and *favorable*, will strengthen a brand.[42] However, it is not clear, for example, how many consumers would be willing to pay a premium for a brand-name diamond.

Marketers have even provided an instant personality or heritage for a new product by employing a symbolic or fictional historical branding strategy. For example, when Brown Forman (**www.brown-forman.com**) entered the microbrewed beer market, it used the brand name "1886" for its new beer, which is the year that one of its other products, Jack Daniel's bourbon, was first distilled.[43] In another vein, marketers are increasingly interested in learning how the experience of consumers visiting their product's Web site impacts on their brand's personality. An exploration of this issue reveals that compared to nonvisitors, visitors to a brand's Web site tend to perceive the brand to be a younger and more modern product, as well as more sincere and trustworthy.[44]

Brand personification

Some marketers find it useful to create a **brand personification**, which tries to recast consumers' perception of the attributes of a product or service into a human-like character. For instance, in focus group research, well-known brands of dishwashing liquid have been likened to "demanding task masters" or "high-energy people." Many consumers express their inner feelings about products or brands in terms of their association with known personalities. Identifying consumers' current brand–personality links and creating personality links for new products are important marketing tasks.

The M&M "people" are a current "fun" example of brand personification (**www.m-ms.com**). It is based on the line of questioning that could ask the following: "If an M&M (or a chocolate-coated peanut variety) was a person, what kind of person would it be?" Additional questioning would be likely to explore how the color of the coating impacts consumers' perceived personality for the "M&M people."

To personify and humanize its model consumer, Celestial Seasonings, Inc. (**www.celestialseasonings.com**), the leading specialty tea maker in the United States, refers in its advertising to "Tracy Jones." And just who is Tracy Jones? According to Celestial Seasonings, she is "female, upscale, well educated, and highly involved in life in every way."[45] In a similar fashion, Mr. Coffee (**www.mrcoffee.com**), a popular brand of automatic-drip coffee makers, unexpectedly found in its focus group research that consumers were referring to Mr. Coffee as if the product were a person (e.g., "he makes good coffee" and "he's got a lot of different models and prices").[46] After careful consideration, the marketers decided to explore the possibility of creating a *brand personification.* Initial consumer research indicated that Mr. Coffee was seen as being "dependable," "friendly," "efficient," "intelligent," and "smart."

Figure 5.8 presents a *brand personality framework* that reflects extensive consumer research designed to pinpoint the structure and nature of a brand's personality. The framework suggests that there are five defining *dimensions* of a brand's personality ("sincerity," "excitement," "competence," "sophistication," and "ruggedness"), and 15 *facets* of personality that flow from the five dimensions (i.e., "down-to-earth," "daring," "reliable," "upper class," and "outdoors").[47] If we carefully review these brand personality dimensions and facets, it appears that this framework tends to accommodate the brand personalities pursued by many consumer products.

It is important to point out that the consumer sometimes develops a relationship with a brand that is similar in certain respects to the relationships they have with others (e.g., friends, family, neighbors). Some consumers, for example, become "brand zealots," and develop a relationship that goes beyond a functional need. An example of this would be VW Beetle owners who give their cars names and who can be seen talking to their vehicles and affectionately stroking them. Another would be the advertising executive who had the Apple Macintosh logo tattooed on this chest (near his heart), or the Harley-Davidson motorcycle owner with a Harley tattoo. While in an "exchange relationship"

A Brand Personality Framework

Source: Jennifer L. Aaker, "Dimension of Brand Personality," *Journal of Marketing Research,* 35 (August 1997): 352. Reprinted by permission of the American Marketing Association.

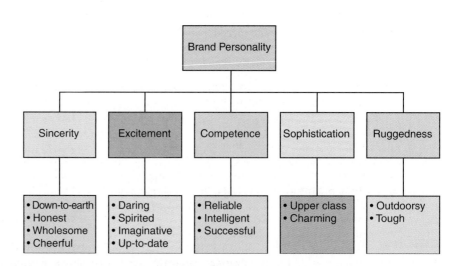

FIGURE 5.8

the consumer gets something back in return, brand zealots develop a "communal relationship" with the product and demonstrate a passion that is typically associated only with close friends and family.[48]

Product personality and gender

A product personality, or persona, frequently endows the product or brand with a gender. For instance, Celestial Seasonings' Tracy Jones was given a feminine persona, whereas Mr. Coffee was given a masculine personality. The assigning of gender as part of a product's personality description is fully consistent with the marketplace reality that products and services, in general, are viewed by consumers as having gender. A study that asked Chinese consumers to categorize various products in terms of gender, found that they perceived coffee and toothpaste to be masculine products, whereas bath soap and shampoo were seen as feminine products.[49]

Armed with knowledge of the perceived gender of a product or a specific brand, marketers are in a better position to select visuals and text copy for various marketing messages.

Product personality and geography

Marketers learned long ago that certain products, in the minds of consumers, possess a strong geographical association (e.g., San Francisco sourdough bread). Consequently, by employing geography in the product's name, the product's manufacturer creates a geographic personality for the product. Such a geographic personality can lead to geographic equity for the brand, meaning that in the consumer's memory, the knowledge of the brand reflects a strong geographic association.

Interestingly, geographic brand names can be either familiar or unfamiliar (or fictitious). For example, take "Philadelphia cream cheese." In fact, it is manufactured in Illinois, even though it uses the name of one of the largest cities in the United States. Still further, although we all know that Arizona is a state, Arizona ice tea is brewed and bottled in the state of New York. Fictitious geographic product names include Hidden Valley salad dressings and Bear Creek soups.[50]

But more important than whether the name is real or fictitious is whether the location and its image add to the product's brand equity.[51] Although Texas' Best Barbecue Sauce may be made in New Jersey, many Americans associate barbecue with Texas. Similarly, the Old El Paso brand of salsa capitalizes on the Mexican influence in the Southwest. The product may be made in Minneapolis, but a brand of salsa named Twin Cities Salsa (e.g., Minneapolis/St. Paul) just doesn't have the same cachet. Table 5.9 provides a list of familiar and not-so-familiar geographic brand names.

Personality and color

Consumers not only ascribe personality traits to products and services, but they also tend to associate personality factors with specific colors. For instance, Coca-Cola (**www.coca cola.com**) is associated with red, which connotes excitement. Blue bottles are often used to sell wine because the color blue appeals particularly to female consumers, and they buy the majority of wine.[52] Yellow is associated with novelty, and black frequently connotes sophistication.[53] For this reason, brands wishing to create a sophisticated persona (such as Pasta LaBella) or an upscale or premium image (e.g., Miller Beers' Miller Reserve) use labeling or packaging that is primarily black. A combination of black and white communicates that a product is carefully engineered, high tech, and sophisticated in design. The IBM Thinkpad has consistently used an all-black case with a red button to house its very successful line of laptops. Nike has used black, white, and a touch of red for selected models of its sport shoes. This color combination seems to imply advanced-performance sports shoes. Recently, M&M/Mars (**www.mmmars.com**) has exploited the folklore that its green M&Ms are

TABLE 5.9	Examples of Geographic Brand Names		
GEOGRAPHIC ORIENTATION	**BRAND NAME**	**PRODUCT**	**LOCALE**
Familiar/Actual	*K.C. Masterpiece*	BBQ Sauce	Oakland, CA
	London Pub	Vinegar	Bloomfield, NJ
	Old El Paso	Salsa	Minneapolis, MN
	Old Milwaukee	Beer	Detroit, MI
	Philadelphia	Cream Cheese	Glenview, IL
	San Francisco Intl	Buns/Rolls	Totowa, NJ
	Arizona Iced Tea	Iced Tea	Lake Success, NY
Unfamiliar/Fictitious	*Bear Creek*	Soup	Harbor City, UT
	Green Forest	Paper Towels	Mexico
	Hidden Valley	Salad Dressing	Oakland, CA
	Italian Village	Ravioli	Secaucus, NJ
	Pepperwood Grove	Wine	Oakville, CA
	Sorrel Ridge	Jam	Port Reading, NJ

Source: K. Damon Aiken, Eric C. Koch, and Robert Mandrigal, "What's in a Name? Explorations in Geographic Equity and Geographic Personality," *American Marketing Association* (Winter 2000): 302.

aphrodisiacs by creating a green female M&M character that it has featured in some of its ads.[54] And although we all know that ketchup is red, Heinz (**www.heinz.com**) developed its green ketchup after doing research with more than 1,000 kids, who helped decide on the product's green color and its packaging (e.g., the bottle is designed to fit smaller hands).[55] A recent print and outdoor advertising campaign for LifeSavers, based on consumer flavor and color research, characterizes *cherry* as "Ms. Popularity," *lime* as "The Outsider," and *sour apple and cherry* (targeted to teens) as "The Troublemaker."[56]

Many fast-food restaurants use combinations of bright colors, like red, yellow, and blue, for their roadside signs and interior designs. These colors have come to be associated with fast service and inexpensive food. In contrast, fine dining restaurants tend to use sophisticated colors like gray, white, shades of tan, or other soft, pale, or muted colors to reflect the feeling of fine, leisurely service. Consumer research sponsored by a marketer of popularly priced casual wear found that dark colors, such as gray, dark blue, and black, were preferred to pastel colors in wintry northeastern and midwestern markets. However, when the multimarket study reached sunny Phoenix, Arizona, a reversal occurred—the darker colors fell into disfavor, and rose, pinks, yellows, and turquoise became the preferred colors. Further research revealed that many people seek to contrast the somber backdrop of the desert with multicolor pastel clothing and home furnishings. Table 5.10 presents a list of various colors, their personality-like meanings, and associated marketing insights.

As part of its *2005 Color Survey*, BuzzBack Market Research asked consumers to look over a palette of 44 color shades and to indicate which one best reflects their nature. The six color shades cited with the greatest frequency were Palace Blue (11 percent), Fiery Red (9 percent), Sunshine (7 percent), Little Boy Blue (6 percent), Sailor Blue (5 percent), and Black Limo (4 percent). Interestingly, while the top selection for males was Palace Blue (17 percent), two top vote gettings among women were Fiery Red and Sunshine (9% each).[57] Table 5.11 presents the associations made by consumers with their "personal shade."

TABLE 5.10	The Personality-like Associations of Selected Colors	
COLOR	**PERSONALITY LINK**	**MARKETING INSIGHTS**
Blue	Commands respect, authority	• America's favored color • IBM holds the title to blue • Associated with club soda • Men seek products packaged in blue • Houses painted blue are avoided • Low-calorie, skim milk • Coffee in a blue can perceived as "mild"
Yellow	Caution, novelty, temporary, warmth	• Eyes register it fastest • Coffee in yellow can taste "weak" • Stops traffic • Sells a house
Green	Secure, natural, relaxed or easygoing, living things	• Good work environment • Associated with vegetables and chewing gum • Canada Dry ginger ale sales increased when it changed sugar-free package from red to green and white
Red	Human, exciting, hot, passionate, strong	• Makes food "smell" better • Coffee in a red can perceived as "rich" • Women have a preference for bluish red • Men have a preference for yellowish red • Coca-Cola "owns" red
Orange	Powerful, affordable, informal	• Draws attention quickly
Brown	Informal and relaxed, masculine, nature	• Coffee in a dark-brown can was "too strong" • Men seek products packaged in brown
White	Goodness, purity, chastity, cleanliness, delicacy, refinement, formality	• Suggests reduced calories • Pure and wholesome food • Clean, bath products, feminine
Black	Sophistication, power, authority, mystery	• Powerful clothing • High-tech electronics
Silver, Gold, Platinum	Regal, wealthy, stately	• Suggests premium price

Source: From Bernice Kanner, "Color Schemes," *New York* magazine, April 3, 1989, 22–23. Reprinted by permission.

self and self-image

Consumers have a variety of enduring images of themselves. These self-images, or perceptions of self, are very closely associated with personality in that individuals tend to buy products and services and patronize retailers whose images or personalities relate in some meaningful way to their own self-images. In essence, consumers seek to depict themselves in their brand choices—they tend to approach products with images that could enhance their self-concept and avoid those products that do not.[58] In this final section, we examine the issue of *one* or *multiple* selves, explore the makeup of the

TABLE 5.11	Consumers' Associations with the Personal Shade	
PALACE BLUE IS. . .		
"calming/peaceful"		27%
FIERY RED IS. . .		
"fiery/hot" & "energetic"		24%
SUNSHINE IS. . .		
"happy/cheerful"		58%
"bright"		30%
"optimistic"		25%
"sunny"		19%
LITTLE BOY BLUE IS. . .		
"calming/peaceful"		28%
a "favorite color"		21%
"easy going/laid back"		16%
"happy/cheerful"		16%
SAILOR BLUE IS. . .		
a "favorite color"		19%
"strong/powerful"		18%
"calming/peaceful"		17%
BLACK LIMO IS. . .		
"dark"		19%
"matches everything/basic"		19%
"mysterious"		14%
"fits my mood"		14%
a "favorite color"		13%
"strong/powerful"		12%

Source: Brandweek, April 4, 2005, 24.

self-image, the notion of **extended self**, and the possibilities or options of *altering the self-image.*

One or multiple selves

Historically, individuals have been thought to have a single self-image and to be interested, as consumers, in products and services that satisfy that single self. However, it is more accurate to think of consumers as having **multiple selves**.[59] This thinking reflects the understanding that a single consumer is likely to act quite differently with different people and in different situations. For instance, a person is likely to behave in different ways with parents, at school, at work, at a museum opening, or with friends at a nightclub. The healthy or normal person is likely to display a somewhat different personality in each of these different situations or social **roles**. In fact, acting exactly the same in all situations or roles and not adapting to the situation at hand may be considered a sign of an abnormal or unhealthy person.

In terms of consumer behavior, the idea that an individual embodies a number of different "selves" (i.e., has multiple self-images) suggests that marketers should target their products and services to consumers *within the context of a particular "self,"* and in certain cases, a choice of different products for different *selves.* (The notion of a consumer having multiple selves or playing multiple roles supports the application of usage situation as a segmentation base discussed in Chapter 3.)

The makeup of the self-image

Consistent with the idea of multiple self-images, each individual has an image of himself or herself as a certain kind of person, with certain traits, skills, habits, possessions, relationships, and ways of behaving. As with other types of images and personality, the individual's self-image is unique, the outgrowth of that person's background and experience. Individuals develop their self-images through interactions with other people—initially their parents, and then other individuals or groups with whom they relate over the years.

Products and brands have symbolic value for individuals, who evaluate them on the basis of their consistency (congruence) with their personal pictures or images of themselves. Some products seem to match one or more of an individual's self-images; others seem totally alien. It is generally believed that consumers attempt to preserve or enhance their self-images by selecting products and brands with "images" or "personalities" that they believe are congruent with their own self-images and avoiding products that are not.[60] This seems to be especially true for women; research reveals that more women than men (77 percent versus 64 percent) feel that the brands they select reflect their personalities.[61]

Given this relationship between brand preference and consumers' self-images, it is natural that consumers use brands to help them in their task of defining themselves. Research indicates that consumers who have strong links to particular brands—a positive self-brand connection—see such brands *as representing an aspect of themselves*. For marketers, such *connections* are certainly an important step in the formation of consumer loyalty and a positive relationship with consumers.[62] Consider the two charts presented in Figure 5.9, which show purchase intent to be strongest when there is a good fit between brand image and self-image.[63]

A variety of different self-images have been recognized in the consumer behavior literature for a long time. In particular, many researchers have depicted some or all of the following kinds of self-image: (1) **actual self-image** (how consumers in fact see themselves), (2) **ideal self-image** (how consumers would like to see themselves), (3) **social self-image** (how consumers feel others see them), and (4) **ideal social self-image** (how consumers would like others to see them).

It also seems useful to think in terms of two other types of self-images—**expected self** and the **"ought-to" self**. The *expected self-image* (how consumers expect to see themselves at some specified future time) is somewhere between the *actual* and *ideal* self-images. It is a future-oriented combination of what is (the actual self-image) and what consumers would like to be (the ideal self-image). As another interesting type of self-image—the *"ought-to" self*—consists of traits or characteristics that an individual believes it is his or her duty or obligation to possess.[64] Examples of this form of self-image might be the striving to achieve a deeper religious understanding or the seeking of a fair and just solution to a challenging ethical problem. Because the expected self and the ought-to self provide consumers with a realistic opportunity to change the self, they are both likely to be more valuable to marketers than the actual or ideal self-image as a guide for designing and promoting products.

In different contexts (i.e., in different situations and/or with respect to different products), consumers might select a different self-image to guide their attitudes or behavior. For instance, with some everyday household products, consumers might be guided by their actual self-image, whereas for some socially enhancing or socially conspicuous products, they might be guided by their social self-image. When it comes to an important and a strong personal goal or wish, like losing weight and feeling better about oneself and one's appearance, an individual might be guided by either their ideal self-images or ideal social self-images.

The concept of self-image has strategic implications for marketers. For example, marketers can segment their markets on the basis of relevant consumer self-images and then position their products or services as symbols of such self-images. Such a strategy is fully consistent with the marketing concept in that the marketer first assesses the needs of a consumer segment (with respect to both the product category and to an appropriate symbol of self-image) and then proceeds to develop and market a product or service that meets both criteria. The importance of marketing cannot be overstated, as brand equity

FIGURE 5.9

Self-Image, Brand Image, and Purchase Intent. (a) Fragrance Commerical: Self-Image and Brand-Image Convergence Among Respondents with Strong Purchase Intent. (b) Fragrance Commercial: Self-Image and Brand-Image Convergence Among Respondents with Weak Purchase Intent.

Source: Abhilasha Mehta, "Using Self-Concept to Assess Advertising Effectiveness," *Journal of Advertising Research* (February 1999): 87.

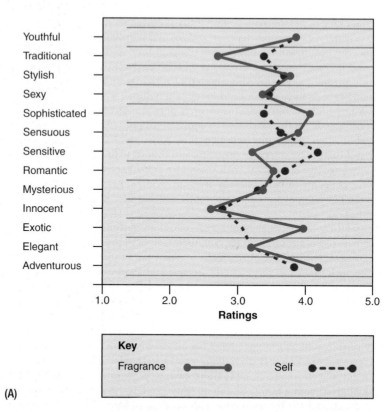

(A)

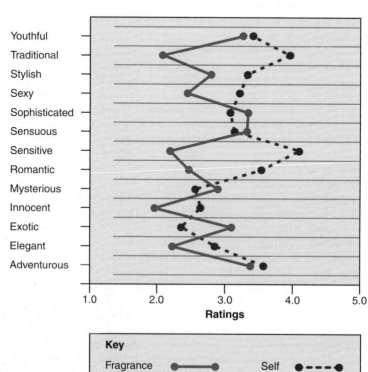

(B)

theory (which focuses on the value inherent in a brand name) postulates that the power of a brand resides in the consumer's mind from both lived (purchase and usage) and mediated (advertising and promotion) experiences.[65]

The extended self

The interrelationship between consumers' self-images and their possessions (i.e., objects they call their own) is an exciting topic. Specifically, consumers' possessions can be seen to confirm or extend their self-images. For instance, acquiring a desired or sought-after pair of "vintage" Levi jeans might serve to expand or enrich a Brazilian teenager's image of self. The teenager might now see herself as being more desirable, more fashionable, and more successful because she has a pair of the sought-after "vintage jeans." In a similar manner, if the gold chain that a college student (let's call him Ted) received as a gift from his grandmother was stolen, Ted is likely to feel diminished in some way. Indeed, the loss of a prized possession may lead Ted to "grieve" and to experience a variety of emotions, such as frustration, loss of control, the feeling of being violated, even the loss of magical protection. Table 5.12 presents sample items from a measurement instrument designed to reflect how particular possessions (e.g., a gold chain) might become part of one's extended self.

The previous examples suggest that much human emotion can be connected to valued possessions. In such cases, possessions are considered extensions of the self. It has been proposed that possessions can extend the self in a number of ways: (1) *actually*, by allowing the person to do things that otherwise would be very difficult or impossible to accomplish (e.g., problem solving by using a computer); (2) *symbolically*, by making the person feel better or "bigger" (receiving an employee award for excellence); (3) by *conferring status or rank* (e.g., among collectors of rare works of art because of the ownership of a particular masterpiece); (4) by *bestowing feelings of immortality* by leaving valued possessions to young family members (this also has the potential of extending the recipients' selves); and (5) by *endowing with magical powers* (e.g., a pair of cuff links inherited from one's grandfather might be perceived as magic amulets bestowing good luck when they are worn).[66]

Altering the self

Sometimes consumers wish to change themselves to become a different or improved self. Clothing, grooming aids or cosmetics, and all kinds of accessories (such as sunglasses, jewelry, tattoos, or even colored contact lenses) offer consumers the opportunity

TABLE 5.12	Sample Items from an Extended Self-Survey[a]

My _____ holds a special place in my life.

My _____ is central to my identity.

I feel emotionally attached to my _____.

My _____ helps me narrow the gap between what I am and try to be.

If my _____ was stolen from me, I would feel as if part of me is missing.

I would be a different person without my _____.

I take good care of my _____.

I trust my _____.

[a]A 6-point agree–disagree scale was used.

Source: Kimberly J. Dodson, "Peak Experiences and Mountain Biking: Incorporating the Bike in the Extended Self," *Advances in Consumer Research*, 1996. Reprinted by permission.

TABLE 5.13	**Sample Items from a Vanity Scale**

PHYSICAL-CONCERN ITEMS

1. The way I look is extremely important to me.
2. I am very concerned with my appearance.
3. It is important that I always look good.

PHYSICAL-VIEW ITEMS

1. People notice how attractive I am.
2. People are envious of my good looks.
3. My body is sexually appealing.

ACHIEVEMENT-CONCERN ITEMS

1. Professional achievements are an obsession with me.
2. Achieving greater success than my peers is important to me.
3. I want my achievements to be recognized by others.

ACHIEVEMENT-VIEW ITEMS

1. My achievements are highly regarded by others.
2. I am a good example of professional success.
3. Others wish they were as successful as me.

Source: Richard G. Netemeyer, Scot Burton, and Donald R. Lichtenstein, "Trait Aspects of Vanity: Measurement and Relevance to Consumer Behavior," *Journal of Consumer Research*, 21 (March 1995): 624. Reprinted by permission of The University of Chicago Press as publisher.

to modify their appearances (to create a "makeover") and thereby to alter their "selves." In using *self-altering products*, consumers are frequently attempting to express their individualism or uniqueness by creating a new self, maintaining the existing self (or preventing the loss of self), and extending the self (modifying or changing the self). Sometimes consumers use self-altering products or services to conform to or take on the appearance of a particular type of person (such as a military person, a physician, a business executive, or a college professor).

Closely related to both self-image and altering the self is the idea of *personal vanity*. As a descriptor of people, vanity is often associated with acting self-important, self-interested, or admiring one's own appearance or achievements. Using a "vanity scale" (Table 5.13), researchers have investigated both *physical vanity* (an excessive concern for and/or a positive — or inflated — view of one's physical appearance) and *achievement vanity* (an excessive concern for and/or a positive or inflated view of one's personal achievements). They have found both these ideas are related to materialism, use of cosmetics, concern with clothing, and country club membership.[67]

There is also research evidence to suggest that self-monitoring may serve as a moderating variable when it comes to how well a person is guided by situational cues regarding social appropriateness. Low self-monitors are individuals who are typically guided by their inner feelings, whereas high self-monitors claim that they act differently in different situations and with different people.[68] Consequently, high self-monitors might be more prone to employ a self-altering product in order to enhance their ideal social self-image.

Altering one's self, particularly one's appearance or body parts, can be accomplished by cosmetics, hair restyling or coloring, getting a tattoo, switching from eyeglasses to contact lenses (or the reverse), undergoing cosmetic surgery, or a "makeover" (see Figure 5.10).

FIGURE 5.10

Source: © The Quaker Oats
Company. Used with permission.
All rights reserved.

Ditched the do.

Lost the leg warmers.

Kept the Quaker Rice Snacks.

Fads come and go, but true goodness lasts forever.
With 70 calories, it's the classic crunch.
Quaker® Rice Snacks. Classic.

**Ad Appealing to the "New You"
or the Altered Self**

virtual personality or self

With the widespread interest in using the Internet as a form of entertainment and as a social
vehicle to meet new people with similar interests, there has been a tremendous growth in
the use of online chat rooms. People who visit chat rooms are able to carry on real-time conversations about themselves and topics of mutual interest with people from all over the
globe. Because at the present time most chats are actually text conversations rather than
live video broadcasts, the participants usually never get to see each other. This creates an
opportunity for chat room participants to try out new identities or to change their identities while online. For instance, one can change from male to female (known as "gender

swapping"); from old to young; from married to single; from white-collar professional to blue-collar worker; or from grossly overweight to svelte. In terms of personality, one can change from mild-mannered to aggressive, or from introvert to extrovert.

The notion of a **virtual personality** or **virtual self** provides an individual with the opportunity to try on different personalities or different identities, much like going to the mall and trying on different outfits in a department or specialty store. If the identity fits, or the personality can be enhanced, the individual may decide to keep the new personality in favor of his or her old personality. From a consumer behavior point of view, it is likely that such opportunities to try out a new personality or alter the self may result in changes in selected forms of purchase behavior. This may in turn offer marketers new opportunities to target various "online selves."

Want to find out about your personality online? One Web site, **www.outofservice.com/ bigfive**, offers Internet users an online test called "The Big Five Personality Test," which takes a few minutes to finish and measures five fundamental dimensions of personality. Give it a try.

SUMMARY

Personality can be described as the psychological characteristics that both determine and reflect how a person responds to his or her environment. Although personality tends to be consistent and enduring, it may change abruptly in response to major life events, as well as gradually over time.

Three theories of personality are prominent in the study of consumer behavior: psychoanalytic theory, neo-Freudian theory, and trait theory. Freud's psychoanalytic theory provides the foundation for the study of motivational research, which operates on the premise that human drives are largely unconscious in nature and serve to motivate many consumer actions. Neo-Freudian theory tends to emphasize the fundamental role of social relationships in the formation and development of personality. Alfred Adler viewed human beings as seeking to overcome feelings of inferiority. Harry Stack Sullivan believed that people attempt to establish significant and rewarding relationships with others. Karen Horney saw individuals as trying to overcome feelings of anxiety and categorized them as compliant, aggressive, or detached.

Trait theory is a major departure from the qualitative (or subjective) approach to personality measurement. It postulates that individuals possess innate psychological traits (e.g., innovativeness, novelty seeking, need for cognition, materialism) to a greater or lesser degree, and that these traits can be measured by specially designed scales or inventories. Because they are simple to use and to score and can be self-administered, personality inventories are the preferred method for many researchers in the assessment of consumer personality. Product and brand personalities represent real opportunities for marketers to take advantage of consumers' connections to various brands they offer. Brands often have personalities—some include "humanlike" traits and even gender. These brand personalities help shape consumer responses, preferences, and loyalties.

Each individual has a perceived self-image (or multiple self-images) as a certain kind of person with certain traits, habits, possessions, relationships, and ways of behaving. Consumers frequently attempt to preserve, enhance, alter, or extend their self-images by purchasing products or services and shopping at stores they perceive as consistent with their relevant self-image(s) and by avoiding products and stores they perceive are not. With the growth of the Internet, there appear to be emerging virtual selves or virtual personalities. Consumer experiences with chat rooms sometimes provide an opportunity to explore new or alternative identities.

DISCUSSION QUESTIONS

1. How would you explain the fact that, although no two individuals have identical personalities, personality is sometimes used in consumer research to identify distinct and sizable market segments?

2. Contrast the major characteristics of the following personality theories: (a) Freudian theory, (b) neo-Freudian theory, and (c) trait theory. In your answer, illustrate how each theory is applied to the understanding of consumer behavior.

3. Describe personality trait theory. Give five examples of how personality traits can be used in consumer research.

4. How can a marketer of cameras use research findings that indicate a target market consists primarily of inner-directed or other-directed consumers? Of consumers who are high (or low) on innovativeness?

5. Describe the type of promotional message that would be most suitable for each of the following personality market segments and give an example of each: (a) highly dogmatic consumers, (b) inner-directed consumers, (c) consumers with high optimum stimulation levels, (d) consumers with a high need for recognition, and (e) consumers who are visualizers versus consumers who are verbalizers.

6. Is there likely to be a difference in personality traits between individuals who readily purchase foreign-made products and those who prefer American-made products? How can marketers use the consumer ethnocentrism scale to segment consumers?

7. A marketer of health foods is attempting to segment a certain market on the basis of consumer self-image. Describe the four types of consumer self-image and discuss which one(s) would be most effective for the stated purpose.

EXERCISES

1. How do your clothing preferences differ from those of your friends? What personality traits might explain why your preferences are different from those of other people?

2. Find three print advertisements based on Freudian personality theory. Discuss how Freudian concepts are used in these ads. Do any of the ads personify a brand? If so, how?

3. Administer the nine items from the materialism scale (listed in Table 5.5) to two of your friends. In your view, are their consumption behaviors consistent with their scores on the scale? Why or why not?

KEY TERMS

- **actual self-image**
- **brand personification**
- **cognitive personality**
- **compulsive consumption**
- **consumer ethnocentrism**
- **consumer innovativeness**
- **consumer innovators**
- **consumer materialism**
- **dogmatism**
- **expected self**
- **extended self**

- **Freudian theory**
- **ideal self-image**
- **ideal social self-image**
- **inner-directedness**
- **multiple selves**
- **need for cognition**
- **neo-Freudian theory**
- **optimum stimulation levels**
- **other-directedness**
- **"ought-to" self**

- **personality**
- **psychoanalytic theory of personality**
- **roles**
- **sensation seeking**
- **social self-image**
- **trait theory**
- **variety- or novelty-seeking**
- **virtual personality or self**
- **visualizers versus verbalizers**

NOTES

1. Amanda B. Diekman and Alice H. Eagly, "Stereotypes as Dynamic Constructs: Women and Men of the Past, Present, and Future," *Personality and Social Psychology Bulletin* 26, no. 10 (October 2000): 1171–1188.

2. Ellen Creager, "Do Snack Foods Such as Nuts and Popcorn Affect Romance?" *The Patriot-News*, Harrisburg, PA, February 14, 2001, E11.

3. For example, see Karen Horney, *The Neurotic Personality of Our Time* (New York: Norton, 1937).

4. Joel B. Cohen, "An Interpersonal Orientation to the Study of Consumer Behavior," *Journal of Marketing Research* 6 (August 1967): 270–278; Arch G. Woodside and Ruth Andress, "CAD Eight Years Later," *Journal of the Academy of Marketing Science* 3 (Summer–Fall 1975): 309–313; see also Jon P. Noerager, "An Assessment of CAD: A Personality Instrument Developed Specifically for Marketing Research," *Journal of Marketing Research* 16 (February 1979): 53–59; and Pradeep K. Tyagi, "Validation of the CAD Instrument: A Replication," in *Advances in Consumer Research*, 10, ed. Richard P. Bogazzio and Alice M. Tybout (Ann Arbor, MI: Association for Consumer Research, 1983), 112–114.

5. Morton I. Jaffe, "Brand-Loyalty/Variety-Seeking and the Consumer's Personality: Comparing Children and Young Adults," in *Proceedings of the Society for Consumer Psychology*, ed. Scott B. MacKenzie and Douglas M. Stayman (La Jolla, CA: American Psychological Association, 1995), 144–151.

6. J. P. Guilford, *Personality* (New York: McGraw-Hill, 1959), 6.

7. Brian Wansink and Sea Bum Park, "Accounting for Tastes: Building Consumer Preference Prototypes," *Journal of Database Marketing* 7, no. 4 (2000): 308–320.

8. Ronald E. Goldsmith and Charles F. Hofacker, "Measuring Consumer Innovativeness," *Journal of the Academy of Marketing Science* 19 (1991): 209–221; Suresh Subramanian and Robert A. Mittelstaedt, "Conceptualizing Innovativeness as a Consumer Trait: Consequences and Alternatives," in *1991 AMA Educators' Proceedings*, ed. Mary C. Gilly and F. Robert Dwyer et al. (Chicago: American Marketing Association, 1991), 352–360; and "Reconceptualizing and Measuring Consumer Innovativeness," in *1992 AMA Educators' Proceedings*, ed. Robert P. Leone and V. Kumor et al. (Chicago: American Marketing Association, 1992), 300–307.

9. Milles Roehrich, "Consumer Innovativenss: Concepts and Measurements," *Journal of Business Research* 57 (June 2004): 671–677.

10. Alka Varma Citrin, David E. Sprott, Steven N. Silverman, and Donald E. Stem, Jr., "From Internet Use to Internet Adoption: Is General Innovativeness Enough?," in *1999 AMA Winter Educators' Conference*, 10, ed. Anil Menon and Arun Sharma (Chicago: American Marketing Association, 1999), 232–233.

11. Gilles Roehrich, "Consumer Innovativeness: Concepts and Measurements," *Journal of Business Research* 6 (June 2004): 671–677; and Angela D'Auria Stanton and Wilbur W. Stanton, "To Click or Not to Click: Personality Characteristics of Internet Versus Non-Internet Purchasers," in *2001 AMA Winter Educators' Conference*, 12, ed. Ram Krishnan and Madhu Viswanathan (Chicago: American Marketing Association, 2001), 161–162.

12. Milton Rokeach, *The Open and Closed Mind* (New York: Basic Books, 1960).

13. Itamar Simonson and Stephen M. Nowlis, "The Role of Explanations and Need for Uniqueness in Consumer Decision Making: Unconventional Choices Based on Reasons," *Journal of Consumer Research* 27 (June 2000): 49–68.

14. Ann Marie Fiore, Leung-Eun Lee, and Grace Kunz, "Individual Differences, Motivations, and Willingness to Use a Mass Customization Option for Fashion Products," *European Journal of Marketing* 38, no. 7 (2004): 835–849.

15. P. S. Raju, "Optimum Stimulation Level: Its Relationship to Personality, Demographics, and Exploratory Behavior," *Journal of Consumer Research* 7 (December 1980): 272–282; Leigh McAlister and Edgar Pessemier, "Variety Seeking Behavior: An Interdisciplinary Review," *Journal of Consumer Research* 9 (December 1982): 311–322; Jan-Benedict, E. M. Steenkamp, and Hans Baumgartner, "The Role of Optimum Stimulation Level in Exploratory Consumer Behavior," *Journal of Consumer Research* 19 (December 1992): 434; Russell G. Wahlers and Michael J. Etzel, "A Consumer Response to Incongruity between Optimal Stimulation and Life Style Satisfaction," in *Advances in Consumer Research*, 12, ed. Elizabeth C. Hirschman and Morris B. Holbrook (Provo, UT: Association for Consumer Research, 1985), 97–101; and Jan-Benedict, E. M. Steenkamp, Frenkel ter Hofstede, and Michael Wedel, "A Cross-National Investigation into the Individual and National Cultural Antecedents of Consumer Innovativeness," *Journal of Marketing* 62 (April 1999): 55–69.

16. Linda McNamara and Mary E. Ballard, "Resting Arousal, Sensation Seeking, and Music Preference," *Genetic, Social, and General Psychology Monographs* 125, no. 3 (1999): 229–250.

17. Elizabeth C. Hirschman, "Innovativeness, Novelty Seeking and Consumer Creativity," *Journal of Consumer Research* 7 (1980): 283–295; Wayne Hoyer and Nancy M. Ridgway, "Variety Seeking as an Explanation for Exploratory Purchase Behavior: A Theoretical Model," in *Advances in Consumer Research*, 17, ed. Thomas C. Kinnear (Provo, UT: Association for Consumer Research, 1984), 114–119; and Minakshi Trivedi, "Using Variety-Seeking-Based Segmentation to Study Promotional Response," *Journal of the Academy of Marketing Science* 27 (Winter 1999), 37–49.

18. Harper A. Roehm, Jr. and Michelle L. Roehm, "Variety-Seeking and Time of Day: Why Leader Brands Hope Young Adults Shop in the Afternoon, but Follower Brands Hope for Morning," *Marketing Letters Boston* 15 (January 2005): 213–221.

19. Barbara E. Kahn, "Dynamic Relationships with Customers: High-Variety Strategies," *Journal of the Academy of Marketing*

Science 26 (Winter 1998): 47–53. Also see J. Jeffrey Inman, "The Role of Sensory-Specific Satiety in Attribute-Level Variety Seeking," *Journal of Consumer Research* 28 (June 2001): 105–120.

20. Minakshi Trivedi and Michael S. Morgan, "Promotional Evaluation and Response among Variety Seeking Segments," *The Journal of Product and Brand Management* 12, no. 6/7 (2003): 408–425.

21. Richard Petty et al., "Personality and Ad Effectiveness: Exploring the Utility of Need for Cognition," in *Advances in Consumer Research*, 15, ed. Michael Houston (Ann Arbor, MI: Association for Consumer Research, 1988), 209–212; and Susan Powell Mantel and Frank R. Kardes, "The Role of Direction of Comparison, Attribute-Based Processing, and Attitude-Based Processing in Consumer Preference," *Journal of Consumer Research* 25 (March 1999): 335–352.

22. Arnold B. Bakker, "Persuasive Communication About AIDS Prevention: Need for Cognition Determines the Impact of Message Format," *AIDS Education and Prevention* 11, no. 2 (1999): 150–162.

23. Yong Zhang and Richard Buda, "Moderating Effects of Need for Cognition on Responses to Positively versus Negatively Framed Advertising Messages," *Journal of Advertising* 28, no. 2 (Summer 1999): 1–15.

24. Ayn E. Crowley and Wayne D. Hoyer, "The Relationship Between Need for Cognition and Other Individual Difference Variables: A Two-Dimensional Framework," in *Advances in Consumer Research*, 16, ed. Thomas K. Srull (Provo, UT: Association for Consumer Research, 1989), 37–43; and James W. Peltier and John A. Schibrowsky, "Need for Cognition, Advertisement Viewing Time and Memory for Advertising Stimuli," *Advances in Consumer Research* 21 (1994): 244–250.

25. Tracy L. Tuten and Michael Bosnjak, "Understanding Differences in Web Usage: The Role of Need for Cognition and the Five Factor Model of Personality," *Social Behavior and Personality* 29, no. 4 (2001): 391–398.

26. Brett A. S. Martin, Michael J. Sherrard, and Daniel Wentzel, "The Role of Sensation Seeking and Need for Cognition on Web-site Evaluations: A Resource-Matching Perspective," *Psychology and Marketing* 22 (December 15, 2004): 109–126.

27. Russell W. Belk, "Three Scales to Measure Constructs Related to Materialism" and "Materialism: Trait Aspects of Living in the Material World," *Journal of Consumer Research* 12 (December 1985): 265–280.

28. Marsha L. Richins and Scott Dawson, "A Consumer Values Orientation for Materialism and Its Measurement: Scale Development and Validation," *Journal of Consumer Research* 19 (December 1992): 303–316; and Jeff Tanner and Jim Roberts, "Materialism Cometh," *Baylor Business Review* (Fall 2000): 8–9.

29. Reto Felix, Roberto Hernandez, and Wolfgang Hinck, "An Empirical Investigation of Materialism in Mexico," in *2000 AMA Educators' Proceedings*, 11, ed. Gregory T. Gundlach and Patrick E. Murphy (Chicago: American Marketing Association, 2000), 279–286.

30. Ronald J. Faber and Thomas C. O'Guinn, "A Clinical Screener for Compulsive Buying," *Journal of Consumer Research* 19 (December 1992): 459–469.

31. Elizabeth C. Hirschman, "The Consciousness of Addiction: Toward a General Theory of Compulsive Consumption," *Journal of Consumer Research* 19 (September 1992): 155–179; and Seung-Hee Lee, Sharron J. Lennon, and Nancy A. Rudd, "Compulsive Consumption Tendencies Among Television Shoppers," *Family and Consumer Sciences Research Journal* 28, no. 4 (June 2000): 463–488; and Booth Moore, "Shopping for a Defense—Consumer-Driven Culture Spills over into the Courtroom," *Houston Chronicle*, July 11, 2001, 8.

32. Kristen Bruinsma and Douglas L. Taren, "Chocolate: Food or Drug?" *Journal of the American Dietetic Association* 99, no. 10 (October 1999): 1249–1256.

33. Ronald J. Faber and Gary A. Christenson, "Can You Buy Happiness?: A Comparison of the Antecedent and Concurrent Moods Associated with the Shopping of Compulsive and Non-Compulsive Buyers," in *1995 Winter Educator's Conference*, 6, ed. David W. Stewart and Naufel J. Vilcassin (Chicago: American Marketing Association, 1995), 378–379.

34. Terence A. Shimp and Subhash Sharma, "Consumer Ethnocentrism: Construction and Validation of the CETSCALE," *Journal of Marketing Research* 24 (August 1987): 280–289; and Richard G. Netemeyer, Srinivas Durvaula, and Donald R. Lichtenstein, "A Cross-National Assessment of the Reliability and Validity of the CETSCALE," *Journal of Marketing Research* 28 (August 1991): 320–327.

35. Osman Mohamad, Zafar U. Ahmed, Earl D. Honeycutt, Jr., and Taizoon Hyder Tyebkhan, "Does 'Made In . . .' Matter to Consumers? A Malaysian Study of Country of Origin Effect," *Multinational Business Review* (Fall 2000): 69–73; and Irvin Clarke, Mahesh N. Shankarmahesh, and John B. Ford, "Consumer Ethnocentrism, Materialism and Values: A Four Country Study," in *2000 AMA Winter Educators' Conference*, 11, ed. John P. Workman and William D. Perreault (Chicago: American Marketing Association, 2000), 102–103.

36. Subhash Sharma, Terence A. Shimp, and Jeongshin Shin, "Consumer Ethnocentrism: A Test of Antecedents and Moderators," *Journal of the Academy of Marketing Science*, 23 (1995): 27.

37. George Balabanis and Adamantios Diamantopoulos, "Domestic Country Bias, Country-of-Origin Effects, and Consumer Ethnocentrism: A Multidimensional Unfolding Approach," *Journal of the Academy of Marketing Science* 32 (Winter 2004): 80–95.

38. Byeong-Joon Moon, "Effects of Consumer Ethnocentrism and Product Knowledge on Consumers' Utilization of Country-of-Origin Information," *Advances in Consumer Research* 31 (2004): 667–673.

39. Jufei Kao, "Is It a Foreign Product? A Scale to Classify Products in an Era of Globalization," *Advances in Consumer Research* 31 (2004): 674–682.

40. David Martin, "Branding: Finding That 'One Thing'," *Brandweek*, February 16, 1998, 18.

41. Subodh Bhat and Srinivas K. Reddy, "Symbolic and Functional Positioning of Brands," *Journal of Consumer Marketing* 15 (1998): 32–43.

42. Traci L. Haigood, "The Brand Personality Effect: An Empirical Investigation," in *1999 AMA Winter Educators' Conference*, 10, ed. Anil Menon and Arun Sharma (Chicago: American Marketing Association, 1999), 149–150; and Traci L. Haigood, "Deconstructing Brand Personality," in *2001 AMA Educators' Proceedings*, 12, ed. Greg W. Marshall and Stephen J. Grove (Chicago: American Marketing Association, 2001), 327–328.

43. Janice S. Griffiths, Mary Zimmer, and Sheniqua K. Little, "The Effect of Reality Engineering on Consumers' Brand Perceptions Using a Fictional Historical Branding Strategy," *American Marketing Association* (Winter 1999): 250–258.

44. Brigitte Muller and Jean-Louis Chandon, "The Impact of Visiting a Brand Website on Brand Personality," *Electonic Markets* 13, no. 3 (2003): 18–29.

45. Tim Triplett, "When Tracy Speaks, Celestial Listens," *Marketing News*, October 24, 1994, 14.

46. David M. Morawski and Lacey J. Zachary, "Making Mr. Coffee," *Quirk's Marketing Research Review* 6 (March 1992): 6–7, 29–33.

47. Jennifer L. Aaker, "Dimension of Brand Personality," *Journal of Marketing Research*, 35 (August 1997): 351–352.

48. Pankaj Aggarwal, "The Effects of Brand Relationship Norms on Consumer Attitudes and Behavior," *Journal of Consumer Research* 31 (June 2004): 87–101.

49. Laura M. Milner and Dale Fodness, "Product Gender Perception: The Case of China," in *1995 Winter Educators' Conference*, 6, ed. David W. Stewart and Naufel J. Vilcassin (Chicago: American Marketing Association, 1995), 331–336.

50. K. Damon Aiken, Eric C. Koch, and Robert Mandrigal, "What's In a Name? Explorations in Geographic Equity and Geographic Personality," in *2000 AMA Winter Educators' Conference*, 11, ed. John P. Workman and William D. Perreault (Chicago: American Marketing Association, 2000), 301–308.

51. Max Blackston, "Observations: Building Brand Equity by Managing the Brand's Relationships," *Journal of Advertising Research* (November/December 2000): 101–105.

52. Elizabeth Jensen, "Blue Bottles, Gimmicky Labels Sell Wine," *Wall Street Journal*, July 7, 1997, B1.

53. Pamela S. Schindler, "Color and Contrast in Magazine Advertising," *Psychology & Marketing* 3 (1986): 69–78.

54. Sally Goll Beatty, "Mars Inc. Dips into Sex to Lure Consumers into Arms of M&Ms," *Wall Street Journal*, January 23, 1997, 9.

55. "Heinz EZ Squirt™ Hits Store Shelves; Industry Watches Unusual Food Phenomenon Unfold," *PR Newswire*, October 17, 2000, 1.

56. Stephanie Thompson, "LifeSavers Effort Gets Personality," *Advertising Age*, January 21, 2002, 42. Also see Lawrence L. Garber, Jr., Eva M. Hyatt, and Richard G. Starr, Jr., "The Effects of Food Color on Perceived Flavor," *Journal of Marketing Theory and Practice* (Fall 2000): 59–72.

57. Becky Ebenkamp (ed.), "Living in Color," *Brandweek*, April 4, 2005, 22–24.

58. Kiran Karande, George M. Zinkhan, and Alyssa Baird Lum, "Brand Personality and Self Concept: A Replication and Extension," *AMA Summer 1997 Conference*, 165–171.

59. Hazel Markus and Paula Nurius, "Possible Selves," *American Psychologist* (1986): 954–969.

60. For a detailed discussion of self-images and congruence, see M. Joseph Sirgy, "Self-Concept in Consumer Behavior: A Critical Review," *Journal of Consumer Research* 9 (December 1992): 287–300; C. B. Claiborne and M. Joseph Sirgy, "Self-Image Congruence as a Model of Consumer Attitude Formation and Behavior: A Conceptual Review and Guide for Future Research," in *Developments in Marketing Science*, 13, ed. B. J. Dunlap (Cullowhee, NC: Academy of Marketing Science, 1990), 1–7; and J. S. Johar and M. Joseph Sirgy, "Value-Expressive versus Utilitarian Advertising Appeals: When and Why to Use Which Appeal," *Journal of Advertising* 20 (September 1991): 23–33.

61. "Sex Appeal," *Brandweek*, April 20, 1998, 26.

62. Susan Fournier, "Consumers and Their Brands: Developing Relationship Theory in Consumer Research," *Journal of Consumer Research* 24 (March 1998); and Kimberly J. Dodson, "Peak Experiences and Mountain Biking: Incorporating the Bike in the Extended Self," in *Advances in Consumer Research*, incomplete vol. 23, ed. Kim P. Cofman and John G. Lynch, Jr. (Provo, UT: Association for Consumer Research 1996), 317–322.

63. Abhilasha Mehta, "Using Self-Concept to Assess Advertising Effectiveness," *Journal of Advertising Research* (February 1999): 81–89.

64. Marlene M. Moretti and E. Tory Higgens, "Internal Representations of Others in Self-Regulation: A New Look at a Classic Issue," *Social Cognition* 17, no. 2 (1999): 186–208.

65. Robert Underwood, Edward Bond, and Robert Baer, "Building Service Brands via Social Identity: Lessons from the Sports Marketplace," *Journal of Marketing Theory and Practice* (Winter 2001): 1–13.

66. Russell W. Belk, "Possessions and the Extended Self," *Journal of Consumer Research* 15 (September 1988): 139–168; and Amy J. Morgan, "The Evolving Self in Consumer Behavior: Exploring Possible Selves," in *Advances in Consumer Research*, 20, ed. Leigh McAlister and Michael L. Rothschild (Provo, UT: Association for Consumer Research, 1992), 429–432.

67. Richard G. Netemeyer, Scot Burton, and Donald R. Lichtenstein, "Trait Aspects of Vanity: Measurement and Relevance to Consumer Behavior," *Journal of Consumer Research* 21 (March 1995): 613.

68. Jennifer L. Aaker, "The Malleable Self: The Role of Self-Expression in Persuasion," *Journal of Marketing Research* XXXVI (February 1999): 45–57.

chapter**six**

> ## Consumer Perception

In 1967, Gablinger's beer was introduced as a "low-calorie" beer. It was promoted as a diet beer with the proposition that heavy beer drinkers (who buy most of the beer sold) would gain less weight drinking this product than they would drinking regular beer. The product failed. Five years later, Miller Lite was introduced as "less filling" under the slogan "everything you want in a beer . . . and less." The product was a great success and paved the way for many other brands of light beer.[1] Miller Lite succeeded because the company's promotion suggested beer drinkers could drink more beer than they already did without feeling full. Gablinger's failed because it told beer drinkers that they would gain less weight while drinking beer (though heavy beer drinkers are usually not concerned with their weight). In reality, in terms of physical product attributes, Gablinger's and Miller Lite were practically identical. It's how the two offerings were perceived by the target audience—how they were "positioned"—that made the difference. Whereas Gablinger's offered consumers a product *attribute* (i.e., less calories), Miller Lite offered them a product *benefit*—a less filling beer that allowed them to drink more beer.

Individuals act and react on the basis of their perceptions, not on the basis of objective reality. For each individual, *reality* is a totally personal phenomenon, based on that person's needs,

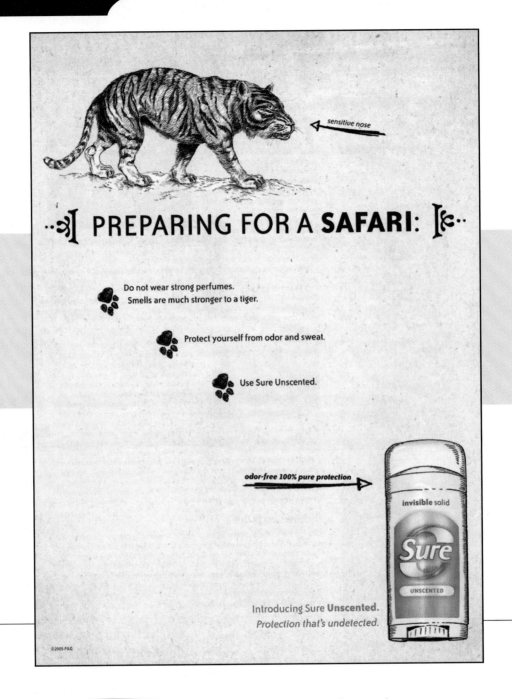

© 2005 P&G

wants, values, and personal experiences. Thus, to the marketer, consumers' perceptions are much more important than their knowledge of objective reality. For if one thinks about it, it's not what actually is so, but what consumers *think* is so, that affects their actions, their buying habits, their leisure habits, and so forth. And, because individuals make decisions and take actions based on what they perceive to be reality, it is important that marketers understand the whole notion of perception and its related concepts to more readily determine what factors influence consumers to buy. Before the introduction of low-calorie beer, consumers had no preconceived view of the product. Because Miller understood the behavior of beer drinkers, it provided the company with a way to interpret the new offering in a manner congruent with their needs, which Gablinger's failed to do earlier for the same product.

This chapter examines the psychological and physiological bases of human perception and discusses the principles that influence our perception and interpretation of the world we see. Knowledge of these principles enables astute marketers to develop advertisements that have a better-than-average chance of being seen and remembered by their target consumers.

elements of perception

Perception is defined as *the process by which an individual selects, organizes, and interprets stimuli into a meaningful and coherent picture of the world*. It can be described as "how we see the world around us." Two individuals may be exposed to the same stimuli under the same apparent conditions, but how each person recognizes, selects, organizes, and interprets these stimuli is a highly individual process based on each person's own needs, values, and expectations. The influence that each of these variables has on the perceptual process and its relevance to marketing will be explored later in the chapter. First, however, we will examine some of the basic concepts that underlie the perceptual process. These will be discussed within the framework of consumer behavior.

Sensation

Sensation is the immediate and direct response of the sensory organs to stimuli. A **stimulus** is any unit of input to any of the senses. Examples of stimuli (i.e., sensory input) include products, packages, brand names, advertisements, and commercials. **Sensory receptors** are the human organs (the eyes, ears, nose, mouth, and skin) that receive sensory inputs. Their sensory functions are to see, hear, smell, taste, and feel. All of these functions are called into play, either singly or in combination, in the evaluation and use of most consumer products. Human sensitivity refers to the experience of sensation. Sensitivity to stimuli varies with the quality of an individual's sensory receptors (e.g., eyesight or hearing) and the amount (or *intensity*) of the stimuli to which he or she is exposed. For example, a blind person may have a more highly developed sense of hearing than the average sighted person and may be able to hear sounds that the average person cannot.

Sensation itself depends on energy change within the environment where the perception occurs (i.e., on differentiation of input). A perfectly bland or unchanging environment, regardless of the strength of the sensory input, provides little or no sensation at all. Thus, a person who lives on a busy street in midtown Manhattan would probably receive little or no sensation from the inputs of such noisy stimuli as horns honking, tires screeching, and fire engines clanging, because such sounds are so commonplace in New York City. In situations in which there is a great deal of sensory input, the senses do not detect small changes or differences in input. Thus, one honking horn more or less would never be noticed on a street with heavy traffic.

As sensory input *decreases*, however, our ability to detect changes in input or intensity *increases*, to the point that we attain maximum sensitivity under conditions of minimal stimulation. This accounts for the statement, "It was so quiet I could hear a pin drop." The ability of the human organism to accommodate itself to varying levels of sensitivity as external conditions vary not only provides more sensitivity when it is needed but also serves to protect us from damaging, disruptive, or irrelevant bombardment when the input level is high.

One researcher pointed out that 83 percent of all communications today appeal to sight; also that smell, not sound, is the second most important sensory input. This study also reported that consumers preferred shoes and belts presented in a scented room rather than a non-scented room, and were also willing to pay higher prices for these products.[2] The importance of smell in communication was strongly supported by two

Americans who developed a scientific explanation as to how people associate memories with smells (and won the 2004 Nobel Prize in Physiology for this work) and other studies demonstrating the impact of fragrance on product and store choices.[3]

The absolute threshold

The lowest level at which an individual can experience a sensation is called the **absolute threshold**. The point at which a person can detect a difference between "something" and "nothing" is that person's absolute threshold for that stimulus. To illustrate, the distance at which a driver can note a specific billboard on a highway is that individual's absolute threshold. Two people riding together may first spot the billboard at different times (i.e., at different distances); thus, they appear to have different absolute thresholds. Under conditions of constant stimulation, such as driving through a "corridor" of billboards, the absolute threshold increases (i.e., the senses tend to become increasingly dulled). After an hour of driving through billboards, it is doubtful that any one billboard will make an impression. Hence, we often speak of "getting used to" a hot bath, a cold shower, or the bright sun. As our exposure to the stimulus increases, we notice it less. In the field of perception, the term *adaptation* refers specifically to "getting used to" certain sensations; that is, becoming accommodated to a certain level of stimulation.

Sensory adaptation is a problem that concerns many national advertisers, which is why they try to change their advertising campaigns regularly. They are concerned that consumers will get so used to their current print ads and TV commercials that they will no longer "see" them; that is, the ads will no longer provide sufficient sensory input to be noted.

In an effort to cut through the advertising clutter and ensure that consumers note their ads, some marketers try to *increase* sensory input. For example, Apple Computer once bought all the advertising space in an issue of *Newsweek* magazine to ensure that readers would note its ads. From time to time, various advertisers have taken all of the bus cards on certain bus routes to advertise their products, ensuring that wherever a rider sits, he or she will be exposed to the ad. Other advertisers try to attract attention by *decreasing* sensory input. For example, some print ads include a lot of empty space in order to accentuate the brand name or product illustration, and some TV ads use silence, the absence of audio sound, to generate attention.

Some marketers seek unusual or technological media in which to place their advertisements in an effort to gain attention. Examples of such media include disks placed in bathroom sinks that play commercials when activated by running water, ads embedded in the floors of supermarkets, and small monitors that display weather and news, as well as advertising, placed in elevators. Researchers have reported that the use of an ambient scent in a retail environment enhances the shopping experience for many consumers and makes the time they spend examining merchandise, waiting in line, and waiting for help seem shorter than it actually is.[4] Some marketers have invested in the development of specially engineered scents to enhance their products and entice consumers to buy. Marketers try to form stronger bonds between young, design-oriented consumers and brands, using the store image itself to give "dimension" to their brands, and present them as "cool." For example, in one store selling sports footwear, the shoes are integrated into a huge sound system in the shape of a wall; in another store selling advertised high-definition TVs, the screens show works of art inside the store.[5]

The differential threshold

The minimal difference that can be detected between two similar stimuli is called the **differential threshold**, or the **just noticeable difference** (the **j.n.d.**). A nineteenth-century German scientist named Ernst Weber discovered that the j.n.d. between two stimuli was not an absolute amount, but an amount relative to the intensity of the first stimulus. **Weber's law**, as it has come to be known, states that the stronger the initial stimulus, the greater the additional intensity needed for the second stimulus to be perceived as different. For example, if the price of a half gallon container of premium, freshly squeezed orange juice is $5.50, most consumers will probably not notice an increase of 25 cents (i.e., the increment would fall below the j.n.d.), and it may take an increase of 50 cents or more before a differential in price would be noticed. However, a 50-cent increase in the price of gasoline would be noticed very quickly by consumers because it is a significant percentage of the initial (base) cost of the gasoline.

According to Weber's law, an additional level of stimulus equivalent to the j.n.d. must be added for the majority of people to perceive a difference between the resulting stimulus and the initial stimulus. Let us say that Goddard's, a 130-year-old manufacturer of fine polishes, wants to improve its silver polish sufficiently to claim that it retards tarnish longer than the leading competitive brand. In a series of experiments, the company determines that the j.n.d. for its present polish (which now gives a shine that lasts about 20 days) is 5 days, or one-fourth longer. That means that the shine given by the improved silver polish must last at least 25 days (or one-fourth) longer if the new polish is to be perceived by the majority of users as, in fact, improved. By finding this j.n.d. of 5 days, the company has isolated the minimum amount of time necessary to make its claim of "lasts longer" believable to the majority of consumers. If it had decided to make the polish effective for 23 days (just 3 extra days of product life), its claim of "lasts longer" would not be perceived as true by most consumers and, from the marketer's point of view, would be "wasted." On the other hand, if the company had decided to make the silver polish effective for 40 days, it would have sacrificed a good deal of repeat purchase frequency. Making the product improvement just equal to the j.n.d. thus becomes the most efficient decision that management can make.

An interesting application of the j.n.d. is the development of new food products. With the public alarm regarding the rapidly rising obesity rates, food marketers are looking for substances that can mimic the creamy and palate-coating food of fatty products such as pudding, cheese, and chocolate.[6] The challenge is to create fat substitutes with taste that is below, or at least not significantly above, consumers' j.n.d. for the original, fatty foods.

Marketing applications of the j.n.d.

Weber's law has important applications in marketing. Manufacturers and marketers endeavor to determine the relevant j.n.d. for their products for two very different reasons: (1) so that negative changes (e.g., reductions in product size or quality, or increases in product price) are not readily discernible to the public (i.e., remain below the j.n.d.), and (2) so that product improvements (e.g., improved or updated packaging, larger size, or lower price) are very apparent to consumers without being wastefully extravagant (i.e., they are at or just above the j.n.d.). For example, some years ago, in an apparent misunderstanding of the j.n.d., a silver polish manufacturer introduced an extension of its silver polish brand that prolonged the shine of the silver by months but raised its product price by merely pennies. By doing so, the company decreased its sales revenue because the new version cannibalized the sales of the old product and, at the same time, was purchased much less frequently than the old version. One marketing expert advised the company to double the price of the new product rather than make it just slightly more expensive than the old one.[7] However, for a nondurable consumer good, a product that has been improved dramatically but is doubled in price is inconsistent with the concept of the j.n.d. A better strategy would have been to introduce several successive versions of the polish; each version with a shine that lasts longer than the previous version (and at or slightly above the j.n.d.) and offered at a higher price (but a price that is lower than the j.n.d.).

When it comes to product improvements, marketers very much want to meet or exceed the consumer's differential threshold; that is, they want consumers to readily perceive any improvements made in the original product. Marketers use the j.n.d. to determine the amount of improvement they should make in their products. Less than the j.n.d. is wasted effort because the improvement will not be perceived; more than the j.n.d. is wasteful because it reduces the level of repeat sales. On the other hand, when it comes to price increases, less than the j.n.d. is desirable because consumers are unlikely to notice it.

Since many routinely purchased consumer goods are relatively inexpensive, companies are reluctant to raise prices when their profit margins on these items are declining.

FIGURE 6.1

Source: Courtesy of General Mills, Inc.

Sequential Changes in the Betty Crocker Symbol Fall Below the j.n.d.

Instead, many marketers decrease the product *quantity* included in the packages, while leaving the prices unchanged—thus, in effect, increasing the per unit price. The manufacturer of Huggies reduced the number of diapers in a package from 240 to 228 (and continued pricing it at $31.99); PepsiCo reduced the weight of one snack food bag from 14.5 ounces to 13.5 ounces (and maintained the price at $3.29), and Poland Spring reduced its water-cooler-sized bottle from 6 to 5 gallons (and maintained the old price at $9.25).[8] The packages for these products remained virtually unchanged. Presumably, the decreases in the number of items or weight of these products reflect j.n.d.-focused research; the reductions in quantity were below most consumers' j.n.d. for these products.

Marketers often want to update their existing package designs without losing the ready recognition of consumers who have been exposed to years of cumulative advertising impact. In such cases, they usually make a number of small changes, each carefully designed to fall below the j.n.d., so that consumers will perceive minimal difference between succeeding versions. For example, Betty Crocker, the General Mills symbol, has been updated seven times from 1936 to 1996 (see Figure 6.1).

When Lexmark International Inc. bought the office supplies and equipment line from IBM in March 1991, it agreed to relinquish the IBM name by 1996. Recognizing the need to build a brand image for Lexmark while moving away from the well-known IBM name, Lexmark officials conducted a four-stage campaign for phasing in the Lexmark name on products. As Figure 6.2 indicates, Stage 1 carried only the IBM name, Stage 2 featured the IBM name and downplayed Lexmark, Stage 3 featured the Lexmark name and downplayed IBM, and Stage 4 features only the Lexmark name. Figure 6.3 shows a Lexmark ad with the transition complete.

Subliminal perception

In Chapter 4 we spoke of people being *motivated* below their level of conscious awareness. People are also *stimulated* below their level of conscious awareness; that is, they can perceive stimuli without being consciously aware that they are doing so. Stimuli that are too weak or too brief to be consciously seen or heard may nevertheless be strong enough to be perceived by one or more receptor cells. This process is called **subliminal perception**

FIGURE 6.2

Source: © Lexmark
International, Inc. Used with
permission.

**Gradual Changes in Brand
Name Below the j.n.d.**

because the stimulus is beneath the threshold, or "limen," of conscious awareness, though obviously not beneath the absolute threshold of the receptors involved. (Perception of stimuli that are above the level of conscious awareness technically is called *supraliminal perception*, though it is usually referred to simply as perception.)

The effectiveness of so-called subliminal advertising was reportedly first tested at a drive-in movie in New Jersey in 1957, where the words "Eat popcorn" and "Drink Coca-Cola" were flashed on the screen during the movie. Exposure times were so short that viewers were unaware of seeing a message. It was reported that during the six-week test period, popcorn sales increased 58 percent and Coca-Cola sales increased 18 percent, but these findings were later reported to be false. Years later, a scientific study found that although the simple subliminal stimulus COKE served to arouse thirst in subjects, the subliminal command DRINK COKE did not have a greater effect, nor did it have any behavioral consequences.[9]

Since the 1950s, there have been sporadic reports of marketers using subliminal messages in their efforts to influence consumption behavior. For example, Disney was

FIGURE 6.3

Source: © Lexmark International, Inc. Used with permission.

Oxymoron: a printer company that helps people print less.

One company will help you print less. Lexmark. We've helped uncomplicate the way the world's biggest businesses print, move and manage information. Go online at **lexmark.com** and see how we can help yours uncomplicate.

LEXMARK

Transition Complete: Lexmark Stands Alone

accused of using subliminal messages in the movies *Aladdin* (where the hero allegedly whispers "good teenagers, take off your clothes" in a subaudible voice), *The Little Mermaid* (where a minister officiating at a wedding ceremony allegedly displays an erection), and *The Lion King* (where the letters "S-E-X" are allegedly formed in a cloud of dust).[10] At times, it has been difficult to separate truth from fiction regarding such alleged manipulations. When some of the subliminal methods were tested methodically using scientific research procedures, the research results did not support the notion that subliminal messages can persuade consumers to act in a given manner.

Evaluating the effectiveness of subliminal persuasion

Despite the many studies undertaken by academicians and researchers since the 1950s, there is no evidence that subliminal advertising persuades people to buy goods or services. A review of the literature indicates that subliminal perception research has been based on two theoretical approaches. According to the first theory, constant repetition of very weak (i.e., subthreshold) stimuli has an incremental effect that enables such stimuli to build response strength over many presentations. This would be the operative theory when weak stimuli are flashed repeatedly on a movie screen or played on a soundtrack or audiocassette. The second approach is based on the theory that subliminal sexual stimuli arouse unconscious sexual motivations. This is the theory behind the use of sexual embeds in print advertising. But no studies have yet indicated that either of these theoretical approaches has been effectively used by advertisers to increase sales. However, there is some indication that subliminal advertising may provide new opportunities for modifying antisocial behavior through public awareness campaigns that call for individuals to make generalized responses to suggestions that enhance their personal performance or improve their attitudes.[11] There is also some (though not definitive) evidence that subliminal methods can indirectly influence attitudes and feelings toward brands.[12]

In summary, although there is some evidence that subliminal stimuli may influence affective reactions, there is no evidence that subliminal stimulation can influence consumption behavior. There continues to be a big gap between perception and persuasion. A recent review of the evidence on subliminal persuasion indicates that the only way for subliminal techniques to have a significant persuasive effect would be through long-term repeated exposure under a limited set of circumstances, which would not be economically feasible or practical within an advertising context.[13]

As to sexual embeds, most researchers are of the opinion that "what you see is what you get"; that is, a vivid imagination can see whatever it wants to see in just about any situation. And that pretty much sums up the whole notion of perception: Individuals see what they want to see (e.g., what they are motivated to see) and what they expect to see. Several studies concerned with public beliefs about subliminal advertising found that a large percentage of Americans know what subliminal advertising is, they believe it is used by advertisers, and that it is effective in persuading consumers to buy.[14] To correct any misperceptions among the public that subliminal advertising does, in fact, exist, the advertising community occasionally sponsors ads like the one depicted in Figure 6.4, which ridicule the notion that subliminal techniques are effective or that they are used in advertising applications. The ethical issues related to subliminal advertising are discussed later in this chapter.

dynamics of perception

The preceding section explained how the individual receives sensations from stimuli in the outside environment and how the human organism adapts to the level and intensity of sensory input. We now come to one of the major principles of perception: Raw sensory input by itself does not produce or explain the coherent picture of the world that most adults possess. Indeed, the study of perception is largely the study of what we subconsciously add to or subtract from raw sensory inputs to produce our own private picture of the world.

Human beings are constantly bombarded with stimuli during every minute and every hour of every day. The sensory world is made up of an almost infinite number of discrete sensations that are constantly and subtly changing. According to the principles of sensation, intensive stimulation "bounces off" most individuals, who subconsciously block (i.e., adapt to) a heavy bombardment of stimuli. Otherwise, the billions of different stimuli to which we are constantly exposed might serve to confuse us and keep us perpetually disoriented in a constantly changing environment. However, neither of these consequences tends to occur, because perception is not a function of sensory input alone. Rather, perception is the result of two different kinds of inputs that interact to form the personal pictures—the perceptions—that each individual experiences.

One type of input is *physical stimuli* from the outside environment; the other type of input is provided by individuals themselves in the form of certain predispositions (expectations, motives, and learning) based on *previous experience*. The combination of these two very different kinds of inputs produces for each of us a very private, very personal picture of the world. Because each person is a unique individual, with unique

FIGURE 6.4

Source: Courtesy of American Association of Advertising Agencies.

Subliminal Embeds Are in the Eye of the Beholder

PEOPLE HAVE BEEN TRYING TO FIND THE BREASTS IN THESE ICE CUBES SINCE 1957.

The advertising industry is sometimes charged with sneaking seductive little pictures into ads.

Supposedly, these pictures can get you to buy a product without your even seeing them.

Consider the photograph above. According to some people, there's a pair of female breasts hidden in the patterns of light refracted by the ice cubes.

Well, if you really searched you probably *could* see the breasts. For that matter, you could also see Millard Fillmore, a stuffed pork chop and a 1946 Dodge.

The point is that so-called "subliminal advertising" simply doesn't exist. Overactive imaginations, however, most certainly do.

So if anyone claims to see breasts in that drink up there, they aren't in the ice cubes.

They're in the eye of the beholder.

ADVERTISING

ANOTHER WORD FOR FREEDOM OF CHOICE.

American Association of Advertising Agencies

experiences, needs, wants, desires, and expectations, it follows that each individual's perceptions are also unique. This explains why no two people see the world in precisely the same way.

Individuals are very selective as to which stimuli they "recognize"; they subconsciously organize the stimuli they do recognize according to widely held psychological principles, and they interpret such stimuli (they give meaning to them) subjectively in accordance with their personal needs, expectations, and experiences. The following sections examine each of these three aspects of perception: the **selection**, **organization**, and **interpretation of stimuli**.

Perceptual selection

Consumers subconsciously exercise a great deal of selectivity as to which aspects of the environment (which stimuli) they perceive. An individual may look at some things, ignore others, and turn away from still others. In actuality, people receive (i.e., perceive) only a small fraction of the stimuli to which they are exposed. Consider, for example, a woman in a supermarket. She may be exposed to over 20,000 products of different colors, sizes, and shapes; to perhaps 100 people (looking, walking, searching, talking); to smells (from fruit, meat, disinfectant, people); to sounds within the store (cash registers ringing, shopping carts rolling, air conditioners humming, and clerks sweeping, mopping aisles, stocking shelves); and to sounds from outside the store (planes passing, cars honking, tires screeching, children shouting, car doors slamming). Yet she manages on a regular basis to visit her local supermarket, select the items she needs, pay for them, and leave, all within a relatively brief period of time, without losing her sanity or her personal orientation to the world around her. This is because she exercises *selectivity* in perception.

Which stimuli get selected depends on two major factors in addition to the nature of the stimulus itself: (1) consumers' *previous experience* as it affects their *expectations* (what they are prepared, or "set," to see) and (2) their *motives* at the time (their needs, desires, interests, and so on). Each of these factors can serve to increase or decrease the probability that a stimulus will be perceived.

Nature of the stimulus

Marketing stimuli include an enormous number of variables that affect the consumer's perception, such as the *nature* of the product, its *physical attributes*, the *package* design, the *brand* name, the *advertisements* and commercials (including copy claims, choice and sex of model, positioning of model, size of ad, typography), the *position* of a print ad or a commercial, and the *editorial* environment.

In general, *contrast* is one of the most attention-compelling attributes of a stimulus. Advertisers often use extreme attention-getting devices to achieve maximum contrast and, thus, penetrate the consumer's perceptual "screen." For example, a number of magazines and newspapers carry ads that readers can unfold to reveal oversized, poster-like advertisements for products ranging from cosmetics to automobiles, because of the "stopping power" of giant ads among more traditional sizes. However, advertising does not have to be unique to achieve a high degree of differentiation; it simply has to contrast with the environment in which it is run. The use of a dramatic image of the product against a white background with little copy in a print advertisement, the absence of sound in a commercial's opening scene, a 60-second commercial within a string of 20-second spots—all offer sufficient contrast from their environments to achieve differentiation and merit the consumer's attention. Figure 6.5 illustrates the attention-getting nature of a dramatic image of a product in an advertisement. In an effort to achieve contrast, some advertisers use splashes of color in black-and-white print ads to highlight the advertised product.

With respect to packaging, astute marketers usually try to differentiate their packages to ensure rapid consumer perception. Since the average package on the supermarket shelf has about 1/10th of a second to make an impression on the consumer, it is important that every aspect of the package—the name, shape, color, label, and copy—provide sufficient sensory stimulation to be noted and remembered.

Expectations

People usually see what they expect to see, and what they expect to see is usually based on familiarity, previous experience, or preconditioned set (**expectations**). In a marketing context, people tend to perceive products and product attributes according to their own expectations. A student who has been told by his friends that a particular professor is interesting and dynamic will probably perceive the professor in that manner when the class begins; a teenager who attends a horror movie that has been billed as terrifying will probably find it so. On the other hand, stimuli that conflict sharply with expectations often receive more attention than those that conform to expectations.

FIGURE 6.5

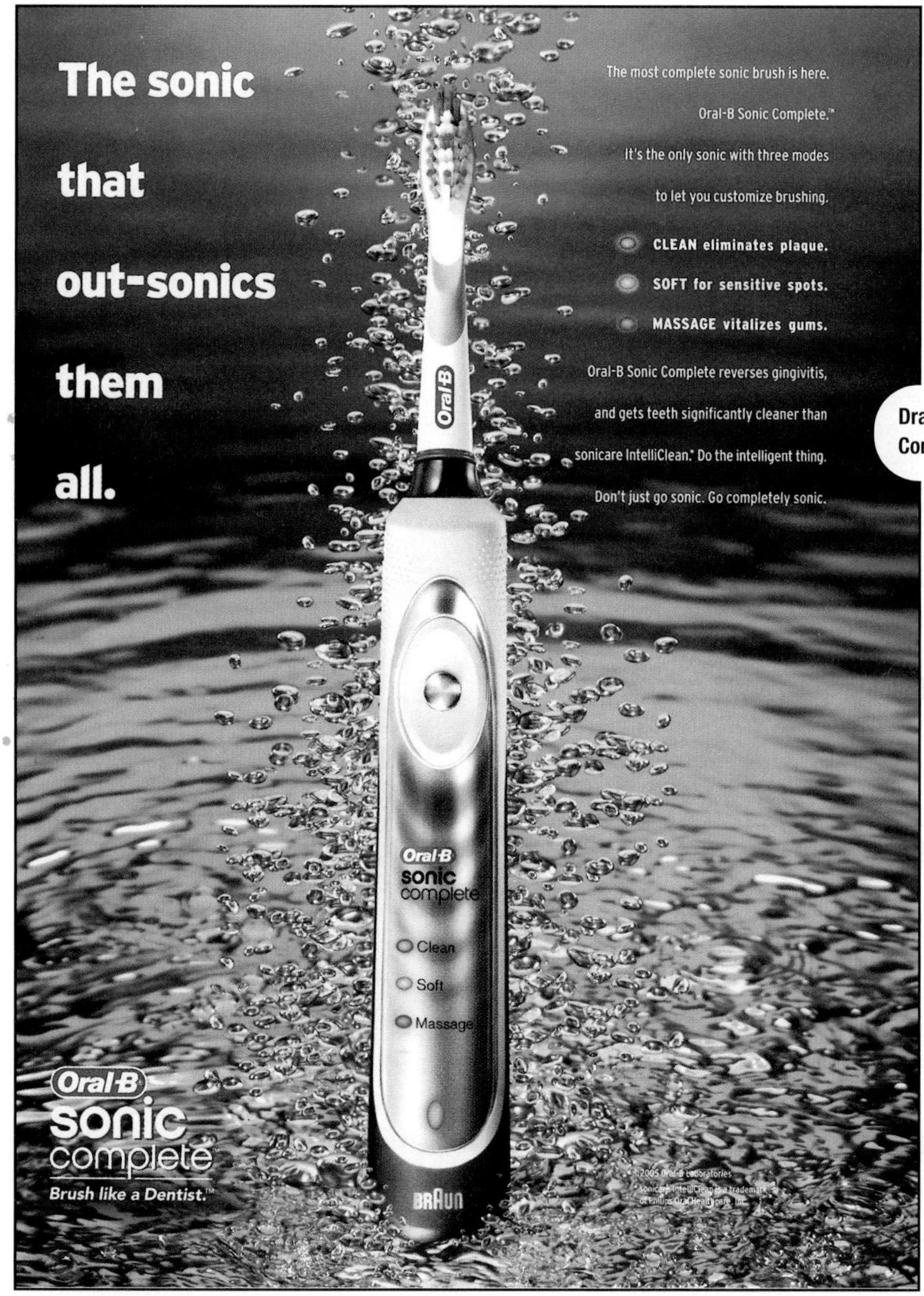
The sonic
that
out-sonics
them
all.
The most complete sonic brush is here.
Oral-B Sonic Complete.™
It's the only sonic with three modes
to let you customize brushing.
CLEAN eliminates plaque.
SOFT for sensitive spots.
MASSAGE vitalizes gums.
Oral-B Sonic Complete reverses gingivitis,
and gets teeth significantly cleaner than
sonicare IntelliClean.* Do the intelligent thing.
Don't just go sonic. Go completely sonic.
Oral-B
sonic
complete
Clean
Soft
Massage
BRAUN
Oral-B
sonic
complete
Brush like a Dentist.™

Source: © The Gillette Company. Used with permission. All rights reserved.

Dramatic Image of a Product Compels Attention

For years, some advertisers have used blatant sexuality in advertisements for products to which sex is not relevant, in the belief that such advertisements would attract a high degree of attention. However, ads with irrelevant sexuality often defeat the marketer's objectives because readers tend to remember the sexual aspects of the ad (e.g., the innuendo or the model), not the product or brand advertised. Nevertheless, some advertisers continue to use erotic appeals in promoting a wide variety of products, from office furniture to jeans. (The use of sex in advertising is discussed in Chapter 9.)

Motives

People tend to perceive the things they need or want; the stronger the need, the greater the tendency to ignore unrelated stimuli in the environment. A student who is looking for a new cell phone provider is more likely to notice and read carefully ads for deals and special offers regarding such services than his roommate, who may be satisfied with his present cellular service. In general, there is a heightened awareness of stimuli that are relevant to one's needs and interests and a decreased awareness of stimuli that are irrelevant to those needs. An individual's perceptual process simply attunes itself more closely to those elements in the environment that are important to him or her. Someone who is overweight is more likely to notice ads for diet foods; a sexually repressed person may perceive sexual symbolism where none exists.

Marketing managers recognize the efficiency of targeting their products to the perceived needs of consumers. For example, a marketer can determine through marketing research what different segments of consumers consider to be the ideal attributes of the product category or what they perceive their needs to be in relation to the product category. The marketer can then segment the market on the basis of those needs and vary the product advertising so that consumers in each segment will perceive the product as meeting their own special needs, wants, or interests.

Selective perception

As the preceding discussion illustrates, the consumer's "selection" of stimuli from the environment is based on the interaction of expectations and motives with the stimulus itself. These factors give rise to four important concepts concerning perception.

Selective Exposure Consumers actively seek out messages that they find pleasant or with which they are sympathetic, and they actively avoid painful or threatening ones. They also selectively expose themselves to advertisements that reassure them of the wisdom of their purchase decisions.

Selective Attention Consumers exercise a great deal of selectivity in terms of the attention they give to commercial stimuli. They have a heightened awareness of stimuli that meet their needs or interests and minimal awareness of stimuli irrelevant to their needs. Thus, consumers are likely to note ads for products that would satisfy their needs and disregard those in which they have no interest. People also vary in terms of the kinds of information in which they are interested and the form of message and type of medium they prefer. Some people are more interested in price, some in appearance, and some in social acceptability. Some people like complex, sophisticated messages; others like simple graphics.

Perceptual Defense Consumers subconsciously screen out stimuli that they find psychologically threatening, even though exposure has already taken place. Thus, threatening or otherwise damaging stimuli are less likely to be consciously perceived than are neutral stimuli at the same level of exposure. Furthermore, individuals sometimes unconsciously distort information that is not consistent with their needs, values, and beliefs. One way to combat *perceptual defense* is to vary and increase the amount of sensory input. For example, since research showed that most Canadian smokers no longer pay attention to the written warning labels on cigarette packs, Canada now requires tobacco firms to feature graphic health warnings on cigarette packs; one such warning shows a damaged brain and warns about strokes; another shows a limp cigarette and states that tobacco can cause impotence.[15]

Perceptual Blocking Consumers protect themselves from being bombarded with stimuli by simply "tuning out"—blocking such stimuli from conscious awareness. They do so out of self-protection because of the visually overwhelming nature of the world in which we live. The popularity of such devices as *TiVo* and *ReplayTV*, which enable viewers to skip over TV commercials with great ease, is, in part, a result of *perceptual blocking*.

Perceptual organization

People do not experience the numerous stimuli they select from the environment as separate and discrete sensations; rather, they tend to organize them into groups and perceive them as unified wholes. Thus, the perceived characteristics of even the simplest stimulus are viewed as a function of the whole to which the stimulus appears to belong. This method of perceptual organization simplifies life considerably for the individual.

The specific principles underlying perceptual organization are often referred to by the name given the school of psychology that first developed it: **Gestalt psychology**. (*Gestalt*, in German, means pattern or configuration.) Three of the most basic principles of perceptual organization are *figure and ground, grouping*, and *closure*.

Figure and ground

As was noted earlier, stimuli that contrast with their environment are more likely to be noticed. A sound must be louder or softer, a color brighter or paler. The simplest visual illustration consists of a figure on a ground (i.e., background). The figure is perceived more clearly because, in contrast to its ground, it appears to be well defined, solid, and in the forefront. The ground is usually perceived as indefinite, hazy, and continuous. The common line that separates the figure and the ground is generally attributed to the figure rather than to the ground, which helps give the figure greater definition. Consider the stimulus of music. People can either "bathe" in music or listen to music. In the first case, music is simply background to other activities; in the second, it is figure. Figure is more clearly perceived because it appears to be dominant; in contrast, ground appears to be subordinate and, therefore, less important. Figure 6.6 presents an ad that stresses *figure* (the product) over *ground* (the hazy, continuous background).

People have a tendency to organize their perceptions into **figure-and-ground** relationships. How a figure–ground pattern is perceived can be influenced by prior pleasant or painful associations with one or the other element in isolation. For example, a short time following the destruction of the World Trade Center on September 11, 2001 by airplanes hijacked by terrorists, a professor in New Jersey came across an ad for Lufthansa (Germany's national airline) that featured a flying jet, photographed from the ground up, between two glass high-rise buildings. Rather than focusing on the brand and the jet (i.e., the "figure"), all the viewer could think about was the two tall glass towers in the background (i.e., the "ground"), and the possibility of the jet crashing into them. When the professor presented the ad to his students, many expressed the same thoughts. Clearly, this figure–ground reversal was the outcome of the painful events that occurred in September 2001.

Advertisers have to plan their advertisements carefully to make sure that the stimulus they want noted is seen as figure and not as ground. The musical background must not overwhelm the jingle; the background of an advertisement must not detract from the product. Print advertisers often silhouette their products against a nondistinct background to make sure that the features they want noted are clearly perceived. We are all familiar with figure–ground reversals, such as the picture of the woman in Figure 6.7. How old would you say she is? Look again very carefully. Depending on how you perceived figure and how you perceived ground, she can be either in her early twenties or her late seventies.

Marketers sometimes run advertisements that confuse the consumer because there is no clear indication of which is figure and which is ground. Of course, in some cases, the blurring of figure and ground is deliberate. The well-known Absolut Vodka campaign, started over 25 years ago, often runs print ads in which the figure (the shape of the Absolut bottle) is poorly delineated against its ground, challenging readers to search for the bottle; the resulting audience "participation" produces more intense ad scrutiny.

Grouping

Individuals tend to group stimuli so that they form a unified picture or impression. The perception of stimuli as groups or chunks of information, rather than as discrete bits of

FIGURE 6.6

Source: © The Gillette
Company. Used with permission.
All rights reserved.

**Product as Figure with a Hazy
(back) Ground.**

information, facilitates their memory and recall. **Grouping** can be used advantageously by marketers to imply certain desired meanings in connection with their products. For example, an advertisement for tea may show a young man and woman sipping tea in a beautifully appointed room before a blazing hearth. The overall mood implied by the grouping of stimuli leads the consumer to associate the drinking of tea with romance, fine living, and winter warmth.

Most of us can remember and repeat our Social Security numbers because we automatically group them into three "*chunks*," rather than try to remember nine separate numbers. Similarly, we recall and repeat our phone number in three segments—the area code, first three digits, and the last four digits. Also, for decades, Americans had five-digit

FIGURE 6.7

Source: American Journal of Psychology by Boring, E. G. Copyright 1930 by Univ. of Illinois Press. Reproduced with permission of Univ. of Illinois Press.

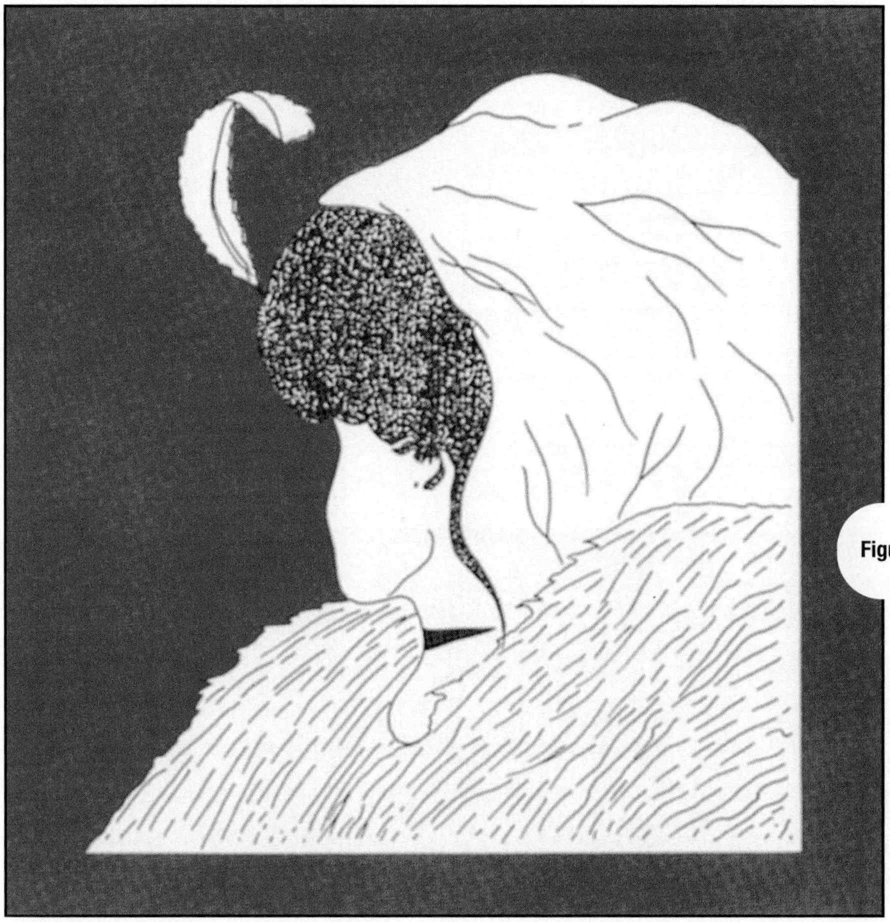

Figure-and-Ground Reversal

zip codes grouped as a single chunk; as four digits are being added to our zip codes, the U.S. Postal Service faces a challenge in getting Americans to recall the extra digits and add a chunk to their recollection of zip codes.

Closure

Individuals have a need for **closure**. They express this need by organizing their perceptions so that they form a complete picture. If the pattern of stimuli to which they are exposed is incomplete, they tend to perceive it, nevertheless, as complete; that is, they consciously or subconsciously fill in the missing pieces. Thus, a circle with a section of its periphery missing is invariably perceived as a circle, not an arc.

Incomplete messages or tasks are better remembered than completed ones. One explanation for this phenomenon is that a person who hears the beginning of a message or who begins a task develops a need to complete it. If he or she is prevented from doing so, a state of tension is created that manifests itself in improved memory for the incomplete task. For example, hearing the beginning of a message leads to the need to hear the rest of it—like waiting for the second shoe to drop.

The need for closure has interesting implications for marketers. Promotional messages in which viewers are required to "fill in" information beg for completion by consumers, and the very act of completion serves to involve them more deeply in the

FIGURE 6.8

Source: Courtesy of Levi
Strauss & Co.

**Using the Need for Closure to
Increase Attention**

message (see Figure 6.8). In a related vein, advertisers have discovered that they can achieve excellent results by using the soundtrack of a frequently viewed television commercial on radio. Consumers who are familiar with the TV commercial perceive the audio track alone as incomplete; in their need for completion, they mentally play back the visual content from memory.

In summary, it is clear that perceptions are not equivalent to the raw sensory input of discrete stimuli, nor to the sum total of discrete stimuli. Rather, people tend to add to or subtract from stimuli to which they are exposed on the basis of their expectations and motives, using generalized principles of organization based on Gestalt theory.

Perceptual interpretation

The preceding discussion has emphasized that perception is a personal phenomenon. People exercise selectivity as to which stimuli they perceive, and they organize these stimuli on the basis of certain psychological principles. The interpretation of stimuli is also uniquely individual, because it is based on what individuals expect to see in light of their previous experiences on the number of plausible explanations they can envision, and on their motives and interests at the time of perception.

Stimuli are often highly ambiguous. Some stimuli are weak because of such factors as poor visibility, brief exposure, high noise level, or constant fluctuation. Even stimuli that are strong tend to fluctuate dramatically because of such factors as different angles of viewing, varying distances, and changing levels of illumination. Consumers usually attribute the sensory input they receive to factors they consider most likely to have caused the specific pattern of stimuli. Past experiences and social interactions help to form certain expectations that provide categories (or alternative explanations) that individuals use in interpreting stimuli.

When stimuli are highly ambiguous, an individual will usually interpret them in such a way that they serve to fulfill personal needs, wishes, interests, and so on. It is this principle that provides the rationale for the projective tests discussed in Chapter 4. Such tests provide ambiguous stimuli (such as incomplete sentences, unclear pictures, untitled cartoons, or ink blots) to respondents who are asked to interpret them. How a person describes a vague illustration, or what meaning the individual ascribes to an ink blot, is a reflection not of the stimulus itself, but of the subject's own needs, wants, and desires. Through the interpretation of ambiguous stimuli, respondents reveal a great deal about themselves.

How close a person's interpretations are to reality, then, depends on the clarity of the stimulus, the past experiences of the perceiver, and his or her motives and interests at the time of perception.

Perceptual distortion

Individuals are subject to a number of influences that tend to distort their perceptions, such as physical appearances, stereotypes, first impressions, jumping to conclusions, and the halo effect.

Physical Appearances   People tend to attribute the qualities they associate with certain people to others who may resemble them, whether or not they consciously recognize the similarity. For this reason, the selection of models for print advertisements and for television commercials can be a key element in their ultimate persuasiveness. Studies have found that attractive models are more persuasive and have a more positive influence on consumer attitudes and behavior than average-looking models; attractive men are perceived as more successful businessmen than average-looking men. Some research suggests that models influence consumers' perceptions of physical attractiveness, and through comparisons, their own self-perceptions.[16] Recent research indicates that using a highly attractive model may not necessarily increase message effectiveness. One study revealed that highly attractive models are perceived as having more expertise regarding enhancement products (e.g., jewelry, lipstick, perfume) but not problem-solving products (e.g., products that correct beauty flaws such as acne or dandruff).[17] Therefore, advertisers must ensure that there is a rational match between the product advertised and the physical attributes of the model used to promote it.

Stereotypes   Individuals tend to carry pictures in their minds of the meanings of various kinds of stimuli. These stereotypes serve as expectations of what specific situations, people, or events will be like, and they are important determinants of how such stimuli are subsequently perceived. Several years ago, an ad for Benetton featuring two men—one black and one white—handcuffed together, which was part of the "united colors of Benetton" campaign promoting racial harmony, produced a public outcry because people perceived it as depicting a white man arresting a black man. Clearly, this perception was the result of stereotypes, since

FIGURE 6.9   *Source:* © DaimlerChrysler Corporation. Used with permission. All rights reserved.

IT'S A BIG FAT JUICY CHEESEBURGER IN A LAND OF TOFU.

The Use of Stereotyped References in Comparing Cars

there was nothing in the ad to indicate that the white person was arresting the black person rather than the other way around. The ad featured in Figure 6.9 contrasts the powerful and rugged Dodge Durango, termed "a big fat juicy cheeseburger" with other, less rugged and "weaker" cars referred to in the ad as the "land of tofu." One Asian student interpreted the ad as contrasting typically American cars with foreign cars manufactured in Southeast Asia, where tofu originated. Clearly, the student was interpreting the ad in terms of stereotypes. One study discovered the stereotypes regarding a product's country-of-origin influenced consumers' purchases, and also that such stereotypes had more impact on an impulse purchase than on a deliberate and planned purchase.[18] The ad for Akteo watches shown in Figure 6.10 is based on the notion that a man's watch reflects his individuality.

First Impressions   First impressions tend to be lasting; yet, in forming such impressions, the perceiver does not yet know which stimuli are relevant, important, or predictive of later behavior. A shampoo commercial effectively used the line, "You'll never have a second chance to make a first impression." Since first impressions are often lasting, introducing a new product before it has been perfected may prove fatal to its ultimate success; subsequent information about its advantages, even if true, will often be negated by the memory of its early performance.

Jumping to Conclusions   Many people tend to jump to conclusions before examining all the relevant evidence. For example, the consumer may hear just the beginning of a commercial message and draw conclusions regarding the product or service being advertised.

FIGURE 6.10

Source: Courtesy of Universal Watch Company.

Ad Depicting Stereotypes

For this reason, many copywriters are careful to give their most persuasive arguments first. A recent study showed that consumers who ate foods with elaborate names such as "succulent Italian seafood filet" rated those foods as more tasty and appealing than those who ate the same foods with such regular names as "seafood filet."[19] Many consumers do not read the volume information on food labels. One study found that consumers purchase packages that they believe contain greater volume, whether or not this is actually so, and that they perceive elongated packaging to contain more volume than round packaging.[20] Clearly, these findings have important implications for package design, advertising, and pricing, and also represent some ethical dilemmas that are discussed later on in this chapter.

Halo Effect   Historically, the halo effect has been used to describe situations in which the evaluation of a single object or person on a multitude of dimensions is based on the evaluation of just one or a few dimensions (e.g., a man is trustworthy, fine, and noble because he looks you in the eye when he speaks). Consumer behaviorists broaden the notion of the halo effect to include the evaluation of multiple objects (e.g., a product line) on the basis of the evaluation of just one dimension (a brand name or a spokesperson). Using this broader definition, marketers take advantage of the halo effect when they extend a brand name associated with one line of products to another. The lucrative field of *licensing* is based on the halo effect. Manufacturers and retailers hope to acquire instant recognition and status for their products by associating them with a well-known name. (Chapter 7 discusses licensing in greater detail.) A recent study discovered that brands are judged more positively than warranted when evaluated alone than when evaluated within a group of other brands.[21] These findings have implications for the placement of brands in stores and the position of a given brand's advertisements in relation to competing ads within a magazine or a commercial break.

Tampering with the perceived halo effect of a product or brand can have disastrous consequences. For example, in an attempt to enhance the image of JW Marriott, the Marriott hotel chain's upscale brand, Marriott took over the Righa Royal Hotel, an upscale hotel in New York City, and renamed it the JW Marriott New York. When the new name signs went up, the company discovered that scores of regular, upscale customers who always stayed at the Righa when visiting New York City canceled their reservations because they did not want to tell colleagues to contact them at the Marriott. The company restored the Righa Hotel name, with the JW Marriott name included in smaller print.[22]

Despite the many subjective influences on perceptual interpretation, individuals usually resolve stimulus ambiguity somewhat "realistically" on the basis of their previous experiences. Only in situations of unusual or changing stimulus conditions do expectations lead to wrong interpretations.

consumer imagery

Consumers have a number of enduring perceptions, or images, that are particularly relevant to the study of consumer behavior. Products and brands have symbolic value for individuals, who evaluate them on the basis of their consistency (congruence) with their personal pictures of themselves. Chapter 5 discussed consumer self-images and how consumers attempt to preserve or enhance their self-images by buying products and using services that they believe are congruent with their self-images and by avoiding those that are not. The following section examines consumers' perceived images of products, brands, services, prices, product quality, retail stores, and manufacturers.

Product positioning

The essence of successful marketing is the image that a product has in the mind of the consumer—that is, its **positioning**. Positioning is more important to the ultimate success of a product than are its actual characteristics, although products that are poorly made will not succeed in the long run on the basis of image alone. The core of effective positioning is a unique position that the product occupies in the mind of the consumer. Most new products fail because they are perceived as "me too" offerings that do not offer potential consumers any advantages or unique benefits over competitive products.

Marketers of different brands in the same category can effectively differentiate their offerings only if they stress the *benefits* that their brands provide rather than their products' physical features. The benefits featured in a product's positioning must reflect attributes that are important to and congruent with the perceptions of the targeted consumer segment. For example, the two energy bars Nutrigrain and Balance are probably quite similar in terms of their nutritional composition and their physical characteristics;

however, each one of the two brands is clearly positioned to offer a distinct benefit. Nutrigrain is positioned as an alternative to unhealthy snack foods in the morning, and Balance is positioned as an energy pickup for the late afternoon.

Positioning strategy is the essence of the marketing mix; it complements the company's definition of the competition, its segmentation strategy, and its selection of target markets. For example, in its positioning as a breakfast food, Nutrigrain competes with other breakfast foods. Through research, the manufacturer has determined the characteristics of people who are concerned about their health and appearance (and yet, eat unhealthy breakfast foods) and the media they read, listen to and watch. The marketers of Balance have determined the characteristics of those who need a pick-me-up in the late afternoon and their media habits, and developed a marketing plan that reflects all these elements.

Positioning conveys the concept, or meaning, of the product or service in terms of how it fulfills a consumer need. A good positioning strategy should have a two-pronged meaning: one that is congruent with the consumer's needs while, at the same time, featuring the brand against its competition. For example, the classic 7-Up slogan "The Un-Cola" was designed to appeal to consumers' desire for an alternative to the most popular soft drink (by using the prefix *un*), while also elevating the product by placing it in the same league with its giant competitor (by using the word *cola*). Also, as demonstrated by 7-Up's change in positioning strategy to "Caffeine—never had it, never will" to depict its core benefit, the same product (or service) can be positioned differently to different market segments or can be repositioned to the same audience, without being physically changed. Procter and Gamble has positioned its SURE deodorant as an essential travel necessity to take on safari—a positioning strategy designed to reach a strong, masculine, adventurous target audience (see Figure 6.11).

The result of successful positioning strategy is a distinctive brand image on which consumers rely in making product choices. A positive brand image also leads to consumer loyalty, positive beliefs about brand value, and a willingness to search for the brand. A positive brand image also promotes consumer interest in future brand promotions and *inoculates* consumers against competitors' marketing activities. An advertiser's positioning strategy affects consumer beliefs about its brand's attributes and the prices consumers are willing to pay.

In today's highly competitive marketplace, a distinctive product image is most important, but also very difficult to create and maintain. As products become more complex and the marketplace more crowded, consumers rely more on the product's image and claimed benefits than on its actual attributes in making purchase decisions. The major positioning strategies are discussed in the following five sections.

Umbrella positioning

This strategy entails creating an overall image of the company around which a lot of products can be featured individually. This strategy is appropriate for very large corporations with diversified product lines. For example, McDonald's positioning approaches over the years include "You deserve a break today at McDonald's," "Nobody can do it like McDonald's can," and "Good times, great taste."

Positioning against the competition

A classic example of positioning against the competition is Wendy's "Where's the beef?" which was used to differentiate the smaller fast-food chain from much larger competitors. Visa's past slogan "We make American Express green with envy" is another good example of this strategy. A Sunkist ad featured a lemon, in the form of a salt shaker, with the caption "Salternative." The Hertz car rental company has run TV ads depicting other car rental companies as lacking in features that Hertz outlets generally possess, such as proximity to passenger terminals at airports (e.g., "Hertz? Not exactly."). Figure 6.12 reminds beer drinkers that Miller Light was the original "less filling" beer and also positions it against Bud Light.

FIGURE 6.11

Source: © Procter & Gamble Company. Used with permission. All rights reserved.

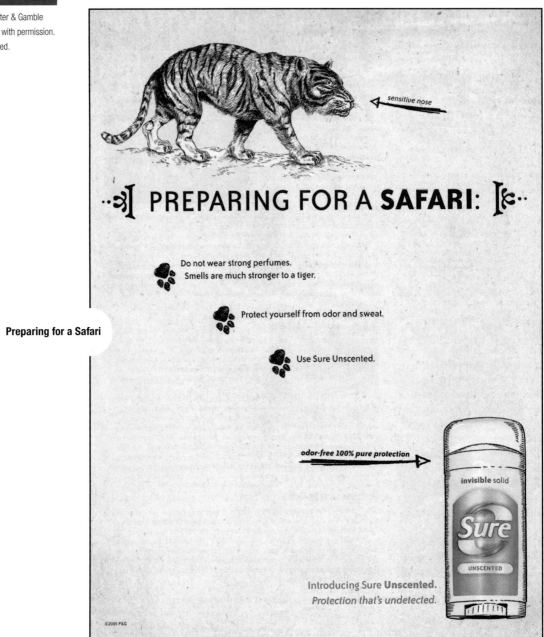

Preparing for a Safari

Positioning based on a specific benefit

FedEx created its highly reliable service image with the slogan "When it absolutely, positively has to be there overnight." Maxwell House Coffee is "good to the last drop." Bounty is "the quicker picker upper." These are examples of slogans that smartly and precisely depict key benefits of the brands they promote and have effectively positioned these brands in the minds of consumers. There are also many examples of products that failed because they were positioned to deliver a benefit that consumers either did not want or did not believe. For example, Gillette's "For Oily Hair Only" shampoo failed because most consumers do not acknowledge that they have oily hair. Effective

FIGURE 6.12

Source: © Miller Brewing
Company. Used with permission.
All rights reserved.

Positioning Against the
Competition

depictions of a core benefit often include memorable imagery (e.g., the old lady featured in Wendy's "Where's the beef?" ad).

Finding an "unowned" position

In highly competitive markets, finding a niche not targeted by other companies is challenging but not impossible. For example, Long Island's *Newsday*, in a reference to two competitive daily newspapers published in New York City (*The Daily News* and the *New York Times*), is positioned as "On top of the news and ahead of the times." A clever approach to finding (or even creating) an "unowned" position was Palmolive's claim to ". . . soften your hands as you do the dishes"; today, even though many people no longer wash dishes by hand, Palmolive positions its dishwashing liquid as "tough on grease, soft on hands."

Filling several positions

Because unfilled gaps or "unowned" perceptual positions present opportunities for competitors, sophisticated marketers create several distinct offerings, often in the form of different brands, to fill several identified niches. For example, Visine's line of eye care offerings include versions for redness relief, eye lubrication, advanced redness relief and lubrication, lubrication and rewetting, and "tears" packaged in a single drop dispenser.[23] Crest Toothpaste's line includes offerings for whitening, tartar protection, multicare, cavity protection, sensitive teeth protection, and refreshing mouth and breath with baking soda. Many of these versions are offered as pastes, gels, liquid gels or striped pastes, in many flavors. There is also a separate line of toothpastes and gels for kids.[24] It would be difficult for a manufacturer to penetrate either the eye care or the toothpaste market with a product that offers a benefit that is not already provided by Visine or Crest, in their respective markets.

Product repositioning

Regardless of how well positioned a product appears to be, the marketer may be forced to reposition it in response to market events, such as a competitor cutting into the brand's market share or too many competitors stressing the same attribute. For example, rather than trying to meet the lower prices of high-quality private-label competition, some premium brand marketers have repositioned their brands to justify their higher prices, playing up brand attributes that had previously been ignored.

Another reason to reposition a product or service is to satisfy changing consumer preferences. For example, for years, GM tried to convince consumers that Oldsmobile is not an "old folks'" car by trying to reposition the car as "not your father's Oldsmobile." However, this effort failed because the "old folks'" image of the brand was very strongly set in the minds of car buyers, and GM discontinued this brand. Following consumers' frantic efforts to cut down on consuming carbohydrates, some brands of orange juice, vegetable juice, and beer were repositioned as products that provide "less carbs." One of the most successful product repositionings is the promotion of Arm & Hammer as America's standard for cleanliness and purity by showing it used as a product for the home, the family, and personal care. The brand's Web site lists about one dozen personal care uses, including using the product as a facial scrub, deodorant, bath soak, and mouth refreshent. The site also lists scores of possible uses of the product in every possible room of a typical house and its outside areas (see Figure 6.13).

Perceptual mapping

The technique of **perceptual mapping** helps marketers to determine just how their products or services appear to consumers in relation to competitive brands on one or more relevant characteristics. It enables them to see gaps in the positioning of all brands in the product or service class and to identify areas in which consumer needs are not being adequately met. For example, if a magazine publisher wants to introduce a new magazine to Generation Y, he may use perceptual mapping to uncover a niche of consumers with a special set of interests that are not being adequately or equally addressed by other magazines targeted to the same demographic segment. This insight allows him to position the new magazine as specifically focused on these interests. Or, a publisher may discover through perceptual mapping that consumers perceive its magazine (let's call it *Splash*) to be very similar in editorial content and format to its closest competitors, *Bash* and *Crash*. By changing the focus of its editorial features to appeal to a new market niche, the publisher can reposition the

FIGURE 6.13

Source: © Church & Dwight Co., Inc., use of Arm & Hammer— "Tour our house" website is with the express written permission of Church & Dwight Co., Inc., Princeton New Jersey.

Product Repositioning

magazine (e.g., from *Splash* to *Fashion Splash*). Figure 6.14 presents this example in a perceptual map.

Positioning of services

Compared with manufacturing firms, service marketers face several unique problems in positioning and promoting their offerings. Because services are intangible, image becomes a key factor in differentiating a service from its competition. Thus, the marketing objective is to enable the consumer to link a specific image with a specific brand name. Many service marketers have developed strategies to provide customers with visual images and tangible reminders of their service offerings. These include delivery vehicles painted in distinct colors, restaurant matchbooks, packaged hotel soaps and shampoos, and a variety of other specialty items. Many service companies feature real service employees in their ads (as tangible cues) and some use people-focused themes to differentiate themselves. For example, the Ritz-Carlton promotes its "guest experience" with the corporate motto "We are ladies and gentlemen serving ladies and gentlemen."

Many service companies market several versions of their service to different market segments by using a differentiated positioning strategy. However, they must be careful to avoid perceptual confusion among their customers. For example, Marriott's Hotels and Resorts brand claims to provide customers with "superior service and genuine care"; the Renaissance Hotels and Resorts brand provides "distinctive décor, imaginative experiences and delights its customers' senses"; the Courtyard brand provides "essential services and amenities to business travelers"; the Residence Inn is

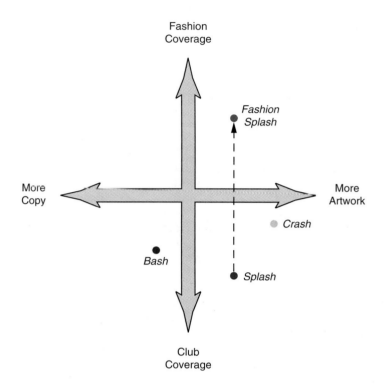

FIGURE 6.14

Perceptual Map of Competitors Facilitates Magazine Repositioning

designed for extended stays; and the Fairfield Inn provides rooms and suites at "prices that will make customers smile."[25] Although distinct brand names are important to all products or services, they are particularly crucial in marketing services due to the abstract and intangible nature of many services. For example, names such as Federal Express (later abbreviated to FedEx) and Humana (a provider of health services) are excellent names because they are distinctive, memorable, and relevant to the services they feature. On the other hand, Allegis—a short-lived brand name aimed at creating a business travel concept by combining United Airlines, Hertz, and Hilton and Westin Hotels under one umbrella—failed because it told consumers nothing about the type of services it offered.[26]

The design of the service environment is an important aspect of service positioning strategy and sharply influences consumer impressions and consumer and employee behavior. The physical environment is particularly important in creating a favorable impression for such services as banks, retail stores, and professional offices, because there are so few objective criteria by which consumers can judge the quality of the services they receive. The service environment conveys the image of the service provider with whom the service is so closely linked. Thus, the Polo Ralph Lauren store in its renovated 1895 mansion on New York's Upper East Side is the embodiment of the image Lauren wants to create for his clothes: traditionalism and Old World values. All the trappings of what one imagines to be the high-class and well-heeled ways of the very, very rich are here, from the baronial, hand-carved staircase lined with "family" portraits to the plush sitting rooms with working fireplaces. The Polo store image artfully extends the image of the clothing it sells and projects an Old World quality of living and shopping that its upscale target market finds appealing.

One study of service environments identified five environmental variables most important to bank customers: (1) privacy (both visually and verbally, with enclosed offices, transaction privacy, etc.); (2) efficiency/convenience (e.g., transaction areas that are easy to find, directional signs); (3) ambient background conditions (temperature, lighting, noise, music); (4) social conditions (the physical appearance of other people in the bank environment, such as bank customers and bank personnel); and (5) aesthetics (e.g., color, style, use of materials, and artwork).[27]

Perceived price

How a consumer perceives a price—as high, as low, as fair—has a strong influence on both purchase intentions and purchase satisfaction. Consider the perception of price fairness, for example. There is some evidence that customers do pay attention to the prices paid by other customers (such as senior citizens, frequent flyers, affinity club members), and that the differential pricing strategies used by some marketers are perceived as unfair by customers not eligible for the special prices. No one is happy knowing he or she paid twice as much for an airline ticket or a theater ticket as the person in the next seat. Perceptions of price unfairness affect consumers' perceptions of product value and, ultimately, their willingness to patronize a store or a service. One study, focused on the special challenges of service industries in pricing intangible products, proposed three types of pricing strategies based on the customer's perception of the value provided by the purchase: *satisfaction-based* pricing, *relationship* pricing, and *efficiency* pricing (see Table 6.1).

Reference prices

Products advertised as "on sale" tend to create enhanced customer perceptions of savings and value. Different formats used in sales advertisements have differing impacts, based on consumer **reference prices**. A reference price is *any price that a consumer uses as a basis for comparison in judging another price.* Reference prices can be external or internal. An advertiser generally uses a higher *external reference price* ("sold elsewhere at . . .") in an ad offering a lower sales price, to persuade the consumer that the product advertised is a really good buy. *Internal reference prices* are those prices (or price ranges) retrieved by the consumer from memory. Internal reference prices play a major role in consumers' evaluations and perceptions of value of an advertised (external) price deal, as well as in the believability of any advertised reference price. However, consumers' internal reference prices change. For example, as the prices of flat-screen TVs declined

TABLE 6.1	Three Pricing Strategies Focused on Perceived Value	
PRICING STRATEGY	**PROVIDES VALUE BY . . .**	**IMPLEMENTED AS . . .**
Satisfaction-based pricing	Recognizing and reducing customers' perceptions of uncertainty, which the intangible nature of services magnifies.	Service guarantees. Benefit-driven pricing. Flat-rate pricing.
Relationship pricing	Encouraging long-term relationships with the company that customers view as beneficial.	Long-term contracts. Price bundling.
Efficiency pricing	Sharing with customers the cost savings that the company has achieved by understanding, managing, and reducing the costs of providing the service.	Cost-leader pricing.

Source: Leonard L. Berry and Yadav S. Manjit, "Capture and Communicate Value in the Pricing of Services," *Sloan Management Review,* Summer 1996, 41–51.

sharply due to competition and manufacturers' abilities to produce them more cheaply, consumers' reference prices for this product have declined as well, and many no longer perceive flat-screen TVs as a luxury product that only few can afford. One study showed that consumers' price reference points include past prices, competitors' prices, and the cost of goods sold. The study also showed that these reference points do not adequately reflect the effects of inflation on costs, and that customers attribute price differentials to profit and fail to consider vendor costs.[28]

Some researchers proposed that two types of utility are associated with consumer purchases. **Acquisition utility** represents the consumer's perceived economic gain or loss associated with a purchase and is a function of product utility and purchase price. **Transaction utility** concerns the perceived pleasure or displeasure associated with the financial aspect of the purchase and is determined by the difference between the internal reference price and the purchase price.[29] For example, if a consumer wants to purchase a television set for which her internal reference price is approximately $500, and she buys a set that is sale-priced at $500, she receives no transaction utility. However, if either her internal reference price is increased or the sales price of the set is decreased, she will receive positive transaction utility, which increases the total utility she experiences with the purchase.

Consumers' perceptions of the credibility and fairness of stated prices is an important factor in overall satisfaction. Although many marketers assume that the traditional phrases "regular price" versus "sale price" have the same meaning for all consumers, this is unlikely given the evidence that perceptions of marketing stimuli vary widely among consumers.[30]

Several studies showed that consumers believe that the selling prices of a product or service are considerably higher than their perceived fair prices.[31] Several studies have investigated the effects on consumer price perceptions of three types of advertised reference prices: plausible low, plausible high, and implausible high. *Plausible low* prices are well within the range of acceptable market prices; *plausible high* are near the outer limits of the range but not beyond the realm of believability, and *implausible high* are well above the consumer's perceived range of acceptable market prices. As long as an advertised reference price is within a given consumer's acceptable price range, it is considered plausible and is assimilated. (See *assimilation-contrast theory* in Chapter 8.) If the advertised reference point is outside the range of acceptable prices (i.e., implausible), it will be *contrasted* and thus will not be perceived as a valid reference point. This will adversely affect both consumer evaluations and the advertiser's image of credibility.[32]

Another study showed that when consumers encounter prices that are significantly different from their expectations, they engage in *dissonance reduction*. That is, they seek additional information to justify the high price or they trivialize their own expectations by, for example, saying that their expectations were unrealistic because it has been a while since they last were in the market to buy the product in question.[33] Table 6.2 depicts the possible changes in the perceptions of consumers who encounter unexpected prices. (The theory of **cognitive dissonance** is fully explored in Chapter 8.)

Perceived quality

Consumers often judge the quality of a product or service on the basis of a variety of informational cues that they associate with the product. Some of these cues are **intrinsic** to the product or service; others are **extrinsic**. Either singly or together, such cues provide the basis for perceptions of product and service quality.

Perceived quality of products

Cues that are *intrinsic* concern physical characteristics of the product itself, such as size, color, flavor, or aroma. In some cases, consumers use physical characteristics (e.g., the flavor of ice cream or cake) to judge product quality. Consumers like to believe that they base their evaluations of product quality on intrinsic cues, because that enables them to justify their product decisions (either positive or negative) as being "rational" or "objective" product choices. More often than not, however, they use extrinsic characteristics to judge quality. For example, though many consumers claim they buy a brand because of its superior taste, they are often unable to identify that brand in blind taste tests. One

TABLE 6.2

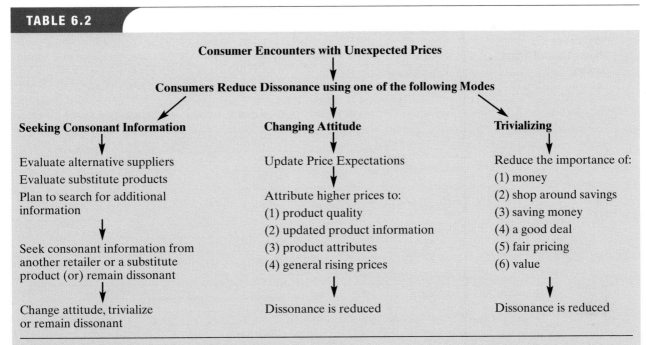

Consumer Encounters with Unexpected Prices

↓

Consumers Reduce Dissonance using one of the following Modes

Seeking Consonant Information	**Changing Attitude**	**Trivializing**
Evaluate alternative suppliers Evaluate substitute products Plan to search for additional information	Update Price Expectations	Reduce the importance of: (1) money (2) shop around savings (3) saving money (4) a good deal (5) fair pricing (6) value
Seek consonant information from another retailer or a substitute product (or) remain dissonant	Attribute higher prices to: (1) product quality (2) updated product information (3) product attributes (4) general rising prices	
Change attitude, trivialize or remain dissonant	Dissonance is reduced	Dissonance is reduced

Source: Joan Lindsey Mulliken, "Beyond Reference Price: Understanding Consumers' Encounters with Unexpected Prices," *Journal of Product and Brand Management*, 12, no. 3, 141.

study discovered that the color of a powdered fruit drink product is a more important determinant than its label and actual taste in determining the consumer's ability to identify the flavor correctly. The study's subjects perceived the purple or grape-colored versions of the powdered product "tart" in flavor and the orange-colored version as "flavorful, sweet, and refreshing."[34] *Consumer Reports* found that consumers often cannot differentiate among various cola beverages and that they base their preferences on such *extrinsic cues* as packaging, pricing, advertising, and even peer pressure.[35] A study reported that both consumers who rated a popcorn's taste as unfavorable and those who rated the same taste as favorable consumed more of the product when the container size was increased.[36] In the absence of actual experience with a product, consumers often evaluate quality on the basis of cues that are external to the product itself, such as price, brand image, manufacturer's image, retail store image, or even the country of origin.

Many consumers use *country-of-origin* stereotypes to evaluate products (e.g., "German engineering is excellent" or "Japanese cars are reliable"). Many consumers believe that a "Made in the U.S.A." label means a product is "superior" or "very good." Yet for food products, a foreign image is often more enticing. For example, Haagen-Dazs, an American-made ice cream, has been incredibly successful with its made-up (and meaningless) Scandinavian-sounding name. The success of Smirnoff vodka, made in Connecticut, can be related to its so-called Russian derivation. Sorbet has become a very popular and chic dessert, now that it is no longer called sherbet. A recent study pointed out that consumers' perceptions of value, risk, trust, attitude towards the brand, satisfaction, familiarity, attachment, and involvement moderate the impact of country-of-origin on perceived quality.[37] Several researchers developed a scale that measures perceptions of brand luxury—a construct that is often related to perceived quality (see Figure 6.15).

Perceived quality of services

It is more difficult for consumers to evaluate the quality of services than the quality of products. This is true because of certain distinctive characteristics of services: They are intangible, they are variable, they are perishable, and they are simultaneously produced and consumed. To overcome the fact that consumers are unable to compare competing

FIGURE 6.15

**Measuring
Perceptions of Brand
Luxury**

Source: Franck Vigneron and
Lester W. Johnson, "Measuring
Perceptions of Brand Luxury,"
Journal of Brand Management,
London, 11, no. 6 (July 2004):
484.

Non-personally-oriented perceptions

Conspicuousness			
	Conspicuous	____:____:____:____:____:____:____	Noticeable
	Popular	____:____:____:____:____:____:____	Elitist*
	Affordable	____:____:____:____:____:____:____	Extremely expensive*
	For wealthy	____:____:____:____:____:____:____	For well-off

Uniqueness			
	Fairly exclusive	____:____:____:____:____:____:____	Very exclusive*
	Precious	____:____:____:____:____:____:____	Valuable
	Rare	____:____:____:____:____:____:____	Uncommon
	Unique	____:____:____:____:____:____:____	Unusual

Quality			
	Crafted	____:____:____:____:____:____:____	Manufactured
	Upmarket	____:____:____:____:____:____:____	Luxurious*
	Best quality	____:____:____:____:____:____:____	Good quality
	Sophisticated	____:____:____:____:____:____:____	Original
	Superior	____:____:____:____:____:____:____	Better

Personally-oriented perceptions

Hedonism			
	Exquisite	____:____:____:____:____:____:____	Tasteful
	Attractive	____:____:____:____:____:____:____	Glamorous*
	Stunning	____:____:____:____:____:____:____	Memorable

Extended self			
	Leading	____:____:____:____:____:____:____	Influential
	Very powerful	____:____:____:____:____:____:____	Fairly powerful
	Rewarding	____:____:____:____:____:____:____	Pleasing
	Successful	____:____:____:____:____:____:____	Well regarded

* Indicates item is reverse-scored

services side-by-side as they do with competing products, consumers rely on surrogate cues (i.e., extrinsic cues) to evaluate service quality. In evaluating a doctor's services, for example, they note the quality of the office and examining room furnishings, the number (and source) of framed degrees on the wall, the pleasantness of the receptionist, and the professionalism of the nurse; all contribute to the consumer's overall evaluation of the quality of a doctor's services.

Because the actual quality of services can vary from day to day, from service employee to service employee, and from customer to customer (e.g., in food, in waitperson service, in haircuts, even in classes taught by the same professor), marketers try to standardize their services in order to provide consistency of quality. The downside of service standardization is the loss of customized services, which many consumers value.

Unlike products, which are first produced, then sold, and then consumed, most services are first sold and then produced and consumed simultaneously. Whereas a defective product is likely to be detected by factory quality control inspectors before it ever reaches the consumer, an inferior service is consumed as it is being produced; thus, there is little opportunity to correct it. For example, a defective haircut is difficult to correct, just as the negative impression caused by an abrupt or careless waiter is difficult to correct.

During peak demand hours, the interactive quality of services often declines, because both the customer and the service provider are hurried and under stress. Without special effort by the service provider to ensure consistency of services during peak hours, service image is likely to decline. Some marketers try to change demand patterns in order to distribute the service more equally over time. Long-distance telephone services, for instance, traditionally have offered a discount on telephone calls placed during off-peak hours (e.g., after 11:00 P.M. or on weekends); some restaurants offer a significantly less expensive "early bird" dinner for consumers who come in before 7:00 P.M. Service providers often try to reduce the perceived waiting time and the likely consequent negative service evaluation by filling the consumer's time. For example, diners may be invited to study the menu while waiting for a table; visitors who wait their turn at an attraction at Disney World are almost always distracted by video presentations or live entertainment.

The most widely accepted framework for researching service quality stems from the premise that a consumer's evaluation of service quality is a function of the magnitude and direction of the gap between the customer's *expectations of service* and the customer's *assessment (perception) of the service actually delivered.*[38] For example, a brand-new graduate student enrolled in an introductory marketing course at a highly reputable university has certain expectations about the intellectual abilities of her classmates, the richness of classroom discussions, and the professor's knowledge and communication skills. At the end of the term, her assessment of the course's quality is based on the differences between her expectations at the start of the term and her perceptions of the course at the end of the semester. If the course falls below her expectations, she will view it as a service of poor quality. If her expectations are exceeded, she will view the course as a high-quality educational experience. Of course, the expectations of a given service vary widely among different consumers of the same service. These expectations stem from word-of-mouth consumers have heard about the service, their past experiences, the promises made about the service in its ads and by its salespersons, the purchase alternatives available, and other situational factors.[39] Based on these factors, the sum total of a consumer's expectations of a service *before* receiving it is termed *predicted service*, services evaluated by the customer at the *end* of the service that significantly exceed the predicted service are perceived as offerings of high quality and generate more customer satisfaction, increased probability of repeat patronage, and favorable word-of-mouth.[40]

The SERVQUAL scale was designed to measure the gap between customers' expectations of services and their perceptions of the actual service delivered, based on the following five dimensions: reliability, responsiveness, assurance, empathy, and tangibility.[41] These dimensions are divided into two groups: the *outcome* dimension (which focuses on the reliable delivery of the core service) and the *process* dimension, which focuses on how the core service is delivered (i.e., the employees' responsiveness, assurance, and empathy in handling customers) and the service's tangible aspects.[42] The process dimension offers the service provider a significant opportunity to exceed customer expectations. For example, although Federal Express provides the same core service as other couriers (the *outcome* dimension), it provides a superior *process* dimension through its advanced tracking system, which can provide customers with instant information about the status of their packages at any time between pickup and delivery; it also provides call centers with knowledgeable, well-trained, and polite employees who can readily answer customers' questions and handle problems. Thus, FedEx uses the process dimension as a method to exceed customers' expectations and has acquired the image of a company that has an important, customer-focused competitive advantage among the many companies providing the same core service. Figure 6.16 shows an ad centered on customer expectations; it also makes the service experience more tangible by depicting the warm interaction between the customer and service employee in a pleasant "homelike" service environment. Table 6.3 depicts the application of the five SERVQUAL dimensions in a study of tourists' perceptions of tour operators.

Perceptions of high service quality and high customer satisfaction lead to higher levels of purchase intentions and repeat buying. Service quality is a determinant of whether the consumer ultimately remains with the company or defects to a competitor. When service quality evaluations are high, customers' behavioral intentions tend to be favorable to the company, and they are likely to remain customers. When service evaluations are low, customer relationships are more likely to weaken, resulting in defection to a competitor. Another issue in the perception of service quality is time. A longitudinal research study using the SERVQUAL scale discovered that consumers' perceptions of service quality declined over time, that favorable perceptions of the service's tangible features declined the least, and that changes in perceptions impacted the intentions to purchase the service again.[43]

Today many services are delivered over the phone or the Internet, without direct visual contact between the customer and the service employee. Under these conditions,

FIGURE 6.16

Source: Courtesy of Country
Inns & Suites.

**Tangible Cues Fulfilling
Customer Expectations in a
Service Ad**

"Guest expectations were met or exceeded more often at Country Inns & Suites By Carlson, than at <u>any other mid-price hotel.</u>"

–2001 Market Metrix Hotel Index (MMHI)

A recent Market Metrix consumer survey awarded Country Inns & Suites the highest rating in providing a comfortable, welcoming and secure environment. They also rated us best in guest satisfaction among all mid-price hotels. But at the end of the day, it's not about surveys or ratings. It's about you. So discover for yourself our special brand of country hospitality at over 300 locations worldwide. 800-456-4000 www.countryinns.com

COUNTRY INNS & SUITES BY CARLSON

"A cozy stay at a comfortable price."

it is more difficult to research the factors that determine the customer's perception of service quality. Because more and more companies, including the manufacturers of many tangible products, use service-focused selling points to promote and differentiate their offerings, such consumer studies are crucial. Call centers are a key point for customer access to the company and also an important source of customer information. One study analyzed voice-to-voice encounters among customers and call-center employees, and developed a scale that measures customers' perceptions of such service experiences and their future intentions regarding the company represented by the call center contacted (see Table 6.4).

TABLE 6.3	Tour Operators Evaluated Under the Five SERVQUAL Dimensions

(1) ASSURANCE DIMENSION:

- being served by the appropriate personnel;
- reinforcement of tourists' confidence;
- experienced and competent tour and hotel escorts; and
- fluent and understandable communication with tourists.

(2) RESPONSIVENESS DIMENSION:

- sincere interest in problem solving;
- provision of adequate information about the service delivered;
- prompt response to tourists' requests;
- provision of information on local entertainment;
- willingness to help tourists; and
- advice on how to use free time.

(3) RELIABILITY DIMENSION:

- easy contact on arrival at airport;
- easy location of and contact with tour and hotel escorts;
- services delivered on time;
- right first time;
- keeping promises;
- insisting on error-free service;
- meeting the tour schedule; and
- no sudden increase in tour cost.

(4) EMPATHY DIMENSION:

- pleasant, friendly personnel;
- understanding of specific needs; and
- cultivation of friendly relationship.

(5) TANGIBLES DIMENSION:

- modern and technologically relevant vehicles;
- appealing accommodation facilities;
- availability of information documents and notes;
- physical appearance of tour and hotel escorts (tidiness etc.); and
- high-quality meals.

Source: Eda Atilgn, Serkan Akinaci, and Safak Aksoy, "Mapping Service Quality in the Tourism Industry," *Managing Service Quality*, 13, no. 5 (2003), 416

Price/quality relationship

Perceived product value has been described as a trade-off between the product's perceived benefits (or quality) and the perceived sacrifice—both monetary and non-monetary—necessary to acquire it. A number of research studies have found that consumers rely on price as an indicator of product quality, that consumers attribute different qualities to identical products that carry different price tags, and that such consumer characteristics as age and income affect the perception of value.[44] One study suggested that consumers using a **price/quality relationship** are actually relying on a well-known (and, hence, more

TABLE 6.4	A Scale Measuring Customers' Perceptions of Call-Center Employees

ATTENTIVENESS

1. The agent did not make an attentive impression.*
2. The agent used short, affirmative words and sounds to indicate that (s)he was really listening.

PERCEPTIVENESS

1. The agent asked for more details and extra information during the conversation.
2. The agent continually attempted to understand what I was saying.
3. The agent paraphrased what had been said adequately.

RESPONSIVENESS

1. The agent offered relevant information to the questions I asked.
2. The agent used full sentences in his or her answers instead of just saying yes or no.
3. The agent did not recognize what information I needed.*

TRUST

1. I believe that this company takes customer calls seriously.
2. I feel that this company does not respond to customer problems with understanding.*
3. This company is ready and willing to offer support to customers.
4. I can count on this company to be sincere.

SATISFACTION

1. I am satisfied with the level of service the agent provided.
2. I am satisfied with the way I was spoken to by the agent.
3. I am satisfied with the information I got from the agent.
4. The telephone call with this agent was a satisfying experience.

CALL INTENTION

1. I will very likely contact this company again.
2. Next time I have any questions I will not hesitate to call again.
3. I would not be willing to discuss problems I have with this company over the phone.*

*Negatively phrased item.

Source: Ko de Ruyter and Martin G. M. Wetzels, *Journal of Service Research*, "The Impact of Perceived Listening Behavior in Voice-to-Voice Service Encounters," February 2000, pp. 276–284, copyright © 2000 by Sage Publications Ltd. Reprinted by permission of Sage Publications.

expensive) brand name as an indicator of quality without actually relying directly on price per se.[45] A later study found out that consumers use price and brand to evaluate the prestige of the product but do not generally use these cues when they evaluate the product's performance.[46] Because price is so often considered an indicator of quality, some product advertisements deliberately emphasize a high price to underscore the marketers' claims of quality. Marketers understand that, at times, products with lower prices may be interpreted as reduced quality. At the same time, when consumers evaluate more concrete attributes of a product, such as performance and durability, they rely less on the price and brand name as indicators of quality than when they evaluate the product's prestige and symbolic value.[47] For these reasons, marketers must understand all the attributes that customers use to evaluate a given product and include all applicable information in order to counter any perceptions of negative quality associated with a lower price.

In most consumption situations, in addition to price, consumers also use such cues as the brand and the store in which the product is bought to evaluate its quality. Consumers use price as a surrogate indicator of quality if they have little information to go on, or if they have little confidence in their own ability to make the product or service choice on other grounds. When the consumer is familiar with a brand name or has experience with a product (or service) or the store where it is purchased, price declines as a determining factor in product evaluation and purchase.

Retail store image

Retail stores have images of their own that serve to influence the perceived quality of products they carry and the decisions of consumers as to where to shop. These images stem from their design and physical environment, their pricing strategies, and product assortments. A study that examined the effects of specific store environmental factors on quality inferences found that consumer perceptions were more heavily influenced by ambient factors (such as the number, type, and behavior of other customers within the store and the sales personnel) than by store design features.[48] Another study discovered that consumers' preferences of apparel stores were determined by the availability of the desired clothing in stock, the outside store appearance, shopping hours, and advertising.[49]

A study of retail store image based on comparative *pricing strategies* found that consumers tend to perceive stores that offer a small discount on a large number of items (i.e., *frequency of price advantage*) as having lower prices overall than competing stores that offer larger discounts on a smaller number of products (i.e., *magnitude of price advantage*). Thus, frequent advertising that presents large numbers of price specials reinforces consumer beliefs about the competitiveness of a store's prices.[50] This finding has important implications for retailers' *positioning strategies*. In times of heavy competition, when it is tempting to hold frequent large sales covering many items, such strategies may result in an unwanted change in store image. For example, Lord & Taylor's in New York City, formerly positioned as an upscale, high-class department store, advertises sales so frequently and fills its aisles with sales racks proclaiming bargain prices, so that its upscale image has been tarnished, and its customer mix has changed. Marketers must also consider how price reductions of *specific* products impact consumers' perceptions. One study pointed out that some poorly chosen price promotions bring about discrepancies between the actual prices in the store and consumers' perceptions of the retailer's *overall store price image*.[51]

The *width of product assortment* also affects retail store image. Grocery retailers, for example, are often reluctant to reduce the number of products they carry out of concern that perceptions of a smaller assortment will reduce the likelihood that consumers will shop in their stores.[52] On the other hand, Whole Foods Markets—a relatively small supermarket chain—has carved itself a profitable niche by carrying a much smaller but highly selective range of products in comparison to conventional supermarkets. Whole Foods stores carry organic (perceived as healthier) products, many of which are bought from mom-and-pop producers; all food products carried are screened for artificial ingredients; and the chain is phasing out all products with hydrogenated fats. The chain has been much more profitable than conventional supermarkets in spite of its limited product assortment.[53] Clearly, the unique benefit that a store provides is more important than the number of items it carries in forming a favorable store image in consumers' minds.

The type of product the consumer wishes to buy influences his or her selection of a retail outlet; conversely, the consumer's evaluation of a product often is influenced by the knowledge of where it was bought. A consumer wishing to buy an elegant dress for a special occasion may go to a store with an elegant, high-fashion image, such as Saks Fifth Avenue. Regardless of what she actually pays for the dress she selects (regular price or marked-down price), she will probably perceive its quality to be high. However, she may perceive the quality of the identical dress to be much lower if she buys it in an off-price store with a low-price image.

Most studies of the effects of extrinsic cues on perceived product quality have focused on just one variable—either price *or* store image. However, when a second extrinsic cue is available (such as price *and* store image), perceived quality is sometimes a function of the interaction of both cues on the consumer. For example, when brand and retailer images become associated, the less favorable image becomes enhanced at the expense of the more favorable image. Thus, when a low-priced store carries a brand with a high-priced image, the image of the store will improve, whereas the image of the brand will be adversely affected. For that reason, marketers of prestigious designer goods often attempt to control the outlets where their products are sold. Also, when upscale stores sell leftover expensive items to discount stores, they remove the designer labels from these goods as part of the agreements they have with the manufacturers of these products.

Fads can have some unforeseen consequences on consumers' store choices. Recently, 99-cent and one-dollar stores, originally the terrain of lower-income consumers, became fashionable among affluent consumers, who bought there such items as beach balls with the logo "99-cents Only" imprinted on them (in giant letters), wines for under $5, and faux-bamboo picture frames. A study of one chain of dollar-stores found that 32 percent of the cars in the chains' parking lots were less than two years old and in excellent condition; in Los Angeles, Mercedes-Benzes, BMWs, and Rolls-Royces were routinely seen in the parking areas of low-status outlets.[54]

Manufacturers' image

Consumer imagery extends beyond perceived price and store image to the producers themselves. Manufacturers who enjoy a favorable image generally find that their new products are accepted more readily than those of manufacturers who have a less favorable or even a "neutral" image. Researchers have found that consumers generally have favorable perceptions of pioneer brands (the first in a product category), even after follower brands become available. They also found a positive correlation between *pioneer brand image* and an individual's *ideal self-image*, which suggests that positive perceptions toward pioneer brands lead to positive purchase intentions.[55] Studies show that consumers choose brands perceived as similar to their own *actual, ideal, social, ideal-social*, and *situational-ideal-social* images. Thus, if a consumer believes that using the brand is fun, she will buy it and use it when she is having fun with her friends and, to her, the brand will be worth what it costs, so long as she perceives it as fun.[56] These findings have important implications regarding the possible perils of repositioning brands.

Some major marketers introduce new products under the guise of supposedly smaller, pioneering (and presumably more forward-thinking) companies. The goal of this so-called *stealth* (or faux) *parentage* is to persuade consumers that the new brands are produced by independent, nonconformist free spirits, rather than by giant corporate entities. Companies sometimes use stealth parentage when they enter a product category totally unrelated to the one with which their corporate name has become synonymous. For example, when Disney Studios—a company with a wholesome, family-focused image—produces films that include violence and sex, it does so under the name Touchstone Pictures.

Today companies are using advertising, exhibits, and sponsorship of community events to enhance their images. Although some marketers argue that product and service advertising do more to boost the corporate image than *institutional* (image) advertising does, others see both types of advertising—product and institutional—as integral and complementary components of a total corporate communications program. When the reputation of Wal-Mart was tarnished by allegations of unfair labor practices, sexual discrimination and the publication of data indicating that the company caused most of America's trade imbalance with China, the company published ads stating that "Wal-Mart Is Working for Everyone." In addition, the company's executives appeared on TV talk shows and met with community groups and government officials to dispel the negative associations. In a further effort to improve its image, Wal-Mart sponsored a new TV reality show, *The Scholar*, on which high school seniors from across the country competed for college scholarships financed by Wal-Mart.[57]

perceived risk

Consumers must constantly make decisions regarding what products or services to buy and where to buy them. Because the outcomes (or consequences) of such decisions are often uncertain, the consumer perceives some degree of "risk" in making a purchase decision. **Perceived risk** is defined as *the uncertainty that consumers face when they cannot foresee the consequences of their purchase decisions.* This definition highlights two relevant dimensions of perceived risk: uncertainty and consequences.

The degree of risk that consumers perceive and their own tolerance for risk taking are factors that influence their purchase strategies. It should be stressed that consumers are influenced by risks that they perceive, whether or not such risks actually exist. Risk that is not perceived—no matter how real or how dangerous—will not influence consumer behavior. The major types of risks that consumers perceive when making product decisions include *functional risk, physical risk, financial risk, social risk, psychological risk,* and *time risk* (see Table 6.5).

Perception of risk varies

Consumer perception of risk varies, depending on the person, the product, the situation, and the culture. The amount of risk perceived depends on the specific consumer. Some consumers tend to perceive high degrees of risk in various consumption situations; others tend to perceive little risk. For example, adolescents who engage in high-risk consumption activities, such as smoking or drug use, obviously have lower perceived risk than those who do not engage in high-risk activities. *High-risk perceivers* are often described as **narrow categorizers** because they limit their choices (e.g., product choices) to a few safe alternatives. They would rather exclude some perfectly good alternatives than chance a poor selection. *Low-risk perceivers* have been described as **broad categorizers** because they tend to make their choices from a much wider range of alternatives. They would rather risk a poor selection than limit the number of alternatives from which they can choose.

An individual's perception of risk varies with product categories. For example, consumers are likely to perceive a higher degree of risk (e.g., functional risk, financial risk, time risk) in the purchase of a plasma television set than in the purchase of an automobile; this type of risk is termed *product-category* perceived risk. Researchers have also identified *product*-specific perceived risk. One study found that consumers perceive service decisions to be riskier than product decisions, particularly in terms of social risk, physical risk, and psychological risk.

TABLE 6.5   **Types of Perceived Risk**

Functional risk is the risk that the product will not perform as expected. ("Can the new PDA operate a full week without needing to be recharged?")

Physical risk is the risk to self and others that the product may pose. ("Is a cellular phone really safe, or does it emit harmful radiation?")

Financial risk is the risk that the product will not be worth its cost. ("Will a new and cheaper model of a Plasma TV monitor become available six months from now?")

Social risk is the risk that a poor product choice may result in social embarrassment. ("Will my classmates laugh at my purple mohawk haircut?")

Psychological risk is the risk that a poor product choice will bruise the consumer's ego. ("Will I be embarrassed when I invite friends to listen to music on my five-year-old stereo?")

Time risk is the risk that the time spent in product search may be wasted if the product does not perform as expected. ("Will I have to go through the shopping effort all over again?")

The degree of risk perceived by a consumer is also affected by the shopping situation (e.g., a traditional bricks-and-mortar retail store, online, catalog, direct-mail solicitations, or door-to-door sales). The sharp increase in mail-order catalog sales in recent years suggests that on the basis of positive experiences and word-of-mouth, consumers now tend to perceive less risk in mail-order shopping than they once did, despite their inability to physically inspect the merchandise before ordering. The findings regarding the impact of perceived risk in shopping online are mixed. While some studies showed that the frequency of shopping online reduced consumers' perceived risk regarding such purchases, other studies showed no correlation between the two factors. Researchers also discovered that consumers' levels of involvement, brand familiarity, and the perceived benefits of shopping online impacted the perceived risk of electronic buying.[58]

How consumers handle risk

Consumers characteristically develop their own strategies for reducing perceived risk. These risk-reduction strategies enable them to act with increased confidence when making product decisions, even though the consequences of such decisions remain somewhat uncertain. Some of the more common risk-reduction strategies are discussed in the following sections.

Consumers seek information

Consumers seek information about the product and product category through word-of-mouth communication (from friends and family and from other people whose opinions they value), from salespeople, and from the general media. They spend more time thinking about their choice and search for more information about the product alternatives when they associate a high degree of risk with the purchase. This strategy is straightforward and logical because the more information the consumer has about the product and the product category, the more predictable the probable consequences and thus, the lower the perceived risk.

Consumers are brand loyal

Consumers avoid risk by remaining loyal to a brand with which they have been satisfied instead of purchasing new or untried brands. High-risk perceivers, for example, are more likely to be loyal to their old brands and less likely to purchase newly introduced products.

Consumers select by brand image

When consumers have had no experience with a product, they tend to "trust" a favored or well-known brand name. Consumers often think well-known brands are better and are worth buying for the implied assurance of quality, dependability, performance, and service. Marketers' promotional efforts supplement the perceived quality of their products by helping to build and sustain a favorable brand image.

Consumers rely on store image

If consumers have no other information about a product, they often trust the judgment of the merchandise buyers of a reputable store and depend on them to have made careful decisions in selecting products for sale. Store image also imparts the implication of product testing and the assurance of service, return privileges, and adjustment in case of dissatisfaction.

Consumers buy the most expensive model

When in doubt, consumers often feel that the most expensive model is probably the best in terms of quality; that is, they equate price with quality. (The price/quality relationship was discussed earlier in this chapter.)

Consumers seek reassurance

Consumers who are uncertain about the wisdom of a product choice seek reassurance through money-back guarantees, government and private laboratory test results, warranties, and prepurchase trial. For example, it is unlikely that anyone would buy a new model car without a test drive. Products that do not easily lend themselves to free or limited trial, such as a refrigerator, present a selling challenge to marketers.

The concept of perceived risk has major implications for the introduction of new products. Because high-risk perceivers are less likely than low-risk perceivers to purchase new or innovative products, it is important for marketers to provide such consumers with persuasive risk-reduction strategies, such as a well-known brand name (sometimes achieved through licensing), distribution through reputable retail outlets, informative advertising, publicity stories in the media, impartial test results, free samples, and money-back guarantees. Also, most stores that carry a number of different brands and models of the same product, as well as manufacturers of such diverse model lines, now offer online consumers quick and easy ways to generate side-by-side comparisons with detailed charts of the features of all the available models.

ethics and consumer perception

The ethical issues related to consumer perception focus on how marketers use the knowledge of perception to manipulate consumers. One technique marketers use is to blur the distinctions between *figure* and *ground*. For example, to combat fast-forwarding by consumers who wish to avoid TV commercials, marketers are increasingly turning to **product placements**, where the line between television shows and ads is virtually non-existent. In ABC's *Extreme Makeover: Home Edition*, Sears' Kenmore appliances and Craftsman tools are the "stars" of the show. Research indicates that many viewers were more likely to shop at Sears after seeing the show. Bags of Doritos and six-packs of Mountain Dew were given to the winners of personal challenge contests on *Survivor*, and the judges of "American Idol" always have a Coca-Cola within easy reach. A new product developed by Burger King went on sale the day after it was featured on *The Apprentice*, and another show of this series focused on developing an ad for Dove Cool Moisture Body Wash. Predictions have indicated that marketers are likely to increase expenditures substantially on such *branded entertainment*. In addition, online editions of newspapers often embed advertisements within the content of news. A newly formed consumer advocacy group, Commercial Alert, is lobbying for legislation that will require advertisers to disclose upfront those ads that are designed as product placements.[59]

Marketers also blend promotion and program content by positioning a TV commercial so close to the storyline of a program that viewers are unaware they are watching an advertisement until they are well into it. Because this was an important factor in advertising to children, the Federal Trade Commission has strictly limited the use of this technique. TV stars or cartoon characters are now prohibited from promoting products during the children's shows in which they appear. Other potential misuses of figure-and-ground are print ads (called *advertorials*) that closely resemble editorial matter, making it increasingly difficult for readers to tell them apart. Thirty-minute commercials (called *infomercials*) appear to the average viewer as documentaries, and thus command more attentive viewing than obvious commercials would receive.

As discussed earlier, marketers use their knowledge of the *just noticeable difference* to ensure that reductions in product quantity or quality and increases in prices go unnoticed by consumers. Marketers can also increase the quantity of the product consumed by the way it is physically packaged or presented. For example, studies showed that: (1) both children and adults consume more juice when the product is presented in short, wide glasses than in tall slender glasses; (2) candies placed in clear jars were eaten much quicker than those presented in opaque jars; (3) sandwiches in transparent wrap generated more consumption than those in opaque wraps; and (4) the visibility and aroma of tempting foods generated greater consumption.[60] Another study demonstrated that the organization of the merchandise, the size of the package, the symmetry of the display and its perceived variety served to impact consumption quantities. The consumer implications of these findings are listed in Table 6.6.[61]

TABLE 6.6	Implications for How Assortment Structure Influences Consumption Quantities				
	ORGANIZATION INFLUENCES CONSUMPTION	**SIZE INFLUENCES CONSUMPTION**	**SYMMETRY INFLUENCES CONSUMPTION**	**PERCEIVED VARIETY PARTIALLY MEDIATES CONSUMPTION**	**CONSUMPTION RULES INFLUENCE CONSUMPTION**
Consumer implications	Organization is relevant for mixed assortments in bowls (or "grab bags"), buffets, potlucks, or dinner table settings. It may also be relevant in retail contexts. Consumers may be able to control consumption by organizing less-structured offerings.	Assortment size or duplication is commonly found in the form of multiple product tastings, multiple offerings of party snacks, duplicate buffet lines, family dinners with multiple dishes, and perhaps even in retail displays. Duplicated offerings can stimulate consumption.	The symmetry of an assortment is an issue wherever multiple units (and perhaps sizes) of options are involved, such as at holiday dinners, toys in play areas, and collectables and collecting. Minimal variation in the size of serving bowls may overstimulate consumption.	People are often surprised at how much they consume, showing that they may have been influenced at a basic or perceptual level.	Large inventory levels in one's home pantry could increase the quantity of food one believes is appropriate for a meal. Health-care professionals and dieticians can stimulate consumption among nutritionally deficient individuals by offering smaller helpings of more items.

Source: Barbara E. Kahn and Brian Wansink, "The Influence of Assortment Structure on Perceived Variety and Consumption Quantities," *Journal of Consumer Research*, 30 (March 2004), 530. Reproduced with permission of the copyright owner. Further reproduction prohibited without permission.

Marketers can also manipulate consumers' perception and behavior by using the physical setting where consumption occurs. It is widely known that supermarkets routinely move products around to encourage consumers to wander around the store, and keep the stores relatively cold because colder temperatures make people hungrier and so they increase their food purchases. (Some nutritionists advise consumers to go food shopping directly after a filling meal.) At DisneyWorld, guests leaving rides, and presumably still under the spell of the thrill and enjoyment experienced, must exit through a corridor of stores featuring merchandise congruent with the themes of the rides.

Marketers can also manipulate consumers' interpretations of marketing stimuli through the context in which they are featured. For example, in QVC's "Extreme Shopping," during which rare and expensive products are offered, consumers perceived $200 art prints as reasonably priced when the prints were shown immediately after much more expensive items.[62] Inadvertently, marketers can also impact the content of news to which consumers are exposed. For example, many marketers carefully screen the context in which their messages are shown, because they recognize that advertisements are perceived more positively when placed within more positive programs. Thus, they may choose not to place ads in news broadcasts or programs that cover serious issues, such as wars and world hunger, where some of the content is bound to be unpleasant.

In 1973, a book entitled *Subliminal Seduction* charged that advertisers were using subliminal embeds in their print ads to persuade consumers to buy their advertised brands. It was alleged, for example, that liquor advertisers were trying to increase the subconscious appeal of their products by embedding sexually suggestive symbols in ice cubes floating in a pictured drink.[63] Subsequently, the Federal Communications Commission (FCC) studied the subject and concluded that subliminal messages, whether effective or not, are intended to deceive consumers and, therefore, contradict the public interest. However, because of the absence of any evidence that subliminal persuasion really works, no state or federal laws have been enacted to restrict the use of subliminal advertising.

Conveying socially undesirable stereotypes in products and advertisements is another ethical dilemma marketers may face. Some years ago, the makers of an American icon—G.I. Joe—introduced a substantially more muscular version of the doll and were subsequently accused of sanctioning the use of muscle-building drugs by teenagers. Similarly, the makers of Barbie—a doll that has gradually become thinner and bustier—were accused of conveying an unrealistic body image to young girls.[64] A recent example of perceived sterotypes in TV ads are ads that portray husbands and fathers as objects of ridicule and scorn (images that the creators of the messages believed to be a clever reversal of traditional sex roles).

SUMMARY

Perception is the process by which individuals select, organize, and interpret stimuli into a meaningful and coherent picture of the world. Perception has strategy implications for marketers because consumers make decisions based on what they perceive rather than on the basis of objective reality.

The lowest level at which an individual can perceive a specific stimulus is that person's absolute threshold. The minimal difference that can be perceived between two stimuli is called the differential threshold or just noticeable difference (j.n.d.). Most stimuli are perceived by consumers above the level of their conscious awareness; however, weak stimuli can be perceived below the level of conscious awareness (i.e., subliminally). Research refutes the notion that subliminal stimuli influence consumer buying decisions.

Consumers' selections of stimuli from the environment are based on the interaction of their expectations and motives with the stimulus itself. The principles of selective perception include the following concepts: selective exposure, selective attention, perceptual defense, and perceptual blocking. People usually perceive things they need or want, and block the perception of unnecessary, unfavorable, or painful stimuli.

Consumers organize their perceptions into unified wholes according to the principles of Gestalt psychology: figure and ground, grouping, and closure. The interpretation of stimuli is highly subjective and is based on what the consumer expects to see in light of previous experience, on motives and interests at the time of perception, and on the clarity of the stimulus itself. Influences that tend to distort objective interpretation include physical appearances, stereotypes, halo effects, irrelevant cues, first impressions, and the tendency to jump to conclusions.

Just as individuals have perceived images of themselves, they also have perceived images of products and brands. The perceived image of a product or service (how it is positioned) is probably more important to its ultimate success

than are its actual physical characteristics. Products and services that are perceived distinctly and favorably have a much better chance of being purchased than products or services with unclear or unfavorable images.

Compared with manufacturing firms, service marketers face several unique problems in positioning and promoting their offerings because services are intangible, inherently variable, perishable, and are simultaneously produced and consumed. Regardless of how well positioned a product or service appears to be, the marketer may be forced to reposition it in response to market events, such as new competitor strategies or changing consumer preferences.

Consumers often judge the quality of a product or service on the basis of a variety of informational cues; some are intrinsic to the product (such as color, size, flavor, and aroma), while others are extrinsic (e.g., price, store image, brand image, and service environment). In the absence of direct experience or other information, consumers often rely on price as an indicator of quality. How a consumer perceives a price—as high, low, or fair—has a strong influence on purchase intentions and satisfaction. Consumers rely on both internal and external reference prices when assessing the fairness of a price.

Consumer imagery also includes perceived images of retail stores that influence the perceived quality of products they carry, as well as decisions as to where to shop. Manufacturers who enjoy a favorable image generally find that their new products are accepted more readily than those of manufacturers with less favorable or even neutral images.

Consumers often perceive risk in making product selections because of uncertainty as to the consequences of their product decisions. The most frequent types of risk that consumers perceive are functional risk, physical risk, financial risk, social risk, psychological risk, and time risk. Consumer strategies for reducing perceived risk include increased information search, brand loyalty, buying a well-known brand, buying from a reputable retailer, buying the most expensive brand, and seeking reassurance in the form of money-back guarantees, warranties, and prepurchase trial. The concept of perceived risk has important implications for marketers, who can facilitate the acceptance of new products by incorporating risk-reduction strategies in their new-product promotional campaigns.

The perception-related ethical issues include blurring the distinction between advertising and the informational or entertainment content of print or electronic media (i.e., figure-and-ground confusion), the large increase in product placements and branded advertising to combat the avoidance by consumers of TV commercials, using the physical environment and stimulus factors to increase consumption, and portraying socially undesirable stereotypes in advertising.

DISCUSSION QUESTIONS

1. How does sensory adaptation affect advertising effectiveness? How can marketers overcome sensory adaptation?

2. Discuss the differences between the absolute threshold and the differential threshold. Which one is more important to marketers? Explain your answer.

3. For each of these products—chocolate bars and bottles of expensive perfume—describe how marketers can apply their knowledge of the differential threshold to packaging, pricing, and promotional claims during periods of (a) rising ingredient and materials costs and (b) increasing competition.

4. Does subliminal advertising work? Support your view.

5. How do advertisers use contrast to make sure that their ads are noticed? Would the lack of contrast between the ad and the medium in which it appears help or hinder the effectiveness of the ad? What are the ethical considerations in employing such strategies?

6. What are the implications of figure–ground relationships for print ads and for online ads? How can the figure–ground construct help or interfere with the communication of advertising messages?

7. Why are marketers sometimes "forced" to reposition their products or services? Illustrate your answers with examples.

8. Why is it more difficult for consumers to evaluate the quality of services than the quality of products?

9. Discuss the roles of extrinsic cues and intrinsic cues in the perceived quality of:
   a. wines.
   b. restaurants.
   c. plasma TV monitors.
   d. graduate education.

EXERCISES

1. Find three print advertisements that use some of the stimulus factors discussed in this chapter to gain attention. For each example, evaluate the effectiveness of the stimulus factors used.

2. Define selective perception, and relate one or two elements of this concept to your own attention patterns in viewing print advertisements and TV commercials.

3. Find an ad or example in print format (e.g., an article) illustrating two of the positioning approaches discussed in this chapter. Evaluate the effectiveness of each ad or example selected.

4. Select a company that produces several versions of the same product under the same brand name (do not use one of the examples discussed in this chapter). Visit the firm's Web site and prepare a list of the product items and the benefits that each item offers to consumers. Are all these benefits believable and will they persuade consumers to buy the different versions of the product? Explain your answers.

5. Construct a two-dimensional perceptual map of your college using the two attributes that were most influential in your selection. Then mark the position of your school on the diagram relative to that of another school you considered. Discuss the implications of this perceptual map for the student recruitment function of the university that you did not choose.

6. Apply two of the concepts used to explain consumers' evaluations of service quality to your evaluation of this course up to this point in the semester.

7. Find a recent article discussing one of the ethical issues discussed in this chapter and present it in class.

KEY TERMS

- **absolute threshold**
- **branded advertising**
- **broad versus narrow categorizers**
- **closure**
- **cognitive dissonance**
- **consumer imagery**
- **differential threshold**
- **expectations**
- **figure and ground**
- **Gestalt psychology**
- **grouping**
- **intrinsic versus extrinsic cues**

- **just noticeable difference (j.n.d.)**
- **perceived price**
- **perceived quality**
- **perceived risk**
- **perception**
- **perceptual blocking**
- **perceptual distortion**
- **perceptual interpretation**
- **perceptual organization**
- **perceptual mapping**
- **positioning**
- **price/quality relationship**

- **product placements**
- **product or service positioning and repositioning**
- **reference prices**
- **selective perception**
- **sensation**
- **sensory adaptation**
- **sensory receptors**
- **stereotypes**
- **subliminal perception**
- **Weber's law**

NOTES

1. Robert McMath and Thomas Forbes, *What Were They Thinking?* (New York: Time Business, Random House, 1998), 13–14.

2. Martin Lindstrom, "Smelling a Branding Opportunity," *Brandweek*, March 14, 2005, 26.

3. Philippa Ward, Barry J. Davies, and Dion Kooijman, "Ambient Smell and the Retail Environment: Retailing Olfaction Research to Consumer Behavior," *Journal of Business and Management* (Summer 2003): 289–303; Daniel Milotic, "The Impact of Fragrance On Consumer Choice," *Journal of Consumer Behaviour* (December 2003): 179; Lawrence K. Altman, "Unravelling Enigma of Smell Wins Nobel for 2 Americans," *The New York Times*, December 5, 2004, A18.

4. Eric R. Spangenberg, Ayn E. Crowley, and Pamela W. Henderson, "Improving the Store Environment: Do Olfactory Cues Affect Evaluations and Behaviors?" *Journal of Marketing* 60 (April 1996): 67–80.

5. Stuart Elliott, "Don't Call It a Store, Call It an Ad With Walls," *The New York Times*, December 7, 2004, 6.

6. Jeffrey Kluger, "Inside the Food Labs," *Time*, October 6, 2003, 56–60; Jon Gertner, "Eat Chocolate, Live Longer?" **www.nytimes.com**, October 10, 2004.

7. Robert McMath and Thomas Forbes, *What Were They Thinking?* 66.

8. Greg Winter, "What Keeps a Bottom Line Healthy? Weight Loss," *New York Times*, January 2, 2001, 1.

9. Sharon E. Beatty and Del I. Hawkins, "Subliminal Stimulation: Some New Data and Interpretation," *Journal of Advertising* 18 (1989): 4–8.

10. Lisa Bannon, "How a Rumor Spread About Subliminal Sex in Disney's *Aladdin*," *Wall Street Journal*, October 24, 1995, A-1; Bruce Orwall, "Disney Recalls *The Rescuers* Video Containing Images of Topless Woman," *Wall Street Journal Interactive Edition*, January 11, 1999.

11. Kathryn T. Theus, "Subliminal Advertising and the Psychology of Processing Unconscious Stimuli: A Review of Research," *Psychology and Marketing* 11, no. 3 (May–June 1994): 271–290. See also Dennis L. Rosen and Surenra N. Singh, "An Investigation of Subliminal Embed Effect on Multiple Measures of Advertising Effectiveness," *Psychology and Marketing* 9, no. 2 (March–April 1992): 157–173.

12. For example, Andrew B. Aylesworth, Ronald C. Goodstein, and Ajay Kalra, "Effects of Archetypal Embeds of Feelings: An Indirect Route to Affecting Attitudes?" *Journal of Advertising* (Fall 1999): 73–81; Nicholas Epley, Kenneth Savitsky, and Robert A. Kachelski, "What Every Skeptic Should Know About Subliminal Persuasion," *Skeptical Inquirer* (September/October 1999): 4–58.

13. Carl L. Witte, Madhavan Parthasarathy, and James W. Gentry, "Subliminal Perception Versus Subliminal Persuasion: A Re-Examination of the Basic Issues," *American Marketing Association* (Summer 1995): 133–138. See also Jack Haberstroh, *Ice Cube Sex: The Truth about Subliminal Advertising* (Notre Dame, IN: Cross Cultural Publications, 1994).

14. Martha Rogers and Christine A. Seiler, "The Answer Is No: A National Survey of Advertising Practitioners and Their Clients about Whether They Use Subliminal Advertising," *Journal of Advertising Research* (March–April 1994): 36–45; Martha Rogers and Kirk H. Smith, "Public Perceptions of Subliminal Advertising: Why Practitioners Shouldn't Ignore

This Issue," *Journal of Advertising Research* (March–April 1993): 10–18. See also Nicolas E. Synodinos, "Subliminal Stimulation: What Does the Public Think about It?" in *Current Issues and Research in Advertising* 11 (1 and 2), eds. James H. Leigh and Claude R. Martin Jr. (1988): 157–187.

15. Keith Naughton, "Gross Out, Smoke Out," *Newsweek*, March 25, 2002, 9.

16. Marsha L. Richins, "Social Comparison and the Idealized Images of Advertising," *Journal of Consumer Research* 18 (June 1991): 71–83. See also Mary C. Martin and James W. Gentry, "Stuck in the Model Trap: The Effects of Beautiful Models in Ads on Female Pre-Adolescents and Adolescents," *Journal of Advertising* 26, no. 2 (Summer 1997): 19–33.

17. Amanda B. Bower and Stacy Landreth, "Is Beauty Best? Highs Versus Normally Attractive Models in Advertising," *Journal of Advertising* 30, no. 1 (Spring 2001): 1–12.

18. Scott S. Liu and Keith F. Johnson, "The Automatic Country-of-Origin Effects on Brand Judgments," *Journal of Advertising* (Spring 2005): 87–98.

19. Brian Wansink, Koert van Ittersum, and James E. Painter, "How Descriptive Food Names Bias Sensory Perceptions in Restaurants," *Food Quality and Preference*, **www.sciencedirect.com**, June 2004.

20. Priya Raghubir and Aradhna Krishna, "Vital Dimensions in Volume Perception: Can the Eye Fool the Stomach?" *JMR, Journal of Marketing Research* (August 1999): 313–326.

21. Steven S. Posavac, David M. Sanbonmatsu, Frank R. Kardes, and Gavan J. Fitzsimons, The Brand Positivity Effect: When Evaluation Confers Preference," *Journal of Consumer Research* (December 2004): 643–652.

22. Joe Sharkey, "Hotels Learn the Importance of Expectations Built into a Brand Name," *New York Times*, June 18, 2002, C12.

23. **http://www.prodhelp.com/eyecare/eye-care_index.shtml**

24. **http://www.crest.com/products/toothpastes.jsp**

25. **http://marriott.com**

26. Leonard L. Berry, Edwin F. Lefkowith, and Terry Clark, "In Services, What's in a Name?" *Harvard Business Review* (September–October 1988): 28–30.

27. Julie Baker, Leonard L. Berry, and A. Parasuraman, "The Marketing Impact of Branch Facility Design," *Journal of Retail Banking* 10, no. 2 (Summer 1988): 33–42.

28. Lesa E. Bolton, Luk Warlop, and Joseph W. Alba, "Consumer Perceptions of Price (Un)Fairness," *Journal of Consumer Research* (March 2003): 474–492.

29. Dhruv Grewal et al., "The Effects of Price Comparison Advertising on Buyers' Perceptions of Acquisition Value, Transaction Value, and Behavioral Intentions," *Journal of Marketing* 62 (April 1998): 46–59.

30. Larry D. Compeau, Joan Lindsey-Mullikin, Dhruv Grewal, and Ross D. Petty, "Consumers' Interpretations of the Semantic Phrases Found in Reference Price Advertisements," *The Journal of Consumer Affairs* (Summer 2004): 178–188.

31. Bolton et al., "Consumer Perceptions of Price (Un)Fairness."

32. Katherine Fraccastoro, Scot Burton, and Abhijit Biswas, "Effective Use of Advertisements Promoting Sales Prices," *Journal of Consumer Marketing* (1993): 61–79.

33. Joan Lindsey-Mullikin, "Beyond Reference Price: Understanding Consumers' Encounters with Unexpected Prices," *The Journal of Product and Brand Management* 12, no. 2/3 (2003): 140–154.

34. Lawrence L. Garber, Jr., Eva M. Hyatt, and Richard G. Starr, Jr., "The Effects of Food Color on Perceived Flavor," *Journal of Marketing Theory and Practice* (Fall 2000): 59–72.

35. Michael J. McCarthy, "Forget the Ads: Cola Is Cola, Magazine Finds," *Wall Street Journal*, February 24, 1991, B1.

36. B. Wansink and S. B. Parker, "At the Movies: How External Cues and Perceived Taste Impact Consumption Volume," *Food Quality and Preference* 12 (2001): 69–74.

37. Ting-Yu Chueh and Danny T. Kao, "The Moderating Effects of Consumer Perception to the Impacts of Country-of-Design on Perceived Quality," *Journal of American Academy of Business* (March 2004): 70.

38. Valarie A. Zeithaml, A. Parasuraman, and Leonard L. Berry, *Delivering Quality Service: Balancing Customer Perceptions and Expectations* (New York: The Free Press, 1990).

39. Valarie A. Zeithaml, Leonard L. Berry, and A. Parasuraman, "The Nature and Determinants of Customer Expectation of Service," *Journal of the Academy of Marketing Science* (Winter 1993): 1–12.

40. Ibid.

41. A. Parasuraman, Leonard L. Berry, and Valarie A. Zeithaml, "Refinement and Reassessment of the SERVQUAL Scale," *Journal of Retailing* 67, no. 4 (Winter 1991): 420–450.

42. A. Parasuraman, Leonard L. Berry, and Valarie A. Zeithaml, "Understanding Customer Expectations of Service," *Sloan Management Review* (Spring 1991): 39–48.

43. Adrian Palmer and Martin O'Neill, "The Effects of Perceptual Processes On the Measurement of Service Quality," *The Journal of Services Marketing* 17, no. 2/3 (2003): 254–275.

44. For example, Kent Monroe, *Pricing: Making Profitable Decisions*, 2d ed. (New York: McGraw Hill, 1990); William Dodds, Kent Monroe, and Dhruv Grewal, "Effects of Price, Brand, and Store Information on Buyers' Product Evaluations," *Journal of Marketing Research* 28 (August 1991): 307–319; Tung Zong Chang and Albert R. Wildt, "Price, Product Information, and Purchase Intention: An Empirical Study," *Journal of the Academy of Marketing Science* 22, no. 1 (1994): 16–27; Indrajit Sinha and Wayne S. DeSasrbo, "An Integrated Approach toward the Spatial Model of Perceived Customer Value," *Journal of Marketing Research* 35 (May 1998): 236–249.

45. Donald R. Liechtenstein, Nancy M. Ridgway, and Richard G. Nitemeyer, "Price Perception and Consumer Shopping Behavior: A Field Study," *Journal of Marketing Research* 30 (May 1993): 242.

46. Merrie Brucks and Valarie A. Zeithaml, "Price and Brand Name as Indicators of Quality Dimensions for Consumer Durables," *Journal of the Academy of Marketing Science* (Summer 2000): 359–374.

47. Ibid.

48. Julie Baker, Dhruv Grewal, and A. Parasuraman, "The Influence of Store Environment on Quality Inferences and Store Image," *Journal of the Academy of Marketing Science* 22, no. 4 (1994): 328–339.

49. V. Ann Paulins and Loren V. Geistfeld, "The Effect of Consumer Perceptions of Store Attributes on Apparel Store Preference," *Journal of Fashion Marketing and Management* 7, no. 4 (2003): 371–386.

50. Joseph W. Alba, Susan M. Broniarczyk, Terence A. Shimp, and Joel E. Urbany, "The Influence of Prior Beliefs, Frequency Cues, and Magnitude Cues on Consumers' Perceptions of Comparative Price Data," *Journal of Consumer Research* 21 (September 1994): 219–235.

51. Kalpesh Kaushik Desai and Debabrata Talukdar, "Relationship Between Product Groups' Price Perceptions, Shopper's Basket Size, and Grocery Store's Overall Store Price Image," *Psychology and Marketing* 20, no. 10 (2003): 903.

52. Susan M. Broniarczyk et al., "Consumers' Perceptions of the Assortment Carried in a Grocery Category: The Impact of Item Reduction," *Journal of Marketing Research* 35 (May 1998): 166–176.

53. Daren Fonda, "Organic Growth," *Time Bonus Section Inside Business* (August 2002): Y1–Y4.

54. Allen Salkin, "Bargain-Hunting in a BMW: The Lure of 99 Cents," *The New York Times*, December 7, 2004, G3.

55. Frank H. Alpert and Michael A. Kamins, "An Empirical Investigation of Consumer Memory, Attitude and Perceptions Toward Pioneer and Follower Brands," *Journal of Marketing* 59 (October 1995): 34–45.

56. Berk Ataman and Burc Ulengin, "A Note on the Effect of Brand Image on Sales," *The Journal of Product and Brand Management* 12, no. 4/5 (2003): 237–251.

57. Nat Ives, "Wal-Mart Turns to Ads to Address Its Critics," **www.nytimes.com**, January 14, 2005; Stuart Elliott,

"Wal-Mart's New Realm: Reality TV," **www.nytimes.com**, June 3, 2005.

58. For example: Wen-yeh Huang, Holly Schrank, and Alan J. Dubinsky, "Effect of Brand Name on Consumers' Risk Perceptions of Online Shopping," *Journal of Consumer Behaviour* (October 2004): 40–51; Guilherme Pires, John Stanton, and Andrew Eckford, "Influences on the Perceived Risk of Purchasing Online," *Journal of Consumer Behaviour* (December 2004): 118–132; Bill Doolin, Stuart Dillon, Fiona Thompson, and James L. Corner, "Perceived Risk, the Internet Shopping Experience and Online Purchasing Behavior: A New Zealand Perspective," *Journal of Global Information Management* (April–June 2005): 66–89.

59. Johnnie L. Roberts, "TV's New Brand of Stars," *Newsweek*, November 22, 2004, 62–64; Stuart Elliott, "Burger King Takes a Product From TV to the Table," **www.nytimes.com**, January 21, 2005; Nat Ives, "Ads Embedded in Online News Raise Questions," **www.nytimes.com**, February 24, 2005; Stuart Elliott, "More Products Get Roles in Shows and Marketers Wonder if They're Getting Their Money's Worth," **www.nytimes.com**, March 29, 2005; Rob Walker, "Soap Opera," **www.nytimes.com**, April 3, 2005.

60. Brian Wansink and Koert van Ittersum, "Bottoms Up! The Influence of Elongation on Pouring and Consumption Value," *Journal of Consumer Research* (December 2003): 455–463; Brian Wansink, "Environmental Factors That Increase the Food Intake and Consumption Volune of Unknowing Consumers," *Annual Reviews* (Nutrition, 2004): 24, 455–479.

61. Barbara E. Kahn and Brian Wansink, "The Influence of Assortment Structure on Perceived Variety and Consumption Quantities," *Journal of Consumer Research* (March 2004): 519–534.

62. Thomas F. Stafford, "Alert or Oblivious? Factors Underlying Consumer Responses to Marketing Stimuli," *Psychology and Marketing* (September 2000): 745–760.

63. Wilson Bryan Key, *Subliminal Seduction* (New York: New American Library, 1973).

64. Natalie Angier, "Drugs, Sports, Body Image and G.I. Joe," *The New York Times*, December 22, 1998, F1.

chapterseven

› Consumer Learning

When Procter & Gamble introduced Crest some fifty years ago as the first toothpaste with fluoride, the product was endorsed by The American Dental Association as the best alternative for preventing teeth decay. Today, under the Crest brand name, P&G markets about one hundred versions of toothpaste, manual and electric toothbrushes, Whitestrips for whitening teeth, and flossing and mouth rinsing products. P&G also combined two of its oldest brands, Cascade dishwashing powder and Dawn liquid dish soap, to create Cascade 2-in-1 Action Packs for the dishwasher. These gelatin packs contain the ingredients of both products, are easier to use, and clean grease better than each of the original products. In 1912, the Oreo cookie was introduced and, for decades, only few and minor variations on the original were offered. But, since 2001, many variations of the cookie's size, filling, and biscuit flavor have been introduced, such as Uh Oh Oreo, Double Delight Peanut Butter & Chocolate Oreo, and Delight Mint 'N Creme Oreo.[1]

All these new products represent *extensions* of highly successful *brands* and follow the principles of *consumer learning*. When Cascade, Dawn, and Oreo were first introduced, they became successful because they worked and effectively fulfilled consumers' needs. Through years of exposure to repeated advertising and

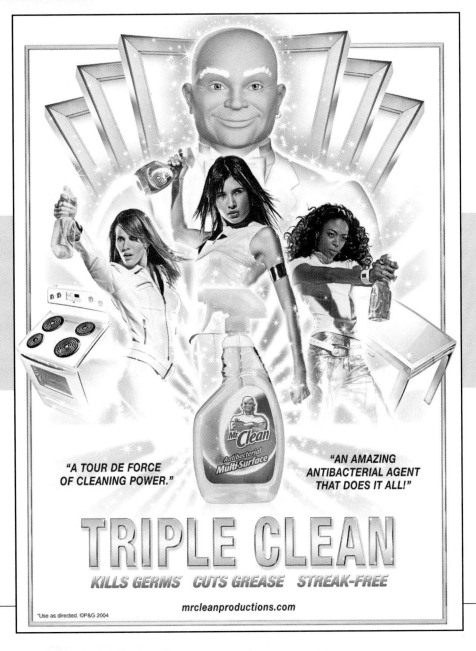

"A TOUR DE FORCE OF CLEANING POWER."

"AN AMAZING ANTIBACTERIAL AGENT THAT DOES IT ALL!"

Mr. Clean
Antibacterial
Multi-Surface

TRIPLE CLEAN

KILLS GERMS *CUTS GREASE* *STREAK-FREE*

mrcleanproductions.com

*Use as directed. ©P&G 2004

reminder advertising, most consumers remember these products and their advertised benefits while shopping. Each time they use them, they are repeatedly rewarded by the superior performances of Crest, Cascade and Dawn, or Oreo's rich and fun-to-take-apart-and-eat quality. When new products carrying the well-known brand names were advertised, consumers immediately *associated* them with the well-established brand names and were eager to try them. When the new products worked well, consumers once again were *rewarded*, they continued to purchase them and became *loyal* to them.

Repeating advertising messages about brands and their benefits, rewarding people for purchase behavior by selling products that provide superior benefits, getting consumers to make associations among different offerings under the same brand name, and developing brand loyalty are all elements of consumer learning. How individuals learn is a matter of great interest and importance to academicians, to psychologists, to consumer researchers, and to marketers.

The reason that marketers are concerned with how individuals learn is that they are vitally interested in teaching them, in their roles as consumers, about products, product attributes, and their potential benefits; where to buy them, how to use them, how to maintain them, and even how to dispose of them. They are also vitally interested in how effectively they have taught consumers to prefer their brands and to differentiate their products from competitive offerings. Marketing strategies are based on communicating with the consumer—directly, through advertisements, and indirectly, through product appearance, packaging, price, and distribution channels. Marketers want their communications to be noted, believed, remembered, and recalled. For these reasons, they are interested in every aspect of the learning process.

However, despite the fact that learning is all-pervasive in our lives, there is no single, universal theory of how people learn. Instead, there are two major schools of thought concerning the learning process: One consists of *behavioral theories,* the other of *cognitive theories.* Cognitive theorists view learning as a function of purely mental processes, whereas behavioral theorists focus almost exclusively on observable behaviors (responses) that occur as the result of exposure to stimuli.

In this chapter, we examine the two general categories of learning theory: **behavioral learning theory** and **cognitive learning theory**. Although these theories differ markedly in a number of essentials, each theory offers insights to marketers on how to shape their messages to consumers to bring about desired purchase behavior. We also discuss how consumers store, retain, and retrieve information, and how learning is measured. We continue with a discussion of how marketers use learning theories in their marketing strategies, and conclude with a discussion of the ethical issues involved with consumer learning and advertising.

the elements of consumer learning

Because not all learning theorists agree on how learning takes place, it is difficult to come up with a generally accepted definition of learning. From a marketing perspective, however, consumer learning can be thought of as *the process by which individuals acquire the purchase and consumption knowledge and experience that they apply to future related behavior.* Several points in this definition are worth noting.

First, consumer learning is a *process;* that is, it continually evolves and changes as a result of newly acquired *knowledge* (which may be gained from reading, from discussions, from observation, from thinking) or from actual *experience.* Both newly acquired knowledge and personal experience serve as *feedback* to the individual and provide the basis for *future behavior* in similar situations.

The role of *experience* in learning does not mean that all learning is deliberately sought. Though much learning is *intentional* (i.e., it is acquired as the result of a careful search for information), a great deal of learning is also *incidental,* acquired by accident or without much effort. For example, some ads may induce learning (e.g., of new products under familiar brand names such as the ones discussed earlier), even though the consumer's attention is elsewhere (on a magazine article rather than the advertisement on the facing page). Other ads are sought out and carefully read by consumers contemplating a major purchase decision.

The term **learning** encompasses the total range of learning, from simple, almost reflexive responses, to the learning of abstract concepts and complex problem solving. Most learning theorists recognize the existence of different types of learning and explain the differences through the use of distinctive models of learning.

Despite their different viewpoints, learning theorists in general agree that in order for learning to occur, certain basic elements must be present. The elements included in most learning theories are *motivation, cues, response,* and *reinforcement.* These concepts are discussed first because they tend to recur in the theories discussed later in this chapter.

Motivation

The concept of **motivation** is important to learning theory. Remember, motivation is based on needs and goals. Motivation acts as a spur to learning. For example, men and women who want to take up bicycle riding for fitness and recreation are motivated to learn all they can about bike riding and also to practice often. They may seek information concerning the prices, quality, and characteristics of bicycles and "learn" which bicycles are the best for the kind of riding that they do. They will also read any articles in their local newspapers about bicycle trails and may seek online information about "active vacations" that involve biking or hiking. Conversely, individuals who are not interested in bike riding are likely to ignore all information related to the activity. The goal object (bicycle riding in order to relax and stay fit) simply has no relevance for them. The degree of relevance, or *involvement,* determines the consumer's level of motivation to search for knowledge or information about a product or service. (*Involvement theory,* as it has come to be known, is discussed later in the chapter.) Uncovering consumer motives is one of the prime tasks of marketers, who then try to teach motivated consumer segments why and how their products will fulfill the consumers' needs.

Cues

If motives serve to stimulate learning, **cues** are the stimuli that give direction to these motives. An advertisement for an exotic trip that includes bike riding may serve as a cue for bike riders, who may suddenly "recognize" that they "need" a vacation. The ad is the cue, or *stimulus,* that suggests a specific way to satisfy a salient motive. In the marketplace, price, styling, packaging, advertising, and store displays all serve as cues to help consumers fulfill their needs in product-specific ways.

Cues serve to direct consumer drives when they are consistent with consumer expectations. Marketers must be careful to provide cues that do not upset those expectations. For example, consumers expect designer clothes to be expensive and to be sold in upscale retail stores. Thus, a high-fashion designer should sell his or her clothes only through exclusive stores and advertise only in upscale fashion magazines. Each aspect of the marketing mix must reinforce the others if cues are to serve as the stimuli that guide consumer actions in the direction desired by the marketer.

Response

How individuals react to a drive or cue—how they behave—constitute their **response**. Learning can occur even when responses are not overt. The automobile manufacturer that provides consistent cues to a consumer may not always succeed in stimulating a purchase. However, if the manufacturer succeeds in forming a favorable image of a particular automobile model in the consumer's mind, it is likely that the consumer will consider that make or model when he or she is ready to buy.

A response is not tied to a need in a one-to-one fashion. Indeed, as was discussed in Chapter 4, a need or motive may evoke a whole variety of responses. For example, there are many ways to respond to the need for physical exercise besides riding bicycles. Cues provide some direction, but there are many cues competing for the consumer's attention. Which response the consumer makes depends heavily on previous learning; that, in turn, depends on how related responses have been reinforced.

FIGURE 7.1

Source: Courtesy of Neutrogena Corporation.

Product Usage Leads to Reinforcement

Reinforcement

Reinforcement increases the likelihood that a specific response will occur in the future as the result of particular cues or stimuli. For example, Figure 7.1 presents a three-step process for facial skin care based on three products (i.e., cues). This ad is instructional and designed to generate consumer learning. If a college student finds that the cleansing routine based on the three products featured in this ad relieves his acne problem, he is likely to continue buying and using these products. Through positive reinforcement, learning has taken place, since the facial cleansing system lived up to expectations. On the other hand, if the products had not provided relief from the problem when first used, the student would have no reason to associate the brand with acne relief in the future. Because of the absence of reinforcement, it is unlikely that he would buy that brand again.

With these basic principles established, we can now discuss some well-known theories or models of how learning occurs.

behavioral learning theories

Behavioral learning theories are sometimes referred to as **stimulus-response theories** because they are based on the premise that observable responses to specific external stimuli signal that learning has taken place. When a person acts (responds) in a predictable way to a known stimulus, he or she is said to have "learned." Behavioral theories are not so much concerned with the *process* of learning as they are with the *inputs* and *outcomes* of learning; that is, in the stimuli that consumers select from the environment and the observable behaviors that result. Two behavioral theories with great relevance to marketing are **classical conditioning** and **instrumental** (or **operant**) **conditioning**.

Classical conditioning

Early classical conditioning theorists regarded all organisms (both animal and human) as relatively passive entities that could be taught certain behaviors through repetition (i.e., *conditioning*). In everyday speech, the word *conditioning* has come to mean a kind of "knee-jerk" (or automatic) response to a situation built up through repeated exposure. If you get a headache every time you think of visiting your Aunt Gertrude, your reaction may be conditioned from years of boring visits with her.

Ivan Pavlov, a Russian physiologist, was the first to describe conditioning and to propose it as a general model of how learning occurs. According to Pavlovian theory, conditioned learning results when a stimulus that is paired with another stimulus that elicits a known response serves to produce the same response when used alone.

Pavlov demonstrated what he meant by **conditioned learning** in his studies with dogs. The dogs were hungry and highly motivated to eat. In his experiments, Pavlov sounded a bell and then immediately applied a meat paste to the dogs' tongues, which caused them to salivate. Learning (conditioning) occurred when, after a sufficient number of repetitions of the bell sound followed almost immediately by the food, the bell sound alone caused the dogs to salivate. The dogs associated the bell sound (the *conditioned* stimulus) with the meat paste (the *unconditioned* stimulus) and, after a number of pairings, gave the same unconditioned response (salivation) to the bell alone as they did to the meat paste. The unconditioned response to the meat paste became the conditioned response to the bell. Figure 7.2A models this relationship. An analogous situation would be one in which the smells of dinner cooking would cause your mouth to water. If you usually listen to the 6 o'clock news while waiting for dinner to be served, you would tend to associate the 6 o'clock news with dinner, so that eventually the sounds of the 6 o'clock news alone might cause your mouth to water, even if dinner was not being prepared and even if you were not hungry. Figure 7.2B diagrams this basic relationship.

In a consumer behavior context, an **unconditioned stimulus** might consist of a well-known brand symbol (such as the Neutrogena name) that implies dermatologists' endorsement and pure (chemically free) products (i.e., containing few potentially irritating ingredients, such as perfume scents commonly added to personal cleansing products). This previously acquired consumer perception of Neutrogena is the *unconditioned response*. **Conditioned stimuli** might consist of new products bearing the well-known symbol (such as the items depicted in Figure 7.1), and the *conditioned response* would be trying these products because of the belief that they embody the same attributes with which the Neutrogena name is associated.

Cognitive associative learning

Contemporary behavioral scientists view classical conditioning as the learning of associations among events that allows the organism to anticipate and "represent" its environment. According to this view, the relationship (or contiguity) between the conditioned stimulus and the unconditioned stimulus (the bell and the meat paste) influenced the dogs' expectations, which in turn influenced their behavior (salivation). Classical conditioning, then, rather than being a reflexive action, is seen as **cognitive associative learning**—not the acquisition of new reflexes, but the acquisition of new knowledge about the world.[2]

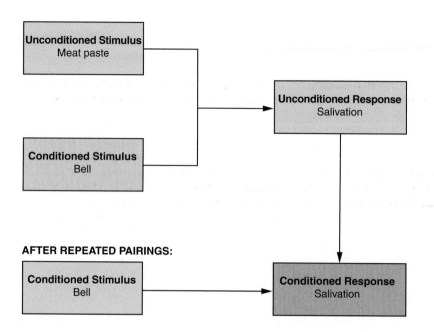

FIGURE 7.2A

Pavlovian Model of Classical Conditioning

FIGURE 7.2B

Analogous Model of Classical Conditioning

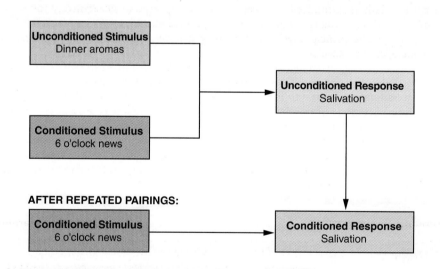

According to some researchers, optimal conditioning—that is, the creation of a strong association between the conditioned stimulus (CS) and the unconditioned stimulus (US)—requires (1) forward conditioning (i.e., the CS should precede the US); (2) repeated pairings of the CS and the US; (3) a CS and US that logically belong together; (4) a CS that is novel and unfamiliar; and (5) a US that is biologically or symbolically salient. This model is known as **neo-Pavlovian conditioning**.

Under neo-Pavlovian theory, the consumer can be viewed as an information seeker who uses logical and perceptual relations among events, along with his or her own preconceptions, to form a sophisticated representation of the world. Conditioning is the learning that results from exposure to relationships among events in the environment; such exposure creates expectations as to the structure of the environment.

Strategic applications of classical conditioning

Three basic concepts derive from classical conditioning: *repetition, stimulus generalization,* and *stimulus discrimination.* Each of these concepts is important to the strategic applications of consumer behavior.

Repetition   **Repetition** increases the strength of the association between a conditioned stimulus and an unconditioned stimulus and slows the process of forgetting. However, research suggests that there is a limit to the amount of repetition that will aid retention. Although some overlearning (i.e., repetition beyond what is necessary for learning) aids retention, at some point an individual can become satiated with numerous exposures, and both attention and retention will decline. This effect, known as **advertising wearout**, can be moderated by varying the advertising message. Some marketers avoid wearout by using *cosmetic variations* in their ads (using different backgrounds, different print types, different advertising spokespersons) while repeating the same advertising theme. For example, the classic, decades-old Absolut Vodka campaign has used the same theme with highly creative and varied backgrounds, relating the product to holidays, trends, and cultural symbols in the United States and across the world (e.g., see Figure 7.3). One study showed that brand familiarity impacted the effectiveness of repeating ads. The effectiveness of repeated ads for an unfamiliar brand declined over time, but when the same advertising was used for a well-known and familiar brand, repetition wearout was postponed.[3]

Substantive variations are changes in advertising content across different versions of an advertisement. For example, the two ads in Figure 7.4 stress two different attributes of the same product. Varied ads provide marketers with several strategic advantages. Consumers exposed to substantively varied ads process more information about product attributes and have more positive thoughts about the product than those exposed to cosmetic variations. Attitudes formed as a result of exposure to substantively varied ads are more resistant to change in the face of competitive attack.

Although the principle of repetition is well established among advertisers, not everyone agrees on how much repetition is enough. Some marketing scholars believe that just three exposures to an advertisement are needed: one to make consumers aware of the product, a second to show consumers the relevance of the product, and a third to remind them of its benefits. This is known as the *three-hit theory.* Others think it may take 11 to 12 repetitions to increase the likelihood that consumers will actually receive the three exposures basic to the so-called three-hit theory.

The effectiveness of repetition is somewhat dependent upon the amount of competitive advertising to which the consumer is exposed. The higher the level of competitive ads, the greater the likelihood that *interference* will occur, causing consumers to forget previous learning that resulted from repetition.

Stimulus Generalization   According to classical conditioning theorists, learning depends not only on repetition but also on the ability of individuals to generalize. Pavlov found, for example, that a dog could learn to salivate not only to the sound of a bell but also to the somewhat similar sound of jangling keys. If we were not capable of **stimulus generalization**—that is, of making the same response to slightly different stimuli—not much learning would take place.

Stimulus generalization explains why some imitative "me-too" products succeed in the marketplace: Consumers confuse them with the original product they have seen advertised. It also explains why manufacturers of private-label brands try to make their packaging closely resemble the national brand leaders. They are hoping that consumers will confuse their packages with the leading brand and buy their product rather than the leading brand. Similarly packaged competitive products result in millions of lost sales for well-positioned and extensively advertised brands.

Product Line, Form, and Category Extensions   The principle of stimulus generalization is applied by marketers to *product line, form,* and *category extensions.* In **product line**

FIGURE 7.3

Source: Under permission by
V&S Vin & Sprit AB (PUBI).
Absolut Country of Sweden
Vodka & Logo, Absolut, Absolut
Bottle Design and Absolut
Calligraphy are the trademarks
owned by V&S Vin & Sprit AB
(PUBI). © 2005 V&S Vin & Sprit
AB. Photographer Shu Akashi.

Absolut Targeting a
Techno-Savvy Consumer

extensions, the marketer adds related products to an already established brand, knowing that the new products are more likely to be adopted when they are associated with a known and trusted brand name (see Figure 7.5).

Marketers also offer **product form extensions**, such as Crest Toothpaste to Crest Whitestrips, Listerine mouthwash to ListerinePaks (see Figure 7.6), and Ivory bath soap to Ivory liquid soap to Ivory shower gel. Marketers also offer **product category extensions** that generally target new market segments (see Figure 7.7).

The success of product extensions depends on a number of factors. If the image of the parent brand is one of quality and the new item is logically linked to the brand, consumers

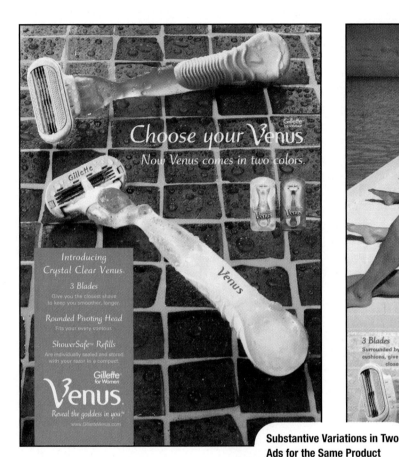

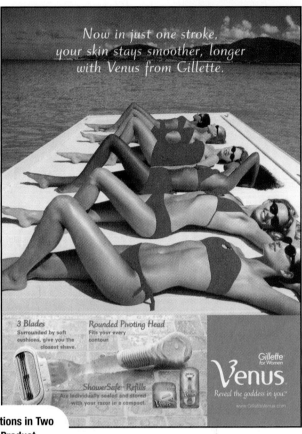

Substantive Variations in Two Ads for the Same Product

are more likely to bring positive associations to the new offerings introduced as product line, form, or category extensions. For example, Tylenol, a highly trusted brand, initially introduced line extensions by making its products available in a number of different forms (tablets, capsules, gelcaps), strengths (regular, extra strength, and children's), and package sizes. It then extended its brand name to a wide range of related remedies for colds, flu, sinus congestion, and allergies, further segmenting the line for adults, children, and infants. The number of different products affiliated with a brand strengthens the brand name, as long as the company maintains a quality image across all brand extensions. Failure to do so, in the long run, is likely to negatively affect consumer confidence and evaluations of all the brand's offerings. One study showed that brands that include diverse products are likely to offer more successful brand extensions than brands that include similar products. The study also confirmed that the likely associations between the benefits offered by the brand and its new extension are the key to consumers' reactions to the brand extension.[4]

Family Branding   **Family branding**—the practice of marketing a whole line of company products under the same brand name—is another strategy that capitalizes on the consumer's ability to generalize favorable brand associations from one product to others. Campbell's, originally a marketer of soups, continues to add new food products to its product line under the Campbell's brand name (such as canned soups, frozen meals, soup to be eaten on-the-go, and tomato juice), thus achieving ready acceptance for the

Source: © Procter & Gamble
Company. Used by permission.
All rights reserved.

FIGURE 7.5

Product Line Extention

new products from satisfied consumers of other Campbell's food products. The Ralph
Lauren designer label on men's and women's clothing helps to achieve ready acceptance for these products in the upscale sportswear market. Clearly, managing a family
brand is more complex than managing a brand that includes only closely related items.
One study demonstrated that consumers are likely to expect variability in the performances of the products under the family brand if the company does not address this
issue in the information provided with new products introduced; the study singles out
the importance of consistent positioning even as the number of offerings under a given
name increases.[5]

FIGURE 7.6

Source: © The Procter & Gamble Company. Used by Permission. Courtesy of Pfizer Consumer Healthcare, Pfizer Inc.

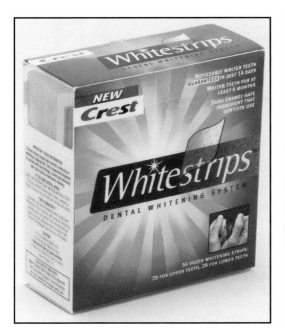

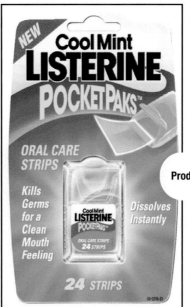

Product Form Extensions

On the other hand, Procter & Gamble (P&G) was built on the strength of its many individual brands in the same product category. For example, the company offers multiple brands of laundry products, of antiperspirants, and of hair care products, including shampoo. Although offering many brands of the same product is expensive, the combined weight of its brands has always provided Procter & Gamble (the **umbrella brand**) with great power in negotiating with advertising media and securing desirable shelf space for its products in the United States and around the world. It also enables the company to effectively combat any competitors who may try to introduce products in markets dominated by P&G.

Donald Trump, the real estate tycoon, made his own surname into a brand name, *Trump,* a name attached to multiple buildings, hotels, and casinos to give consumers feelings of confidence in their quality. He extended this brand into television with his highly successful reality show *The Apprentice,* which has itself developed brand extensions. Real estate developers offer Mr. Trump a percentage in their new developments in return for the use of his name. However, he has to be vigilant that the Trump name is not attached to inferior buildings or hotels or TV shows because the brand would lose its carefully built up quality image.

Retail private branding often achieves the same effect as family branding. For example, Wal-Mart used to advertise that its stores carried only "brands you trust." Now, the name Wal-Mart itself has become a "brand" that consumers have confidence in, and the name confers brand value on Wal-Mart's store brands.

Licensing   **Licensing**—allowing a well-known brand name to be affixed to products of another manufacturer—is a marketing strategy that operates on the principle of *stimulus generalization.* The names of designers, manufacturers, celebrities, corporations, and even cartoon characters are attached for a fee (i.e., "rented") to a variety of products, enabling the licensees to achieve instant recognition and implied quality for the licensed products. Some successful licensors include Liz Claiborne, Tommy Hilfiger, Calvin Klein, and Christian Dior, whose names appear on an exceptionally wide variety of products, from sheets to shoes and luggage to perfume. Figure 7.8 shows an ad for eyeglasses bearing the name of the well-known shoe manufacturer Kenneth Cole.

FIGURE 7.7

Source: Courtesy of Neutrogena Corporation.

Product Category Extensions

Corporations also license their names and trademarks, usually for some form of brand extension, where the name of the corporation is licensed to the maker of a related product and thereby enters a new product category (e.g., Godiva chocolates licensed its name for Godiva liqueur). Corporations also license their names for purely promotional licensing, in which popular company logos (such as "Always Coca-Cola") are stamped on clothing, toys, coffee mugs, and the like. The Vatican Library licenses its name for a variety of products from luggage to bed linens, and the Mormon Church has expanded its licensing activities to apparel and home decorating items.

FIGURE 7.8

Source: Courtesy of Kenneth
Cole Productions, Inc.

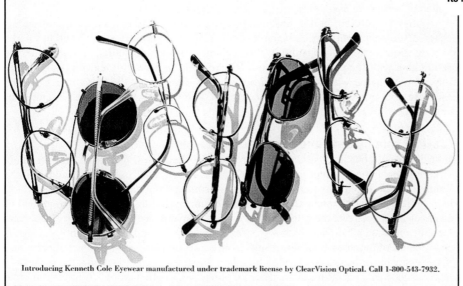

No matter what your point of view, we hope you see things our way.

— Kenneth Cole

**Shoe Manufacturer Licenses
Its Name**

Introducing Kenneth Cole Eyewear manufactured under trademark license by ClearVision Optical. Call 1-800-543-7932.

The increase in licensing has made *counterfeiting* a booming business, as counterfeiters add well-known licensor names to a variety of products without benefit of contract or quality control. Aside from the loss of sales revenue because of counterfeiting, the authentic brands also suffer the consequences associated with zero quality control over counterfeit products that bear their names. It is also increasingly difficult to identify fakes of such expensive and upscale goods as Christian Dior bags, Gucci shoes, and Chanel No. 5 perfume. Many firms are now legally pursuing retailers that sell counterfeit branded goods; many also are employing specialized technology to make their products more counterfeit-proof.[6]

Stimulus Discrimination **Stimulus discrimination** is the opposite of stimulus generalization and results in the selection of a specific stimulus from among similar stimuli. The consumer's ability to discriminate among similar stimuli is the basis of positioning strategy (discussed in Chapter 6), which seeks to establish a unique image for a brand in the consumer's mind.

Positioning In our over-communicated society, the key to stimulus discrimination is effective **positioning**, a major competitive advantage. The image—or position—that a product or service holds in the mind of the consumer is critical to its success. When a marketer targets consumers with a strong communications program that stresses the unique ways in which its product will satisfy the consumer's needs, it wants the consumer to differentiate its product from among competitive products on the shelf. Unlike the imitator who hopes consumers will *generalize* their perceptions and attribute special characteristics of the market leader's products to its own products, market leaders want the consumer to *discriminate* among similar stimuli. Major marketers are constantly vigilant concerning store brand look-alikes, and they quickly file suit against retailers that they believe are cannibalizing their sales. They want their products to be recognized as uniquely fulfilling consumers' needs. Studies have shown that the favorable attitudes resulting from effective positioning and stimulus discrimination are usually retained long enough to influence future purchase behavior.[7]

Product Differentiation Most product differentiation strategies are designed to distinguish a product or brand from that of competitors on the basis of an attribute that is relevant, meaningful, and valuable to consumers. However, many marketers also successfully differentiate their brands on an attribute that may actually be irrelevant to creating the implied benefit, such as a noncontributing ingredient or a color.

It often is quite difficult to unseat a brand leader once stimulus discrimination has occurred. One explanation is that the leader is usually first in the market and has had a longer period to "teach" consumers (through advertising and selling) to associate the brand name with the product. In general, the longer the period of learning—of associating a brand name with a specific product—the more likely the consumer is to discriminate and the less likely to generalize the stimulus. Figure 7.9 is an example of stimulus discrimination.

Classical conditioning and consumer behavior

The principles of classical conditioning provide the theoretical underpinnings for many marketing applications. Repetition, stimulus generalization, and stimulus discrimination are all major applied concepts that help to explain consumer behavior in the marketplace. However, they do not explain all behavioral consumer learning. Although a great deal of consumer behavior (e.g., the purchase of branded convenience goods) is shaped to some extent by repeated advertising messages stressing a unique competitive advantage, a significant amount of purchase behavior results from careful evaluation of product alternatives. Our assessments of products are often based on the degree of satisfaction—the rewards— we experience as a result of making specific purchases; in other words, from instrumental conditioning.

Instrumental conditioning

Like classical conditioning, **instrumental conditioning** requires a link between a stimulus and a response. However, in instrumental conditioning, the stimulus that results in the most satisfactory response is the one that is learned.

Instrumental learning theorists believe that learning occurs through a trial-and-error process, with habits formed as a result of rewards received for certain responses or behaviors. This model of learning applies to many situations in which consumers learn about products, services, and retail stores. For example, consumers learn which stores carry the type of clothing they prefer at prices they can afford to pay by shopping in a number of

FIGURE 7.9

Source: © Farmland Dairies
LLC. Used with permission.

Stimulus Discrimination

stores. Once they find a store that carries clothing that meets their needs, they are likely to patronize that store to the exclusion of others. Every time they purchase a shirt or a sweater there that they really like, their store loyalty is rewarded (*reinforced*), and their patronage of that store is more likely to be repeated. Whereas classical conditioning is useful in explaining how consumers learn very simple kinds of behaviors, instrumental conditioning is more helpful in explaining complex, goal-directed activities.

The name most closely associated with instrumental (*operant*) conditioning is that of the American psychologist B. F. Skinner. According to Skinner, most individual learning occurs in a controlled environment in which individuals are "rewarded" for choosing an appropriate behavior. In consumer behavior terms, instrumental conditioning suggests that consumers learn by means of a trial-and-error process in which some purchase behaviors result in more favorable outcomes (i.e., rewards) than other purchase behaviors. A favorable experience is "instrumental" in teaching the individual to repeat a specific behavior.

Like Pavlov, Skinner developed his model of learning by working with animals. Small animals, such as rats and pigeons, were placed in his "Skinner box"; if they made appropriate movements (e.g., if they depressed levers or pecked keys), they received food (a positive reinforcement). Skinner and his many adherents have done amazing things with this simple learning model, including teaching pigeons to play Ping-Pong and even to dance. In a marketing context, the consumer who tries several brands and styles of jeans before finding a style that fits her figure (positive reinforcement) has engaged in instrumental learning. Presumably, the brand that fits best is the one she will continue to buy. This model of instrumental conditioning is presented in Figure 7.10.

Reinforcement of behavior

Skinner distinguished two types of reinforcement (or reward) that influence the likelihood that a response will be repeated. The first type, **positive reinforcement**, consists of events that strengthen the likelihood of a specific response. Using a shampoo that leaves your hair feeling silky and clean is likely to result in a repeat purchase of the shampoo. **Negative reinforcement** is an unpleasant or negative outcome that also serves to encourage a specific behavior. An advertisement that shows a model with wrinkled skin is designed to encourage consumers to buy and use the advertised skin cream.

Fear appeals in ad messages are examples of negative reinforcement. Many life insurance advertisements rely on negative reinforcement to encourage the purchase of life insurance. The ads warn husbands of the dire consequences to their wives and children in the event of their sudden death. Marketers of headache remedies use negative reinforcement when they illustrate the unpleasant symptoms of an unrelieved headache, as do marketers of mouthwash when they show the loneliness suffered by someone with bad breath. In each of these cases, the consumer is encouraged to avoid the negative consequences by buying the advertised product.

Either positive or negative reinforcement can be used to elicit a desired response. However, negative reinforcement should not be confused with punishment, which is

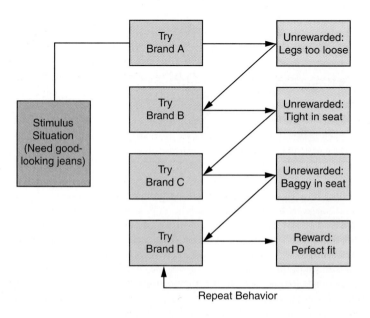

A Model of Instrumental Conditioning

FIGURE 7.10

designed to *discourage* behavior. For example, parking tickets are not negative rein-forcement; they are a form of "punishment" designed to discourage drivers from parking illegally.

Extinction and Forgetting   When a learned response is no longer reinforced, it diminishes to the point of *extinction,* that is, to the point at which the link between the stimulus and the expected reward is eliminated. If a consumer is no longer satisfied with the service a retail store provides, the link between the stimulus (the store) and the response (expected satisfaction) is no longer reinforced, and there is little likeli-hood that the consumer will return. When behavior is no longer reinforced, it is "unlearned." There is a difference, however, between extinction and *forgetting.* A couple who have not visited a once-favorite restaurant for a very long time may sim-ply forget how much they used to enjoy eating there and not think to return. Thus, their behavior is unlearned because of lack of use rather than lack of reinforcement. Forgetting is often related to the passage of time; this is known as the process of *decay.* Marketers can overcome forgetting through repetition, and can combat extinction through the deliberate enhancement of consumer satisfaction. Sometimes, marketers may cause extinction deliberately and "undo" a previously learned association. For example, a large car service in New York City known for many years as Tel Aviv Car Service is now advertising itself as the "Dial 7s" car service in reference to its phone number (consisting of seven consecutive sevens) and, quite possibly, to undo its associ-ation in the consumer's mind with Israeli ownership.

Strategic applications of instrumental conditioning

Marketers effectively utilize the concepts of consumer instrumental learning when they provide positive reinforcement by assuring customer satisfaction with the product, the service, and the total buying experience.

Customer Satisfaction (Reinforcement)   The objective of all marketing efforts should be to maximize customer satisfaction. Marketers must be certain to provide the best pos-sible product for the money and to avoid raising consumer expectations for product (or service) performance beyond what the product can deliver. Aside from the experience of using the product itself, consumers can receive reinforcement from other elements in the purchase situation, such as the environment in which the transaction or service takes place, the attention and service provided by employees, and the amenities provided. For example, an upscale beauty salon, in addition to a beautiful environment, may offer coffee and soft drinks to waiting clients and provide free local telephone service at each hairdressing station. Even if the styling outcome is not so great, the client may feel so pampered with the atmosphere and service that she looks forward to her next visit. On the other hand, even with the other positive reinforcements in place, if the salon's employees are so busy talking with each other while the service is being rendered that the client feels ignored, she is not likely to return.

Recent data from the American Customer Satisfaction Index—the benchmark source regarding customer satisfaction with businesses—illustrate that many companies wrongly assume that lower prices and more diverse product lines make customers more satisfied. Instead, it appears that companies that create personal connections with customers, and also offer diverse product lines and competitive prices, are the ones providing the best reinforcement, resulting in satisfaction and repeat patronage.[8] Some hotels offer reinforcements in the form of small amenities, such as chocolates on the pillow or bottled water on the dresser; others send platters of fruit or even bottles of wine to returning guests to show their appreciation for continued patronage. Most frequent shopper programs are based on enhancing positive reinforcement and encour-aging continued patronage. The more a consumer uses the service, the greater the rewards. Kellogg's provides a frequent user program by including coupons on the top of its cereal boxes that can be accumulated and exchanged for various premiums, such as a coffee mug or denim shirt emblazoned with the company's logo.

Relationship marketing—developing a close personalized relationship with customers—is another form of nonproduct reinforcement. Knowing that she will be advised of a forthcoming sale or that selected merchandise will be set aside for her next visit cements the loyalty that a consumer may have for a retail store. The ability to telephone his "personal" banker to transfer funds between accounts or to make other banking transactions without coming into the bank reinforces the satisfaction a consumer may have with his bank. Service companies are particularly vulnerable to interruptions in customer reinforcement because of service failures that cannot be controlled in advance. As a result, astute service providers have implemented *service recovery* measures that provide extra rewards to customers who have experienced service failures. Studies indicate that customers who emotionally bonded with the service provider were less forgiving than other customers because they felt truly "betrayed," and that the effectiveness of service recovery measures had the strongest impact on loyal customers.[9]

Reinforcement Schedules Marketers have found that product quality must be consistently high and provide satisfaction to the customer with each use for desired consumer behavior to continue. However, they have also discovered that some nonproduct rewards do not have to be offered each time the transaction takes place; even an occasional reward provides reinforcement and encourages consumer patronage. For example, airlines may occasionally upgrade a passenger at the gate, or a clothing discounter may from time to time announce a one-hour sale over the store sound system. The promise of possibly receiving a reward provides positive reinforcement and encourages consumer patronage.

Marketers have identified three types of reinforcement schedules: *total* (or continuous) reinforcement, *systematic* (fixed ratio) reinforcement, and *random* (variable ratio) reinforcement. An example of a total (or continuous) reinforcement schedule is the free after-dinner drink or fruit plate always served to patrons at certain restaurants. Needless to say, the basic product or service rendered is expected to provide total satisfaction (reinforcement) each time it is used.

A *fixed ratio* reinforcement schedule provides reinforcement every "*n*th" time the product or service is purchased (say, every third time). For example, a retailer may send a credit voucher to account holders every three months based on a percentage of the previous quarter's purchases. A *variable ratio* reinforcement schedule rewards consumers on a random basis or on an average frequency basis (such as every third or tenth transaction). Gambling casinos operate on the basis of variable ratios. People pour money into slot machines (which are programmed to pay off on a variable ratio), hoping for the big win. Variable ratios tend to engender high rates of desired behavior and are somewhat resistant to extinction—perhaps because, for many consumers, hope springs eternal. Other examples of variable ratio schedules include lotteries, sweepstakes, door prizes, and contests that require certain consumer behaviors for eligibility.

Shaping Reinforcement performed *before* the desired consumer behavior actually takes place is called **shaping**. Shaping increases the probabilities that certain desired consumer behavior will occur. For example, retailers recognize that they must first attract customers to their stores before they can expect them to do the bulk of their shopping there. Many retailers provide some form of preliminary reinforcement (shaping) to encourage consumers to visit only their store. For example, some retailers offer loss leaders—popular products at severely discounted prices—to the first hundred or so customers to arrive, since those customers are likely to stay to do much of their shopping. By reinforcing the behavior that's needed to enable the desired consumer behavior to take place, marketers increase the probability that the desired behavior will occur. Car dealers recognize that in order to sell new model cars, they must first encourage people to visit their showrooms and to test-drive their cars. Hopefully, the test-drive will result in a sale. Using shaping principles, many car dealers encourage showroom visits by providing small gifts (such as key chains and DVDs), larger gifts (e.g., a $10 check) to test-drive the car, and a rebate check upon placement of an order. They use a multi-step shaping process to achieve desired consumer learning.

Massed versus distributed learning

As illustrated previously, *timing* has an important influence on consumer learning. Should a learning schedule be spread out over a period of time (*distributed learning,*) or should it be "bunched up" all at once (*massed learning*)? The question is an important one for advertisers planning a media schedule, because massed advertising produces more initial learning, whereas a distributed schedule usually results in learning that persists longer. When advertisers want an immediate impact (e.g., to introduce a new product or to counter a competitor's blitz campaign), they generally use a massed schedule to hasten consumer learning. However, when the goal is long-term repeat buying on a regular basis, a distributed schedule is preferable. A distributed schedule, with ads repeated on a regular basis, usually results in more long-term learning and is relatively immune to extinction.

Modeling or observational learning

Learning theorists have noted that a considerable amount of learning takes place in the absence of direct reinforcement, either positive or negative, through a process psychologists call **modeling** or **observational learning** (also called *vicarious learning*). Consumers often observe how others behave in response to certain situations (stimuli) and the ensuing results (reinforcement) that occur, and they imitate (model) the positively reinforced behavior when faced with similar situations. Modeling is *the process through which individuals learn behavior by observing the behavior of others and the consequences of such behavior.* Their role models are usually people they admire because of such traits as appearance, accomplishment, skill, and even social class.

Advertisers recognize the importance of observational learning in their selection of models—whether celebrities or unknowns. If a teenager sees an ad that depicts social success as the outcome of using a certain brand of shampoo, she will want to buy it. If her brother sees a commercial that shows a muscular young athlete eating Wheaties—"the breakfast of champions"—he will want to eat it, too. Indeed, vicarious (or observational) learning is the basis of much of today's advertising. Consumer models with whom the target audience can identify are shown achieving positive outcomes to common problem situations through the use of the advertised product. Children learn much of their social behavior and consumer behavior by observing their older siblings or their parents. They imitate the behavior of those they see rewarded, expecting to be rewarded similarly if they adopt the same behavior.

Sometimes ads depict negative consequences for certain types of behavior. This is particularly true of public policy ads, which may show the negative consequences of smoking, of driving too fast, or of taking drugs. By observing the actions of others and the resulting consequences, consumers learn vicariously to recognize appropriate and inappropriate behavior.

cognitive learning theory

Not all learning takes place as the result of repeated trials. A considerable amount of learning takes place as the result of consumer thinking and problem solving. Sudden learning is also a reality. When confronted with a problem, we sometimes see the solution instantly. More often, however, we are likely to search for information on which to base a decision, and we carefully evaluate what we learn in order to make the best decision possible for our purposes.

Learning based on mental activity is called **cognitive learning**. Cognitive learning theory holds that the kind of learning most characteristic of human beings is *problem solving,* which enables individuals to gain some control over their environment. Unlike behavioral learning theory, cognitive theory holds that learning involves complex *mental processing of information.* Instead of stressing the importance of repetition or the association of a reward with a specific response, cognitive theorists emphasize the role of motivation and mental processes in producing a desired response.

Information processing

Just as a computer processes information received as input, so too does the human mind process the information it receives as input. **Information processing** is related to both the consumer's cognitive ability and the complexity of the information to be processed. Consumers process product information by attributes, brands, comparisons between brands, or a combination of these factors. Although the attributes included in the brand's message and the number of available alternatives influence the intensity or degree of information processing, consumers with higher cognitive ability apparently acquire more product information and are more capable of integrating information on several product attributes than consumers with lesser ability.

Individuals also differ in terms of **imagery**—that is, in their ability to form mental images—and these differences influence their ability to recall information. Individual differences in imagery processing can be measured with tests of *imagery vividness* (the ability to evoke clear images), *processing style* (preference for and frequency of visual versus verbal processing), and *daydream (fantasy) content* and *frequency.*[10]

The more experience a consumer has with a product category, the greater his or her ability to make use of product information. Greater familiarity with the product category also increases cognitive ability and learning during a new purchase decision, particularly with regard to technical information. Some consumers learn by analogy; that is, they transfer knowledge about products they are familiar with to new or unfamiliar products in order to enhance their understanding. One study found that when people exerted more cognitive effort in processing information about a product, they experienced a process-induced negative effect toward that alternative and were more likely to choose a product that required less effort to evaluate. However, the negative effect did not influence product choice for a clearly superior product.[11]

How consumers store, retain, and retrieve information

Of central importance to the processing of information is the human memory. A basic research concern of most cognitive scientists is discovering how information gets stored in memory, how it is retained, and how it is retrieved.

Because information processing occurs in stages, it is generally believed that there are separate and sequential "storehouses" in memory where information is kept temporarily before further processing: a *sensory store,* a *short-term store,* and a *long-term store.*

Sensory Store All data come to us through our senses; however, the senses do not transmit whole images as a camera does. Instead, each sense receives a fragmented piece of information (such as the smell, color, shape, and feel of a flower) and transmits it to the brain in parallel, where the perceptions of a single instant are synchronized and perceived as a single image, in a single moment of time. The image of a sensory input lasts for just a second or two in the mind's **sensory store**. If it is not processed, it is lost immediately. As noted in Chapter 6, we are constantly bombarded with stimuli from the environment and subconsciously block out a great deal of information that we do not "need" or cannot use. For marketers, this means that although it is relatively easy to get information into the consumer's sensory store, it is difficult to make a lasting impression. Furthermore, the brain automatically and subconsciously "tags" all perceptions with a value, either positive or negative; this evaluation, added to the initial perception in the first microsecond of cognition, tends to remain unless further information is processed. This would explain why first impressions tend to last and why it is hazardous for a marketer to introduce a product prematurely into the marketplace.

Short-term Store The **short-term store** (known as "working memory") is the stage of real memory in which information is processed and held for just a brief period. Anyone who has ever looked up a number in a telephone book, only to forget it just before dialing, knows how briefly information lasts in short-term storage. If information in the short-term store undergoes the process known as *rehearsal* (i.e., the silent, mental repetition of

FIGURE 7.11

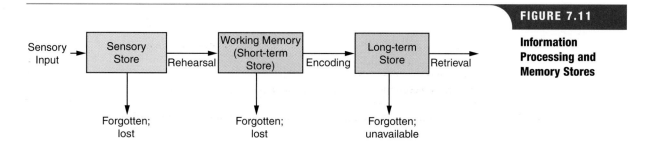

information), it is then transferred to the long-term store. The transfer process takes from 2 to 10 seconds. If information is not rehearsed and transferred, it is lost in about 30 seconds or less. The amount of information that can be held in short-term storage is limited to about four or five items.

Long-term Store   In contrast to the short-term store, where information lasts only a few seconds, the **long-term store** retains information for relatively extended periods of time. Although it is possible to forget something within a few minutes after the information has reached long-term storage, it is more common for data in long-term storage to last for days, weeks, or even years. Almost all of us, for example, can remember the name of our first-grade teacher. Figure 7.11 depicts the transfer of information received by the sensory store, through the short-term store, to long-term storage.

Rehearsal and Encoding   The amount of information available for delivery from short-term storage to long-term storage depends on the amount of **rehearsal** it is given. Failure to rehearse an input, either by repeating it or by relating it to other data, can result in fading and eventual loss of the information. Information can also be lost because of competition for attention. For example, if the short-term store receives a great number of inputs simultaneously from the sensory store, its capacity may be reduced to only two or three pieces of information.

The purpose of rehearsal is to hold information in short-term storage long enough for encoding to take place. **Encoding** is the process by which we select a word or visual image to represent a perceived object. Marketers, for example, help consumers encode brands by using brand symbols. Kellogg's uses Tony the Tiger on its Frosted Flakes; the Green Giant Company has its Jolly Green Giant. Dell Computer turns the *e* in its logo on its side for quick name recognition; Microsoft uses a stylized window, presumably on the world.

"Learning" a picture takes less time than learning verbal information, but both types of information are important in forming an overall mental image. A print ad with both an illustration and body copy is more likely to be encoded and stored than an illustration without verbal information. A study that compared the effects of visual and verbal advertising found that, when advertising copy and illustrations focus on different product attributes, the illustrations disproportionately influence consumer inferences.[12] Another study found that high-imagery copy had greater recall than low-imagery copy, whether or not it was accompanied by an illustration; for low-imagery copy, however, illustrations were an important factor in audience recall.[13]

Researchers have found that the encoding of a commercial is related to the context of the TV program during (or adjacent to) which it is shown. Some parts of a program may require viewers to commit a larger portion of their cognitive resources to processing (e.g., when a dramatic event takes place versus a casual conversation). When viewers commit more cognitive resources to the program itself, they encode and store less of the information conveyed by a commercial. This suggests that commercials requiring relatively little cognitive processing may be more effective within or adjacent to a dramatic program setting than commercials requiring more elaborate processing.[14] Viewers who are very involved with a television show respond more positively to commercials adjacent to that show and have more positive purchase intentions. Men and women exhibit different encoding patterns. For example, although women are more likely than men to recall TV commercials depicting a social relationship theme, there is no difference in recall among men and women for commercials that focus on the product itself.[15]

When consumers are presented with too much information (called **information overload**), they may encounter difficulty in encoding and storing it all. Often, it is difficult for consumers to remember product information from ads for new brands in heavily advertised categories. Consumers can become cognitively overloaded when they are given a lot of information in a limited time. The result of this overload is confusion, resulting in poor purchase decisions.

Retention Information does not just sit in long-term storage waiting to be retrieved. Instead, information is constantly organized and reorganized as new links between chunks of information are forged. In fact, many information-processing theorists view the long-term store as a network consisting of nodes (i.e., concepts), with links between and among them. As individuals gain more knowledge about a subject, they expand their network of relationships and sometimes their search for additional information. This process is known as *activation,* which involves relating new data to old to make the material more meaningful. Consumer memory for the name of a product may also be activated by relating it to the spokesperson used in its advertising. For many people, Michael Jordan means Nike sneakers. The total package of associations brought to mind when a cue is activated is called a *schema.*

Product information stored in memory tends to be brand based, and consumers interpret new information in a manner consistent with the way in which it is already organized. Consumers are confronted with thousands of new products each year, and their information search is often dependent upon how similar or dissimilar (discrepant) these products are to product categories already stored in memory. Therefore, consumers are more likely to recall the information they receive on new products bearing a familiar brand name, and their memory is less affected by exposure to competitive ads.

One study demonstrated that *brand imprinting*—messages that merely establish the brand's identity—conducted before the presentation of the brand's benefits facilitates consumer learning and retention of information about the brand.[16] Studies also showed that a brand's *sound symbolism* (a theory suggesting that the *sounds* of words convey meanings) and the brand's *linguistic characteristics* (e.g., unusual spelling) impacted the encoding and retention of the brand name.[17]

Consumers recode what they have already encoded to include larger amounts of information (called **chunking**). Marketers should research the kinds and numbers of groupings (chunks) of information that consumers can handle. When the chunks offered in an advertisement do not match those in the consumer's frame of reference, information recall may be hampered. The extent of prior knowledge is also an important consideration. Knowledgeable consumers can take in more complex chunks of information than those who are less knowledgeable about the product category. Thus, the amount and type of technological information contained in a computer ad can be much more detailed in a magazine such as *PC Magazine* or *Wired* than in a general-interest magazine such as *Time.*

Information is stored in long-term memory in two ways: *episodically* (by the order in which it is acquired) and *semantically* (according to significant concepts). We may remember having gone to a movie last Saturday because of our ability to store data episodically, and we may remember the plot, the stars, and the director because of our ability to store data semantically. Learning theorists believe that memories stored semantically are organized into frameworks by which we integrate new data with previous experience. For information about a new brand or model of printer to enter our memory, for example, we would have to relate it to our previous experience with printers in terms of such qualities as speed, print quality, resolution, and memory.

Retrieval   **Retrieval** is the *process by which we recover information from long-term storage.* For example, when we are unable to remember something with which we are very familiar, we are experiencing a failure of the retrieval system. Marketers maintain that consumers tend to remember the product's benefits rather than its attributes, suggesting that advertising messages are most effective when they link the product's attributes with the benefits that consumers seek from the product; this view is consistent with the previous discussion of product positioning strategies (Chapter 6). Consumers are likely to spend time interpreting and elaborating on information they find relevant to their needs and to activate such relevant knowledge from long-term memory.

Incongruent (or unexpected) message elements pierce consumers' perceptual screens and improve the memorability of an ad when these elements are relevant to the advertising message. For example, an ad for a brand of stain-resistant, easy-to-clean carpet shows an elegantly dressed couple in a beautiful dining room setting where the man inadvertently knocks the food, the flowers, and the china crashing to the floor. The elegance of the actors and the upscale setting make the accident totally incongruous and unexpected, whereas the message remains highly relevant: The mess can be cleaned up easily without leaving a stain on the carpet.

Incongruent elements that are not relevant to an ad also pierce the consumer's perceptual screen but provide no memorability for the product. An ad showing a nude woman sitting on a piece of office furniture would very likely attract readers' attention, but would provide no memorability for the product or the advertiser because of the irrelevance of the nudity to the advertising message. One study discovered that false cues in post-experience advertising influence recollection. Also, when the false verbal cues and picture appeared together they were more likely to be integrated into memory than false verbal cues without pictures.[18]

Interference   The greater the number of competitive ads in a product category, the lower the recall of brand claims in a specific ad. These **interference effects** are caused by confusion with competing ads, and make information retrieval difficult. Ads can also act as retrieval cues for a competitive brand. An example of such consumer confusion occurred when consumers attributed the long-running and attention-getting television campaign featuring the Eveready Energizer Bunny to the leader in the field, Duracell. Advertisements for competing brands or for other products made by the same manufacturer can lower the consumer's ability to remember advertised brand information. Such effects occur in response to even a small amount of advertising for similar products.

The level of interference experienced can depend on the consumer's previous experiences, prior knowledge of brand attribute information, and the amount of brand information available at the time of choice. There are actually two kinds of interference: *New learning* can interfere with the retrieval of previously stored material, and *old learning* can interfere with the recall of recently learned material. With both kinds of interference, the problem is the similarity of old and new information. Advertising that creates a distinctive brand image can assist in the retention and retrieval of message contents.

Limited and extensive information processing

For a long time, consumer researchers believed that all consumers passed through a complex series of mental and behavioral stages in arriving at a purchase decision. These stages ranged from awareness (exposure to information) to evaluation (preference, attitude formation), to behavior (purchase), to final evaluation (adoption or rejection). This same series of stages is often presented as the *consumer adoption process* (discussed in Chapter 15).

A number of models have been developed over the years to express the same notion of sequential processing of information by consumers (see Table 7.1). Initially, marketing scholars believed that extensive and complex processing of information by consumers was applicable to all purchase decisions. However, on the basis of their own subjective experiences as consumers, some theorists began to realize that there were

TABLE 7.1	Models of Cognitive Learning				
	PROMOTIONAL MODEL	**TRICOMPONENT MODEL**	**DECISION-MAKING MODEL**	**INNOVATION ADOPTION MODEL**	**INNOVATION DECISION PROCESS**
	Attention	Cognitive	Awareness Knowledge	Awareness	Knowledge
Sequential Stages of Processing	Interest Desire	Affective	Evaluation	Interest Evaluation	Persuasion
	Action	Conative	Purchase Postpurchase Evaluation	Trial Adoption	Decision Confirmation

some purchase situations that simply did not call for extensive information processing and evaluation; that sometimes consumers simply went from awareness of a need to a routine purchase, without a great deal of information search and mental evaluation. Such purchases were considered of minimal personal relevance, as opposed to highly relevant, search-oriented purchases. Purchases of minimal personal importance were called *low-involvement purchases,* and complex, search-oriented purchases were considered *high-involvement purchases.* The following section describes the development of **involvement theory** and discusses its applications to marketing strategy.

Involvement theory

Involvement theory developed from a stream of research called **hemispheral lateralization,** or split-brain theory. The basic premise of *split-brain theory* is that the right and left hemispheres of the brain "specialize" in the kinds of information they process. The left hemisphere is primarily responsible for cognitive activities such as reading, speaking, and attributional information processing. Individuals who are exposed to verbal information cognitively analyze the information through left-brain processing and form mental images. Unlike the left hemisphere, the right hemisphere of the brain is concerned with nonverbal, timeless, pictorial, and holistic information. Put another way, the left side of the brain is rational, active, and realistic; the right side is emotional, metaphoric, impulsive, and intuitive.[19] Figure 7.12 shows an ad literally depicting split-brain theory.

Involvement theory and media strategy

Building on the notion of hemispheral lateralization, a pioneer consumer researcher theorized that individuals *passively* process and store right-brain (nonverbal, pictorial) information—that is, without active involvement.[20] Because TV is primarily a pictorial medium, TV viewing was considered a right-brain activity (passive and holistic processing of images viewed on the screen), and TV itself was therefore considered a low-involvement medium. This research concluded that **passive learning** occurs through repeated exposures to a TV commercial (i.e., low-involvement information processing) and produces changes in consumer behavior (e.g., product purchases) *prior* to changes in the consumer's attitude toward the product. This view contradicts the models presented in Table 7.1, all of which maintain that cognitive evaluation and favorable attitude toward a product take place before the actual purchase behavior.

To extend this line of reasoning, cognitive (verbal) information is processed by the left side of the brain; thus, print media (e.g., newspapers and magazines) and interactive media (the Internet) are considered high-involvement media. According to this theory, print advertising is processed in the complex sequence of cognitive stages

FIGURE 7.12

Source: Courtesy of American Airlines. Image © Abrams Lacagnina/Getty Images/The Image Bank.

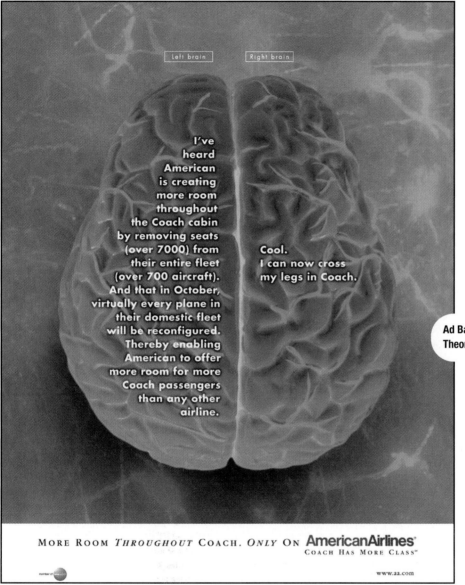

Ad Based on Split-Brain Theory

depicted in classic models of information processing (i.e., high-involvement information processing).

The right-brain theory of passive processing of information is consistent with classical conditioning. Through repetition, the product is paired with a visual image (e.g., a distinctive package) to produce the desired response: purchase of the advertised brand. According to this theory, in situations of passive learning (generated by low-involvement media), repetition is the key factor in producing purchase behavior. In marketing terms, the theory suggests that television commercials are most effective when they are of short duration and repeated frequently, thus ensuring brand familiarity without provoking detailed evaluation of the message content.

The right-brain processing theory stresses the importance of the *visual component* of advertising, including the creative use of symbols. Under this theory, highly visual TV commercials, packaging, and in-store displays generate familiarity with the brand and induce purchase behavior. Pictorial cues are more effective at generating recall and familiarity with the product, whereas verbal cues (which trigger left-brain processing) generate cognitive activity that encourages consumers to evaluate the advantages and disadvantages of the product.

There are limitations to the application of split-brain theory to media strategy. Although the right and left hemispheres of the brain process different types of cues, they do not operate independently of each other but work together to process information. Some individuals are *integrated processors* (they readily engage both hemispheres during information processing). Integrated processors have better overall recall of both the verbal and the visual portions of print ads than individuals who exhibit right or left hemispheral processing.

Involvement theory and consumer relevance

From the conceptualization of high- and low-involvement media, involvement theory next focused on the consumer's involvement with products and purchases. It was briefly hypothesized that there are high- and low-involvement consumers; then, that there are high- and low-involvement purchases. These two approaches led to the notion that a consumer's level of involvement depends on the degree of personal relevance that the product holds for that consumer. Under this definition, high-involvement purchases are those that are very important to the consumer (e.g., in terms of perceived risk) and thus provoke extensive problem solving (information processing). An automobile and a dandruff shampoo both may represent high-involvement purchases under this scenario—the automobile because of high perceived financial risk, the shampoo because of high perceived social risk. Low-involvement purchases are purchases that are not very important to the consumer, hold little relevance, and have little perceived risk, and, thus, provoke very limited information processing. Highly involved consumers find fewer brands acceptable (they are called **narrow categorizers**); uninvolved consumers are likely to be receptive to a greater number of advertising messages regarding the purchase and will consider more brands (they are **broad categorizers**).

Central and peripheral routes to persuasion

The theory of **central** and **peripheral routes to persuasion** illustrates the concepts of extensive and limited problem solving for high- and low-involvement purchase situations. The major premise of this theory is that consumers are more likely to carefully evaluate the merits and weaknesses of a product when the purchase is of high relevance to them. Conversely, the likelihood is great that consumers will engage in very limited information search and evaluation when the purchase holds little relevance or importance for them. Thus, for high-involvement purchases, the *central route to persuasion*—which requires considered thought and cognitive processing—is likely to be the most effective marketing strategy. For low-involvement purchases, the *peripheral route to persuasion* is likely to be more effective. In this instance, because the consumer is less motivated to exert cognitive effort, learning is more likely to occur through repetition, the passive processing of visual cues, and holistic perception.

Various researchers have addressed the relationship between the theory of central and peripheral routes to persuasion and consumer information processing. Numerous studies have found that high involvement with a product produces more extensive processing of information, including extensive information search on the Internet.[21] It is apparent that highly involved consumers use more attributes to evaluate brands, whereas less involved consumers apply very simple decision rules. In marketing to highly involved consumers, the quality of the argument presented in the persuasive message, rather than merely the imagery of the promotional message, has the greater impact on the consumption decision.

Many studies investigated the relationship between the level of information processing and the product and promotional elements of the marketing mix. For example, one study found that comparative ads (see Chapter 9) are more likely to be processed centrally (purposeful processing of message arguments), whereas noncomparative ads are commonly processed peripherally (with little message elaboration and a response derived from other executional elements in the ad).[22] Another study found that the use of metaphors and figures of speech that deviate from the expected in print ads places added processing demands on the readers and increases the ad's persuasiveness and memorability. The metaphors examined in this study were such slogans as "It forced other car makers into the copier business" (Mercury Sable) and "In the Caribbean, there's no such thing as a party of one" (Malibu Caribbean Rum).[23] Another study demonstrated that the correlation between a consumer's product involvement and objective product knowledge is higher for utilitarian products than in products designed to bring about pleasure (termed *hedonic products*); in the case of hedonic products, the correlation between subjective knowledge and product involvement is higher than for utilitarian products.[24] Assuming that *subjective knowledge* is the result of interpreting the imagery presented in the ad while *objective knowledge* is the outcome of the factual information that the ad provides, marketers should consider the degree of the product's utilitarianism in selecting either the central or peripheral route in promoting that product.

The Elaboration Likelihood Model   The **elaboration likelihood model (ELM)** suggests that a person's level of involvement during message processing is a critical factor in determining which route to persuasion is likely to be effective. For example, as the message becomes more personally relevant (i.e., as involvement increases), people are more willing to expend the cognitive effort required to process the message arguments. Thus, when involvement is high, consumers follow the central route and base their attitudes or choices on the message arguments. When involvement is low, they follow the peripheral route and rely more heavily on other message elements (such as spokespersons or background music) to form attitudes or make product choices.

Measures of involvement

Given that involvement theory evolved from the notion of high- and low-involvement media, to high- and low-involvement consumers, to high- and low-involvement products and purchases, to appropriate methods of persuasion in situations of high and low product relevance, it is not surprising to find there is great variation in the conceptualization and measurement of involvement itself. Researchers have defined and conceptualized involvement in a variety of ways, including ego involvement, commitment, communications involvement, purchase importance, extent of information search, persons, products, situations, and purchase decisions.[25] Some studies have tried to differentiate between *brand* involvement and *product* involvement.[26]

The lack of a clear definition about the essential components of involvement poses some measurement problems. Researchers who regard involvement as a cognitive state are concerned with the measurement of ego involvement, risk perception, and purchase importance. Researchers who focus on the behavioral aspects of involvement measure such factors as the search for and evaluation of product information. Others argue that involvement should be measured by the degree of importance the product has to the buyer.

Because of the many different dimensions and conceptualizations of involvement, it makes the most sense to develop self-administered measures that assess the consumer's cognitions or behaviors regarding a particular product or product category, and where involvement is measured on a continuum rather than as a dichotomy consisting of two mutually exclusive categories of "high" and "low" involvement. Table 7.2 presents a semantic differential scale designed to measure involvement. Table 7.3 shows a personal involvement inventory developed to measure a consumer's "enduring involvement" with a product.

Marketing applications of involvement

Involvement theory has a number of strategic applications for the marketer. For example, the left-brain (cognitive processing)/right-brain (passive processing) paradigm seems to have strong implications for the content, length, and presentation of both print, television, and interactive advertisements. There is evidence that people process information extensively when the purchase is of high personal relevance and engage in

TABLE 7.2	Measuring Involvement on a Semantic Differential Scale

To Me, [Insert Product or Product Category] Is:

	1	2	3	4	5	6	7	
1. Important	—	—	—	—	—	—	—	Unimportant
2. Interesting	—	—	—	—	—	—	—	Boring
3. Relevant	—	—	—	—	—	—	—	Irrelevant
4. Exciting	—	—	—	—	—	—	—	Unexciting
5. Meaningful	—	—	—	—	—	—	—	Meaningless
6. Appealing	—	—	—	—	—	—	—	Unappealing
7. Fascinating	—	—	—	—	—	—	—	Ordinary
8. Priceless	—	—	—	—	—	—	—	Worthless
9. Involving	—	—	—	—	—	—	—	Uninvolving
10. Necessary	—	—	—	—	—	—	—	Unnecessary

Source: Adapted from Judith Lynne Zaichowsky, "The Personal Involvement Inventory: Reduction, Revision, and Application to Advertising," *Journal of Advertising,* 23, 4 (December 1994): 59–70. Reprinted by permission.

limited information processing when the purchase is of low personal relevance. Uninvolved consumers appear to be susceptible to different kinds of persuasion than highly involved consumers. Therefore, for high-involvement purchases, marketers should use arguments stressing the strong, solid, high-quality attributes of their products, thus using the central (or highly cognitive) route. For low-involvement purchases, marketers should use the peripheral route to persuasion, focusing on the method of presentation rather than on the content of the message (e.g., through the use of celebrity spokespersons or highly visual and symbolic advertisements).

Marketers can take steps to increase customer involvement with their ads. For example, advertisers can use sensory appeals, unusual stimuli, and celebrity endorsers to generate more attention for their messages. Since highly involved consumers are more likely to engage in long-term relationships with products and brands, marketers should simultaneously increase customer involvement levels and create bonds with their

TABLE 7.3	Product Involvement Inventory Measuring Consumers' Enduring Involvement with Products

1. I would be interested in reading about this product.
2. I would read a *Consumer Reports* article about this product.
3. I have compared product characteristics among brands.
4. I usually pay attention to ads for this product.
5. I usually talk about this product with other people.
6. I usually seek advice from other people prior to purchasing this product.
7. I usually take many factors into account before purchasing this product.
8. I usually spend a lot of time choosing what kind to buy.

Source: Edward F. McQuarrie and J. Michael Munson, "A Revised Product Involvement Inventory: Improved Usability and Validity," *Diversity in Consumer Behavior: Advances in Consumer Research,* vol. 19 (Provo, UT: Association for Consumer Research, 1992), pp. 108–115. Reprinted by permission.

customers.[27] Of course, the best strategy for increasing the personal relevance of products to consumers is the same as the core of modern marketing itself: Provide benefits that are important and relevant to customers, improve the product and add benefits as competition intensifies, and focus on forging *bonds* and *relationships* with customers rather than just engaging in *transactions.*

measures of consumer learning

For many marketers, the dual goals of consumer learning are increased market share and brand-loyal consumers. These goals are interdependent: Brand-loyal customers provide the basis for a stable and growing market share, and brands with larger market shares have proportionately larger groups of loyal buyers. Marketers focus their promotional budgets on trying to teach consumers that their brands are best and that their products will best solve the consumers' problems and satisfy their needs. Thus, it is important for the marketer to measure how effectively consumers have "learned" its message. The following sections will examine various measures of consumer learning: *recognition* and *recall measures, cognitive measures,* and the *attitudinal and behavioral measures of brand loyalty.*

Recognition and recall measures

Recognition and **recall tests** are conducted to determine whether consumers remember seeing an ad, the extent to which they have read it or seen it and can recall its content, their resulting attitudes toward the product and the brand, and their purchase intentions. Recognition tests are based on *aided recall,* whereas recall tests use *unaided recall.* In recognition tests, the consumer is shown an ad and asked whether he or she remembers seeing it and can remember any of its salient points. In recall tests, the consumer is asked whether he or she has read a specific magazine or watched a specific television show, and if so, can recall any ads or commercials seen, the product advertised, the brand, and any salient points about the product.

A number of syndicated research services conduct recognition and recall tests, such as the Starch Readership Service, which evaluates the effectiveness of magazine advertisements. After qualifying as having read a given issue of a magazine, respondents are presented with the magazine and asked to point out which ads they *noted,* which they *associated with the advertiser,* and which they *read most.* They are also asked which parts of the ads they *noted* and *read most.* An advertiser can gauge the effectiveness of a given ad by comparing its readership recognition scores to similar-sized ads, to competitive ads, and to the company's own prior ads. Figure 7.13 shows an example of a "Starched" ad. A recent study using Starch readership scores demonstrated that consumers received more information from advertisements for *shopping products* (e.g., high-priced clothing and accessories) than from ads for *convenience goods* (e.g., low-priced items purchased routinely) and, surprisingly, from ads for *search products* (e.g., very expensive, durable items purchased infrequently following an extensive information search). These findings show that marketers may be under-informing consumers when advertising search products.[28]

Cognitive responses to advertising

Another measure of consumer learning is the degree to which consumers accurately comprehend the intended advertising message. **Comprehension** is a function of the message characteristics, the consumer's opportunity and ability to process the information, and the consumer's motivation (or level of involvement). To ensure a high level of comprehension, many marketers conduct **copy testing** either *before* the advertising is actually run (called **pretesting**) or *after* it appears (**posttesting**). Pretests are used to determine which, if any, elements of an advertising message should be revised before major media expenses are

FIGURE 7.13

Source: Courtesy of Buick.

Starch Readership Scores Measure Learning Through Ad Recognition Tests

incurred. Posttests are used to evaluate the effectiveness of an ad that has already run and to identify which elements, if any, should be changed to improve the impact and memorability of future ads.

Attitudinal and behavioral measures of brand loyalty

Brand loyalty is the ultimate desired outcome of consumer learning. However, there is no single definition of this concept. The varied definitions of brand loyalty reflect the models presented earlier in Table 7.1. They are summarized in Table 7.4, together with their shortcomings and weaknesses in the context of potential competitive responses.

TABLE 7.4	Definitions of Brand Loyalty and Their Shortcomings	
STAGE	**IDENTIFYING MARKER**	**VULNERABILITIES**
Cognitive	Loyalty to information such as price, features, and so forth.	Actual or imagined better competitive features or price through communications (e.g., advertising) and vicarious or personal experience. Deterioration in brand features or price. Variety seeking and voluntary trial.
Affective	Loyalty to a liking: "I buy it because I like it."	Cognitively induced dissatisfaction. Enhanced liking for competitive brands, perhaps conveyed through imagery and association. Variety seeking and voluntary trial. Deteriorating performance.
Conative	Loyalty to an intention: "I'm committed to buying it."	Persuasive counterargumentative competitive messages. Induced trial (e.g., coupons, sampling, point-of-purchase promotions). Deteriorating performance.
Action	Loyalty to action, coupled with the overcoming of obstacles.	Induced unavailability (e.g., stocklifts—purchasing the entire inventory of a competitor's product from a merchant). Increased obstacles generally. Deteriorating performance.

Source: Reprinted with permission from 1999 Special Issue of Journal of Marketing, published by the American Marketing Association, Richard L. Oliver, 1999, vol. 63, 33–34.

Marketers agree that brand loyalty consists of both attitudes and actual behaviors toward a brand and that both must be measured. **Attitudinal measures** are concerned with consumers' overall feelings about the product and the brand (i.e., evaluation), and their purchase intentions. **Behavioral measures** are based on observable responses to promotional stimuli—repeat purchase behavior rather than attitude toward the product or brand. A recent study pointed out that marketers must distinguish between two attitudinal measures of brand loyalty (see Table 7.5); the study demonstrated that the degree of commitment toward buying the brand and the propensity to be brand loyal are two *separate* dimensions but did not conclusively determine which construct is more useful for explaining buying behavior.[29]

Behavioral scientists who favor the theory of instrumental conditioning believe that brand loyalty results from an initial product trial that is reinforced through satisfaction, leading to repeat purchase. *Cognitive* researchers, on the other hand, emphasize the role of mental processes in building brand loyalty. They believe that consumers engage in extensive problem-solving behavior involving brand and attribute comparisons, leading to a strong brand preference and repeat purchase behavior. Therefore, brand loyalty is the synergy among such attitudinal components as perceived product superiority, customer satisfaction and the purchase behavior itself.

Recently, brain imaging technologies, commonly used in medicine, were used to study brand loyalty and yielded some fascinating results. Brain scans of some Japanese women taken while they were answering questions about everyday events showed similar patterns, but these patterns became distinctive when women who were brand loyal to a given store responded to the statement "this is the perfect store for me."

The brain scans of consumers who were split as to whether they prefer Coke or Pepsi and were given blind taste tests indicated that two different brain regions were at play. When the subjects tasted either of the soft drinks, their brain's reward system was activated. But when these persons were told which brand they were drinking, their brains' memory region (where information regarding brand loyalty is stored) was activated and overrode the preferences the participants indicated after tasting the soft drink, but before knowing which brand they had tasted.[30]

Behavioral definitions (such as frequency of purchase or proportion of total purchases) lack precision, because they do not distinguish between the "real" brand-loyal

TABLE 7.5	Two Distinct Attitudinal Measures of Brand Loyalty

MEASURE DESCRIPTION

ATTITUDE TOWARD THE ACT OF PURCHASING THE BRAND

Using a scale from 1 to 5, please tell me how committed you are to purchasing your preferred brand of directory advertising.

x_1 Uncommitted	1	2	3	4	5	Committed

Purchasing advertising with my preferred brand of directory in the next issue would be:

x_2 Bad	1	2	3	4	5	Good
x_3 Unpleasant	1	2	3	4	5	Pleasant
x_4 Unfavorable	1	2	3	4	5	Favorable
x_5 Negative	1	2	3	4	5	Positive
x_6 Undesirable	1	2	3	4	5	Desirable
x_7 Unwise	1	2	3	4	5	Wise
x_8 Unlikely	1	2	3	4	5	Likely

x_9 I would recommend my main brand to other people.

Unlikely	1	2	3	4	5	Likely

PROPENSITY TO BE LOYAL

x_1 I would rather stick with a brand I usually buy than try something I am not very sure of.

x_2 If I like a brand, I rarely switch from it just to try something different.

x_3 I rarely introduce new brands and products to my colleagues.

x_4 I rarely take chances by buying unfamiliar brands even if it means sacrificing variety.

x_5 I buy the same brands even if they are only average.

x_6 I would rather wait for others to try a new brand than try it myself.

x_7 I would rather stick to well-known brands when purchasing directory advertising.

Behavioral loyalty includes the dimensions of preference and allegiance. It was operationalized as the amount of money spent on the preferred brand (preference) over time (allegiance).

Source: Rebekah Bennett and Sharyn Rundle-Thiele, "A Comparison of Attitudinal Loyalty Measurement Approaches," *Journal of Brand Management* (January 2002): 193–209. Reprinted by permission.

buyer who is intentionally faithful and the spurious brand-loyal buyer who repeats a brand purchase out of mere habit or because it is the only one available at the store. Often consumers buy from a mix of brands within their acceptable range (i.e., their **evoked set**, see Chapter 16). The greater the number of acceptable brands in a specific product category, the less likely the consumer is to be brand loyal to one specific brand. Conversely, products having few competitors, as well as those purchased with great frequency, are likely to have greater brand loyalty. Thus, a more favorable attitude toward a brand, service, or store, compared to potential alternatives, together with repeat patronage, are seen as the requisite components of customer loyalty. A recent study related the attitudinal and purchase aspects of brand loyalty to market share and the relative prices of brands. The study showed that brand trust and brand affect, combined, determine purchase loyalty and attitudinal loyalty. Purchase loyalty leads to a higher market share, and attitudinal loyalty often enables the marketer to charge a higher price for the brand relative to competition.[31]

An integrated conceptual framework views consumer loyalty as the function of three groups of influences: (1) consumer drivers (i.e., personal degree of risk aversion or variety seeking); (2) brand drivers (i.e., the brand's reputation and availability of substitute brands); and (3) social drivers (i.e., social group influences and peers' recommendations). These influences produce four types of loyalty: (1) *no loyalty*—no purchase at all and no cognitive attachment to the brand; (2) *covetous loyalty*—no purchase but strong attachment and predisposition towards the brand that was developed from the person's social environment; (3) *inertia loyalty*—purchasing the brand because of habit and convenience but without any emotional attachment to the brand; and (4) *premium loyalty*—high attachment to the brand and high repeat purchase.[32] This framework also reflects a correlation among consumer involvement and the cognitive and behavioral dimensions of brand loyalty. Due to social perceptions regarding the importance of a car, and the symbolism of a particular car brand (e.g., Mercedes) as representing prestige and achievement, consumers may become involved with and attached to the brand without purchasing it (covetous loyalty), but may purchase the brand when they have the money to do so. Low involvement leads to exposure and brand awareness and then to brand habit (inertia loyalty). Consumers operating in this condition perceive little differentiation among brands and buy the brand repeatedly due to familiarity and convenience. On the other hand, premium loyalty represents truly brand-loyal consumers who have a strong commitment to the brand, are less likely to switch to other brands in spite of the persuasive promotional efforts of competitors, and may even go out of their way to obtain the strongly preferred brand.

Loyalty programs are generally designed with the intention of forming and maintaining brand loyalty. One study showed that brand managers believe that all reward programs impact incremental purchases and that low and moderate reward programs are the most cost-effective. The study proposed three types of brand-loyalty reward programs (see Table 7.6).[33] This research illustrates the options of tailoring loyalty programs to the purchase patterns of different market segments and the importance of doing so.

Unlike tangible products, where switching to another brand is relatively easy, it is often difficult to switch to another "brand" of service. For example, it is costly and time consuming to transfer one's business to a new attorney or accountant or even to get used

TABLE 7.6   Three Brand-Loyalty Reward Programs

REWARD PROGRAM	MEMBERSHIP NEWSLETTER	DISCOUNT COUPONS	PRODUCT LINE MERCHANDISE
Low	A quarterly one-page newsletter with information concerning new and existing products in the product line.	Coupons included in the newsletter for a $0.25 discount off any product in the product line.	Receive product line merchandise (e.g., coffee mugs or T-shirts) with 20 proofs of purchase and a $5.00 postage and handling fee.
Moderate	A quarterly full-color booklet with recipes and information concerning new and existing products in the product line.	Coupons included in the booklet for a $0.50 discount off any product in the product line.	Receive product line merchandise (e.g., coffee mugs or T-shirts) with 20 proofs of purchase.
High	A monthly full-color booklet with recipes, games and puzzles, and information concerning new and existing products in the product line.	Coupons included in the booklet for a $1.00 discount off any product in the product line.	Receive product line merchandise (e.g., coffee mugs or T-shirts) with 10 proofs of purchase.

Source: Brian Wansink, "Developing a Cost-Effective Brand Loyalty Program," *Journal of Advertising Research* 43 (3) (September 2003): 305.

to a new hair stylist. One study showed that the reasons that cause customers to switch service providers play a role in their loyalty behaviors toward subsequent providers. Thus, service marketers should research past customer behavior and use these data to increase the loyalty of new customers.[34]

Brand equity

The term **brand equity** refers to the value inherent in a well-known brand name. This value stems from the consumer's perception of the brand's superiority, the social esteem that using it provides, and the customer's trust and identification with the brand. For many companies, their most valuable assets are their brand names. Well-known brand names are referred to as **megabrands**. Among the best-known brands are Coca-Cola, Campbell's Soup, Hallmark Cards, and United Parcel Service. Their names have become "cultural icons" and enjoy powerful advantages over the competition.

Because of the escalation of new-product costs and the high rate of new-product failures, many companies prefer to leverage their brand equity through brand extensions rather than risk launching a new brand. Brand equity facilitates the acceptance of new products and the allocation of preferred shelf space, and enhances perceived value, perceived quality, and premium pricing options. Brand equity is most important for low-involvement purchases, such as inexpensive consumer goods that are bought routinely and with little processing of cognitive information. A study found that very strong brand cues, such as the ones conveyed by brands with high equity, may actually "block" the learning of quality-related cues for specific product attributes.[35] Thus, competitors of a strong brand will find it difficult to "teach" brand-loyal customers about the benefits of their brands.

Because a brand that has been promoted heavily in the past retains a cumulative level of name recognition, companies buy, sell, and rent (i.e., license) their brand names, knowing that it is easier for a new company to buy, rather than to create, a brand name that has enduring strength. Brand equity enables companies to charge a price premium—an additional amount over and above the price of an identical store brand. A relatively new strategy among some marketers is **co-branding** (also called double branding). The basis of co-branding, in which two brand names are featured on a single product, is to use another product's brand equity to enhance the primary brand's equity. For example, Cranberry Newtons is a product of Nabisco and Ocean Spray, bearing both brand names. Some experts believe that using a second brand's equity may imply that the host brand can no longer stand on its own. Others question whether a co-branded product causes consumer confusion as to who actually makes the product, and whether the host brand can survive if the second brand endorsement is taken away.

Brand equity reflects brand loyalty, which, as presented here, is a *learned* construct and one of the most important applications of learning theory to consumption behavior. Brand loyalty and brand equity lead to increased market share and greater profits. To marketers, the major function of learning theory is to teach consumers that their product is best, to encourage repeat purchase, and, ultimately, to develop loyalty to the brand name and brand equity for the company.

ethics and consumer learning

Previously, we discussed the ethics involved in using such factors as motivation and perception to arouse consumer needs and influence their cognitions of marketing offerings, with the assumptions that such influences will lead to purchase behavior. This section discusses the ethics of using the *elements of learning* to lead consumers to engage in *undesirable* behaviors. For example, behavioral, cognitive, and observational learning can sometimes lead to undesirable behavior after a person observes a particular behavior in an advertisement or commercial, and develops a cognition based on the ad, which subsequently leads to undesirable behavior. In trying to illustrate that some ads may bring about undesirable, although unintended, behavior, a New Jersey professor showed his students a magazine ad featuring a fit, smiling young man on a sidewalk in New York City with yellow cabs, pedestrians, and buildings in the background. The bright red headline read "Just once a day!" All other copy elements of the ad were concealed in order to disguise the actual product advertised. When the professor asked his students to guess what kind of product the ad was promoting, the consensus of the guesses was that the ad was for some kind of a pill, probably a vitamin. In fact, the ad was for a medication that is used as part of an HIV therapy by persons who are HIV positive. Since visual images are very persuasive, is it possible that the fit young man and the bright red caption "Just once a day!" conveys to young adults that being HIV positive is an easily "manageable" condition, and that one can engage in unsafe sex? And, if a study indicates that such a perception is indeed created by the ad, what should the marketer do? Clearly, featuring an individual who looks *unhealthy* in an ad for a pharmaceutical designed to control a serious medical condition will not be effective. The caption is an accurate representation of how often this drug should be taken (in combination, of course, with other drugs). This example demonstrates how difficult it is to develop advertisements that are free of any cues that may unintentionally cause *some* persons to draw the wrong conclusions and engage in undesirable behavior.

Since children are more likely than adults to imitate behavior they see (observational learning) on TV with little or no evaluative judgment, there are many ethical concerns regarding advertising to children. Advertising to children is subject to self-regulation according to guidelines developed by the Children's Advertising Review Unit (CARU) of the Council of Better Business Bureaus. Among others, the guidelines state that product presentations or claims must not mislead children about the product's performance or benefits, exploit the child's imagination or create unrealistic expectations, that products be shown in safe situations and the ads must refrain from encouraging behavior that is inappropriate for children. Following the direction of stimulus–response theory that children may easily form associations between stimuli and outcomes, the guidelines also include directions for avoiding ads that (1) encourage children to pressure their parents to buy the products advertised, and (2) compel children to feel that ownership of a given product will make them more accepted by peers. In relation to loyalty-building measures such as kid's clubs, premiums, and sweepstakes, the guidelines recognize that children may not always understand the true purpose of such measures and so they direct marketers to take steps not to exploit children with such programs.[36]

CARU's new releases illustrate many possible misuses in advertising to children and also the effectiveness of self-regulation. For example, in response to CARU's routine monitoring of children's advertising and CARU's subsequent request, a marketer of cotton candy machines agreed to modify a TV commercial that featured children operating an electrical candy machine without parental supervision and while dancing or talking on the phone.

After viewing a commercial showing Oreo cookies going into a toaster and popping out as KoolStuf pastries, a four-year-old child inserted Oreos into a toaster and, when they did not pop out, tried to retrieve them with a pair of scissors. The child's mother complained to CARU, which brought it to the attention of Oreo's marketer, who subsequently agreed to modify the commercial. Procter & Gamble agreed to modify a TV spot for Pringles that CARU believed encouraged excessive consumption of the snack food.[37]

Currently, a major concern regarding the impact of marketing on children's behavior is whether food marketers "teach" children to eat more than they should and thus cause the surging obesity and health problems among young consumers. Some consumer advocacy groups have called for the regulation of food marketing targeted to children; the food marketers and CARU believe that CARU's current guidelines already address this issue.[38] Clearly, there are merits to the argument that, ultimately, any consumption behavior, including excessive eating, is the responsibility of adult individuals and not the marketer who produced the food. As a society, we have not always accepted this position; for example, smokers are allowed to sue tobacco companies. However, it must always be remembered that children are a vulnerable population. Fearing that "McDonald's-made-me-fat" lawsuits will gain momentum, the food companies are now pursuing legislation that will not allow obese persons to sue them for personal damages.[39]

The principle of stimulus generalization can also be used to confuse consumers and alter intended consumption behavior. In most drugstores, less expensive brands of personal care products such as shampoo, dental floss, skin care lotions, and soap come in packages that are extremely similar to instantly recognized and more expensive premium brands of these products, and are deliberately placed right next to them on the shelf. Consumers can easily be confused by such displays and also by brand names or logos similar to those of premium offerings. Therefore, the marketers of premium brands often secure legal protection (in the form of patents or trademarks) for their brand names, packages and visual identities.

SUMMARY

Consumer learning is the process by which individuals acquire the purchase and consumption knowledge and experience they apply to future related behavior. Although some learning is intentional, much learning is incidental. Basic elements that contribute to an understanding of learning are motivation, cues, response, and reinforcement.

There are two schools of thought as to how individuals learn—behavioral theories and cognitive theories. Both contribute to an understanding of consumer behavior. Behavioral theorists view learning as observable responses to stimuli, whereas cognitive theorists believe that learning is a function of mental processing.

Three major *behavioral learning theories* are classical conditioning, instrumental conditioning, and observational (vicarious) learning. The principles of classical conditioning that provide theoretical underpinnings for many marketing applications include repetition, stimulus generalization, and stimulus discrimination. Neo-Pavlovian theories view traditional classical conditioning as cognitive associative learning rather than as reflexive action.

Instrumental learning theorists believe that learning occurs through a trial-and-error process in which positive outcomes (i.e., rewards) result in repeat behavior. Both positive and negative reinforcement can be used to encourage the desired behavior. Reinforcement schedules can be total (consistent) or partial (fixed ratio or random). The timing of repetitions influences how long the learned material is retained. Massed repetitions produce more initial learning than distributed repetitions; however, learning usually persists longer with distributed (i.e., spread out) reinforcement schedules.

Cognitive learning theory holds that the kind of learning most characteristic of humans is problem solving. Cognitive theorists are concerned with how information is processed by the human mind: how it is stored, retained, and retrieved. A simple model of the structure and operation of memory suggests the existence of three separate storage units: the sensory store, short-term store (or working memory), and long-term store. The processes of memory include rehearsal, encoding, storage, and retrieval.

Involvement theory proposes that people engage in limited information processing in situations of low importance or relevance to them and in extensive information processing in situations of high relevance. Hemispheral lateralization (i.e., split-brain) theory gave rise to the theory that television is a low-involvement medium that results in passive learning and that print and interactive media encourage more cognitive information processing.

Measures of consumer learning include recall and recognition tests, cognitive responses to advertising, and attitudinal and behavioral measures of brand loyalty. A basic issue among researchers is whether to define brand loyalty in terms of the consumer's behavior or the consumer's attitude toward the brand. Brand equity refers to the inherent value a brand name has in the marketplace.

Brand loyalty consists of both attitudes and actual behaviors toward a brand and both must be measured. For marketers, the major reasons for understanding how consumers learn are to teach them that their brand is best and to develop brand loyalty.

The ethical issues regarding consumer learning are centered on potential misuses of behavioral, cognitive, and observational learning. Most importantly, these issues involve targeting children and young adults and, albeit unintentionally, "teaching" them to engage in socially undesirable behaviors.

DISCUSSION QUESTIONS

1. How can the principles of (a) classical conditioning theory and (b) instrumental conditioning theory be applied to the development of marketing strategies?

2. Describe in learning terms the conditions under which family branding is a good policy and those under which it is not.

3. Neutrogena, the cosmetics company, offers a line of shaving products for men. How can the company use stimulus generalization to market these products? Is instrumental conditioning applicable to this marketing situation? If so, how?

4. Which theory of learning (classical conditioning, instrumental conditioning, observational learning, or cognitive learning) best explains the following consumption behaviors: (a) buying a six-pack of Gatorade, (b) preferring to purchase jeans at a Diesel Store, (c) buying a digital camera for the first time, (d) buying a new car, and (e) switching from one cellular phone service to another? Explain your choices.

5. a. Define the following memory structures: sensory store, short-term store (working memory), and long-term store. Discuss how each of these concepts can be used in the development of an advertising strategy.

   b. How does information overload affect the consumer's ability to comprehend an ad and store it in his or her memory?

6. Discuss the differences between low- and high-involvement media. How would you apply the knowledge of hemispheral lateralization to the design of TV commercials and print advertisements?

7. Why are both attitudinal and behavioral measures important in measuring brand loyalty?

8. What is the relationship between brand loyalty and brand equity? What role do concepts play in the development of marketing strategies?

9. How can marketers use measures of recognition and recall to study the extent of consumer learning?

EXERCISES

1. Imagine you are the instructor in this course and that you are trying to increase student participation in class discussions. How would you use reinforcement to achieve your objective?

2. Visit a supermarket. Can you identify any packages where you think the marketer's knowledge of stimulus generalization or stimulus discrimination was incorpo-rated into the package design? Note these examples and present them in class.

3. Visit the news section at **www.caru.org**. Select three of the press releases featured there (other than the ones discussed in this chapter) and illustrate how they depict the ethics of applying learning theory in advertising to children.

KEY TERMS

- **advertising wearout**
- **behavioral learning theory**
- **behavioral response**
- **brand equity**
- **brand loyalty**
- **broad categorizers versus narrow categorizers**
- **central and peripheral routes to persuasion**
- **chunking**
- **classical conditioning**
- **co-branding**

- **cognitive associative learning**
- **cognitive learning theory**
- **comprehension**
- **conditioned learning**
- **conditioned versus unconditioned stimuli**
- **copy testing**
- **cues**
- **elaboration likelihood model (ELM)**
- **encoding**
- **evoked set**

- **family branding**
- **hemispheral lateralization**
- **imagery**
- **information overload**
- **information processing**
- **instrumental learning**
- **interference effects**
- **involvement theory**
- **learning**
- **licensing**
- **massed versus distributed learning**

- **megabrands**
- **modeling, observational, and vicarious learning**
- **motivation**
- **negative reinforcement**
- **neo-Pavlovian conditioning**
- **operant learning**
- **passive learning**

- **positioning**
- **positive reinforcement**
- **pretesting and posttesting**
- **product category, product form and product line extensions**
- **recognition and recall tests**
- **rehearsal**
- **reinforcement**

- **repetition**
- **retrieval**
- **sensory, short-term, and long-term stores**
- **shaping**
- **stimulus discrimination**
- **stimulus generalization**
- **stimulus-response theories**

NOTES

1. **www.crest.com**, David Barboza, "Permutations Push Oreo Far Beyond Cookie Aisle," *The New York Times,* C2; and Micheline Maynard, "Wrapping Familiar Name Brand Around a New Product," *The New York Times,* May 22, 2004, C1.

2. N. J. Mackintosh, *Conditioning and Associative Learning* (New York: Oxford University Press, 1983), 10.

3. Margaret C. Campbell and Kevin Lane Keller, "Brand Familiarity and Advertising Repetition Effects," *Journal of Consumer Research* (September 2003): 292+.

4. Tom Meyvis and Chris Janiszewski, "When Are Broader Brands Stronger Brands? An Accessibility Perspective on the Success of Brand Extensions," *Journal of Consumer Research* (September 2004): 346–358.

5. Zeynep Gurhan-Canli, "The Effect of Expected Variability of Product Quality and Attribute Uniqueness on Family Brand Evaluations," *Journal of Consumer Research* (June 2003): 105+.

6. Ken Bensinger, "Can You Spot the Fake?" *Wall Street Journal,* February 16, 2001, W1, W14.

7. For example, Randi Priluck Grossman and Brian D. Till, "The Persistence of Classically Conditioned Brand Attitudes," *Journal of Advertising* 27, no. 1 (Spring 1998): 23–31.

8. William Taylor "Companies Find They Cannot Buy Love with Bargains," *The New York Times,* August 4, 2004, C5.

9. Anna A. Mattila, "The Impact of Service Failures on Customer Loyalty: The Moderating Role of Effective Commitment," *International Journal of Service Industry Management* 15, no. 2 (2004): 134+; and Tina L. Robbins and Janis L. Miller, "Considering Customer Loyalty in Developing Service Recovery Strategies," *Journal of Business Strategies* (Fall 2004): 95–110.

10. Michael D. Johnson and Claes Fornell, "The Nature and Methodological Implications of the Cognitive Representation of Products," *Journal of Consumer Research* 14 (September 1987): 214–227.

11. Ellen C. Garbarino and Julie A. Edell, "Cognitive Effort, Affect, and Choice," *Journal of Consumer Research* 24 (September 1997): 147–158.

12. Ruth Ann Smith, "The Effects of Visual and Verbal Advertising Information on Consumers' Inferences," *Journal of Advertising* 20, no. 4 (December 1991): 13–23.

13. H. Rao Unnava and Robert E. Burnkrant, "An Imagery-Processing View of the Role of Pictures in Print Advertisements," *Journal of Marketing Research* 28 (May 1991): 226–231.

14. Kenneth R. Lord and Robert E. Burnkrant, "Television Program Elaboration Effects on Commercial Processing," in *Advances in Consumer Research,* vol. 15, ed. Michael Houston (Provo, UT: Association for Consumer Research, 1988), 213–218.

15. Joan Meyers-Levy and Durairaj Maheswaran, "Exploring Differences in Males' and Females' Processing Strategies," *Journal of Consumer Research* 18 (June 1991): 63–70.

16. William E. Baker, "Does Brand Imprinting in Memory Increase Brand Information Retention?" *Psychology & Marketing* (December 2003): 1119+.

17. Tina M. Lowery, L. J. Shrum, and Tony M. Dubitsky, "The Relation Between Brand-Name Linguistic Characteristics and Brand-Name Memory," *Journal of Advertising* (Fall 2003): 7–18; and Eric Yorkston and Geeta Menon, "A Sound Idea: Phonetic Effects of Brand Names on Consumer Judgments," *Journal of Consumer Research* (June 2004): 43–52.

18. Kathryn A. Braun-LaTour, Michael S. LaTour, Jacqueline E. Pickrell, and Elizabeth F. Loftus, "How and When Advertising Can Influence Memory for Consumer Experience," *Journal of Advertising* (Winter 2004): 7–26.

19. Flemming Hansen, "Hemispheral Lateralization: Implications for Understanding Consumer Behavior," *Journal of Consumer Research* 8 (June 1981): 23–36; Peter H. Lindzay and Donald Norman, *Human Information Processing* (New York: Academic Press, 1977); and Merlin C. Wittrock, *The Human Brain* (Upper Saddle River, NJ: Prentice Hall, 1977).

20. Herbert E. Krugman, "The Impact of Television Advertising: Learning Without Involvement," *Public Opinion Quarterly* 29 (Fall 1965): 349–356; "Brain Wave Measures of Media

Involvement," *Journal of Advertising Research* 11 (February 1971): 3–10; and "Memory Without Recall, Exposure Without Perception," *Journal of Advertising Research,* Classics 1 (September 1982): 80–85.

21. See, for example, Richard E. Petty and John T. Cacioppo, "Issues Involvement Can Increase or Decrease Persuasion by Enhancing Message-Relevant Cognitive Responses," *Journal of Personality and Social Psychology* 37 (1979): 1915–1926; Cacioppo and Petty, "The Need for Cognition," *Journal of Personality and Social Psychology* 42 (1982): 116–131; Cacioppo, Petty, and Katherine J. Morris, "Effects of Need for Cognition on Message Evaluation, Recall and Persuasion," *Journal of Personality and Social Psychology* 45 (1983): 805–818; and Liping A. Cai, Ruomei Feng, and Deborah Breiter, "Tourist Purchase Decision Involvement and Information Preferences," *Journal of Vacation Marketing* (March 2004): 138–149.

22. Sanjay Putrevu and Kenneth R. Lord, "Comparative and Noncomparative Advertising: Attitudinal Effects Under Cognitive and Affective Involvement Conditions," *Journal of Advertising* 23, no. 2 (June 1994): 77–91.

23. Mark Toncar and James Munch, "Consumer Responses to Tropes in Print Advertising," *Journal of Advertising* (Spring 2001): 55–65.

24. Chan-Wook Park and Byeong-Joon Moon, "The Relationship Between Product Involvement and Product Knowledge: Moderating Roles of Product Type and Product Knowledge Type," *Psychology & Marketing* (November 2003): 977+.

25. Theo B. C. Poiesz and J. P. M. de Bont, "Do We Need Involvement to Understand Consumer Behavior?" *Advances in Consumer Research,* vol. 22, 1995, 448–452. See also the following articles in *Advances in Consumer Research,* vol. 11, ed. Thomas C. Kinnear (Provo, UT: Association for Consumer Research, 1984); James A. Muncy and Shelby D. Hunt, "Consumer Involvement: Definitional Issues and Research Directions," 193–196; John H. Antil, "Conceptualization and Operationalization of Involvement," 203–209; and Michael L. Rothschild, "Perspectives on Involvement: Current Problems and Future Directions," 216–217. Judith L. Zaichkowsky, "Conceptualizing Involvement," *Journal of Advertising* 15, no. 2 (1986): 4–34.

26. For example: Banwari Mittal and Myung Soo Lee, "Separating Brand Choice Involvement from Product Involvement via Consumer Involvement Profiles," in *Advances in Consumer Research,* vol. 15, ed. Michael Houston (Provo, UT: Association for Consumer Research, 1988), 43–49.

27. Many studies had demonstrated the relationship between level of involvement and long-term relationships between customers and marketers. For example: Sajeev Varki and Shirley Wong, "Consumer Involvement in Relationship Marketing of Services," *Journal of Service Research* (August 2003): 83+.

28. George R. Franke, Bruce A. Huhmann, and David L. Mothersbaugh, "Information Content and Consumer Readership of Print Ads: A Comparison of Search and Experience Products," *Academy of Marketing Science Journal* (Winter 2004): 20+.

29. Rebekah Bennett and Sharyn Rundle-Thiele, "A Comparison of Attitudinal Loyalty Measurement Approaches," *Journal of Brand Management* (January 2002): 193–209.

30. Sandra Blakeslee, "If You Have a 'Buy Button' in Your Brain, What Pushes It?" *The New York Times,* October 19, 2004, F5.

31. Arjun Chaudhuri and Morris B. Holbrook, "The Chain of Effects from Brand Trust and Brand Affect to Brand Performance: The Role of Brand Loyalty," *Journal of Marketing* (April 2001): 81–93.

32. Spiros Gounaris and Vlasis Stathakopoulos, "Antecedents and Consequences of Brand Loyalty: An Empirical Study," *Journal of Brand Management* (April 2004): 283–307.

33. Brian Wansink, "Developing a Cost-effective Brand Loyalty Program," *Journal of Advertising Research* (September 2003): 301–307.

34. Jaishankar Ganesh, Mark J. Arnold, and Kristy E. Reynolds, "Understanding the Customer Base of Service Providers: An Examination of the Differences Between Switchers and Stayers," *Journal of Marketing* (July 2000): 65–87.

35. Stijn M. J. Van Osselaer and Joseph W. Alba, "Consumer Learning and Brand Equity," *Journal of Consumer Research* 27 (June 2000): 1–16.

36. "Self-Regulatory Guidelines for Children's Advertising," **www.caru.org**

37. CARU New Releases: "Roseart Supports CARU and Children's Safety . . . " (January 5, 2005); "Nabisco Puts Safety First in TV Ads" (October 4, 2000); "Procter and Gamble Works With CARU On Pringles Commercial" (April 15, 2004). **http://www.caru.org/news/index.asp**

38. "NARC White Paper: Guidelines for Food Advertising Self-Regulation," **http://www.narcpartners.org/reports/whitepaper.asp**

39. Melanie Warner, "The Food Industry Empire Strikes Back" (July 5, 2005) **www.nytonline.com**

chaptereight

› Consumer Attitude Formation and Change

As consumers, each of us has a vast number of attitudes toward products, services, advertisements, direct mail, the Internet, and retail stores. Whenever we are asked whether we like or dislike a product (e.g., a Samsung HDTV set), a service (e.g., satellite TV from Direct TV), a particular retailer (e.g., Wal-Mart), a specific direct marketer (e.g., **www.Buy.com**), or an advertising theme (e.g., "Chrysler—inspiration comes standard"), we are being asked to express our **attitudes**.

Within the context of consumer behavior, an appreciation of prevailing attitudes has considerable strategic merit. For instance, there has been very rapid growth in the sales of natural ingredient bath, body, and cosmetic products throughout the world. This trend seems linked to the currently popular attitude that things "natural" are good and things "synthetic" are bad. Yet, in reality, the positive attitude favoring things natural is not based on any systematic evidence that natural cosmetic products are any safer or better for consumers.

To get at the heart of what is driving consumers' behavior, *attitude research* has been used to study a wide range of strategic marketing questions. For example, attitude research is frequently undertaken to determine whether consumers will accept a proposed new-product idea, to gauge why a firm's target audience has

Introducing PūR water.
(And ice too.)

Kenmore peace of mind.

Kenmore is now offering PūR Ultimate water filtration. And no one else has it. Why use those heavy pitchers that take up space in your refrigerator? A built-in PūR water filter gives you bottled-water quality through the door. And that includes ice, too. So treat your family to a better drink of water. For more information call 1-888-KENMORE, or visit kenmore.com. Kenmore. Ideas for the good life.

SEARS
Good life. Great prices.

not reacted more favorably to its new promotional theme, or to learn how target customers are likely to react to a proposed change in the firm's packaging design. To illustrate, major athletic shoe marketers such as Nike (**www.nike.com**) or Reebok (**www.reebok.com**) frequently conduct research among target consumers of the different types of athletic footwear products that they market. They seek attitudes of target consumers with respect to size, fit, comfort, and fashion elements of their footwear, as well as test reactions to potential new designs or functional features. They also regularly gauge reactions to their latest advertising and other marketing messages designed to form and change consumer attitudes. All these marketing activities are related to the important task of impacting consumers' attitudes.

In this chapter we will discuss the reasons why attitude research has had such a pervasive impact on consumer behavior. We also will discuss the properties that have made attitudes so attractive to consumer researchers, as well as some of the common frustrations encountered in attitude research. Particular attention will be paid to the central topics of attitude formation, attitude change, and related strategic marketing issues.

what are attitudes?

Consumer researchers assess attitudes by asking questions or making inferences from behavior. For example, if a researcher determines from questioning a consumer that she consistently buys Secret deodorant (**www.secret-deodorant.com**) and even recommends the product to friends, the researcher is likely to infer that the consumer possesses a positive attitude toward this brand of deodorant. This example illustrates that attitudes are not directly observable but must be inferred from what people say or what they do.

Moreover, the illustration suggests that a whole universe of consumer behaviors—consistency of purchases, recommendations to others, top rankings, beliefs, evaluations, and intentions are related to attitudes. What, then, are attitudes? In a consumer behavior context, an *attitude is a learned predisposition to behave in a consistently favorable or unfavorable way with respect to a given object.* Each part of this definition describes an important property of an attitude and is critical to understanding the role of attitudes in consumer behavior.

The attitude "object"

The word *object* in our consumer-oriented definition of attitude should be interpreted broadly to include specific consumption- or marketing-related concepts, such as product, product category, brand, service, possessions, product use, causes or issues, people, advertisement, Internet site, price, medium, or retailer. There is general agreement that an attitude "can be conceptualized as a summary evaluation of an object."[1]

In conducting attitude research, we tend to be *object specific.* For example, if we were interested in learning consumers' attitudes toward three major brands of popularly priced watches, our "object" might include Seiko, Fossil, and Casio; if we were examining consumer attitudes toward major brands of computer printers, our "object" might include HP, Dell, Brother, Canon, OKI, Lexmark, and Epson.

Attitudes are a learned predisposition

There is general agreement that attitudes are *learned.* This means that attitudes relevant to purchase behavior are formed as a result of direct experience with the product, word-of-mouth information acquired from others, or exposure to mass-media advertising, the Internet, and various forms of direct marketing (e.g., a retailer's catalog). It is important to remember that although attitudes may result from behavior, they are not synonymous with behavior. Instead, they reflect either a favorable or an unfavorable evaluation of the attitude object. As *learned predispositions,* attitudes have a motivational quality; that is, they might propel a consumer *toward* a particular behavior or repel the consumer *away* from a particular behavior.

Attitudes have consistency

Another characteristic of attitudes is that they are relatively consistent with the behavior they reflect. However, despite their *consistency,* attitudes are not necessarily permanent; they do change. (Attitude change is explored later in this chapter.)

It is important to illustrate what we mean by consistency. Normally, we expect consumers' behavior to correspond with their attitudes. For example, if a Canadian consumer reported preferring German over Japanese automobiles, we would expect that the individual would be more likely to buy a German brand when his current vehicle needed to be replaced. In other words, when consumers are free to act as they wish, we anticipate that their actions will be consistent with their attitudes. However, circumstances often preclude consistency between attitudes and behavior. For example, in the case of our Canadian consumer, the matter of affordability may intervene, and the consumer would find a particular Japanese car to be a more cost-effective choice than a German car. Therefore, we must consider possible *situational* influences on consumer attitudes and behavior.

Attitudes occur within a situation

It is not immediately evident from our definition that attitudes occur within and are affected by the *situation*.[2] By "situation," we mean events or circumstances that, at a particular point in time, influence the relationship between an attitude and behavior. A specific situation can cause consumers to behave in ways seemingly inconsistent with their attitudes. For instance, let us assume that Brad purchases a different brand of toothpaste each time he runs low. Although his brand-switching behavior may seem to reflect a negative attitude or dissatisfaction with the brands he tries, it actually may be influenced by a specific situation, for example, his wish to economize. Thus, he will buy whatever is the least expensive brand, and it is not a matter of a negative attitude.[3]

The opposite can also be true. If Sheryl stays at a Holiday Inn each time she goes out of town for business, we may erroneously infer that she has a particularly favorable attitude toward Holiday Inn. On the contrary, Sheryl may find Holiday Inn to be "just okay." However, because she owns her own business and travels at her own expense, she may feel that Holiday Inn is "good enough," given that she may be paying less than she would be paying if she stayed at a Marriott, Sheraton, or Hilton hotel.

Indeed, consumers can have a variety of attitudes toward a particular object, each corresponding to a particular situation or application. For instance, Saul may feel its alright to have a station wagon to drive the kids to their afterschool and weekend activities; or even to take his college-age daughter back and forth each year, with all her stuff, to State College, some two hundred and fifty miles away. However, when it comes to his growing interest in off-road driving, Saul feels strongly that only a high-quality sports utility vehicle (SUV) would provide the appropriate features to enable him to safely pursue his growing interest. So recently when it came time to replace the family's old station wagon, he opted for a new SUV, one that provided the "right" feature set to ensure his off-road interests.

It is important to understand how consumer attitudes vary from situation to situation. For instance, it is useful to know whether consumer preferences for various brands of SUVs (e.g., Honda Pilot, Jeep Liberty, and Ford Explorer) might depend on the anticipated driving task or most common driving situation (i.e., storage capacity, car pooling, and off-road driving). In Saul's case, his attitude and decision-making process lead him to select a Jeep 4x4. He feels it provides a win-win situation—in that the Jeep 4x4 would satisfy his need to car pool and transport his daughter to college, as well as his interest in off-road driving (Figure 8.1).

Clearly, when measuring attitudes, it is important to consider the situation in which the behavior takes place, or we can misinterpret the relationship between attitude and behavior. Table 8.1 presents additional examples of specific situations that might influence consumer attitudes toward specific brands of products or services.

structural models of attitudes

Motivated by a desire to understand the relationship between attitudes and behavior, psychologists have sought to construct models that capture the underlying dimensions of an attitude.[4] To this end, the focus has been on specifying the

FIGURE 8.1

Source: © DaimlerChrysler Corporation. Used by permission. All rights reserved.

Jeep's 4x4 SUV with Trail Rated™ System

TABLE 8.1	Examples of How Situations Might Influence Attitudes	
PRODUCT/SERVICE	**SITUATION**	**ATTITUDE**
Claritan	Runny nose due to allergies	"I've got to stop my nose from running because I've got a date in two hours."
Hyundai Automobile	Buying a new car	"With my son starting college in the fall, I don't want to spend a lot of money on a car."
Northwestern Mutual	Life insurance	"Now that I've just become a father, I want to make sure that my family is provided for."
The New York Times	Need a job	"I graduated college last month, spent three weeks in Europe, and now it's time to find a job."
American Airlines	Family wedding	"My cousin is getting married and I want to be there."
Starbucks	Need to stay awake	"I have to pull an 'all-nighter' to finish this paper that has to be submitted by 9:00 A.M."
Softsoap Pump Soap	Messy bathroom counter	"I'm tired of cleaning soap off of the bathroom counter."

composition of an attitude to better explain or predict behavior. The following section examines several important attitude models: the *tricomponent attitude model,* the *multiattribute attitude models,* the *trying-to-consume model,* and the *attitude-toward-the-ad models.* Each of these models provides a somewhat different perspective on the number of component parts of an attitude and how those parts are arranged or interrelated.

Tricomponent attitude model

According to the **tricomponent attitude model**, attitudes consist of three major components: a *cognitive* component, an *affective* component, and a *conative* component (see Figure 8.2).[5]

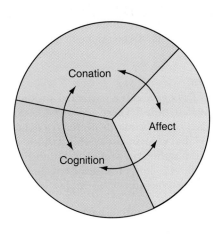

A Simple Representation of the Tricomponent Attitude Model

FIGURE 8.2

FIGURE 8.3	A Consumer's Belief System for Two Methods of Broadband Internet Access

Product	BROADBAND INTERNET ACCESS							
Brand	Cable Internet Access				DSL Internet Access			
Attributes	Speed	Availability	Reliability	Other Features	Speed	Availability	Reliability	Other Features
Beliefs	Faster than DSL	Offered now by my cable company	As reliable as my cable TV	No choice of provider and slows down when lots of subscribers are online	Slower than a cable modem but faster than dial-up service	Offered now by my local telephone company	Can be spotty	Bandwidth varies less than with a cable connection but can be more difficult to install and troubleshoot
Evaluations	(++++)	(+++)	(+++)	(−)	(++)	(+++)	(−)	(+)

Source: Adapted from Todd Spangler, "Crossing the Broadband Divide," *PC Magazine*, February 12, 2001, 92–103.

The cognitive component

The first part of the tricomponent attitude model consists of a person's *cognitions,* that is, the knowledge and perceptions that are acquired by a combination of direct experience with the *attitude object* and related information from various sources. This knowledge and resulting perceptions commonly take the form of *beliefs;* that is, the consumer believes that the attitude object possesses various attributes and that specific behavior will lead to specific outcomes.

Although it captures only a part of Steve's belief system about two types of broadband Internet connections (e.g., cable and DSL), Figure 8.3 illustrates the composition of a consumer's belief system about these two alternatives. Steve's belief system for both types of connections consists of the same basic four attributes: speed, availability, reliability, and "other" features. However, Steve has somewhat different beliefs about the two broadband alternatives with respect to these attributes. For instance, he knows from friends that the local cable company's broadband connection is much faster than DSL, but he does not like the fact that he will also have to begin subscribing to cable TV if he does not want to pay an extra $20 a month for the broadband Internet connection. Steve is thinking of asking a few of his friends about the differences between cable and DSL broadband Internet service and will also go online to a number of Web sites that discuss this topic (e.g., **www.cnet.com**).

The affective component

A consumer's *emotions* or *feelings* about a particular product or brand constitute the *affective component* of an attitude.[6] These emotions and feelings are frequently treated by consumer researchers as primarily *evaluative* in nature; that is, they capture an individual's direct or global assessment of the attitude object (i.e., the extent to which the individual rates the attitude object as "favorable" or "unfavorable," "good" or "bad"). To illustrate, Table 8.2 shows a series of evaluative (affective) scale items that might be used to assess consumers' attitudes toward Old Spice aftershave (**www.oldspice.com**).

Affect-laden experiences also manifest themselves as *emotionally charged states* (e.g., happiness, sadness, shame, disgust, anger, distress, guilt, or surprise). Research indicates that such emotional states may enhance or amplify positive or negative

TABLE 8.2	**Selected Evaluative Scale Used to Gauge Consumers's Attitudes Toward Old Spice Aftershave**

Compared to other aftershaves, Old Spice aftershave is:

Refreshing	[1]	[2]	[3]	[4]	[5]	[6]	[7]	Not refreshing
Positive	[1]	[2]	[3]	[4]	[5]	[6]	[7]	Negative
Pleasant	[1]	[2]	[3]	[4]	[5]	[6]	[7]	Unpleasant
Appealing to others	[1]	[2]	[3]	[4]	[5]	[6]	[7]	Unappealing to others

experiences and that later recollections of such experiences may impact what comes to mind and how the individual acts.[7] For instance, a person visiting a shopping center is likely to be influenced by his or her emotional state at the time. If the shopper is feeling particularly joyous at the moment, a positive response to the shopping center may be amplified. The emotionally enhanced response to the shopping center may lead the shopper to recall with great pleasure the time spent at the shopping center. It also may influence the individual shopper to persuade friends and acquaintances to visit the same shopping center and to make the personal decision to revisit the center.

In addition to using direct or global evaluative measures of an attitude object, consumer researchers can also use a battery of affective response scales (e.g., that measure feelings and emotions) to construct a picture of consumers' overall feelings about a product, service, or ad. Table 8.3 gives an example of a five-point scale that measures affective responses.

The conative component

Conation, the final component of the tricomponent attitude model, is concerned with the *likelihood* or *tendency* that an individual will undertake a specific action or behave in a

TABLE 8.3	**Measuring Consumers' Feelings and Emotions with Regard to Using Old Spice Aftershave**

For the past 30 days you have had a chance to try Old Spice Aftershave. We would appreciate it if you would identify how your face felt after using the product during this 30-day trial period. For each of the words below, we would appreciate it if you would mark an "X" in the box corresponding to how your face felt after using Old Spice Aftershave during the past 30 days.

	VERY				**NOT AT ALL**
Relaxed	[]	[]	[]	[]	[]
Attractive looking	[]	[]	[]	[]	[]
Tight	[]	[]	[]	[]	[]
Smooth	[]	[]	[]	[]	[]
Supple	[]	[]	[]	[]	[]
Clean	[]	[]	[]	[]	[]
Refreshed	[]	[]	[]	[]	[]
Younger	[]	[]	[]	[]	[]
Revived	[]	[]	[]	[]	[]
Renewed	[]	[]	[]	[]	[]

TABLE 8.4	Two Examples of Intention-to-Buy Scales

Which of the following statements best describes the chance that you will buy Old Spice Aftershave the next time you purchase an aftershave product?

_____ I definitely will buy it.

_____ I probably will buy it.

_____ I am uncertain whether I will buy it.

_____ I probably will not buy it.

_____ I definitely will not buy it.

How likely are you to buy Old Spice Aftershave during the next three months?

_____ Very likely

_____ Likcly

_____ Unlikely

_____ Very unlikely

particular way with regard to the attitude object. According to some interpretations, the conative component may include the actual behavior itself.

In marketing and consumer research, the conative component is frequently treated as an expression of the consumer's *intention to buy.* Buyer intention scales are used to assess the likelihood of a consumer purchasing a product or behaving in a certain way. Table 8.4 provides several examples of common **intention-to-buy scales**. Interestingly, consumers who are asked to respond to an intention-to-buy question appear to be more likely to actually make a brand purchase for positively evaluated brands (e.g., "I will buy it"), as contrasted to consumers who are not asked to respond to an intention question.[8] This suggests that a positive brand commitment in the form of a positive answer to an attitude intention question impacts in a positive way on the actual brand purchase.

Multiattribute attitude models

Multiattribute attitude models portray consumers' attitudes with regard to an attitude object (e.g., a product, a service, a direct-mail catalog, or a cause or an issue) as a function of consumers' perception and assessment of the key attributes or beliefs held with regard to the particular attitude object. Although there are many variations of this type of attitude model, we have selected the following three models to briefly consider here: the *attitude-toward-object model,* the *attitude-toward-behavior model,* and the *theory-of-reasoned-action model.*

The attitude-toward-object model

The **attitude-toward-object model** is especially suitable for measuring attitudes toward a *product* (or *service*) category or specific *brands.*[9] According to this model, the consumer's attitude toward a product or specific brands of a product is a function of the presence (or absence) and evaluation of certain product-specific beliefs and/or attributes. In other words, consumers generally have favorable attitudes toward those brands that they believe have an adequate level of attributes that they evaluate as positive, and they have unfavorable attitudes toward those brands they feel do not have an adequate level of desired attributes or have too many negative or undesired attributes. As an illustration, we return to the broadband Internet connection example (see Figure 8.3). Each alternative has a different "mix" of features (a "feature set"). The defining features might include speed, reliability, cost, availability of 24/7 technical assistance, maximum file size that can be e-mailed, and so on. For instance, one of the two types of connections might be found to excel on core features, whereas the other may be really good on a few of the core

TABLE 8.5	A Scale Used to Measure Attitude Toward Brands for 8- to 12-Year-Olds			
	DEFINITELY DISAGREE	**DISAGREE**	**AGREE**	**DEFINITELY AGREE**
Kellogg's—I like it.	❏	❏	❏	❏
Kellogg's—It is fun.	❏	❏	❏	❏
Kellogg's—It is great.	❏	❏	❏	❏
Kellogg's—It is useful.	❏	❏	❏	❏
Kellogg's—I like it very much.	❏	❏	❏	❏
Kellogg's—It is practical/handy.	❏	❏	❏	❏
Kellogg's—It is useless.	❏	❏	❏	❏

Source: Claude Pecheux and Christian Derbaix, "Children and Attitude Toward the Brand. A New Measurement Scale," *Journal of Advertising Research* (July/August 1999): 19–27.

features but offer more additional features. It is also possible that neither the cable nor the DSL carriers may be more than "second rate." However, what consumers will purchase is likely to be a function "how much they know," "what they feel are important features for them," and in the current example, their "awareness as to which type of broadband service possesses (or lacks) the valued attributes."

Conducting consumer attitude research with children, especially gauging their attitudes toward products and brands, is an ongoing challenge. What is needed are new and effective measurement approaches that allow children to express their attitudes toward brands. To this end, researchers have labored to develop an especially simple and short attitude measurement instrument for questioning children between 8 and 12 years of age. In the case of the example presented in Table 8.5, the questionnaire is set up to assess children's attitudes toward the Kellogg's brand.[10]

The attitude-toward-behavior model

The **attitude-toward-behavior model** is designed to capture the individual's *attitude toward behaving* or *acting* with respect to an object rather than the attitude toward the object itself.[11] The appeal of the attitude-toward-behavior model is that it seems to correspond somewhat more closely to actual behavior than does the attitude-toward-object model. For instance, knowing Sam's attitude about the act of purchasing a Rolex wristwatch (i.e., his attitude toward the *behavior*) reveals more about the potential act of purchasing than does simply knowing his attitude toward expensive watches or specifically Rolex watches (i.e., the attitude toward the *object*). This seems logical, for a consumer might have a positive attitude toward an expensive Rolex wristwatch but a negative attitude as to his prospects for purchasing such an expensive wristwatch.

A recent study conducted in Taiwan examined the relationship between consumer characteristics and attitude toward the behavior of online shopping. The researcher found that attitudes toward online shopping are significantly different based on various consumer behavior factors. For example, the research identified the following nine benefits of online shopping: (1) effectiveness and modern, (2) purchase convenience, (3) information abundance, (4) multiform and safety, (5) service quality, (6) delivery speed, (7) homepage design, (8) selection freedom, and (9) company name familiarity. These nine attributes were selected because they tend to reflect consumers' attitude toward online shopping.[12] The researcher goes on to explore a model (see Figure 8.4) that suggests that *consumer characteristics* (on the left-side of the model) impact *attitudes toward online shopping* (in the middle of the model—the nine attitudinal attributes listed above) and the *rating of the online shopping experience* (on the right-side of the model).

FIGURE 8.4

Consumer Characteristics, Attitude, and Online Shopping

Source: Shwu-Ing Wu, "The Relationship Between Consumer Characteristics and Attitude Toward Online Shopping," *Marketing Intelligence and Planning* 21, no. 7 (2003): 40.

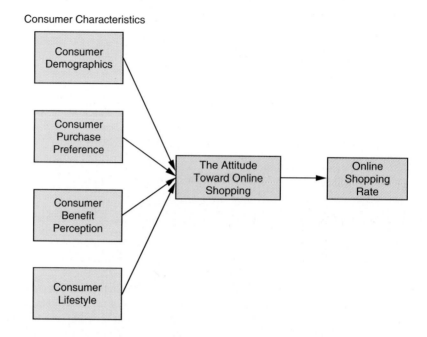

Consumer Characteristics

Theory-of-reasoned-action model

The **theory-of-reasoned-action model** represents a comprehensive integration of attitude components into a structure that is designed to lead to both better explanation and better predictions of behavior. Like the basic tricomponent attitude model, the theory-of-reasoned-action model incorporates a *cognitive* component, an *affective* component, and a *conative* component; however, these are arranged in a pattern different from that of the tricomponent model (see Figure 8.5).

In accordance with this expanded model, to understand *intention* we also need to measure the *subjective norms* that influence an individual's intention to act. A subjective norm can be measured directly by assessing a consumer's feelings as to what relevant others (family, friends, roommates, coworkers) would think of the action being contemplated; that is, would they look favorably or unfavorably on the anticipated action? For example, if an undergraduate student was considering cutting her hair shorter and dying it red and stopped to ask herself what her parents or boyfriend would think of such behavior (i.e., approve or disapprove), such a reflection would constitute her subjective norm.

Consumer researchers can get behind the *subjective norm* to the underlying factors that are likely to produce it. They accomplish this by assessing the *normative beliefs* that the individual attributes to relevant others, as well as the individual's *motivation to comply* with each of the relevant others. For instance, consider the undergraduate student contemplating cutting her hair shorter and dying it red. To understand her subjective norm about the desired purchase, we would have to identify her relevant others (parents and boyfriend); her beliefs about how each would respond to her short red hair (e.g., "Mom would consider the shorter hair as too 'boyish,' but my boyfriend would love it"); and, finally, her motivation to comply with her parents and/or her boyfriend.[13] A recent study also indicates that incorporating the consumer's emotional experience into the multiattribute model has the potential of enhancing the predictability of motives and preferences.[14]

Theory of trying-to-consume model

There has been an effort underway to extend attitude models so that they might better accommodate consumers' goals as expressed by their "trying" to consume.[15] The **theory of trying to consume** is designed to account for the many cases in which the action or

FIGURE 8.5

**A Simplified Version
of the Theory of
Reasoned Action**

Source: Adapted from Icek Ajzen
and Martin Fishbein,
*Understanding Attitudes and
Predicting Social Behavior* (Upper
Saddle River, NJ: Prentice Hall,
1980), 84. © 1980. Adapted by
permission of Prentice Hall, Inc.

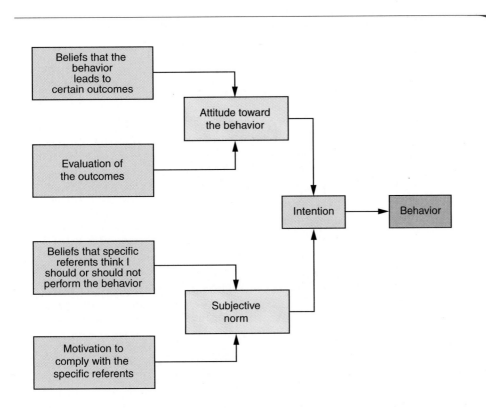

outcome is not certain but instead reflects the consumer's attempts to consume (i.e., purchase). In trying to consume, there are often *personal impediments* (a consumer is trying to find just the right shoes to go with a newly purchased dress for under $100 or trying to lose weight but loves chocolate bars) and/or *environmental impediments* (only the first 50 in line will be able to purchase this $200 MP3 player for the special Saturday 8:00 A.M. to 9:00 A.M. price of $99) that might prevent the desired action or outcome from occurring. Again, the key point is that in these cases of trying, the outcome (e.g., purchase, possession, use, or action) is not and cannot be assumed to be certain. Table 8.6 lists a few examples of possible personal and environmental impediments that might negatively impact the outcome for a consumer trying to consume. Researchers have recently extended this inquiry by examining those situations in which consumers do *not* try to consume—that is, *fail to try to consume.* In this case, consumers appear to (1) fail to see or are ignorant of their options and (2) make a conscious effort not to consume; that is, they might seek to self-sacrifice or defer gratification to some future time.[16]

Attitude-toward-the-ad models

In an effort to understand the impact of advertising or some other promotional vehicle (e.g., a catalog) on consumer attitudes toward particular products or brands, considerable attention has been paid to developing what has been referred to as **attitude-toward-the-ad models**.

Figure 8.6 presents a schematic of some of the basic relationships described by an attitude-toward-the-ad model. As the model depicts, the consumer forms various feelings (affects) and judgments (cognitions) as the result of exposure to an ad. These feelings and judgments in turn affect the consumer's *attitude toward the ad* and *beliefs about the brand* secured from exposure to the ad. Finally, the consumer's attitude toward the ad and beliefs about the brand influence his or her *attitude toward the brand.*[17]

Research among Asian Indian U.S. immigrants have explored attitudes toward 12 advertisements and purchase intention of six different products that the ads feature.

TABLE 8.6	**Selected Examples of Potential Impediments That Might Impact on Trying**

Potential Personal Impediments

"I wonder whether my hair will be long enough by the time of my wedding so that I can have the hairdo I want."

"I want to try to lose 2 inches off my waist by my birthday."

"I'm going to try to get us tickets for the Rolling Stones concert for our anniversary."

"I'm going to attempt to give up smoking by my birthday."

"I am going to increase how often I run two miles from three to five times a week."

"Tonight I'm not going to have dessert at the restaurant."

Potential Environmental Impediments

"The first 1,000 people at the baseball game will receive a team cap."

"Sorry, the car you ordered didn't come in from Japan on the ship that docked yesterday."

"There are only two cases of Chardonnay in our stockroom. You better come in sometime today."

"I am sorry. We cannot serve you. We are closing the restaurant because of an electrical problem."

The study found a positive relationship between attitude toward the advertisement and purchase intention for each of the advertised products; that is, if consumers "like" the ad, they are more likely to purchase the product.[18]

Finally, consumer socialization has also shown itself to be an important determinant of a consumer's attitudes toward advertising. One study, for example, found that parental communication, peer communication, social utility of advertising, amount of television watched, gender, and race were all associated with attitude toward advertising. African Americans and women were found to have more positive attitudes toward advertising.[19]

A Conception of the Relationship Among Elements in an Attitude-Toward-the-Ad Model

Source: Inspired by and based on Julie A. Edell and Marian Chapman Burke, "The Power of Feelings in Understanding Advertising Effects," *Journal of Consumer Research* 14 (December 1987): 431. Reprinted by permission of University of Chicago Press as publisher.

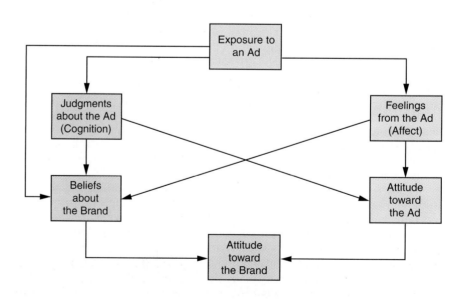

FIGURE 8.6

attitude formation

How do people, especially young people, form their initial *general* attitudes toward "things"? Consider their attitudes toward clothing they wear, for example, underwear, casual wear, and business attire. On a more specific level, how do they form attitudes toward Fruit of the Loom or Calvin Klein underwear, or Levi's or Gap casual wear, or Anne Klein or Emporium Armani business clothing? Also, what about where such clothing is purchased? Would they buy their underwear, casual wear, and business clothing at Wal-Mart, Sears, JC Penney, or Macy's? How do family members and friends, admired celebrities, mass-media advertisements, even cultural memberships, influence the formation of their attitudes concerning consuming or not consuming each of these types of apparel items? Why do some attitudes seem to persist indefinitely while others change fairly often? The answers to such questions are of vital importance to marketers, for without knowing how attitudes are formed, they are unable to understand or to influence consumer attitudes or behavior.

Our examination of attitude formation is divided into three areas: *how attitudes are learned,* the *sources of influence* on attitude formation, and the impact of *personality* on attitude formation.

How attitudes are learned

When we speak of the formation of an attitude, we refer to the shift from having no attitude toward a given object (e.g., an MP3 player) to having *some* attitude toward it (e.g., having an MP3 player is great when you want to listen to music while on a treadmill at the gym). The shift from no attitude to an attitude (i.e., the *attitude formation*) is a result of learning (see Chapter 7 for detailed exploration of consumer behavior and learning theories).

Consumers often purchase new products that are associated with a favorably viewed brand name. Their favorable attitude toward the brand name is frequently the result of repeated satisfaction with other products produced by the same company. In terms of *classical conditioning,* an established brand name is an *unconditioned* stimulus that through past positive reinforcement resulted in a favorable brand attitude. A new product, yet to be linked to the established brand, would be the *conditioned* stimulus. To illustrate, by giving its Secret Platinum and Olay conditioners the benefit of two well-known and respected family names (i.e., Secret and Olay), P&G is expecting on a transfer of the favorable attitude already associated with these two brand names to the new product (see Figure 8.7). They are counting on stimulus generalization from the two brand names to the new product. Research suggests that the "fit" between a parent brand (e.g., in this case both Secret and Olay) and a brand extension (e.g., in this case Secret Platinum and Olay conditioners) is a function of two factors: (1) the similarity between the preexisting product categories already associated with the parent brands (i.e., mostly products related to skin care) and the new extension and (2) the fit or match between the images of the parent brands and the new extension.[20]

Sometimes attitudes *follow* the purchase and consumption of a product. For example, a consumer may purchase a brand-name product *without* having a prior attitude toward it because it is the only product of its kind available (e.g., the last bottle of aspirin in a gas station mini-mart). Consumers also make trial purchases of new brands from product categories in which they have little personal involvement (see Chapter 7). If they find the purchased brand to be satisfactory, then they are likely to develop a favorable attitude toward it.

In situations in which consumers seek to solve a problem or satisfy a need, they are likely to form attitudes (either positive or negative) about products on the basis of information exposure and their own cognition (knowledge and beliefs). In general, the more information consumers have about a product or service, the more likely they are to form attitudes about it, either positive or negative. However, regardless of available information, consumers are not always ready or willing to process product-related

FIGURE 8.7

Source: © Procter & Gamble
Company. Used with permission.
All rights reserved.

**Attitudes Are Formed Through
Association with Favorable
Brand Names**

information. Furthermore, consumers often use only a limited amount of the information. Specifically, only two or three important beliefs about a product are likely to dominate in the formation of attitudes and that less important beliefs provide little additional input.[21] This suggests that marketers should fight off the impulse to include *all* the features of their products and services in their ads; rather, they should focus on the few key points that are at the heart of what distinguishes their product from the competition.

Sources of influence on attitude formation

The formation of consumer attitudes is strongly influenced by *personal experience,* the *influence* of family and friends, *direct marketing, mass media,* and the *Internet.*

A primary means by which attitudes toward goods and services are formed is through the consumer's direct experience in trying and evaluating them.[22] Recognizing the importance of direct experience, marketers frequently attempt to stimulate trial of new products by offering cents-off coupons or even free samples. Figure 8.8 illustrates this strategy; the ad for Wrigley's Cool Green Apple Free Gum includes a trial coupon for a pack of gum (which would make one of the two packs free). In such cases, the marketer's objective is to get consumers to try and evaluate the product. If a product proves to be to their liking, then it is likely that consumers will form a positive attitude and be more likely to repurchase the product. In addition, from the information on the coupon the marketer is able to create a database of interested consumers.

As we come in contact with others, especially family, close friends, and admired individuals (e.g., a respected teacher), we form attitudes that influence our lives.[23] The family is an extremely important source of influence on the formation of attitudes, for it is the family that provides us with many of our basic values and a wide range of less central beliefs. For instance, young children who are rewarded for good behavior with sweet foods and candy often retain a taste for (and positive attitude toward) sweets as adults.

Marketers are increasingly using highly focused direct-marketing programs to target small consumer niches with products and services that fit their interests and lifestyles. (Niche marketing is sometimes called *micromarketing.*) Marketers very carefully target customers on the basis of their demographic, psychographic, or geo-demographic profiles with highly personalized product offerings (e.g., watches for left-handed people) and messages that show they understand their special needs and desires. Direct-marketing efforts have an excellent chance of favorably influencing target consumers' attitudes, because the products and services offered and the promotional messages conveyed are very carefully designed to address the individual segment's needs and concerns and, thus, are able to achieve a higher "hit rate" than mass marketing.

In countries where people have easy access to newspapers and a variety of general and special-interest magazines and television channels, consumers are constantly exposed to new ideas, products, opinions, and advertisements. These mass-media communications provide an important source of information that influences the formation of consumer attitudes. Other research indicates that for consumers who lack direct experience with a product, exposure to an emotionally appealing advertising message is more likely to create an attitude toward the product than for consumers who have beforehand secured direct experience with the product category.[24] The net implications of these findings appear to be that emotional appeals are most effective with consumers who lack product experience.

Still another issue with regard to evaluating the impact of advertising messages on attitude formation is the level of realism that is provided. Research has shown that attitudes that develop through *direct experience* (e.g., product usage) tend to be more confidently held, more enduring, and more resistant to attack than those developed via *indirect experience* (e.g., reading a print ad). And just as television provided the advertiser with more realism than is possible in a radio or print ad, the Internet has an even greater ability to provide telepresence, which is the simulated perception of direct experience. The Internet also has the ability to provide the "flow experience," which is a cognitive state occurring when the individual is so involved in an activity that nothing else matters. Research on telepresence suggests that "perceptions of telepresence grew stronger as levels of interactivity and levels of vividness (i.e., the way an environment presents information to the senses) of web sites increased."[25]

FIGURE 8.8

Source: © Wm. Wrigley Jr. Company. Used with permission. All rights reserved.

Wrigley's Extra Cool Green Apple

Personality factors

Personality also plays a critical role in attitude formation. For example, individuals with a *high need for cognition* (i.e., those who crave information and enjoy thinking) are likely to form positive attitudes in response to ads or direct mail that are rich in product-related information. On the other hand, consumers who are relatively *low in need for cognition* are more likely to form positive attitudes in response to ads that feature an attractive model or well-known celebrity. In a similar fashion, attitudes toward new products and new consumption situations are strongly influenced by specific personality characteristics of consumers.

strategies of attitude change

It is important to recognize that much of what has been said about *attitude formation* is also basically true of attitude change. That is, attitude changes are *learned;* they are influenced by *personal experience* and other *sources of information,* and *personality* affects both the receptivity and the speed with which attitudes are likely to be altered.

Altering consumer attitudes is a key strategy consideration for most marketers. For marketers who are fortunate enough to be market leaders and to enjoy a significant amount of customer goodwill and loyalty, the overriding goal is to fortify the existing positive attitudes of customers so that they will not succumb to competitors' special offers and other inducements designed to win them over. For instance, in many product categories (e.g., crayons, in which Crayola has been the leader, or baking soda, in which Arm & Hammer has dominated), most competitors take aim at the market leaders when developing their marketing strategies. Their objective is to change the attitudes of the market leaders' customers and win them over. Among the *attitude-change strategies* that are available to them are (1) changing the consumer's basic motivational function, (2) associating the product with an admired group or event, (3) resolving two conflicting attitudes, (4) altering components of the multiattribute model, and (5) changing consumer beliefs about competitors' brands.

Changing the basic motivational function

An effective strategy for changing consumer attitudes toward a product or brand is to make particular needs prominent. One method for changing motivation is known as the **functional approach**.[26] According to this approach, attitudes can be classified in terms of four functions: the **utilitarian function**, the **ego-defensive function**, the **value-expressive function**, and the **knowledge function**.

The utilitarian function

We hold certain brand attitudes partly because of a brand's utility. When a product has been useful or helped us in the past, our attitude toward it tends to be favorable. One way of changing attitudes in favor of a product is by showing people that it can serve a utilitarian purpose that they may not have considered. For example, the ad for Lysol (Figure 8.9) points out that this product kills harmful germs.

The ego-defensive function

Most people want to protect their self-images from inner feelings of doubt—they want to replace their uncertainty with a sense of security and personal confidence.[27] Ads for cosmetics and fashion clothing, by acknowledging this need, increase both their relevance to the consumer and the likelihood of a favorable attitude change by offering reassurance to the consumer's self-concept. For example, the ad in Figure 8.10 for Dressbarn, a retailer of fashion clothing, stresses in its headline: "When I believe in myself, everything becomes possible." Another example would be the ongoing advertising campaign for the Zippo lighter, designed to counter the trend toward disposable lighters. In an effort to equate the long-lasting relationship a consumer can have with his Zippo lighter with other things in life, the campaign uses headlines such as "True love is not disposable" (the ad shows a Zippo with an engraved love poem).[28]

The value-expressive function

Attitudes are an expression or reflection of the consumer's general values, lifestyle, and outlook. If a consumer segment generally holds a positive attitude toward owning the latest designer jeans, then their attitudes toward new brands of designer jeans are likely to reflect that orientation. Similarly, if a segment of consumers has a positive

FIGURE 8.9

Source: © Reckiti Benckiser Inc. Used with permission. All rights reserved.

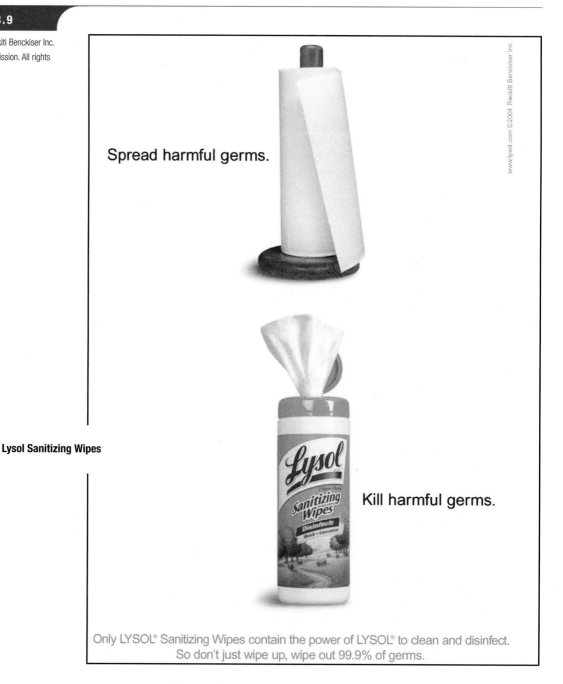

Lysol Sanitizing Wipes

attitude toward being "high tech," then their attitudes toward thin wall-mountable HDTV sets are likely to reflect this viewpoint. Thus, by knowing target consumers' attitudes, marketers can better anticipate their values, lifestyle, or outlook and can reflect these characteristics in their advertising and direct-marketing efforts. The advertisement for Timberland in Figure 8.11 addresses target consumers' attitudes and outlooks.

The knowledge function

Individuals generally have a strong need to know and understand the people and things they encounter. The consumer's "need to know," a cognitive need, is important

Source: © dressbarn. Used with permission. All rights reserved. **FIGURE 8.10**

Dressbarn Uses Ego-Defensive Appeal

to marketers concerned with product positioning. Indeed, many product and brand positionings are attempts to satisfy the *need to know* and to improve the consumer's attitudes toward the brand by emphasizing its advantages over competitive brands. For instance, a message for a new OTC allergy medication might point out how it is superior to other OTC allergy medications in alleviating the symptoms of allergies. The message might even use a bar graph to contrast its allergy symptom relief abilities to other leading allergy medications. Figure 8.12 is an ad for General Mills' Milk'n Cereal bars that focus on the product information panel for the two products. In addition, the ad goes on to state that they are "50% larger, twice the calcium, and three times the iron of Kellogg's bars." An important characteristic of the advertising is its appeal and usefulness to consumers' *need to know.*

Combining several functions

Because different consumers may like or dislike the same product or service for different reasons, a functional framework for examining attitudes can be very useful. For instance, three consumers may all have positive attitudes toward Suave hair care products. However, one may be responding solely to the fact that the products work well (the utilitarian function); the second may have the inner confidence to agree with the point "When you know beautiful hair doesn't have to cost a fortune" (an ego-defensive function). The third consumer's favorable attitudes might reflect the realization that Suave has for many years stressed value (equal or better products for less)—the *knowledge function.*

Source: © 2005 The Timberland Company. All rights reserved.

FIGURE 8.11

Timberland Titan

Associating the product with a special group, event, or cause

Attitudes are related, at least in part, to certain groups, social events, or causes. It is possible to alter attitudes toward companies and their products, services, and brands by pointing out their relationships to particular social groups, events, or causes. Ben & Jerry's ice cream factory, for example, may be the number-one tourist attraction in the State of Vermont but, more importantly, the company is well recognized for giving approximately 7.5 percent of its pretax profits to a variety of causes (see **www.benjerry.com**), for establishing employee-led community action teams that work on local public service projects, and for distributing small grants to community groups within the State of Vermont.

FIGURE 8.12

Source: Honey Nut Cheerios®
bar is a registered trademark of
General Mills and is used with
permission.

NOT ALL CEREAL BARS ARE CREATED EQUAL.

You want your kids to have all the advantages. So give them a cereal bar that has plenty of them. A Milk 'n Cereal bar, only from General Mills. For real cereal nutrition, all you have to do is look for the 🅖.

50% larger, twice the calcium, and three times the iron of Kellogg's bars.

*Vitamin and mineral nutrition of other Kellogg's varieties varies.

© 2004 General Mills
Kellogg's Frosted Flakes is a registered trademark of Kellogg Company

General Mills Uses a Knowledge Appeal in Helping Target Consumers Formulate an Attitude

Companies regularly include mention in their advertising of the civic and public acts that they sponsor to let the public know about the good that they are trying to do. For instance, Folgers® coffee sponsors a program "Wakin' up the Music," which supports a music appreciation program for youngsters in grades K–3, created by the GRAMMY® Foundation. Similarly, Crest sponsors a program that promotes good oral care to children through the Boys and Girls Clubs of America. Figure 8.13 presents an ad highlighting the benefits of McDonalds' ongoing charity—Ronald McDonald Houses.

Recent research into brand-cause alliances have investigated the relationship between the "cause" and the "sponsor." For instance, one study found that while both the

FIGURE 8.13

Source: © McDonald's Corporation. "Used with permission from McDonald's Corporation."

McDonald's Demonstrates Its Ongoing Commitment to Ronald McDonald Houses

brand and the cause benefit from such alliances, a *low familiar cause* benefitted more from its association with a positive brand than did a *highly familiar cause*.[29] The results of another study further suggests that if corporate sponsors fail to explicitly indicate their motives for a company-cause or a product-cause association, it is likely that consumers will form their own motives for the association between the company, product or service, and the cause.[30] This finding seems to indicate that it is likely to be a good idea for a sponsor to reveal to target consumers the reasoning behind their sponsorship, so that consumers know the sponsor's motives rather than form their own potentially inaccurate or negative motives.

Resolving two conflicting attitudes

Attitude-change strategies can sometimes resolve actual or potential conflict between two attitudes. Specifically, if consumers can be made to see that their negative attitude toward a product, a specific brand, or its attributes is really not in conflict with another attitude, they may be induced to change their evaluation of the brand (i.e., moving from negative to positive).

For example, Stanley is a serious amateur photographer who has been thinking of moving from 35 mm photography into the realm of medium-format photography in order to take advantage of the larger negative size. However, with the growth of digital photography, Stanley is unsure of whether his move to the medium format will be worthwhile. Stanley loves the idea of having a bigger negative to work with in his darkroom (attitude 1), but he may feel that purchasing a medium-format camera is an unwise investment because these cameras may be supplanted in the near future by digital photography (attitude 2). However, if Stanley learns that Mamiya offers a medium-format camera that offers both a film capability and a digital capability, and even has recently introduced an entirely digital medium-format camera, he might change his mind and thereby resolve his conflicting attitudes. Finally, Figure 8.14 is an ad for Seventh Generation's line of natural dishwashing and laundry detergents. The company points out that their products are as affective as synthetic chemical cleaning agents and are safer because they are all natural. For a person who cares about both the affectiveness and environmental safety of the cleaning products they use, Seventh Generation is attempting to resolve what might otherwise be conflicting attitudes.

Altering components of the multiattribute model

Earlier in this chapter we discussed a number of multiattribute attitude models. These models have implications for attitude-change strategies; specifically, they provide us with additional insights as to how to bring about attitude change: (1) changing the relative evaluation of attributes, (2) changing brand beliefs, (3) adding an attribute, and (4) changing the overall brand rating.

Changing the relative evaluation of attributes

The overall market for many product categories is often set out so that different consumer segments are offered different brands with different features or benefits. For instance, within a product category such as dishwashing liquids, there are brands such as Dawn that stress potency and brands such as Dove that stress gentleness. These two brands of dishwashing liquids have historically appealed to different segments of the overall dishwashing liquid market. Similarly, when it comes to coffee, the market can be divided into regular coffee and decaffeinated coffee, or when it comes to headache remedies, there is the division between aspirin (e.g., Bayer) and acetaminophen (e.g., Tylenol).

In general, when a product category is naturally divided according to distinct product features or benefits that appeal to a particular segment of consumers, marketers usually have an opportunity to persuade consumers to "cross over," that is, to persuade consumers who prefer one version of the product (e.g., standard bifocal eyeglass lenses) to shift their favorable attitudes toward another version of the product (e.g., progressive bifocal lenses).

Changing brand beliefs

A second cognitive-oriented strategy for changing attitudes concentrates on changing beliefs or perceptions about the brand itself. This is by far the most common form of advertising appeal. Advertisers constantly are reminding us that their product has "more" or is "better" or "best" in terms of some important product attribute. As a variation on this theme of "more," ads for Palmolive dishwashing liquid are designed to *extend* consumers' brand attitudes with regard to the product's gentleness by suggesting

FIGURE 8.14

Source: © Seventh
Generation, Inc.

**Seventh Generation Offers
Information That Helps Resolve
Two Conflicting Attitudes**

that it be used for hand washing of fine clothing items. Figure 8.15 presents an ad for Bush's Baked Beans that makes the point that "We couldn't make our secret family recipe any better, so we made it easier" (by placing it in a microwavable cup). In a similar fashion, Paul Mitchell hair care products have challenged the notion that hair damaged by chemicals, the environment, or heat cannot be helped. Paul Mitchell claims that the use of their Super Strong™ hair care products can strengthen damaged hair over 50 percent.

Within the context of brand beliefs, there are forces working to stop or slow down attitude change. For instance, consumers frequently resist evidence that challenges a strongly held attitude or belief and tend to interpret any ambiguous information in ways that reinforce their preexisting attitudes.[31] Therefore, information suggesting a change in attitude needs to be compelling and repeated enough to overcome the natural resistance to letting go of established attitudes.

FIGURE 8.15

Source: © Bush Brothers & Company.

WE COULDN'T MAKE OUR SECRET FAMILY RECIPE
ANY BETTER, SO WE MADE IT EASIER.

Same great secret family recipe, now in a handy new microwavable cup.
www.bushbeans.com   ©2004 Bush Brothers & Company

Changing Attitudes by Altering Beliefs About a Brand

Adding an attribute

Another cognitive strategy consists of *adding an attribute.* This can be accomplished either by adding an attribute that previously has been ignored or one that represents an improvement or technological innovation.

The first route, adding a previously ignored attribute, is illustrated by the point that yogurt has more potassium than a banana (a fruit associated with a high quantity of potassium). For consumers interested in increasing their intake of potassium, the comparison of yogurt and bananas has the power of enhancing their attitudes toward yogurt.

The second route of adding an attribute that reflects an actual product change or technological innovation is easier to accomplish than stressing a previously ignored attribute. To illustrate, Kenmore has introduced a refrigerator with PūR, an advanced and unique

FIGURE 8.16

Source: © Sears Brands, LLC. Used with permission. All rights reserved.

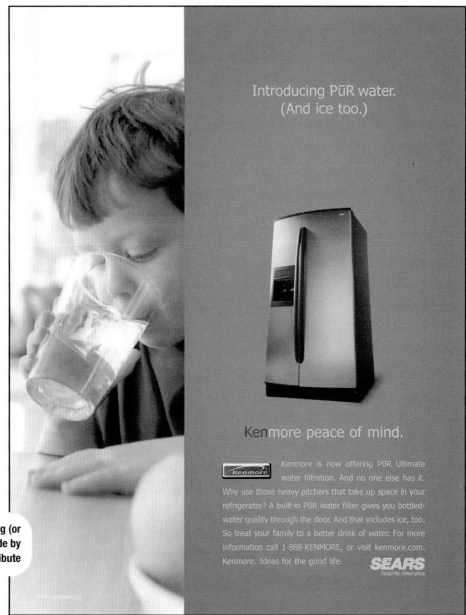

Kenmore Is Changing (or Enhancing) an Attitude by Adding an Attribute

water filtration system (Figure 8.16). This is a powerful and attractive feature for a refrigerator, a feature that reflects Kenmore's continued efforts to create innovative products.

Sometimes eliminating a characteristic or feature has the same enhancing outcome as adding a characteristic or attribute. For instance, a number of skin care or deodorant manufacturers offer versions of their products that are unscented (i.e., *deleting an ingredient*). Indeed, Dove also markets an unscented version of its original Dove product.

Changing the overall brand rating

Still another cognitive-oriented strategy consists of attempting to alter consumers' *overall assessment of the brand* directly, without attempting to improve or change their evaluation of any single brand attribute. Such a strategy frequently relies on some form of global statement that "this is the largest-selling brand" or "the one all others try to imitate," or a similar claim that sets the brand apart from all its competitors. For instance, an advertisement announcing that the Chrysler 300C is "the most awarded new car ever" is the type of information that can increase consumers' positive attitudes, and also stimulate positive word-of-mouth, and even the purchase of a Chrysler 300C.

Changing beliefs about competitors' brands

Another approach to attitude-change strategy involves changing consumer beliefs about the *attributes of competitive* brands or product categories. For instance, a Motrin advertisement makes a dramatic assertion of product superiority over Advil and Aleve by claiming that "no other works faster or stronger on muscle pain." Similarly, Clorox Clean-Up that claims that Mr. Clean cannot remove certain types of tough stains that Clorox Clean-Up can. The main message is to proffer the insight that Clorex Clean-Up is a superior product to Mr. Clean's product (a principal competitor). While potentially very effective, such comparative advertising can boomerang by giving visibility to a competing brand and their claims. (Chapter 9 discusses comparative advertising in greater depth.)

The elaboration likelihood model (ELM)

Compared to the various specific strategies of attitude change that we have reviewed, the **elaboration likelihood model (ELM)** proposes the more global view that consumer attitudes are changed by two distinctly different "routes to persuasion": a central route or a peripheral route (see also Chapter 7).[32] The *central route* is particularly relevant to attitude change when a consumer's motivation or ability to assess the attitude object is *high;* that is, attitude change occurs because the consumer actively seeks out information relevant to the attitude object itself. When consumers are willing to exert the effort to comprehend, learn, or evaluate the available information about the attitude object, learning and attitude change occur via the central route.

In contrast, when a consumer's motivation or assessment skills are low (e.g., low involvement), learning and attitude change tend to occur via the *peripheral route* without the consumer focusing on information relevant to the attitude object itself. In such cases, attitude change often is an outcome of secondary inducements (e.g., cents-off coupons, free samples, beautiful background scenery, great packaging, or the encouragement of a celebrity endorsement). Research indicates that even in low-involvement conditions (e.g., such as exposure to most advertising), in which both central and secondary inducements are initially equal in their ability to evoke similar attitudes, it is the central inducement that has the greatest "staying power"—that is, over time it is more persistent. Additionally, for subjects low in product knowledge, advertisements with terminology result in the consumer having a better attitude toward the brand and the ad.[33]

An offshoot of the elaboration likehood model is the *dual mediation model* (DMM). The DMM model adds a link between attitude towards the ad and brand cognitions.[34] It acknowledges the possibility that the central route to persuasion could be influenced by a peripheral cue (i.e., attitude towards the ad). Thus, this model demonstrated the interrelationship between the central and peripheral processes.

behavior can precede or follow attitude formation

Our discussion of attitude formation and attitude change has stressed the traditional "rational" view that consumers develop their attitudes before taking action (e.g., "Know what you are doing before you do it"). There are alternatives to this "attitude precedes behavior" perspective, alternatives that, on careful analysis, are likely to be just as logical and rational. For example, *cognitive dissonance theory* and *attribution theory* each provide a different explanation as to why behavior might precede attitude formation.

Cognitive dissonance theory

According to **cognitive dissonance theory**, discomfort or dissonance occurs when a consumer holds conflicting thoughts about a belief or an attitude object. For instance, when consumers have made a commitment—made a down payment or placed an order for a product, particularly an expensive one such as an automobile or a personal computer—they often begin to feel cognitive dissonance *when they think of the unique, positive qualities of the brands not selected ("left behind")*. When cognitive dissonance occurs after a purchase, it is called *postpurchase dissonance.* Because purchase decisions often require some amount of compromise, postpurchase dissonance is quite normal. Nevertheless, it is likely to leave consumers with an uneasy feeling about their prior beliefs or actions—a feeling that they would seek to resolve by changing their attitudes to conform with their behavior.[35]

Thus, in the case of postpurchase dissonance, attitude change is frequently an *outcome* of an action or behavior. The conflicting thoughts and dissonant information following a purchase are prime factors that induce consumers to change their attitudes so that they will be consonant with their actual purchase behavior.

What makes postpurchase dissonance relevant to marketing strategists is the premise that *dissonance* propels consumers to reduce the unpleasant feelings created by the rival thoughts. A variety of tactics are open to consumers to reduce postpurchase dissonance. The consumer can rationalize the decision as being wise, seek out advertisements that support the choice (while avoiding dissonance-creating competitive ads), try to "sell" friends on the positive features of the brand (i.e., *"the consumer as a sales agent"*), or look to known satisfied owners for reassurance. For example, consider the response of a young man who just purchased an engagement ring for his girlfriend to the following ad headline he spots in a magazine: "How can you make two months' salary last forever?" This thought is likely to catch his attention. It says to him that although an engagement ring costs a great deal of money, it lasts forever because the future bride will cherish it for the rest of her life. Such an ad exposure is bound to help him reduce any lingering dissonance that he might have about how much he just spent on the ring.

While it has traditionally been viewed that with respect to a particular purchase, cognitive dissonance was something that a consumer either had or did not have, a recent study found that there can exist different types and levels of dissonance. The research studied consumer durable purchases, and found three distinct segments of consumers: a high dissonance segment, a low dissonance segment, and a "concerned about needing the purchase" segment.[36]

In addition to such consumer-initiated tactics for reducing postpurchase uncertainty, marketers can help consumers relieve their dissonance by including messages in their advertising specifically aimed at reinforcing consumers' decisions by complimenting their wisdom, offering stronger guarantees or warranties, increasing the number and effectiveness of its services, or providing detailed brochures on how to use its products correctly. However, with respect to product and service advertisements, there is evidence that as many as 75 percent of Americans feel that advertisers, on purpose, stretch the truth about their products in their advertising.[37]

Attribution theory

As a group of loosely interrelated social psychological principles, **attribution theory** attempts to explain how people assign causality (e.g., blame or credit) to events on the basis of either their own behavior or the behavior of others.[38] In other words, a person might say, "I contributed to UNICEF because it really helps people in need," or "She tried to persuade me to buy that unknown brand of DVD player because she'd make a bigger commission." In attribution theory, the underlying question is why: "Why did I do this?" "Why did she try to get me to switch brands?" This process of making inferences about one's own or another's behavior is a major component of attitude formation and change.

Attribution theory is certainly part of our everyday life, as companies continue to have their names on football stadiums and sponsor all types of charitable events. Research results indicate that the better the "match" between a sponsor and an event, the more positive the outcome is likely to be. Still further, there is evidence to suggest that consumers are willing to reward high-effort firms (i.e., they will pay more and/or evaluate the product higher) if they feel that the company has made an extra effort to make a better product or provide better consumer services.[39]

Self-perception theory

Of the various perspectives on attribution theory that have been proposed, **self-perception theory**—individuals' inferences or judgments as to the causes of their own behavior—is a good beginning point for a discussion of attribution.

In terms of consumer behavior, self-perception theory suggests that attitudes develop as consumers *look at and make judgments about their own behavior.* Simply stated, if a young Wall Street banker observes that he routinely purchases *The Wall Street Journal* on his way to the office, he is apt to conclude that he likes *The Wall Street Journal* (i.e., he has a positive attitude toward this newspaper).[40] Drawing inferences from one's own behavior is not always as simple or as clear-cut as the newspaper example might suggest. To appreciate the complexity of self-perception theory, it is useful to distinguish between **internal and external attributions**. Let us assume that Dana has just finished using a popular computer photoediting software (e.g., Adobe's Photoshop) for the first time and that her digital photographs were well received when they were shown to the members of the photography club that she belongs to. After receiving the compliments, she says to herself, "I'm really a natural at editing my digital photos," this statement would be an example of an *internal attribution*. It is an internal attribution because she is giving herself credit for the outcome (e.g., her ability, her skill, or her effort). That is, she is saying, "These photos are good because of me." On the other hand, if Dana concluded that the successful digital photoediting was due to factors beyond her control (e.g., a user-friendly photoediting program, the assistance of another club member, or just "luck"), this would be an example of an *external attribution*. In such a case, she might be saying, "My great photos are beginner's luck."

This distinction between internal and external attributions can be of strategic marketing importance. For instance, it would generally be in the best interests of the firm that produces the photoediting software if users, especially inexperienced users, *internalized* their successful use of the software package. If they internalized such a positive experience, it is more likely that they will repeat the behavior and become a satisfied regular user. Alternatively, however, if they were to *externalize* their success, it would be preferable that they attribute it to the particular software rather than to an incidental environmental factor such as "beginner's luck" or another's "foolproof" instructions. Additionally, recent studies suggest that when advertisers accurately target their message to consumers, with the proper cognitive generalizations about the self ("self-schema"), the consumer perceives the argument quality of the ad as being higher, and therefore has a more favorable attitude towards the message.[41]

According to the principle of **defensive attribution**, consumers are likely to accept credit personally for success (internal attribution) and to credit failure to others or to outside events (external attribution). For this reason, it is crucial that marketers offer uniformly high-quality products that allow consumers to perceive themselves as the reason for the success; that is, "I'm competent." Moreover, a company's advertising should serve to reassure consumers, particularly inexperienced ones, that its products will not let them down but will make them heroes instead.

Foot-in-the-door Technique Self-perception theorists have explored situations in which consumer compliance with a minor request affects subsequent compliance with a more substantial request. This strategy, which is commonly referred to as the **foot-in-the-door technique**, is based on the premise that individuals look at their prior behavior (e.g., compliance with a minor request) and conclude that they are the kind of person who says "yes" to such requests (i.e., an internal attribution). Such self-attribution serves to increase the likelihood that they will agree to a similar more substantial request. Someone who donates twenty-five dollars to the American Heart Association might be persuaded to donate a much larger amount when properly approached. The initial donation is, in effect, the *foot in the door.*

Research into the foot-in-the-door technique has concentrated on understanding how specific incentives (e.g., cents-off coupons of varying amounts) ultimately influence consumer attitudes and subsequent purchase behavior. It appears that different-size incentives create different degrees of internal attribution, which, in turn, lead to different amounts of attitude change. For instance, individuals who try a brand without any inducements or individuals who buy a brand repeatedly are more likely to infer increasingly positive attitudes toward the brand from their respective behaviors (e.g., "I buy this brand because I like it"). In contrast, individuals who try a free sample are less committed to changing their attitudes toward the brand ("I tried this brand because it was free").

Thus, contrary to what might be expected, it is not the biggest incentive that is most likely to lead to positive attitude change. If an incentive is too big, marketers run the risk that consumers might externalize the cause of their behavior to the incentive and be *less* likely to change their attitudes and *less* likely to make future purchases of the brand. Instead, what seems most effective is a *moderate* incentive, one that is just big enough to stimulate initial purchase of the brand but still small enough to encourage consumers to internalize their positive usage experience and allow a positive attitude change to occur.[42]

In contrast with the foot-in-the-door technique is the **door-in-the-face technique**, in which a large, costly first request that is probably refused is followed by a second, more realistic, less costly request. Under certain situations, this technique may prove more effective than the foot-in-the-door technique.[43]

Attributions toward others

In addition to understanding self-perception theory, it is important to understand **attributions toward others** because of the variety of potential applications to consumer behavior and marketing. As already suggested, every time a person asks "why?" about a statement or action of another or "others"—a family member, a friend, a salesperson, a direct marketer, a shipping company—attribution theory is relevant. To illustrate, in evaluating the words or deeds of others, say, a salesperson, a consumer tries to determine if the salesperson's motives are in the consumer's best interests. If the salesperson's motives are viewed as favorable to the consumer, the consumer is likely to respond favorably. Otherwise, the consumer is likely to reject the salesperson's words and go elsewhere to make a purchase. In another case, a consumer orders a new digital camera from a major direct marketer such as **Buy.com** or **Newegg.com**. Because the consumer wants it immediately, she agrees to pay an extra $8 to $15 for next-day delivery by FedEx or UPS. If on the next day the package with the digital camera fails to show up as expected, the consumer has two possible "others" to which she might attribute the failure—that is, the direct marketer (failing to get the product out on time) or the delivery service (failing to get the package to the consumer on time). In addition, she might blame them both (a dual failure); or if the weather was really bad, she might conclude that it was the bad weather (an attribution that neither of them was at fault).[44]

Attributions toward things

Consumer researchers also are interested in consumers' **attributions toward things** because products (or services) can readily be thought of as "things." It is in the area of judging product performance that consumers are most likely to form product attributions. Specifically, they want to find out why a product meets or fails to meet their expectations. In this regard, they could attribute the product's successful performance (or failure) to the product itself, to themselves, to other people or situations, or to some combination of these factors.[45] To recap an earlier example, when Dana edited a set of challenging digital photos, she could attribute her success to the Photoshop software (product attribution), to her own skill (self or internal attribution), or to a fellow photo club member who helped her (external attribution).

How we test our attributions

After making initial attributions about a product's performance or a person's words or actions, we often attempt to determine whether the inference we made is correct. According to a leading attribution theorist, individuals acquire conviction about particular observations by acting like "naive scientists," that is, by collecting additional information in an attempt to confirm (or disconfirm) prior inferences. In collecting such information, consumers often use the following criteria:[46]

1. Distinctiveness—The consumer attributes an action to a particular product or person if the action occurs when the product (or person) is present and does not occur in its absence.

2. Consistency over time—Whenever the person or product is present, the consumer's inference or reaction must be the same, or nearly so.

3. Consistency over modality—The inference or reaction must be the same, even when the situation in which it occurs varies.

4. Consensus—The action is perceived in the same way by other consumers.

To illustrate how the process of testing our attributions work, Figure 8.17 provides three scenarios that depict (for three of the four "attributions testing criteria"), how people might use information to determine why a corporation has given a grant for an after-school program to benefit public school children, and whether the giving is either internally or externally driven or caused.

Consensus	Distinctiveness	Consistency	Resulting attribution
High *Many groups support the after-school program*	**High** *The corporation supports only the school*	**High** *The corporation supports the school regularly*	→ **External influence** *Support of the school is related to the quality of the school*
Low *Only the corporation supports the after-school program*	**Low** *The corporation supports several schools and other programs*	**High** *The corporation supports the school regularly*	→ **Internal disposition** *Support of the school is related to the benevolence of the corporation*
Either **High or Low**	**Either** **High or Low**	**Low** *The corporation gave a grant to the school only once*	→ **External influence** *Support of the school is related to an undefined aspect of the particular situation that occurred at the time of the grant*

Testing Attributions of a Corporate Grant to Support an After-School Program

Source: Andrea M. Sjovall and Andrew C. Talk, "From Actions to Impressions: Cognitive Attribution Theory and the Formation of Corporate Reputation," *Corporate Reputation Review* 7 (Fall 2004): 277.

FIGURE 8.17

The following example illustrates how each of these criteria might be used to make inferences about product performance and people's actions.

If Mike, a city bus driver who loves do-it-yourself projects, observes that the edges on wooden tables that he builds seem to be smoother when using his new DeWalt router (**www.dewalt.com**), he is likely to credit the new DeWalt power tool with the improved appearance of his tables (i.e., distinctiveness). Furthermore, if Mike finds that his new DeWalt router produces the same high-quality results each time he uses it, he will tend to be more confident about his initial observation (i.e., the inference has consistency over time). Similarly, he will also be more confident if he finds that his satisfaction with the DeWalt power tool extends across a wide range of other related tasks, from making dovetail joints for drawers to cutting patterns in wood (i.e., consistency over modality). Finally, Mike will have still more confidence in his inferences to the extent that his friends who own DeWalt routers also have similar experiences (i.e., consensus).

Much like Mike, we go about gathering additional information from our experiences with people and things, and we use this information to test our initial inferences.

SUMMARY

An attitude is a learned predisposition to behave in a consistently favorable or unfavorable way with respect to a given object (e.g., a product category, a brand, a service, an advertisement, a Web site, or a retail establishment). Each property of this definition is critical to understanding why and how attitudes are relevant in consumer behavior and marketing.

Of considerable importance in understanding the role of attitudes in consumer behavior is an appreciation of the structure and composition of an attitude. Four broad categories of attitude models have received attention: tricomponent attitude model, multiattribute attitude model, trying-to-consume attitude model, and attitude-toward-the-ad model.

The tricomponent model of attitudes consists of three parts: a cognitive component, an affective component, and a conative component. The cognitive component captures a consumer's knowledge and perceptions (i.e., beliefs) about products and services. The affective component focuses on a consumer's emotions or feelings with respect to a particular product or service. Evaluative in nature, the affective component determines an individual's overall assessment of the attitude object in terms of some kind of favorableness rating. The conative component is concerned with the likelihood that a consumer will act in a specific fashion with respect to the attitude object. In marketing and consumer behavior, the conative component is frequently treated as an expression of the consumer's intention to buy.

Multiattribute attitude models (i.e., attitude-toward-object, attitude-toward-behavior, and the theory-of-reasoned-action models) have received much attention from consumer researchers. As a group, these models examine consumer beliefs about specific product attributes (e.g., product or brand features or benefits). Recently, there has been an effort to better accommodate consumers' goals as expressed by their "trying to consume" (i.e., a goal the consumer is trying or planning to accomplish). The theory of trying is designed to account for the many cases in which the action or outcome is not certain. The attitude-toward-the-ad models examine the influence of advertisements on the consumer's attitudes toward the brand.

How consumer attitudes are formed and how they are changed are two closely related issues of considerable concern to marketing practitioners. When it comes to attitude formation, it is useful to remember that attitudes are learned and that different learning theories provide unique insights as to how attitudes initially may be formed. Attitude formation is facilitated by direct personal experience and influenced by the ideas and experiences of friends and family members and exposure to mass media. In addition, it is likely that an individual's personality plays a role in attitude formation.

These same factors also have an impact on attitude change; that is, attitude changes are learned, and they are influenced by personal experiences and the information gained from various personal and impersonal sources. The consumer's own personality affects both the acceptance and the speed with which attitudes are likely to be altered.

Strategies of attitude change can be classified into six distinct categories: (1) changing the basic motivational function, (2) associating the attitude object with a specific group or event, (3) relating the attitude object to conflicting attitudes, (4) altering components of the multiattribute model, (5) changing beliefs about competitors' brands, and (6) the elaboration likelihood model. Each of these strategies provides the marketer with alternative ways of changing consumers' existing attitudes.

Most discussions of attitude formation and attitude change stress the traditional view that consumers develop attitudes before they act. However, this may not always, or even usually, be true. Both cognitive dissonance theory and attribution theory provide alternative explanations of attitude formation and change that suggest that behavior might precede attitudes. Cognitive dissonance theory suggests that the conflicting thoughts, or dissonant information, following a purchase decision might propel consumers to change their attitudes to make them consonant with their actions. Attribution theory focuses on how people assign causality to events and how they form or alter attitudes as an outcome of assessing their own behavior or the behavior of other people or things.

DISCUSSION QUESTIONS

1. Explain how situational factors are likely to influence the degree of consistency between attitudes and behavior.

2. Because attitudes are learned predispositions to respond, why don't marketers and consumer researchers just measure purchase behavior and forget attitudes?

3. Explain a person's attitude toward visiting Disney World in terms of the tricomponent attitude model.

4. How can the marketer of a "nicotine patch" (a device that assists individuals to quit smoking) use the *theory of trying* to segment its market? Using this theory, identify two segments that the marketer should target and propose product positioning approaches to be directed at each of the two segments.

5. Explain how the product manager of a breakfast cereal might change consumer attitudes toward the company's brand by (a) changing beliefs about the brand, (b) changing beliefs about competing brands, (c) changing the relative evaluation of attributes, and (d) adding an attribute.

6. The Department of Transportation of a large city is planning an advertising campaign that encourages people to switch from private cars to mass transit. Give examples of how the department can use the following strategies to change commuters' attitudes: (a) changing the basic motivational function, (b) changing beliefs about public transportation, (c) using self-perception theory, and (d) using cognitive dissonance.

7. The Saturn Corporation is faced with the problem that many consumers perceive compact and midsize American cars to be of poorer quality than comparable Japanese cars. Assuming that Saturn produces cars that are of equal or better quality than Japanese cars, how can the company persuade consumers of this fact?

8. Should the marketer of a popular computer graphics program prefer consumers to make internal or external attributions? Explain your answer.

9. A college student has just purchased a new personal computer. What factors might cause the student to experience postpurchase dissonance? How might the student try to overcome it? How can the retailer who sold the computer help reduce the student's dissonance? How can the computer's manufacturer help?

EXERCISES

1. Find two print ads, one illustrating the use of the affective component and the other illustrating the cognitive component. Discuss each ad in the context of the tricomponent model. In your view, why has each marketer taken the approach it did in each of these ads?

2. What sources influenced your attitude about this course before classes started? Has your initial attitude changed since the course started? If so, how?

3. Describe a situation in which you acquired an attitude toward a new product through exposure to an advertisement for that product. Describe a situation in which you formed an attitude toward a product or brand on the basis of personal influence.

4. Find advertisements that illustrate each of the four motivational functions of attitudes. Distinguish between ads that are designed to reinforce an existing attitude and those aimed at changing an attitude.

5. Think back to the time when you were selecting a college. Did you experience dissonance immediately after you made a decision? Why or why not? If you did experience dissonance, how did you resolve it?

KEY TERMS

- attitudes
- attitude-toward-behavior model
- attitude-toward-object model
- attitude-toward-the-ad models
- attributions toward others
- attributions toward things
- attribution theory
- cognitive dissonance theory
- defensive attribution

- door-in-the-face technique
- ego-defensive function
- elaboration likelihood model (ELM)
- foot-in-the-door technique
- functional approach
- intention-to-buy scales
- internal and external attributions
- knowledge function

- multiattribute attitude models
- self-perception theory
- theory of reasoned action
- theory of trying to consume
- tricomponent attitude model
- utilitarian function
- value-expressive function

NOTES

1. Naresh K. Malhotra, "Attitude and Affect: New Frontiers of Research in the 21st Century," *Journal of Business Research* 58 (April 2005): 477–482.

2. See, for example, Gordon R. Foxall, M. Mirella, and Yani-de-Soriano, "Situational Influences on Consumers' Attitudes and Behavior," *Journal of Business Research* 58 (April 2005): 518–525.

3. Jack Neff, "Suave Strokes," *Advertising Age,* August 20, 2001, 12.

4. Richard J. Lutz, "The Role of Attitude Theory in Marketing," in Harold H. Kassarjian and Thomas S. Robertson, eds., *Perspectives in Consumer Behavior,* 4th ed. (Upper Saddle River, NJ: Prentice-Hall, 1991), 317–339.

5. Pamela E. Grimm, "A_b Components' Impact on Brand Preference," *Journal of Business Research* 58 (April 2005): 508–517.

6. See, for example, Chris T. Allen, Karen A. Machleit, Susan Schultz Kleine, and Arti Sahni Notani, "A Place for Emotion in Attitude Models," *Journal of Business Research* 58 (April 2005): 494–499.

7. Joel B. Cohen and Charles S. Areni, "Affect and Consumer Behavior," in Harold H. Kassarjian and Thomas S. Robertson, eds., *Perspectives in Consumer Behavior,* 188–240; and Madeline Johnson and George M. Zinkhan, "Emotional Responses to a Professional Service Encounter," *Journal of Service Marketing* 5 (Spring 1991): 5–16. Also see John Kim, Jeen-Su Iim, and Mukesh Bhargava, "The Role of Affect in Attitude Formation: A Classical Condition Approach," *Journal of the Academy of Marketing Science* 26 (1998): 143–152.

8. Jaideep Sengupta, "Perspectives on Attitude Strength" (a special session summary), in Joseph W. Alba and J. Wesley Hutchinson, eds., *Advances in Consumer Research, 25*

(Provo, UT: Association for Consumer Research, 1998), 63–64.

9. Martin Fishbein, "An Investigation of the Relationships Between Beliefs About an Object and the Attitude Toward the Object," *Human Relations* 16 (1963): 233–240; and Martin Fishbein, "A Behavioral Theory Approach to the Relations Between Beliefs About an Object and the Attitude Toward the Object," in Martin Fishbein, ed., *Readings in Attitude Theory and Measurement* (New York: Wiley, 1967), 389–400.

10. Claude Pecheux and Christian Derbaix, "Children and Attitude Toward the Brand: A New Measurement Scale," *Journal of Advertising Research* (July/August 1999): 19–27.

11. Icek Ajzen and Martin Fishbein, *Understanding Attitudes and Predicting Social Behavior* (Upper Saddle River, NJ: Prentice-Hall, 1980); and Martin Fishbein and Icek Ajzen, *Belief, Attitude, Intentions, and Behavior* (Reading, MA: Addison-Wesley, 1975), 62–63. Also see Robert E. Burnkrant, H. Rao Unnava, and Thomas J. Page, Jr., "Effects of Experience on Attitude Structure," in Rebecca H. Holman and Michael R. Solomon, eds., *Advances in Consumer Research,* 18 (Provo, UT: Association for Consumer Research, 1991), 28–29.

12. Shwu-Ing Wu, "The Relationship between Consumer Characteristics and Attitude toward Online Shopping," *Marketing Intelligence and Planning* 21, no. 1, (2003): 37–44.

13. Terence A. Shimp and Alican Kavas, "The Theory of Reasoned Action Applied to Coupon Usage," *Journal of Consumer Research* 11 (December 1984): 795–809; Blair H. Sheppard, Jon Hartwick, and Paul R. Warshaw, "The Theory of Reasoned Action: A Meta-Analysis of Past Research

with Recommendations for Modifications and Future Research," *Journal of Consumer Research* 15 (September 1986): 325–343; Sharon E. Beatly and Lynn R. Kahle, "Alternative Hierarchies of the Attitude-Behavior Relationship: The Impact of Brand Commitment and Habit," *Journal of the Academy of Marketing Science* 16 (Summer 1988):1–10; Richard P. Bagozzi, Hans Baumgartner, and Youjae Yi, "Coupon Usage and the Theory of Reasoned Action," in Rebecca H. Holman and Michael R. Solomon, eds., *Advances in Consumer Research,* 18 (Provo, UT: Association for Consumer Research, 1991), 24–27; Hee Sun Park, "Relationships Among Attitudes and Subjective Norms: Testing the Theory of Reasoned Action Across Cultures," *Communication Studies* 51, no. 2 (Summer 2000): 162–175; and Hung-Pin Shih, "An Empirical Study on Predicting User Acceptance of e-Shopping on the Web," *Information & Management (Amsterdam)* 41 (January 2004): 351.

14. Chris T. Allen, Karen A. Machleit, Susan Schultz Kleine, and Arti Sahni Notani, "A Place for Emotion in Attitude Models," *Journal of Business Research* 58 (April 2005): 494–499.

15. Richard P. Bagozzi and Paul R. Warshaw, "Trying to Consume," *Journal of Consumer Research* 17 (September 1990): 127–140; Richard P. Bagozzi, Fred D. Davis, and Paul R. Warshaw, "Development and Test of a Theory of Technological Learning and Usage," *Human Relations* 45, no. 7 (July 1992): 659–686; and Anil Mathur, "From Intentions to Behavior: The Role of Trying and Control," in Barbara B. Stern and George M. Zinkan, eds., *1995 AMA Educators' Proceedings* (Chicago: American Marketing Association, 1995), 374–375.

16. Stephen J. Gould, Franklin S. Houston, and Jonel Mundt, "Failing to Try to Consume: A Reversal of the Usual Consumer Research Perspective," in Merrie Brucks and Deborah J. MacInnis, eds., *Advances in Consumer Research* (Provo, UT: Association for Consumer Research, 1997), 211–216.

17. Rajeev Batra and Michael L. Ray, "Affective Responses Mediating Acceptance of Advertising," *Journal of Consumer Research* 13 (September 1986): 236–239; Julie A. Edell and Marian Chapman Burke, "The Power of Feelings in Understanding Advertising Effects," *Journal of Consumer Research* 14 (December 1987): 421–433; and Marian Chapman Burke and Julie A. Edell, "The Impact of Feelings on Ad-Based Affect and Cognition," *Journal of Marketing Research* 26 (February 1989): 69–83.

18. Durriya Z. Khairullah and Zahid Y. Khairullah, "Relationships Between Acculturation, Attitude Toward the Advertisement, and Purchase Intention of Asian-Indian Immigrants," *International Journal of Commerce and Management* 9, no. 3/4 (1999): 46–65.

19. Alan J. Bush, Rachel Smith, and Craig Martin, "The Influence of Consumer Socialization Variables on Attitude Toward Advertising: A Comparison of African-Americans and Caucasians," *Journal of Advertising* 28, no. 3 (Fall 1999): 13–24.

20. Subodh Bhat and Srinivas K. Reddy, "Investigating the Dimensions of the Fit Between a Brand and Its Extensions," *1997 AMA Winter Educators' Conference Proceedings,* 8 (Chicago: American Marketing Association, 1997), 186–194.

21. Morris B. Holbrook, David A. Velez, and Gerard J. Tabouret, "Attitude Structure and Search: An Integrative Model of Importance-Directed Information Processing," in Kent B. Monroe, ed., *Advances in Consumer Research,* 8 (Ann Arbor, MI: Association for Consumer Research, 1981), 35–41.

22. Richard P. Bagozzi, Hans Baumgartner, and Youjae Yi, "Coupon Usage and the Theory of Reasoned Action," in Rebecca H. Holman and Michael R. Solomon, eds., *Advances in Consumer Research,* 18 (Provo, UT: Association for Consumer Research, 1991), 24–27.

23. For an interesting article on the impact of social interaction on attitude development, see Daniel J. Howard and Charles Gengler, "Emotional Contagion Effects on Product Attitudes," *Journal of Consumer Research* 28 (September 2001): 189–201.

24. Haksik Lee, Gilbert D. Harrell, and Cornelia L. Droge, "Product Experiences and Hierarchy of Advertising Effects," in *2000 AMA Winter Educators' Conference,* 11, eds. John P. Workman and William D. Perreault (Chicago: American Marketing Association, 2000), 41–42.

25. James R. Coyle and Esther Thorson, "The Effects of Progressive Levels of Interactivity and Vividness in Web Marketing Sites," *Journal of Advertising* 30, no. 3 (Fall 2001): 65–77; and Lynn C. Dailey and C. Edward Heath, "Creating the Flow Experience Online: The Role of Web Atmospherics," in *2000 AMA Winter Educators' Conference,* 11, eds. John P. Workman and William D. Perreault (Chicago: American Marketing Association, 2000), 58.

26. Daniel Katz, "The Functional Approach to the Study of Attitudes," *Public Opinion Quarterly* 24 (Summer 1960): 163–191; Sharon Shavitt, "Products, Personality and Situations in Attitude Functions: Implications for Consumer Behavior," in Thomas K. Srull, ed., *Advances in Consumer Research,* 16 (Provo, UT: Association for Consumer Research, 1989), 300–305; and Richard Ennis and Mark P. Zanna, "Attitudes, Advertising, and Automobiles: A Functional Approach," in Leigh McAlister and Michael L. Rothschild, eds., *Advances in Consumer Research,* 20 (Provo, UT: Association for Consumer Research, 1992), 662–666.

27. Maria Knight Lapinski and Franklin J. Boster, "Modeling the Ego-Defensive Function of Attitudes," *Communication Monographs* 68, no. 3 (September 2001): 314–324.

28. Cara Beardi, "Zippo's Eternal Flame," *Advertising Age,* August 13, 2001, 4.

29. Barbara A. Lafferty and Ronald E. Goldsmith, "Cause-Brand Alliances: Does the Cause Help the Brand or Does the Brand Help the Cause?," *Journal of Business Reasearch* 58 (April 2005): 423–429.

30. Nora J. Rifon, Sejung Marina Choi, Carrie S. Tripble, and Hairong Li, "Congruence Effects in Sponsorship," *Journal of Advertising* 33 (Spring 2004): 29–42.

31. Geoffrey L. Cohen, Joshua Aronson, and Claude M. Steele, "When Beliefs Yield to Evidence: Reducing Biased Evaluation by Affirming the Self," *Personality and Social Psychology Bulletin* 26, no. 9 (September 2000): 1151–1164.

32. Richard E. Petty, et al., "Theories of Attitude Change," in Harold Kassarjian and Thomas Robertson, eds., *Handbook of Consumer Theory and Research* (Upper Saddle River, NJ: Prentice Hall, 1991); and Richard E. Petty, John T. Cacioppo, and David Schumann, "Central and Peripheral Routes to Advertising Effectiveness: The Moderating Role of Involvement," *Journal of Consumer Research* 10 (September 1983): 135–146. Also see Curtis P. Haugtvedt and Alan J. Strathman, "Situational Product Relevance and Attitude Persistence," in Marvin E. Goldberg, Gerald Gorn, and Richard W. Pollay, eds., *Advances in Consumer Research,* 17 (Provo, UT: Association for Consumer Research, 1990), 766–769; and Scott B. Mackenzie and Richard A. Spreng, "How Does Motivation Moderate the Impact of Central and Peripheral Processing on Brand Attitudes and Intentions?" *Journal of Consumer Research* 18 (March 1992): 519–529.

33. Shin-Chieh Chuang and Chia-Ching Tsai, "The Impact of Consumer Product Knowledge on the Effect of Terminology in Advertising," *Journal of the American Academy of Business* 6 (March 2005): 154–158, and Jaideep Sgupta, Ronald C. Goldstein, and David S. Boninger, "All Cues Are Not Created Equal: Obtaining Attitude Persistence Under Low-Involvement Conditions," *Journal of Consumer Research* 23 (March 1997): 351–361.

34. Keith S. Coulter and Girish N. Punj, "The Effects of Cognitive Resource Requirements, Availability, and Argument Quality on Brand Attitudes," *Journal of Advertising* 33 (Winter 2004): 53–64.

35. See, for example, David C. Matz and Wendy Wood, "Cognitive Dissonance in Groups," *Journal of Personality and Social Psychology* 88 (January 2005): 22–37; Jillian C. Sweeney and Tanya Mukhopadhyay, "Cognitive Dissonance After Purchase: A Comparison of Bricks and Mortar and Online Retail Purchase Situations," *American Marketing Association Conference Proceedings: 2004 AMA Winter Educators' Conference, Chicago,* 15, 190–191; Martin O'Neill and Adrian Palmer, "Cognitive Dissonance and the Stability of Service Quality Perceptions," *The Journal of Services Marketing* 18 no. 6/7 (2004): 433–449; Robert A Wicklund and Jack W. Brehm, "Internalization of Multiple Perpectives or Dissonance Reduction?," *Theory & Psychology (London)* 14 (June 2004): 355–371, and Alex R. Zablah, Danny N. Bellenger, and Westley J. Johnson, "Customer Relationship Management Implementation Gaps," *The Journal of Personal Selling & Sales Management* 24 (Fall 2004): 279–295.

36. Geoffrey N. Soutar and Jillian C. Sweeney, "Are There Cognitive Dissonance Segments?" *Australian Journal of Management* 28 (December 2003): 227–239.

37. Phil Lampert, "Cognitive Dissonance," *Progressive Grocer* 83 (May 15, 2004): 16.

38. Edward E. Jones, et al., *Attribution: Perceiving the Causes of Behavior* (Morristown, NJ: General Learning Press, 1972); and Bernard Weiner, "Attributional Thoughts About Consumer Behavior," *Journal of Consumer Research* 27, no. 3 (December 2000): 382–387.

39. Op. Cit, Rifon, and others, "Congruence Effects in Sponsorship," 29; and Andrea C. Morales, "Giving Firms an 'E' for Effort: Consumer Responses to High-Effort Firms," *Journal of Consumer Research* 3 (March 2005): 806–812.

40. Chris T. Allen and William R. Dillon, "Self-Perception Development and Consumer Choice Criteria: Is There a Linkage?" in Richard P. Bagozzi and Alice M. Tybout, eds., *Advances in Consumer Research,* 10 (Ann Arbor, MI: Association for Consumer Research, 1983), 45–50.

41. S. Christian Wheeler, Richard E. Petty, and George Y. Bizer, "Self-Schema Matching and Attitude Change: Situational and Dispositional Determinants of Message Elaboration," *Journal of Consumer Research* 31 (March 2005): 787–797.

42. See, for example, Leslie Lazar Kanuk, *Mail Questionnaire Response Behavior as a Function of Motivational Treatment* (New York: CUNY, 1974).

43. Angelos Rodafinos, Arso Vucevic, and Georgios D. Sideridis, "The Effectiveness of Compliance Techniques: Foot in the Door Versus Door in the Face," *The Journal of Social Psychology* 145 (April 2005): 237–239.

44. John R. O'Malley, Jr., "Consumer Attributions of Product Failures to Channel Members," in Kim P. Corfman and John F. Lynch, Jr., eds., *Advances in Consumer Research,* 23 (Provo, UT: Association for Consumer Research, 1996), 342–345. Also see Charmine Hartel, Janet R. Mccoll-Kennedy, and Lyn McDonald, "Incorporating Attributional Theory and the Theory of Reasoned Action Within an Affective Events Theory Framework to Produce a Contingency Predictive Model of Consumer Reactions to

Organizational Mishaps," in Joseph W. Alba and J. Wesley Hutchinson, eds., *Advances in Consumer Research,* 25 (Provo, UT: Association for Consumer Research, 1998), 428–432.

45. Valerie S. Folkes, "Consumer Reactions to Product Failure: Attributional Approach," *Journal of Consumer Research* 10 (March 1984): 398–409; and "Recent Attribution

Research in Consumer Behavior: A Review and New Dimensions," *Journal of Consumer Research* 14 (March 1988): 548–565.

46. Harold H. Kelley, "Attribution Theory in Social Psychology," in David Levine, ed., *Nebraska Symposium on Motivation*, 15 (Lincoln: University of Nebraska Press, 1967), 197.

chapter**nine**

› **Communication and Consumer Behavior**

When you watch TV today, like so many other Americans, you probably have cable or satellite service with access to hundreds of channels. You may also have the ability to order movies and other programs on-demand or have a digital video recorder (DVR) provided by your cable service or that you purchased from TiVo or ReplayTV. If you have a DVR, you can "time shift" by recording programs and watching them at your convenience and skip through commercials easily. The programs and commercials broadcast to you on the network, local, and cable channels are the same as those transmitted to your next-door neighbor. Your household may even be one of the few thousand families declared as "representative" of the nation by the Nielsen Media Research company and the programs that you and other members of your family watch and the precise durations of these viewings, including all "channel surfing" activities, are transmitted to Nielsen via your telephone or broadband connection at least once a day. In turn, Nielsen uses the information it receives from its "Nielsen Families" to estimate the number of viewers of all TV programs each day and conclude, for example, that *American Idol* was the most-watched program one week, a position perhaps occupied by *CSI* during another week. Nielsen's ratings also determine the prices that broadcasters charge advertisers for 30-second spots.

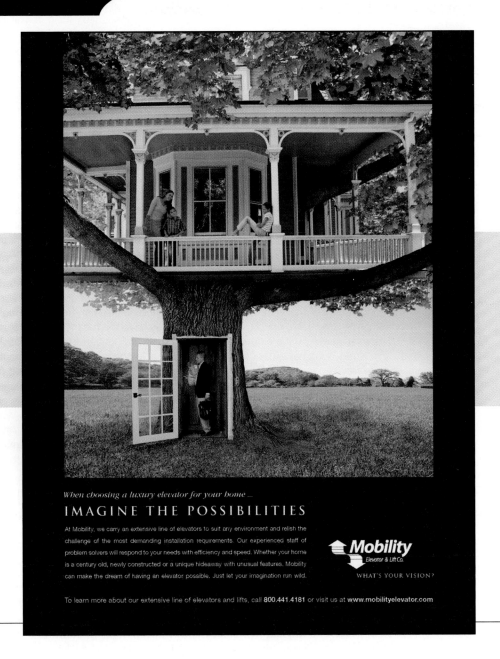

When choosing a luxury elevator for your home ...

IMAGINE THE POSSIBILITIES

At Mobility, we carry an extensive line of elevators to suit any environment and relish the challenge of the most demanding installation requirements. Our experienced staff of problem solvers will respond to your needs with efficiency and speed. Whether your home is a century old, newly constructed or a unique hideaway with unusual features. Mobility can make the dream of having an elevator possible. Just let your imagination run wild.

Mobility
Elevator & Lift Co.

WHAT'S YOUR VISION?

To learn more about our extensive line of elevators and lifts, call **800.441.4181** or visit us at **www.mobilityelevator.com**

For example, on the basis of Nielsen's estimates, a 30-second spot on the 2005 Super Bowl program cost 2.4 million dollars.[1]

Let's fast-forward into the future, say, five years from now (perhaps even less). Then, if you do not own a dog, you will not see ads for Puppy Chow, and if you are an apartment dweller, you will not have to watch commercials for lawn mowers or snow blowers. And if you would like to go on a virtual test-drive while receiving an ad for a Mercedes, you will be able to do so by pressing a button on your remote control.[2]

Your viewing habits will still be closely monitored, but in more sophisticated ways. Your cable provider may give you an upgrade or other incentive if you agree to be part of a group whose viewing habits are used for research purposes (i.e., for determining ratings and advertising rates). Or, Nielsen or another company may pay you to carry a Portable People Meter (PPM)—a small device that you will clip to your belt, wear all day, and plug into a cradle at night that will transmit the data the device had collected. That data will include not only what you had seen on TV that day but also all the ads you were exposed to on the radio, in stores, in the newspapers or magazines that you had read, and the Web sites you visited. If you drove your car that day and your PPM was equipped with a GPS, it will also record the ads posted on every billboard that you passed.[3]

Clearly, communications are undergoing a vast change. Communications are the link between the individual and society. This chapter is the bridge between the characteristics of individuals (covered in Chapters 3 through 8) and the small groups and larger society in which they operate. Communication is the tool that marketers use to persuade consumers to act in a desired way (e.g., to vote, to make a purchase, to make a donation, to patronize a retail store). Today, the media and communications models that have been used for decades are undergoing fundamental changes. Advertisers are unhappy with the current broadcast media because there are many more channels, thus they are reaching smaller and more fragmented audiences and getting less "eyeballs" for the money they spend for TV ads. Consumers can avoid commercials with increasing ease, and advertising messages reach many people who are not interested in the products advertised. Advertisers complain that the Nielsen ratings do not accurately reflect the ethnic composition of the United States population and do not monitor TV viewing via DVRs and other means. Cable operators realize that they have the means to monitor media viewing more accurately but are deeply aware of the privacy concerns of their subscribers. The TV networks, who have lost vast audiences to cable channels, realize that continuing to provide free programming underwritten by advertising revenues generated from reaching massive audiences of prime-time shows—a model in place since the early 1950s—may no longer be feasible. The networks, cable companies, and advertisers agree that the new communications model consists of smaller groups of consumers who are already interested in the products advertised, and to whom they must provide more interactive and enticing ways of viewing their promotional messages.[4] In short, driven by technology, mass communication is going through the greatest changes since the development of spoken and written language.

components of communication

Although there are many ways to define communication, most marketers agree that **communication** is *the transmission of a message from a sender to a receiver via a medium (or channel) of transmission.* In addition to these four basic components—sender, receiver, medium, and message—the fifth essential component of communication is *feedback,* which alerts the sender as to whether the intended message was, in fact, received. Figure 9.1 depicts this basic communications model.

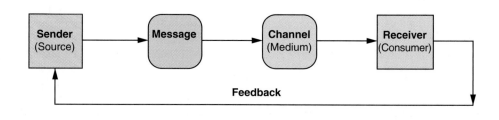

Basic Communication Model

FIGURE 9.1

The sender

The sender, as the initiator of the communication, can be a formal or an informal source. A **formal communications source** is likely to represent either a for-profit (commercial) or a not-for-profit organization (see Figure 9.2); an **informal source** can be a parent or friend who gives product information or advice. Consumers often rely on informal communications sources in making purchase decisions because, unlike formal sources, the sender is perceived as having nothing to gain from the receiver's subsequent actions. For that reason, marketers must always encourage and even initiate positive **word-of-mouth communications** about their products and services.

Not-for-Profit Advertising

Source: © The Breast Cancer Research Foundation. Used with permission. All rights reserved. (www.bcrfcure.org).

FIGURE 9.2

The receiver

The **receiver** of formal marketing communications is likely to be a targeted prospect or a customer (e.g., a member of the marketer's target audience). *Intermediary* and *unintended* audiences are also likely to receive marketers' communications. Examples of intermediary audiences are wholesalers, distributors, and retailers, who receive trade advertising from marketers designed to persuade them to order and stock merchandise, and relevant professionals (such as architects or physicians), who are sent *professional advertising* in the hopes that they will specify or prescribe the marketer's products. Unintended audiences include everyone who is exposed to the message who is not specifically targeted by the sender. Unintended receivers of marketing communications often include publics that are important to the marketer, such as shareholders, creditors, suppliers, employees, bankers, and the local community. It is important to remember that the audience—no matter how large or how diverse—is composed of *individual receivers,* each of whom interprets the message according to his or her own personal perceptions and experiences.

The medium

The **medium**, or communications channel, can be **impersonal** (e.g., a mass medium) or **interpersonal** (a formal conversation between a salesperson and a customer, or an informal conversation between two or more people that takes place face-to-face, by telephone, by mail, or online).

Mass media are generally classified as *print* (newspapers, magazines, billboards), *broadcast* (radio, television), or *electronic* (primarily the Internet). New modes of *interactive communication* that permit the receivers of communication messages to provide direct feedback are beginning to blur the distinction between interpersonal and impersonal communications. For example, most companies encourage consumers to visit their Web sites to find out more about the product or service being advertised or to order online, but not all visitors receive the same message. The information visitors see on the site and the ordering links to which they are routed depend on their selections (in the form of clicking patterns) during that visit or even past visits to the site. **Direct marketers**—often called *database marketers*—also seek individual responses from advertisements they place in all the mass media: broadcast, print, and online, as well as from **direct mail**. Home shopping networks are expanding dramatically as consumers demonstrate their enthusiasm for TV and online shopping. Direct marketers use data regarding recent buying behavior of their customers to generate purchases from subsequent customers.

The message

The **message** can be **verbal** (spoken or written), **nonverbal** (a photograph, an illustration, or a symbol), or a combination of the two. A verbal message, whether it is spoken or written, can usually contain more specific product (or service) information than a nonverbal message. However, a verbal message combined with a nonverbal message is often more persuasive than either would be alone (see Figure 9.3).

Nonverbal information takes place in both interpersonal channels and impersonal channels and often takes the form of symbolic communication. Marketers often try to develop logos or symbols that are associated exclusively with their products and that achieve high recognition. The Coca-Cola Company, for example, has trademarked both the word *Coke* in a specific typographic style and the shape of the traditional Coke bottle, and both are instantly recognizable to consumers as symbols of the company's best-selling soft drink.[5] In 1994, the Supreme Court ruled that even a color that distinguishes a product (and serves no other function) can be registered as a trademark.[6]

FIGURE 9.3

Source: © Dell.

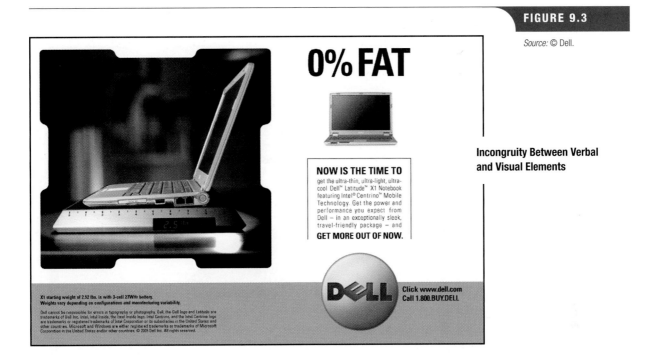

Incongruity Between Verbal and Visual Elements

Figure 9.4 depicts an ad portraying nonverbal, symbolic communications (in the form of hand gestures) in three different cultures.

Feedback

Feedback is an essential component of both interpersonal and impersonal communications. Prompt feedback permits the sender to reinforce, to change, or to modify the message to ensure that it is understood in the intended way. Generally, it is easier to obtain feedback (both verbal and nonverbal) from interpersonal communications than impersonal communications. For example, a good salesperson usually is alert to nonverbal feedback provided by the prospective consumer. Such feedback may take the form of facial expressions (a smile, a frown, a look of total boredom, an expression of disbelief) or body movements (finger tapping, head nodding, head shaking, or clenched hands). Because of the high cost of space and time in impersonal media, it is very important for sponsors of impersonal communications to devise methods to obtain feedback as promptly as possible, so that they may revise a message if its meaning is not being received as intended. (An expanded discussion of *feedback* can be found later in the chapter.)

An excellent example of marketing based on shoppers' feedback, in the form of "body language," is the selling method employed at the rapidly growing Diesel jeans chain. Unlike other clothing stores, Diesel stores are not user-friendly because the company believes that a disoriented customer is the best prospect. Diesel stores feature loud techno music and large TV screens playing videos unrelated to the merchandise sold. There are no signs directing customers to different departments, no obvious salespeople, and jeans items have strange names accompanied by confusing charts intended to explain the clothing options. In the midst of this chaos, young and hip-looking salespeople, who are trained to spot "wayward-looking," overwhelmed, and confused shoppers, "rescue" them by becoming their "shopping friends" and, of course, sell them as many pairs of jeans as possible.[7]

FIGURE 9.4

Source: © HSBC North America Holdings Inc. Used with permission. All rights reserved. (www.hsbc.com).

Nonverbal Communication

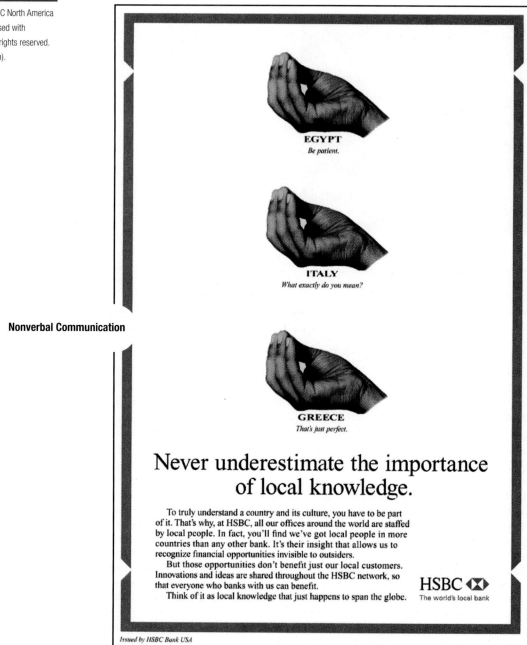

the communications process

In general, a company's marketing communications are designed to make the consumer aware of the product or service, induce purchase or commitment, create a positive attitude toward the product, give the product a symbolic meaning, or show how it can solve the consumer's problem better than a competitive product (or service).

The message initiator (source)

The sponsor (initiator) of the message first must decide to whom the message should be sent and what meaning it should convey. Then the sponsor must *encode* the message in such a way that its meaning is interpreted by the targeted audience in precisely the intended way.

The sources of *impersonal communications* usually are organizations (either for-profit or not-for-profit) that develop and transmit appropriate messages through special departments (e.g., marketing or public relations) or spokespersons. The targets, or receivers, of such messages usually are a specific audience or several audiences that the organization is trying to inform, influence, or persuade. For example, AOL wants to attract both online users and advertisers; a museum may wish to target both donors and visitors; and a mail-order company may want to persuade consumers to call a toll-free number for a copy of its catalog.

Marketers have a large arsenal from which to draw in encoding their messages: They can use words, pictures, symbols, spokespersons, and special channels. They can buy space or time in carefully selected media to advertise or broadcast their message, or they can try to have their message appear in space or time usually reserved for editorial messages. (The latter, called **publicity**, usually is the result of public relations efforts and tends to be more believable because its commercial origins and intent are not readily apparent.)

Credibility

The *credibility of the source* affects the *decoding* of the message. The sponsor of the communications—and his or her perceived honesty and objectivity—have an enormous influence on how the communication is accepted by the receiver(s). When the source is well respected and highly thought of by the intended audience, the message is much more likely to be believed. Conversely, a message from a source considered unreliable or untrustworthy is likely to be received with skepticism and may be rejected.

Credibility is built on a number of factors, of which the most important are the perceived intentions of the source. Receivers ask themselves, "Just what does he (or she) stand to gain if I do what is suggested?" If the receiver perceives any type of personal gain for the message sponsor as a result of the proposed action or advice, the message itself becomes suspect: "He wants me to buy that product just to earn a commission."

Credibility of Informal Sources   One of the major reasons that informal sources such as friends, neighbors, and relatives have a strong influence on a receiver's behavior is simply that they are perceived as having nothing to gain from their purchase recommendation. That is why word-of-mouth communication is so effective. Interestingly enough, informal communications sources, called **opinion leaders**, often do profit psychologically, if not tangibly, by providing product information to others. A person may obtain a great deal of ego satisfaction by providing solicited as well as unsolicited information and advice to friends. This ego gratification may actually improve the quality of the information provided, because the opinion leader often deliberately seeks out the latest detailed information in order to enhance his or her position as "expert" in a particular product category. The fact that the opinion leader does not receive material gain from the recommended action increases the likelihood that the advice will be seriously considered.

Clever marketers initiate **word-of-mouth** (WOM) campaigns. Many firms enlist typical consumers to serve as their **buzz agents**, who agree to bring products they are promoting to gatherings of family and friends, read books they are promoting on mass transit with the title clearly visible, suggest to store owners who do not carry a given product that they should do so, and talk other consumers into trying certain products during shopping trips. Generally, these "agents" do not receive direct payment from the companies they represent, although they often receive free samples. They are motivated by having been identified by the marketers as opinion leaders, and they get an ego boost by appearing so knowledgeable to their peers and having access to new products before others do.[8]

Although marketers had long-ago recognized the perils of *negative* word-of-mouth that can result in unfounded rumors about products (see Chapter 15), today they are more acutely concerned about this issue than ever before. Digital technologies now enable disgruntled consumers to reach millions of people easily through chat rooms and their own Web sites and describe their often-exaggerated negative experiences with products and services. Persistent critics of marketers who initiate bad publicity online are called **determined detractors**. Many companies have been subject to such online attacks; perhaps the best-known example is the individual who ate nothing but McDonald's food for thirty days and produced an extremely critical documentary about this company entitled *Super Size Me.*[9]

Some of the factors that motivate consumers to engage in word-of-mouth are: consumer involvement with the product or message, self-involvement, alleviating postpurchase uncertainty and dissonance (by convincing others to make a similar purchase), seeking information, and concern for others A recent study identified the following factors as the primary motives behind **WOM**: venting negative feelings, concern for others, extraversion and positive self-enhancement, social benefits, economic incentives, helping the company, and advice seeking.[10]

Credibility of Formal Sources   Not-for-profit sources generally have more credibility than for-profit (commercial) sources. Formal sources that are perceived to be "neutral"—such as *Consumer Reports* or newspaper articles—have greater credibility than commercial sources because of the perception that they are more objective in their product assessments. That is why publicity is so valuable to a manufacturer: Citations of a product in an editorial context, rather than in a paid advertisement, give the reader much more confidence in the message. A recent study found that the publicity surrounding the Super Bowl increased viewers' attention to and recall of the advertisements shown during the game.[11]

Because consumers recognize that the intentions of commercial sources (e.g., manufacturers, service companies, financial institutions, retailers) are clearly profit oriented, they judge commercial **source credibility** on such factors as past performance, reputation, the kind and quality of service they are known to render, the quality and image of other products they manufacture, the image and attractiveness of the spokesperson used, the type of retail outlets through which they sell, and their position in the community (e.g., evidence of their commitment to such issues as social responsibility or equal employment). Many Starbucks' ads stress social responsibility.

Firms with well-established reputations generally have an easier time selling their products than do firms with lesser reputations. The ability of a quality image to invoke credibility is one of the reasons for the growth of family brands. Manufacturers with favorable brand images prefer to give their new products the existing brand name in order to obtain ready acceptance from consumers. Furthermore, a quality image permits a company to experiment more freely in many more areas of marketing than would otherwise be considered prudent, such as freestanding retail outlets, new price levels, and innovative promotional techniques. Recognizing that a manufacturer with a good reputation generally has high credibility among consumers, many companies spend a sizable part of their advertising budget on **institutional advertising**, which is designed to promote a favorable company image rather than to promote specific products.

In a crowded marketplace, many companies try to distinguish themselves and increase their credibility by being "good corporate citizens." These firms often engage in **cause-related marketing**, where they contribute a portion of the revenues they receive from selling certain products to such causes as helping people inflicted with incurable diseases or hurt by inclement weather. For example, fashion designers such as Armani and Ralph Lauren have donated selected portions of their sales to AIDS research and other charities. To acknowledge National Breast Cancer Awareness Month in October, many beauty and cosmetics companies earmark a portion of the selling price of their "pink-ribbon" products to breast cancer charities.

Following the December 2004 tsunami in Southeast Asia, several designers sold tsunami-relief T-shirts; many others encouraged consumers to make donations to a fund that was set up to help the storm's victims and even included links to this fund in their Web sites. Other kinds of corporate-sponsored special events include marching bands, fireworks displays, parades, laser shows, and traveling art exhibits. The nature and quality of these sponsorships constitute a subtle message to the consumer: "We're a great (kind, good-natured, socially responsible) company; we deserve your business."

Credibility of Spokespersons and Endorsers   Consumers sometimes regard the spokesperson who gives the product message as the source (or initiator) of the message. Thus, the "pitchman" (whether male or female) who appears in person or in a commercial or advertisement has a major influence on message credibility.

Many studies have investigated the relationship between the effectiveness of the message and the spokesperson or endorser employed. Here are some of the key findings of this body of research:

- The effectiveness of the spokesperson is related to the message itself. For example, when message comprehension is low, receivers rely on the spokesperson's credibility in forming attitudes toward the product, but when comprehension (and, thus, systematic information processing) is high, the expertise of the spokesperson has far less impact on a receiver's attitudes.[12]

- The synergy between the endorser and the type of product or service advertised is an important factor. Figure 9.5 gives the educational credentials of an employee endorsing his company's product. One study found that, for attractiveness-related products (such as cosmetics), a physically attractive celebrity spokesperson significantly enhanced message credibility and attitude toward the ad; for attractiveness-unrelated products (e.g., a camera), an attractive endorser had little or no effect. This suggests a "match-up" hypothesis for celebrity advertising.[13] Another study found that a celebrity endorser was more effective in terms of source credibility and consumer attitudes toward the ad for a hedonistic and "experiential" service (e.g., a restaurant) than for a utilitarian service (e.g., a bank).[14] When a celebrity endorser has damaged his or her credentials through engaging in scandalous behavior, the marketer immediately disassociates itself from the endorser in question.

- Endorsers who have demographic characteristics (e.g., age, social class, and ethnicity) that are similar to those of the target audience are viewed as more credible and persuasive than those that do not. Also, consumers with strong ethnic identification are more likely to be persuaded by endorsers with similar ethnicity than individuals with weaker ethnic identification.[15]

- The endorser's credibility is not a substitute for corporate credibility. One study discovered that although the endorser's credibility strongly impacted the audience's *attitudes toward the ad,* the perceived corporate credibility had a strong impact on *attitudes toward the advertised brand.*[16] This study supports the development of multiple measures to evaluate the credibility and persuasiveness of advertising messages, such as attitudes toward the ad, attitudes toward the brand, and consumer purchase intentions.

- Marketers who use celebrities to give testimonials or endorse products must be sure that the specific wording of the endorsement lies within the recognized competence of the spokesperson. A tennis star can believably endorse a brand of analgesic with comments about how it relieves sore muscle pain; however, a recitation of medical evidence supporting the brand's superiority over other brands is beyond his or her expected knowledge and expertise, and thus may reduce (rather than enhance) message credibility. Somewhat surprisingly, one study of advertising agencies found that none of the agencies surveyed had a written strategy regarding the selection of celebrity endorsers. The study's authors recommended a long list of factors to be considered in selecting celebrity endorsers, such as a careful match with the target audience, product and brand, the celebrity's overall image, prior endorsements, trustworthiness, familiarity, expertise, profession, physical attractiveness, and whether the celebrity is a brand user.[17]

FIGURE 9.5

Source: © Coors Brewing
Company. Golden, Colorado.

**Employee's Educational
Credentials Add Credibility**

Keith Villa, Ph.D.
Coors Master Brewer

The **Master Brewer** and
his **Tasteful Brew.**

COORS™
Master Brewers
TASTE
GUARANTEE

Like other beer lovers, Keith Villa knows
that Aspen Edge™ has more taste.* But
unlike other beer lovers, Keith knows
exactly why. As a Ph.D. holder in brewing
and as the Master Brewer of Aspen Edge,
Keith can explain that Aspen Edge is made
from a special blend of pale and caramel
malts, using old-world techniques combined
with a new high-tech method for brewing
low-carb beer to create a complex taste of
malts, a delicate taste of hops, and a clean
finish. More simply stated, Aspen Edge is
a high-quality, balanced-tasting, low-carb
beer that is crisp, smooth, and full of
flavor. That's a mouthful. And in this
case, one mouthful deserves another.
So go ahead. Try Aspen Edge. And see
what Keith is talking about.

*Testing conducted by Guideline Associates, NY, 2004.

AVERAGE ANALYSIS PER 12 FL. OZ. SERVING OF ASPEN EDGE LAGER:
94 CALORIES, 2.6 GRAMS OF CARBOHYDRATES, 0.7 GRAMS OF PROTEIN,
AND 0.0 GRAMS OF FAT.

ASPEN
EDGE.

ASPEN
EDGE.
CRAFTED BY
Coors Master Brewers

In interpersonal communications, consumers are more likely to be persuaded by
salespersons who engender confidence and who give the impression of honesty and
integrity. Consumer confidence in a salesperson is created in diverse ways, whether warranted or not. A salesperson who "looks you in the eye" often is perceived as more honest than one who evades direct eye contact. For many products, a sales representative
who dresses well and drives an expensive, late-model car may have more credibility than
one without such outward signs of success (and inferred representation of a best-selling
product). For some products, however, a salesperson may achieve more credibility by
dressing in the role of an expert. For example, a man selling home improvements may

achieve more credibility by looking like someone who just climbed off a roof or out of a basement than by looking like a banker.

Message Credibility   The reputation of the retailer who sells the product has a major influence on message credibility. Products sold by well-known quality stores seem to carry the added endorsement (and implicit guarantee) of the store itself (e.g., "If Macy's carries it, it must be good."). The aura of credibility generated by reputable retail advertising reinforces the manufacturer's message as well. That is why so many national ads (i.e., manufacturer-initiated ads) carry the line, "Sold at better stores everywhere."

The reputation of the medium that carries the advertisement also enhances the credibility of the message. For example, the image of a prestige magazine like *Fortune* confers added status on the products advertised within. The reputation of the medium for honesty and objectivity also affects the believability of the advertising. Consumers often think that a medium they respect would not accept advertising for products it did not "know" were good. Because specialization in an area implies knowledge and expertise, consumers tend to regard advertising they see in special-interest magazines with more credibility than those they note in general-interest magazines. However, following such revelations that a highly visible media commentator was paid by the government to promote a particular view regarding education, that a reporter in a presidential news conference was actually "planted" there in order to ask friendly questions, and that a national magazine published questionable accusations that American soldiers desecrated a Koran, a majority of Americans have begun to question seriously the credibility of the media.[18]

Consumers today have more media options than ever before in new forms of media (such as the Web) and traditional media in new forms (such as online editions of well-established newspapers), but there is no single answer as to which medium has the most credibility. One study discovered that individuals interested in politics are shifting from television to the Web for political information.[19] Another study reported that the public generally considers opinion polls reported in traditional news media as more credible than online polls;[20] still another study reported that cable television newscasts are viewed as the most credible, and that differences in the perceived credibility of various media were related to the consumer's age.[21] As the number and types of media continue to evolve and grow, print, broadcast, and digital media executives should survey their audiences periodically on such factors as perceived fairness, balance, and accuracy in order to maximize their credibility with audiences and their attractiveness to advertisers.

The consumer's previous experience with the product or the retailer has a major impact on the credibility of the message. Fulfilled product expectations tend to increase the credibility accorded future messages by the same advertiser; unfulfilled product claims or disappointing product experiences tend to reduce the credibility of future messages. Thus, the key basis for message credibility is the ability of the product, service, or brand to deliver consistent quality, value, and satisfaction to consumers.

Effects of Time on Source Credibility: The Sleeper Effect   The persuasive effects of high-credibility sources do not endure over time. Although a high-credibility source is initially more influential than a low-credibility source, research suggests that both positive and negative credibility effects tend to disappear after six weeks or so. This phenomenon has been termed the **sleeper effect**.[22] Consumers simply forget the source of the message faster than they forget the message itself. The sleeper effect is caused by *disassociation* (i.e., the consumer disassociates the message from its source) over time, leaving just the message content. The theory of ***differential decay*** suggests that the memory of a negative cue (e.g., a low-credibility source) simply decays faster than the message itself, leaving behind the primary message content.[23] However, reintroduction of the same or similar message by the source serves to jog the audience's memory, and the original effect remanifests itself; that is, the high-credibility source remains more persuasive than the low-credibility source. The implication for marketers who use high-credibility spokespersons is that they must repeat the same series of ads or commercials regularly in order to maintain a high level of persuasiveness. Somewhat surprisingly, the sleeper effect supports the use of negative attack advertising in political campaigns. The results of a study applying the sleeper effect to political advertising showed that the effectiveness of the attack ad increases considerably over a period of weeks, while the audience's initial negative perception of the political assailant as having low credibility fades and has only a temporary negative impact on the ad.[24] However, this logic must not be extended to advertising and marketers must not assume that consumers who become aware of a brand through a loud and intrusive ad campaign will continue to remember the brand favorably and forget the negative experience of watching the ads that made them aware of the brand.[25]

The target audience (receivers)

Receivers decode the messages they receive on the basis of their personal experiences and personal characteristics. If Joe Brown, a college freshman attempting to purchase a textbook online, receives shoddy service and delayed delivery from an online retailer claiming to sell textbooks at discounted prices, he will be reluctant to use this outlet again. Instead, he will probably use a reputable online book seller (such as **Amazon.com**), from whom many of his classmates reported prompt and reliable service, even though the book costs slightly more there than at the other discount seller. The selection of the online retailer is based on Joe's and his classmates' experiences.

A number of factors affect the *decoding* and *comprehension* of persuasive messages, including the receiver's personal characteristics, involvement with the product or product category, the congruency of the message with the medium, and the receiver's mood.

Personal characteristics and comprehension

The amount of meaning accurately derived from the message is a function of the message characteristics, the receiver's opportunity and ability to process the message, and the receiver's motivation. In fact, all of an individual's personal characteristics (described in earlier chapters) influence the accuracy with which the individual decodes a message. A person's demographics (such as age, gender, marital status), sociocultural memberships (social class, race, religion), and lifestyle are key determinants in how a message is interpreted. A bachelor may interpret a friendly comment from his unmarried neighbor as a "come-on"; a student may interpret a professor's easygoing manner as an indication of "relaxed" grading rigor. Personality, attitudes, and prior learning all affect how a message is decoded. Perception, based as it is on expectations, motivation, and past experience, certainly influences message interpretation. Clearly, not everyone reads and understands the marketing communications they receive in the same way that the sender intended.

For example, one study, focused on gender-based differences in responding to charity ads, reported that women found altruistic appeals that stressed helping others more persuasive, whereas men tended to choose self-oriented themes that stressed helping oneself.[26] Another study discovered that persons who view themselves as more individualistic and unique and who tend to enjoy effortful thinking (i.e., they are high in the personality trait termed *need for cognition*) were more likely to be persuaded by comparative advertising than persons who possess lower levels of these personality traits.[27] Other researchers discovered that persons with a high need for cognition are more persuaded by messages that consist of high-quality arguments followed by implicit, rather than explicit, conclusions.[28] Another study found that the level of confidence that people have in their evaluations of an ad influence the type of ad they prefer; persons who were highly confident in their judgments were more persuaded by strong ads, rather than comparable weak ads, for a given product.[29]

Involvement and congruency

A person's level of involvement (see Chapter 7) plays a key role in how much attention is paid to the message and how carefully it is decoded. People who have little interest (i.e., a low level of involvement) in golf, for example, may not pay much attention to an ad for a specially designed putter; people who are very interested (highly involved) in golf may read every word of a highly technical advertisement describing the new golf club. Thus, a target audience's level of involvement is an important consideration in the design and content of persuasive communications. One study discovered a relationship between level of involvement and the style and context of an ad. Subjects with low involvement with the product preferred messages placed within a congruent context (e.g., a humorous ad within a humorous TV series) while persons highly involved with the product preferred messages that contrasted the style of ad and the context within which it was placed (e.g., a humorous ad within a rational context such as a TV documentary).[30] Another study showed that the congruency between the nature of the television program and the advertisement affected the level of viewer recall. Cognitively involving commercials shown in a cognitively involving program context had higher recall than low-involvement commercials placed within an affective program context.[31]

Mood

Mood, or affect, plays a significant role in how a message is decoded. A consumer's mood (e.g., cheerfulness or unhappiness) affects the way in which an advertisement is perceived, recalled, and acted upon. Marketers of many image-centered products such as perfume, fashion, and liquor have found that appeals focused on emotions and feelings associated with these products are more effective than rational appeals depicting the product's benefits. However, some advertisers have used emotional appeals effectively for technologically complex products. For example, Apple Computer encourages consumers to "Think Different"; Intel uses the "Intel Inside" theme to differentiate its product. After the September 11, 2001 terrorist attacks, many marketers adapted the mood of their advertising to reflect the newly somber, patriotic spirit of the country.

Many studies have investigated the impact of mood on message comprehension and effectiveness. In one study, the subjects' moods were manipulated by showing humorous ads (generating a positive mood) to some subjects and informational ads (generating a neutral mood) to other subjects. The study found that a positive mood enhanced the learning of brand names and the product categories to which they belong.[32] The consumer's mood is influenced by the *content* of the ad and by the *context* in which the advertising message appears (such as the accompanying TV program or adjacent newspaper story); these in turn affect the consumer's evaluation and recall of the message. One study showed that consumers with low familiarity with a service category prefer ads based on story appeals rather than lists of attributes and that such appeals work better when the receivers are in a happy mood while decoding the message.[33]

Barriers to communication

Various "barriers" to communication may affect the accuracy with which consumers interpret messages. These include selective perception and psychological noise.

Selective Exposure to Messages   Consumers selectively perceive advertising messages. They read carefully ads for products they are interested in and tend to ignore advertisements that have no special interest or relevance to them. Furthermore, technology provides consumers with increasingly sophisticated means to control their exposure to media. TV remote controls offer viewers the ability to "wander" among program offerings with ease (often referred to as *grazing*), to *zap* commercials by muting the audio, and to *channel surf*—switch channels to check out other program offerings during commercial breaks. Some marketers try to overcome channel surfing during commercials by *roadblocking* (i.e., playing the same commercial simultaneously on competing channels).

The VCR enables viewers to fast-forward (*zip*) through commercials of prerecorded programs. The majority of consumers zip indiscriminately through videotapes to avoid all commercials, without first evaluating the commercials they *zap*. More recently, digital video recorders and services such as *TiVo* and *ReplayTV* allow consumers not only to watch programs whenever they want, but also to skip commercials easily. In response, worried broadcasters have increased their *product placements* and expenditures on *branded entertainment* (see Chapter 6) and have sought other means to make it more difficult for consumers to avoid exposure to TV commercials. The growth of satellite radio allows consumers to avoid hearing radio ads. Caller ID, phone answering machines, the government's "do not call" list, and other devices allow consumers to screen out tele-marketing and other unsolicited contacts from marketers.

Psychological Noise Just as telephone static can impair reception of a message, so too can **psychological noise** (e.g., competing advertising messages or distracting thoughts). A viewer faced with the clutter of nine successive commercial messages during a program break may actually receive and retain almost nothing of what he has seen. Similarly, an exec-utive planning a department meeting while driving to work may be too engrossed in her thoughts to "hear" a radio commercial. On a more familiar level, a student daydreaming about a Saturday night date may simply not "hear" a direct question by the professor. The student is just as much a victim of noise—albeit psychological noise—as another student who literally cannot hear a question because of construction noise from the building next door. There are various strategies that marketers use to overcome psychological noise:

- Repeated exposure to an advertising message (through *repetition* or *redundancy* of the advertising appeal) helps surmount psychological noise and facilitates message reception. Thus, repeating an ad several times is a must. (The effects of repetition on learning were discussed in Chapter 7.) The principle of redundancy also is seen in advertisements that use both illustrations and copy to emphasize the same points. To achieve more advertising redundancy, many marketers now place their messages in such places as video games, movie theaters, elevators, floors in supermarkets, and even public restrooms.

- Copywriters often use *contrast* to break through the psychological noise and adver-tising clutter. Contrast (discussed in Chapter 6) entails using features within the message itself to attract additional attention. Such strategies include featuring an unexpected outcome, increasing the amount of sensory input (such as color, scent, or sound), and using tested message appeals that tend to attract more attention.

- Broadcasters and marketers also use *teasers* to overcome noise. For example, trivia quizzes shown at the beginning of a commercial break are designed to engage view-ers in sticking with the channel in order to find out at the end of the break whether their own answers were right.

- Thanks to new technologies, marketers can now place customized ads on such devices as cell phones and addressable cable TV boxes; they can get consumers to register for promotional messages and giveaways more easily, and engage con-sumers with the product before the sales pitch.[34]

- The Web provides marketers with more options, and many advertisers have shifted considerable sums from TV to Internet advertising. Online, marketers can place ads that consumers' PCs will automatically retrieve from the Internet, in such formats as *floater ads* that sometimes replace the more commonly used *pop-ups,* and in Web sites that use programming from TV.[35] In fact, some large marketers like Pepsi, Unilever, and GE have implemented campaigns that run only online and that gen-erally are more innovative and significantly cheaper than TV advertisements.[36]

Of course, the most effective way to ensure that a promotional message stands out and is received and decoded appropriately by the target audience is through effective *positioning* and a *unique selling proposition.* Advertisements for products that are per-ceived to provide better value than competitive products are more likely to be received in their intended ways than other promotional messages within the advertising clutter.

Feedback—the receiver's response

Since marketing communications are usually designed to persuade a target audience to act in a desired way (e.g., to purchase a specific brand or product, to vote for a presiden-tial candidate, to pay income taxes early), the ultimate test of marketing communications is the receiver's response. For this reason, it is essential for the sender to obtain **feedback** as promptly and as accurately as possible. Only through feedback can the sender determine whether and how well the message has been received.

As noted earlier, an important advantage of interpersonal communications is the ability to obtain immediate feedback through verbal as well as nonverbal cues. Experienced speakers are very attentive to feedback and constantly modify their messages based on what they see and hear from the audience. Immediate feedback is the factor that makes personal selling so effective. It enables the salesperson to tailor the sales pitch to the expressed needs and observed reactions of each prospect. Similarly, it enables a political candidate to stress specific aspects of his or her platform selectively in response to questions posed by prospective voters in face-to-face meetings. Immediate feedback in the form of inattention serves to alert the college professor to jolt a dozing class awake; thus, the professor may make a deliberately provocative statement such as: "This material will probably appear in your final exam."

Obtaining feedback is as important in *impersonal* (mass) communications as it is in *interpersonal* communications. Indeed, because of the high costs of advertising space and time in mass media, many marketers consider impersonal communications feedback to be even more essential. The organization that initiates the message must develop some method for determining *a priori* whether its mass communications are received by the intended audience, understood in the intended way, and effective in achieving the intended objectives.

Unlike interpersonal communications feedback, mass communications feedback is rarely direct; instead, it is usually inferred. Senders infer how persuasive their messages are from the resulting action (or inaction) of the targeted audience. Receivers buy (or do not buy) the advertised product; they renew (or do not renew) their magazine subscriptions; they vote (or do not vote) for the political candidate. Another type of feedback that companies seek from mass audiences is the degree of customer satisfaction (or dissatisfaction) with a product purchase. They try to discover and correct as swiftly as possible any problems with the product in order to retain their brand's image of reliability. Many companies have established 24-hour hot lines to encourage comments and questions from their consumers and they also solicit consumer feedback through online contact. Figure 9.6 shows a comprehensive model of the options and relationships among the basic communications elements discussed above.

Advertising effectiveness research

In evaluating the impact of their advertising, marketers must measure the *persuasion effects* (i.e., was the message received, understood, and interpreted correctly?) and the *sales effects* (i.e., did the ad increase sales?) of their advertising messages. Advertisers gauge the *persuasion effects* of their messages by conducting audience research to find out which media are read, which television programs are viewed, and which advertisements were remembered by their target audience(s). Should feedback indicate that the audience does not note or miscomprehends an ad, an alert sponsor modifies or revises the message so that the intended communication does, in fact, take place.

Unlike interpersonal communications between, say, a retail salesperson and a customer, in which the feedback (e.g., the customer's purchase or nonpurchase) is immediate, impersonal communications feedback is much less timely. Therefore, the *sales effects* of mass communications are difficult to assess (although retailers usually can assess the effectiveness of their morning newspaper ads by midday on the basis of sales activity for the advertised product). A widely used method of measuring the sales effects of food and other packaged goods advertising is based on the Universal Product Code (UPC), which is tied to computerized cash registers. Supermarket scanner data can be combined with data from other sources (e.g., media and promotional information) to measure the correlation between advertisements, special promotions, and sales.

Generally, persuasion effects are measured through *exposure, attention, interpretation,* and *recall.* Selected measures of these factors are described below.

FIGURE 9.6   **Comprehensive Communication Model**

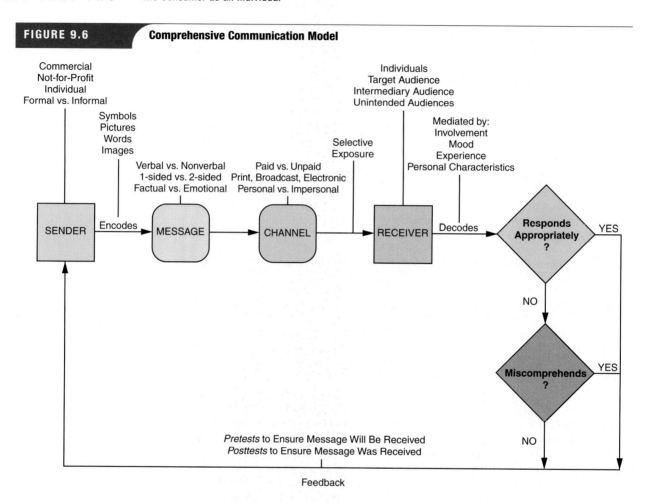

Media and Message Exposure Measures   Some of these measures assess *how many* consumers received the message and others focus on *who* received it. Data collected via both types of measures are offered for sale by syndicated services. For example, comScore Media Metrix measures the sizes of Internet audiences, their demographic characteristics and also segments these groups according to their purchasing power. Mediamark Research Inc. (MRI) provides, for a given magazine, data on its *circulation* as well as a descriptive *audience profile* (a breakdown of its readers by gender, median age, and household income). The weekly Nielsen Ratings rank TV programs by the size of their audiences. A "top ranking" means that the program was watched by more people than any other program at that time during the week. In order to measure who watched a given program, some of the households in the Nielsen sample are also equipped with *People Meters*—small boxes that are placed on or near each TV set in the household. The boxes have buttons and lights that are assigned to each household member. When a viewer begins watching TV, he or she pushes the assigned button, which changes the indicator light from red to green. When viewers finish watching, they push their button again (and the indicator changes back to red). To measure the audiences of local TV, Nielsen uses *diaries* in which viewers record the programs watched each day and who in the household watched each program.[37] As discussed earlier, some companies are developing *Portable People Meters* that will measure a person's total exposure to all communications and advertising and transmit this data daily to advertisers and broadcasters.

Message Attention and Interpretation Measures   Physiological measures track bodily responses to stimuli. For example, Perception Research Services uses *eye tracking*—a method where a camera tracks the movement of the eye across store shelves and gauges to which labels or brands respondents paid more attention. The Capita Research Group uses *brain wave analysis* that tracks the degree of attention paid to the components of viewed advertisements through monitoring electrical impulses produced by the viewer's brain.[38] In *theater tests,* TV programs or commercials are shown in a theater setting and viewers use dials (located in their armrests) to indicate their levels of interest or disinterest during the showing of the program or advertisement. *Web site usability tests* allow researchers to "peek over the shoulders" of visitors to record how quickly they find specific information, which components of the site draw more attention, and which parts lead to more clicks. The *Starch Readership Survey* (discussed in Chapter 7) is a measure of attention as well as recall.

Sophisticated physiological techniques can be used to measure the degrees of consumer arousal and involvement but do not assess the reasons behind their levels of engagement with the messages tested. Generally, researchers use *attitudinal measures,* placed within *copy pretests* or *posttests* to assess whether respondents like the message, understand it correctly, and regard it as effective and persuasive. Researchers are also interested in measuring the emotions and feelings provoked by ads. One study tested the use of *Facial Electromyography* (Facial EMG)—a method that tracks the electrical activity and subtle movements of facial muscles—to gauge the emotions generated by different types of TV commercials. This research concluded that facial EMG is more effective in measuring emotional responses than self-reported cognitive responses because it goes beyond the biases and limitations of the commonly used (but much cheaper and easier to administer) *self-report technique.*[39]

Message Recall Measures   In addition to the *recall and recognition* measures discussed in Chapter 7, researchers use *day-after recall tests* in which viewers of TV shows or listeners to radio broadcasts are interviewed a day after watching or listening to a given program. Participants are asked to describe which commercials they recall. The recall of a commercial and its central theme is evidence of its attention-getting and persuasive power.

designing persuasive communications

In order to create persuasive communications, the sponsor (who may be an individual, a for-profit company, or a not-for-profit organization) must first establish the objectives of the communication, then select the appropriate audiences for the message and the appropriate media through which to reach them, and then design (encode) the message in a manner that is appropriate to each medium and to each audience. As noted earlier, the communications strategy should also include an *a priori* feedback mechanism that alerts the sponsor to any need for modifications or adjustments to the media or the message.

Communications strategy

In developing its communications strategy, the sponsor must establish the primary communications objectives. These might consist of creating awareness of a service, promoting sales of a product, encouraging (or discouraging) certain practices, attracting retail patronage, reducing postpurchase dissonance, creating goodwill or a favorable image, or any combination of these and other communications objectives.

There are numerous models claiming to depict how persuasive communications work. The *cognitive models* depict a process in which exposure to a message leads to interest and desire for the product and, ultimately, to buying behavior. For many decades, this general model had been widely adopted by advertisers. A more recent and sophisticated model of advertising is shown in Figure 9.7. The authors of this paradigm maintain

FIGURE 9.7

The Three Phases and Flow of the Perception/Experience/ Memory Model of Advertising

Source: Bruce F. Hall, "A New Model for Measuring Advertising Effectiveness," *Journal of Advertising Research* (March/April 2002): 23–31.

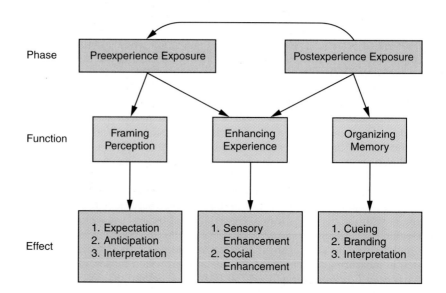

that it reflects the interrelationship among the key factors of persuasion—*perception, experience,* and *memory*—in a manner more consistent with how the human mind really works than the older cognitive models, and that advertising messages based on this model are more likely to generate consumption behavior.[40] The existence of these and many other models that claim to explain how persuasion works reflects the complexity of human information processing and the resulting challenges faced by advertisers trying to influence consumption behavior.

Target audience

An essential component of a communications strategy is selecting the appropriate audience. It is important to remember that an audience is made up of individuals—in many cases, great numbers of individuals. Because each individual has his or her own traits, characteristics, interests, needs, experience, and knowledge, it is essential for the sender to segment the audience into groups that are homogeneous in terms of some relevant characteristic. Segmentation enables the sender to create specific messages for each target group and to run them in specific media that are seen, heard, or read by the relevant target group. It is unlikely that a marketer could develop a single message that would appeal simultaneously to its total audience. Efforts to use "universal" appeals phrased in simple language that everyone can understand invariably result in unsuccessful advertisements to which few people relate.

Companies that have many diverse audiences sometimes find it useful to develop a communications strategy that consists of an overall (or umbrella) communications message to all their audiences, from which they spin off a series of related messages targeted directly to the specific interests of individual segments. In addition, to maintain positive communications with all of their publics, most large organizations have public relations departments or employ public relations consultants to broadcast favorable information about the company and to suppress unfavorable information.

Media strategy

Media strategy is an essential component of a communications plan. It calls for the placement of ads in the specific media read, viewed, or heard by each targeted audience. To accomplish this, advertisers develop, through research, a **consumer profile** of their target customers that includes the specific media they read or watch. Media organizations regularly research their own audiences in order to develop descriptive **audience profiles**. A cost-effective media choice is one that closely matches the advertiser's consumer profile to a medium's audience profile.

Before selecting specific media vehicles, advertisers must select general media categories that will enhance the message they want to convey. Which media categories the marketer selects depends on the product or service to be advertised, the market segments to be reached, and the marketer's advertising objectives. Rather than select one media category to the exclusion of others, many advertisers use a multimedia campaign strategy, with one primary media category carrying the major burden of the campaign and other categories providing supplemental support.

The Web is the newest advertising medium, and using it to communicate effectively with customers still represents a challenge to marketers. A recent study identified three groups of factors that marketers should consider when building a Web site: (1) providing information search tools such as easy site navigation, complete product information, and ability to customize the content; (2) incorporating designs that enhance the enjoyment of the site's users (such as attractive visuals and colors); and (3) providing tools that support the transaction such as security, ease of entering the information, stating the rules of the transaction clearly, providing the company information, and quick response time.[41] Table 9.1 compares the potential persuasive impact of major advertising media along the dimensions of *targeting precision* (i.e., the ability to reach exclusively the intended audience), constructing a *persuasive message,* degree of *psychological noise, feedback,* and relative *cost.*

Message strategies

The message is the thought, idea, attitude, image, or other information that the sender wishes to convey to the intended audience. In trying to encode the message in a form that will enable the audience to understand its precise meaning, the sender must know exactly what he or she is trying to say and why (what the objectives are and what the message is intended to accomplish). The sender must also know the target audience's personal characteristics in terms of education, interests, needs, and experience. The sender must then design a message strategy through words and/or pictures that will be perceived and accurately interpreted (decoded) by the targeted audience. One study developed a list of message elements designed to appeal to three personality types, defined as the *righteous buyer* (who looks to recommendations from independent sources such as *Consumer Reports*), the *social buyer* (who relies on the recommendations of friends, on celebrity endorsements, and testimonials), and the *pragmatic buyer* (who looks for the best value for the money, though not necessarily the least expensive).[42]

Involvement theory

Involvement theory (see Chapter 7) suggests that individuals are more likely to devote active cognitive effort to evaluating the pros and cons of a product in a high-involvement purchase situation and more likely to focus on peripheral message cues in low-involvement situations. The *Elaboration Likelihood Model* (ELM) proposes that, for high-involvement products, marketers should follow the **central route to persuasion**; that is, they should present advertisements with strong, well-documented, issue-relevant arguments that encourage cognitive processing. When involvement is low, marketers should follow the **peripheral route to persuasion** by emphasizing non-content visual or symbolic material (e.g., background scenery, music, or celebrity spokespersons) that provide the consumer with pleasant, indirect associations with the product and provoke favorable inferences about its merits. A recent study discovered that the level of involvement and the focus of the ad determined its persuasive effectiveness. Highly involved consumers were more influenced by ads stressing the *outcome* of using the product and less involved consumers were more influenced by ads portraying the *process* of using it.[43]

TABLE 9.1	Persuasive Capabilities and Limitations of Major Advertising Media				
	TARGETING PRECISION	**MESSAGE DEVELOPMENT AND EXECUTION**	**DEGREE OF PSYCHOLOGICAL NOISE**	**OBTAINING FEEDBACK**	**RELATIVE COST**
Newspapers	Access to large audiences. Not very selective in reaching consumers with specific demographics. Effective for reaching local consumers.	Flexible. Messages can be designed and published quickly. Limited production quality and short message life.	High clutter. Many messages competing for attention.	Sales volume. Redemptions of special promotions and level of store traffic provide immediate feedback.	Determined by size of ad and the medium's circulation. Affordable for local businesses. Permits joint (cooperative) advertising by national manufacturers and local sellers.
Magazines	High geographic and demographic selectivity. *Selective binding*[a] allows more precise targeting of subscribers with the desired demographics.	High quality of production. High credibility of ads in special-interest magazines. Long message life and pass-along readership. Long lead time required.	High clutter. Some magazines may not guarantee ad placement in a particular position within the magazine.	Delayed and indirect feedback, such as the Starch scores that measure recall and attention.	Determined by cost of page and circulation. Top magazines charge very high rates.
Television	Reaches very large audiences. Many programs lack audience selectivity.	Appeals to several senses. Enables messages that draw attention and generate emotion. Short-duration messages must be repeated. Long lead time.	High clutter. Viewers can avoid message exposures by channel surfing or using advanced technologies such as TiVo.	Day-after recall tests measure how many consumers were exposed to the message and, to a lesser degree, their characteristics.	Very high costs based on how many consumers watch a given program.
Radio	High geographic and demographic audience selectivity.	Audio messages only. Short exposure. Relatively short lead time.	High clutter. Listeners can easily switch among stations during commercials.	Delayed feedback, such as day-after recall tests.	Based on size of the audience reached. Local radio may be relatively inexpensive.
Internet	Potential for great audience selectivity. Audience may be demographically skewed. Enables tracking customers and building databases. Privacy issues make targeting more difficult.	Increasingly more advanced messages can be designed and shown relatively quickly. Marketers recognize that their home pages are advertisements and must be designed as persuasive tools.	Very high degree of clutter. Visitors can easily escape promotional messages. Banner ads and home pages can reinforce and expand promotional messages featured in other media.	Interactive medium with potential for gathering immediate feedback. Click rates on ads do not measure their impact accurately (since exposure to the brands featured occurs even without a click).	Great variation in establishing advertising rates since there is no standard measure of the impact of online advertising.

(Continued)

TABLE 9.1 Continued

	TARGETING PRECISION	MESSAGE DEVELOPMENT AND EXECUTION	DEGREE OF PSYCHOLOGICAL NOISE	OBTAINING FEEDBACK	RELATIVE COST
Direct Mail[b]	High audience selectivity. Enables personalization. Perceived by many as "junk mail" and discarded.	Enables novel, visually appealing, and dramatic messages (including the addition of sensory inputs).	No competing messages within the mailing.	Easy to measure feedback through limited pretests and cost-per-inquiry and cost-per-order. Delayed feedback.	Relatively high cost per person per mailing due to "junk mail" image.
Direct Marketing[c]	Marketers can build and constantly refine an electronic database of qualified buyers based on inquiries and direct orders. Permits the development of highly selective customer segments. Privacy concerns makes this practice difficult.	A function of the medium used to solicit the direct response from the customer.	Can be relatively free of clutter, even in media where there is generally a lot of noise. For example, infomercials provide advertisers with a "clutter-free" environment.	Generates measurable responses and enables marketers to measure the profitability of their efforts directly.	Determined through such variables as cost-per-inquiry, cost-per-sale, and revenue-per-advertisement.

Notes: [a]Selective binding is a technique that enables publishers to narrowly segment their subscription bases. When readers subscribe, they are asked to provide demographic information, which the publisher enters into a database. Through a sophisticated computerized system, the publisher is able to select specific subscribers, based on reader demographic profiles, to receive special sections that are bound into a limited number of magazines.
[b]Direct mail includes catalogs, letters, brochures, promotional offers, and any materials mailed directly to customers at their homes or offices.
[c]Direct marketing is not a medium but an interactive marketing technique that uses various media (such as mail, print, broadcast, telephone, and cyberspace) for the purpose of soliciting a direct response from a consumer. Electronic shopping (through home-shopping TV channels or interactive cable) is also considered direct marketing.

Message structure and presentation

Some of the decisions that marketers must make in designing the message include the use of *resonance, positive* or *negative message framing, one-sided* or *two-sided messages, comparative advertising,* and the *order* of presentation.

Resonance

Advertising resonance is defined as wordplay, often used to create a double meaning used in combination with a relevant picture. Examples of advertising resonance include the phrase "absolut masterpiece" appearing next to a bottle of Absolut Vodka, and Pepsi's slogan "hit the beach topless" next to a Pepsi bottle cap lying in the sand. By using resonance in ads marketers can improve the chances that their ads will be noticed by consumers and create favorable and lasting impressions. A recent study tested the effectiveness of metaphors and puns, such as a car seat with a package of motion sickness remedy serving as the seat belt's buckle. The study concluded that using rhetorical figures and symbols in ads increased the recall and memory of these messages; these findings are consistent with data from Starch Readership Surveys (see Chapter 7) showing that consumers are more likely to read ads that employ resonance than those that do not.[44]

Message framing

Should a marketer stress the benefits to be gained by using a specific product (**positive message framing**) or the benefits to be lost by not using the product (**negative message framing**)? Research suggests that the appropriate message framing decision depends on the consumer's attitudes and characteristics as well as the product itself. For example, one study found that persons with a low need for cognition were more likely to be persuaded by negatively framed messages.[45] Another study found that an individual's self-image impacts the type of framing that he or she finds more persuasive. Individuals with an independent self-image (i.e., who view themselves as defined by unique characteristics) were more persuaded by messages stressing an approach goal (positive framing), and those with an interdependent self-view (i.e., who view themselves as defined by others) found messages that stress avoidance goals more convincing (negative framing).[46]

A study of a credit card company's customers who had not used their cards in the preceding three months found that negative message framing (i.e., what the consumer might lose by not using the credit card) had a much stronger effect on subsequent usage behavior than positive message framing.[47] A study of advertised products that enabled the early detection of disease indicated that positively framed anecdotal messages were less persuasive than negatively framed anecdotal messages.[48] A recent study discovered that negative message framing was more effective than positive framing when respondents had less opportunity to process the information in the ad, but less effective when respondents had more opportunity to process the ad's content.[49]

One-sided versus two-sided messages

Should marketers tell their audiences only the good points about their products, or should they also tell them the bad (or the commonplace)? Should they pretend that their products are the only ones of their kind, or should they acknowledge competing products? These are very real strategy questions that marketers face every day, and the answers depend on the nature of the audience and the nature of the competition.

If the audience is friendly (e.g., if it uses the advertiser's products), if it initially favors the communicator's position, or if it is not likely to hear an opposing argument, then a *one-sided (supportive) message* that stresses only favorable information is most effective. However, if the audience is critical or unfriendly (e.g., if it uses competitive products), if it is well educated, or if it is likely to hear opposing claims, then a *two-sided (refutational) message* is likely to be more effective. Two-sided advertising messages tend to be more credible than one-sided advertising messages because they acknowledge that the advertised brand has shortcomings. Two-sided messages can also be very effective when consumers are likely to see competitors' negative counterclaims or when consumer attitudes toward the brand are already negative.

Some marketers stress only positive factors about their products and pretend that competition does not exist. However, when competition does exist and when it is likely to be vocal, such advertisers tend to lose credibility with the consumer. The credibility of an advertised claim can often be enhanced by actually disclaiming superiority of some product features in relation to a competing brand or by not claiming that the product is a universal cure. For example, an ad for Rogaine noted that, at the conclusion of a 12-month clinical test, almost half the men using the product experienced modest to dense hair regrowth, about a third experienced minimal hair regrowth, and about one-sixth had no regrowth whatever (see Figure 9.8). The admission that the product did not always work enhanced the credibility of the ad. In political marketing, a candidate will sometimes argue in generalities that a particular course of action is the correct one but give no details with which the audience can analyze, discuss, or rebut the argument (a one-sided argument). Using a two-sided argument, the candidate may say something favorable about the reasonableness of an opponent's position before attacking it, thus gaining credibility by appearing objective, open-minded, and fair in examining the issues.

Comparative advertising

Comparative advertising is a widely used marketing strategy in which a marketer claims product superiority for its brand over one or more explicitly named or implicitly identified competitors, either on an overall basis or on selected product attributes. Comparative advertising is useful for product positioning, for target market selection, and for brand-positioning strategies.

Source: Courtesy of Pfizer
Consumer Healthcare, Pfizer Inc.

FIGURE 9.8

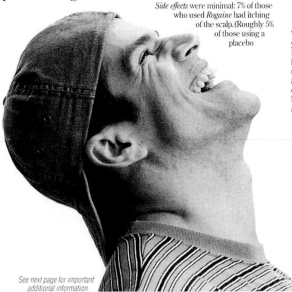

John's losing his hair.
His mission: get it back.

ASAP!
But how?
Weaving? No.
Transplant?
Not for him.
A hairpiece?
Never, never.
What John really
wants is his
own hair back.
And now he's learned,
**for male pattern
baldness, only**
Rogaine® **has been
proven to regrow hair.**

Normal hair grows and rests in cycles. The exact mechanism by which *Rogaine*® Topical Solution (minoxidil topical solution 2%) stimulates hair growth is unknown. But many scientists believe that *Rogaine* works, in part, by taking advantage of the existing hair's growth cycle. Prolong the growth cycle so that more hairs grow longer and thicker at the same time, and you may see improved scalp coverage.

Will *Rogaine* work for you?

Dermatologists conducted 12-month clinical tests. After 4 months, 26% of patients using *Rogaine* reported moderate to dense hair regrowth, compared with 11% of those using a placebo (a similar solution without minoxidil — the active ingredient in *Rogaine*). After 1 year of use, almost half of the men who continued using *Rogaine* in the study rated their regrowth as moderate (40%) to dense (8%). Thirty-six percent reported minimal regrowth. The rest (16%) had no regrowth.

Side effects were minimal: 7% of those who used *Rogaine* had itching of the scalp. (Roughly 5% of those using a placebo

reported the same minor irritations.) *Rogaine* should only be applied to a normal, healthy scalp (not sunburned or irritated).

Make a commitment to see results.

Studies indicate that *at least 4 months of twice-daily treatment with* Rogaine *are usually necessary before there is evidence of regrowth.* So why not make it part of your normal routine when you wake up and go to bed, like brushing your teeth.

As you'd expect, if you're younger, have been losing your hair for a shorter period of time, and have less initial hair loss, you're more likely to have a better response.

Rogaine is a treatment, not a cure. So further progress is only possible by using it continuously. If you stop using it, you will probably shed the newly regrown hair within a few months.

Get your free Information Kit, plus a $10 incentive to see a doctor.

Why wait? Find out whether *Rogaine* is for you. Call 1-800-965-1199 for a free Information Kit about the product and how to use it. **And because** *Rogaine* **requires a prescription,** we'll include a list of nearby dermatologists or other doctors experienced in treating hair loss, plus a $10 incentive to visit a doctor soon.

Call

1-800-965-1199

for your free Information Kit
on *Rogaine* and a $10
incentive to see a doctor.

Rogaine®
TOPICAL SOLUTION minoxidil 2%

See next page for important additional information.

©1994 The Upjohn Company USJ 2659 00 January 1995

Two-Sided Appeal

Some critics of the technique maintain that comparative ads often assist recall of the competitor's brand at the expense of the advertised brand. However, the wide use of comparative advertising and research into its strategic effects do not support this view. Studies have found that comparative ads are capable of exerting more positive effects on brand attitudes, purchase intentions, and actual purchase than noncomparative advertisements.[50] Studies of comparative advertising found that comparative ads elicited higher levels of cognitive processing, had better recall, and were perceived as more relevant than noncomparative ads.[51] A study that tested the degree of negativity in comparative messages (by using positive, negative, and mildly negative comparative messages) for several products reported that negative elements in an ad contributed to its effectiveness as long as they were believable or were offset by some elements that made the ad appear neutral.[52] These studies and many others support the view that, if used properly and in the right context, comparative marketing is a highly effective positioning strategy.

There has been considerable concern expressed regarding the ability of comparative advertising to mislead consumers, including several legal actions against companies by the Federal Trade Commission. A recent study advocates the development of specific measures designed to gauge a comparative ad's ability to mislead consumers.

Overall, comparative advertising has been used more in the United States than in other countries. However, one study of American and Thai consumers discovered that the persuasive ability of comparative ads was related to the two personality traits—*self-construal* (the degree to which people view themselves as autonomous and independent) and *need for cognition*—in the same way in both countries.[53] Another study compared American and Korean consumers and demonstrated that cultural values were more important in influencing reactions to comparative ads than reactions to noncomparative ads, and also that *need for cognition* impacted the persuasiveness of comparative ads for both groups.[54]

Order effects

Is it best to present your commercial first or last? Should you give the bad news first or last? Communications researchers have found that the **order** in which a message is presented affects audience receptivity. For this reason, politicians and other professional communicators often jockey for position when they address an audience sequentially; they are aware that the first and last speeches are more likely to be retained in the audience's memory than those in between. On TV, the position of a commercial in a commercial pod can be critical. The commercials shown first are recalled the best, whereas those in the middle are recalled the least.

When just two competing messages are presented, one after the other, the evidence as to which position is more effective is somewhat conflicting. Some researchers have found that the material presented first produces a greater effect (*primacy effect*), whereas others have found that the material presented last is more effective (*recency effect*.) Magazine publishers recognize the impact of **order effects** by charging more for ads on the front, back, and inside covers of magazines than for the inside magazine pages because of their greater visibility and recall.

Order is also important in listing product benefits within an ad. If audience interest is low, the most important point should be made first to attract attention. However, if interest is high, it is not necessary to pique curiosity, so product benefits can be arranged in ascending order, with the most important point mentioned last. When both favorable information and unfavorable information are to be presented (as in an annual stockholders' report), placing the favorable material first often produces greater tolerance for the unfavorable news. It also produces greater acceptance and better understanding of the total message. A recent study found that revealing the brand name at the onset of a message enhances brand recall and message persuasiveness.[55]

Repetition

Repetition is an important factor in learning. Thus, it is not surprising that repetition, or frequency of the ad, affects persuasion, ad recall, brand-name recall, and brand preferences. Multiple message exposures give consumers more opportunity to internalize product attributes, to develop more or stronger cue associations, to develop more positive attitudes, and an increased willingness to resist competitive counterpersuasion efforts. In low-involvement situations, individuals are more likely to regard message claims that are repeated frequently as more truthful than those repeated with less frequency. Different ads depicting different applications of the same promotional theme enhance the memorability of the brand advertised.

Advertising appeals

Sometimes objective, *factual appeals* are more effective in persuading a target audience; at other times *emotional appeals* are more effective. It depends on the kind of audience to be reached and their degree of involvement in the product category. In general, however, logical, reason-why appeals are more effective in persuading educated audiences, and emotional appeals are more effective in persuading less-educated consumers. The following section examines the effectiveness of several frequently used emotional appeals.

Fear   Fear is an effective appeal often used in marketing communications. Some researchers have found a negative relationship between the intensity of fear appeals and their ability to persuade, so that strong fear appeals tend to be less effective than mild fear appeals. A number of explanations have been offered for this phenomenon. Strong fear appeals concerning a highly relevant topic (such as cigarette smoking) cause the individual to experience cognitive dissonance, which is resolved either by rejecting the practice or by rejecting the unwelcome information. Because giving up a comfortable habit is difficult, consumers more readily reject the threat. This they do by a variety of techniques, including denial of its validity ("There still is no real proof that smoking causes cancer"), the belief that they are immune to personal disaster ("It can't happen to me"), and a diffusing process that robs the claim of its true significance ("I play it safe by smoking only filter cigarettes"). Therefore, marketers should use reasonable but not extreme fear appeals and also recognize that fear appeals are not always appropriate. For example, a study of warning information labels affixed to full-fat, reduced-fat, and nonfat products concluded that, for products with credible and familiar risks, information labels were more effective than warning labels because they do not arouse *psychological reactance.*[56] (See Chapter 4.) Another study of adolescent responses to fear communications found that adolescents are more persuaded to avoid drug use by messages that depict negative social consequences of drug use rather than physical threats to their bodies.[57] A five-month study of high school students discovered that short-term cosmetic fear appeals (such as yellow teeth or bad breath) used in ads to stop or reduce smoking were more persuasive for males, while long-term health fear appeals (such as getting cancer later in life) were more persuasive for females.[58]

There is no single explanation of the relationship between fear appeals and persuasiveness. One theory proposes that individuals cognitively appraise the available information regarding the severity of the threat, then they appraise the likelihood that the threat will occur; they evaluate whether coping behavior can eliminate the threat's danger, and if so, whether they have the ability to perform the coping behavior. This theory is called the *Ordered Protection Motivation* (OPM) model. The study also found that the personality variable "sensation seeking" affected the processing of fear appeals. A high sensation seeker is more likely to use drugs and also to react negatively to fear-focused antidrug messages, feeling that he or she is immortal.[59]

Marketers must also consider that the mention of possibly detrimental side effects of using a product while proclaiming its benefits may result in negative attitudes toward the product itself. For that reason, when the benefits of a new pharmaceutical are discussed by actors in a TV ad, the negative side effects—which the company is required to mention—are usually rapidly intoned by a voice-over while the actors cheerfully repeat the drug's benefits.

Humor   Many marketers use humorous appeals in the belief that humor will increase the acceptance and persuasiveness of their advertising communications. By some estimates, up to 24 percent of TV ads in the United States use humor, but there are some risks associated with using this appeal. For example, the effects of humorous ads vary by the audience's demographics, level of involvement (humor is more effective for promoting low-involvement products), and attitudes (humor is more effective when the audience already has positive attitudes toward the brand).[60] Table 9.2 summarizes some research findings on the impact of humor on advertising.

Marketers believe that younger, better-educated, upscale, and professional people tend to be receptive audiences for humorous messages (see Figure 9.9). A study of how humor actually works within ads discovered that surprise is almost always needed to generate humor and that the effectiveness of humorous ads is also influenced by such

TABLE 9.2	**Impact of Humor on Advertising**

- *Humor attracts attention.*
- *Humor does not harm comprehension.* (In some cases it may even aid comprehension.)
- *Humor is not more effective at increasing persuasion.*
- *Humor does not enhance source credibility.*
- *Humor enhances liking.*
- *Humor that is relevant to the product is superior to humor that is unrelated to the product.*
- *Audience demographic factors (e.g., gender, ethnicity, age) affect the response to humorous advertising appeals.*
- *The nature of the product affects the appropriateness of a humorous treatment.*
- *Humor is more effective with existing products than with new products.*
- *Humor is more appropriate for low-involvement products and feeling-oriented products than for high-involvement products.*

Source: Marc G. Weinberger and Charles S. Gulas, "The Impact of Humor in Advertising: A Review," *Journal of Advertising* 21, 4 (December 1992): 35–59. Reprinted by permission.

message elements as warmth and playfulness.[61] A recent study developed a measure of a personality trait named *need for humor* (NFH) that is focused on a person's tendency to enjoy, engage, or seek out amusement and suggested that these cognitive factors can better explain how consumers respond to humorous advertisements.[62]

Abrasive Advertising How effective can unpleasant or annoying ads be? Studies of the *sleeper effect,* discussed earlier, suggest that the memory of an unpleasant commercial that antagonizes listeners or viewers may dissipate over time, leaving only the brand name in the minds of consumers.

All of us have at one time or another been repelled by so-called *agony commercials,* which depict in diagrammatic detail the internal and intestinal effects of heartburn, indigestion, clogged sinus cavities, hammer-induced headaches, and the like. Nevertheless, pharmaceutical companies often run such commercials with great success because they appeal to a certain segment of the population that suffers from ailments that are not visible and thus elicit little sympathy from family and friends. Their complaints are legitimized by commercials with which they immediately identify. With the sponsor's credibility established ("They really understand the misery I'm going through"), the message itself tends to be highly persuasive in getting consumers to buy the advertised product.

Sex in Advertising In our highly permissive society, sensual advertising seems to permeate the print media and the airwaves. Advertisers are increasingly trying to provoke attention with suggestive illustrations, crude language, and nudity in their efforts to appear "hip" and contemporary. In today's advertising, there is a lot of explicit and daring sexual imagery, extending far beyond the traditional product categories of fashion and fragrance into such categories as shampoo, beer, cars, and home construction.

There is little doubt that sexual themes have attention-getting value, but studies show that they rarely encourage actual consumption behavior. A widely quoted study that examined the effects of sexual advertising appeals on cognitive processing and communications effectiveness found that sexual appeals interfere with message comprehension, particularly when there is substantial information to be processed. It also found that more product-related thinking occurs in response to nonsexual appeals and that visual sexual elements in an ad are more likely to be processed than its verbal content, drawing

FIGURE 9.9

Source: Client: Mobility Elevator and Lift Co. – West Caldwell, NJ Agency: BrandStreet Advertising – Montclair, NJ Creative Director: David Frank, Co-Creative Director: Joe Gugliuzza, Copywriter: James A. Cotter, Photography/Photo Illustration: John Halpern. Used with permission.

Humorous Appeal: Upward Mobility

cognitive processing away from product or message evaluation.[63] Some researchers have concluded that nudity may negatively impact the product message.[64] These and other findings support the theory that sexual advertising appeals often detract from the processing of message content.

The type of interest that sexual advertising evokes often stops exactly where it starts—with sex. If a sexually suggestive or explicit illustration is not relevant to the product advertised, it has little effect on consumers' buying intentions. This highlights the potential risk of sexually-oriented advertising: The advertiser may be giving up persuasiveness to achieve "stopping power." When using sex to promote a product, the advertiser must be sure that the product, the ad, the target audience, and the use of sexual themes and elements all work together. When sex is relevant to the product, it can be an extremely potent copy theme. For example, the advertisers of fragrances for either men or women often use highly romantic or suggestive visuals in their ads, implying that the use of the fragrance will result in a meaningful or sultry romance.

Audience Participation   Earlier we spoke about the importance of feedback in the communications process. The provision of feedback changes the communications process from one-way to two-way communication. This is important to senders because it enables them to determine whether and how well communication has taken place. But feedback also is important to receivers because it enables them to participate, to be involved, to experience in some way the message itself. Participation by the receiver reinforces the message. An experienced communicator asks questions and opinions of an audience to draw them into the discussion. Many professors use the participative approach in classrooms rather than the more sterile lecture format because they recognize that student participation tends to facilitate internalization of the information covered.

Although participation is easily accomplished in interpersonal and online communications, it takes a great deal of ingenuity to achieve in impersonal communications.

marketing communication and ethics

The keys to effective marketing communications are developing the right persuasive message and delivering it to the right audience. The corresponding ethical issues focus on (1) identifying and locating specific audiences and (2) the contents of the promotional messages they are sent.

Precision targeting

The consumer's loss of privacy is an increasingly problematic ethical issue as marketers manage to identify and reach out to increasingly smaller audiences through innovative media. As evident from discussions throughout this chapter, it is apparent that the old *broadcasting* model—where large audiences are reached with the same electronic or print messages—is rapidly becoming obsolete. Advertisers are increasingly adopting *narrowcasting*—a technique that allows them to send very directed messages to very small audiences on an ongoing basis. **Narrowcasting** is made possible through the efforts of sophisticated data providers who compile individual profiles from census data, tax records, credit card companies, banks, direct-mail responses, surveys and product warranty cards completed by consumers, and from internal sales records provided by companies. Sophisticated analysis of such data enables the compilation of extremely specialized lists of consumers. For example, a marketer can purchase a list of left-handed people with a specified income who own pets and are of Hispanic origin. Based on these characteristics, the marketer can develop and deliver a highly targeted and persuasive message designed specifically for this very narrow group.

Narrowcasting was used extensively in the swing state of Ohio during the 2004 presidential elections, where campaign workers received daily lists of voters with very specific characteristics and the issues that these individuals were likely to be concerned about. The campaign workers were also equipped with Palm Pilots where short audiovisual, precisely targeted messages, developed on the basis of specific voters' characteristics, were stored and shown to these voters by the campaign workers who visited them.[65] Narrowcasting is made possible because people who buy products (generally with credit cards), fill out census surveys, and file taxes have inadvertently yielded their privacy rights regarding their demographics and consumption habits.

Another ethical issue of targeted communications is reaching and possibly manipulating consumers who are, according to some, less capable of making sound consumption decisions. Public complaints have been made regarding the targeting of ads to students in classrooms through such media as Whittle Communication's Channel One (a closed-circuit TV offered free to public schools), and through the provision of materials and programs that marketers provide to students as "educational" tools when, in fact, they include a lot of persuasive advertising.

Marketers can learn not only *who* you are (e.g., your personal characteristics) and *what* specific purchases you make, but now they can also learn *where* you are at any given moment because your cell phone, mobile e-mail device, or the GPS integrated into your car or sports-watch serve as sort of "electronic bracelets" that monitor your movements. In one futuristic movie thriller set in 2054, the hero passes a billboard featuring the American Express card, which, upon scanning his eye retina, becomes a hologram (presumably only visible to him) portraying his picture and personal data and urging him to use the card. He then enters a Gap store where he is met by voices greeting him by name, asking how he liked his previous purchases, and suggesting items that he may like based on his past purchases. Although such scanning and recognition devices are not yet widespread, if you travel abroad and have a cell phone with a roaming service, upon landing at your destination your phone is likely to include a message welcoming you to that destination and offering you additional services designed for travelers. Clearly, in the not-too-distant future, when you drive a car equipped with a GPS with the radio on, the commercial that you will hear may alert you to, say, a McDonald's two exits down next to the highway; that ad will not be the same as the one heard by another driver in a different location and listening to the same radio station. In fact, some companies use cabs equipped with GPS and advertising billboards on their roofs to create ever-changing advertising messages; the changing ad displays correspond to the businesses the cabs pass as they travel.[66] Once again, more sophisticated media to reach consumers results in loss of consumers' privacy.

The contents of promotional messages

The ethical issues related to the content of marketing communications include the accuracy of the information provided, the impact of values portrayed in ads, and the potential misuse of promotional messages' persuasive abilities. Regarding accuracy, a toothpaste ad stating that "brand A is the best" is considered an acceptable form of advertising "puffery" because consumers generally understand that there is no credible way to determine what "best" means. A toothpaste ad stating that the brand was "endorsed by the American Dental Association" is an objective statement because it includes information that is easy to verify. However, is an ad stating that the brand "provides more cavity protection than any other toothpaste" permissible advertising puffery, or is it false or misleading? The answer depends on how most reasonable consumers are likely to interpret the ad. Do they believe that there is a scientific way to measure the degree of cavity protection and that the maker of the brand has conducted a scientific study of all brands of toothpaste on the market and whether the study proved the ad's claim? It is clear that determining how most reasonable consumers are likely to interpret the ad is a complex undertaking, and therefore there is no definitive answer to the question "At what point does puffery become deceptive?"

Truth-in-advertising laws protect consumers from false advertisements. Over time, the Federal Trade Commission (FTC) has developed guidelines as to what constitutes **deceptive advertising** and they hold marketers responsible for determining their ads' potential to mislead consumers. While the FTC is responsible for stopping false or misleading ads, it is apparent that such ads continue to exist. For example, the FTC's Web site has featured a "Red Flag" button alerting consumers that "misleading weight loss advertising is everywhere" and also warning them to beware of weight loss claims that are too good to be true, such as claims that the product causes "substantial weight loss no matter how much the consumer eats" or promising "a weight loss of two pounds or more a week for a month or more without dieting or exercise."[67] The FTC encourages and investigates complaints by consumers and companies regarding false or misleading ads, but its public advice for consumers regarding weight loss products illustrates that it cannot locate and stop all misleading ads. The FTC can also require companies that have misled consumers through their advertising to run **corrective advertising**. For example, years ago Listerine's maker was forced to correct the claim that the product prevents colds.

In addition to the FTC, the National Advertising Review Council (NARC) is the self-regulatory group that monitors complaints from companies and consumers regarding truth in advertising and often determines what ads can or cannot state. For example, NARC determined that Colgate-Palmolive provided supportive evidence to the claim that its Oxy-Plus product "blasts away grease faster" than P&G's Ultra Dawn, but decided that there was no evidence supporting GlaxoSmithKline's claim that Super PoliGrip provides the "strongest hold ever," a claim that the company subsequently withdrew. NARC also supported a challenge of promotions for cancer treatment claiming that "Chemotherapy doesn't work for everyone."[68] In some cases, powerful companies can persuade media to stop running ads they deem deceptive. For example, Anheuser-Busch persuaded ABC, CBS, and NBC to stop running Miller Beer ads depicting consumers comparing beers and saying that the Miller beers have more flavor, on the grounds that these comparisons were flawed.[69]

The potential manipulative impact of promotional messages on children was explored earlier (see Chapter 7). There is a consensus that even if children understand the purpose of promotional messages, marketers must take special care in advertising to children because of the amount of time children spend viewing TV and spend online. As discussed in Chapter 7, CARU has developed specific guidelines regarding truth and accuracy in advertisements directed at the young, and the organization regularly monitors such communications.[70] Studies also show that parents significantly influence children's understanding and processing of advertisements.[71] Generally, advertising to children in the United States is less regulated than in European countries.

Since advertising is part of our culture, the cumulative persuasive impact of promotional messages on societal values must be considered. By itself, one tasteless ad has little impact on our values. However, cumulatively, such ads may persuade consumers to act unwisely or develop undesirable attitudes. For example, repeated exposure to ads depicting perfectly tanned persons is likely to result in excessive sun bathing or tanning via ultraviolet light, despite the fact that it has been documented that such practices significantly increase the chances of developing cancer. Interestingly, not all ads that promote a practice that may negatively impact one's health are treated the same way. For example, although it is known that tanning causes cancer, we have accepted ads portraying perfectly tanned models without criticism. On the other hand, the Food and Drug Administration (FDA) has alerted marketers of HIV medications to the fact that some of their ads, which often show healthy-looking persons involved in rigorous physical activity, may be conveying the notion that since the drugs can restore one's health, they implicitly encourage unsafe sex.[72]

Following considerable research, it is now generally accepted that repeated exposure to very thin "ideal" figures in promotional messages leads to negative self-perceptions (particularly in women) and is partially responsible for the increase in eating-related disorders. Marketers now recognize that ads focused on beauty and attractiveness, especially if they stress the importance of these attributes over other personal characteristics, are likely to be scrutinized by the media, consumers, advocacy groups, or religious organizations. Subsequently, numerous advertisements now portray more realistic-looking models and some beauty-products ads integrate the notion that although the "outside" is important, the person's self-worth or "true beauty" comes from "within."

Although many ads portray values or behaviors that many consumers find distasteful or wrong, the importance of public scrutiny must not be underestimated. For example, the broadcast of the 2004 Super Bowl included many ads portraying crude humor and gags that were later criticized by many (and also amplified by the coincidental "wardrobe malfunction" of a female entertainer during the half-time show). As a result, advertisers during the 2005 Super Bowl broadcast took special care to develop ads that were more mainstream and traditional, not an easy task since Super Bowl ads—expected to be creative and unique—are the most analyzed group of ads in American broadcasting.[73]

SUMMARY

This chapter has described how the consumer receives and is influenced by marketing communications. There are five basic components of communication: the sender, the receiver, the medium, the message, and feedback (the receiver's response). In the communications process, the sender encodes the message using words, pictures, symbols, or spokespersons and sends it through a selected channel (or medium). The receiver decodes (interprets) the message based on his or her personal characteristics and experience, and responds (or does not respond) based on such factors as selective exposure, selective perception, comprehension, and psychological noise.

There are two types of communications: interpersonal and impersonal (or mass) communications. Interpersonal communications occur on a personal level between two or more people and may be verbal or nonverbal, formal or informal. In mass communications, there is no direct contact between source and receiver. Interpersonal communications take place in person, by telephone, by mail, on the Web or e-mail; mass communications occur through such impersonal media as television, radio, newspapers, and magazines. Feedback is an essential component of all types of communications because it provides the sender with some notion as to whether and how well the message has been received.

The credibility of the source, a vital element in message persuasiveness, often is based on the source's perceived intentions. Informal sources and neutral or editorial sources are considered to be highly objective and, thus, highly credible. The credibility of a commercial source is more problematic and usually is based on a composite evaluation of its reputation, expertise, and knowledge and that of the medium in which it advertises, the retail channel, and company spokespersons.

Media selection depends on the product, the audience, and the advertising objectives of the campaign. Each medium has advantages and shortcomings that must be weighed in the selection of media for an advertising campaign. Following the emergence of new technologies, many advertisers are now developing more customized communications that can reach consumers via media with narrowcasting, rather than broadcasting, capabilities.

The manner in which a message is presented influences its impact. For example, one-sided messages are more effective in some situations and with some audiences; two-sided messages are more effective with others. High-involvement products (those with great relevance to a consumer segment) are best advertised through the central route to persuasion, which encourages active cognitive effort. Low-involvement products are best promoted through peripheral cues, such as background scenery, music, or celebrity spokespersons.

Marketers can either use objective, factual appeals or emotional appeals. The emotional appeals most frequently used in advertising include fear, humor, and sexual appeals. Audience participation is a very effective communications strategy because it encourages internalization of the advertising message.

The ethical issues related to marketing communications include invasion of consumer privacy, the potential manipulation of consumers who are less capable of making wise decisions due to age or other demographic factors, the distinction between advertising puffery and deception, misleading advertising, and the cumulative persuasive impact of messages that portray socially undesirable behavior or values.

DISCUSSION QUESTIONS

1. Explain the differences between feedback from interpersonal communications and feedback from impersonal communications. How can the marketer obtain and use each kind of feedback?

2. List and discuss the effects of psychological noise on the communications process. What strategies can a marketer use to overcome psychological noise?

3. List and discuss factors that affect the credibility of formal communications sources of product information. What factors influence the perceived credibility of an informal communications source?

4. What are the implications of the sleeper effect for the selection of spokespersons and the scheduling of advertising messages?

5. Should marketers use more body copy than artwork in print ads? Explain your answer.

6. For what kinds of audiences would you consider using comparative advertising? Why?

EXERCISES

1. Bring two print advertisements to class: one illustrating a one-sided message and the other a two-sided message. Which of the measures discussed in the chapter would you use to evaluate the effectiveness of each ad? Explain your answers.

2. Find one example of each of the following two advertising appeals: fear and sex. One example must be a print ad and the other a TV commercial. Analyze the placement of each ad in the medium where it appeared according to the media selection criteria presented in Table 9.1.

3. Watch one hour of TV on a single channel during prime time and also tape the broadcast. Immediately after watching the broadcast, list all the commercials you can recall seeing. For each commercial, identify (a) the message framing approach used, and (b) whether the message was one-sided or two-sided. Compare your list with the actual taped broadcast. Explain any discrepancies between your recollections and the actual broadcast on the basis of concepts discussed in this chapter.

4. For three of the commercials you watched in the preceding exercise, identify whether the marketer used the central or peripheral route to persuasion. Explain your answer and speculate on why each marketer chose the approach it used to advertise the product or service.

5. Find an example of a promotional message delivered by narrowcasting and discuss it along the ethical issues discussed in this chapter.

6. Find an example of an advertisement that, in your view, depicts a socially undesirable practice and explain why.

KEY TERMS

- **advertising resonance**
- **audience versus consumer profiles**
- **broadcasting versus narrowcasting**
- **buzz-agents**
- **cause-related marketing**
- **central versus peripheral routes to persuasion**
- **communication**
- **comparative advertising**
- **corrective advertising**
- **deceptive advertising**
- **direct marketing versus direct mail**
- **Federal Trade Commission**
- **feedback**
- **formal versus informal communications sources**
- **institutional advertising**
- **interpersonal versus impersonal communications**
- **one-sided versus two-sided messages**
- **opinion leaders**
- **order effects**
- **positive versus negative framing strategies**
- **psychological noise**
- **publicity**
- **repetition**
- **resonance**
- **sleeper effect**
- **source credibility**
- **target audience**
- **truth-in-advertising laws**
- **verbal versus nonverbal messages**
- **word-of-mouth communications**

NOTES

1. Lorne Manly, "The Future of the 30-Second Spot," March 27, 2005, **www.nytimes.com**; Jon Gertner, "Our Ratings, Ourselves," April 10, 2005, **www.nytimes.com**; Steven Levy, "Television Reload," *Newsweek,* May 30, 2005, 49–62.

2. Ibid.

3. Ibid.

4. Ibid.

5. For an empirical analysis of some 200 logos designed to achieve corporate image and communication goals, see Pamela W. Henderson and Joseph A. Cote, "Guidelines for Selecting or Modifying Logos," *Journal of Marketing* (April 1998): 14–30.

6. Linda Greenhouse, "High Court Ruling Upholds Trademarking of a Color," *New York Times,* March 29, 1994, D1.

7. Warren St. John, "A Store Lures Guys Who Are Graduating from Chinos," *New York Times on the Web,* July 14, 2002.

8. Rob Walker, "The Hidden (in Plain Sight) Persuaders," December 5, 2004, **www.nytimes.com**

9. Nat Ives, "Marketing's Flip Side: The 'Determined Detractor'," *The New York Times,* December 27, 2004, C1.

10. Thorsten Hennig-Thurau, Kevin P. Gwinner, Gianfranco Walsh, and Dwayne D. Gremler, "Electronic Word-of-Mouth Via Consumer-Opinion Platforms: What Motivates Consumers to Articulate Themselves on the Internet?" *Journal of Interactive Marketing* (Winter 2004): 38–52.

11. Hyun Seung Jin, "Compounding Consumer Interest: Effects of Advertising Campaign Publicity on the Ability to Recall Subsequent Advertisements," *Journal of Advertising* (Winter 2003/2004): 29–42.

12. S. Ratneshwar and Shelly Chaiken, "Comprehension's Role in Persuasion: The Case of Its Moderating Effect on the Persuasive Impact of Source Cues," *Journal of Consumer Research* 18 (June 1991): 52–62.

13. Michael A. Kamins, "An Investigation into the 'Match Up' Hypothesis in Celebrity Advertising: When Beauty May Be Only Skin Deep," *Journal of Advertising* 19, no. 1 (1990): 4–13. See also Marsha L. Richins, "Social Comparison and the Idealized Images of Advertising," *Journal of Consumer Research* 18 (June 1991): 71–83.

14. Marla Royne Stafford, Thomas F. Stafford, and Ellen Day, "A Contingency Approach: The Effects of Spokesperson Type and Service Type on Service Advertising," *Journal of Advertising* (Summer 2000): 17–32.

15. Laura M. Arpan, "When in Rome? The Effects of Spokesperson Ethnicity on Audience Evaluation of Crisis," *The Journal of Business Communication* (July 2002): 314–339; Osei Appiah, "Ethnic Identification and Adolescents' Evaluations of Advertisements," *Journal of Advertising Research* (September/October 2001): 7–22; Oscar W. DeShields, Jr. and Ali Kara, "The Persuasive Effect of Spokesperson Similarity Moderated by Source Credibility," *2000 American Marketing Association Education Proceedings,* (2000) vol. 11, 132–143.

16. Ronald E. Goldsmith, Barbara A. Lafferty, and Stephen J. Newell, "The Impact of Corporate Credibility and Celebrity Credibility on Consumer Reaction to Advertisements and Brands," *Journal of Advertising* (Fall 2000): 43–54.

17. B. Zafer Erdogan, Michael J. Baker, and Stephen Tagg, "Selecting Celebrity Endorsers: The Practitioner's Perspective," *Journal of Advertising Research* (May/June 2001): 39–48.

18. Stuart Elliott, "Agency Admits Errors in Deal With TV Host," January 20, 2005, **www.nytimes.com**; Frank Rich, "The White House Stages Its 'Daily Show'," February 20, 2005, **www.nytimes.com**; Patrick D. Healy, "Believe It: The Media's Credibility Headache Gets Worse," May 22, 2005, **www.nytimes.com**

19. Thomas J. Robinson and Barbara K. Kaye, "Using Is Believing: The Influence of Reliance on the Credibility of Online Political Information Among Politically Interested Internet Users," *Journalism and Mass Communication Quarterly* (Winter 2000): 865–879.

20. Sung Tae Kim, David Weaver, and Lars Willnat, "Media Reporting and Perceived Credibility of Online Polls," *Journalism and Mass Communication Quarterly* (Winter 2000): 846–864.

21. Mineabere Ibelema and Lary Powell, "Cable Television News Viewed as Most Credible," *Newspaper Research Journal* (Winter 2001): 41–51.

22. Carl I. Hovland, Arthur A. Lumsdaine, and Fred D. Sheffield, *Experiments on Mass Communication* (New York: Wiley, 1949): 182–200.

23. See Joseph W. Alba, Howard Marmorstein, and Amitava Chattopadhyay, "Transitions in Preference over Time: The Effects of Memory on Message Persuasiveness," *Journal of Marketing Research* 29 (November 1992): 414.

24. Ruth Ann Weaver Lariscy and Spencer F. Tinkham, "The Sleeper Effect and Negative Political Advertising," *Journal of Advertising* (Winter 1999): 13–30.

25. Kartik Pashupati, " 'I Know This Brand, But Did I Like the Ad?' An Investigation of the Familiarity-Based Sleeper Effect," *Psychology & Marketing* (November 2003): 1017–1028.

26. Frédéric F. Brunel and Michelle R. Nelson, "Explaining Gender Responses to 'Help-Self' and 'Help-Others' Charity Ads Appeals: The Mediating Role of World-Views," *Journal of Advertising* (Fall 2000): 15–27.

27. Kawpong Polyorat and Dana L Alden, "Self-Construal and Need-for-Cognition Effects on Brand Attitudes and Purchase Intentions in Response to Comparative Advertising in Thailand and the United States," *Journal of Advertising* (Spring 2005): 37–49.

28. Bred A. S. Martin, Bodo Lang, and Stephanie Wong, "Conclusion Explicitness in Advertising: The Moderating Role of Need for Cognition (NFC) and Argument Quality (AQ) on Persuasion," *Journal of Advertising* (Winter 2003/2004): 57–66.

29. Pablo Brioni, Richard E. Petty, and Zakary L. Tormala, "Self-Validation of Cognitive Responses to Advertisements," *Journal of Consumer Research* (March 2004): 559–574.

30. Patrick De Pelsmacker, Maggie Geuens, and Pascal Anckaert, "Media Context and Advertising Effectiveness: The Role of Context Appreciation and Context/Ad Similarity," *Journal of Advertising* (Summer 2002): 49–61.

31. Andrew Sharma, "Recall of Television Commercials as a Function of Viewing Context: The Impact of Program-Commercial Congruity on Commercial Messages," *Journal of General Psychology* (October 2000): 383–396.

32. Angela Y. Lee and Brian Sternthal, "The Effects of Positive Mood on Memory," *Journal of Consumer Research* (September 1999): 115–129.

33. Anna S. Mattila, "The Role of Narratives in the Advertising of Experiential Services," *Journal of Service Research* (August 2000): 35–45.

34. Brian Steinberg and Suzanne Vranica, "The Ad World's Message for 2005: Stealth," *The Wall Street Journal,* December 30, 2004, B1.

35. Jonathan Miller, "Floater Ads, the Cousins to Pop-Ups, Evade the Blockers," February 24, 2005, **www.nytimes.com**; Nat Ives, "As TV Moves to the Web, Marketers Follow," May 27, 2005, **www.nytimes.com**; Louise Story, "Marketers See Opportunity as a Web Tool Gains Users," July 5, 2005, **www.nytimes.com**

36. Stuart Elliott, "Pepsi One Goes on a Television-Free, Celebrity-Free Commercial Diet," March 16, 2005, **www.nytimes.com**; Stuart Elliott, "Advertisers Want Something Different," May 23, 2005, **www.nytimes.com**; Stuart Elliott, "I Can't Believe It's Not a TV Ad!" July 26, 2005, **www.nytimes.com**

37. **www.nielsenmedia.com**, **www.comscore.com**, **www.mediamark.com**

38. **www.prresearch.com**; "Market Research: What's On Your Mind?" *American Demographics* (April 2000).

39. Richard H. Hazlett and Sasha Yassky, "Emotional Response to Television Commercials: Facial EMG vs. Self Reports," *Journal of Advertising Research* (March/April 1999): 7–23.

40. Bruce F. Hall, "A New Model for Measuring Advertising Effectiveness," *Journal of Advertising Research* (March/April 2002): 23–31.

41. Sang M. Lee, Pairin Katerattanakul, and Soongoo Hong, "Framework for User Perception of Effective E-Tail Web Sites," *Journal of Electronic Commerce* (January–March 2005): 13–35.

42. Gary Hennerberg, "The Righteous, Social, and Pragmatic Buyer," *Direct Marketing* (May 1993): 31–34.

43. Jennifer Edson Escalas and Mary Frances Luce, "Understanding the Effects of Process-Focused versus Outcome-Focused Thought in Response to Advertising," *Journal of Consumer Research* (September 2004): 274–286.

44. Edward F. McQuarrie and David Glen Mick, "Visual and Verbal Rhetorical Figures under Directed Processing versus Incidental Exposure to Advertising," *Journal of Consumer Research* (March 2003): 579–588.

45. Richard Buda and Bruce H. Charnov, "Message Processing in Realistic Recruitment Practices," *Journal of Managerial Issues* (Fall 2003): 302+.

46. Jennifer L. Aaker and Angela Y. Lee, " 'I' Seek Pleasure and 'We' Avoid Pains: The Role of Self-Regulatory Goals in Information Processing and Persuasion," *Journal of Consumer Research* (June 2001): 33–49.

47. Yoav Ganzach and Nili Karsahi, "Message Framing and Buying Behavior: A Field Experiment," *Journal of Business Research* 32 (1995): 11–17.

48. Dena Cox and Anthony D. Cox, "Communicating the Consequences of Early Detection: The Role of Evidence and Framing," *Journal of Marketing* (July 2001): 91–103.

49. Baba Shiv, Julie A. Edell Britton, and John W. Payne, "Does Elaboration Increase or Decrease the Effectiveness of Negatively versus Positively Framed Messages?" *Journal of Consumer Research* (June 2004): 199–209.

50. Randall L. Rose, Paul W. Miniard, Michael J. Barone, Kenneth C. Manning, and Brian D. Till, "When Persuasion Goes Undetected: The Case of Comparative Advertising," *Journal of Marketing Research* 30 (August 1993): 315–330; see also Cornelia Pechmann and S. Ratneshwar, "The Use of Comparative Advertising for Brand Positioning: Association versus Differentiation," *Journal of Consumer Research* 18 (September 1991): 145–160; and Cornelia Pechmann and David W. Stewart, "The Effects of Comparative Advertising on Attention, Memory, and Purchase Intentions," *Journal of Consumer Research* 17 (September 1990): 180–191.

51. Darrel D. Muehling, Jeffrey J. Stoltman, and Sanford Grossbart, "The Impact of Comparative Advertising on Levels of Message Involvement," *Journal of Advertising* 19, no. 4 (1990): 41–50; see also Jerry B. Gotlieb and Dan Sarel, "Comparative Advertising Effectiveness: The Role of Involvement and Source Credibility," *Journal of Advertising* 20, no. 1 (1991): 38–45.

52. Kenneth C. Manning, Paul W. Miniard, Michael J. Barone, and Randall L. Rose, "Understanding the Mental Representations Created by Comparative Advertising," *Journal of Advertising* (Summer 2001): 27–39.

53. Kawpong Polyorat and Dana L Alden, "Self-Construal and Need-for-Cognition Effects on Brand Attitudes and Purchase Intentions in Response to Comparative Advertising in Thailand and the United States," *Journal of Advertising* (Spring 2005): 37–49.

54. Yung Kyun Choi and Gordon E. Miracle, "The Effectiveness of Comparative Advertising in Korea and the United States," *Journal of Advertising* (Winter 2004): 75–88.

55. William E. Baker, Heather Honea, and Cristel Antonia Russell, "Do Not Wait to Reveal the Brand Name: The Effect of Brand-Name Placement on Television Advertising Effectiveness," *Journal of Advertising* (Fall 2004): 77–86.

56. Brad J. Bushman, "Effects of Warning and Information Labels on Consumption of Full Fat, Reduced Fat, and No Fat Products," *Journal of Applied Psychology* 83, no. 1 (1998): 97–101.

57. Denise D. Schoenbachler and Tommy E. Whittler, "Adolescent Processing of Social and Physical Threat Communications," *Journal of Advertising* 35, no. 4 (Winter 1996): 37–54.

58. Karen H. Smith and Mary Ann Stutts, "Effects of Short-Term Cosmetic Versus Long-Term Health Fear Appeals in Anti-Smoking Advertisements on the Smoking Behaviour of Adolescents," *Journal of Consumer Behaviour* (December 2003): 157+.

59. James B. Hunt, John F. Tanner, Jr., and David R. Eppright, "Forty Years of Fear Appeal Research: Support for the Ordered Protection Motivation Model," *American Marketing Association* 6 (Winter 1995): 147–153.

60. Dana L. Alden, Ashesh Mukherjee, and Wayne D. Hoyer, "The Effects of Incongruity, Surprise and Positive Moderators on Perceived Humor in Advertising," *Journal of Advertising* (Summer 2000): 1–15.

61. Ibid.

62. Thomas W. Cline, Moses B. Altsech, and James J. Kellaris, "When Does Humor Enhance or Inhibit Ad Responses?: The Moderating Role of the Need for Humor," *Journal of Advertising* (Fall 2003): 31–46.

63. Jessica Severn, George E. Belch, and Michael A. Belch, "The Effects of Sexual and Non-Sexual Advertising Appeals and Information Level on Cognitive Processing and Communication Effectiveness," *Journal of Advertising* 19, no. 1 (1990): 14–22.

64. Michael S. LaTour, Robert E. Pitts, and David C. Snook Luther, "Female Nudity, Arousal, and Ad Response: An Experimental Investigation," *Journal of Advertising* 19, no. 4 (1990): 51–62.

65. PBS TV, *Frontline,* "The Persuaders," November 4 2005, transcript at: **http://www.pbs.org/wgbh/pages/frontline/shows/persuaders/etc/script.html**

66. "Outdoor Interactive—Electronic Changing Ads on Top of Cabs," *American Demographics* (August 1, 2001).

67. **www.ftc.gov/bcp/conline/edcams/redflag/falseclaims**

68. Nat Ives, "Advertisers Have a Deep Concern for the Truth, Especially When It Comes to a Rival's Claim," *The New York Times,* September 21, 2004, C4.

69. Ibid.

70. "Self-Regulatory Guidelines for Children's Advertising," **www.caru.org**

71. For example, Albert Caruana and Rosella Vassallo, "Children's Perception of Their Influence over Purchases: The Role of Parental Communication Patterns," *Journal of Consumer Marketing* 20, no. 1 (2003): 55–67.

72. "FDA Faults 'Misleading' Drug-Ad Images," *The Wall Street Journal,* May 4, 2001, B8.

73. Stuart Elliott, "Emphasizing Taste, and Not Just in Beer, at Super Bowl," *The New York Times,* January 26, 2005, C1.

PART 3 DISCUSSES CONSUMERS IN THEIR OWN CULTURAL AND SOCIAL MILIEUS

The five chapters in Part III are designed to provide the reader with a detailed picture of the social and cultural dimensions of consumer behavior. Chapters 10 through 14 explain how these factors affect the attitudes and behavior of individuals in the United States and the world beyond, and demonstrate how an in-depth knowledge of social and behavioral concepts enable marketers to achieve their marketing objectives.

chapterten

❯ Reference Groups and Family Influences

With the exception of those very few people who are classified as hermits, most individuals interact with other people on a daily basis, especially with members of their own families.

In the first part of this chapter, we will consider how group involvements and memberships influence our actions as consumers—that is, impact consumers' decision making, shopping activities, and actual consumption. The second part of this chapter deals with how the family influences its members' consumer behavior. For instance, a child learning the uses and value of money is often a "family matter"; so are decisions about a new car, a vacation trip, or whether to go to a local or an out-of-town college. The family commonly provides the opportunity for product exposure and trial and imparts consumption values to its members. As a major consumption group, the family is also a prime target for many products and services.

This chapter begins with a discussion of the basic concepts of group dynamics and how reference groups both directly and indirectly influence consumer behavior. We then examine some basic family concepts. Next we discuss family consumer decision

making and consumption behavior; last we explore the marketing implications of the family life cycle. (The four chapters that follow discuss other social and societal *groupings* that influence consumer buying processes: social class, culture, subculture, and cross-cultural exposure.)

what is a group?

A **group** may be defined as two or more people who interact to accomplish either individual or mutual goals. The broad scope of this definition includes an intimate group of two neighbors who each summer Saturday drive to the local golf course to play a round of golf and a larger, more formal group, such as a local scuba diving club, whose members are mutually interested in scuba equipment, scuba training, and scuba diving trips and vacations. Also, included in this definition, is a kind of "one-sided grouping" in which an individual consumer observes the appearance or actions of others, who unknowingly serve as consumption-related role models.

Sometimes groups are classified by membership status. A group to which a person either belongs or would qualify for membership in is called a *membership group*. For example, the group of men with whom a young executive plays poker weekly would be considered, for him, a membership group. There are also groups in which an individual is not likely to receive membership, despite acting like a member by adopting the group's values, attitudes, and behavior. This is considered a **symbolic group**. For instance, professional tennis players may constitute a symbolic group for an amateur tennis player who identifies with certain players by imitating their behavior whenever possible (e.g., by purchasing a specific brand of tennis racket or tennis sneaker). However, the amateur tennis player does not (and probably never will) qualify for membership as a professional tennis player because she has neither the skills nor the opportunity to compete professionally.

understanding the power of reference groups

Within the context of consumer behavior, the concept of reference groups is an extremely important and powerful idea. A **reference group** is any person or group that serves as a point of comparison (or reference) for an individual in forming either general or specific values, attitudes, or a specific guide for behavior. This basic concept provides a valuable perspective for understanding the impact of other people on an individual's consumption beliefs, attitudes, and behavior. It also provides insight into the methods marketers sometimes use to effect desired changes in consumer behavior.

From a marketing perspective, *reference groups* are groups that serve as *frames of reference* for individuals in their purchase or consumption decisions. The usefulness of this concept is enhanced by the fact that it places no restrictions on group size or membership, nor does it require that consumers identify with a tangible group (i.e., the group can be symbolic such as owners of successful small businesses, leading corporate chief executive officers, country music stars, or baseball celebrities).

Reference groups that influence general or broadly defined values or behavior are called **normative reference groups**. An example of a child's normative reference group is the immediate family, which is likely to play an important role in molding the child's general consumer values and behavior (such as which foods to select for good nutrition, appropriate ways to dress for specific occasions, how and where to shop, or what constitutes "good" value).

Reference groups that serve as benchmarks for specific or narrowly defined attitudes or behavior are called **comparative reference groups**. A comparative reference group might be a neighboring family whose lifestyle appears to be admirable and worthy of imitation (the way they maintain their home, their choice of home furnishings and cars, their taste in clothing, or the number and types of vacations they take).

Both normative and comparative reference groups are important. Normative reference groups influence the development of a basic code of behavior; comparative reference groups influence the expression of specific consumer attitudes and behavior. It is likely that the specific influences of comparative reference groups, to some measure, depend on the basic values and behavior patterns established early in a person's development by normative reference groups.

A broadened perspective on reference groups

The meaning of "reference group" has changed over the years. As originally used, reference groups were narrowly defined to include only those groups with which a person interacted on a direct basis (such as family and close friends). However, the concept gradually has broadened to include both direct and indirect and individual or group influences. **Indirect reference groups** consist of those individuals or groups with whom a person does not have direct face-to-face contact, such as movie stars, sports heroes, political leaders, TV personalities, or even well-dressed and interesting-looking people on the street. It is the power of the indirect reference group that helps sell Jimmy Buffet's record albums, T-shirts, mugs, jewelry, and other "parrothead" (i.e., Buffet fans) merchandise (**www.margaritaville. com**).

Referents a person might use in evaluating his or her own general or specific attitudes or behavior vary from one individual to several family members, to a broader kinship or from a voluntary association to a social class, a profession, an ethnic group, a community, an age category, or even a nation or culture. As Figure 10.1 indicates, the major societal groupings that influence an individual's consumer behavior are family, friends, social class, various subcultures, one's own culture, and even other cultures. For instance, within the scope of selected subcultures, we would include various age categories (seniors or young adults) that might serve as a reference group for their own or others' behavior.

Factors that affect reference group influence

The degree of influence that a reference group exerts on an individual's behavior usually depends on the nature of the individual and the product and on specific social factors.

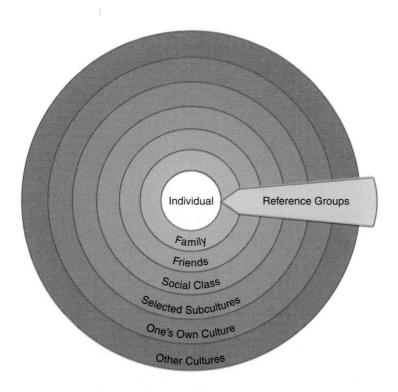

**Major Consumer
Reference Groups**

FIGURE 10.1

TABLE 10.1	Selective Factors That Positively Influence Conformity
CHARACTERISTICS	**POSITIVE (+) EFFECT**
Task/situational characteristics	Difficulty/complexity
	Ambiguity/subjectivity
Brand characteristics	No information
	Limited choice
	Prior conformity
	Crisis/emergency
Group characteristics	Attractiveness
	Expertise
	Credibility
	Clarity of group goals
	Likely future interaction with group
	Past success
Personal characteristics	Tendency to conform
	Need for affiliation
	Need to be liked
	Desire for control
	Fear of negative evaluation

Source: Based on Dana-Nicoleta Lascu and George Zinkhan, "Consumer Conformity: Review and Applications for Marketing Theory and Practice," *Journal of Marketing Theory and Practice* (Summer 1999): 1–12.

This section discusses how and why some of these factors influence consumer behavior. Table 10.1 presents a broad view of the factors that influence conformity.

Information and experience

An individual who has firsthand experience with a product or service, or can easily obtain full information about it, is less likely to be influenced by the advice or example of others. On the other hand, a person who has little or no experience with a product or service and does not expect to have access to objective information about it (e.g., a person who believes that advertising may be misleading or deceptive) is more likely to seek out the advice or example of others. For instance, when a young corporate sales rep wants to impress his client, he may take her to a restaurant that he knows from experience to be good or to one that has been highly recommended by the local newspaper's Dining Out Guide. If he has neither personal experience nor information he regards as valid, he may seek the advice of a friend or a parent or imitate the behavior of others by taking her to a restaurant he knows is frequented by young business executives whom he admires.

It is important to note that many consumers today feel bombarded with advertising, and feel that it is frequently both intrusive and downright sneaky. They also find fault with guerrilla marketing tactics in which an employee on a manufacturer's payroll poses as a consumer at an event or in a chat room for the purpose of "talking up" the product. As a result, sales of high-tech items like TiVo and other digital video recorders have skyrocketed, as consumers use such devices to zip past commercials, and computer users are purchasing anti-spyware and anti-adware programs to stop sneak attacks on their PCs.[1]

Credibility, attractiveness, and power of the reference group

A reference group that is perceived as credible, attractive, or powerful can induce consumer attitude and behavior change. For example, when consumers are concerned with obtaining accurate information about the performance or quality of a product or service, they are likely to be persuaded by those whom they consider trustworthy and knowledgeable. That is, they are more likely to be persuaded by sources with *high credibility*.

When consumers are primarily concerned with the acceptance or approval of others they like, with whom they identify, or those who offer them status or other benefits, they are likely to adopt their product, brand, or other behavioral characteristics. When consumers are primarily concerned with the power that a person or group can exert over them, they might choose products or services that conform to the norms of that person or group in order to avoid ridicule or punishment. However, unlike other reference groups that consumers follow because they are credible or because they are attractive, *power groups* are not as likely to cause attitude change. Individuals may conform to the behavior of a powerful person or group but are not as likely to experience a change in their own attitudes.

Different reference groups may influence the beliefs, attitudes, and behavior of an individual at different points in time or under different circumstances. For example, the dress habits of a young staff member working for a conservative law firm may vary, depending on her place and role. She may conform to the dress code of her office by wearing conservative clothing and skirts or dresses that do not end above the knee by day and drastically alter her mode of dress after work by wearing more trendy, flamboyant, revealing styles.

Conspicuousness of the product

The potential influence of a reference group on a purchase decision varies according to how visually or verbally conspicuous the product is to others. A visually *conspicuous product* is one that will stand out and be noticed (such as a luxury item or novelty product); a verbally conspicuous product may be highly interesting, or it may be easily described to others. Products that are especially conspicuous and status revealing (a new automobile, fashion clothing, sleek laptop computer, or home furniture) are most likely to be purchased with an eye to the reactions of relevant others. Privately consumed products that are less conspicuous (shaving cream or bath soap) are less likely to be purchased with a reference group in mind.

Walk down any street in America (and almost anywhere else) and you are likely to see someone wearing a hat, T-shirt, or jacket emblazoned with the logo of a favorite sports team. Similarly, while in a car, just look at the license plates of other cars on the road. It will not be long before you start seeing license plates containing the name and logo of universities, favorite sports teams, environmental groups, and many other institutions and causes. Research has found that among those attending a sporting event (e.g., baseball or basketball game), the more an individual identifies with a particular team, the greater the likelihood that he or she will purchase the products of the companies that sponsor that team (e.g., a particular brand of beer, hot dogs, or newspapers).[2]

Reference groups and consumer conformity

Marketers may have divergent goals with regard to **consumer conformity**. Some marketers, especially market leaders, are interested in the ability of reference groups to change consumer attitudes and behavior by encouraging *conformity*. To be capable of such influence, a reference group must accomplish the following:

1. *Inform or make the individual aware of a specific product or brand*
2. *Provide the individual with the opportunity to compare his or her own thinking with the attitudes and behavior of the group*
3. *Influence the individual to adopt attitudes and behavior that are consistent with the norms of the group*
4. *Legitimize the decision to use the same products as the group*

In contrast, marketers, especially those responsible for a new brand or a brand that is not the market leader, may wish to elect a strategy that asks consumers to strike out and be different and not just *follow the crowd* when making a purchase decision.

In reality the nonconformity appeal can be thought of as a request to shift one's reference (attitudes or behavior) from one grouping (brand A users) to another reference (non–brand A users or brand B users).

selected consumer-related reference groups

As already mentioned, consumers are potentially influenced by a diverse range of people that they come in contact with or observe. We will consider the following five specific reference groups because they give us a kind of cross section of the types of groups that influence consumers' attitudes and behavior: (1) friendship groups, (2) shopping groups, (3) work groups, (4) virtual groups or communities, and (5) consumer-action groups. The family, possibly the most compelling reference group for consumer behavior, will be fully covered in the second part of this chapter.

Friendship groups

Friendship groups are typically classified as **informal groups** because they are usually unstructured and lack specific authority levels. In terms of relative influence, after an individual's family, his or her friends are most likely to influence the individual's purchase decisions.

Seeking and maintaining friendships is a basic drive for most people. Friends fulfill a wide range of needs: They provide companionship, security, and opportunities to discuss problems that an individual may be reluctant to discuss with family members. Friendships are also a sign of maturity and independence, for they represent a breaking away from the family and the forming of social ties with the outside world.

The opinions and preferences of friends are an important influence in determining the products or brands a consumer ultimately selects. Marketers of products such as brand-name clothing, fine jewelry, snack foods, and alcoholic beverages recognize the power of peer group influence and frequently depict friendship situations in their ads.

Shopping groups

Two or more people who shop together, whether for food, clothing, or simply to pass the time, can be called a **shopping group**. Such groups are often offshoots of family or friendship groups and, therefore, they function as what has been referred to as *purchase pals*.[3] The motivations for shopping with a purchase pal range from a primarily social motive (to share time together and enjoy lunch after shopping), to help to reduce the risk when making an important decision (having someone along whose expertise will reduce the chance of making an incorrect purchase). In instances where none of the members of the shopping group knows much about the product under consideration (such as an expensive home entertainment center), a shopping group may form for defensive reasons; members may feel more confident with a collective decision.

A special type of shopping group is the in-home shopping party, which typically consists of a group that gathers together in the home of a friend to attend a "party" devoted to demonstrating and evaluating a specific line of products. The in-home party approach provides marketers with an opportunity to demonstrate the features of their products simultaneously to a group of potential customers. Early purchasers tend to create a bandwagon effect: Undecided guests often overcome a reluctance to buy when they see their friends make positive purchase decisions. Furthermore, some of the guests may feel obliged to buy because they are in the home of the sponsoring host or hostess. Given the spirit and excitement of "consumer gatherings" or "parties," Tupperware, for example, generates 90 percent of its $1 billion in annual sales from such consumer parties.[4]

A customer *referral program* is an element of shopping behavior, which takes into account group dynamics, in that it focuses on member-get-member (MGM) campaigns. More specifically, a current customer is asked to persuade others to become customers (or members). For example, a warehouse membership club (e.g., Costco or Sam's Club) might offer a reward to a current member who convinces a nonmember to join—or the reward might be divided among the two parties. Such programs may only reward the current customer (member) for finding a new customer, may only reward the new customer, or may reward both parties (either equally or unequally). While both current and potential members were found to prefer campaigns in which they got 100 percent of the reward, current members found a 50/50 distribution to be more appropriate when the "new" member was required to make a substantial financial investment in order to join.[5]

Work groups

The sheer amount of time that people spend at their jobs, frequently more than 35 hours per week, provides ample opportunity for work groups to serve as a major influence on the consumption behavior of members.

Both the formal work group and the informal friendship-work group can influence consumer behavior. The *formal work group* consists of individuals who work together as part of a team and, thus, have a sustained opportunity to influence each other's consumption-related attitudes and actions. Informal friendship-work groups consist of people who have become friends as a result of working for the same firm, whether or not they work together as a team. Members of informal work groups may influence the consumption behavior of other members during coffee or lunch breaks or at after-work meetings.

Recognizing that work groups influence consumers' brand choices and that many women now work outside of their homes, firms that in the past sold their products exclusively through direct calls on women in their homes now are redirecting their sales efforts to offices and plants during lunch-hour visits. For instance, Avon (**www.avon.com**) and Tupperware (**www.tupperware.com**), two leading direct-to-home marketers, encourage their sales representatives to reach working women at their places of employment.

Virtual groups or communities

Thanks to computers and the Internet, we are witnessing the emergence of a new type of group—virtual groups or communities. Both adults and children are turning on their computers, logging onto the Web, and visiting special-interest Web sites, often with chat rooms. If you're an amateur photographer, you can chat online with other amateur photographers; if you're a stamp collector, you can chat online with others who share your interest. Local newspapers everywhere run stories from time to time about singles who met online, typically accompanied by a picture of their wedding. An Internet provider such as America Online even lets its members create *Buddy Lists*,™ so when they sign onto AOL they immediately know which of their friends are currently online and can send and receive instant messages. An elderly person in Minneapolis, for example, might not make it to the local senior citizen center when it's freezing outside and snowing, but he or she can always log on.

Whereas 50 years ago the definition of a community stressed the notion of geographic proximity and face-to-face relationships, today's communities are much more broadly defined as "sets of social relations among people." In this spirit, there is also rather wide-scale access to what is known as "Internet communities" or "virtual communities." These terms refer to Web-based consumer groups (e.g., **www.well.com**, **www.ivillage.com**, and **www.icq.com**). These communities provide their members with access to extensive amounts of information, fellowship, and social interaction covering an extremely wide range of topics and issues (e.g., vegetarianism, cooking, collecting, trading, finance, filmmaking, romance, politics, technology, art, hobbies, spiritualism, age grouping, online game playing, voice-video chats, free e-mail, tech assistance, travel and vacations, educational opportunities, living with illnesses, and a host of lifestyle options). Virtual communities provide an opportunity for a marketer to address consumers with a particular common interest, which can be one of the primary pleasures a consumer has online, and also have the ability to enhance the consumption experience (via discussion with others).

The exchange of knowledge that can take place within a virtual community can help a good product sell faster and a poor product fail faster. Indeed, there are a number of "knowledge exchanges" that permit registered members and others to ask questions of experts on subjects germane to that exchange. And some virtual communities, hosted by a commercial source, are aimed at particular ethnic groups and contain online content targeted to a distinct ethnic community. Startec Global Communications Corporation (**www.startec.com**) already operates virtual communities for Arab, Iranian, Turkish, Indian, and Chinese consumers. Its DragonSurf.com site, for instance, concentrates on the needs and interests of young, educated Chinese Web surfers in China and elsewhere around the world.[6]

When visiting such communities, it does not matter if you are tall or short, thin or fat, handsome or plain-looking. On the Internet, people are free to express their thoughts, to be emotional and intimate with those they do not know and have never met, and even to escape from those they normally interact with by spending time on the Internet. The anonymity of the Web gives its users the freedom to express whatever views they wish and to also benefit from savoring the views of others. Because of this anonymity, Internet users can say things to others that they would not say in face-to-face interactions. Communicating over the Internet permits people to explore the boundaries of their personalities (see the related discussion in Chapter 5) and to shift from one persona to another. For example, investigators have found that there are a surprisingly large number of men who adopt female persona online ("gender swapping").[7] Some community Web sites have attempted to control what is deemed appropriate action by instituting codes of behavior. For example, fans of the canceled TV program *Dr. Quinn, Medicine Woman* are not only part of an e-mail discussion list, but also new members are sent a "conduct code" when they subscribe.[8]

Some researchers have come to the conclusion that the Internet, for many Americans, has become "indispensable," and that it is often the small things that the Internet is used for, on a daily basis, that makes it such an integral part of people's lives (e.g., following a stock portfolio, communicating with friends, shopping online for "stuff"). In the United States, the number of individuals using the Internet grew 50 percent from 2000 to 2003 (to 126 million users in 2003); during this same time frame, for example, the use of online banking went from 24 percent to 60 percent of Internet users, and the gathering of health information rose from 46 percent to 76 percent of Internet users.[9]

Brand communities

The next step in the evolution of interactive marketing, beyond advances in relationship marketing (discussed earlier in Chapter 7), is the establishment of *brand communities*. As one recent newspaper article noted, "There is a definite feeling among marketers that if you want to build up loyalty to your brand, your product has to have an active social life."[10] Examples of such brand communities include a group of runners who get together at the Niketown store in Boston on Wednesday evenings for a run (**www.nike.com**), Saturn automobile reunions and barbeques (**www.saturn.com**), and Harley-Davidson owner groups (**www.harleydavidson.com**). A *brand communiy* has been defined as "a specialized, non-geographically bound community, based on a structured set of social relationships among admirers of a brand . . . it is marked by a shared consciousness, rituals and traditions, and a sense of moral responsibility."[11] It is this sense of community, for example, that causes Saab owners (**www.saabusa.com**) to beep or flash their lights at another Saab on the road (i.e., a greeting ritual).

Consider how Jeep has developed its brand community. The company offers multiple opportunities for Jeep owners to get to know each other, get to know their vehicles, and get to know the company. Jeep (**www.jeep.com**) conducts Jeep Jamborees (regional rallies that concentrate on off-road driving), Camp Jeep (national rallies offering off-road driving and product-related activities), and Jeep 101 (an off-road driving course with product-related activities and displays). At both Camp Jeep and Jeep 101 there are "camp counselors" who provide participants with free beverages, free product information, and free off-road trail recommendations.[12] The result is that Jeep has fostered involvement in its brand community, so that a bond exists between the Jeep owner and (1) the product, (2) the brand, (3) the company, and (4) other Jeep owners. The brand community is, therefore, "customer centric"; it is the customer experience that provides meaning to the brand community rather than the brand itself. Consider the following comment from a Jeep owner attending Jeep 101:[13]

> *I've been very happy. I get a lot of communications from Jeep, which I've been so impressed with. Usually you buy a car and then you're a forgotten soul. It's kinda like they want you to be part of the family. As soon as I got the invitation for Jeep 101, I registered. I was very excited. But I was nervous. I didn't think I would end up driving. I was very relieved to see someone in the car with you, 'cause it gave you the confidence to do what you're supposed to. Otherwise, I had visions of abandoning the truck on the hill and saying "I can't do it!" I thought I might wimp out, but I didn't.*

Another example of a brand community is one centered around the Apple Newton (a *personal digital assistance* device — PDA) introduced by Apple in 1993 and discontinued in 1998. As an Apple product, the Newton was the product of a company that stressed uniqueness and nonconformity. At the height of its popularity, there were almost 200,000 Apple Newton users, and to this day many have refused to switch to alternatives such as the Palm Pilot (which was introduced in 1996). While no company is writing new software for the Newton and service is hard to obtain, there are still thousands of Apple Newton users who would rather fight than switch. Indeed, some of the new applications and some of the repair servicing is today being performed by diehard Newton users. When reading the comments of the Apple Newton brand community, religious, magical, and even supernatural motifs are common in their narratives, as "are strong elements of survival, the miraculous, and the return of the creator." Consider the following comment by a product user regarding the morale of the Apple Newton community:[14]

> *I think morale is still pretty high . . . I think it's the fact that we are all united. I think the unity is a big thing because the list is so big. The other thing is that whenever people, like someone from the outside, actually see what the Newton can do, they are impressed. Every story that I've ever read that someone [demonstrated] the system to some new person, it's like, "Hey, wow, what's that? You can do this on this? Where can I buy one of those?" . . . So everyone is still amazed that the product has been going for so long.*

Marketers sometime design a specific product or service to create a sense of community or take advantage of a preexisting relationship (e.g., an offer to members of a family and relatives, or friends, or even people doing business with each other). For example, Verizon Wireless has created special programs for "calling communities" that includes calling with the "community" (or "network") at a reduced or even no costs (when calls are made between callers in the program, such as two Verizon wireless customers).

Consumer-action groups

A particular kind of consumer group—a **consumer-action group**—has emerged in response to the consumerist movement. Today there are a very large number of such groups dedicated to providing consumers with assistance in their effort to make the right purchase decisions, consume products and services in a healthy and responsible manner, and generally add to the overall quality of their lives (see Figure 10.2). The following are just a few examples of the diverse range of consumer concerns being addressed by private and public consumer-action groups: neighborhood crime watch, youth development, forests and wildlife concerns, children and advertising, race and ethnicity, community volunteerism, legal assistance, public health, disaster relief, energy conservation, education, smoking, the environment, access to telecommunications, science in the public interest, credit counseling, privacy issues, and children and the Internet.

Consumer-action groups can be divided into two broad categories: (1) those that organize to correct a specific consumer abuse and then disband and (2) those that

FIGURE 10.2

Source: Courtesy of FoA.
(www.friendsofanimals.org).

A Consumer Action Group Appealing for Involvement

LIKE HUMANS, WOLVES LIVE IN FAMILIES.

LIKE HUMANS, WOLVES NEED FRIENDS.

WOLVES DISPLAY A HIGH DEGREE OF INTELLIGENCE, EXPRESSIVENESS AND OTHER CHARACTERISTICS THAT ENABLE THEM TO MAINTAIN SOPHISTICATED, FAMILY-BASED SOCIAL BONDS. BUT WITHOUT FRIENDS LOOKING OUT FOR THEM, THESE FAMILIES WILL BE BROKEN APART. TO LEARN HOW YOU CAN BECOME A FRIEND AND HELP FRIENDS OF ANIMALS PROTECT ALASKA'S WOLVES, PLEASE CALL 203.656.1522 OR VISIT WWW.FRIENDSOFANIMALS.ORG. BE A FRIEND FOR LIFE.

Friends of Animals

organize to address broader, more pervasive problem areas and operate over an extended or indefinite period of time. A group of irate parents who band together to protest the opening of an adult X-rated video rental store in their neighborhood or a group of neighbors who attend a meeting of the local highway department to demand that additional stop signs be placed on specific corners in their residential neighborhood are examples of temporary, cause-specific consumer-action groups. An example of an enduring consumer-action group is Mothers Against Drunk Driving (MADD), a group founded in 1980 and operating today throughout the United States within local community groups. MADD representatives serve on numerous public advisory boards and help establish local task forces to combat drunk driving. Additionally, the organization supports actions to restrict alcoholic beverage advertising and is opposed in general to any advertising and products that may have a negative impact on youth.

The overriding objective of many consumer-action groups is to bring sufficient pressure to bear on selected members of the business community to make them correct perceived consumer abuses. Examples might include an attempt to ban gas-guzzling SUVs and/or genetically altered foods.[15]

celebrity and other reference group appeals

Appeals by celebrities and other similar reference groups are used very effectively by advertisers to communicate with their markets. Celebrities can be a powerful force in creating interest or actions with regard to purchasing or using selected goods and services. This identification may be based on admiration (of an athlete), on aspiration (of a celebrity or a way of life), on empathy (with a person or a situation), or on recognition (of a person—real or stereotypical—or of a situation). In some cases, the prospective consumer may think, "If she uses it, it must be good. If I use it, I'll be like her." In other cases, the prospective consumer says to himself, "He has the same problems that I have. What worked for him will work for me." Today even mainstream companies are targeting extreme sports (e.g., skateboarding, snowboarding) as a way to reach consumers.[16]

Five major types of reference group appeals in common marketing usage are *celebrity appeals, expert appeals, common-man appeals, executive and employee appeals,* and *trade or spokes-character appeals.* These appeals, as well as less frequently employed appeals, are often operationalized in the form of testimonials or endorsements. In the case of the common man, they may be presented as *slice-of-life* commercials.

Celebrities

Celebrities, particularly movie stars, TV personalities, popular entertainers, and sports icons, provide a very common type of reference group appeal. Indeed, it has been estimated that 25 percent of U.S. commercials include celebrity endorsers.[17] To their loyal followers and to much of the general public, celebrities represent an idealization of life that most people imagine that they would love to live. Advertisers spend enormous sums of money to have celebrities promote their products, with the expectation that the reading or viewing audience will react positively to the celebrity's association with their products. One discussion about celebrity endorsers noted that "famous people hold the viewer's attention," and this is why the TV chef Emeril Lagasse appears in TV commercials for a new Crest toothpaste, Whitening Expressions, and former NFL quarterback Joe Montana is part of an $11 million ad campaign for McCormick's Grill Mates line of spice rubs and marinades.[18]

Michael Jordan has been a particularly powerful product endorser. He has assisted many firms, whose products he promotes, to substantially increase their stock market value. Indeed, as a sign of Michael Jordon celebrity power, he is under contract to Nike until the year 2023.[19] In the same vein, Tiger Woods has a five-year agreement with Buick, estimated at $30 million, and his $40 million deal with Nike is expected to double because he has switched to Nike brand golf balls.[20] Finally, the soccer star David Beckham, who went from Manchester United to play for Real Madrid, has recently signed an agreement with Gillette worth $68 million.[21]

A firm that decides to employ a celebrity to promote its product or service has the choice of using the celebrity to give a **testimonial** or an **endorsement** as an **actor** in a commercial or as a company **spokesperson**. Table 10.2 distinguishes among these different types of celebrity appeals, and Table 10.3 lists the top ten international sponsorship deals with sports personalities, July 2003 to June 2004. Figure 10.3 presents the findings of a study that explored what marketing practitioners in the United Kingdom look for in

TABLE 10.2	Types of Celebrity Appeals
TYPES	**DEFINITION**
Testimonial	Based on personal usage, a celebrity attests to the quality of the product or service.
Endorsement	Celebrity lends his or her name and appears on behalf of a product or service with which he or she may or may not be an expert.
Actor	Celebrity presents a product or service as part of character endorsement.
Spokesperson	Celebrity represents the brand or company over an extended period of time.

selecting a celebrity endorser. What is apparent is that the importance of certain celebrity characteristics varies depending on whether the product being promoted is technical (e.g., PCs) or nontechnical (e.g., jeans) in nature. Specifically, for a product like a PC the "trustworthiness" of a celebrity is considered to be most important, whereas for a clothing item like jeans the "physical attractiveness" of the celebrity is viewed as most important.

Of all the benefits that a celebrity might contribute to a firm's advertising program—fame, talent, credibility, or charisma—celebrity credibility with the consumer audience is the most important. By **celebrity credibility** we mean the audience's perception of both the celebrity's *expertise* (how much the celebrity knows about the product area) and *trustworthiness* (how honest the celebrity is about what he or she says about the product).[22] To illustrate, when a celebrity endorses only one product, consumers are likely to perceive the product in a highly favorable light and indicate a greater intention to purchase it. In contrast, when a celebrity endorses a variety of products, his or her perceived credibility is reduced because of the apparent economic motivation underlying the celebrity's efforts.[23] Figure 10.4 presents International Soccer Star David Beckham as an endorser for Gillette.

A recent study that examined the impact of celebrity athlete endorsers on teens found that such endorsers had a positive influence on favorable word-of-mouth (W-O-M)

TABLE 10.3	Top 10 International Sponsorship Deals with Sports Personalities July 2003–June 2004		
RANK	**PERSONALITY**	**SPONSOR**	**VALUE OF DEAL ($MIL)**
1	David Beckham (soccer)	Gillette	$68
2	Serena Williams (tennis)	Nike	$60
3	David Beckham (soccer)	Pepsi	$25.5
4	Tiger Woods (golf)	Accenture	$18
5	Andre Agassi (tennis)	24Hour Fitness	$15
6	Ha Seung-jin (basketball)	Nike	$10+
7	David Beckham (soccer)	Adidas	$10+
8	Yao Ming (basketball)	McDonald's	$10+
9	Francesco Totti (soccer)	Pepsi	$10+
10	Ronaldhino (soccer)	Pepsi	$10+

Source: From Ben Pincus, "Saving Face of Sponsorship," *Brand Strategy* (September 2004): 55; (as cited) *The World Sponsorship Monitor* (includes renewals and new deals).

FIGURE 10.3

Importance of Celebrity Characteristics According to Product Types

Source: From "Selecting Celebrity Endorsers: The Practitioner's Perspective," by B. Zafer Erdogan, Michael J. Baker, and Stephen Tagg in Journal of Advertising Research, May–June 2001. Reprinted by permission.

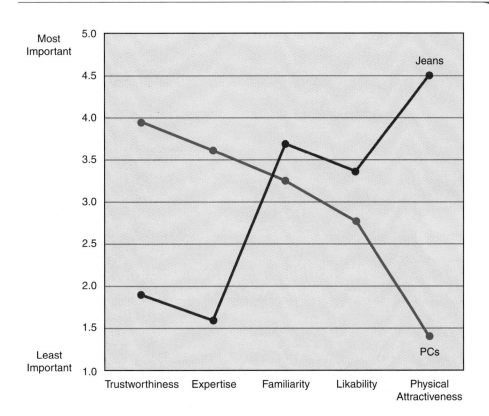

and increase brand loyalty. Moreover, the research found that female teens tended to spread more favorable W-O-M about a product or brand endorsed by their favorite celebrity athlete than did male teens. The females were also more likely to agree that males who had athlete role models had influenced them to purchase certain brands.[24]

Not all companies feel that using celebrity endorsers is the best way to advertise. Some companies avoid celebrities because they fear that if the celebrity gets involved in some undesirable act or event (e.g., an ugly matrimonial problem, a scandal, or a criminal case), the news or press coverage will negatively impact the sale of the endorsed brand. For example, researchers recently compiled a list of 48 undesirable events occurring between 1980 and 1994 that involved celebrity endorsers hired by publicly traded companies. The list included such notables as Mike Tyson, Michael Jackson, and Jennifer Capriati.[25]

The expert

A second type of reference group appeal used by marketers is the *expert,* a person who, because of his or her occupation, special training, or experience, is in a unique position to help the prospective consumer evaluate the product or service that the advertisement promotes. For example, an advertisement for a quality frying pan may feature the endorsement of a chef, an ad for fishing tackle may contain the endorsement of a professional fishing guide, or an ad for an allergy medication may contain the endorsement of a professional golfer.

The "common man"

A reference group appeal that uses the testimonials of satisfied customers is known as the *common-man* approach. The advantage of the common-man appeal is that it demonstrates

Source: © The Gillette Company. Used with permission. All rights reserved.

FIGURE 10.4

Celebrity Endorsement

to prospective customers that someone just like them uses and is satisfied with the product or service being advertised. The common-man appeal is especially effective in public health announcements (such as antismoking or high blood pressure messages), for most people seem to identify with people like themselves when it comes to such messages.[26]

Many television commercials show a typical person or family solving a problem by using the advertised product or service. These commercials are known as *slice-of-life commercials* because they focus on real-life situations with which the viewer can identify. For example, one commercial focuses on how a laundry detergent can deodorize clothes; another talks about how a certain breakfast cereal provides enough energy to get an individual through a hectic morning. When viewers identify with the situation, they are likely to adopt the solution that worked in the TV commercial.

The executive and employee spokesperson

During the past two decades, an increasing number of firms have used their top executives as spokespersons in consumer ads. The popularity of this type of advertising probably is due to the success and publicity received by a number of executive spokespersons. For instance, early in the history of this type of advertising, Lee Iacocca, former CEO of Chrysler, was a highly effective corporate spokesperson in persuading consumers that Chrysler automobiles were worthy of their purchase consideration. Similarly, Frank Perdue (Perdue chickens) was after many years replaced as the spokesperson for his company and products by his son. Like celebrity spokespersons, executive spokespersons seem to be admired by the general population because of their achievements and the status implicitly conferred on business leaders in the United States. The appearance of a company's chief executive in its advertising seems to imply that someone at the top is watching over the consumers' best interests, and it encourages consumers to have more confidence in the firm's products or services.

To apply a more grass roots approach to such promotional programs, some companies feature employees rather than top executives in selected advertising campaigns. Figure 10.5 shows an example from GM's Mr. Goodwrench advertising program modules that were used to depict employees. The heart of the program is to put a face on Mr. Goodwrench. Mr. Goodwrench is your technician at your local GM dealership.

Trade or spokes-characters

Trade or spokes-characters (e.g., M&M People, Tony the Tiger, or Capt'n Crunch), as well as familiar cartoon characters (Ninja Turtles, Mr. Magoo, Bart Simpson), serve as quasi-celebrity endorsers. These trade spokes-characters present an idealized image and dispense information that can be very important for the product or service that they "work for." Figure 10.6 shows Kellogg's Tony the Tiger trade character promoting his own whole grain cereal, and Table 10.4 presents some of the most frequently identified spokes-characters.

With few exceptions, trade characters serve as exclusive spokespersons for a particular product or service. They sometimes provide a kind of personality for the product or service and make the product appear friendlier (Ronald McDonald). Betty Crocker now even has her own Web site to offer recipes, personalized weekly menus, and household hints (**www.bettycrocker.com**). This Web site is the modern-day extension of the fact that Betty Crocker started answering letters from consumers in the 1920s and got her own toll-free telephone number in 1980. According to the company, the purpose of the Web site "is not to push Betty Crocker, not to sell products, but to provide content that offers ideas and solves problems, so people consider the site a valuable resource."[27]

A recent study examined a finding of prior research, that a spokes-character can create a perception of trust. The research found that spokes-character expertise (e.g., Toucan Sam is the expert for Kellogg's Fruit Loops) and spokes-character nostalgia (e.g., some companies have reintroduced spokes-characters from the past) favorably affect spokes-character trust, which, in turn, favorably affects attitude toward the brand. Still further, for consumers with less brand experience, spokes-character features (e.g., expertise and nostalgia) result in more favorable brand attitudes, while for consumers with brand experience, spokes-character features tend to have little effect on brand attitudes.[28]

Other reference group appeals

A variety of other promotional strategies can function creatively as frames of reference for consumers. Respected retailers and the editorial content of selected special-interest magazines can also function as frames of reference that influence consumer attitudes and behavior. For instance, a customer might feel that if a leading fashion-oriented store such as Neiman Marcus depicts Calvin Klein dresses on its Web site (**www.neimanmarcus.com**), then such clothing must be acceptable and in good taste. Similarly, a regular reader of *GQ* might see unstructured and relaxed sport coats as appropriate to wear to work if the magazine were to feature them in office surroundings. In these two instances, the retailer and the magazine are functioning as frames of reference that influence consumer behavior.

FIGURE 10.5

Source: Courtesy of General Motors Corporation.

Employees as Spokesperson for a Firm's Products or Services

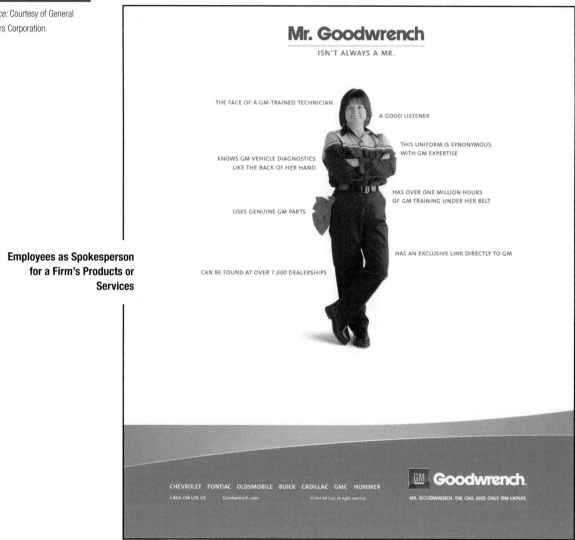

Finally, *seals of approval* and even objective product ratings can serve as positive endorsements that encourage consumers to act favorably toward certain products. For instance, many parents of young children look for the American Dental Association's seal of approval before selecting a brand of toothpaste. A high rating by an objective rating magazine, such as *Consumer Reports,* can also serve as an endorsement for a brand.

The remainder of this chapter concentrates on the family—arguably the most important group influencing human behavior in general and consumer behavior in particular.

the family is a concept in flux

Although the term **family** is a basic concept, it is not easy to define because family composition and structure, as well as the roles played by family members, are almost always in transition. Traditionally, however, *family* is defined as *two or more persons related by blood, marriage, or adoption who reside together.* In a more dynamic sense, the individuals who constitute a family might be described as members of the most basic social

group who live together and interact to satisfy their personal and mutual needs. Today in the United States, 68 percent of the 111.3 million households are families.[29] According to many sources, the *family* remains the central or dominant institution in providing for the welfare of its members and is the major household consumer and consuming unit.

Although families sometimes are referred to as households, not all households are families. For example, a household might include individuals who are not related by blood, marriage, or adoption, such as unmarried couples, family friends, roommates, or boarders. However, within the context of consumer behavior, households and families usually are treated as synonymous, and we will continue this convention.

In most Western societies, three types of families dominate: the married couple, the nuclear family, and the extended family. The simplest type of family, in number of members, is the *married couple*—a husband and a wife. As a household unit, the married couple generally is representative of either new marrieds who have not yet started a family or older couples who have already raised their children.

A husband and wife and one or more children constitute a **nuclear family**. This type of family is still commonplace but has been on the decline. The nuclear family,

Source: © Kellogg Company. Used with permission. All rights reserved.

FIGURE 10.6

A Well Established Trade or Spokes-Character

together with at least one grandparent living within the household, is called an **extended family**. Within the past 30 years the incidence of the extended family has also declined because of the geographic mobility that splits up families. Moreover, because of divorce, separation, and out-of-wedlock births, there has been a rapid increase in the number of **single-parent family** households consisting of one parent and at least one child.

Not surprisingly, the type of family that is most typical can vary considerably from culture to culture. For instance, in an individualistic society such as that in Canada, the nuclear family is most common. In a kinship culture (with extended families), such as that in Thailand, a family would commonly include a head of household, married adult children, and grandchildren.[30]

TABLE 10.4	Most Frequently Identified Spokes-Characters	

MOST FREQUENTLY IDENTIFIED SPOKES-CHARACTERS		
SPOKES-CHARACTER	**ENDORSED BRAND**	**RESPONDENTS**
Poppin Fresh Pillsbury Doughboy	Pillsbury Products	30
Tony the Tiger	Kellogg's Frosted Flakes Cereal	26
Energizer Bunny	Energizer Batteries	17
M&M's Characters	M&M's Chocolate Candy	9
Snuggle Bear	Snuggle Fabric Softener	7
Keebler Elves	Keebler Snacks	6
Mr. Mini-Wheat	Kellogg's Frosted Mini-Wheats Cereal	5
The Geico Gecko	Geico Insurance	4
Toucan Sam	Fruit Loops Cereal	4

Notes: Spokes-characters identified by three respondents or less include: Lucky Charms Leprechaun; Cingular X-Man; Aflac Duck; Joe Camel; Aunt Jemima; Kool-Aid Man; Trix Bunny; Mr. Clean; Chester Cheetah; Snap, Crackle, and Pop; Captain Crunch; Sony's Blue Alien; Honeycomb Cereal Kid; Cheerios Bee; Jack $$$ the Box: Charlie Tuna; Buddy Lee; Morton Salt Girl; Elsie the Cow; Chevron Car; Michelin Man; Mrs. Butterworth; Hamburger Helper Glove; and Scrubbing Bubbles.

Source: Judith A. Garretson and Ronald W. Niedrich, "Spokes-Characters: Creating Character Trust and Positive Brand Attitudes, *Journal of Advertising* 33 (Summer 2004).

The changing U.S. family

Important demographic changes reflect the dynamic nature of the family. For example, about 55 percent of career women who are 35 years old are childless, between a third and half of 40-year-old career women have no children, and the number of childless women between the ages of 40 and 44 has doubled during the past 20 years.[31] Moreover, 49 percent of female corporate executives earning $100,000 or more annually are childless (but only 10 percent of high-income male executives have no children).

With the huge number of wives and mothers employed outside the home, studies have examined the question of whether an employed wife behaves at home the same as a nonworking wife. Research results indicate that there is little to no difference between working and nonworking wives with respect to their purchases of time-saving goods; indeed, nonworking wives are even more likely to buy time-saving durables (i.e., if they are doing the domestic work themselves, they want to save time). Additionally, a husbands' behavior with respect to household chores remained the same whether the wife was or was not employed, and the ultimate responsibility for household management still belonged to the wife. Evidence also indicates that the more traditional the division of household labor in a household, the higher the marital satisfaction is of the man (husband) and the lower the satisfaction of the woman (wife). Interestingly, though, husbands of working wives make fewer decisions by themselves.[32]

There is no doubt that the "typical" or "traditional" family or household has changed. Although families represented 81 percent of households in 1970, by 2003 this percentage was reduced to 68 percent, and households consisting of married couples with children under 18 went from 40.3 percent in 1970 to just 23.3 percent in 2003, and "not married, no children" households (i.e., nonfamily households) rose from almost 19 percent in 1970 to 32 percent in 2003, making nonfamily households more numerous than married couples with children households (see Figure 10.7). During this same time frame, the percentage of family households with no spouse present rose significantly from 11 to 16 percent, and people living alone grew from 17 percent in 1970 to 26 percent in 2003. Also, while in 1970, 65 percent of men and

FIGURE 10.7

Evidence of the Dynamic Nature of U.S. Households

Source: U.S. Census Bureau, "American's Families and Living Arrangements: 2003," November 2004, 4, accessed at www.census.gov/prod/ 2004pubs/p20–553.pdf

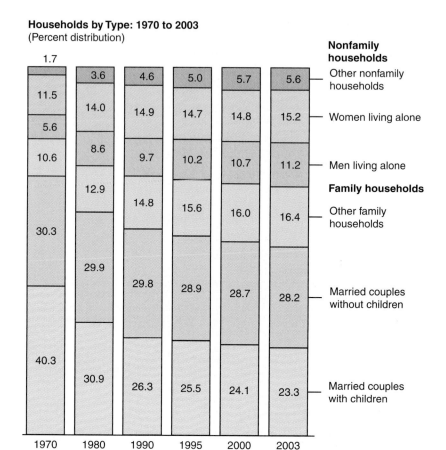

Households by Type: 1970 to 2003
(Percent distribution)

60 percent of women age 15 and older were married, by 2003 these figures were reduced to 55 percent of men and 52 percent of women; during this same time period, the percentage of men and women either separated or divorced almost tripled. Still further, households have decreased in size. The percent of households with five or more people dropped from 21 percent in 1970 to just under 10 percent in 2003, while households with only one or two members grew from 46 percent to 60 percent over the same period of time (see Figure 10.8).[33] Because of these changes in family dynamics, companies such as American Greetings sell Mother's Day cards for single moms, divorced moms, stepmothers, foster mothers, caregivers, guardians, and others who play a maternal role.

Attitudes with respect to children and child-rearing have also been changing. Consider the information presented in Table 10.5, which compares the attitudes toward children of Gen-Xers (those adults born roughly between 1965 and 1978), Baby Boomers (those adults born roughly between 1946 and 1964), and Pre-Boomers (those adults born roughly between 1938 and 1945). The results, for example, show that while 37 percent of Gen-Xers "believe preschool kids suffer if mother works," 46 percent of Baby Boomers and 57 percent of Pre-Boomers share this view.[34]

As yet another example of how family dynamics and child-rearing has been changing, consider the family meal. At one time, family mealtime was an opportunity for parents to interact with their children and to discuss various topics—it was an important part of the socialization process. However, in North America, the importance of family mealtime has decreased, often due to family member schedules. So family mealtime is being replaced with the child eating the meal in a bedroom, family room, or living room—someplace where the child can be in front of a television set, and be influenced by programming and commercials.

FIGURE 10.8

Households by Size: 1970 to 2003

Source: U.S. Census Bureau, "American's Families and Living Arrangements: 2003," November 2004, 5, accessed at www.census.gov/prod/2004pubs/p20–553.pdf

Households by Size: 1970 to 2003
(Percent distribution)

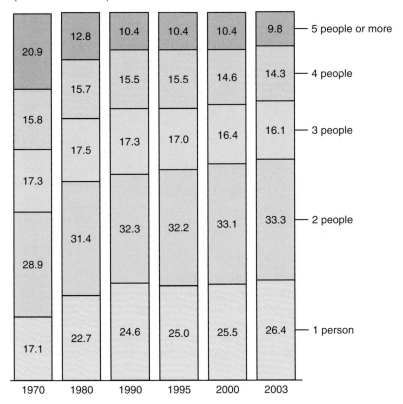

TABLE 10.5	How Different Generations Feel About Children		
	GEN-XERS	**BABY BOOMERS**	**PRE-BOOMERS**
Ideal number of children is two	52%	55%	50%
Ideal number of children is three	27%	21%	30%
Favor spanking to discipline a child	74%	76%	76%
Favor sex ed in public schools	91%	87%	80%
Believe preschool kids suffer if mother works	37%	46%	57%
Believe it's better for the man to work and the woman to tend home	29%	37%	64%
Believe a working mother doesn't hurt children	67%	63%	52%
Believe a wife should help husband put career first	12%	15%	32%
I spend too little time with my kids	45%	46%	25%
Divorce laws should be tougher	50%	52%	59%

Source: Pamela Paul, "Meet the Parents," *American Demographics* (January 2002): 46. Reprinted by permission of Primedia.

FIGURE 10.9

How the "Average" Family Spends Its Money

Source: Reprinted with permission from the February 7, 2005 issue of Advertising Age. © Crain Communications Inc. 2005.

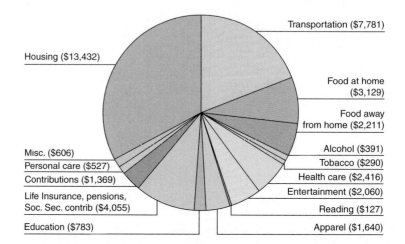

The average U.S. household spent $40,817 in 2003. What got bought:

Transportation ($7,781)
Housing ($13,432)
Food at home ($3,129)
Food away from home ($2,211)
Alcohol ($391)
Tobacco ($290)
Health care ($2,416)
Entertainment ($2,060)
Reading ($127)
Apparel ($1,640)
Education ($783)
Life Insurance, pensions, Soc. Sec. contrib ($4,055)
Contributions ($1,369)
Personal care ($527)
Misc. ($606)

Ever-changing household spending patterns

The past 50 years have witnessed some dramatic changes in how families spend their incomes. While the average American family's spending on goods and services in 2003 was $40,817, food accounted for only 13¢ out of every dollar, down from 32¢ in 1950, while 41 percent of food spending in 2003 went for restaurant dining and takeout food—up from 21 percent in 1960. At the same time, the amount families spent on apparel and shoes decreased from 12 percent in 1950 to 4 percent in 2003. And in 2004, one in 17 Americans bought a new car, versus one in 25 in 1960.[35] Figure 10.9 presents how the "average" U.S. family spent its money in 2003. The chart reveals that the seven biggest expenditure areas are: housing, transportation, life insurance and related security and saving programs, food at home, health care, food away from home, and entertainment. The total of these seven expenditure areas constitute a major portion of a family's or household's entire annual expenditures.

socialization of family members

The **socialization of family members**, ranging from young children to adults, is a central family function. In the case of young children, this process includes imparting to children the basic values and modes of behavior consistent with the culture. These generally include moral and religious principles, interpersonal skills, dress and grooming standards, appropriate manners and speech, and the selection of suitable educational and occupational or career goals. Table 10.6 presents the results of a study by SmartGirl Internette (**www.smartgirl.org**) that looks at the household chores performed by girls 11 to 17 years of age. The findings indicate that nearly 40 percent of the girls in this age category claim to perform all of these household chores.

Other research indicates that Dutch juveniles spend most of their leisure time with their family, whereas older children spend most of their leisure time with peers.[36] The transition period between these two age groups was 13, with 13-year-olds dividing their leisure time between parents, peers, and being alone. The results further indicate that 14- and 15-year-old boys, especially from the higher social classes, were strongly focused on peer groups, whereas girls the same age preferred dyadic friendships.

Parental socialization responsibility seems to be constantly expanding. For instance, parents are often anxious to see their young children possess adequate computer skills,

TABLE 10.6	Household Chores Performed by Girls Age 11 to 17	
CHORE		**% WHO SAY THEY PERFORM IT**
Picking things up in my room		95%
Picking things up around the house		84%
Vacuuming		72%
Washing/drying the dishes		66%
Loading or unloading the dishwasher		65%
Doing laundry		61%
Sweeping		55%
Dusting		55%
Cleaning the bathtub, shower, or sink		54%
Washing the windows or mirrors		48%
Cleaning the kitchen		46%
Cleaning the toilet		41%
Mopping the bathroom or kitchen floor		39%
Ironing		37%

Source: Marketing to Women, January 2002, p. 3. (**http://www.smartgirl.org**).

almost before they are able to talk or walk—as early as 12 months after their birth. In general, parents' intensive interest in seeing that their young children are learning new skills and preparing for the challenges that they will face in what they see as a "competitive world." To this end, many parents want their young children to learn computer skills, be "reading ready," and are proud parents when their young child can operate the DVD player better than they can. Marketers of educational products and aids seek to provide parents with a flow of products that enable them to assist their children to be better achievers (see Figure 10.10).

Another sign of parents' constant pressure to help their young children secure an "advantage" or "keep ahead" are the demanding daily schedules that rule the lives of many children (e.g., daily preschool classes, after-school classes, play dates, weekend enrichment, and/or sports programs). Such hectic schedules foster a concentration on competition and results and not on having fun or on being creative. In contrast, as kids their parents might have built forts out of blankets or pillows. However, with the structured activities of today and with the child constantly surrounded by media, there is little opportunity for the child to explore his or her world in such an imaginative fashion.[37]

Marketers frequently target parents looking for assistance in the task of socializing their children. To this end, marketers are sensitive to the fact that the socialization of young children provides an opportunity to establish a foundation on which later experiences continue to build throughout life. These experiences are reinforced and modified as the child grows into adolescence, the teenage years, and eventually into adulthood.

Consumer socialization of children

The aspect of childhood socialization that is particularly relevant to the study of consumer behavior is **consumer socialization**, which is defined as the *process by which children acquire the skills, knowledge, attitudes, and experiences necessary to function as consumers.* A variety of studies have focused on how children develop consumption skills. Many preadolescent children acquire their *consumer behavior norms* through observation of their parents and older siblings, who function as role models and sources of cues for basic

FIGURE 10.10

Source: Excerpted from BRAIN QUEST. Copyright © 2005 by Workman Publishing Co., Inc., New York. All rights reserved.

Parents Seeks Products that Help Their Children Succeed and Excel

consumption learning. In contrast, adolescents and teenagers are likely to look to their friends for models of acceptable consumption behavior.[38] Other research has shown that younger children generally also react positively to advertisements employing a spokesperson who seems to fulfill a parental role, whereas teens often like products for the simple reason that their parents disapprove of them.[39]

Shared shopping experiences (i.e., coshopping when mother and child shop together) also give children the opportunity to acquire in-store shopping skills. Possibly because of their more harried lifestyles, working mothers are more likely to undertake coshopping with their children than are nonworking mothers. Coshopping is a way of spending time with one's children while at the same time accomplishing a necessary task.

Consumer socialization also serves as a tool by which parents influence other aspects of the socialization process. For instance, parents frequently use the promise or reward of material goods as a device to modify or control a child's behavior. A mother may reward her child with a gift when the child does something to please her, or she may withhold or remove it when the child disobeys. Research conducted by one of the authors supports this behavior-controlling function. Specifically, adolescents reported that their parents frequently used the promise of chocolate candy as a means of controlling their behavior (e.g., getting them to complete homework or to clean their rooms).

It is important to mention that consumer socialization of children does not function identically in all cultures. For example, research indicates that American mothers emphasize autonomy more than Japanese mothers and want their children to develop independent consumption skills at an early age. In contrast, Japanese mothers maintain greater control over their children's consumption and, therefore, their offspring's understanding of how advertising works and other consumer-related skills develop at a somewhat later age.[40]

There is research evidence to suggest that a child's age and sex, family size, social class, and race are important factors in the consumer socialization process. For example, parents have been found to be more active in the consumer socialization of their daughters than their sons (e.g., parents coshop more often with their daughters). Still further, wealthier parents appear to engage in more deliberate consumer training than those in lower socioeconomic groups (e.g., coshopping, talking about how buying decisions are made).[41]

Adult consumer socialization

The socialization process is not confined to childhood; rather, it is an ongoing process. It is now accepted that socialization begins in early childhood and extends throughout a person's entire life. For example, when a newly married couple establishes their own household, their adjustment to living and consuming together is part of this continuing process. Similarly, the adjustment of a middle-aged couple who decide to move from Chicago to Miami is also part of the ongoing socialization process. Even a family that is welcoming a pet into their home as a new family member must face the challenge of socializing the pet so that it fits into the family environment. Recent survey research reveals that pet owners commonly treat their pets as full-fledged family members. For instance, 58 percent of those surveyed indicated that they have sent or received a holiday card from their dog or cat; and 78 percent regularly talk in a different voice ("I wov you") to their pets.[42]

Intergenerational socialization

It appears that it is quite common for certain product loyalties or brand preferences to be transferred from one generation to another—*intergenerational brand transfer*—maybe for even three or four generations within the same family.[43] For instance, specific brand preferences for products such as peanut butter, mayonnaise, ketchup, coffee, and canned soup are all product categories that are frequently passed on from one generation to another generation. The following are selected verbatims from research with college-aged consumers as to how they feel about product usage extending over several generations:[44]

> *My mother stills buys almost every brand that her mother did. She is scared to try any-thing else, for it will not meet the standards, and (she) would feel bad not buying something that has been with her so long. (Respondent is an Italian American male in his early twenties.)*
>
> *I find it hard to break away from the things I've been using since I was little, like Vaseline products, Ivory soap, Lipton tea, and cornflakes. I live on campus so I have to do my own shopping, and when I do I see a lot of my mother in myself. I buy things I'm accustomed to using . . . products my mother buys for the house. (Respondent is West Indian American female.)*

FIGURE 10.11

A Simple Model of the Socialization Process

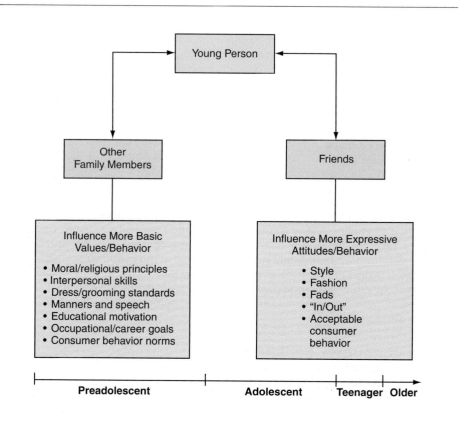

Figure 10.11 presents a simple model of the socialization process that focuses on the socialization of young children but that can be extended to family members of all ages. Note that the arrows run both ways between the young person and other family members and between the young person and his or her friends. This two-directional arrow signifies that socialization is really a "two-way street," one in which the young person is both socialized and influences those who are doing the socializing. Supporting this view is the reality that children of all ages often influence the opinions and behavior of their parents. As an example, research with elementary school-aged children has found that parental warmth relates positively to (1) the extent to which a child's interest in the Internet serves as a catalyst for increased parental Internet interest, (2) how much the child teaches a parent about the Internet, and (3) whether the child acts as the parent's Internet agent (e.g., the child shops for the parent on the Internet).[45] Because children are often more comfortable than their parents with digital and electronic media, they are often the ones in the family who do the teaching. Another research study examined the influence of family on consumer innovativeness, and found that the perceptions of adult children regarding their parent's innovativeness influences their own innovativeness.[46]

other functions of the family

Three other basic functions provided by the family are particularly relevant to a discussion of consumer behavior. These include economic well-being, emotional support, and suitable family lifestyles.

Economic well-being

Although families in the affluent nations of North America, Europe, and Asia are no longer formed primarily for economic security, providing financial means to its dependents is unquestionably a basic family function. How the family divides its responsibilities for providing economic well-being has changed considerably during the past 30 years. No longer are the traditional roles of husband as economic provider and wife as homemaker and child-rearer still valid. For instance, it is very common for married women with children in the United States and other industrial countries to be employed outside the home and for their husbands to share household responsibilities. In part, this may be why more than 70 percent of women in the United States who are over the age of 18 claim that it is more difficult to be a mother now than it was 20 or 30 years ago.[47] However, the increased contributions of working mothers to the family's total income, according to some sociologists, has had mostly a positive net effect. The positive effects included greater marital stability and greater marital equality.[48]

The economic role of children also has changed. Today, despite the fact that many teenage children work, they rarely assist the family financially. Instead, many teenagers are expected to pay for their own amusements; others contribute to the costs of their formal education and prepare themselves to be financially independent. It is of interest to note when parents are involved in a college student's acquisition of a credit card, credit card balances tend to be lower.[49]

Emotional support

The provision of emotional nourishment (including love, affection, and intimacy) to its members is an important core function of the contemporary family. In fulfilling this function, the family provides support and encouragement and assists its members in coping with decision making and with personal or social problems. To make it easier for working parents to show their love, affection, and support to their children, greeting card companies have been increasingly creating cards for parents to give to their children (or vice versa).

The *San Francisco Chronicle* asked its younger readers: "What is the key to happiness?" Many responses dealt specifically with the child's family:[50]

> *My key to happiness is to be with my family, because they're the only ones that understand my feelings, and also they're the only ones that care for me.*
> *The key to happiness is when my dad is making me laugh.*
> *The key to my happiness is my family, because they love and trust me.*
> *My family is a very good family. My mom and dad are very nice and listen to me.*
> *My sisters both have babies, so I'm even happier than I was before. Also, my grandpa lives with us. That's my key to happiness.*

If the family cannot provide adequate assistance when it is needed, it may turn to a counselor, psychologist, or other helping professional as an alternative. For instance, in most communities, educational and psychological centers are available that are designed to assist parents who want to help their children improve their learning and communication skills or to generally better adjust to their environments.

Suitable family lifestyles

Another important family function in terms of consumer behavior is the establishment of a suitable *lifestyle* for the family. Upbringing, experience, and the personal and jointly held goals of the spouses determine the importance placed on education or career, on reading, on television viewing, on the learning of computer skills, on the frequency and quality of dining out, and on the selection of other entertainment and recreational activities. Researchers have identified a shift in the nature of family "togetherness." Whereas a family being together once meant doing things together,

FIGURE 10.12

Source: © Brunswick Boat Group. Used with permission. All rights reserved.

An Ad Telling Target Readers of the Importance of Quality Family Time

today it often means being in the same household and each person doing his or her own thing.[51]

Family lifestyle commitments, including the allocation of time, are greatly influencing consumption patterns. For example, a series of diverse pressures on moms has reduced the time that they have available for household chores and has created a market for convenience products and fast-food restaurants. Also, with both parents working, an increased emphasis is being placed on the notion of "quality time" rather than on the "quantity of time" spent with children and other family members. Realizing the importance of quality family time, Bayliner is telling its target audience about how owning a family boat adds to the family's happiness (see Figure 10.12).

family decision making and consumption-related roles

Although many marketers recognize the family as the basic consumer decision-making unit, they most frequently examine the attitudes and behavior of the one family member whom they believe to be the major *decision maker.* In some cases, they also examine the attitudes and behavior of the person most likely to be the primary *user* of the product or service. For instance, in the case of men's underwear, which is frequently purchased by women for their husbands and unmarried sons, it is commonplace to seek the views of both the men who wear the underwear and the women who buy it. By considering both the likely user and the likely purchaser, the marketer obtains a richer picture of the consumption process.

Key family consumption roles

For a family to function as a cohesive unit, tasks such as doing the laundry, preparing meals, setting the dinner table, taking out the garbage, and walking the dog must be carried out by one or more family members. In a dynamic society, family-related duties are constantly changing (such as the greater performance of household tasks by men). However, we can identify eight distinct roles in the *family decision-making process,* as presented in Table 10.7. A look at these roles provides further insight into how family members interact in their various consumption-related roles.

The number and identity of the family members who fill these roles vary from family to family and from product to product. In some cases, a single family member will independently assume a number of roles; in other cases, a single role will be performed jointly by two or more family members. In still other cases, one or more of these basic roles may not be required. For example, a family member may be walking down the cookie aisle at a local supermarket when she picks out an interesting new fat-free cookie. Her selection does not directly involve the influence of other family members. She is the *decider,* the *buyer* and, in a sense, the *gatekeeper*; however, she may or may not be the sole consumer (or user). Products may be consumed by a single family member (deodorant, razor),

TABLE 10.7	The Eight Roles in the Family Decision-Making Process
ROLE	**DESCRIPTION**
Influencers	Family member(s) who provide information to other members about a product or service
Gatekeepers	Family member(s) who control the flow of information about a product or service into the family
Deciders	Family member(s) with the power to determine unilaterally or jointly whether to shop for, purchase, use, consume, or dispose of a specific product or service
Buyers	Family member(s) who make the actual purchase of a particular product or service
Preparers	Family member(s) who transform the product into a form suitable for consumption by other family members
Users	Family member(s) who use or consume a particular product or service
Maintainers	Family member(s) who service or repair the product so that it will provide continued satisfaction
Disposers	Family member(s) who initiate or carry out the disposal or discontinuation of a particular product or service

consumed or used directly by two or more family members (orange juice, shampoo), or consumed indirectly by the entire family (central air conditioning, HDTV set, or art glass collection).

Dynamics of husband–wife decision making

Marketers are interested in the relative amount of influence that a husband and a wife have when it comes to family consumption choices. The relative influence of husbands and wives can be classified as: **husband dominated**, **wife dominated**, **joint** (either equal or syncratic), and **autonomic** (either solitary or unilateral).[52]

The relative influence of a husband and wife on a particular consumer decision depends in part on the product and service category. For instance, during the 1950s, the purchase of a new automobile was strongly husband dominated, whereas food and financial banking decisions more often were wife dominated. Fifty years later, the purchase of the family's principal automobile is still often husband dominated in many households. However, in other contexts or situations (e.g., a car to transport the children around or a car for a working mother), female car buyers are a segment to which many car manufacturers are currently receiving a great deal of marketing attention. Also, in the case of financial decision making, there has been a general trend over the past decade to have the female head of household make financial decisions.[53]

Husband–wife decision making also appears to be related to cultural influence. Research comparing husband–wife decision-making patterns in the People's Republic of China and in the United States reveals that among Chinese there were substantially fewer "joint" decisions and more "husband-dominated" decisions for many household purchases.[54] However, when limiting the comparison to urban and rural Chinese households (i.e., a "within-China" comparison), the research showed that in a larger city such as Beijing, married couples were more likely than rural couples to share equally in purchase decisions. Still further, because of China's "one child" policy and the ensuing custom of treating a single child as a "little emperor," many of the parents' purchase decisions are influenced by the input of their child.[55]

In another recent cross-cultural study, husband–wife decision making was studied among three groups: Asian Indians living in India, Asian Indians living in the United States, and American nationals. Results show a decrease in husband-dominated decisions and an increase in wife-dominated decisions, going from Asian Indians in India, to Asian Indians in the United States, to American nationals. This pattern seems to indicate the impact of assimilation on decision making.[56]

The expanding role of children in family decision making

Over the past several decades, there has been a trend toward children playing a more active role in what the family buys, as well as in the family decision-making process. This shift in influence has occurred as a result of families having fewer children (which increases the influence of each child), more dual-income couples who can afford to permit their children to make a greater number of the choices, and the encouragement by the media to allow children to "express themselves." Still further, single-parent households often push their children toward household participation and self-reliance. As one example of children's influence, kids in supermarkets with a parent make an average of 15 requests, of which about half are typically granted.[57] Table 10.8 enumerates some of the tactics employed by children to influence their parents, and Table 10.9 presents the amount of influence children perceive they have with respect to their family's purchasing of a variety of items. As Table 10.9 indicates, children's influence was claimed to be higher when the purchase was for themselves, although many claimed to be influential in the purchase of "family products," such as meals, vacations, and automobiles.

Still other research reveals that children have considerable influence on family decision making with respect to eating. The research found that about 17 percent of

TABLE 10.8	Tactics Used by Children to Influence Their Parents
Pressure tactics	The child makes demands, uses threats, or intimidation to persuade you to comply with his/her request
Upward appeal	The child seeks to persuade you, saying that the request was approved or supported by an older member of the family, a teacher, or even a family friend
Exchange tactics	The child makes an explicit or implicit promise to give you some sort of service such as washing the car, cleaning the house, or taking care of the baby, in return for a favor
Coalition tactics	The child seeks the aid of others to persuade you to comply with his/her request or uses the support of others as an argument for you to agree with him/her
Ingratiating tactics	The child seeks to get you in a good mood or think favorably of him or her before asking you to comply with a request
Rational persuasion	The child uses logical arguments and factual evidence to persuade you to agree with his/her request
Inspirational appeals	The child makes an emotional appeal or proposal that arouses enthusiasm by appealing to your values and ideals
Consultation tactics	The child seeks your involvement in making a decision

Source: "Tactics Used by Children to Influence Their Parents," Joyantha S. Wimalasir–Journal of Consumer Marketing (2004, Vol. 21, No. 4) © MCB UP Limited **http://www.emeraldinsight.com/msq.htm**.

the 9- to 12-year-old children studied considered themselves to be the main decision maker with respect to the decision to go to a restaurant, whereas 40 percent thought of themselves as the main decision maker with respect to the choice of restaurants.[58] Interestingly, some 30 percent of the parents of these children felt that their offspring were the main decision makers in deciding to eat out, and almost an equal number, 29 percent, felt that the child (or children) also was the main decision

TABLE 10.9	Items Children Perceive Themselves to Have Influenced the Purchase Of	
		%
Casual clothes for me		91
Trainers for me		88
CDs for me		84
Sweets for me		83
Computers for me		83
Soft drinks for me		80
School shoes for me		80
A family trip to the cinema		73
Food for me for lunch at the weekend		73
A holiday I would go on with the family		63
Going out for a family meal		52
A family car		37

Source: Julie Tinson and Clive Nancarrow, *International Journal of Market Research* 47, no. 1 (2005): 22.

TABLE 10.10	Who Makes the Decision to Go to a Restaurant? Children's Perceptions by Family Type			
	CHILD	**FATHER**	**MOTHER**	**TOTAL**
Traditional	12.0	52.0	36.0	100% 75.8
Nontraditional	25.0	12.5	62.5	100% 24.2
Total	15.2	42.4	42.4	100% 100%

Source: Reprinted from the Journal of Business Research, 54, JoAnne Labrecque and Line Ricard, Children's Influence on Family Decision Making: A Restaurant Study, © November 2001, p. 175, with permission from Elsevier.

maker with regard to which restaurant was patronized. Additionally, in traditional families, children most often felt that it was the father who makes the decision to go to a restaurant, whereas in nontraditional families it was most often the mother (see Table 10.10). The results also reveal that in nontraditional households a child was twice as likely to make the decision to go to a restaurant than in a traditional household.

There is also research evidence supporting the notion that the extent to which children influence a family's purchases is related to family communication patterns. As might be expected, children's influence has been found to be highest in families where the parents are *pluralistic parents* (i.e., parents who encourage children to speak up and express their individual preferences on purchases) and *consensual parents* (i.e., parents who encourage children to seek harmony, but are nevertheless open to the children's veiwpoint on purchases), because such parents allow their children a significantly greater amount of influence than do *protective parents* (i.e., parents who stress that children should not stress their own preferences, but rather go along with the parents judgment on what is to be purchased).[59]

Still further, there is research that has explored the notion of the *teen Internet maven*—teenagers who spend considerable time on the Internet and know how to search for and find information, and respond to requests from others to provide information (this is a variation on the *market maven* discussed in Chapter 15). It has been shown that teen Internet mavens contribute significantly to the family's decision making.[60] Specifically, they perceive themselves to be more influential in researching and evaluating family purchases; indeed, their parents tend to concur that they are more influential with regard to family decision making.

Finally, advertisers have long recognized the importance of children's "pester power," and therefore encourage children to "pester" their parents to purchase what they see in ads. A recent study of the strategies children use to influence their parents' food-purchasing decisions began with the proposed framework that there are four types of influence: individual differences, interpersonal influences, environmental influences, and societal influences that children employ to influence their parents so that food-purchase decisions reflect their choices or preferences. This framework is depicted in Figure 10.13. This research goes on to reveal that ten-year-old French Canadian children (living in Montreal) considered it important to eat foods similar to those eaten by others, to eat in front of the television, to suggest that the family eat foods advertised on TV, and to develop strategies to influence parental food-purchasing decisions. Still further, it was more important for boys than for girls to select foods eaten by others, and boys were more likely to eat in front of the TV and to eat in their bedrooms. The strategies used by children to influence their parents' food-purchasing decisions, included such persuasive strategies as: stating their preferences

FIGURE 10.13

Conceptual Framework Related to Factors Explaining the Development of Strategies by Ten-Year-Old Children to Influence Parental Decisions on Food Purchasing

Source: Marie Marquis, "Strategies for Influencing Parental Decisions on Food Purchasing," *Journal of Consumer Marketing* 21, no. 2 (2004): 135.

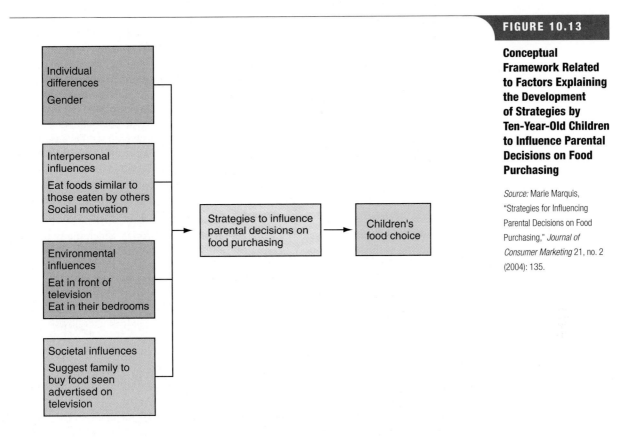

or begging; and emotional strategies, such as asking repetitively for a product (in a way that irritates the parents).[61] An additional point must be made about children and TV viewing—networks today try to promote the branding process because it can change a child from a viewer into a consumer likely to purchase the advertised product. As examples of how this may be accomplished, Nickelodeon has an agreement with Gateway, the computer manufacturer, to offer Rugrats and Blue's Clues editions of its Astro computer, and General Motors has a deal with Nickelodeon that includes using some Nickelodeon programming in its in-vehicle entertainment systems. Still further, research conducted by J.D. Power and Associates found that 78 percent of parents claimed that they had had discussions with their children while shopping for a new vehicle.[62]

the family life cycle

Sociologists and consumer researchers have long been attracted to the concept of the **family life cycle (FLC)** as a means of depicting what was once a rather steady and predictable series of stages through which most families progressed. However, with the advent of many diverse family and lifestyle arrangements, what was the rule has been on the decline. This decline in the percentage of families that progress through a traditional FLC (to be explored shortly) seems to be caused by a host of societal factors, including an increasing divorce rate, the explosive number of out-of-wedlock births, and the 35-year decline in the number of extended families that transpired as many young families moved to advance their job and career opportunities.

The notion of the FLC remains a useful marketing tool when one keeps in mind that there are family and lifestyle arrangements that are not fully accounted for by the traditional representation. FLC analysis enables marketers to segment families in terms of a series of stages spanning the life course of a family unit. The FLC is a composite variable created by systematically combining such commonly used demographic variables as *marital status, size of family, age of family members* (focusing on the age of the oldest or youngest child), and *employment status* of the head of household. The ages of the parents and the relative amount of disposable income usually are inferred from the stage in the family life cycle.

To reflect the current realities of a wide range of family and lifestyle arrangements, our treatment of the FLC concept is divided into two sections. The first section considers the traditional FLC schema. This model is increasingly being challenged because it fails to account for various important family living arrangements. To rectify these limitations, the second section focuses on alternative FLC stages, including increasingly important nontraditional family structures.

Traditional family life cycle

The **traditional family life cycle** is a progression of stages through which many families pass, starting with bachelorhood, moving on to marriage (and the creation of the basic family unit), then to family growth (with the birth of children), to family contraction (as grown children leave the household), and ending with the dissolution of the basic unit (due to the death of one spouse). Although different researchers have expressed various preferences in terms of the number of FLC stages, the traditional FLC models proposed over the years can be synthesized into just five basic stages, as follows:

> *Stage I: Bachelorhood—young single adult living apart from parents*
> *Stage II: Honeymooners—young married couple*
> *Stage III: Parenthood—married couple with at least one child living at home*
> *Stage IV: Postparenthood—an older married couple with no children living at home*
> *Stage V: Dissolution—one surviving spouse*

The following discussion examines the five stages in detail and shows how they lend themselves to market segmentation strategies.

Stage I: bachelorhood

The first FLC stage consists of young single men and women who have established households apart from their parents. Although most members of this FLC stage are fully employed, many are college or graduate students who have left their parents' homes. Young single adults are apt to spend their incomes on rent, basic home furnishings, the purchase and maintenance of automobiles, travel and entertainment, and clothing and accessories. Members of the bachelorhood stage frequently have sufficient disposable income to indulge themselves. Marketers target singles for a wide variety of products and services.

In most large cities, there are travel agents, housing developments, health clubs, sports clubs, and other service and product marketers that find this FLC stage a lucrative target niche. *Meeting, dating,* and *mating* are prominent concerns of many young adults who typically are beginning their working lives after recently completing college or some other form of career or job training. It is relatively easy to reach this segment because many special-interest publications target singles. For example, *GQ, Details,* and *Playboy* are directed to a young, sophisticated, single male audience, whereas *Cosmopolitan, Allure,* and *Glamour* are directed to young single females.

It is interesting to note how the perceptions of 18- to 29-year-olds have been changing with respect to marriage. Whereas in 1991, 72 percent of this group felt that a happy marriage is part of the good life, by 1996 the number had risen to 86 percent. This growth in percentage is higher than for any other age group of U.S. adults.[63]

Marriage marks the transition from the bachelorhood stage to the honeymooner stage. Engaged and soon-to-be-married couples tend to have a combined income that is more than the average U.S. household); therefore, they are often the target for many products and services (the bridal industry is more than a $30-billion-a-year market—

FIGURE 10.14

Source: © Bed Bath & Beyond
Inc. and it's subsidiaries. Used
with permission.

Targeting the "To Be Married"
Market

Imagine a registry that includes everything on your wish list, from the finest china to a huge assortment
of professional cookware to a luxurious collection of bed linens.

That dream becomes a reality with the Bed Bath & Beyond® Bridal and Gift Registry. For more information
visit any of our stores, *call* 1–800–GO BEYOND® or go *online* at www.bedbathandbeyond.com

The Bridal & Gift Registry

BED BATH & **BEYOND**®

www.bedbathandbeyond.com

see Figure 10.14). And they want their wedding to be special, which explains the recent
trend in wedding sites that are far from home—an exotic Carribean island or a major
European capital city.

Stage II: honeymooners

The *honeymoon* stage starts immediately after the marriage vows are taken and generally continues until the arrival of the couple's first child. This FLC stage serves as a
period of adjustment to married life. Because many young husbands and wives both
work, these couples have available a combined income that often permits a lifestyle that
provides them with the opportunities of more indulgent purchasing of possessions or
allows them to save or invest their extra income.

Honeymooners have considerable start-up expenses when establishing a new home (major and minor appliances, bedroom and living room furniture, carpeting, drapes, dishes, and a host of utensils and accessory items). During this stage, the advice and experience of other married couples are likely to be important to newlyweds. Also important as sources of new product information are the so-called shelter magazines, such as *Better Homes and Gardens* and *Metropolitan Home*.

Stage III: parenthood

When a couple has its first child, the honeymoon is considered over. The *parenthood* stage (sometimes called the full-nest stage) usually extends over more than a 20-year period. Because of its long duration, this stage can be divided into shorter phases: the preschool phase, the elementary school phase, the high school phase, and the college phase. Throughout these parenthood phases, the interrelationships of family members and the structure of the family gradually change. Furthermore, the financial resources of the family change significantly, as one (or both) parents progress in a career and as child-rearing and educational responsibilities gradually increase and finally decrease as children become self-supporting.

Parents, especially Baby Boomers (born between 1946 and 1964) and Generation X (born between 1965 and 1978) who are parents, make up the majority of parents in U.S. households. These parents tend to be better educated, more affluent, and more socially aware than previous generations of parents. Their children often become the focus of their lives, and they spend money accordingly. Therefore, it is not surprising that affluent parents today believe that *"If you don't buy the good brand for your kid, you're really being an unfit parent,"* and this attitude has created a market for $150 to $400 diaper bags, $1,000 high chairs, and limited-edition, leather-lined baby strollers for $2,000.

Many magazines cater to the information and entertainment needs of parents and children. For example, there are many other special-interest publications, such as *Humpty Dumpty,* designed for the young child just learning to read; *Scholastic Magazine,* for the elementary school pupil; *Boy's Life,* for young boys; and *American Girl, Seventeen,* and *Glamour* for teen and young adult girls interested in fashion. In addition, a relatively new magazine, *Cookie,* is targeting the parents in the more than 22 million U.S. homes, with annual incomes in excess of $75,000, who have children under 10 years of age.[64]

Stage IV: postparenthood

Because parenthood extends over many years, it is only natural to find that *postparenthood,* when all the children have left home, is traumatic for some parents and liberating for others. This so-called *empty-nest stage* signifies for many parents almost a "rebirth," a time for doing all the things they could not do while the children were at home and they had to worry about soaring educational expenses. For the mother, it may be a time to further her education, to enter or reenter the job market, or to seek new interests. For the father, it is a time to indulge in new hobbies. For both, it is the time to travel, to entertain, perhaps to refurnish their home, or to sell it in favor of a new home or condominium.

It is during this stage that married couples tend to be most comfortable financially. Today's empty nesters have more leisure time. They travel more frequently, take extended vacations, and are likely to purchase a second home in a warmer climate. They have higher disposable incomes because of savings and investments, and they have fewer expenses (no mortgage or college tuition bills). They look forward to being involved grandparents. For this reason, families in the postparenthood stage are an important market for luxury goods, new automobiles, expensive furniture, and vacations to faraway places.

Consider Baby Boomers, who make up a large percentage of the 70 million Americans who are grandparents; they are spending about $35 billion annually on their grandchildren, account for 25 percent of all toy purchases, an average spending of $500 a year per grandchild (although one-third spend over $2,400 a year per grandchild).[65]

Many empty nesters retire while they are still in good health. Retirement provides the opportunity to pursue new interests, to travel, and to fulfill unsatisfied needs. Hotels,

FIGURE 10.15

Source: © Rarity Communities, Inc. Used with permission. All rights reserved.

Community Developers Target Members of the Postparenthood Stage of FLC

airlines, and car-leasing companies have responded to this market with discounts to consumers over 60; some airlines have established special travel clubs with unlimited mileage for a flat fee. Adult communities have sprung up in many parts of the nation (see Figure 10.15). Of course, for older retired couples who do not have adequate savings or income, retirement is far different and very restrictive. On the other hand, there are subsegments of older individuals who do *not* wish to retire—they simply love what they do at work too much to think of retiring. Older consumers tend to use television as an important source of information and entertainment. They favor programs that provide the opportunity to "keep up with what's happening," especially news and public affairs programs. In addition, a number of special-interest magazines cater exclusively to this market, such as *Modern Maturity*. (Chapter 13 contains a more detailed discussion of the older consumer as a subcultural market segment.)

Stage V: dissolution

Dissolution of the basic family unit occurs with the death of one spouse. When the surviving spouse is in good health, is working or has adequate savings, and has supportive family and friends, the adjustment is easier. The surviving spouse (usually, the wife) often tends to follow a more economical lifestyle. Many surviving spouses seek each other out for companionship; others enter into second (or third and even fourth) marriages.

Marketing and the traditional FLC

Whereas the foregoing discussion of the traditional family life cycle concept indicated the types of products and services that a household or family might be most interested in at each stage, it is also possible to trace how the FLC concept impacts a single product or service over time. An example is a study that employed an eight-stage FLC schema to investigate how consumers choose a bank.[66] As part of the research, the 3,100 respondents were asked to rate the relative importance of 18 product/service characteristics that might impact on their choice of a bank. The research reveals that a convenient location is very important to all respondents (i.e., it was always ranked either first or second), but other bank attributes tended to be much more important to some FLC segments than others. For instance, "fast service" was ranked fifth by bachelor stage individuals and twelfth or thirteenth by full-nest II, empty-nest I, and empty-nest II respondents.

Modifications—the nontraditional FLC

As we already noted, the traditional FLC model has lost its ability to fully represent the progression of stages through which current family and lifestyle arrangements move. To compensate for these limitations, consumer researchers have been attempting to search out expanded FLC models that better reflect diversity of family and lifestyle arrangements.[67] Figure 10.16 presents an FLC model that depicts along the main horizontal row

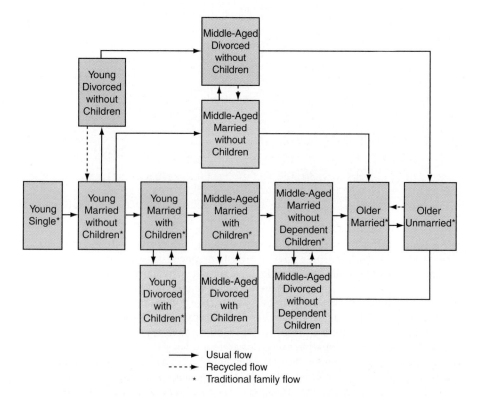

An Extended Family Life Cycle Schema Accounts for Alternative Consumer Lifestyle Realities

Source: Patrick E. Murphy and William A. Staples, "A Modern-Sized Family Life Cycle," *Journal of Consumer Research*, 6 June 1979, 17. Reprinted by permission of The University of Chicago Press as publisher.

FIGURE 10.16

the stages of the traditional FLC and above and below the main horizontal row are selected alternative FLC stages that account for some important nontraditional family households that marketers are increasingly targeting. The underlying sociodemographic forces that drive this expanded FLC model include divorce and later marriages, with and without the presence of children. Although somewhat greater reality is provided by this modified FLC model, it only recognizes families that started in marriage, ignoring such single-parent households as unwed mothers and families formed because a single person or single persons adopt a child.

Nontraditional FLC stages

Table 10.11 presents an extensive categorization of nontraditional FLC stages that are derived from the dynamic sociodemographic forces operating during the past 30 years or so. These nontraditional stages include not only family households but also nonfamily households: those consisting of a single individual and those consisting of two or more unrelated individuals. At one time, nonfamily households were so uncommon that it was not really important whether they were considered or not. However, as Table 10.12 reveals, over 30 percent of all households are currently nonfamily households (i.e., men or women living

---

TABLE 10.11   **Noteworthy Nontraditional FLC Stages**

ALTERNATIVE FLC STAGES	DEFINITION/COMMENTARY
FAMILY HOUSEHOLDS	
Childless couples	It is increasingly acceptable for married couples to elect not to have children. Contributing forces are more career-oriented married women and delayed marriages.
Couples who marry later in life (in their late 30s or later)	More career-oriented men and women and greater occurrence of couples living together. Likely to have fewer or even no children.
Couples who have first child later in life (in their late 30s or later)	Likely to have fewer children. Stress quality lifestyle: "Only the best is good enough."
Single parents I	High divorce rates (about 50 percent) contribute to a portion of singleparent households.
Single parents II	Young man or woman who has one or more children out of wedlock.
Single parents III	A single person who adopts one or more children.
Extended family	Young single-adult children who return home to avoid the expenses of living alone while establishing their careers. Divorced daughter or son and grandchild(ren) return home to parents. Frail elderly parents who move in with children. Newlyweds living with in-laws.
NONFAMILY HOUSEHOLDS	
Unmarried couples	Increased acceptance of heterosexual and homosexual couples.
Divorced persons (no children)	High divorce rate contributes to dissolution of households before children are born.
Single persons (most are young)	Primarily a result of delaying first marriage; also, men and women who never marry.
Widowed persons (most are elderly)	Longer life expectancy, especially for women, means more over-75 single-person households.

TABLE 10.12	Family and Nonfamily Households	
	NUMBER OF HOUSEHOLDS BY TYPE IN 2000 (IN 000S)	DISTRIBUTION OF HOUSEHOLDS BY TYPE
ALL HOUSEHOLDS	111,278	100.0%
FAMILY HOUSEHOLDS	75,596	67.9%
Married couples	57,320	51.5%
With own children under 18	27,059	24.3%
Female householder (no husband present)	13,620	12.2%
NONFAMILY HOUSEHOLDS	35,682	32.0%
Householder living alone	29,377	26.4%
Average household size = 2.57		
Average family size = 3.19		

Source: U.S. Census Bureau (**www.census.gov/prod/2004pubs/p20–553.pdf**)

alone or with another person as an unmarried couple). The table points out how FLC stages have shifted so that today nonfamily households actually outnumber married couples with children, the once stereotypical family.

Consumption in nontraditional families

When households undergo status changes (divorce, temporary retirement, a new person moving into the household, or the death of a spouse), they often undergo spontaneous changes in consumption-related preferences and, thus, become attractive targets for many marketers. For example, divorce often requires that one (or both) former spouses find a new residence, get new telephones (with new telephone numbers), buy new furniture, and perhaps find a job. These requirements mean that a divorced person might need to contact real estate agents, call the local and long-distance telephone companies, visit furniture stores, and possibly contact a personnel agency or career consultant. There are also the special needs of the children who are experiencing the divorce.

In another sphere, the substantial increase in dual-income households (in which both the husband and wife work) has also tended to muddy the lifestyle assumptions implicit in the traditional FLC. Most dual-income families have children (the majority of those children are between 11 and 20 years of age). The most affluent dual-income segment is, not surprisingly, the "crowded nesters." This dual-income couple, with an adult child living at home, has the advantage of an additional potential source of income to contribute to the general well-being of the household.

The side-by-side existence of traditional and nontraditional FLC stages is another example of our recurring observation that the contemporary marketplace is complex in its diversity, and it is a challenge to segment and serve.

SUMMARY

Almost all individuals regularly interact with other people who directly or indirectly influence their purchase decisions. Thus, the study of groups and their impact on the individual is of great importance to marketers concerned with influencing consumer behavior.

Consumer reference groups are groups that serve as frames of reference for individuals in their purchase decisions. Examples of reference groups include (1) friendship groups, (2) shopping groups, (3) work groups, (4) virtual groups or communities, and (5) consumer-action groups. Reference groups that influence general values or behavior are called normative reference groups; those that influence specific attitudes are called comparative reference groups. The concept of consumer reference groups has been broadened to include groups with which consumers have no direct face-to-face contact, such as celebrities, political figures, and social classes.

The credibility, attractiveness, and power of the reference group affect the degree of influence it has. Reference group appeals are used very effectively by some advertisers in promoting their goods and services because they subtly induce the prospective consumer to identify with the pictured user of the product.

The five types of reference group appeals most commonly used in marketing are celebrities, experts, the common man, the executive and employee spokesperson, and the trade spokes-character. Celebrities are used to give testimonials or endorsements as actors or as company spokespersons. Experts may be recognized experts in the product category or actors playing the part of experts (e.g., an automobile mechanic). The common-man approach is designed to show that individuals who are just like the prospect are satisfied with the advertised product. Increasingly, firms are using their top executives as spokespersons because their appearance in company advertisements seems to imply that someone at the top is watching over the consumer's interest.

For many consumers their family is their primary reference group for many attitudes and behaviors. The family is the prime target market for most products and product categories. As the most basic membership group, families are defined as two or more persons related by blood, marriage, or adoption who reside together. There are three types of families: married couples, nuclear families, and extended families. Socialization is a core function of the family. Other functions of the family are the provision of economic and emotional support and the pursuit of a suitable lifestyle for its members.

The members of a family assume specific roles in their everyday functioning; such roles or tasks extend to the realm of consumer purchase decisions. Key consumer-related roles of family members include influencers, gatekeepers, deciders, buyers, preparers, users, maintainers, and disposers. A family's decision-making style often is influenced by its lifestyle, roles, and cultural factors.

The majority of consumer studies classify family consumption decisions as husband-dominated, wife-dominated, joint, or autonomic decisions. The extent and nature of husband–wife influence in family decisions depend, in part, on the specific product or service and selected cultural influences.

Classification of families by stage in the family life cycle (FLC) provides valuable insights into family consumption-related behavior. The traditional FLC begins with bachelorhood, moves on to marriage, then to an expanding family, to a contracting family, and to an end with the death of a spouse. Dynamic sociodemographic changes in society have resulted in many nontraditional stages that a family or nonfamily household might pass through (such as childless couples, couples marrying later in life, single parents, unmarried couples, or single-person households). These nontraditional stages are becoming increasingly important to marketers in terms of specific market niches.

DISCUSSION QUESTIONS

1. As a marketing consultant, you have been asked to evaluate a new promotional campaign for a large retail chain. The campaign strategy is aimed at increasing group shopping. What recommendations would you make?

2. Many celebrities who are considered to be persuasive role models often appear in TV beer commercials. Does the use of such celebrities in beer advertising constitute an unethical marketing practice? Discuss.

3. You are the marketing vice president of a large soft-drink company. Your company's advertising agency is in the process of negotiating a contract to employ a superstar female singer to promote your product. Discuss the reference group factors that you would raise before the celebrity is hired.

4. How does the family influence the consumer socialization of children? What role does television advertising play in consumer socialization?

5. As a marketing consultant, you were retained by the Walt Disney Company to design a study investigating how families make vacation decisions. Whom, within the family, would you interview? What kind of questions would you ask? How would you assess the relative power of each family member in making vacation-related decisions?

6. Which of the five stages of the traditional family life cycle constitute the most lucrative segment(s) for the following products and services: (a) telephone party lines, (b) a Club Med vacation, (c) Domino's pizza, (d) compact disc players, (e) mutual funds, and (f) motor homes? Explain your answers.

7. As the marketing manager of a high-quality, fairly expensive line of frozen dinners, how would you use the nonfamily household information listed in Table 10.11 to segment the market and position your product?

8. A domestic airline's frequent-flyer program states that award tickets are transferable only to family members. As the airline executive charged with reevaluating this policy, how would you use the census data listed in Table 10.12 to decide whether or not to change the present policy?

EXERCISES

1. Prepare a list of formal and informal groups to which you belong and give examples of purchases for which each served as a reference group. In which of the groups you listed is the pressure to conform the greatest? Why?

2. With a paper and pencil, spend one hour watching a network television channel during prime time. Record the total number of commercials that aired. For each commercial using a celebrity endorser, record the celebrity's name, the product or service advertised, and whether the celebrity was used in a testimonial, as an endorser, as an actor, or as a spokesperson.

3. Think of a recent major purchase your family has made. Analyze the roles performed by the various family members in terms of the following consumption roles: influencers, gatekeepers, deciders, buyers, preparers, users, maintainers, and disposers.

4. Select three product categories and compare the brands you prefer to those your parents prefer. To what extent are the preferences similar? Discuss the similarities in the context of consumer socialization.

5. Identify one traditional family and one nontraditional family (or household) featured in a TV sitcom or series. (The two families households can be featured in the same or in different TV shows.) Classify the traditional group into one stage of the traditional FLC. Classify the nontraditional group into one of the categories described in Table 10.11. Select two characters of the same gender and approximate age, one from each group, and compare their consumption behavior (such as clothes, furniture, or stated or implied attitudes toward spending money).

KEY TERMS

- **actor**
- **autonomic (unilateral) decisions**
- **celebrity credibility**
- **comparative reference groups**
- **consumer-action group**
- **consumer conformity**
- **consumer socialization**
- **endorsement**
- **extended family**

- **family**
- **family life cycle (FLC)**
- **group**
- **husband-dominated decisions**
- **indirect reference groups**
- **informal groups**
- **joint (syncratic) decisions**
- **normative reference groups**
- **nuclear family**

- **reference group**
- **shopping group**
- **single-parent family**
- **socialization of family members**
- **spokesperson**
- **symbolic group**
- **testimonial**
- **traditional family life cycle**
- **wife-dominated decisions**

NOTES

1. Josh Linkner, "Please Remove Your Sneakers," *Brandweek,* April 18, 2005, 28.

2. Robert Madrigal, "The Influence of Social Alliances with Sports Teams on Intentions to Purchase Corporate Sponsors' Products," *Journal of Advertising* 29 (Winter 2000): 13–24.

3. Pamela Kicker and Cathy L. Hartman, "Purchase Pal Use: Why Buyers Choose to Shop with Others," in *1993 AMA Winter Educators' Proceedings,* 4, eds. Rajan Varadarajan and Bernard Jaworski (Chicago: American Marketing Association, 1993), 378–384.

4. Eve M. Kahn and Julie Lasky, "Out of the Pantry and Partying On," *New York Times,* November 8, 2001, F9.

5. Peeter W. J. Verleigh, Ad Th. H. Pruyn, and Kim A. Peters, "Turning Shoppers into Sellers: Two Experiments on Member-Get-Member Campaigns," *Advances in Consumer Research* 30 (2003): 346.

6. "Startec Acquires Chinese Web Community," *PR Newswire,* March 7, 2000, 1.

7. "Is the Net Redefining Our Identity?" *Business Week,* May 12, 1997, 100–101.

8. Elizabeth Bird, "Chatting on Cynthia's Porch: Creating Community in an E-Mail Fan Group," *Southern Communication Journal* 65, no. 1 (Fall 1999): 49–65.

9. Donna L. Hoffman, Thomas P. Novak, and Alladi Venkatesh, "Has the Internet Become Indispensable?," *Communications of the ACM* 47 (July 2004): 37–42.

10. Kendra Nordin, *Christian Science Monitor,* February 26, 2001, 16.

11. Albert M. Muniz, Jr. and Thomas C. O'Guinn, "Brand Community," *Journal of Consumer Research* 27 (March 2001): 412–432.

12. James H. McAlexander, John W. Schouten, and Harold F. Koenig, "Building Brand Community," *Journal of Marketing* 66 (January 2002): 38–54.

13. Ibid., 46.

14. Albert M. Muniz, Jr. and Hope Jensen Schau, "Religiosity in the Abandoned Apple Newton Brand Community," *Journal of Consumer Research* 31 (March 2005): 737–747.

15. For example, see Robert V. Kozinets and Jay M. Handelman, "Adversaries of Consumption: Consumer Movements, Activism, and Ideology," *Journal of Consumer Research* 31 (December 2004): 691–704; and Jill Gabrielle Klein, N. Craig Smith, and Andrew John, "Why We Boycott: Consumer Motivations for Boycott Participation," *Journal of Marketing* 68 (July 2004): 92–109.

16. Barry Janoff, "Lights, Camera, Action Sports!," *Brandweek,* February 28, 2005, 26–30.

17. Zafer Erdogan, Michael J. Baker, and Stephen Tagg, "Selecting Celebrity Endorsers: The Practitioner's Perspective," *Journal of Advertising Research* (May/June 2001): 39–48.

18. Sarah Ellison, "Crest Spices Up Toothpaste War With New Tastes," *The Wall Street Journal,* September 15, 2003, B1; and Sonia Reyes, "McCormick Seasons Grill with Saucy New Effort," *Brandweek,* March 21, 2005, 8.

19. Lynette Knowles Mathur, Ike Mathur, and Nanda Rangan, "The Wealth Effects Associated with a Celebrity Endorser: The Michael Jordan Phenomenon," *Journal of Advertising Research* 37, no. 3 (May–June 1997): 25; and Jeff Manning, "Jordan, Nike Linked Until 2023," *The Oregonian,* January 14, 1999, D1.

20. David Nielsen, "Tiger on Verge of Becoming No. 1 Pitchman in Sports," *Cincinnati Post,* June 21, 2000, 8B.

21. Ben Pincus, "Saving Face of Sponsorship," *Brand Strategy,* September 2004, 54–55.

22. Roobina Ohanian, "The Impact of Celebrity Spokespersons: Perceived Image on Consumers' Intention to Purchase," *Journal of Advertising Research* (February–March 1991): 46–54.

23. Carolyn Tripp, Thomas D. Jensen, and Les Carlson, "The Effects of Multiple Product Endorsements by Celebrities on Consumers' Attitudes and Intentions," *Journal of Consumer Research* 20 (March 1994): 535–547; and David C. Bojanic, Patricia K. Voli, and James B. Hunt, "Can Consumers Match Celebrity Endorsers with Products?" in *Developments in Marketing Science,* ed. Robert L. King (Richmond, VA: Academy of Marketing Science, 1991), 303–307.

24. Alan J. Bush, Craig A. Martin, and Victoria D. Bush, "Sports Celebrity Influence on the Behavioral Intentions of Generation Y," *Journal of Advertising Research* (March 2004): 108–118.

25. Richard Morin, "When Celebrity Endorsers Go Bad," *The Washington Post,* February 3, 2002, B5

26. "Study Identifies Qualities of Effective Public Health Service Announcements," *Marketing News,* April 1981, 7.

27. Stuart Elliott, "Betty Crocker Sets Up House in Cyberspace," *New York Times,* August 11, 1997, B1, B8.

28. Judith A. Garretson and Ronald W. Niedrich, "Spokes-Characters: Creating Character Trust and Positive Brand Attitudes," *Journal of Advertising* 33 (Summer 2004): 25–36.

29. U.S. Census Bureau, "America's Families and Living Arrangements: 2003," November 2004, accessed at **www.census.gov/prod/2004pubs/p20-553.pdf**

30. Terry L. Childers and Akshay R. Rao, "The Influence of Familial and Peer-Based Reference Groups on Consumer Decisions," *Journal of Consumer Research* 19 (September 1992): 198–211.

31. Maureen Dowd, "The Baby Bust," *New York Times,* April 10, 2001, A27; and Nancy Gibbs, "Making Time for a Baby," *Time Magazine* 159, no. 15 (April 15, 2002): 48–54.

32. James W. Gentry and Lee Phillip McGinnis, "Doing Gender in the Family: Household Production Issues," *Advances in Consumer Research* 30 (2003): 309–313.

33. Op. cit. U.S. Census Bureau, "American's Families and Living Arrangements: 2003," November 2004, accessed at **www.census.gov/prod/2004pubs/p20-553.pdf**

34. Pamela Paul, "Meet the Parents," *American Demographics* (January 2002): 43–47.

35. Bradley Johnson, "Families Spend Less on Food as They Pursue House, Car Dreams," *Advertising Age,* February 7, 2005, 34.

36. Elke Zeijl, Yolanda te Poel, Manuela du Bois-Reymond, Janita Ravesloot, and Jacqueline J. Meulman, "The Role of Parents and Peers in the Leisure Activities of Young Adolescents," *Journal of Leisure Research* 32, no. 3 (2000): 281–302.

37. Pamela Kruger, "Why Johnny Can't Play," *Fast Company,* August 2000, 271–272. See also Daniel Thomas Cook, *The Co-modifiction of Childhood: The Children's Clothing Industry and the Rise of the Child Consumer,* Durham: Duke University Press, 2004.

38. Deborah Roedder John, "Consumer Socialization of Children: A Retrospective Look at Twenty-Five Years of Research," *Journal of Consumer Research* 26 (December 1999): 183–213.

39. Amy Rummel, John Howard, Jennifer M. Swinton, and D. Bradley Seymour, "You Can't Have That! A Study of Reactance Effects and Children's Consumer Behavior," *Journal of Marketing Theory and Practice* (Winter 2000): 38–45.

40. Gregory M. Rose, "Consumer Socialization, Parental Style, and Developmental Timetables in the United States and Japan," *Journal of Marketing* 63 (July 1999): 105–119.

41. Sabrina Neeley, "Influences on Consumer Socialization," *Young Consumers,* Quarter 1, 2005, 63–69.

42. John Fetto, "'Woof Woof' Means,'I Love You,' " *American Demographics,* February 2002, 11.

43. See, for example, Carter A. Mandrik, Edward F. Fern, and Yeqing Bao, "Intergenerational Influence in Mothers and Young Adult Daughters," *Advances in Consumer Research* 31 (2004): 697–699.

44. Barbara Olsen, "Brand Loyalty and Lineage: Exploring New Dimensions for Research," in *Advances in Consumer Research,* 20, eds. Leigh McAlister and Michael L. Rothschild (Provo, UT: Association for Consumer Research, 1993), 575–579; Marilyn Lavin, "Husband-Dominant, Wife-Dominant, Joint," *Journal of Consumer Marketing* 10 (1993): 33–42; and Vern L. Bengtson, "Beyond the Nuclear Family: The Increasing Importance of Multigenerational Bond," *Journal of Marriage and Family* (February 2001): 1–16.

45. Sanford Grossbart, Stephanie McConnell Hughes, Cara Okleshen, Stephanie Nelson, Les Carlson, Russell N. Laczniak, and Darrel Muehling, "Parents, Children, and the Internet: Socialization Perspectives," in *2001 AMA Winter Educators' Conference,* 12, eds. Ram Krishnan and Madhu Viswanathan (Chicago: American Marketing Association, 2001), 379–385.

46. June Cotte and Stacy L. Wood, "Families and Innovative Consumer Behavior: A Triadic Analysis of Sibling and Parental Influence," *Journal of Consumer Research* 31 (June 2004): 78–86.

47. Kevin Heubusch, "A Tough Job Gets Tougher," *American Demographics* (September 1997): 39.

48. Lynn White and Stacy J. Rogers, "Economic Circumstances and Family Outcomes: A Review of the 1990s," *Journal of Marriage and the Family* 62 (November 2000): 1035–1051.

49. Todd Starr Palmer, Mary Beth Pinto, and Diane H. Parente, "College Students' Credit Card Debt and the Role of Parental Involvement: Implications for Public Policy," *Journal of Public Policy and Marketing* 20, no. 1 (Spring 2001): 105–113.

50. Janice Greene, "Dogs, Dads and Laughter Bring Happiness to Kids," *San Francisco Chronicle,* November 2, 2001, 2.

51. Leah Haran, "Families Together Differently Today," *Advertising Age,* October 23, 1995, 1, 12.

52. Kim P. Corfman, "Perceptions of Relative Influence: Formation and Measurement," *Journal of Marketing Research* 28 (May 1991): 125–136. Also, for additional articles on family decision-making roles and structures, see Christina Kwai-Choi and Roger Marshall, "Who Do We Ask and When: A Pilot Study About Research in Family Decision Making," in *Developments in Marketing Science,* 16, eds. Michael Levy and Dhruv Grewal (Coral Gables, FL: Academy of Marketing Science, 1993), 30–35.

53. Joan Raymond, "For Richer and for Poorer," *American Demographics,* July 2000, 58–64.

54. John B. Ford, Michael S. LaTour, and Tony L. Henthorne, "Perception of Marital Roles in Purchase Decision Processes: A Cross-Cultural Study," *Journal of the Academy of Marketing Science* 23, no. 2 (1995): 120–131; and Tony L. Henthorne, Michael S. LaTour, and Robert Matthews, "Perception of Marital Roles in Purchase Decision Making: A Study of Japanese Couples," *Proceedings* (Chicago: American Marketing Association, 1995), 321–322.

55. James U. McNeal and Chyon-Hwa Yeh, "Development of Consumer Behavior Patterns among Chinese Children," *Journal of Consumer Marketing* 14 (1997): 45–59.

56. Gopala Ganesh, "Spousal Influence in Consumer Decisions: A Study of Cultural Assimilation," *Journal of Consumer Marketing* 14 (1997): 132–145.

57. Joyantha S. Wimalasiri, "A Cross-National Study on Children's Purchasing Behavior and Parental Response," *Journal of Consumer Marketing* 21, no. 4 (2004): 274–284; Michael J. Dotson and Eva M. Hyatt, "Major Influence Factors in Children's Consumer Socialization," *Journal of Consumer Marketing* 22, no. 1 (2005): 35–42; Aviv Shoham, "He Said, She Said . . . They Said: Parents' and Children's Assessment of Children's Influence on Family Consumption Decisions," *Journal of Consumer Marketing* 22, no. 3 (2005): 152–160, and L.A. Flurry and Alvin C. Burns, "Children's Influence in Purchase Decisions: A Social Power Theory Approach," *Journal of Business Research* 58 (May 2005): 593–601.

58. J. Labrecque and L. Ricard, "Children's Influence on Family Decision-Making: A Restaurant Study," *Journal of Business Research* 54 (November 2001): 173–176.

59. Avis Shoham, Gregory M. Rose, and Aysen Bakir, "The Effect of Family Communication Patterns on Mothers' and Fathers' Perceived Influence in Family Decision Making," *Advances in Consumer Behavior* 31 (2004): 692.

60. Michael A. Belch, Kathleen A. Krentler, and Laura A. Willis-Flurry, "Teen Internet Mavens: Influence in Family Decision Making," *Journal of Business Research* 58 (May 2005): 569–575.

61. N. Marie Marquis, "Strategies for Influencing Parental Decisions on Food Purchasing," *Journal of Consumer Marketing* 21, no. 2 (2004): 134–143.

62. O. Elizabeth Preston and Cindy L. White, "Commodifying Kids: Branded Identities and the Selling of Adspace on Kids' Networks," *Communication Quarterly* 52 (Spring 2004): 115–128; and John Consoli, "Nick Buy is

Unexpected Turn for Chevy Uplander," *Brandweek,* May 9, 2005, 7.

63. "Romantic Resurgence," *American Demographics,* August 1997, 35.

64. Stephanie Thompson, "Million-Dollar Baby," *Advertising Age,* May 30, 2005, 1, 50.

65. Sarah-Jane Muskett and Sharon Wolf, "Boomers As Grandparents," *QRCA Views* (Summer 2004): 64–68.

66. Rajshekhar G. Javalgi and Paul Dion, "A Life Cycle Segmentation Approach to Marketing Financial Products and Services," *The Services Industries Journal* 19, no. 3 (July 1999): 74–96.

67. Charles M. Schaninger and William D. Danko, "A Conceptual and Empirical Comparison of Alternative Household Life Cycle Models," *Journal of Consumer Research* 19 (March 1993): 580–594.

chapter**eleven**

❯ **Social Class and
Consumer Behavior**

S ome form of class structure or social stratification has existed in
all societies throughout the history of human existence. In contemporary societies, an indication that social classes exist is the
common reality that people who are better educated or have more
prestigious occupations such as physicians and lawyers often are
more highly valued than those who are truck drivers and farmhands.
This is so, even though all four occupations are necessary for a society's well-being. Moreover, as will be discussed later, a wide range
of differences in values, attitudes, and behavior exists among members of different social classes.

The major topics that will be explored in this chapter are a definition of social class and how it is measured, lifestyle profiles of the
social classes, social-class mobility, geodemographic clustering,
the affluent and nonaffluent consumer, the presence of a "techno-
class," and how social-class-linked attitudes and behavior influence
selected aspects of consumer behavior.

BRIDGING THE GAP BETWEEN
DECADENCE AND VIRTUE

THE RITZ-CARLTON GOLF CLUB & SPA®
JUPITER

Sipping mojitos on your lanai beside the Jack Nicklaus Signature Golf Course, it is tempting to forget you have made a purely practical choice. For a fraction of what you might have paid for a traditional second home in the Palm Beaches, your Club Home includes Spa and Clubhouse privileges, Ritz-Carlton service, twice-daily housekeeping, 35 days in residence annually and reciprocal stays in Aspen, Bachelor Gulch and the Caribbean;* not to mention, landscape maintenance by those fellows so valiantly ignoring the aroma of sizzling sirloins adrift on the breeze from your outdoor kitchen. Honestly, is anything better for one's self-esteem than the exercise of common sense?

Refundable Non-Resident Social & Spa Memberships from $45,000 and refundable Non-Resident Golf Memberships from $185,000. Fractional Ownership Real Estate from $237,000. For more information telephone 800.278.2107, E-mail us at inquiry@ritzcarltonclub.com or visit our sales center at 106 Ritz-Carlton Club Drive, off Donald Ross Road in Jupiter.**

ASPEN HIGHLANDS   ST. THOMAS   BACHELOR GULCH   JUPITER   WWW.RITZCARLTONCLUB.COM

THIS ADVERTISING MATERIAL IS BEING USED FOR THE PURPOSE OF SOLICITING SALES OF FRACTIONAL OWNERSHIP INTERESTS.
*Subject to The Ritz-Carlton Club Membership Program Reservation Procedures and the Multisite Public Offering of The Ritz-Carlton Club. **Prices are subject to change. 05-0323

what is social class?

Although **social class** can be thought of as a continuum—a range of social positions on which each member of society can be placed—researchers have preferred to divide the continuum into a small number of specific social classes, or *strata*. Within this framework, the concept of social class is used to assign individuals or families to a social-class category. Consistent with this practice, social class is defined as *the division of members of a society into a hierarchy of distinct status classes, so that members of each class have relatively the same status and members of all other classes have either more or less status.*

To appreciate more fully the nature and complexity of social class, we will briefly consider several underlying concepts pertinent to this definition.

Social class and social status

Researchers often measure social class in terms of **social status**; that is, they define each social class by the amount of status the members of that class have in comparison with members of other social classes. In social-class research (sometimes called *social stratification*), *status is frequently thought of as the relative rankings of members of each social class in terms of specific status factors*. For example, relative *wealth* (amount of economic assets), *power* (the degree of personal choice or influence over others), and *prestige* (the degree of recognition received from others) are three status factors frequently used when estimating social class.

To secure an understanding of how status operates within the minds of consumers, researchers have explored the idea of *social comparison theory*. According to this social-psychological concept, individuals quite normally compare their own material possessions with those owned by others in order to determine their relative social standing. This is especially important in a marketing society where status is often associated with consumers' purchasing power (or how much can be purchased). Simply stated, individuals with more purchasing power or a greater ability to make purchases have more status. Those who have more restrictions on what they can or cannot buy have less status. Because visible or conspicuous possessions are easy to spot, they especially serve as markers or indicators of one's own status and the status of others. Not surprisingly, research confirmed that a key ingredient of status is a consumer's possessions compared with others' similar possessions (possibly one's home versus another person's home).[1] In making such a comparison, an individual consumer might decide to compare himself with someone who is worse off (i.e., a downward comparison) in order to bolster his self-esteem; or alternatively, a consumer might elect to *compare upward* with another consumer "with more" or some idealized media image (e.g., a beautiful home in a magazine advertisement), which is likely to make the consumer feel somewhat inferior.

The dynamics of status consumption

A related concept is *status consumption*—which is the process by which consumers endeavor to increase their social standing through conspicuous consumption and possessions.[2] A number of research studies validated a status consumption scale (see Table 11.1). The development of such measures are important, for as the market for luxury or status products continues to grow, there is an even greater need for marketers to identify and understand which consumers especially seek out status-enhancing possessions, as well as the relationship between status consumption and social class.[3]

It is important to mention that a recent study in Australia examined the two interrelated concepts of status consumption and conspicuous consumption with respect to fashion clothing and sunglasses (both products that are visible or conspicuous to others

TABLE 11.1	**A Five-Question Status Consumption Scale**[a]

1. I would buy a product just because it has status.
2. I am interested in new products with status.
3. I would pay more for a product if it had status.
4. The status of a product is irrelevant to me (negatively worded).
5. A product is more valuable to me if it has some snob appeal.

[a]Each of the five items is measured on 7-point Likert (agree–disagree) scale.
Source: Jacqueline K. Eastman, Ronald E. Goldsmith, and Leisa Reinecke Flynn, "Status Consumption in Consumer Behavior: Scale Development and Validation," *Journal of Marketing Theory and Practice* (Summer 1999): 44.

and capable of providing the possessor with "status"). The research found that *status consumption* (i.e., gauges the degree to which a consumer is likely to consume for status) and *conspicuous consumption* (i.e., measures the extent to which a consumer is to consume conspicuously) are different consumer measures, yet they are related in that they both are impacted by interpersonal or word-of-mouth communication. The research also revealed that females were more prone than males to conspicuously consume; whereas only status consumption was affected by self-monitoring (i.e., the tendency for consumers to use products as "props").[4]

Although *social comparison theory* and its related activity of *status consumption* (and possibly conspicuous consumption) status have the potential of being very enlightening about status and how it operates, consumer and marketing researchers most often approach the actual study of status in terms of one or more of the following convenient demographic (more precisely socioeconomic) variables: *family income, occupational status or prestige,* and *educational attainment.* These socioeconomic variables, as expressions of status, are used by marketing practitioners on a daily basis to measure social class.

Social class is hierarchical and a form of segmentation

Social-class categories usually are ranked in a hierarchy, ranging from low to high status. Thus, members of a specific social class perceive members of other social classes as having either more or less status than they do. To many people, therefore, social-class categories suggest that others are either equal to them (about the same social class), superior to them (higher social class), or inferior to them (lower social class).

Within this context, social-class membership serves consumers as a frame of reference (or a reference group) for the development of their attitudes and behavior. In the context of reference groups, members of a specific social class may be expected to turn most often to other members of the same class for cues (or clues) regarding appropriate behavior. In other cases, members of a particular social class (e.g., upper-lower class) may aspire to advance their social-class standing by emulating the behavior of members of the middle class. To accomplish this goal, they might read middle-class magazines, do "middle-class things" (such as visit museums and advance their education), and hang out at middle-class restaurants so that they can observe middle-class behavior.[5]

The hierarchical aspect of social class is important to marketers. Consumers may purchase certain products because these products are favored by members of either their own or a higher social class (e.g., a high-priced Swiss wristwatch), and consumers may avoid other products because they perceive the products to be "lower-class" products (e.g., a "no-name" brand of sneaker). Thus, the various social-class strata provide a natural basis for market segmentation for many products and services. In many instances, consumer researchers have been able to relate aspects of product usage to social-class membership. For example, when it comes to the consumption of instant coffee throughout Europe, it appears that for German consumers instant coffee tends to be a particularly upmarket or upscale product; and in contrast, for French consumers instant coffee is a particularly downmarket or downscale product.[6]

The classification of society's members into a small number of social classes has also enabled researchers to note the existence of shared values, attitudes, and behavioral patterns among members within each social class and differing values, attitudes, and behavior *between* social classes. Consumer researchers have been able to relate social-class standing to consumer attitudes concerning specific products and to examine social-class influences on the actual consumption of products.

Social-class categories

Little agreement exists among sociologists on how many distinct class divisions are necessary to adequately describe the class structure of the United States. Most early studies divided the members of specific communities into five or six social-class groups. However, other researchers have found nine-, four-, three-, and even two-class schemas suitable for their purposes. The choice of how many separate classes to use depends on the amount of detail that the researcher believes is necessary to explain adequately the attitudes or behavior under study. Marketers are interested in the social-class structures of communities that are potential markets for their products and in the specific social-class level of their potential customers. Table 11.2 illustrates the number and diversity of social-class schemas, while Table 11.3 provides a sense of the distribution of the U.S. population according to a five-category subdivision.

TABLE 11.2	**Variations in the Number and Types of Social-Class Categories**

Two-Category Social-Class Schemas
- *Blue collar, white collar*
- *Lower, upper*
- *Lower, middle*

Three-Category Social-Class Schemas
- *Blue collar, gray collar, white collar*
- *Lower, middle, upper*

Four-Category Social-Class Schemas
- *Lower, lower-middle, upper-middle, upper*

Five-Category Social-Class Schemas
- *Lower, working class, lower-middle, upper-middle, upper*
- *Lower, lower-middle, middle, upper-middle, upper*

Six-Category Social-Class Schemas
- *Lower-lower, upper-lower, lower-middle, upper-middle, lower-upper, upper-upper*

Seven-Category Social-Class Schemas
- *Real lower-lower, a lower group of people but not the lowest, working class, middle class, upper-middle, lower-upper, upper-upper*

Nine-Category Social-Class Schemas
- *Lower-lower, middle-lower, upper-lower, lower-middle, middle-middle, upper-middle, lower-upper, middle-upper, upper-upper*

TABLE 11.3	Percent Distribution of Five-Category Social-Class Measure

SOCIAL CLASSES	PERCENTAGE
Upper	4.3
Upper-middle	13.8
Middle	32.8
Working	32.3
Lower	16.8
Total percentage	100.0

Source: Eugene Sivadas, George Mathew, and David J. Curry, "A Preliminary Examination of the Continued Significance of Social Class to Marketing: A Geodemographic Replication," *Journal of Consumer Marketing* 14, no. 6 (1997): 469. Reprinted by permission.

Table 11.3 also reveals the small size of the upper class, which is the reason why most mass marketers simply ignore it (or combine it with the upper-middle class). On the other hand, its small size and highly cultivated tastes make the upper class a particularly desirable target market for specialty firms with a specific expertise and the ability to cater to the small number of particularly affluent consumers (see Figure 11.1).

the measurement of social class

There is no general agreement on how to measure social class. To a great extent, researchers are uncertain about the underlying dimensions of social-class structure. To attempt to resolve this dilemma, researchers have used a wide range of measurement techniques that they believe give a fair approximation of social class.

Systematic approaches for measuring social class fall into the following broad categories: **subjective measures**, **reputational measures**, and **objective measures** of social class.

Subjective measures

In the *subjective* approach to measuring social class, individuals are asked to estimate their own social-class positions. Typical of this approach is the following question:

Which one of the following four categories best describes your social class: the lower class, the lower-middle class, the upper-middle class, or the upper class?

Lower class	[ ]
Lower-middle class	[ ]
Upper-middle class	[ ]
Upper class	[ ]
Do not know/refuse to answer	[ ]

The resulting classification of social-class membership is based on the participants' self-perceptions or self-images. Social class is treated as a personal phenomenon, one that reflects an individual's sense of belonging or identification with others. This feeling of social-group membership is often referred to as **class consciousness**.

FIGURE 11.1

Source: © 2005, DC Ranch
L.L.C. The DC Ranch & Silverleaf
names & related marks are
registered trademarks.
(www.silverleaf.com)

Featuring a Particularly
Upscale Residence and
Lifestyle

BRIDGING THE GAP BETWEEN
DECADENCE *AND* VIRTUE

THE RITZ-CARLTON GOLF CLUB & SPA®
JUPITER

Sipping mojitos on your lanai beside the Jack Nicklaus Signature Golf Course, it is tempting to forget you have made a purely practical choice. For a fraction of what you might have paid for a traditional second home in the Palm Beaches, your Club Home includes Spa and Clubhouse privileges, Ritz-Carlton service, twice-daily housekeeping, 35 days in residence annually and reciprocal stays in Aspen, Bachelor Gulch and the Caribbean;* not to mention, landscape maintenance by those fellows so valiantly ignoring the aroma of sizzling sirloins adrift on the breeze from your outdoor kitchen. Honestly, is anything better for one's self-esteem than the exercise of common sense?

Refundable Non-Resident Social & Spa Memberships from $45,000 and refundable Non-Resident Golf Memberships from $185,000. Fractional Ownership Real Estate from $237,000.* For more information telephone 800.278.2107, E-mail us at inquiry@ritzcarltonclub.com or visit our sales center at 106 Ritz-Carlton Club Drive, off Donald Ross Road in Jupiter.

ASPEN HIGHLANDS   ST. THOMAS   BACHELOR GULCH   JUPITER   WWW.RITZCARLTONCLUB.COM

THIS ADVERTISING MATERIAL IS BEING USED FOR THE PURPOSE OF SOLICITING SALES OF FRACTIONAL OWNERSHIP INTERESTS.
*Subject to The Ritz-Carlton Club Membership Program Reservation Procedures and the Multisite Public Offering of The Ritz-Carlton Club. **Prices are subject to change. 05-0323

Subjective measures of social-class membership tend to produce an overabundance of people who classify themselves as middle class (thus, understating the number of people—the "fringe people"—who would, perhaps, be more correctly classified as either lower or upper class).[7] Moreover, it is likely that the subjective perception of one's social-class membership, as a reflection of one's self-image, is related to product usage and consumption preferences (see Chapter 5). This is not only an American phenomenon. Every year in Japan, a "Life of the Nation" survey asks citizens to place themselves into one of five social-class categories: upper, upper-middle, middle-middle, lower-middle, and lower class. Whereas in the late 1950s over 70 percent of respondents placed themselves into one of the three middle-class categories, by the late 1960s, and continuing on through today, close to 90 percent categorize themselves as "middle class."[8] Again, this demonstrates the tendency for consumers to report seeing themselves as "middle class."

Reputational measures

The *reputational* approach for measuring social class requires selected community informants to make initial judgments concerning the social-class membership of others within the community. The final task of assigning community members to social-class positions, however, belongs to the trained researcher.

Sociologists have used the reputational approach to obtain a better understanding of the specific class structures of communities under study. Consumer researchers, however, are concerned with the measurement of social class to understand markets and consumption behavior better, not social structure. In keeping with this more focused goal, the reputational approach has proved to be impractical.

Objective measures

In contrast to the subjective and reputational methods, which require people to envision their own class standing or that of other community members, *objective* measures consist of selected demographic or socioeconomic variables concerning the individual(s) under study. These variables are measured through questionnaires that ask respondents several factual questions about themselves, their families, or their places of residence. When selecting objective measures of social class, most researchers favor one or more of the following variables: occupation, amount of income, and education. To these socioeconomic factors they sometimes add geodemographic clustering data in the form of zip code and residence-neighborhood information. These socioeconomic indicators are especially important as a means of locating concentrations of consumers with specific social-class membership.

Socioeconomic measures of social class are of considerable value to marketers concerned with segmenting markets. Marketing managers who have developed socioeconomic profiles of their target markets can locate these markets (i.e., identify and measure them) by studying the socioeconomic data periodically issued by the United States Bureau of the Census and numerous commercial geodemographic data services. To reach a desired target market, marketers match the *socioeconomic profiles* of their target audiences to the *audience profiles* of selected advertising media. Socioeconomic audience profiles are regularly developed and routinely made available to potential advertisers by most of the mass media (see Table 11.4). Readers' median income data for a selection of print media are presented in Table 11.5.

Objective measures of social class fall into two basic categories: **single-variable indexes** and **composite-variable indexes**.

Single-variable indexes

A single-variable index uses just one socioeconomic variable to evaluate social-class membership. Some of the variables that are used for this purpose are discussed next.

Occupation   Occupation is a widely accepted and probably the best-documented measure of social class because it reflects occupational status.[9] The importance of occupation as a social-class indicator is dramatized by the frequency with which people ask others they meet for the first time, "What do you do for a living?" The response to this question serves as a guide in sizing up (or evaluating and forming opinions of) others.

More important, marketers frequently think in terms of specific occupations when defining a target market for their products (such as "Accountants are our best customers for late Spring—after April 15th—Caribbean Island vacations") or broader occupational categories ("We target our ultra-deluxe 7-day cruises to

TABLE 11.4	Socioeconomic Profile of *GQ* Readers		
Subscription:	587,917	72%	
Newsstand:	227,960	28%	
Total Average Paid Circulation:	**815,877**	**100%**	
	AUD (000)	**COMP**	**INDEX**
Total Adults	**4,743**	**100%**	
Men	3,346	71%	147
Women	1,397	29%	57
Age			
18–24	1,009	21%	165
18–34	2,610	55%	175
18–49	4,174	88%	142
25–49	3,165	67%	136
Median Age: 33.5			
Marital Status			
Single	2,982	63%	145
Married	1,761	37%	66
Education			
Attended/Graduated College	3,444	73%	140
Graduated College+	1,536	32%	131
Income			
HHI $50,000+	2,993	63%	123
HHI $100,000+	1,086	23%	129
Median HHI: $65,450			

Source: ABC December 2004; MRI Fall 2004, updated April 2005, see: **http://www.condenastmediakit.com/gq/circulation.cfm**

executives and professionals"). Still further, the likelihood that particular occupations would be receptive to certain products or services often provides the basis for an occupational screener requirement for participation in focus groups or survey research and for marketers to select occupational databases to target with direct-marketing campaigns (e.g., a list of male college professors teaching in the San Francisco, California area).

Figure 11.2 presents findings from a continuing survey undertaken by the Gallup organization that estimates the relative honesty and perceived ethical standards that people assign to a sample of basic occupational titles. Because this ranking is based more on respect or societal prestige (a form of status) than on wealth, it is not surprising that the rankings (i.e., from top to bottom) does *not* seem to suggest that occupations toward the top half of the figure earn higher incomes or require more formal education than those toward the bottom half.

Within the domain of occupational status, there has also been an increasing trend toward self-employment among business and professional people. Specifically, it appears that business executives and professionals who are self-employed or entrepreneurs are substantially more likely to be *very wealthy* than their counterparts who work for someone else.[10] This link between self-employment and higher incomes is consistent with the trend of increasing numbers of business school graduates seeking to work for themselves rather than going to work for a "big business."

TABLE 11.5	Readers' Median Household Income for Selected Publications

NEWSPAPER/MAGAZINE	MEDIAN HOUSEHOLD INCOME
Conde Nast Traveler	$104,984
Wine Spectator	103,785
Delta's SKY Magazine	102,620
Yachting	87,717
Barron's	87,371
Money	86,461
Golf Digest	84,389
Business Week	81,381
Coastal Living	81,178
Motor Boating	78,942
PC Magazine	74,099
Consumer Reports	74,028
O, The Oprah Magazine	68,373
Newsweek	66,234
Sports Illustrated	64,026
Popular Photography & Imaging	60,742
Psychology Today	60,422
American Photo	59,985
Glamour	57,865
Country Living	56,443
Entertainment Weekly	56,006
Modern Bride	54,281
Town & Country	54,120
Family Circle	53,617
AARP The Magazine	48,457
Star	45,171
Scholastic Parent & Child	42,499
Essence	39,448
Soap Opera Weekly	37,706

Source: From *2005 Magazine Audience Estimates* (New York: Mediamark Research, Inc.). Reprinted by permission.

Still further, it is also noteworthy to keep in mind that although the status of a particular occupation may change significantly over time, evidence suggests that when it comes to the status of some 40 occupations (studied between 1976 and 2000) a high degree of *status consistency* was found.[11] Specifically, certain occupations (e.g., U.S. Supreme Court justices and physicians) were consistently ranked high over the many years of the research, whereas other occupations (e.g., farmhands and taxi drivers) were consistently ranked low during the same period of time.

Education The level of a person's formal education is another commonly accepted approximation of social-class standing. Generally speaking, the more education a person has, the more likely it is that the person is well paid (or has a higher income) and has

FIGURE 11.2

Occupational Rankings in Terms of Honesty and Ethical Standards

Question: Please tell me how you would rate the honesty and ethical standards of people in these different fields—very high, high, average, low, or very low?

Source: The Gallup Poll Monthly, November 2004. Reprinted by permission. At http://www.gallup.com/poll/content/default.aspx?ci=1654

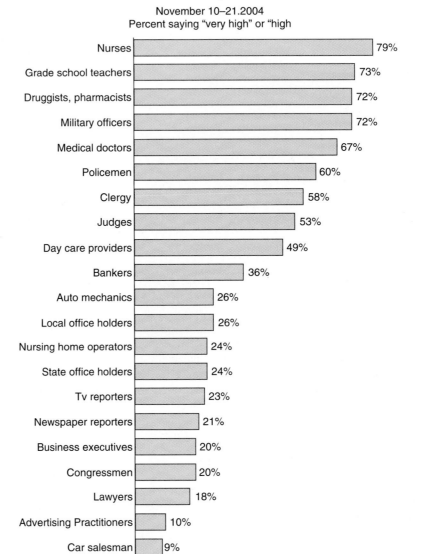

November 10–21.2004
Percent saying "very high" or "high

Nurses	79%
Grade school teachers	73%
Druggists, pharmacists	72%
Military officers	72%
Medical doctors	67%
Policemen	60%
Clergy	58%
Judges	53%
Day care providers	49%
Bankers	36%
Auto mechanics	26%
Local office holders	26%
Nursing home operators	24%
State office holders	24%
Tv reporters	23%
Newspaper reporters	21%
Business executives	20%
Congressmen	20%
Lawyers	18%
Advertising Practitioners	10%
Car salesman	9%

an admired or respected position (high occupational status).[12] Using U.S. census data, Table 11.6 supports the close relationship between educational attainment and amount of household income.

Research has shown that different social classes often approach the notion of a college degree very differently. For example, students at the most selective universities in the country are often the sons and daughters of upper-class Americans, while lower-class children are often encouraged to "get a good job." In a recent series of articles on social class, a 50-year-old man whose father was a factory worker, was quoted as saying: "The whole concept of life was that you should get a good job in the factory . . . if I'd said I wanted to go to college, it would have been like saying I wanted to grow gills and breathe underwater."[13] Almost one in three Americans in their mid-20s today is a college dropout (compared to one in five in the late 1960s), and most are members of poor and working-class families. In contrast, the children of the middle and upper-classes more often stay in college until they graduate "because they can hardly imagine doing otherwise."[14]

TABLE 11.6	The Relationship Between Formal Education and Family Income						
	TOTAL	**LESS THAN 9TH GRADE**	**SOME HIGH SCHOOL**	**HIGH SCHOOL GRADUATE**	**SOME COLLEGE (NO DEGREE)**	**ASSOCIATES DEGREE**	**BACHELOR'S DEGREE OR MORE**
All Households[a]	100%	100%	100%	100%	100%	100%	100%
Under $15,000	8.8	24.5	19.7	10.2	6.6	5.2	2.9
$15,000 to $24,999	10.9	25.3	20.6	13.7	9.6	6.6	3.7
$25,000 to $34,999	11.7	17.8	18.6	14.3	12.5	10.4	5.2
$35,000 to $49,999	15.6	16.2	17.9	18.8	17.0	17.2	10.0
$50,000 to $74,999	21.1	9.5	14.6	22.9	24.5	25.5	20.3
$75,000 to $99,999	13.6	3.9	4.8	11.2	14.9	18.3	18.8
$100,000 and over	18.3	2.7	3.9	8.9	14.8	16.8	39.1
Number of families (000)	70,722	4,306	6,176	21,769	12,627	5,956	19,887
Median income	$51,407	$25,077	$29,512	$43,870	$53,809	$60,033	$84,836

[a]Persons 25 years old and over

Source: U.S. Census Bureau, Statistical Abstract of the United States: 2004–2005; accessed at **www.census.gov/prod/www/statistical-abstract-04.html**

Income   Individual or family income is another socioeconomic variable frequently used to approximate social-class standing. Researchers who favor income as a measure of social class use either *amount* or *source* of income. Table 11.7 illustrates the types of categories used for each of these income variables. Available research suggests that income works best in accounting for leisure consumption when measured in terms of ("engaging in" or "doing or not doing") a particular leisure activity (such as snow skiing, bowling, or playing basketball or golf).[15]

A recent effort to differentiate between "income" and "wealth" points up that: (1) Wealth, not income, is the primary driver to financial freedom—wealth, not income, is a function of savings, so to achieve wealth you have to increase your net worth, and not just your income; (2) Wealth and money are not the same—wealth deals with the creation of resources and money deals more with consumption; (3) For wealth you need to network and build personal alliances, because a great deal of the information needed to create wealth is passed along via such relationships; and (4) You need to find ways to minimize your taxes, because taxes reduce your ability to create wealth.[16]

TABLE 11.7	Typical Categories Used for Assessing Amount or Source of Income
AMOUNT OF INCOME	**SOURCE OF INCOME**
Under $25,000 per year	Public welfare
$25,000 to $49,999	Private financial assistance
$50,000 to $74,999	Wages (hourly)
$75,000 to $99,999	Salary (yearly)
$100,000 to $124,999	Profits or fees
$125,000 to $149,999	Earned wealth
$150,000 to $174,999	Inherited wealth, interest, dividends, royalties
$175,000 to $199,999	
$200,000 and over	

TABLE 11.8	Distribution of Income Growth to Income Group, 1979–2000
INCOME GROUP (HOUSEHOLDS)	**SHARE OF INCOME GROWTH, 1979–2000**
Poorest 20%	0.8%
Middle 20%	5.1
Richest 20%	74.0
80–85%	21.5
95–99%	14.1
Richest 1%	38.4

Source: Michael D. Yates, "A Statistical Portrait of the U.S. Working Class," *Monthly Review* 56 (April 2005): 20.

It is important to point out that the distribution of income and net worth in the United States has become more unbalanced over the past few decades. For example, in the year 2001, the richest 1 percent of households possessed almost 34 percent of all net worth, while the bottom 90 percent of all households had 28.5 percent. It is accurate to state that the trend has been that the rich get richer, and the poor get poorer. Table 11.8, which presents the distribution of income growth to income group from 1979 to 2000, clearly shows that while the income of the richest 1 percent of all households grew 38.4 percent during this time period, the income growth for the poorest 20 percent of households was less than 1 percent.[17]

Although income is a popular estimate of social-class standing, not all consumer researchers agree that it is an appropriate index of social class. Some argue that a blue-collar electrician and a white-collar administrative assistant may both earn $57,000 a year, yet because of (or as a reflection of) social-class differences, each will spend that income in a different way. How they decide to spend their incomes reflects different values. Within this context, it is the difference in values that is an important discriminant of social class between people, not the amount of income they earn.

Substantiating the importance of consumers' personal values, rather than amount of income, is the observation that affluence may be more a function of attitude or behavior than of income level.[18] These "adaptational affluent" consumers represent a broad segment who do not have the income needed to be considered affluent in today's society, yet they desire to have the best. They buy less but buy better quality, assigning priorities and gradually working their way toward having everything they want.

Researchers have explored the question of how envious the "have-nots" are of what the "haves" possess. As revealed by Figure 11.3, the 18- to 34-year-old age group is most jealous of what their neighbors have and, across all age categories, money was the most coveted item, with "good health or physical appearance" and "physical fitness" ranking a distant second and third.[19]

Other Variables Quality of neighborhood and dollar value of residence are rarely used as sole measures of social class. However, they are used informally to support or verify social-class membership assigned on the basis of occupational status or income.

Finally, possessions have been used by sociologists as an index of social class.[20] The best-known and most elaborate rating scheme for evaluating possessions is **Chapin's Social Status Scale**, which focuses on the presence of certain items of furniture and accessories in the living room (types of floor or floor covering, drapes, fireplace, library table, telephone, or bookcases) and the condition of the room (cleanliness, organization, or general atmosphere).[21] Conclusions are drawn about a family's social class on the basis of such observations. To illustrate how home decorations reflect social-class standing, lower-class families are likely to place their television sets in the living room and bedrooms, whereas middle- and upper-class families usually place their television sets in one or more of the following rooms: bedrooms, family room, or a media room (*but **not** in*

FIGURE 11.3

Covert Thy Neighbor's Goods

Source: Christopher Reynolds, "Up on the Envy Meter," *American Demographics.* June 2004, 7.

THE YOUNG AND THE GREEN
Green—with envy,that is. We found that younger people admit to jealousy far more frequently than older folks do. Money is naturally where most of us break the 10th commandment (Thou shalt not covet thy neighbor's, goods). Among most age groups, except younger respondents, friends are most often the primary target of envy. Young adults most want what celebs have.
WHEN YOU HAVE FOUND YOURSELF WANTING POSSESSIONS, PERSONAL TRAITS, OR LIFESTYLES THAT OTHER PEOPLE HAVE, WOULD YOU SAY THAT THE OTHER PEOPLE WERE MOST OFTEN"?

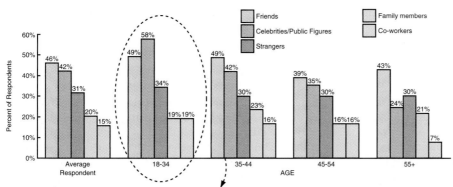

The younger demographic's desire for the things that celebrities and public figures have overshadows any other group's covetous nature.

Source: *American Demographics*/Harris Interactive

the living room). The marketing implications of such insights suggest that advertisements for television sets targeted at lower-class consumers should show the set in a living room, whereas advertisements directed to middle- or upper-class consumers should show the set in a bedroom, a family room, or a media room.

Composite-variable indexes

Composite indexes systematically combine a number of socioeconomic factors to form one overall measure of social-class standing. Such indexes are of interest to consumer researchers because they may better reflect the complexity of social class than single-variable indexes. For instance, research exploring consumers' perceptions of mail and phone order shopping reveals that the *higher* the socioeconomic status (in terms of a composite of income, occupational status, and education), the more positive are the consumers' ratings of mail and phone order buying, relative to in-store shopping.[22] The same research also found that downscale consumers (a composite of lower scores on the three variables) were less positive toward magazine and catalog shopping and more positive toward in-store shopping than more upscale socioeconomic groupings. Armed with such information, retailers such as Kmart, Wal-Mart, and Target that especially target *working-class* consumers would have a real challenge using direct-marketing catalogs and telephone-selling approaches. In contrast, retailers concentrating on upscale consumers, such as Neiman Marcus and Saks, have been especially effective in developing catalog programs targeted to specific segments of affluent or upscale consumers.

Two of the more important composite indexes are the **Index of Status Characteristics** and the **Socioeconomic Status Score**:

1. Index of Status Characteristics. *A classic composite measure of social class is Warner's Index of Status Characteristics (ISC).*[23] *The ISC is a weighted measure of the following socioeconomic variables: occupation, source of income (not amount of income), house type, and dwelling area (quality of neighborhood).*

2. Socioeconomic Status Scores. *The United States Bureau of the Census developed the Socioeconomic Status Score (SES), which combines three basic socioeconomic variables: occupation, family income, and educational attainment.*[24]

lifestyle profiles of the social classes

Consumer research has found evidence that within each of the social classes, there is a constellation of specific lifestyle factors (shared beliefs, attitudes, activities, and behaviors) that tends to distinguish the members of each class from the members of all other social classes.

To capture the lifestyle composition of the various social-class groupings, Table 11.9 presents a consolidated portrait, pieced together from numerous sources, of the members of the following six social classes: upper-upper class, lower-upper class, upper-middle class, lower-middle class, upper-lower class, and lower-lower class. Each of these profiles is only a generalized picture of the class. People in any class may possess values, attitudes, and behavioral patterns that are a hybrid of two or more classes.

China: pursuing a middle-class lifestyle

In recent years, established marketers from all over the world have singled out China as a highly desirable growth market for their brands. These marketers have been anxious to satisfy China's rapidly expanding urban middle class's appetite for consumer goods. Specifically, the wealthiest 20 percent of urban Chinese households (about 80 million people) constitutes a highly attractive market. These relatively affluent urban Chinese consumers are primarily composed of the two following segments: (1) "little rich"—those 15 percent with annual household income of about $3,200, and (2) "yuppies"—those 5 percent with annual household income of about $9,500.[25] Although household incomes between $3,200 and $9,500, on first glance, do not seem like much, this conclusion can be a real error. With small families and housing and other costs subsidized by the government, an urban Chinese family is able to have a relatively good lifestyle on a relatively small income. The "secret" is that a fairly large amount of a family's income is discretionary income (i.e., income that can be spent on a wide range of nonnecessities).

It is of interest to note that it has only been since the late 1990s that local brands have existed in China. And while multinational companies have targeted China's middle class, local brands have made huge inroads in the past few years with the rest of China's population.. These local brands are often the equal of Western brands in terms of reliability and functionality, and they tend to be far less expensive. With the exception of Proctor & Gamble, large local brands tend to outspend multinationals with respect to consumer advertising.[26]

social-class mobility

Social-class membership in the United States is not as hard and fixed as it is in some other countries and cultures. Although individuals can move either up or down in social-class standing from the class position held by their parents, Americans have primarily thought in terms of **upward mobility** because of the availability of free education and opportunities for self-development and self-advancement. Indeed, the classic Horatio Alger tale of a penniless young orphan who managed to achieve great success in business and in life is depicted over and over again in American novels, movies, and television shows. Today many young men and women with ambition to get ahead dream of going to college and eventually starting their own successful businesses.

Because upward mobility has commonly been attainable in American society, the higher social classes often become reference groups for ambitious men and women of lower social status. Familiar examples of upward mobility are the new management trainee who strives to dress like the boss, the middle manager who aspires to belong to the status country club, or the graduate of a municipal college who wants to send his daughter to Stanford.

TABLE 11.9	**Social-Class Profiles**

The Upper-Upper Class—Country Club Establishment
- *Small number of well-established families*
- *Belong to best country clubs and sponsor major charity events*
- *Serve as trustees for local colleges and hospitals*
- *Prominent physicians and lawyers*
- *May be heads of major financial institutions, owners of major long-established firms*
- *Accustomed to wealth, so do not spend money conspicuously*

The Lower-Upper Class—New Wealth
- *Not quite accepted by the upper crust of society*
- *Represent "new money"*
- *Successful business executives*
- *Conspicuous users of their new wealth*

The Upper-Middle Class—Achieving Professionals
- *Have neither family status nor unusual wealth*
- *Career oriented*
- *Young successful professionals, corporate managers, and business owners*
- *Most are college graduates, many with advanced degrees*
- *Active in professional, community, and social activities*
- *Have a keen interest in obtaining the "better things in life"*
- *Their homes serve as symbols of their achievements*
- *Consumption is often conspicuous*
- *Very child oriented*

The Lower-Middle Class—Faithful Followers
- *Primarily nonmanagerial white-collar workers and highly paid blue-collar workers*
- *Want to achieve respectability and be accepted as good citizens*
- *Want their children to be well-behaved*
- *Tend to be churchgoers and are often involved in church-sponsored activities*
- *Prefer a neat and clean appearance and tend to avoid faddish or highly styled clothing*
- *Constitute a major market for do-it-yourself products*

The Upper-Lower Class—Security-Minded Majority
- *The largest social-class segment*
- *Solidly blue collar*
- *Strive for security (sometimes gained from union membership)*
- *View work as a means to "buy" enjoyment*
- *Want children to behave properly*
- *High wage earners in this group may spend impulsively*
- *Interested in items that enhance their leisure time (e.g., TV sets, hunting equipment)*
- *Husbands typically have a strong "macho" self-image*
- *Males are sports fans, heavy smokers, beer drinkers*

The Lower-Lower Class—Rock Bottom
- *Poorly educated, unskilled laborers*
- *Often out of work*
- *Children are often poorly treated*
- *Tend to live a day-to-day existence*

Recognizing that individuals often aspire to the lifestyle and possessions enjoyed by members of a higher social class, marketers frequently incorporate the symbols of higher-class membership, both as products and props in advertisements targeted to lower social-class audiences. For example, ads often present or display marketers' products within an upper-class setting.

Sometimes a more direct appeal to consumers' sense of having products that are normally restricted to members of other social classes is an effective message. For instance, if a direct marketer of consumer electronics were to promote a top-of-the-line HDTV set (such as a high-end Hitachi 42-inch plasma set), usually purchased by ultra-wealthy home owners, as "now it's your turn to have what families living in the big houses have enjoyed" (it's been marked down to about 50 percent of the original price), this would be a marketing message that encourages household consumers to have a "dream TV" in their homes.

Another characteristic of social-class mobility is that products and services traditionally within the realm of one social class may filter down to lower social classes. For instance, plastic surgery was once affordable only for movie stars and other wealthy consumers. Today, however, consumers of all economic strata undergo cosmetic procedures.

Some signs of downward mobility

Although the United States is frequently associated with *upward mobility,* because it was the "rule" for much of its history that each generation within a family tended to "do better" than the last generation, there now are signs of some **downward mobility**. Social commentators have suggested that some young adults (such as members of the X-Generation described in Chapter 13) are not only likely to find it difficult to "do better" than their successful parents (e.g., to get better jobs, own homes, have more disposable income, and have more savings) but also may *not* even do as well as their parents.

There is some evidence of such a slide in social-class mobility. Specifically, researchers have found that the odds that young men's income will reach middle-class levels by the time they reach their thirtieth birthday have been slowly declining.[27] This regressive pattern holds true, regardless of race, parents' income, and young persons' educational level.

Is horatio alger dead?

While many Americans still believe in the Horatio Alger rags-to-riches story, there is a growing body of evidence that social mobility in America is not what it used to be. For example, income inequality is rising to levels not seen since the 1880s—the Gilded Age, and the gap between the rich and the poor has widened since 1970. While the income of households in the top fifth grew 70 percent between 1979 and 2000, the real income of households in the bottom fifth rose only 6.4 percent. Although most Americans find little wrong with income inequality, as long as there still exists plenty of social mobility, there are signs that social mobility is falling. One recent study examined 2,749 father-and-son pairs and found that few sons ever got to move up the class ladder. Another research effort found that out of over six thousand American families studied, 42 percent of the individuals born into the poorest fifth ended up there, at the bottom, with another 24 percent moving up only slightly, to the next-to-bottom group. Only 10 percent of adult men born into the bottom quarter ever made it to the top quarter. It has been reported that currently, a child born into poverty in Europe or Canada has a better chance at prosperity than one born in the United States, and that "Americans are no more or less likely to rise above, or fall below, their parents' economic class than they were 35 years ago."[28] Still further, a recent article commented that:

> So it appears that while it is easier for a few high achievers to scale the summits of wealth, for many others it has become harder to move up from one economic class to another. Americans are arguably more likely than they were 30 years ago to end up in the class into which they were born.[29]

geodemographic clustering

In recent years, traditional social-class measures have been enhanced by linking consumer-related geographic and socioeconomic data to create more powerful **geodemographic clusters**. The underlying rationale for geodemographic clustering is that "birds of a feather flock together." This is to say that families of similar socioeconomic backgrounds tend to reside in the same neighborhoods or communities—that is, "they cluster together." Furthermore, throughout a large and diversified country, like the United States, there are dispersed communities made up of similar people with similar geographic profiles. Employing a variety of consumer research methodologies, these communities can be defined, then they can be identified or located in terms of their zip codes and/or postal routes. Still further, they can be "added together" or combined to create a considerably larger "geodemographic cluster" (often given a distinctive name). These larger clusters can then be marketed to (often using direct marketing).

One of the most popular clustering services is **PRIZM NE** (i.e., "new edition") from Claritas (**www.claritas.com**), which identifies a variety of socioeconomic and demographic factors (education, income, occupation, family life cycle, ethnicity, housing, and urbanization) drawn from U.S. census data. This material is combined with survey and panel data on actual consumer behavior (e.g., product purchase and usage, mail-order buying, and media-exposure habits) to locate concentrations of consumers with similar characteristics. Experts point to the benefits of marketing to consumer clusters:

> *America has become a nation of such diversity that the clusters are essential to finding people most interested in your products and services. For consumers, the value of clusters is that they don't have to wade through a lot of junk mail that misses the target. What's the point of an apartment dweller getting a pitch for buying a lawn mower?*[30]

PRIZM NE assigns every one of the microneighborhoods in the United States (zip code + 4 areas) to one of 66 PRIZM NE clusters, which can be further collapsed into 15 groups (U1—Urban Uptown through T4—Rustic Living). Table 11.10 shows eight examples of PRIZM NE cluster segments drawn from specific socioeconomic categories. Marketers can superimpose these geodemographic clusters onto a host of product and service usage data, media-exposure data, and lifestyle data (such as VALS, discussed in Chapter 5) to create a sharp, refined picture of their target markets. To illustrate the usefulness of such information, Table 11.11 presents an overview profile of the "Up-and-Comers" PRIZM NE cluster.

the affluent consumer

Affluent households constitute an especially attractive target segment because its members have incomes that provide them with a disproportionately larger share of all discretionary income—the "extras" that allow the purchase of luxury cruises, foreign sports cars, time-sharing ski-resort condos, fine jewelry, and ready access to home PCs, laptops, and surfing on the Internet. It has also been pointed out there is a strong positive relationship between health and economic status—that is, "the healthiest people are those who are economically advantaged" and "poverty is bad for you."[31] Indeed, higher income and more highly educated people are less likely to die of heart disease, strokes, diabetes, and many types of cancer, and affluent Americans live longer and in better health than middle-class Americans, who live longer and in better health than individuals at the bottom.[32] Conversely, evidence suggests that children of the affluent may have problems with substance abuse, anxiety, and depression, which can be caused by excessive pressures to achieve and isolation from parents (both physically and emotionally).[33]

The wealth of Americans grew dramatically during the 1990s partially due to the longest bull market in U.S. history. By 2004, the total personal wealth of American households was a record $48.5 trillion, a gain of 8.8 percent over 2003.[34] From 2002 to 2004, the number of high net worth individuals (HNWIs) in North America, that is, individuals with a minimum net worth of $1 million, grew by 9.7 percent, for a total

TABLE 11.10 Sample PRIZM Cluster Segments Drawn from All 62 Clusters to Reflect a Range of Socioeconomic Groups

CODES	CLUSTER NUMBER	CLUSTER NICKNAME/ DESCRIPTION	PERCENT OF U.S. HOUSEHOLDS	MEDIAN HOUSEHOLD INCOME	KEY EDUCATION LEVEL	KEY OCCUPATIONAL LEVEL	PREDOMINANT AGE RANGE(S)
S1 Elite Suburbs (Suburban)	01	Upper Crust/ Privileged superrich families	1.51%	$103,735	College grad+	Professional	45+
U1 Urban Uptown (Urban)	04	Young Digerati/ Tech-Savvy singles and couples	1.26%	$79,151	College grad+	Professional	25–44
S2 The Affluentials (Suburban)	15	Pools & Patios/ Mature Empty Nest Couples	1.22%	$66,885	College grad+	Professional and white collar	45+
T2 Country Comfort (Rural)	32	New Homesteaders/ Young, middle-class families	1.73%	$53,627	High school	White collar, blue collar, service	25–44
C2 City Centers (Urban)	27	Middleburg Managers/Empty nesters settled in nesters satellite communities	1.87%	$47,331	High school/ college	Professional and white collar	55+
T3 Middle American (Rural)	43	Heartlanders/ Middle age couples with working class jobs	1.93%	$39,957	High school	Blue collar and farm	45+
C3 Micro-City Blues (Urban)	53	Mobility Blues/ Young singles and single parents in satellite cities	1.29%	$28,173	High school	Blue collar and service	<35
U3 Urban Core	61	City Roots/ Lower income retirees, many Hispanic and African-American	1.2%	$25,639	Elementary/ High school	Blue collar, white collar, service	65+

Source: Claritas, Inc. Accessed at **www.claritas.com**

TABLE 11.11	A Profile of PRIZM NE Cluster: "Up-and-Comers" (Cluster 24)
SOCIOECONOMIC FACTORS	**CHARACTERISTIC OF THE CLUSTER**
Percent of U.S. households	1.23%
Predominant age range	<35
Social group	City Centers
Lifestage group	Young Achievers
Ethnic diversity	White, Asian
Family types	Mixed
Education levels	H.S./College
Employment levels	Professional, white-collar
Housing types	Renters
Income	Midscale
Lifestyle Traits	
Use Internet for job search	
Shop at Ann Taylor	
Read *Shape*	
Watch MTV	
Drive a Mitsubishi Eclipse	

Source: Claritas, Inc., accessed at **www.clusterbigip1.claritas.com/claritas/Default.jsp?main=3&submenu=seg&subcat=segprizmne**

HNWI population of 2.7 million.[35] The affluent market is increasingly attracting marketers. Whirlpool Corporation, for example, the leading home appliance manufacturer in the United States, realizes that as more and more consumers own household appliances, it can no longer rely on volume to increase profits. So the firm now focuses on upscale products that are so profitable they can sell fewer appliances and still make more money. Its Duet line, a $2,200 washer-dryer set, sold so well in the first six months after its introduction that Whirlpool had to double its sales projections.[36]

According to the Census Bureau, one out of every four households in the United States can now be classified as "mass affluent," which is defined as people living in households with annual incomes of at least $75,000. In 1980, this number was one out of every seven households. And "mass affluent" households are different than less- or non-affluent households. For example, as depicted in Figure 11.4, they place more importance on friendships, leisure time, and hobbies, and less importance on money and religion.[37]

While the affluent market is most often defined by income or net worth, one research study explored this market to examine whether such a definition was sufficient. The study proposed that an operational definition of "affluent" should also include both lifestyle and psychographic factors because the heads of affluent households have a tendency to behave and think affluently. Using a richer mix of factors, researchers have been able to reclassify about one-third of the households, and to create a more useful definition for "affluent consumers."[38]

For over 25 years, Mendelsohn Media Research has conducted an annual study of the **affluent market** (currently defined in terms of three affluent segments: those with household incomes of $75,000 to $99,999 per year—the "least affluent," those with incomes of $100,000 to $199,999 per year—the "medium affluent," and those with incomes of $200,000 or more per year—the "most affluent"). Of the approximately $6.62 trillion in 2004 total household income in the United States, these "affluent households" ($75,000+) account for $4.0 trillion, or about 60 percent. Although it consists of only 26 percent of total

FIGURE 11.4

Importance of Various Aspects of Life Mass Affluents vs. Non-Affluents

Source: Raksha Arora, "Affluent Americans: Priorities of the Prosperous," *Gallup Poll News Service,* February 8, 2005, 2.

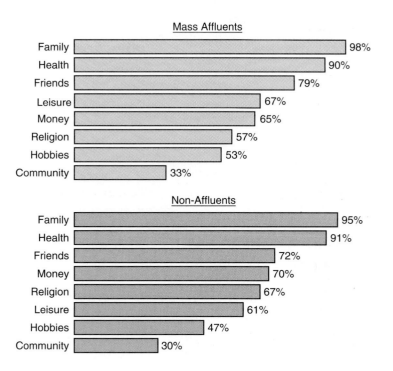

U.S. households, this upscale market segment consumed more wine (2.4 drinks per week per adult), took more domestic airline flights (7.1 flights annually per adult), owned more vehicles (2.5 per household), and held more securities ($270,300 per household) than nonaffluent households. The average household income for these consumers is $134,800, and 59 percent of this group are employed in either a professional or managerial capacity.[39] Figure 11.5 presents additional information as to average household expenditures for selected purchases for the three affluent segments. The results reveal that although the first two segments of affluent consumers certainly spend ample amounts purchasing a wide variety of products, in most cases the "most affluent" purchasers spend significantly more. For instance, when it comes to desktop, laptop, and handheld computers, the "least affluent" spent $1,469 and the "medium affluent" spent $1,716, whereas the "most affluent" spent $2,617. Figure 11.6 presents some further insights about this much sought after market segment in terms of a comparison of the sports participation of the three segments of affluent consumers. The results reveal that the "most affluent" are more likely than members of the two other affluent consumer segments to participate in a sampling of sports.[40] An examination of these two figures explains why marketers are so eager to target affluent consumers.

Still further, a growing subcategory of the affluent overall affluent market are the *millionaires.* As already cited, there are currently approximately 2.7 million individuals or families with a net worth that is at least $1 million. Contrary to common stereotypes, these millionaires are quite similar to nonmillionaires. They are typically first-generation wealthy, often working for themselves in "ordinary" nonglamour businesses. They work hard and frequently live in nonpretentious homes, often next door to nonmillionaires.

In the United Kingdom, the affluent are often empty nesters with high disposable incomes and small or paid-off mortgages. They have an abundance of money, but are time poor and are interested in improving the quality of their lives with overseas vacations and sports cars.[41] Moreover, researchers who have examined affluent consumers, in both the United Kingdom and United States, have found that they are likely to focus on

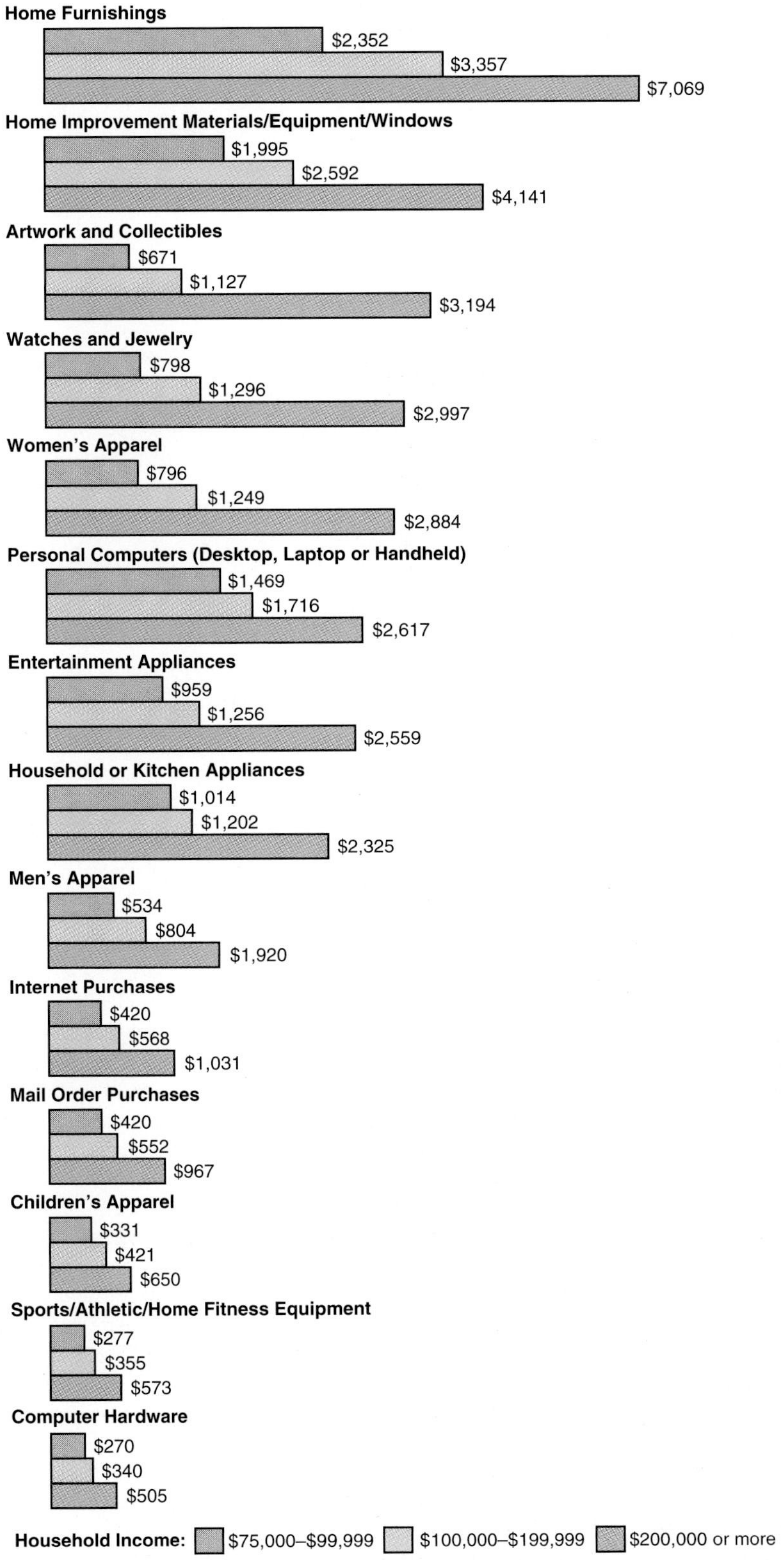

FIGURE 11.5

Three Segments of Affluent Consumers' Average Household Expenditures (among purchasing households)

Source: 2004 Mendelsohn Affluent Survey (New York: Mendelsohn Media Research, Inc., 2002), 11.

Home Furnishings
- $2,352
- $3,357
- $7,069

Home Improvement Materials/Equipment/Windows
- $1,995
- $2,592
- $4,141

Artwork and Collectibles
- $671
- $1,127
- $3,194

Watches and Jewelry
- $798
- $1,296
- $2,997

Women's Apparel
- $796
- $1,249
- $2,884

Personal Computers (Desktop, Laptop or Handheld)
- $1,469
- $1,716
- $2,617

Entertainment Appliances
- $959
- $1,256
- $2,559

Household or Kitchen Appliances
- $1,014
- $1,202
- $2,325

Men's Apparel
- $534
- $804
- $1,920

Internet Purchases
- $420
- $568
- $1,031

Mail Order Purchases
- $420
- $552
- $967

Children's Apparel
- $331
- $421
- $650

Sports/Athletic/Home Fitness Equipment
- $277
- $355
- $573

Computer Hardware
- $270
- $340
- $505

Household Income: ☐ $75,000–$99,999 ☐ $100,000–$199,999 ☐ $200,000 or more

FIGURE 11.6

Affluent Consumers' Participation in Selected Sports (number of days in past year, indexed to each of the three income segments)

Source: 2004 Mendelsohn Affluent Survey (New York: Mendelsohn Media Research, Inc., 2002).

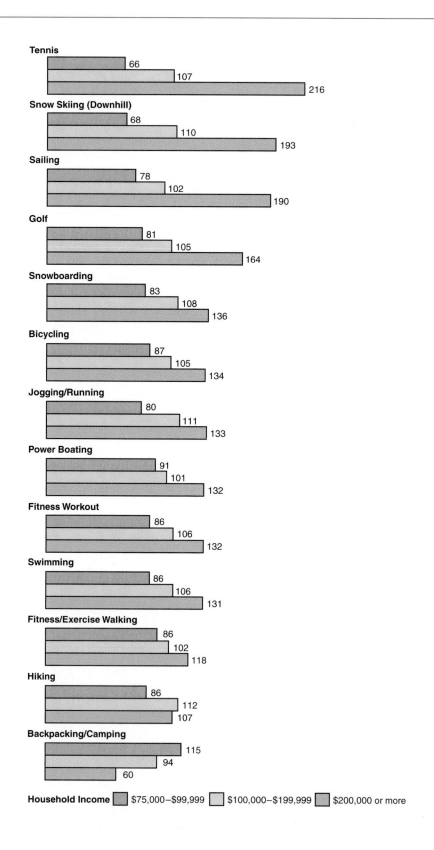

saving or reducing time and effort and, not unsurprisingly, are willing to pay for many things that provide such convenience.[42]

The media exposure of the affluent consumer

As might be expected, the media habits of the affluent differ from those of the general population.[43] For example, those households earning more than $75,000 a year view *less* TV per day than less affluent households. A profile of the media habits of $75,000-plus affluent adult householders shows they read 5.9 different publications; they listen to 11.9 hours of weekday radio and watch 24.3 hours of TV per week; and 88 percent of them view cable TV. Magazines that cater to the tastes and interests of the affluent include *Architectural Digest, Condé Nast Traveler, Gourmet, Southern Accents,* and *Town & Country.* Table 11.12 presents a selection of magazines and reveals the median household incomes of their readers who have incomes of $75,000 or more. (See Table 11.5 for a more general selection of print media and corresponding median incomes.)

Traditionally, when Nielsen Media Research provided information on TV viewership, the company's highest household income category had been $75,000-plus. Recently, though, Nielsen has begun providing demographic data for households earning $100,000-plus, which permits advertisers and television stations to gain new insights into the TV habits of more affluent Americans.[44]

TABLE 11.12	**Mendelsohn Affluent Survey 2004 Audiences: Male and Female Heads of Household**
	MEDIAN HOUSEHOLD INCOME
Total	$107,400
Allure	$120,200
Architectural Digest	$128,000
Boating	$115,600
Bon Appétit	$120,700
BusinessWeek	$128,100
Cigar Aficionado	$137,500
Condé Nast Traveler	$131,100
Elle	$115,900
Esquire	$119,200
Fortune	$129,700
Golf Magazine	$119,600
GQ Gentlemen's Quarterly	$121,100
House & Garden	$110,400
Martha Stewart Living	$113,000
National Geographic	$111,800
Newsweek	$116,500
Self	$112,800
Southern Accents	$123,500
Town & Country	$118,300
Travel + Leisure	$124,200
U.S. News & World Report	$115,800
Vanity Fair	$123,500
Vogue	$119,500
W	$119,400

Segmenting the affluent market

In addition to Mendelsohn Media Research's division of the overall affluent consumer market into three subsegments, it is recognized that affluent consumers can be "re-segmented" or further defined in terms of various other factors. That is contrary to popular stereotypes, the wealth in America is not found only behind "the tall, cloistered walls of suburban country clubs, but is spread among niches, including Asian immigrants, single women, and young Cuban Americans, to name a few."[45]

Because not all affluent consumers share the same lifestyles (i.e., activities, interests, and opinions), various marketers have tried to isolate meaningful segments of the affluent market. One scheme, for example, has divided the affluent into two groups—the *upbeat enjoyers* who live for today and the *financial positives* who are conservative and look for value. Still further, it has been commented that "most people who have money are fairly conservative, and have accumulated wealth because they are very good savers."[46]

To assist the many marketers interested in reaching subsegments of the affluent market, Mediamark Research (MRI) has developed an affluent market-segmentation schema that they call the *Upper Deck* consumers (defined as the top 10 percent of households in terms of income).[47] Table 11.13 presents, identifies, and defines each of the five segments that constitute the Upper Deck consumers.

Armed with such affluent lifestyle segments, MRI provides its clients with profiles of users of a variety of goods and services frequently targeted to the affluent consumer and specifically to five segments of the Upper Deck. For instance, when it comes to leisure activities, members of the *Well-feathered nest segment* are more likely to be out flying a kite than members of the other four Upper Deck consumers, the *No strings attached segment* are more interested in going to live theater performances, the *Nanny's in charge segment* would rather attend a country music performance, the *Two career segment* are more likely to engage in model making, and members of the *Good life segment* are most interested in birdwatching.[48] What we have is different segments of the affluent consumer market interested in different leisure activities. This type of information is of considerable interest to marketers who always want to target their marketing messages to the most suitable segment of consumers.

TABLE 11.13	**Upper Deck Consumers Segments—Top 10 Percent of Household in Terms of Income**	
SEGMENT NAME	**SEGMENT SIZE**	**SEGMENT DESCRIPTION**
Well-feathered nests	38.0% of Upper Deck	*Households that have at least one high-income earner and children present*
No strings attached	34.0% of Upper Deck	*Households that have at least one high-income earner and no children*
Nanny's in charge	07.4% of Upper Deck	*Households that have two or more earners, none earning high incomes, and children present*
Two careers	10.3% of Upper Deck	*Households that have two or more earners, neither earning high incomes, and no children present*
The good life	10.2% of Upper Deck	*Households that have a high degree of affluence with no person employed or with the head of household not employed*

Source: The Upper Deck (Mediamark Research, Inc., 2004).

middle-class consumers

It is not easy to define the boundaries of what is meant by "middle class." Although the U.S. Bureau of the Census does *not* have a definition of middle class, there have nevertheless been many attempts to define it. For instance, "middle market" has been defined as the "middle" 50 percent of household incomes—that is, about 56 million households earning between $22,500 and $80,000.[49] Still another definition of "middle class" envisions households composed of college-educated adults, who in some way use computers to make a living, are involved in their children's education, and are confident that they can maintain the quality of their family's life.[50]

For many marketers "middle class" can be thought of as including households that range from lower-middle to middle-middle class in terms of some acceptable variable or combination of variables (e.g., income, education, and/or occupation). This view of middle class does *not* include the upper-middle class, which over the years has increasingly been treated as a segment of affluent consumers.

A recent article differentiated between the children of middle-class parents and those from working-class and poor families. Working-class families often teach their children, at an early age, to do what they are told and to manage their own free time. In contrast, middle-class parents actively play a role in shaping their kids' activities, want their children to get involved in extracurricular activities that will add to their talents, and encourage them to speak up and negotiate with figures of authority.[51]

The dynamic nature of social class in the United States has been working against the middle class. In particular, there is mounting evidence that the middle-class American is slowly disappearing. It appears that middle-class consumers are increasingly moving upstream to the ranks of the upper-middle class, and another smaller segment is losing ground and slipping backward to the ranks of the working class—creating a distribution that looks like an "hourglass."[52]

Although the middle class has been shrinking in the United States, there has been a fairly rapid increase in the number of middle-class consumers in select Asian and Eastern European countries. For example, within the past few years, Tropicana and other fruit juice companies have been successfully positioning their products to the expanding middle-class Indian consumers who are seeking more health-oriented products.[53] Similarly, American, Japanese, amd Korean automobile manufacturers are now manufacturing cars, trucks, and motorcyles in China, hoping that China's growing middle class will be attracted to purchasing its vehicles.

Moving up to more "near" luxuries

Adding to the challenge of defining "middle class" is the reality that luxury and technological products have been becoming more affordable for more consumers (often because of the introduction of near-luxury models by major luxury-brand firms and/or the downward price trend for many technology products) and, therefore, more middle-class consumers have access to products and brands that were once considered beyond their reach.[54]

Additionally, evidence suggests that some middle-class consumers are willing to pinch pennies on certain purchases in order to splurge on others. For example, a household might buy groceries at Wal-Mart and clothes at Target in order to afford luxury or near-luxury goods that satisfy emotional needs, such as a BMW. The luxury product purchased might even be premium food for their dog. One study found that people generally trade up in two to five categories, but at the same time they trade down in 20. For example, they might want the least expensive airfare they can get for a vacation trip to Hawaii, but they want to stay at a luxury resort hotel when they get there.

Still further, while high-end retailers still consider their primary customer base to be the affluent, they are realizing that middle-class customers have been purchasing more high-style items, often at not-so-high prices. Consequently, traditional marketers of luxury products have been expanding their offerings to more affordable merchandise. For example, this "massification of luxury" includes Tiffany offering sterling silver cuff links for $90, and Coach selling a collection of vintage wristlets in leather and in its signature fabric for $78. It is believed that a crucial factor in the growth of upscale retailers over the next few years will be how well they cater to middle-class buyers.[55]

However, companies offering "luxury to the masses" must be careful how they position their products. Many loyal Jaguar owners, for example, "went through the roof" when the company introduced the entry-level X-Type, and Jaguar's loyalty rate dove to 38 percent from 85 percent over the past few years. Trying to bring a luxury automobile to the masses appears to have been a flawed strategy for Jaguar.[56] And companies such as Coach, J. Crew, and Godiva, realizing that they have made their offerings more accessible to the less than affluent marketplace, have been introducing high-priced collections in order to pull up their elite images.[57] These firms realize that if one of their products slips into the mass market, they will need a new product to take its place in the luxury market. As an example, Godiva now sells its $100 a pound "G" line only during holiday seasons and only at select stores.[58]

the working class and other nonaffluent consumers

Although many advertisers would prefer to show their products as part of an affluent lifestyle, working-class or blue-collar people represent a vast group of consumers that marketers cannot ignore. In fact, households earning less than $40,000 control somewhere near 30 percent of the total income in the United States. Lower-income or **downscale consumers** (frequently defined as having household incomes of $35,000 or less) may actually be more brand loyal than wealthier consumers, because they cannot afford to make mistakes by switching to unfamiliar brands.

Understanding the importance of speaking to (not *at*) the downscale consumers, companies such as RC Cola, MasterCard, and McDonald's target "average Joes" (and Janes) with ads reflecting the modest lifestyles of some of their customers.[59] For instance, marketers need to be sensitive to the reality that downscale consumers often spend a higher percentage of their available incomes on food than do their middle-class counterparts. Moreover, food is a particularly important purchase area for low-income consumers because it represents an area of "indulgence." For this reason, they periodically trade-up the foods they purchase—especially favorite ethnic and natural foods—"where taste and authenticity matter."[60] Still further, a British writer, reflecting on a trend toward super-sized fast-food offerings in the United Kingdom noted that "It isn't the wealthy middle classes . . . that are generally obese—it's the under-class . . . with little budget, knowledge of diet . . . that is suffering."[61]

When discussing the lower social classes, it is important to note the plight of those often on the bottom rung of the ladder—illegal immigrants. Over 5 million Mexicans, for example, are currently living in the United States, with over 400,000 more coming here annually. They often take jobs that pay extremely low wages and require a long work week. For example, a recent newspaper article chronicled the experiences of a man who came, illegally, from Mexico to New York City. To earn $600 a week he must work at least 10 hours a day, six days a week, and can be fired at any time and for any reason. He pays $500 a month to rent space in a 9' x 9' room in an apartment that he shares with nine other Mexicans, consisting of three families. While his children were born here and are therefore eligible for medical assistance, he and his wife are not. His biggest obstacle is his illegal status—he is without rights, without security, and without a way to improve his future.[62]

recognizing the "techno-class"

The degree of literacy, familiarity, and competency with technology, especially computers and the Internet, appears to be a new basis for a kind of "class standing," or status or prestige. Those who are unfamiliar with or lack computer skills are being referred to as "technologically underclassed."[63] Educators, business leaders, and government officials have warned that the inability to adequately use technology is negatively impacting lifestyles and the quality of life of those who are not computer literate.

Not wanting to see their children left out of the "sweep of computer technology," parents in all social-class groupings are seeking out early computer exposure for their children. Either based on their positive experiences using computers (or possibly on fears produced as the result of a lack of personal computer experience), parents sense that an understanding of computers is a necessary tool of competitive achievement and success. At the other end of the life and age spectrum, even 55-year-old professionals, who were initially reluctant to "learn computers," are now seeking personal computer training—they no longer want to be left out, nor do they want to be further embarrassed by having to admit that they "don't know computers."

Consumers throughout the world have come to believe that it is critical to acquire a functional understanding of computers in order to ensure that they do not become obsolete or hinder themselves socially or professionally. In this sense, there is a technological class structure that centers around the amount of computer skills that one possesses. It appears that those without necessary computer skills will increasingly find themselves to be "underclassed" and "disadvantaged."

The geek gets status

The importance of the computer and the prominent role it now plays in our lives has resulted in somewhat of a reversal of fortune, in that the "geek" is now often viewed by his or her peers as "friendly and fun." The increasingly positive image of geeks has made them and their lifestyles the target of marketers' messages designed to appeal to their great appetite for novel technological products (see Figure 11.7).

Indeed, according to a recent British National Opinion Poll (NOP) of 7- to 16-year-olds, "computer geeks are now the coolest kids in class."[64] The poll found that the archetypical geek is most typically a 14- to 16-year-old boy who is the family computer expert, and he is willing to teach his parents, siblings, and teachers about computers. Interestingly, in an environment where children naturally take to computers, it is often the parents who find themselves technologically disenfranchised. To remedy this situation, some schools are offering classes to bring parents up to speed in the use of computers.[65]

selected consumer behavior applications of social class

Social-class profiles provide a broad picture of the values, attitudes, and behavior that distinguish the members of various social classes. This section focuses on specific consumer research that relates social class to the development of marketing strategy.

Clothing, fashion, and shopping

A Greek philosopher once said, "Know, first, who you are; and then adorn yourself accordingly."[66] This bit of wisdom is relevant to clothing marketers today, because most people dress to fit their self-image, which includes their perceptions of their own social-class membership. However, for many consumers, the notion of "keeping up with the Joneses" (i.e., trying to be like one's neighbors) has been replaced by looking to more upscale reference groups that they would like to emulate (most often, people earning substantially more than they do).

Members of specific social classes differ in terms of what they consider fashionable or in good taste. For instance, lower-middle-class consumers have a strong preference for T-shirts, caps, and other clothing that offer an *external point of identification,* such as the name of an admired person or group (the Dallas Cowboys), a respected company or brand name (Mustang), or a valued trademark (FUBU). These consumers are prime targets for licensed goods (with well-known logos). In contrast, upper-class consumers are likely to buy clothing that is free from such supporting associations. Upper-class consumers also seek clothing with a more subtle look, such as the kind of sportswear found in an L.L. Bean, Land's End, or Talbots catalog, rather than designer jeans.

Social class is also an important variable in determining where a consumer shops. People tend to avoid stores that have the image of appealing to a social class very different from their own. In the past, some mass merchandisers who tried to appeal to a higher class of consumers

FIGURE 11.7

Source: © Yamaha Electronics Corporation, USA. Used with permission. All rights reserved.

Appealing to the Geek-Oriented Consumer

found themselves alienating their traditional customers. This implies that retailers should pay attention to the social class of their customer base and the social class of their store appeal to ensure that they send the appropriate message through advertising. For instance, Gap rolled out the Old Navy clothing stores in an effort to attract working-class families who usually purchased their casual and active wear clothing from general merchandise retailers such as Kmart, Wal-Mart, or Target. For Gap, trading down to the lower-income consumer with Old Navy has resulted in bigger sales, more leverage with suppliers, and increased traffic volume. It let Gap create a "knock-off" of itself before anybody else got the chance.[67] However, in creating a lower-price alternative to itself, Gap has also tended to cannibalize itself—shifting loyal Gap customers to the Old Navy outlets. Different department stores also target different social-class consumers. For example, Neiman Marcus and Nordstrom target upscale consumers, whereas JCPenney and Dillards are appealing to middle-class shoppers, and Kmart and Wal-Mart tend to target more of a working-class customer.

In exploring the social-class image or perception of retailers, researchers have discovered that consumers rate shirts purchased at Nordstrom, for example, to have higher status than shirts sold at Kmart.[68] In another study examining the social-class perceptions of five retail stores among whites, Korean Americans, and African Americans, researchers found that both whites and Koreans perceived JCPenney to be more lower-middle class in its appeal than did African American consumers.[69] Moreover, Korean respondents imagined Dillards, Nordstrom, and Macy's to each be in a lower social-class position than the social-class perceptions of whites and African American consumers. All three subcultural groups, however, had a similar social-class image of Wal-Mart—that is, as a "lower-middle" or "upper-lower" class store.

In a recent study, young Americans from 14 to 30 years of age were asked to indicate which adjective best described their "personal style" (i.e., multiple answers were accepted). While 66 percent of respondents checked-off "natural," males were much more likely to also check "sporty" (36% to 22%), while females were more likely to check "romantic" (30% to 9%) and/or alluring (40% to 21%). Interestingly, some study participants, who were asked to indicate their personal style on more than one occasion, checked different styles on different days, which suggests that some young people frequently try to reinvent themselves.[70] Table 11.14 presents the results of this study.

The pursuit of leisure

Social-class membership is also closely related to the choice of recreational and leisure-time activities. For instance, upper-class consumers are likely to attend the theater and concerts, to play bridge, and to attend college football games. Lower-class consumers tend to be avid television watchers and fishing enthusiasts, and they enjoy drive-in movies and baseball games. Furthermore, the lower-class consumer spends more time on commercial types of activities (bowling, playing pool or billiards, or visiting taverns) and craft activities (model building, painting, and woodworking projects) rather than cerebral activities (reading, visiting museums). In any case, whether we are describing middle-class or working-class consumers, there appears to be a trend toward more spending on "experiences" that bring the family together (family vacations or activities) and less spending on "things."[71]

Over the past decade or so, however, a number of changes are increasingly being observed that point to a further blurring of social-class lines with regard to leisure interests, especially with regard to arts and media preference. More specifically, only with the

TABLE 11.14	**Which of the Following Best Defines Your Personal Style?**					
Sporty (outdoorsy, athetic)	26%	36%	22%	31%	20%	33%
Preppy (monograms, polos, stripes)	25	29	24	32	23	20
Gothic (dark, Medieval)	9	8	9	12	7	8
Trendy (magazine cover)	34	36	33	30	36	38
Natural (easy, casual, comfortable)	66	63	67	71	60	72
Romantic (feminine, soft, flowing)	24	9	30	25	23	25
Dramatic (bold, creative, colorful)	30	24	33	41	28	21
Classic/conservative (tailored, elegant)	29	31	28	27	31	26
Alluring (chic, sexy, edgy)	35	21	40	34	37	33
Other	13	15	13	19	13	5
I don't have a personal style	5	3	6	8	4	3

Note: Look-Look polled 328 respondents ages 14–30, both trendsetting & mainstream. Subjects were asked to choose all answers that apply.
Source: Becky Ebenkamp. "Style:" It's a 'Natural' Fact," *Brandweem.* March 7, 2005, 22.

increased numbers of the suburban middle-class viewers could wrestling have become one of cable TV's most popular programming areas. Similarly, the presumedly sophisticated consumers who read magazines such as *The New Yorker* also like to attend theme parks and shoot billiards.[72] Figure 11.8 presents these and other preferences in terms of a perceptual map of 100 arts, media, and leisure pursuits.

Saving, spending, and credit

Saving, spending, and credit card usage all seem to be related to social-class standing. Upper-class consumers are more future oriented and confident of their financial acumen; they are more willing to invest in insurance, stocks, and real estate. In comparison, lower-class consumers are generally more concerned with immediate gratification; when they do save, they are primarily interested in safety and security. Therefore, it is not surprising that when it comes to bank credit card usage, members of the lower social classes tend to use their bank credit cards for installment purchases, whereas members of the upper social classes pay their credit card bills in full each month. In other words, lower-class purchasers tend to use their credit cards to "buy now and pay later" for things they might not otherwise be able to afford, whereas upper-class purchasers use their credit cards as a convenient substitute for cash.

A recent study examined the role of empowerment and disempowerment as a central phenomenon of social class among working-class and young professionals (25–30 years of age) in Sydney, Australia. The study focused on money management, and financial planning practices and priorities. As shown in Figure 11.9, young professionals perceived themselves to be empowered in the sense that they could achieve whatever they set their minds to, and they were disciplined and results oriented. Working-class participants, in contrast, perceived themselves as being average, were more likely to describe a range of personal weaknesses (e.g., "I can never finish things") and, unlike the young professionals, had a strong uncertainty about the future.[73]

Social class and communication

Social-class groupings differ in terms of their media habits and in how they transmit and receive communications. Knowledge of these differences is invaluable to marketers who segment their markets on the basis of social class.

When it comes to describing their world, lower-class consumers tend to portray it in rather personal and concrete terms, whereas middle-class consumers are able to describe their experiences from a number of different perspectives. A simple example illustrates that members of different social classes tend to see the world differently. The following responses to a question asking where the respondent usually purchases gasoline were received:

> *Upper-middle-class answer: At Mobil or Shell.*
> *Lower-middle-class answer: At the station on Main and Fifth Street.*
> *Lower-class answer: At Ed's.*

Such variations in response indicate that middle-class consumers have a broader or more general view of the world, while lower-class consumers tend to have a narrow or personal view—seeing the world through their own immediate experiences.

Regional differences in terminology, choice of words and phrases, and patterns of usage also tend to increase as we move down the social-class ladder. Therefore, in creating messages targeted to the lower classes, marketers try to word advertisements to reflect particular regional preferences that exist (e.g., the children's game hopscotch is called "potsy" in Manhattan and "blue sky" in Chicago).

Selective exposure to various types of mass media differs by social class. In the selection of specific television programs and program types, higher-social-class members tend to prefer current events and drama, whereas lower-class individuals tend to prefer soap operas, quiz shows, and situation comedies. Higher-class consumers tend to have greater exposure to magazines and newspapers than do their lower-class counterparts. Lower-class consumers are likely to have greater exposure to publications that dramatize romance and the

Source: Michael J. Weiss, Morris B. Holbrook, and John Habich, "Death of the Arts Snob?" *American Demographics,* June 2001, 44. All rights reserved. Reprinted by permission.

FIGURE 11.8

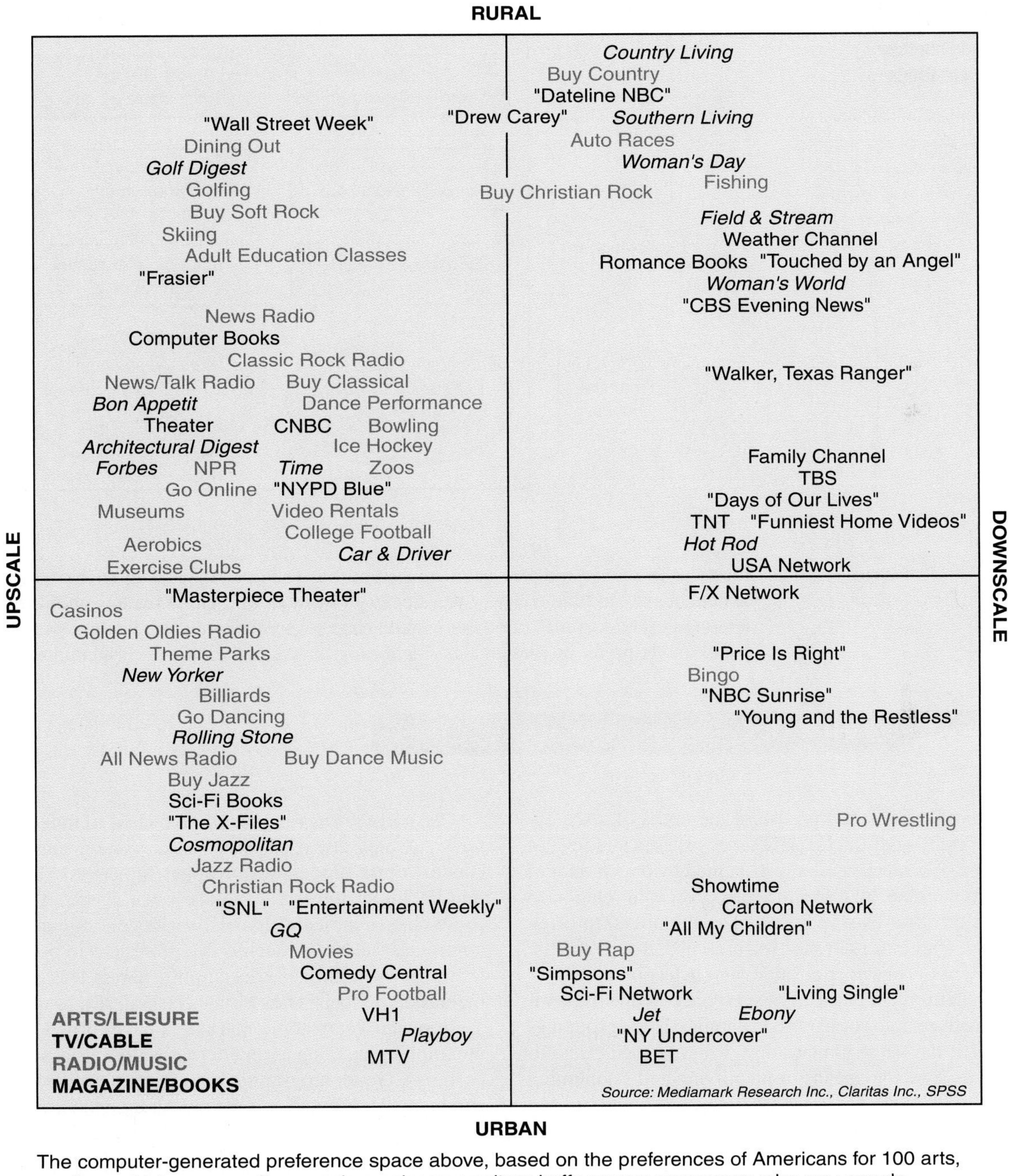

RURAL

Country Living
Buy Country
"Dateline NBC"
"Drew Carey"   *Southern Living*
Auto Races
Woman's Day
Buy Christian Rock   Fishing

"Wall Street Week"
Dining Out
Golf Digest
Golfing
Buy Soft Rock
Skiing
Adult Education Classes
"Frasier"

Field & Stream
Weather Channel
Romance Books   "Touched by an Angel"
Woman's World
"CBS Evening News"

News Radio
Computer Books
Classic Rock Radio
News/Talk Radio   Buy Classical
Bon Appetit   Dance Performance
Theater   CNBC   Bowling
Architectural Digest   Ice Hockey
Forbes   NPR   *Time*   Zoos
Go Online   "NYPD Blue"
Museums   Video Rentals
College Football
Aerobics   *Car & Driver*
Exercise Clubs

"Walker, Texas Ranger"

Family Channel
TBS
"Days of Our Lives"
TNT   "Funniest Home Videos"
Hot Rod
USA Network

UPSCALE

DOWNSCALE

"Masterpiece Theater"
Casinos
Golden Oldies Radio
Theme Parks
New Yorker
Billiards
Go Dancing
Rolling Stone
All News Radio   Buy Dance Music
Buy Jazz
Sci-Fi Books
"The X-Files"
Cosmopolitan
Jazz Radio
Christian Rock Radio
"SNL"   "Entertainment Weekly"
GQ
Movies
Comedy Central
Pro Football
VH1
Playboy
MTV

F/X Network

"Price Is Right"
Bingo
"NBC Sunrise"
"Young and the Restless"

Pro Wrestling

Showtime
Cartoon Network
"All My Children"
Buy Rap
"Simpsons"
Sci-Fi Network   "Living Single"
Jet   *Ebony*
"NY Undercover"
BET

ARTS/LEISURE
TV/CABLE
RADIO/MUSIC
MAGAZINE/BOOKS

Source: Mediamark Research Inc., Claritas Inc., SPSS

URBAN

The computer-generated preference space above, based on the preferences of Americans for 100 arts, media, and leisure pursuits, reveals omnivorous culture buffs among consumers who are upscale, downscale, urban, or rural.

Preferences of Americans for 100 Arts, Media, and Leisure Pursuits

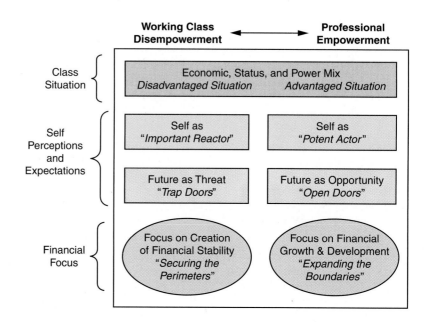

FIGURE 11.9

Class Situations, Self-Perceptions, and Financial Orientations

Source: Paul C. Henry, "Social Class, Market Situation, and Consumers' Metaphors of (Dis)Empowerment," *Journal of Consumer Research* 31 (March 2005): 769

lifestyles of movie and television celebrities. For example, magazines such as *True Story* appeal heavily to blue-collar or working-class women, who enjoy reading about the problems, fame, and fortunes of others. Middle-class consumers are more likely to read a newspaper and to prefer movies and late-night programs than their lower-class counterparts.[74]

SUMMARY

Social stratification, the division of members of a society into a hierarchy of distinct social classes, exists in all societies and cultures. Social class usually is defined by the amount of status that members of a specific class possess in relation to members of other classes. Social-class membership often serves as a frame of reference (a reference group) for the development of consumer attitudes and behavior.

The measurement of social class is concerned with classifying individuals into social-class groupings. These groupings are of particular value to marketers, who use social classification as an effective means of identifying and segmenting target markets. There are three basic methods for measuring social class: subjective measurement, reputational measurement, and objective measurement. Subjective measures rely on an individual's self-perception; reputational measures rely on an individual's perceptions of others; and objective measures use specific socioeconomic measures, either alone (as a single-variable index) or in combination with others (as a composite-variable index). Composite-variable indexes, such as the Index of Status Characteristics and the Socioeconomic Status Score, combine a number of socioeconomic factors to form one overall measure of social-class standing.

Class structures range from two-class to nine-class systems. A frequently used classification system consists of six classes: upper-upper, lower-upper, upper-middle, lower-middle, upper-lower, and lower-lower classes. Profiles of these classes indicate that the socioeconomic differences among classes are reflected in differences in attitudes, in leisure activities, and in consumption habits. This is why segmentation by social class is of special interest to marketers.

In recent years, some marketers have turned to geodemographic clustering as an alternative to a strict social-class typology. Geodemographic clustering is a technique that combines geographic and socioeconomic factors to locate concentrations of consumers with particular characteristics. Particular attention currently is being directed to affluent consumers, who represent the fastest-growing segment in our population; however, some marketers are finding it extremely profitable to cater to the needs of nonaffluent consumers.

Research has revealed social-class differences in clothing habits, home decoration, and leisure activities, as well as saving, spending, and credit habits. Thus, astute marketers tailor specific product and promotional strategies to each social-class target segment.

DISCUSSION QUESTIONS

1. Marketing researchers generally use the objective method to measure social class rather than the subjective or reputational methods. Why is the objective method preferred by researchers?

2. Under what circumstances would you expect income to be a better predictor of consumer behavior than a composite measure of social class (e.g., based on income, education, and occupation)? When would you expect the composite social-class measure to be superior?

3. Describe the correlation between social status (or prestige) and income. Which is a more useful segmentation variable? Discuss.

4. Which status-related variable—occupation, education, or income—is the most appropriate segmentation base for: (a) expensive vacations, (b) opera subscriptions, (c) *People* magazine subscriptions, (d) fat-free foods, (e) personal computers, (f) pocket-size cellular telephones, and (g) health clubs?

5. Consider the Rolex watch, which has a retail price range starting at about $2,000 for a stainless-steel model to thousands of dollars for a solid-gold model. How might the Rolex company use geodemographic clustering in its marketing efforts?

6. How would you use the research evidence on affluent households presented in this chapter to segment the market for (a) home exercise equipment, (b) vacations, and (c) banking services?

7. How can a marketer use knowledge of consumer behavior to develop financial services for affluent consumers? For downscale consumers?

8. You are the owner of two furniture stores, one catering to upper-middle-class consumers and the other to lower-class consumers. How do social-class differences influence each store's (a) product lines and styles, (b) advertising media selection, (c) the copy and communications style used in the ads, and (d) payment policies?

EXERCISES

1. Copy the list of occupations in Figure 11.2 and ask students majoring in areas other than marketing (both business and nonbusiness) to rank the relative prestige of these occupations. Are any differences in the rankings related to the students' majors? Explain.

2. Find three print ads in one of the publications listed in Table 11.5. Using the social-class characteristics listed in Table 11.9, identify the social class targeted by each ad and evaluate the effectiveness of the advertising appeals used.

3. Select two households featured in two different TV series or sitcoms. Classify each household into one of the social classes discussed in the text and analyze its lifestyle and consumption behavior.

KEY TERMS

- **affluent market**
- **chapin's social status scale**
- **class consciousness**
- **composite-variable indexes**
- **downscale consumers**
- **downward mobility**

- **geodemographic clusters**
- **index of status characteristics**
- **objective measures**
- **PRIZM NE**
- **reputational measures**
- **single-variable index**

- **social class**
- **social status**
- **socioeconomic status score**
- **subjective measures**
- **upward mobility**

NOTES

1. Shaun Saunders, "Fromm's Marketing Character and Rokeach Values," *Social Behavior and Personality,* 29, no. 2 (2001): 191–196.

2. Jacqueline K. Eastman, Ronald E. Goldsmith, and Leisa Reinecke Flynn, "Status Consumption in Consumer Behavior: Scale Development and Validation," *Journal*

of Marketing Theory and Practice (Summer 1999): 41–52.

3. Ibid., 43.

4. Aron O'Cass and Emily McEwen, "Exploring Consumer Status and Conspicuous Consumption," *Journal of Consumer Behaviour (London)* 4 (October 2004): 25–39.

5. Douglas B. Holt, "Does Cultural Capital Structure American Consumption?" *Journal of Consumer Research* 25 (June 1998): 19.

6. "Brand Stats: Market Focus—Instant Coffee," *Brand Strategy (London),* May 10, 2005, 50.

7. Malcolm M. Knapp, "Believing 'Myth of the Middle Class' Can Be Costly Misreading of Consumer Spending," *Nation's Restaurant News,* January 1, 2001, 36.

8. Takashina Shuji, "The New Inequality," *Japan Echo,* August 2000, 38–39.

9. Rebecca Piirto Heath, "The New Working Class," *American Demographics,* January 1998, 52.

10. John P. Dickson and R. Bruce Lind, "The Stability of Occupational Prestige as a Key Variable in Determining Social Class Structure: A Longitudinal Study 1976–2000," in *2001 AMA Winter Educators' Conference,* 12, eds. Ram Krishnan and Madhu Viswanathan (Chicago: American Marketing Association, 2001), 38–44.

11. Rebecca Piirto Heath, "Life on Easy Street," *American Demographics,* April 1997, 33–38.

12. Diane Crispell, "The Real Middle Americans," *American Demographics,* October 1994, 28–35.

13. Tamar Lewin, "A Marriage of Unequals," *The New York Times,* May 19, 2005, A1, 14–15.

14. David Leonhardt, "The College Dropout Boom," *The New York Times,* May 24, 2005, A1, 18–19.

15. Eugene Sivadas, George Mathew, and David J. Curry, "A Preliminary Examination of the Continued Significance of Social Class to Marketing: A Geodemographic Replication," *Journal of Consumer Marketing* 14, no. 6 (1997): 469.

16. David Hinson, "Closing the Wealth Gap; How African-Americans Can Sustain a Middle-Class Lifestyle," *Network Journal* 11 (February 29, 2004): 8.

17. Michael D. Yates, "A Statistical Portrait of the U.S. Working Class," *Monthly Review* 56 (April 2005): 12–31.

18. Dennis Rodkin, "Wealthy Attitude Wins over Healthy Wallet: Consumers Prove Affluence Is a State of Mind," *Advertising Age,* July 9, 1990, S4, S6.

19. Christopher Reynolds, "Up on the Envy Meter," *American Demographics,* June 2004, 6–7.

20. Janeen Arnold Costa and Russell W. Belk, "Nouveaux Riches as Quintessential Americans: Case Studies of Consumption in an Extended Family," *Advances in Nonprofit Marketing,* 3 (Greenwich, CT: JAI Press, 1990), 83–140.

21. F. Stuart Chapin, *Contemporary American Institutions* (New York: Harper, 1935), 373–397.

22. Robert B. Settle, Pamela L. Alreck, and Denny E. McCorkle, "Consumer Perceptions of Mail Phone Order Shopping Media," *Journal of Direct Marketing* 8 (Summer 1994): 30–45.

23. W. Lloyd Warner, Marchia Meeker, and Kenneth Eells, *Social Class in America: Manual of Procedure for the Measurement of Social Status* (New York: Harper & Brothers, 1960).

24. *Methodology and Scores of Socioeconomic Status,* Working Paper No. 15 (Washington, DC: U.S. Bureau of the Census, 1963).

25. Geng Cui and Quiming Liu, "Executive Insights: Emerging Market Segments in a Transitional Economy: A Study of Urban Consumers in China," *Journal of International Marketing* 9, no. 1 (2001): 84–106.

26. Tom Doctoroff, "Brands to Watch," *Campaign,* February 18, 2005, 31.

27. Randy Kennedy, "For Middle Class, New York Shrinks as Home Prices Soar," *New York Times,* April 1, 1998, A1, B6; "Two Tier Marketing," *Business Week,* March 17, 1997, 82–90; and Keith Bradsher, "America's Opportunity Gap," *New York Times,* June 4, 1995, 4.

28. "Special Report: Ever Higher Society, Ever Harder to Ascend—Meritocracy in America," *The Economist,* 374, January 1, 2005, 35–37; Arthur Cordell, "Rich Poor Gap in the US," *The Wall Street Journal,* May 13, 2005, 19; and Debra Branch McBrier and George Wilson, "Going Down?," *Work and Occupations* 31 (August 2004): 283–322.

29. Janny Scott and David Leonhardt, "Class in America: Shadowy Lines That Still Divide," *The New York Times,* May 15, 2005, A1, 26–29.

30. Lynn Kahle, "Zip Decoder Giving a Salesclerk Your Postal Code Is Only the First Step for Marketers to Sort the Citizenry into 'Clusters,' the Better for Firms to Know and Target Their Customers," *The Oregonian,* December 21, 1999, C01. Also, examine Peter Duchessi, Charles M. Schaninger, and Thomas Nowak, "Creating Cluster-Specific Purchase Profiles from Point-of-Sale Scanner Data and Geodemographic Clusters: Improving Category Management at a Major US Grocery Chain," *Journal of Consumer Behavior (London)* 4 (December 2004): 97–117.

31. Paul Bruder, "Economic Health: The Key Ingredient in the Personal Health of Global Communities," *Hospital Topics* 79, no. 1 (Winter 2001): 32–35.

32. Janny Scott, "In America, Living Better and Living Longer Is a Major Factor in Health Care and the Gaps Are Widening," *International Herald Tribune,* May 17, 2005, 2.

33. Suniya S. Luthar and Shawn J. Latendresse, "Children of the Affluent; Challenges to Well-Being," *Current Directions in Psychological Science* 14 (February 2005): 49.

34. "Kudlow's Money Politic$," March 11, 2005, access at **http://lkmp.blogspot.com/2005/03/wealth-of-nations.html**

35. Merrill Lynch and Capgemini "World Wealth Report, 2005," accessed at **www.capgemini.com/resources/ thought_leadership/world_wealth_report_2005**

36. Lisa Singhania, "Whirlpool Looks to Innovation to Boost Appliance Sales," *The Grand Rapids Press,* February 6, 2000,

F1; and Gregory L. White and Shirley Leung, "Stepping Up: Middle Market Shrinks as Americans Migrate Toward the High End—Shifting Consumer Values Create 'Hourglass' Effect'; Quality Gets Easier to Sell—Six Air Bags, 22 Bath Towels," *Wall Street Journal,* March 29, 2002, A1.

37. Raksha Arora, "Affluent Americans: Priorities of the Prosperous," *Gallup Poll News Service,* February 8, 2005, 1–4.

38. Michael R. Hyman, Gopala Ganesh, and Shaun McQuitty, "Augmenting the Household Affluence Construct," *Journal of Marketing Theory and Practice* 10 (Summer 2002): 13–31.

39. "The 2004 Mendelsohn Affluent Survey," Mendelsohn Media Research, Inc., 2004.

40. Ibid.

41. Geoffrey Holliman, "Once a Teenager, Now Affluent and Best Not Ignored," *Marketing,* December 2, 1999, 22.

42. Martha R. McEnally and Charles Bodkin, "A Comparison of Convenience Orientation Between U.S. and U.K. Households," in *2001 AMA Winter Educators' Conference,* 12, eds. Ram Krishnan and Madhu Viswanathan (Chicago: American Marketing Association, 2001), 332–338.

43. Op. cit., The Mendelsohn Affluent Survey, 2004.

44. Joe Mandese, "In Search of Affluent Viewers," *TelevisionWeek (Chicago),* 23, January 12, 2004, 47.

45. "Marketing to Affluents: Hidden Pockets of Wealth," *Advertising Age,* July 9, 1990, S1.

46. Jeanie Casison, "Wealthy and Wise," *Incentive,* January 1999, 78–81.

47. *The Upper Deck* (Mediamark Research, Inc., 2004).

48. Ibid.

49. Adopted from "CPS Annual Demographic Survey, March 2005, Supplement," accessed at **http://pubdb3.census.gov/macro/032004/hhincnew01_001.htm**

50. Debra Goldman, "Paradox of Pleasure," *American Demographics,* May 1999, 50–53; and, for a discussion of the growth of the middle class in the United States after WWII, see Shelley Nickles, "More is Better: Mass Consumption, Gender, and Class Identity in Postwar America," *American Quarterly* 54 (December 2002): 581–622.

51. Tamar Lewin, "Up From the Holler: Living in Two Worlds, At Home in Neither; Class Matters," *The New York Times,* May 19, 2005, A14.

52. White and Leung, "Stepping Up," A1.

53. Rasul Bailay, "Juice Processors See Fruitful Future in India—Companies Hope to Lure Country's Middle Class—'The Taste of Good Health'," *Wall Street Journal,* November 17, 2000, 28; and Clay Chandler, "GM to Make Small Cars in China; Buick Sail, Similar to Opel, Will Be Aimed at Middle Class," *The Washington Post,* October 24, 2000, E1.

54. W. Michael Cox, "The Low Cost of Living," *The Voluntaryist,* October 1999, 3.

55. Lorrie Grant, "Scrimping to Splurge: Value-Conscious Middle-Class Buyers Pinch Pennies to Afford Luxuries," *USA Today,* January 28, 2005, B1; Tiffany Meyers, "Marketers Learn Luxury Isn't Simply for the Very Wealthy," *Advertising Age,* September 13, 2004, S2–S3; and "America Loves to Trade Up," *Home Textiles Today* 25 (January 26, 2004): 4.

56. Jean Halliday and Lisa Sanders, "Jaguar Hunts for Marketing Panacea," *Advertising Age,* November 8, 2004, 1 & 64.

57. Stephanie Thompson, "Marketers Hike Prices to Restake Luxury Claims," *Advertising Age,* November 15, 2004, 12.

58. Jennifer Steinhauer, "When the Joneses Wear Jeans," *The New York Times,* May 29, 2005, A1, 16–17.

59. Karen Benezra, "Hardworking RC Cola," *Brandweek,* May 25, 1998, 18–19.

60. "Small Budgets Yield Big Clout for Food Companies—10.1 Million Low Income Consumers Can't (or Shouldn't) Be Ignored," *PR Newswire,* August 22, 2002, 1.

61. George Pitcher, "Being Super-Sized Boils Down to Personal Choice," *Marketing Week (London),* October 7, 2004, 33.

62. Anthony DePalma, "15 Years on the Bottom Rung," *The New York Times,* May 26, 2005, A1, 20–21.

63. Steve Rosenbush, "Techno Leaders Warn of a 'Great Divide'," *USA Today,* June 17, 1998, B1.

64. "Computer Geeks Now the Cool Kids in Class," *The Press* (Christchurch, New Zealand), July 20, 2000, 31.

65. Sophia Lezin Jones, "Parent Technology Nights: Classes to Help Boost Computer Savvy Riverside Elementary Moms, Dads Invited," *The Atlanta Journal—Constitution,* October 19, 1999, JJ1.

66. Epictetus, "Discourses" (second century) in *The Enchiridon,* 2nd ed., trans. Thomas Higginson (Indianapolis: Bobbs-Merrill, 1955).

67. Mike Duff, "Old Navy: The Master of Downmarket Apparel Dollars," *DSN Retailing Today,* May 8, 2000, 89–90.

68. D. F. Baugh, and L. L. Davis. "The Effect of Store Image on Consumers' Perceptions of Designer and Private Label Clothing," *Clothing and Textiles Research Journal* 7, no. 3 (1989): 15–21.

69. Youn-Kyung Kim and Seunghae Han, "Perceived Images of Retail Stores and Brands: Comparison Among Three Ethnic Consumer Groups," *Journal of Family and Consumer Sciences* 92, no. 3 (2000): 58–61.

70. Becky Ebenkam, "Style: It's a Natural Fact," *Brandweek,* March 7, 2005, 22.

71. Christina Duff, "Indulging in Inconspicuous Consumption," *Wall Street Journal,* April 14, 1997, B1, B2; and Christina Duff, "Two Family Budgets: Different Means, Similar Ends," *Wall Street Journal,* April 14, 1997, B1, B2.

72. Michael J. Weiss, Morris B. Holbrook, and John Habich, "Death of the Arts Snob?" *American Demographics,* June 2001, 40–42.

73. Paul C. Henry, "Social Class, Market Situation, and Consumers' Metaphors of (Dis)Empowerment," *Journal of Consumer Research* 31 (March 2005): 766–778.

74. Kim and Han, "Perceived Images of Retail Store Brands," 59.

chaptertwelve

> ## The Influence of Culture on Consumer Behavior

The study of culture is a challenging undertaking because its primary focus is on the broadest component of social behavior—*an entire society.* In contrast to the psychologist, who is principally concerned with the study of individual behavior, or the sociologist, who is concerned with the study of groups, the anthropologist is primarily interested in identifying the very fabric of society itself.

This chapter explores the basic concepts of culture, with particular emphasis on the role that culture plays in influencing consumer behavior. We will first consider the specific dimensions of culture that make it a powerful force in regulating human behavior. After reviewing several measurement approaches that researchers use to understand the impact of culture on consumption behavior, we will show how a variety of core American cultural values influence consumer behavior.

This chapter is concerned with the general aspects of culture; the following two chapters focus on subculture and on cross-culture and show how marketers can use such knowledge to shape and modify their marketing strategies.

LIKE TO CUSTOMIZE?

Do a different kind of combo meal. Do Wendy's® Combo Choices.

Pick any combo and choose from any of five delicious sides at no extra cost. **Do what tastes right.**™

At participating locations.

© 2006 Oldemark LLC.

what is culture?

Given the broad and pervasive nature of **culture**, its study generally requires a detailed examination of the character of the total society, including such factors as language, knowledge, laws, religions, food customs, music, art, technology, work patterns, products, and other artifacts that give a society its distinctive flavor. In a sense, culture is a society's personality. For this reason, it is not easy to define its boundaries.

Because our objective is to understand the influence of culture on consumer behavior, we define culture as the *sum total of learned beliefs, values, and customs that serve to direct the consumer behavior of members of a particular society.*

The *belief* and *value* components of our definition refer to the accumulated feelings and priorities that individuals have about "things" and possessions. More precisely, *beliefs* consist of the very large number of mental or verbal statements (i.e., "I believe . . . ") that reflect a person's particular knowledge and assessment of something (another person, a store, a product, a brand). *Values* also are beliefs. Values differ from other beliefs, however, because they meet the following criteria: (1) They are relatively few in number; (2) they serve as a guide for culturally appropriate behavior; (3) they are enduring or difficult to change; (4) they are not tied to specific objects or situations; and (5) they are widely accepted by the members of a society.

Therefore, in a broad sense, both values and beliefs are mental images that affect a wide range of specific attitudes that, in turn, influence the way a person is likely to respond in a specific situation. For example, the criteria a person uses to evaluate alternative brands in a product category (such as Samsung versus Panasonic HDTV sets), or his or her eventual preference for one of these brands over the other, are influenced by both a person's general values (perceptions as to what constitutes quality and the meaning of country of origin) and specific beliefs (particular perceptions about the quality of South Korean-made versus Japanese-made televisions).

In contrast to beliefs and values, customs are *overt modes of behavior that constitute culturally approved or acceptable ways of behaving in specific situations.* Customs consist of everyday or routine behavior. For example, a consumer's routine behavior, such as adding a diet sweetener to coffee, putting ketchup on scrambled eggs, putting mustard on frankfurters, and having a pasta dish *before* rather than *with* the main course of a meal, are customs. Thus, whereas beliefs and values are guides for behavior, customs are *usual and acceptable ways of behaving.*

By our definition, it is easy to see how an understanding of various cultures of a society helps marketers predict consumer acceptance of their products.

the invisible hand of culture

The impact of culture is so natural and automatic that its influence on behavior is usually taken for granted. For instance, when consumer researchers ask people why they do certain things, they frequently answer, "Because it's the right thing to do." This seemingly superficial response partially reflects the ingrained influence of culture on our behavior. Often it is only when we are exposed to people with different cultural values or customs (as when visiting a different region or a different country) that we become aware of how culture has molded our own behavior. Thus, a true appreciation of the influence that culture has on our daily life requires some knowledge of at least one other society with different cultural characteristics. For example, to understand that brushing our teeth twice a day with flavored toothpaste is a cultural phenomenon requires some awareness that members of another society either do not brush their teeth at all or do so in a distinctly different manner than our own society.

Perhaps the following statement expresses it best:

Consumers both view themselves in the context of their culture and react to their environment based upon the cultural framework that they bring to that experience. Each individual perceives the world through his own cultural lens.[1]

Culture can exist and sometimes reveal itself at different perceived or subjective levels.[2] For those of us interested in consumer behavior, we would be most concerned with three "levels" of subjective culture that are especially revelvant to the exploration of consumer behavior and formation of marketing strategy. The first-level can be thought of as the *supranational level;* it reflects the underlying dimensions of culture that impact multiple cultures or different societies (i.e., cross-national or cross-cultural boundaries). For instance, it might reflect regional character (e.g., people living in several nations in a particular region of Europe), or racial and religious similarities or differences, or shared or different languages (mostly the concern of Chapter 14). The second level is concerned with *national level* factors, such as shared core values, customs, personalities, and predispositional factors that tend to capture the essence of the "national character" of the citizens of a particular country (mostly the content of this chapter). Finally, *group level* factors are concerned with various subdivisions of a country or society. They might include subcultures' difference (see Chapter 13), and membership and reference group differences (see Chapter 10). Table 12.1 summarizes this discussion, whereas Figure 12.1 presents a model depicting the role that subjective culture (on the left side of the model) plays in determining our beliefs, practices, and values, which in turn impact our social norms, attitudes, behavioral intentions, and, ultimately, our behavior (see the discussion of such attitude models in Chapter 8).

culture satisfies needs

Culture exists to satisfy the needs of the people within a society. It offers order, direction, and guidance in all phases of human problem solving by providing "tried-and-true" methods of satisfying physiological, personal, and social needs. For example, culture provides standards and "rules" about when to eat ("not between meals"); where to eat ("in a busy restaurant, because the food is likely to be good"); what is appropriate to eat for breakfast (eggs and toast), lunch (a sandwich), dinner ("something hot and good and healthy"), and snacks ("something with quick energy, but not too many calories"); and what to serve to guests at a dinner party ("a formal sit-down meal"), at a picnic (barbecued "franks and hamburgers"), or at a wedding (champagne). Culture is also associated with what a

TABLE 12.1	Three Levels of Subjective Culture—Supranational, National, and Groups
LEVELS	**DEFINITION/DIMENSIONS**
Level 1: Supranational	Subjective cultural differences that cross national boundaries or can be seen to be present in more than one country
	Composed of the following consumer behavior relevant factors: regional makeup, ethnic-racial composition of population, language and symbolisms meaning
Level 2: National	Shared cultural characters (national character or identity) that uniquely or specifically define the citizens of particular countries
Level 3: Group	Cultural divisions or grouping (especially subcultures) that contain various collections of individuals (e.g., families, work groups, shopping groups, friendship groups)

Inspired and adapted from: Elena Karahanna, J. Roberto Evaristo, and Mark Strite, "Levels of Culture and Individual Behavior: An Integrative Perspective," *Journal of Global Information Management* 13 (April–June 2005): 5.

FIGURE 12.1

A Theoretical Model of Culture's Influence on Behavior

Source: Elena Karahanna, J. Roberto Evaristo, and Mark Strite, "Levels of Culture and Individual Behavior: An Integrative Perspective," *Journal of Global Information Management* 13 (April–June 2005): 8.

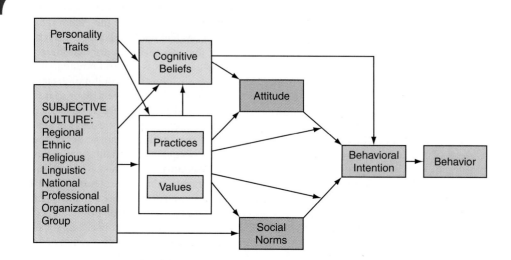

society's members consider to be a necessity and what they view as a luxury. For instance, 55 percent of American adults consider a microwave to be a necessity, and 36 percent consider a remote control for a TV or VCR to be a necessity.[3]

Similarly, culture also provides insights as to suitable dress for specific occasions (such as what to wear around the house, what to wear to school, to work, to church, at a fast-food restaurant, or to a movie theater). Dress codes have shifted dramatically; people are dressing more casually most of the time. Today, only a few big-city restaurants and clubs have business dress requirements. With the relaxed dress code in the corporate work environment, fewer men are wearing dress shirts, ties, and business suits, and fewer women are wearing dresses, suits, and panty hose. In their place casual slacks, sports shirts and blouses, jeans, and the emerging category of "dress casual" have been increasing in sales.

Soft-drink companies would prefer that consumers received their morning "jolt" of caffeine from one of their products rather than from coffee. Because most Americans do not consider soda a suitable breakfast beverage, the real challenge for soft-drink companies is to overcome culture, not competition. Indeed, coffee has been challenged on all fronts by juices, milk, teas (hot and iced), a host of different types of soft drinks, and now even caffeinated waters. Not resting on their "cultural advantage" as a breakfast drink and the namesake of the "coffee break," coffee marketers have been fighting back by targeting gourmet and specialty coffees (e.g., espresso, cappuccino, and café mocha) to young adults (those 18 to 24 years of age). These efforts have been paying off as young adults (an important segment of the soft-drink market) have been responding positively to gourmet coffees.

Cultural beliefs, values, and customs continue to be followed as long as they yield satisfaction. When a specific standard no longer satisfies the members of a society, however, it is modified or replaced, so that the resulting standard is more in line with current needs and desires. For instance, it was once considered a sign of a fine hotel that it provided down or goose feather pillows in rooms. Today, with so many guests allergic to such materials, synthetic polyfill pillows are becoming more the rule. Thus, culture gradually but continually evolves to meet the needs of society.

culture is learned

Unlike innate biological characteristics (e.g., sex, skin, hair color, or intelligence), culture is learned. At an early age, we begin to acquire from our social environment a set of beliefs, values, and customs that make up our culture. For children, the learning of these acceptable cultural values and customs is reinforced by the process of playing with their toys. As children play, they act out and rehearse important cultural lessons and situations. This cultural learning prepares them for later real-life circumstances.

How culture is learned

Anthropologists have identified three distinct forms of cultural learning: *formal learning,* in which adults and older siblings teach a young family member "how to behave"; *informal learning,* in which a child learns primarily by imitating the behavior of selected others, such as family, friends, or TV heroes; and *technical learning,* in which teachers instruct the child in an educational environment about what should be done, how it should be done, and why it should be done. Although a firm's advertising can influence all three types of cultural learning, it is likely that many product advertisements enhance informal cultural learning by providing the audience with a model of behavior to imitate. This is especially true for visible or conspicuous products that are evaluated in public settings (such as designer clothing, cell phones, or status golf clubs), where peer influence is likely to play an important role. Additionally, "not only are cultural values cited in advertising copy, they also are often coded in the visual imagery, colors, movements, music, and other nonverbal elements of an advertisement."[4]

The repetition of advertising messages creates and reinforces cultural beliefs and values. For example, many advertisers continually stress the same selected benefits of their products or services. Ads for wireless phone service often stress the clarity of their connection, or the nationwide coverage of their service, or the free long distance calling, as well as the flexibility of their pricing plans. It is difficult to say whether wireless phone subscribers *inherently* desire these benefits from their wireless service providers or whether, after several years of cumulative exposure to advertising appeals stressing these benefits, they have been taught by marketers to desire them. In a sense, although specific product advertising may reinforce the benefits that consumers want from the product (as determined by consumer behavior research), such advertising also "teaches" future generations of consumers to expect the same benefits from the product category.

Figure 12.2 shows that cultural meaning moves from the culturally constituted world to consumer goods and from there to the individual consumer by means of various *consumption-related vehicles* (e.g., advertising or observing or imitating others' behavior). Imagine the ever-popular T-shirt and how it can furnish cultural meaning and identity for wearers. T-shirts can function as *trophies* (as proof of participation in sports or travel) or as self-proclaimed labels of *belonging to a cultural category* ("World Series Attendee"). T-shirts can also be used as a means of *self-expression,* which may provide wearers with the additional benefit of serving as a "topic" initiating social dialogue with others. Still further, although we might expect that a New York T-shirt would be worn by a person who has been to New York (or has received it as a gift from someone else who has visited New York), this is not necessarily so. In such a world of "virtual identities," consumers can now just buy a New York T-shirt at a local retailer and create the impression that they have been there.

Enculturation and acculturation

When discussing the acquisition of culture, anthropologists often distinguish between the learning of one's own, or native, culture and the learning of some "new" (other) culture. The learning of one's own culture is known as **enculturation**. The learning of a new or foreign culture is known as **acculturation**. In Chapter 14, we will see that acculturation is an important concept for marketers who plan to sell their products in foreign or multinational markets. In such cases, marketers must study the specific culture(s) of their potential target markets to determine whether their products will be acceptable to its members and, if so, how they can best communicate the characteristics of their products to persuade the target market to buy.

FIGURE 12.2

The Movement of Cultural Meaning

Source: Grant McCracken, "Culture and Consumption: A Theoretical Account of the Structure and Movement of the Cultural Meaning of Consumer Goods," *Journal of Consumer Research,* 13 (June 1986): 72. Reprinted by permission of The University of Chicago Press as publishers.

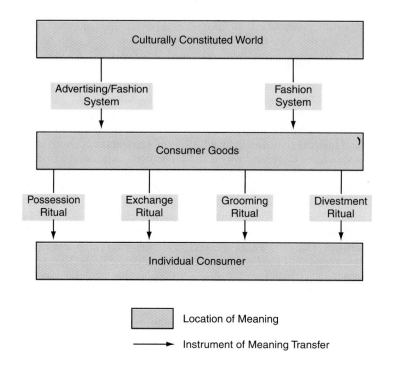

Language and symbols

To acquire a common culture, the members of a society must be able to communicate with each other through a common language. Without a common language, shared meaning could not exist and true communication would not take place (see Chapter 9).

To communicate effectively with their audiences, marketers must use appropriate **symbols** to convey desired product images or characteristics. These symbols can be verbal or nonverbal. Verbal symbols may include a television announcement or an advertisement in a magazine. Nonverbal communication includes the use of such symbols as figures, colors, shapes, and even textures to lend additional meaning to print or broadcast advertisements, to trademarks, and to packaging or product designs (see Figure 12.3).

Basically, the symbolic nature of human language sets it apart from all other animal communication. A symbol is anything that stands for something else. Any word is a symbol. The word *razor* calls forth a specific image related to an individual's own knowledge and experience (possibly either a shaving-related image or a Motorola cell phone-related image). The word *tsunami* calls forth the notion of waves and water and also has the power to stir us emotionally, arousing feelings of danger and the need for protection and safety. Similarly, the word *mercedes* has symbolic meaning: To some it suggests a fine luxury automobile; to others it implies wealth and status; to still others it reminds them of a woman named Mercedes.

Because the human mind can process symbols, it is possible, for example, for a person to "experience" cognitively a visualization for a product, like the advertisement for a skin moisturizing gel, which contrasts two scenes—one of a parched desert without the gel and one of a rich green landscape with the gel. Such a comparison presents the idea that a skin-moisturizing gel will transform a person's dry skin to a comfortable moist state. The capacity to learn symbolically is primarily a human phenomenon; most other animals learn by direct experience. Clearly, the ability of humans to understand symbolically how a product, service, or idea can satisfy their needs makes it easier for marketers to sell the features and benefits of their offerings. Through a shared language and culture, individuals already know what the image means; thus, an association can be made without actively thinking about it.

FIGURE 12.3

Source: © Wm. Wrigley
Jr. Company. Used with
permission. All rights reserved.

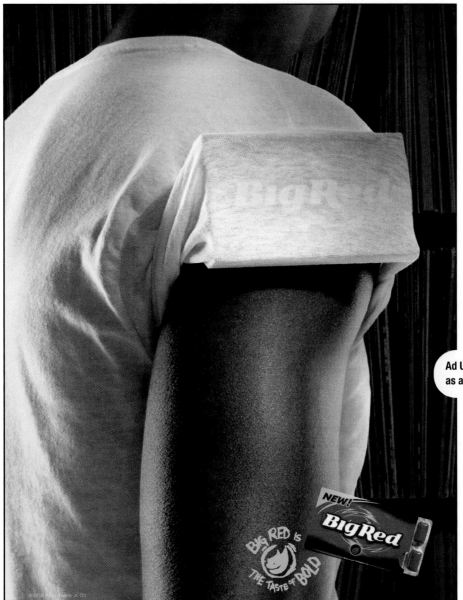

**Ad Using Visual Imagery
as a Symbol**

A symbol may have several, even contradictory, meanings, so the advertiser must ascertain exactly what the symbol is communicating to its intended audience. For example, the advertiser who uses a trademark depicting an old craftsman to symbolize careful workmanship may instead be communicating an image of outmoded methods and lack of style. The marketer who uses slang in an advertisement to attract a teenage audience must do so with great care; slang that is misused or outdated will symbolically date the marketer's firm and product.

Price and channels of distribution also are significant symbols of the marketer and the marketer's product. For example, price often implies quality to potential buyers. For certain products (such as clothing), the type of store in which the product is sold also is an important symbol of quality. In fact, all the elements of the marketing mix—the product, its promotion, price, and the stores at which it is available—are symbols that communicate ranges of quality to potential buyers.

Ritual

In addition to language and symbols, culture includes various ritualized experiences and behaviors that until recently have been largely neglected by consumer researchers. A **ritual** is a type of symbolic activity consisting of a series of steps (multiple behaviors) occurring in a fixed sequence and repeated over time.[5]

In practice, rituals extend over the human life cycle from birth to death, including a host of intermediate events (such as confirmation, graduations, and marriage). These rituals can be very public, elaborate, religious, or civil ceremonies, or they can be as mundane as an individual's grooming behavior or flossing. Ritualized behavior is typically rather formal and often is scripted behavior (as a religious service requiring a prayer book or the code of proper conduct in a court of law). It is also likely to occur repeatedly over time (such as singing the national anthem before a basketball game).

Most important from the standpoint of marketers is the fact that rituals tend to be replete with ritual artifacts (products) that are associated with or somehow enhance the performance of the ritual. For instance, turkey, stuffing, and other various food items are linked to the ritual of a Thanksgiving Day, New Year's Day, or other holiday celebrations; other rituals (such as a graduation, a wedding or wedding anniversary, a Tuesday night card game, or a Saturday morning visit to the hair salon) have their own specific artifacts associated with them. For special occasions, such as wedding anniversaries, some types of artifacts are perceived as more appropriate as gifts than others, for example, jewelry rather than everyday household items (Table 12.2).

In addition to a ritual, which is the way that something is traditionally done, there is also *ritualistic behavior,* which can be defined as any behavior that is made into a ritual. For example, a tennis player may bounce the ball a few times or swing the arm holding the tennis racket in a big arc once or twice before every serve. Table 12.3 describes a young woman's ritualistic behavior with respect to facial beauty care.

TABLE 12.2	Selected Rituals and Associated Artifacts
SELECTED RITUALS	**TYPICAL ARTIFACTS**
Wedding	White gown (something old, something new, something borrowed, something blue)
Birth of child	U.S. savings bond, silver baby spoon
Birthday	Card, present, cake with candles
50th wedding anniversary	Catered party, card and gift, display of photos of the couple's life together
Graduation	Pen, U.S. savings bond, card, wristwatch
Valentine's Day	Candy, card, flowers
New Year's Eve	Champagne, party, fancy dress
Thanksgiving	Prepare a turkey meal for family and friends
Going to the gym	Towel, exercise clothes, water, portable tape player
Sunday football	Beer, potato chips, pretzels
Super Bowl party	Same as Sunday football (just more)
Starting a new job	Get a haircut, buy some new clothing
Getting a job promotion	Taken out to lunch by coworkers, receive token gift
Retirement	Company party, watch, plaque
Death	Send a card, give to charity in the name of the deceased

TABLE 12.3	**Facial Beauty Ritual of a Young TV Advertising Sales Representative**

1. I pull my hair back with a headband.
2. I take all my makeup off with L'Oréal eye makeup remover.
3. Next, I use a Q-tip with some moisturizer around my eyes to make sure all eye makeup is removed.
4. I wash my face with Noxzema facial wash.
5. I apply Clinique Dramatically Different Lotion to my face, neck, and throat.
6. If I have a blemish, I apply Clearasil Treatment to the area to dry it out.
7. Twice weekly (or as necessary) I use Aapri Facial Scrub to remove dry and dead skin.
8. Once a week I apply Clinique Clarifying Lotion 2 with a cotton ball to my face and throat to remove deep-down dirt and oils.
9. Once every three months I get a professional salon facial to deep-clean my pores.

Culture is shared

To be considered a cultural characteristic, a particular belief, value, or practice must be shared by a significant portion of the society. Thus, culture frequently is viewed as group *customs* that link together the members of a society. Of course, common language is the critical cultural component that makes it possible for people to share values, experiences, and customs.

Various social institutions within a society transmit the elements of culture and make the sharing of culture a reality. Chief among such institutions is the *family,* which serves as the primary agent for enculturation—the passing along of basic cultural beliefs, values, and customs to society's newest members. A vital part of the enculturation role of the family is the consumer socialization of the young (see Chapter 10). This includes teaching such basic consumer-related values and skills as the meaning of money; the relationship between price and quality; the establishment of product tastes, preferences, and habits; and appropriate methods of response to various promotional messages.

In addition to the family, two other institutions traditionally share much of the responsibility for the transfer of selected aspects of culture: *educational institutions* and *houses of worship.* Educational institutions specifically are charged with imparting basic learning skills, history, patriotism, citizenship, and the technical training needed to prepare people for significant roles within society. Religious institutions provide and perpetuate religious consciousness, spiritual guidance, and moral training. Although the young receive much of their consumer training within the family setting, the educational and religious systems reinforce this training by teaching economic and ethical concepts.

A fourth, frequently overlooked, social institution that plays a major role in the transfer of culture throughout society is the mass media. Given the extensive exposure of the American population to both print and broadcast media, as well as the easily ingested, entertaining format in which the contents of such media usually are presented, it is not surprising that the mass media are powerful vehicles for imparting a wide range of cultural values.

We are exposed daily to advertising, an important component of the media. Advertising not only underwrites, or makes economically feasible, the editorial or programming contents of the media, but it also transmits much about our culture. Without advertising, it would be almost impossible to disseminate information about products, ideas, and causes.

Consumers receive important cultural information from advertising. For example, it has been hypothesized that one of the roles of advertising in sophisticated magazines such as *Vogue* (**www.vogue.com**), *Bon Appetit* (**www. epicurious.com/bonappetit**), and

Architectural Digest (**www.architecturaldigest.com**) is to instruct readers how to dress, how to decorate their homes, and what foods and wines to serve guests, or in other words, what types of behavior are most appropriate to their particular social class. Thus, although the scope of advertising is often considered to be limited to influencing the demand for specific products or services, in a cultural context, advertising has the expanded mission of reinforcing established cultural values and aiding in the dissemination of new tastes, habits, and customs. In planning their advertising, marketers should recognize that advertising is an important agent for social change in our society.

culture is dynamic

To fulfill its need-gratifying role, culture continually must evolve if it is to function in the best interests of a society. For this reason, the marketer must carefully monitor the sociocultural environment in order to market an existing product more effectively or to develop promising new products.

This is not an easy task because many factors are likely to produce cultural changes within a given society (new technology, population shifts, resource shortages, wars, changing values, and customs borrowed from other cultures). For example, major ongoing cultural changes in American society reflect the expanded career options open to women. Today, most women work outside the home, frequently in careers that once were considered exclusively male oriented. These career women are increasingly not waiting for marriage or a man to buy them luxury items—such as fur coats, expensive wristwatches, and diamond rings. More and more such women are saying, "I earn a good living, why wait? I will buy it for myself."

The changing nature of culture means that marketers have to consistently reconsider *why* consumers are now doing what they do, *who* the purchasers and the users of their products are (males only, females only, or both), *when* they do their shopping, *how* and *where* they can be reached by the media, and *what* new product and service needs are emerging. Marketers who monitor cultural changes also often find new opportunities to increase corporate profitability. For example, marketers of such products and services as life insurance, financial and investment advice, casual clothing, toy electric trains, and cigars are among those who have attempted to take advantage of shifts in what is feminine and how to communicate with female consumers. As yet another example, "design has (re)emerged as a major force in American consumers' lives." Since today even basic consumer goods deliver on their promises of performance, design has become a way for a company to differentiate its products.[6] If all MP3 players, for example, sound great, then why not purchase the one that looks the "coolest," which is probably the iPod. One writer has recently described the period we are now living in "as the age of aesthetics," wherein the way things look, feel, and smell have come to matter—not just among the upper-middle classes but among all consumers.[7]

A recently longitudinal study of how women have been depicted in *Fortune* magazine serves as yet another example of how culture is dynamic. The study employed content analysis (discussed later in this chapter) as its methodology, and concluded that the changes in advertising tended to reflect the changing role of women during the decade starting in 1990.[8] In particular, the research reveals a fourfold increase in the number of women as the "figure" (i.e., presented in the foreground of the print advertisement) compared to men. Women were also substantially more likely to be portrayed as being a "professional."

Insights about cultural change are also secured from lists that trend observers create as to "what's hot" and "what's not." Table 12.4 presents an example of such a comparison. Specifically, this one tells potential vistors to France that small, lesser-known cities are "in," whereas Paris is "out"; similarly, expensive or upscale hotels are also "out," while small inns are "in." Such lists often reflect the dynamic nature of a particular society or culture.

TABLE 12.4	What Is IN and What Is OUT When Visiting France
IN	**OUT**
Lesser-known cities	Paris
Languedoc	Provence
Recreational travel	Luxury travel
Small inns	Upscale hotels
Living in France	Visiting France
Driving	Riding the rails
Bringing your cell phone	Using a phone card
Packing light	Packing heavy

Source: Kery Carr, "France Travel Trends—What's In & What's Out for 2005," accessed at
http://gofrance.about.com/odissuesnewsshottopics/a/inandout.htm

the measurement of culture

A wide range of measurement techniques are used in the study of culture. Some of these techniques were described in Chapter 2. For example, the projective tests used by psychologists to study motivation and personality and the attitude measurement techniques used by social psychologists and sociologists are relatively popular tools in the study of culture.

In addition, *content analysis, consumer fieldwork,* and *value measurement instruments* are three research approaches that are frequently used to examine culture and to spot cultural trends. There are also several commercial services that track emerging values and social trends for businesses and governmental agencies.

Content analysis

Conclusions about a society, or specific aspects of a society, or a comparison of two or more societies sometimes can be drawn from examining the content of particular messages. **Content analysis**, as the name implies, focuses on the content of verbal, written, and pictorial communications (such as the copy and art composition of an ad).

Content analysis can be used as a relatively objective means of determining what social and cultural changes have occurred in a specific society or as a way of contrasting aspects of two different societies. A content analysis of more than 250 ads appearing in eight issues of *Seventeen* magazine, four Japanese issues, and four American issues, found that teenage girls are portrayed differently. The research concluded that these "differences correspond to each country's central concepts of self and society." Whereas American teen girls are often associated with images of "independence and determination," Japanese teen girls are most often portrayed with a "happy, playful, childlike girlish image."[9] In another content analysis study—this one comparing American and Chinese television commercials targeted to children—the research revealed that 82 percent of the Chinese ads aimed at children were for food products, whereas 56 percent of the ads directed at American children were for toys.[10]

Content analysis is useful to both marketers and public policymakers interested in comparing the advertising claims of competitors within a specific industry, as well as for evaluating the nature of advertising claims targeted to specific audiences (e.g., women, the elderly, or children).

Consumer fieldwork

When examining a specific society, anthropologists frequently immerse themselves in the environment under study through **consumer fieldwork**. As trained researchers, they are likely to select a small sample of people from a particular society and carefully observe their behavior. Based on their observations, researchers draw conclusions about the values, beliefs, and customs of the society under investigation. For example, if researchers were interested in how men select neckties, they might position trained observers in department and clothing stores and note how neckties are selected (solid versus patterned, striped versus paisley, and so on). The researchers also may be interested in the degree of search that accompanies the choice, that is, how often consumers tend to take a necktie off the display, examine it, compare it to other neckties in the store, and place it back again before selecting the necktie that they finally purchase.

The distinct characteristics of **field observation** are that (1) it takes place within a natural environment; (2) it is performed sometimes without the subject's awareness; and (3) it focuses on observation of behavior. Because the emphasis is on a natural environment and observable behavior, field observation concerned with consumer behavior often focuses on in-store shopping behavior and, less frequently, on in-home preparation and consumption.

In some cases, instead of just observing behavior, researchers become **participant-observers** (i.e., they become active members of the environment that they are studying). For example, if researchers were interested in examining how consumers select computer software, they might take a sales position in a computer superstore to observe directly and even to interact with customers in the transaction process.

Today, there are consumer research firms that specialize in studying consumer rituals and values. These firms often videotape subjects at work, at home, in their cars, and in public places. For instance, researchers might ask a teenager why he's buying a certain backpack, and you might not get a useful response. Rather, watching a teenager as he shops for that backpack, and you might "learn a few things." This type of research, used by Nissan in the 1990s when it was designing its line of Infinity automobiles, discovered that the Japanese notion of luxury was very different than the American version—whereas the Japanese crave simplicity, Americans crave visible opulence.[11]

Both field observation and participant-observer research require highly skilled researchers who can separate their own preferences and emotions from what they actually observe in their professional roles. Both techniques provide valuable insight that might not easily be obtained through survey research that simply asks consumers questions about their behavior.

In addition to fieldwork methods, depth interviews and focus-group sessions (see Chapter 2) are also often used by marketers to get a "first look" at an emerging social or cultural change. In the relatively informal atmosphere of focus group discussions, consumers are apt to reveal attitudes or behavior that may signal a shift in values that, in turn, may affect the long-run market acceptance of a product or service. For instance, focus group studies can be used to identify marketing programs that reinforce established customer loyalty and goodwill (or relationship marketing). A common thread running throughout these studies showed that established customers, especially for services (such as investment and banking services), want to have their loyalty acknowledged in the form of *personalized services*. These observations have led various service and product companies to refine or establish loyalty programs that are more personalized in the way that they treat their established customers (e.g., by recognizing the individuality of such core customers). This is just one of numerous examples showing how focus groups and depth interviews are used to spot social trends.

Value measurement survey instruments

Anthropologists have traditionally observed the behavior of members of a specific society and inferred from such behavior the dominant or underlying values of the society. In recent years, however, there has been a gradual shift to measuring values directly by means of survey (questionnaire) research. Researchers use data collection instruments called *value instruments* to ask people how they feel about such basic personal and social concepts as freedom, comfort, national security, and peace.

A variety of popular value instruments have been used in consumer behavior studies, including the **Rokeach Value Survey**, the *List of Values (LOV)*, and the *Values and Lifestyles—VALS* (discussed in Chapter 3). The widely used Rokeach Value Survey is a self-administered value inventory that is divided into two parts, each part measuring different

TABLE 12.5	The Rokeach Value Survey Instrument

TERMINAL VALUES	INSTRUMENTAL VALUES
A Comfortable Life (a prosperous life)	Ambitious (hardworking, aspiring)
An Exciting Life (a stimulating, active life)	Broad-Minded (open-minded)
A World at Peace (free of war and conflict)	Capable (competent, effective)
Equality (brotherhood, equal opportunity for all)	Cheerful (lighthearted, joyful)
Freedom (independence and free choice)	Clean (neat, tidy)
Happiness (contentedness)	Courageous (standing up for your beliefs)
National Security (protection from attack)	Forgiving (willing to pardon others)
Pleasure (an enjoyable life)	Helpful (working for the welfare of others)
Salvation (saved, eternal life)	Honest (sincere, truthful)
Social Recognition (respect and admiration)	Imaginative (daring, creative)
True Friendship (close companionship)	Independent (self-reliant, self-sufficient)
Wisdom (a mature understanding of life)	Intellectual (intelligent, reflective)
A World of Beauty (beauty of nature and the arts)	Logical (consistent, rational)
Family Security (taking care of loved ones)	Loving (affectionate, tender)
Mature Love (sexual and spiritual intimacy)	Obedient (dutiful, respectful)
Self-Respect (self-esteem)	Polite (courteous, well-mannered)
A Sense of Accomplishment (lasting contribution)	Responsible (dependable, reliable)
Inner Harmony (freedom from inner conflict)	Self-Controlled (restrained, self-disciplined)

Source: Modified and reproduced by special permission of the publisher, Consulting Psychologists Press, Inc., Palo Alto, CA 94303 from *Rokeach Value Survey* by Milton Research. Copyright 1983 by Milton Rokeach. All rights reserved. Further reproduction is prohibited without the publisher's written consent.

but complementary types of personal values (see Table 12.5). The first part consists of 18 *terminal value* items, which are designed to measure the relative importance of end states of existence (or personal goals). The second part consists of 18 *instrumental value* items, which measure basic approaches an individual might take to reach end-state values. Thus, the first half of the measurement instrument deals with ends, and the second half considers means.

Using the Rokeach Value Survey, adult Brazilians were categorized into six distinctive value segments.[12] For example, Segment A (representing 13 percent of the sample) was most concerned with "world peace," followed by "inner harmony" and "true friendship." Members of this segment were found to be especially involved in domestic-oriented activities (such as gardening, reading, and going out with the family to visit relatives). Because of their less materialistic and nonhedonistic orientation, this segment also may be the least prone to experiment with new products. In contrast, Segment B (representing 9 percent of the sample) was most concerned with self-centered values such as self-respect, a comfortable life, pleasure, an exciting life, a sense of accomplishment, and social recognition. They were least concerned with values related to the family, such as friendship, love, and equality. These self-centered, achievement-oriented pleasure seekers were expected to prefer provocative clothes in the latest fashion, to enjoy an active lifestyle, and be more likely to try new products.

The LOV scale is a related measurement instrument that is also designed to be used in surveying consumers' personal values. The LOV scale asks consumers to identify their two most important values from a nine-value list (such as "warm relationships with others," "a sense of belonging," or "a sense of accomplishment") that is based on the terminal values of the Rokeach Value Survey.[13]

american core values

What is the American culture? In this section, we identify a number of **core values** that both affect and reflect the character of American society. This is a difficult undertaking for several reasons. First, the United States is a diverse country, consisting of a good number of **subcultures** (religious, ethnic, regional, racial, and economic groups), each of which interprets and responds to society's basic beliefs and values in its own specific way. Second, America is a dynamic society that has undergone an almost constant change in response to the development of new technology. This element of rapid change makes it especially difficult to monitor changes in cultural values. Finally, the existence of contradictory values in American society is somewhat confusing. For instance, Americans traditionally embrace freedom of choice and individualism, yet simultaneously they show great tendencies to conform (in dress, in furnishings, and in fads) to the rest of society. In the context of consumer behavior, Americans like to have a wide choice of products and prefer those that uniquely express what they envison to be their personal lifestyles. Yet, there is often a considerable amount of implicit pressure to conform to the values of family members, friends, and other socially important groups. It is difficult to reconcile these seemingly inconsistent values; their existence, however, demonstrates that America is a complex society with numerous paradoxes.

When selecting the specific core values to be examined, we were guided by three criteria:

1. The value must be pervasive. *A significant portion of the American people must accept the value and use it as a guide for their attitudes and actions.*

2. The value must be enduring. *The specific value must have influenced the actions of the American people over an extended period of time (as distinguished from a short-run trend).*

3. The value must be consumer related. *The specific value must provide insights that help us to understand the consumption actions of the American people.*

Meeting these criteria are a number of basic values that expert observers of the American scene consider the "building blocks" of that rather elusive concept called the "American character."

Achievement and success

In a broad cultural context, achievement is a major American value, with historical roots that can be traced to the traditional religious belief in the Protestant work ethic, which considers hard work to be wholesome, spiritually rewarding, and an appropriate end in itself. Indeed, substantial research evidence shows that the achievement orientation is closely associated with the technical development and general economic growth of American society.[14]

Individuals who consider a "sense of accomplishment" an important personal value tend to be achievers who strive hard for success. Although historically associated with men, especially male business executives, today *achievement* is very important for women, who are increasingly enrolled in undergraduate and graduate business programs and are more commonly seeking top-level business careers.

A recent study that examined the interplay between the Internet and personal values found that those individuals scoring high in "sense of accomplishment" were more likely to use the Internet for learning or gathering information, making reservations or researching travel, work/business, buying goods or services, looking up stock quotes, and participating in online auctions by buying or selling products. Conversely, Internet activities not associated with a high "sense of accomplishment" included surfing the Web, communication with others in chat rooms, and gathering product or retail store information.[15]

Success is a closely related American cultural theme. However, achievement and success do differ. Specifically, achievement is its own direct reward (it is implicitly satisfying to the individual achiever), whereas success implies an extrinsic reward (such as luxury possessions, financial compensation, or status improvement). Moreover, it is the widespread embracing of achievement and success that has led to the great success and progress of the United States.[16] A recent study examining what influences college students' choice of major found that the most important influence for incoming freshmen was interest in the subject. However, while for female students the next most influential factor was aptitude in the subject, for male students it was "the major's potential for career advancement, and job opportunites and the level of compensation in the field."[17]

Both achievement and success influence consumption. They often serve as social and moral justification for the acquisition of goods and services. For example, "You owe it to yourself," "You worked for it," and "You deserve it" are popular achievement themes used by advertisers to coax consumers into purchasing their products. Regardless of gender, achievement-oriented people often enjoy conspicuous consumption because it allows them to display symbols of their personal achievement. When it comes to personal development and preparation for future careers, the themes of achievement and success are also especially appropriate.

Activity

Americans attach an extraordinary amount of importance to being *active* or *involved*. Keeping busy is widely accepted as a healthy and even necessary part of the American lifestyle. The hectic nature of American life is attested to by foreign visitors, who frequently comment that they cannot understand why Americans are always "on the run" and seemingly unable to relax. It is easy to identify ads in the mass media for products and services that are designed to assist consumers in dealing with their hectic or "overful" lives (see Figure 12.4).

The premium placed on activity has had both positive and negative effects on the popularity of various products. For example, a principal reason for the enormous growth of fast-food chains, such as McDonald's and Kentucky Fried Chicken, is that so many people want quick, prepared meals when they are away from the house. Americans rarely eat a full breakfast because they usually are too rushed in the morning to prepare and consume a traditional morning meal.

Research suggests that "being busy," in and of itself, is not enough and not necessarily healthy. For example, some researchers have reported that although it is important for elderly people to "keep busy," it is important that the activities they engage in be fulfilling. Similarly, it is being questioned whether keeping young children busy all the time is healthy for them—it's been suggested that kids need time to relax![18]

Efficiency and practicality

With a basic philosophy of down-to-earth pragmatism, Americans pride themselves on being efficient and practical. When it comes to *efficiency,* they admire anything that saves time and effort. In terms of *practicality,* they generally are receptive to any new product that makes tasks easier and can help solve problems. For example, today it is possible for manufacturers of many product categories to offer the public a wide range of interchangeable components. Thus, a consumer can design his or her own customized wall unit from such standard components as compatible metals and woods, legs, door facings, and style panels at a cost not much higher than a completely standardized unit. The capacity of manufacturers to create mass-produced components offers consumers the practical option of a customized product at a reasonable price. If you are unfamiliar with such furniture, just browse through an IKEA catalog or the "virtual catalog" on the IKEA Web site (**www.ikea.com**). As another example, if you go to the Dell Computer Web site (**www.dell.com**) you can observe the myriad of ways in which almost any model of a Dell computer can be customized by the purchaser (e.g., memory upgrades, video card upgrades, hard drive size upgrades, software upgrades, etc.).

Source: © The Golden Grain Company. Used with permission. All rights reserved.

FIGURE 12.4

Ad Offering Assistance to Busy-Active Consumers

Another illustration of Americans' attentiveness to efficiency and practicality is the extreme importance attached to *time.* Americans seem to be convinced that "time waits for no one," which is reflected in their habitual attention to being prompt. Another sign of America's preoccupation with time is the belief that time is in increasingly short supply. Americans place a great deal of importance on getting there first, on the value of time itself, on the notion that time is money, on the importance of not wasting time, and on identifying "more" time. In our attempt to get more and more out of each day, one author has concluded that we may become trapped in a vicious circle in which we feel as if we are getting less and less out of each day.[19]

The frequency with which Americans look at their watches and the importance attached to having an accurate timepiece tend to support the American value of *punctuality*.

Progress

Progress is another watchword of American society. Americans respond favorably to the promise of progress. Receptivity to progress appears to be closely linked to the other core values already examined (*achievement, success, efficiency,* and *practicality*) and to the central belief that people can always improve themselves, that tomorrow should be better than today. In a consumption-oriented society, such as that of the United States, progress often means the acceptance of change, new products, or services designed to fulfill previously undersatisfied or unsatisfied needs. A new type of counselor, the "life coach" or "personal coach," works with individuals in order to help them improve themselves and seek "fulfillment and balance in careers, family, health, and hobbies." The coach tracks the client's progress and tries to keep the client heading in the direction of his or her fulfillment. Ideally, the coach makes the client excited about prospects for the future.

In the name of progress, Americans appear to be receptive to product claims that stress "new," "improved," "longer-lasting," "speedier," "quicker," "smoother and closer," and "increased strength" (see Figure 12.5).

Material comfort

For most Americans (even young children), *material comfort* signifies the attainment of "the good life," a life that may include a new car, a dishwasher, an air conditioner, a hot tub, and an almost infinite variety of other convenience-oriented and pleasure-providing goods and services. It appears that consumers' idea of material comfort is largely a *relative* view; that is, consumers tend to define their own satisfaction with the amount of material goods they have in terms of a comparison of what they have to what others have. If a comparison suggests that they have more than others do, then they are more likely to be satisfied.[20] On the other hand, as many popular songs point out, the ownership of material goods does not always lead to happiness. For instance, many people, especially affluent people, might be willing to trade money for more free time to spend with family and friends.

Vivre (**www.vivre.com**) offers a mail-order and online catalog aimed at "connecting luxury brands with affluent shoppers that is dedicated to providing material comfort for its customers." Consider how the company responds to the question "What is Vivre?" (taken from its Web site):

> One might consider Vivre to be a revival of the classic "first floor" of a department store, which traditionally displayed only the best of the best to a discriminating clientele. Likewise, Vivre presents only that which is deemed to be relevant, inspiring and exquisitely crafted. With a modern sensibility, the resulting treasure trove is delivered to doorsteps in the form of a glossy catalog . . . and to desktops via a full-service e-commerce website. Therein shoppers will find the best of the world at their fingertips.
>
> By presenting each season's collection in a lifestyle context, we create an emotional connection with our customers, who rely upon us to offer an edited collection of the very best of each season. By interspersing our selections with editorial and advice, we create an inspirational shopping experience—one where Vivre is considered to be a trusted advisor to "A Beautiful Life."[21]

Material comfort has often been associated with "bigger quantities of things" or "more of something." Recently, however, there has been a noticeable shift away from such a "more is better" viewpoint to a "better is better" vision—one that stresses better quality and better design. Americans today increasingly want *better,* and *better looking,* products. Such a state of affairs has been referred to as "the design economy"—that is, an economy that is based on the interaction of four elements: sustained prosperity, ongoing technology, a culture open to change, and marketing expertise.[22] Consider, for example, how the famous designer, Michael Graves, has helped Target (mass-merchandise retailer) accomplish its goal of being a standout provider of finely designed products at mass-market prices.

FIGURE 12.5

Source: © Church & Dwight Co., Inc. Use of Arm & Hammer— "The new Look of Clean" is with the express written permission of Church & Dwight Co., Inc., Princeton, New Jersey.

Progress Is a Popular and Winning Appeal

Individualism

Americans value "being themselves." Self-reliance, self-interest, self-confidence, self-esteem, and self-fulfillment are all exceedingly popular expressions of *individualism*. Striving for individualism seems to be linked to the rejection of dependency; that is, it is better to rely on oneself than on others. American "rugged individualism" is a form of individualism. It is based on the notion of self-reliance with competition (i.e., we try to meet our needs through personal effort, and in a way that outperforms our peers). Still further, solo performance, to the rugged individualist, is more important than teamwork—tasks should be accomplished alone, and victory should be earned alone.[23] Table 12.6 presents an interesting elaboration of the concept of "rugged individualism." Please examine it.

In terms of consumer behavior, an appeal to individualism frequently takes the form of reinforcing the consumer's sense of identity with products or services that both

TABLE 12.6	An Elaboration of the Cultural Dynamics of the "Rugged Individual"	
LABEL	**DEFINITION**	**IMAGERY**
Competition against self/Competition against others	Sees both self-weakness and others' strengths as foes to overcome.	Transforming self from a weakling to a warrior.
Manual labor/ Purchased labor	The choice to make or buy competitive equipment.	Becoming completely self-sufficient.
Solo performance/ Team work	Accomplishing goals by self or as a team.	The solo performer as the ideal.
Technology and machines/Aesthetics and fashion	Exaltation to utility, denigration of beauty.	Aesthetics as a seductive siren.
Instrumentalism/ Anthropomorphism	The extended self as alive, nonself as target or tool.	Dog as partner, deer as prey.
Nature/Culture	Culture as inadequate for testing manhood; nature as both refuge and providing ground.	The wilderness as heaven and hell.
Individual freedom/ Rule of law	Any form of government is restrictive of personal freedom and therefore undesirable.	The warrior as the quintessence of selfhood, the embodiment of freedom, and the exemplar of natural law.

Source: Elizabeth C. Hirschman, "Men, Dogs, Guns, and Cars: The Semiotics of Rugged Individualism," *Journal of Advertising* 32 (Spring 2003): 11.

reflect and emphasize that identity. For example, advertisements for high-style clothing and cosmetics usually promise that their products will enhance the consumer's exclusive or distinctive character and set him or her apart from others.

Freedom

Freedom is another very strong American value, with historical roots in such democratic ideals as freedom of speech, freedom of the press, and freedom of worship. As an outgrowth of these beliefs in freedom, Americans have a strong preference for *freedom of choice,* the opportunity to choose from a wide range of alternatives. This preference is reflected in the large number of competitive brands and product variations that can be found on the shelves of the modern supermarket or department store. For many products, consumers can select from a wide variety of sizes, colors, flavors, features, styles, and even special ingredients. It also explains why many companies offer consumers many choices (see Figure 12.6).

However, there are decision-making situations when consumers are faced with too many choices. In such cases they may feel overwhelmed by the shear number of choices and respond by running away from the stressful situation (see Chapter 16). Research with English consumers found that many of the respondents reported feeling bewildered and irritated by the fact that they were being offered "too much choice."[24]

External conformity

Although Americans deeply embrace freedom of choice and individualism, they nevertheless accept the reality of conformity. *External conformity* is a necessary process by which the individual adapts to society.

FIGURE 12.6

Source: Courtesy of Wendy's
International, Inc.

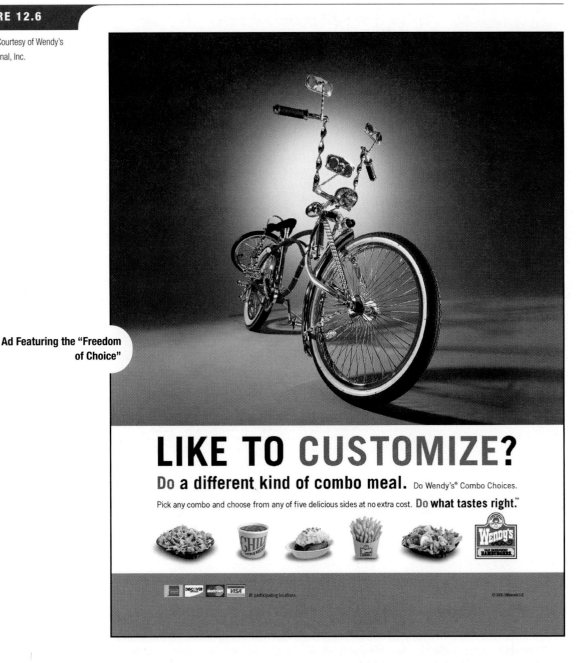

Ad Featuring the "Freedom
of Choice"

In the realm of consumer behavior, conformity (or uniformity) takes the form of standardized goods and services. Standardized products have been made possible by mass production. The availability of a wide choice of standardized products places the consumer in the unique position of being *individualistic* (by selecting specific products that close friends do not have) or of *conforming* (by purchasing a similar or identical product). In this context, individualism and conformity exist side by side as choices for the consumer.

An interesting example of the "Ping-Pong" relationship between seeking individualism and accepting conformity is the widespread acceptance of more casual dressing in the workplace. For instance, male and female executives are conforming less to workplace dress codes (i.e., there are more "total" dress options open to business executives). For instance, some male executives are wearing casual slacks and sport shirts to work; others are wearing blazers and slacks rather than business suits. Greater personal confidence and an emphasis on comfort appear to be the reasons that many executives are wearing less traditional business attire. Nevertheless, in some companies the appearance of male executives in blue blazers and gray slacks does seem like a "business uniform" (which is a kind of conformity). Consumer research examining the types of clothing that men and women wear to the office suggests that the majority of American workers are wearing some type of casual clothing to work.[25] For men, it is commonly "everyday casual" (jeans, shorts, T-shirts, etc.); for women it is "casual" (casual pants with or without a jacket, sweaters, separates, and pantsuits). Moreover, more than 50 percent of workers surveyed feel that it increases their productivity to wear casual clothing to work.

Humanitarianism

Americans are often generous when it comes to giving to those in need. They support with a passion many humane and charitable causes, and they sympathize with the underdog who must overcome adversity to get ahead. They also tend to be charitable and willing to come to the aid of people who are less fortunate than they are. To make the study of charitable giving more fruitful, consumer researchers have validated two scales that deal with *attitudes toward helping others* (AHO) and *attitudes toward charitable organizations* (ACO).[26] Table 12.7 presents the nine-item scale used to measure AHO and ACO.

Within the context of making charitable decisions, the Web site of the Planned Giving Design Center (**www.pgdc.net**) assists charities in their efforts to establish and cultivate relationships with professionals who advise clients in a position to make charitable contributions (e.g., lawyers, financial planners, trust officers).[27] Other Web sites are designed to provide individual givers with assistance in donating to specific charities (e.g., **www.charityguide.org**, **www.guidestar.org**, and **www.charitynavigator.org**).

Beyond charitable giving, other social issues have an impact on both what consumers buy and where they invest. For example, some investors prefer mutual funds that screen companies for such social concerns as military contracts, pollution problems, and equal opportunity employment. Investments in socially conscious mutual funds are now

---

TABLE 12.7	A Scale to Measure Attitude Toward Helping Others (AHO) and Attitude Toward Charitable Organizations (ACO)

SCALE ITEM

Attitude Toward Helping Others (AHO)

People should be willing to help others who are less fortunate.

Helping troubled people with their problems is very important to me.

People should be more charitable toward others in society.

People in need should receive support from others.

Attitude Toward Charitable Organizations (ACO)

The money given to charities goes to good causes.

Much of the money donated to charity is wasted. (R)

My image of charitable organizations is positive.

Charitable organizations have been quite successful in helping the needy.

Charity organizations perform a useful function for society.

Note: (R) = reverse scored.

Sources: Deborah J. Webb, Corliss L. Green, and Thomas G. Brashear, "Development and Validation of Scales to Measure Attitudes Influencing Monetary Donations to Charitable Organizations," *Journal of the Academy of Marketing Science* 28, no. 12 (Spring 2000): 299–309. Reprinted by permission of the publisher.

Elizabeth C. Hirschman, "Men, Dogs, Guns, and Cars: The Seminotics of Rugged Individualism," *Journal of Advertising* 32 (Spring 2003): 9–22.

quite commonplace. Many companies try to appeal to consumers by emphasizing their concern for environmental or social issues.

Youthfulness

Americans tend to place an almost sacred value on *youthfulness*. This emphasis is a reflection of America's rapid technological development. In an atmosphere where "new" is constantly stressed, "old" is often equated with being outdated. This is in contrast to traditional European, African, and Asian societies, in which the elderly are revered for having the wisdom of experience that comes with age.

Youthfulness should not be confused with youth, which describes an age grouping. Americans are preoccupied with *looking* and *acting* young, regardless of their chronological age. For Americans, youthfulness is a state of mind and a state of being, sometimes expressed as being "young at heart," "young in spirit," or "young in appearance."

A great deal of advertising is directed to creating a sense of urgency about retaining one's youth and fearing aging.[28] Hand-cream ads talk about "young hands"; skin-treatment ads state "I dreaded turning $30^1/_4$"; fragrance and makeup ads stress looking "sexy and young" or "denying your age"; detergent ads ask the reader, "Can you match their hands with their ages?" These advertising themes, which promise the consumer the benefits of youthfulness, reflect the high premium Americans place on appearing and acting young.

Fitness and health

Americans' preoccupation with *fitness* and *health* has emerged as a core value. This value has manifested itself in a number of ways, including tennis, racquetball, and jogging, and the continued increases in sales of vitamins. Added to these trends is an enhanced consciousness on the part of Americans that "You are what you eat." It has been suggested that the fitness boom of the 1980s was a result of a perceived lack of social control in America—people just felt anxious, insecure, and had self-doubts. A person feeling a lack of external self-control turns inward—if you can't control the world, you can control and change your own body through exercise.[29]

Fitness and health have increasingly become lifestyle choices for many consumers. Therefore, it is not suprising to find an almost constant stream of new products and services designed to assist health-focused consumers to achieve a healthier lifestyle (see Figure 12.7). This trend has stimulated Reebok to open a series of exercise–retail complexes that seek to build a cultural connection with consumers that goes beyond the normal marketing approach. Traditional food manufacturers have begun modifying their ingredients to cater to the health conscious consumer. Frozen dinners have become more nutritious in recent years, and manufacturers of traditional "junk food" are trying to make it more healthful. "Light" or "fat-free" versions of snack chips or pretzels, along with "low-sodium," "no-cholesterol," "no-preservative" snack products, are an attempt to provide consumers with tasty and healthy options. There are even Web sites for the fitness-minded consumer (see **www.fitnessonline.com**) offering workout tips, nutritional information, and fitness-related products and services. And the *Wall Street Journal* has reported that 100 million Americans sought health information over the Internet in the year 2000—up 30 million from the prior year.

Although there is no denying the "fitness and healthy living" trend in American society, there is evidence that consumers find it difficult "to be good" in terms of their personal health. For instance, people miss their desserts. Research suggests that more than 75 percent of American consumers think about dessert between one and eight times a day. The main activities that seem to put people in the mood for desserts are exercise, working, entertainment, eating, and studying.[30] Also, many Americans are unwilling to compromise on flavor for health benefits, with the result being a kind of reverse trend toward full-flavored, rich foods. This countertrend reveals the diversity of preferences that exist side by side within the marketplace.[31] It points out that low-fat, low-cholesterol, and low-carb food products are not for everyone. Moreover, it suggests that there is an important market segment whose members seek to indulge their taste buds

FIGURE 12.7

Source: © The Quaker Oats
Company. Used with permission.
All rights reserved.

HALF THE SUGAR,
FULL OF FLAVOR.
A NEW QUAKER OATMEAL.

**Ad Pointing Up the Importance
of Making "Healthy Choices"**

and their waistlines. Indeed, the World Health Organization has released a report stating
that obesity is an increasing problem in both developed and developing countries.[32]

Core values are not only an american phenomenon

The cultural values just examined are not all uniquely or originally American. Some may
have originally been borrowed, particularly from European society, as people emigrated
to the United States. Some values that originated in America are now part of the fabric of
other societies. For example, there is evidence that the good life may be nearly a universal
notion and that global brands are used as an external sign of attaining the good life.[33]

In addition, not all Americans necessarily accept each of these values. However, as a
whole, these values do account for much of the American character. Table 12.8 summarizes
a number of American core values and indicates their relevance to consumer behavior.

TABLE 12.8	Summary of American Core Values	
VALUE	**GENERAL FEATURES**	**RELEVANCE TO CONSUMER BEHAVIOR**
Achievement and Success Activity	Hard work is good; success flows from hard work. Keeping busy is healthy and natural.	Acts as a justification for acquisition of goods ("You deserve it"). Stimulates interest in products that are time-savers and enhance leisure time.
Efficiency and Practicality	Admiration of things that solve problems (e.g., saves time and effort). People can improve themselves; tomorrow should be better than today.	Stimulates purchase of products that function well and save time. Stimulates desire for new products that fulfill unsatisfied needs; ready acceptance of products that claim to be "new and improved."
Material Comfort	"The good life."	Fosters acceptance of convenience and luxury products that make life more comfortable and enjoyable.
Individualism	Being oneself (e.g., self-reliance, self-interest, self-esteem).	Stimulates acceptance of customized or unique products that enable a person to "express his or her own personality."
Freedom	Freedom of choice.	Fosters interest in wide product lines and differentiated products.
External Conformity	Uniformity of observable behavior; desire for acceptance.	Stimulates interest in products that are used or owned by others in the same social group.
Humanitarianism	Caring for others, particularly the underdog.	Stimulates patronage of firms that compete with market leaders.
Youthfulness	A state of mind that stresses being "young at heart" and having a youthful appearance.	Stimulates acceptance of products that provide the illusion of maintaining or fostering youthfulness.
Fitness and Health	Caring about one's body, including the desire to be physically fit and healthy.	Stimulates acceptance of food products, activities, and equipment perceived to maintain or increase physical fitness.

toward a shopping culture

It appears that the role that shopping plays in the American life has been elevated to the point that the American culture has become a *shopping culture* (which is a parallel perspective to the commonly held view that America's culture is a *consumer culture*). One authority has even noted that shopping has remade our culture and now defines the way we understand the world around us—"shopping is what we do to create value in our lives."[34] Making this possible is the reality that great shopping experiences are no longer just for the rich, as consumers from all walks of life can enjoy the low prices found in discount stores. Still further, shopping "has become an increasingly acceptable and popular pastime even for younger, single guys." Specifically, men between 25 and 49 years of age now account for over half of all male buying power, and this market is expected to grow to $6.7 trillion by 2009, an increase of almost 25 percent. A recent study found that one in four men under age 40 claim to shop frequently, compared to less than 20 percent of men in their 40s and 50s.[35]

Much of this "shop to you drop" mentality has propelled shopping to the "all American" pastime, an obsession that is driving an increasing number of Americans to be in credit card debt. It appears that consumers' credit card usage is more and more defining the meaning of a *consumption lifestyle,* one that unfortunately fosters consumers' attainment through their consumption of unfulfilling possessions and burdensome debt.[36]

SUMMARY

The study of culture is the study of all aspects of a society. It is the language, knowledge, laws, and customs that give that society its distinctive character and personality. In the context of consumer behavior, culture is defined as the sum total of learned beliefs, values, and customs that serve to regulate the consumer behavior of members of a particular society. Beliefs and values are guides for consumer behavior; customs are usual and accepted ways of behaving.

The impact of culture on society is so natural and so ingrained that its influence on behavior is rarely noted. Yet, culture offers order, direction, and guidance to members of society in all phases of human problem solving. Culture is dynamic and gradually and continually evolves to meet the needs of society.

Culture is learned as part of social experience. Children acquire from their environment a set of beliefs, values, and customs that constitutes culture (i.e., they are encultured). These are acquired through formal learning, informal learning, and technical learning. Advertising enhances formal learning by reinforcing desired modes of behavior and expectations; it enhances informal learning by providing models for behavior.

Culture is communicated to members of society through a common language and through commonly shared symbols. Because the human mind has the ability to absorb and to process symbolic communication, marketers can successfully promote both tangible and intangible products and product concepts to consumers through mass media.

All the elements in the marketing mix serve to communicate symbolically with the audience. Products project an image of their own; so does promotion. Price and retail outlets symbolically convey images concerning the quality of the product.

The elements of culture are transmitted by three pervasive social institutions: the family, the church, and the school. A fourth social institution that plays a major role in the transmission of culture is the mass media, both through editorial content and through advertising.

A wide range of measurement techniques is used to study culture. The range includes projective techniques, attitude measurement methods, field observation, participant observation, content analysis, and value measurement survey techniques.

A number of core values of the American people are relevant to the study of consumer behavior. These include achievement and success, activity, efficiency and practicality, progress, material comfort, individualism, freedom, conformity, humanitarianism, youthfulness, and fitness and health.

Because each of these values varies in importance to the members of our society, each provides an effective basis for segmenting consumer markets.

DISCUSSION QUESTIONS

1. Distinguish among beliefs, values, and customs. Illustrate how the clothing a person wears at different times or for different occasions is influenced by customs.

2. A manufacturer of fat-free granola bars is considering targeting school-age children by positioning its product as a healthy, nutritious snack food. How can an understanding of the three forms of cultural learning be used in developing an effective strategy to target the intended market?

3. The Citrus Growers of America is planning a promotional campaign to encourage the drinking of orange and grapefruit juice in situations in which many consumers normally consume soft drinks. Using the Rokeach Value Survey (Table 12.5), identify relevant cultural, consumption-specific, and product-specific values for citrus juices as an alternative to soft drinks. What are the implications of these values for an advertising campaign designed to increase the consumption of citrus juices?

4. For each of the following products and activities:
   a. Identify the core values most relevant to their purchase and use.
   b. Determine whether these values encourage or discourage use or ownership.

c. Determine whether these core values are shifting and, if so, in what direction. The products and activities are:

1. Donating money to charities
2. Donating blood
3. Compact disk players
4. Telephone answering machines
5. Toothpaste
6. Diet soft drinks
7. Foreign travel
8. Suntan lotion
9. Cellular phones
10. Interactive TV home-shopping services
11. Fat-free foods
12. Products in recyclable packaging

EXERCISES

1. Identify a singer or singing group whose music you like and discuss the symbolic function of the clothes that person (or group) wears.

2. Think of various routines in your everyday life (such as grooming or food preparation). Identify one ritual and describe it. In your view, is this ritual shared by others? If so, to what extent? What are the implications of your ritualistic behavior to the marketer(s) of the product(s) you use during your routine?

3. a. Summarize an episode of a weekly television series that you watched recently. Describe how the program transmitted cultural beliefs, values, and customs.

   b. Select and describe three commercials that were broadcast during the program mentioned in 3a. Do these commercials create or reflect cultural values? Explain your answer.

4. a. Find two different advertisements for deodorants in two magazines that are targeted to different audiences. Content-analyze the written and pictorial aspects of each ad, using any core values discussed in this chapter. How are these values portrayed to the target audiences?

   b. Identify symbols used in these ads and discuss their effectiveness in conveying the desired product image or characteristics

KEY TERMS

- **acculturation**
- **consumer fieldwork**
- **content analysis**
- **core values**

- **culture**
- **enculturation**
- **field observation**
- **participant-observers**

- **ritual**
- **rokeach value survey**
- **subcultures**
- **symbols**

NOTES

1. Linda C. Ueltschy and Robert F. Krampf, "Cultural Sensitivity to Satisfaction and Service Quality Measures," *Journal of Marketing Theory and Practice* (Summer 2001): 14–31.

2. Elena Karahanna, J. Roberto Evaristo, and Mark Strite, "Levels of Culture and Individual Behavior: An Integrative Perspective," *Journal of Global Information Management* 13 (April–June 2005): 1–20.

3. "Demo Memo," *American Demographics*, February 1998, 41.

4. Elizabeth C. Hirschman, "Men, Dogs, Guns, and Cars: The Semiotics of Rugged Individualism," *Journal of Advertising* 32 (Spring 2003): 9–22.

5. Dennis W. Rook, "The Ritual Dimension of Consumer Behavior," *Journal of Consumer Research* 12 (December 1985): 251–264.

6. Andrew Zolli, "Why Design Matters More," *American Demographics,* October 2004, 52–53.

7. Virginia Postrel, *The Substance of Style: How the Rise of Aesthetic Value Is Remaking Commerce, Culture, and Consciousness* (New York: HaperCollins, 2003).

8. Jeff Strieter and Jerald Weaver, "A Longitudinal Study of the Depiction of Women in a United States Business

Publication," *The Journal of the American Academy of Business* 7 (September 2005): 229–235.

9. Michael L. Maynard and Charles R. Taylor, "Girlish Images Across Cultures: Analyzing Japanese Versus U.S. *Seventeen* Magazine Ads," *Journal of Advertising* 28, no. 1 (Spring 1999): 39–45.

10. Mindy F. Ji and James U. McNeal, "How Chinese Children's Commercials Differ from Those of the United States: A Content Analysis," *Journal of Advertising* 30, no. 3 (Fall 2001): 79–92.

11. Lawrence Osborne, "Consuming Rituals of the Suburban Tribe," *New York Times Magazine*, January 13, 2002, 28–31; Margaret Littman, "Science Shopping," *Crain's Chicago Business,* January 11, 1999, 3; and Marvin Matises, "Top of Mind: Send Ethnographers into New-SKU Jungle," *Brandweek*, September 25, 2000, 32–33.

12. Wagner A. Kamakura and Jose Afonso Mazzon, "Value Segmentation: A Model for the Measurement of Values and Value Systems," *Journal of Consumer Research* 18 (September 1991): 208–218.

13. Lynn R. Kahle, ed., *Social Values and Social Change: Adaption of Life in America* (New York: Praeger, 1983); Sharon E. Beatty et al., "Alternative Measurement Approaches to Consumer Values: The List of Values and the Rokeach Value Survey," *Psychology & Marketing* 2 (1985): 181–200; and Lynn R. Kahle, Roger P. McIntyre, Reid P. Claxton, and David B. Jones, "Empirical Relationships Between Cognitive Style and LOV: Implications for Values and Value Systems," in *Advances in Consumer Research,* vol. 22, ed. Frank R. Kardes and Mita Sujan (Provo, UT: Association for Consumer Research 1995), 141–146.

14. David C. McClelland, *The Achieving Society* (New York: Free Press, 1961), 150–151.

15. Leon G. Schiffman, Elaine Sherman, and Mary M. Long, "Toward a Better Understanding of the Interplay of Personal Values and the Internet," *Psychology and Marketing* 20 (February 2003): 169–186.

16. Lawrence E. Harrison, "Culture Matters," *The National Interest* 60 (Summer 2000): 55–65.

17. Charles A. Malgwi, Martha A. Howe, and Priscilla A. Burnaby, "Influences on Students' Choice of College Major," *Journal of Education for Business* 80 (May/June 2005): 275–282.

18. "Just Keeping Busy in Old Age Isn't the Key to Actively Enjoying Life; Seniors: The Quality and Purpose of Their Activities Determine Whether the Elderly Are Just Going Through the Motions or Truly Fulfilled, a Researcher Has Found," *The Los Angeles Times*, November 26, 1999, 5C; and Evelyn Petersen, "Being Busy All The Time Isn't Healthy Series: Booked Solid," *Syracuse Herald American,* October 17, 1999, A13.

19. Peter Rojas, "Time-Out Guide," *Red Herring*, December 1999, 114.

20. Ramesh Venkat and Harold J. Ogden, "Material Satisfaction: The Effects of Social Comparison and Attribution," in *1995 AMA Educators' Proceedings,* eds. Barbara B. Stern and George M. Zinkan (Chicago: American Marketing Association, 1995), 314–349.

21. "Vivre, A Beautiful Life," accessed at **www.vive.com**.

22. Frank Gibney, Jr. and Belinda Luscombe, "The Redesigning of America," *Time,* June 26, 2000, unnumbered insert section.

23. Op. cit., Hirschman, 2003.

24. Virginia Matthews, "Simplicity Is the Consumer's Choice: Marketing Product Innovation: Shoppers Complain of Confusion as Companies Blitz Them with a Host of New Products, Writes Virginia Matthews," *Financial Times* (*London*), December 10, 1999, 16.

25. "Casual Clothes Are Workplace Trend," *Brandweek,* July 18, 1994, 17. Also, see Ellen Neuborne, "Fashion on Menu at T.G.I. Friday's," *USA Today*, February 27, 1996, B1.

26. Deborah J. Webb, Corliss L. Green, and Thomas G. Brashear, "Development and Validation of Scales to Measure Attitudes Influencing Monetary Donations to Charitable Organizations," *Journal of the Academy of Marketing Science* 28, no. 2 (Spring 2000): 299–309.

27. George R. Reis, "Building Bridges," *Fund Raising Management* 30, no. 6 (August 1999): 19–23.

28. Richard A. Lee "The Youth Bias in Advertising," *American Demographics,* January 1997, 47–50.

29. Barbara J. Phillips, "Working Out: Consumers and the Culture of Exercise," *Journal of Popular Culture* 38 (February 2005): 525–551.

30. "The Big Scoop on Just Desserts," *Advertising Age,* October 2, 1995, 3.

31. Sean Mehegan, "As Indulgence Roars Back with a Vengeance, Low-Fat Candies Beat a Strategic Retreat," *Brandweek,* March 2, 1998, 12.

32. Jeffrey A. Tannenbaum, "Fat-Free Store Pushes to Gain Weight in U.S.—Small New York Firm Targets Shrinking Market," *Asian Wall Street Journal,* February 14, 2001, N5; and Normita Thongtham, "You Are What You Eat," *The Bangkok Post,* March 2, 2002, 1.

33. George M. Zinkhan and Penelope J. Prenshaw, "Good Life Images and Brand Name Associations: Evidence from Asia, America, and Europe," in *Advances in Consumer Research,* vol. 21, eds. Chris T. Allen and Deborah Roedder John (Provo, UT: Association for Consumer Research, 1994), 496–500.

34. Juliet Schor, "Point of Purchase: How Shopping Changed American Culture," *Contemporary Sociology* 34 (January 2005): 43–44.

35. Christine Van Dusen, "Shopping: It's More of a Man's World These Days," *The Atlanta Journal-Constitution,* April 1, 2005, F1.

36. Matthew J. Bernthal, David Crockett, and Randall L. Rose, "Credit Cards as Lifestyle Facilitators," *Journal of Consumer Research* 32 (June 2005): 130–145.

chapterthirteen

› Subcultures and Consumer Behavior

Culture has a potent influence on all consumer behavior. Individuals are brought up to follow the beliefs, values, and customs of their society and to avoid behavior that is judged unacceptable or considered taboo. In addition to segmenting in terms of cultural factors, marketers also segment overall societies into smaller subgroups (subcultures) that consist of people who are similar in terms of their ethnic origin, their customs, and the ways they behave. These subcultures provide important marketing opportunities for astute marketing strategists.

Our discussion of subcultures, therefore, has a narrower focus than the discussion of culture. Instead of examining the dominant beliefs, values, and customs that exist within an entire society, this chapter explores the marketing opportunities created by the existence of certain beliefs, values, and customs shared by members of specific subcultural groups within a society.

These subcultural divisions are based on a variety of sociocultural and demographic variables, such as nationality, religion, geographic locality, race, age, and sex.

All that... and then some.

**Immerse yourself in
family fun & culture
in Wisconsin.**

If you're looking for a fantastic family getaway, it's
right next door - in Wisconsin. We've got the most
amazing indoor water parks, ethnic festivals, and
art and cultural exhibits – including America's *only*
Black Holocaust Museum.

For free getaway information, call 1 800-432-TRIP
or visit travelwisconsin.com

WISCONSIN
travelwisconsin.com

what is subculture?

The members of a specific **subculture** possess beliefs, values, and customs that set them apart from other members of the same society. In addition, they adhere to most of the dominant cultural beliefs, values, and behavioral patterns of the larger society. We define subculture, then, as *a distinct cultural group that exists as an identifiable segment within a larger, more complex society.*

Thus, the cultural profile of a society or nation is a composite of two distinct elements: (1) the unique beliefs, values, and customs subscribed to by members of specific subcultures; and (2) the central or core cultural themes that are shared by most of the population, regardless of specific subcultural memberships. Figure 13.1 presents a simple model of the relationship between two subcultural groups (Hispanic Americans and African Americans) and the larger or "more general" culture. As the figure depicts, each subculture has its own unique traits, yet both groups share the dominant traits of the overall American culture.

Let us look at it in another way: Each American is, in large part, a product of the "American way of life." Each American, however, is at the same time a member of various subcultures. For example, a 10-year-old girl may simultaneously be African American, Baptist, a preteen, and a Texan. We would expect that membership in each different subculture would provide its own set of specific beliefs, values, attitudes, and customs. Table 13.1 lists typical subcultural categories and corresponding examples of specific subcultural groups. This list is by no means exhaustive: Electricians, Democrats, Cub Scouts, and millionaires—in fact, any group that shares common beliefs and customs—may be classified as a subculture.

Subcultural analysis enables the marketing manager to focus on sizable and natural market segments. When carrying out such analyses, the marketer must determine whether the beliefs, values, and customs shared by members of a specific subgroup make them desirable candidates for special marketing attention. Subcultures, therefore, are relevant units of analysis for market research. And these subcultures are dynamic—for example, the different ethnic groups that comprise the U.S. population have been changing and will continue to change in size and economic power in the coming years. More specifically, the white (non-Hispanic) population of the United States, which made up 71 percent of Americans in the year 2000 (date of the last U.S. Census), is projected to represent about 53 percent of the U.S. population by the year 2050.[1] Frequently a "window on the future," the State of California has estimated that the state's multicultural or combined minority population is now the state's majority population.

A recent study of ethnic media usage in California also found that over 80 percent of Asian American, African American, and Hispanic American respondents claimed to

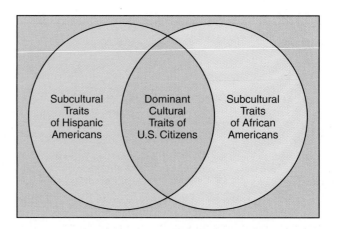

Relationship Between Culture and Subculture

FIGURE 13.1

TABLE 13.1	Examples of Major Subcultural Categories

CATEGORIES	EXAMPLES
Nationality (i.e., birthplace of ancestors)	Greek, Italian, Russian
Religion	Catholic, Hindu, Mormon
Geographic region	Eastern, Southern Southwestern
Race	African American, Asian, Caucasian
Age	Teenager, Xers, elderly
Gender	Female, male
Occupation	Bus driver, cook, scientist
Social class	Lower, middle, upper

get information from ethnic television, radio, and publications. Furthermore, 68 percent preferred ethnic-language TV stations over English channels for news, and 40 percent reported paying greater attention to ethnic language ads than English-language ads.[2]

The following sections examine a number of important subcultural categories: nationality, religion, geographic location, race, age, and sex. (Occupational and social-class subgroups were discussed in detail in Chapter 11.)

nationality subcultures

For many people, **nationality** is an important subcultural reference that guides what they value and what they buy. This is especially true for the population of a country like the United States that has a history of attracting people from all over the globe. Supporting this pattern are the results of the 2000 U.S. Census, which found that about one in ten Americans is foreign born.[3] It has also been reported that Queens County (one of the five boroughs that make up the City of New York) is the most multicultural county in America, and that 46 percent of its residents were born outside of the United States.[4] For these Americans, as well as Americans born in the United States, there is frequently a strong sense of identification and pride in the language and customs of their ancestors.

When it comes to consumer behavior, this ancestral pride is manifested most strongly in the consumption of ethnic foods, in travel to the "homeland," and in the purchase of numerous cultural artifacts (ethnic clothing, art, music, foreign-language newspapers). Interest in these goods and services has expanded rapidly as younger Americans attempt to better understand and more closely associate with their ethnic roots. To illustrate the importance of ethnic origin as a subcultural market segment, the next section examines the **Hispanic American subculture**.

Hispanic subcultures

The 2000 U.S. Census found that the number of Hispanic Americans (of all races) had grown by 58 percent during the decade of the 1990s (compared to an overall U.S. population growth of 13.2 percent). And, according to the Census Bureau, in July of 2002 Hispanics replaced African Americans as the largest minority group in the United States (see Table 13.2). Hispanics are currently 14 percent of the U.S. population, and their number is estimated to reach 24 percent of the population by the year 2050, giving the United States a Hispanic population of over 100 million.[5] These Hispanic Americans had an estimated purchasing power in 2004 of $687 billion, which is expected to climb to $992 billion by 2009.[6] In contrast to other American population segments, Hispanic Americans are younger—in 2005 almost 38 percent of Hispanics are 19 years old or younger, whereas only 28 percent of the U.S. population is 19 or younger. The median age

TABLE 13.2	Hispanics Become the Largest Minority Group in the United States			
	POPULATION, IN MILLIONS		PERCENTAGE CHANGE	PERCENTAGE OF THE POPULATION, JULY 2001
	JULY 2001*	APRIL 2000		
Total population	284.8	281.4	1.2%	100.0%
Hispanic (of any race)	37.0	35.3	4.7	13.0
One race	280.7	277.5	1.2	98.6
White	230.3	228.1	1.0	80.9
Non-Hispanic white	196.2	195.6	0.3	68.9
Black or African American	36.2	35.7	1.5	12.7
American Indian or Alaska Native	2.7	2.7	2.3	1.0
Asian	11.0	10.6	3.7	3.9
Native Hawaiian/ Pacific Islander	0.5	0.5	3.0	0.2
Two or more races	4.1	3.9	4.6	1.4
				*Estimated

Source: "Largest Minority Group: Hispanics," *The New York Times*, January 22, 2003, A17.

for Hispanics is 26 years of age, whereas the median age for the rest of America is 35 years of age.[7] Hispanic Americans also tend to be members of larger families (average Hispanic household size is 3.5 people compared to an average U.S. household size of 2.6 people).[8] They are also more likely to live in an extended family household consisting of several generations of family members. Not only are Hispanic households more likely than black or non-Hispanic American white families to contain children, but also Hispanics spend more time caring for their children.[9]

As of this writing, 88 percent of all Hispanics under the age of 18 living in the United States were born here. And by 2020, only 34 percent of Hispanics living here will be foreign-born first generation, 36 percent will be U.S. born second-generation children of immigrants, and 30 percent will be third-generation children of U.S. born Hispanics.[10] In terms of acculturation, only 20 percent of the Hispanic/Latino market has recently migrated to the United States and speak only Spanish. Of the remaining 80 percent, 20 percent speak only English and 60 percent speak both Spanish and English.

Of the more than 41 million Hispanics currently living in the United States, the most recent Census found that 77 percent live in the seven states that have a Hispanic population of one million or more (California, Texas, New York, Florida, Illinois, Arizona, and New Jersey). Still further, while Hispanics represented 42 percent of New Mexico's total population, the highest percentage of any state, some counties in North Carolina, Georgia, Iowa, Arkansas, Minnesota, and Nebraska are between 6 and 25 percent Hispanic.[11] Table 13.3 presents the 25 largest U.S. Hispanic markets, the Hispanic population of each, and the Hispanic percentage of the total residents of that market.

This subcultural group can be considered as a single market, based on a common language and culture, or as separate subcultural markets that correspond to different Hispanic countries of origin. There are 12 Hispanic subgroups identified in the United

TABLE 13.3	Top 25 U.S. Hispanic Markets		
RANK	**MARKET**	**HISPANIC POPULATION**	**HISPANIC % OF TOTAL**
1	Los Angeles	7,811,100	44.5
2	New York	4,316,400	20.5
3	Chicago	1,838,000	19.0
4	Miami	1,836,800	43.1
5	Houston	1,822,600	33.4
6	Dallas-Fort Worth	1,509,700	23.5
7	San Francisco	1,491,800	21.3
8	San Antonio	1,293,700	60.3
9	Phoenix	1,208,000	27.2
10	McAllen, Texas	1,142,000	94.8
11	San Diego	927,600	31.2
12	Fresno-Visalia, Calif.	893,000	50.7
13	Sacramento, Calif.	892,400	24.1
14	El Paso, Texas	782,500	87.7
15	Albuquerque, N.M.	740,700	41.6
16	Denver	740,600	19.7
17	Washington	545,200	9.0
18	Philadelphia	534,300	6.9
19	Austin, Texas	471,700	29.0
20	Las Vegas	438,800	26.0
21	Atlanta	433,600	7.5
22	Orlando	432,200	13.2
23	Boston	417,700	6.6
24	Tampa, Fla.	415,400	10.4
25	Tucson-Nogales, Ariz.	385,900	35.4

Source: "Hispanic Fact Pack, 2004 Edition," *A Supplement to Advertising Age*, 40.

States. The three largest Hispanic subcultural groups consist of Mexican Americans (about 58.5 percent of total Hispanic Americans), Puerto Ricans (approximately 9.6 percent of the total), and Cubans (about 3.5 percent of the total). These subcultures are heavily concentrated geographically, with more than 70 percent of their members residing in California, Texas, New York, and Florida; Los Angeles alone is home to one-fifth of the Hispanic population of the United States. Also, whereas more than 60 percent of all Mexican Americans (the largest Hispanic group) were born in the United States, 72 percent of Cuban Americans were born in Cuba.[12]

Understanding hispanic consumer behavior

Available evidence indicates that Hispanic and Anglo consumers differ in terms of a variety of important buyer behavior variables. For instance, Hispanic consumers have a strong preference for well-established brands and traditionally prefer to shop at smaller stores. In the New York metropolitan area, for example, Hispanic consumers spend a substantial portion of their food budgets in *bodegas* (relatively small food specialty stores), despite the fact that supermarket prices generally are lower. Table 13.4 presents these and other distinctive characteristics of the overall Hispanic market.

TABLE 13.4	**Traditional Characteristics of the Hispanic American Market**

Prefer well-known or familiar brands

Buy brands perceived to be more prestigious

Are fashion conscious

Historically prefer to shop at smaller personal stores

Buy brands advertised by their ethnic-group stores

Tend not to be impulse buyers (i.e., are deliberate)

Increasingly clipping and using cents-off coupons

Likely to buy what their parents bought

Prefer fresh to frozen or prepared items

Tend to be negative about marketing practices and government intervention in business

Although mindful of their tradition, Hispanic Americans, like other major subcultural groups, are a dynamic and evolving portion of the overall society. For this reason, a growing number of Hispanic consumers are shifting their food shopping to nonethnic, large, American-style supermarkets. They appear to be engaged in a process of acculturation; that is, they are gradually adopting the consumption patterns of the majority of U.S. consumers. Similarly, when it comes to clothes shopping, Hispanic youths are more fashion conscious and are more likely to seek out and be loyal to well-known brands and to generally like the act of shopping more than their non-Hispanic counterparts.[13] While about half of Hispanic Americans have a computer at home (as compared to about three-quarters of the U.S. population), and only about 35 percent have Internet access at home (as compared to about 65 percent of the U.S. population), the number of Hispanic households with computers with Internet access has been increasing annually.[14] Perhaps one of the reasons why Mattel has introduced a Spanish-language "Barbie" site targeted to young girls (**www.barbielatina.com**) is because of the increasing number of Hispanic households with personal computers and Internet connections.[15]

Defining and segmenting the hispanic market

Marketers who are targeting the diversity within the Hispanic subcultures are concerned with finding the best ways to define and segment this overall subculture. In terms of definition, Table 13.5 presents six variables marketers have used to determine who is Hispanic. Of these measures, the combination of *self-identification* and *degree of identification* are particularly appealing, because they permit consumers to define or label themselves. Research shows that those who strongly identify with being Hispanic (*Strong Hispanic Identifiers*) are more frequent users of Spanish-language media, are more brand loyal, are more likely to buy prestige brands, are more likely to seek the advice of another and to more often be influenced by friends or family, and are more likely to buy brands advertised to Hispanics than Weak Hispanic Identifiers.[16] This pattern suggests that the degree of Hispanic identification is a useful segmentation variable.

Some marketers feel that it is worthwhile to target each Hispanic American market separately. Other marketers, especially larger marketers, have been targeting the Hispanic market as a single market, using Spanish-language mass media. For instance, to cater to the Hispanic market, Toyota launched an interactive soccer game on its Spanish-language Web site (**www.toyota.com/español**), which asked the player to defend their Corolla.[17] Johnson & Johnson has outfitted a 53 foot trailer as a six-room home (including life-size cutouts of family members) and has sent it on a cross-country tour, making stops at 100 Wal-Marts and 20 Hispanic fiestas. Individuals visiting the trailer learn about 15 different J&J brands and will receive free product samples.[18] While the Spanish language is often regarded as the bridge that links the various Hispanic subcultures,

TABLE 13.5	Ways in Which "Hispanic" Has Been Defined
NAME OF INDICATOR	**NATURE/SCOPE AND COMMENTARY**
Spanish surname	Not a definitive; since a non-Hispanic person might have a Spanish surname, or a Hispanic person might have a non-Spanish surname.
Country of origin	The birthplace of persons born in the United States of Hispanic parents (e.g., of Puerto Rican parentage) would not reveal their Hispanic background.
Country of family ancestry	Includes those individuals who may not be Hispanic despite coming from a particular Spanish-Latin country (e.g., people of German parentage who may be brought up in a Latin country).
Spanish spoken at home	A significant minority of Hispanic households may speak English at home, yet consider themselves to be culturally Hispanic.
Self-identification	It is reasonable that if an adequate number of self-report choices are offered, a person might identify himself or herself as "Hispanic."
Degree of identification	This measure captures the "degree" of personal identification as "Hispanic" and augments the self-identification measure.

nevertheless, there is considerable variation among Hispanics regarding their language preferences (such as Spanish only, Spanish preferred, English only, or English preferred). This language categorization provides still another basis for segmenting the Hispanic American market. Available research indicates that Hispanic Americans spend the most time with mass media in the first language that they learn to speak. So those whose first language is Spanish tend to prefer TV, radio, magazines, and newspapers in Spanish (see Figure 13.2), whereas those Hispanic Americans who first learn English prefer their media exposure to be in English.[19] For instance, supporting this point of view, the number of Spanish-language stations is growing; Discovery Communications launched two new networks—Discovery Kids en Espanol and Discovery Viajar y Vivir (Travel and Living).[20] With respect to the medium of radio, Clear Channel Radio recently flipped a general market to a Spanish-language format radio station in Atlanta and went from a 1.6 to an 11.3 share among listeners 18 to 34 years old.[21] Table 13.6 presents the language preferences of Hispanic Americans, 18 years of age and older, with respect to language usage. Note that in all categories, a smaller than average percentage of 18- to 24-year-olds prefer "only Spanish."

Recently, Cohorts, Inc., a Denver company that provides information to database marketers, developed a segmentation scheme for the Hispanic market that contains 19 lifestyle segments. These segments ranged from "Affluent Grandparents" (successful, dual-income couples) to "Latinos with Roommates" (less-educated single Latinos with roommates). Table 13.7 presents a brief profile of six of the 19 segments, including median age, median income, and size.

religious subcultures

The United States reportedly has more than 200 different organized **religious subcultures**. Of this number, Protestant denominations, Roman Catholicism, and Judaism are the principal organized religious faiths. The members of all these religious groups at times are

FIGURE 13.2

Source: Copyright © State Farm Mutual Automobile Insurance Company, 2005. Used by permission

Ad Targeting Hispanic American Consumers

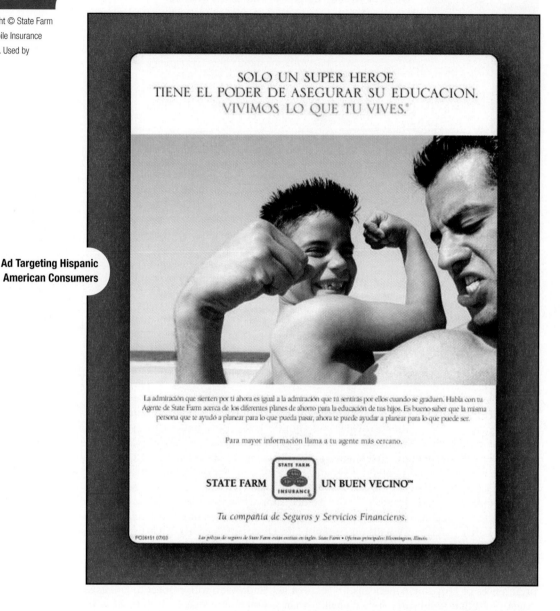

likely to make purchase decisions that are influenced by their religious identity. Commonly, consumer behavior is directly affected by religion in terms of products that are *symbolically* and *ritualistically* associated with the celebration of various religious holidays. For example, Christmas has become the major gift-purchasing season of the year.

Consider born-again Christians, the fastest-growing religious affiliation in America. Members of this group are generally defined as individuals "who follow literal interpretations of the Bible and acknowledge being born again through religious conversion." These consumers make up about 72 million of the 235 million Christians in the United States. Religion is part of their daily activity, and their interests and opinions are often tied to their religion. From a marketer's perspective, born-again Christians tend to be fiercely loyal to a brand that supports their causes and viewpoint.[22]

Religious requirements or practices sometimes take on an expanded meaning beyond their original purpose. For instance, dietary laws for an observant Jewish

TABLE 13.6	Selected Dimensions of Language Usage by U.S. Hispanic Adults						
	ALL HISPANIC ADULTS	**% BY AGE GROUP**					
		18–24	**25–34**	**35–44**	**45–54**	**55–64**	**65+**
SPEAK AT HOME:							
Only English	12.3	10.1	13.2	12.1	13.9	13.5	10.8
Mostly Eng., some Span.	20.9	22.9	19.6	19.1	25.8	15.6	23.7
Eng. & Span. equally	15.8	19.4	8.2	16.3	16.1	32.8	15.6
Mostly Span., some Eng.	29.8	35.2	31.3	31.2	26.7	20.3	22.5
Only Spanish	20.4	12.4	27.2	20.4	17.2	16.2	24.2
SPEAK OUTSIDE THE HOME:							
Only English	16.7	23.3	13.3	16.1	17.2	17.0	13.6
Mostly Eng., some Span.	32.0	33.5	29.5	34.4	37.5	27.0	27.4
Eng. & Span. equally	8.3	12.1	2.3	7.7	9.1	17.8	11.3
Mostly Span., some Eng.	24.9	19.1	35.0	23.0	20.8	21.0	17.5
Only Spanish	14.0	8.1	16.1	15.8	14.0	12.0	17.4
PREFER SPEAKING IN:							
Only English	17.2	24.8	17.0	13.6	16.3	17.4	11.5
Mostly Eng., some Span.	27.4	31.9	20.3	31.3	21.7	40.5	27.6
Mostly Span., some Eng.	24.5	23.9	26.8	23.2	32.3	13.9	19.2
Only Spanish	25.4	14.6	32.2	27.0	24.1	22.0	27.0
PREFER READING IN:							
Only English	33.2	38.0	28.2	28.2	36.5	49.0	31.5
Mostly Eng., some Span.	21.8	25.3	17.6	25.0	23.2	17.1	22.8
Mostly Span., some Eng.	16.7	14.5	22.9	17.7	12.6	10.3	10.3
Only Spanish	24.4	18.5	29.3	25.6	23.4	21.3	21.2
PREFER WATCHING TV IN:							
Only English	25.9	30.3	22.1	24.7	22.5	38.5	25.7
Mostly Eng., some Span.	29.9	32.3	26.9	25.7	42.0	29.5	26.8
Mostly Span., some Eng.	25.8	23.3	29.2	31.6	21.4	14.4	22.5
Only Spanish	13.8	7.7	19.0	13.6	10.6	14.6	14.5
PREFER LISTENING RADIO IN:							
Only English	23.4	31.3	20.9	23.5	19.0	24.2	20.6
Mostly Eng., some Span.	21.0	24.0	17.3	22.1	23.4	24.7	16.9
Mostly Span., some Eng.	25.6	24.8	28.0	22.7	31.0	19.4	24.4
Only Spanish	25.0	15.2	30.2	26.8	22.8	25.9	27.2

Source: "Hispanic Fact Pack, 2004 Edition," *Advertising Age*, 42 (Data from Simmons Market Research Bureau's Fall 2005 Full-Year National Consumer Study).

family represent an obligation, so there are toothpastes and artificial sweeteners that are kosher for Passover. The *U* and *K* marks on food packaging are symbols that the food meets Jewish dietary laws. For nonobservant Jews and an increasing number of non-Jews, however, these marks often signify that the food is pure and wholesome — a kind of "Jewish *Good Housekeeping* Seal of Approval." In response to the broader meaning given to kosher-certified products, a number of national brands, such as Coors beer and Pepperidge Farm cookies, have secured kosher certification for their

TABLE 13.7	Illustrative Segments from Segmentation Research of the Hispanic Market			
HISPANIC COHORT SEGMENT NAME	**DESCRIPTION**	**HISPANIC MEDIAN AGE**	**HISPANIC MEDIAN INCOME**	**HISPANIC POPULATION SIZE AND %**
Married Couples				
Manuel y Beatriz	*Affluent Grandparents* Successful, dual-income couples who are financially secure and enjoy upscale activities, lots of travel and doting on their grandchildren.	62	$113,000	415K 4.1%
Raul y Cristina	*Professional Couples* Educated, dual-income, childless couples who have connoisseur tastes, enjoy the latest in fashion and high-tech, and focus on staying fit and building their investment portfolio.	31	$74,000	473K 4.7%
Single Females				
Andrea	*Educated Career-Oriented Moms* Better-educated single mothers who juggle their jobs with the demands of parenthood.	31	$52,000	618K 6.1%
Isabel	*Successful Career Women* Childless, well-acculturated fashion-conscious professionals who are pursuing careers, sophisticated tastes and fitness.	35	$67,000	348K 3.5%
Single Males				
Felipe	*Career-Oriented Single Guys* Educated, career-oriented, fitness-minded single men with busy lifestyles who enjoy designer clothing, cars and high-tech gadgets.	28	$58,000	550K 5.5%
Pablo	*Young Latinos* Less-educated, single Latino guys who enjoy living on the edge. They're into sports, cool cars, music and electronics. They share their homes with another adult who has children.	28	$36,000	873K 8.6%

Source: Cohorts, Inc., accessed at **www.cohorts.com/hispanic1.html**.

products. Indeed, most Kosher food is consumed by non-Jews.[23] A kosher Manhattan steak house, the Prime Grill, claims that about half of its clientele are non-Jews, and that its success is based on the fact that it has a fine dining menu (without "Jewish types of food") that "just happens to be kosher."[24] Packaging and print ads for food items that are kosher often display a *K* or a *U* inside a circle and sometimes the word *parve.* This word tells the shopper that the product is kosher and that it can be eaten with either meat or dairy products (but not both). Targeting specific religious groups with specially designed marketing programs can be really profitable. For instance, the Shaklee Corporation, a multilevel marketer of the Shaklee Performance drink mix, recruits salespeople from a variety of different religious groups (e.g., Hasidic Jews, Amish, and Mennonites) to sell its products to members of their communities.[25] It is likely that such shared religious identity and membership aid a salesperson in his or her effort to communicate with and persuade potential customers.

geographic and regional subcultures

The United States is a large country, one that enjoys a wide range of climatic and geographic conditions. Given the country's size and physical diversity, it is only natural that many Americans have a sense of **regional** identification and use this identification as a way of describing others (such as "he is a true Southerner"). These labels often assist us in developing a mental picture and supporting *stereotype* of the person in question.

Anyone who has traveled across the United States has probably noted many regional differences in consumption behavior, especially when it comes to food and drink. For example, a *mug* of black coffee typifies the West, while a *cup* of coffee with milk and sugar is preferred in the East. There also are geographic differences in the consumption of a staple food such as bread. Specifically, in the South and Midwest, soft white bread is preferred, whereas on the East and West coasts, firmer breads (rye, whole wheat, and French and Italian breads) are favored. Regional differences also include brand preferences. Why do you suppose Skippy is the best-selling brand of peanut butter on both the East and West coasts, while Peter Pan sells best in the South and Jif sells best in the Midwest?[26]

Consumer research studies document regional differences in consumption patterns. For instance, Table 13.8 illustrates that differences in product purchase, ownership, or usage levels occur between major metropolitan areas. This distribution helps redefine local markets in terms of specific urban lifestyles. Still further, Table 13.9 reveals that San Francisco leads the nation's 10 largest markets when it comes to ordering anything from

TABLE 13.8	**Product Purchase/Usage by Leading Metropolitan Market**	
PRODUCT PURCHASE/USAGE	**HIGHEST PURCHASE/USAGE**	**LOWEST PURCHASE/USAGE**
Body power	New York	San Francisco
Energy drinks	San Francisco	Philadelphia
Artificial sweetener	Los Angeles	Dallas-Forth Worth
Total beer/ale	Chicago	Philadelphia
Ground coffee	Boston	Los Angeles
Gasoline	Dallas-Fort Worth	New York
Jams and jellies	Cleveland	San Francisco
Hair growth products	New York	Boston
Attend an auto show	Detroit	Washington, DC
Grated cheese	Philadelphia	Los Angeles
Attend a movie once a month	Boston	Dallas-Fort Worth
Own a mountain bike	San Francisco	New York
Boxed chocolates	Chicago	Dallas-Fort Worth
Personally have a valid passport	San Francisco	Cleveland
Vegetarian frozen burger	Boston	Dallas-Fort Worth

Source: Doublebase Mediamark Research, Inc. 2005 Doublebase Report. All rights reserved. Reprinted by permission.

TABLE 13.9	Ranking of Leading Metropolitan Markets in Terms of Ordering Anything from Amazon.com During the Past 12 Months
MARKET	**U.S. AVERAGE = 100**
San Francisco	203
Washington, DC	168
Boston	152
New York	138
Philadelphia	114
Chicago	114
Los Angeles	92
Dallas-Fort Worth	83
Detroit	82
Cleveland	69

Source: Doublebase Mediamark Research, Inc. 2005 Doublebase Report. All rights reserved. Reprinted by permission.

Amazon.com during a past 12 month period. An examination of this table and the other evidence presented here supports marketers who argue that it is important to take geographic consumption patterns into account when planning marketing and promotional efforts.

In general, large metropolitan areas, with a substantial number of affluent middle-age households, dominate many, but not all, consumer-spending categories. Two examples are the San Jose, California, metro area, which leads in apparel purchasing, and Nassau-Suffolk counties in New York, which lead in purchasing of insurance and pension programs.[27]

racial subcultures

The major **racial subcultures** in the United States are Caucasian, African American, Asian American, and American Indian. Although differences in lifestyles and consumer-spending patterns exist among these groups, the vast majority of racially oriented consumer research has focused on consumer differences between African Americans and Caucasians. More recently, particular research attention has been given to Asian American consumers.

The african american consumer

The U.S. Census Bureau estimates the African American population of the United States to be more than 39 million people, or more than 13 percent of the U.S. population.[28] While the overall U.S. population grew 13 percent between 1990 and 2000, the African American population in the U.S. grew by 21 percent.[29] As such, **African American consumers** currently constitute the second largest minority in the United States. With a purchasing power currently estimated to be $723 billion, and expected to grow to $965 billion by 2010, more than half of African American consumers are less than 35 years of age.[30] However, this important subcultural grouping is frequently portrayed as a single, undifferentiated African American market, consisting of consumers who have a uniform set of consumer needs. In reality they are a diverse group, consisting of numerous subgroups, each with distinctive backgrounds, needs, interests, and opinions. For example, in addition to the African Americans who have been in the United States for many generations, there are Caribbean Americans, from such islands as Jamaica and Haiti, who have recently immigrated to the United States.[31] Therefore, just as the white majority has been divided into a variety of market segments, each with its own distinctive needs and tastes, so, too, can the African American market be segmented.

Consumer behavior characteristics of african american consumers

Although there are many similarities between African Americans and the rest of America in terms of consumer behavior, there are also some meaningful differences in terms of product preferences and brand purchase patterns. African American consumers tend to prefer popular or leading brands, are brand loyal, and are unlikely to purchase private-label and generic products. One study, for example, found that almost two-thirds of African Americans are willing to pay more to get "the best," even if the brand or product is not widely recognized (only 51 percent of whites were reported to feel this way), and African Americans have been reported to buy high fashions and name brands "as signals of their success."[32] Still further, African American consumers tend to make more trips during the course of a week to the grocery store (2.2 trips versus 1.8 trips for the average shopper), and they also spend more per week ($94 versus $85 for the average shopper) than other consumers.[33]

African Americans account for over 30 percent of spending in the $4 billion hair care market, and they spend more on telephone services than any other consumer segment. Still further, they spend an average of $1,427 annually on clothing for themselves, which is $458 more than all U.S. consumers.[34] Similarly, African American teens spend more on clothing and fine jewelry than all U.S. teens.

Some meaningful differences exist among Anglo-White, African American, and Hispanic American consumers in the purchase, ownership, and use of a diverse group of products (see Table 13.10). For marketers, these findings confirm the wisdom of targeting racial market segments.

Reaching the african american audience

A question of central importance to marketers is how to best reach *African American consumers*. Traditionally, marketers have subscribed to one of two distinct marketing strategies. Some have followed the policy of running all their advertising in general mass media in the belief that African Americans have the same media habits as whites; others have followed the policy of running additional advertising in selected media directed exclusively to African Americans.

Both strategies may be appropriate in specific situations and for specific product categories. For products of very broad appeal (as aspirin or toothpaste), it is possible that the mass media (primarily television) may effectively reach all relevant consumers, including African American and white. For other products (such as personal grooming products or food products), marketers may find that mass media do not communicate effectively with the African American market. Because the media habits of African American consumers differ from those of the general population, media specifically targeted to African Americans are likely to be more effective. The notion that African Americans have cultural values subtly different from the U.S. population as a whole is supported by a Yankelovich survey in which a majority of African Americans believe that most advertising is designed for white people.[35] Furthermore, a recent study of ethnic identification found that African American adolescents with a stronger sense of black ethnic identity tend to identify more closely with black models or characters appearing in ads than do African American adolescents with weaker ethnic identification.[36] Research studies have also concluded that the socializing effects of the media may be greater for African Americans than for Caucasians. For example, while 7.5 hours a day is the average daily TV viewing for all TV households in America, African American households average 10 hours of TV per day, and both children and adolescents often use television as a source of guidance (e.g., African American adolescents use TV to learn about occupations and to learn dating behavior).[37] Other research reveals that African American adults tend to

TABLE 13.10	Comparison of Purchase Patterns of Anglo-White, African American, and Hispanic American Households		
PRODUCT/ACTIVITY	**ANGLO-WHITE**	**AFRICAN AMERICAN**	**HISPANIC AMERICAN**
Dental floss	102*	86	91
Mouthwash	97	122	102
Hand and body cream	97	118	100
Vitamin and dieting supplements	103	77	86
Energy drinks	93	137	161
Car rental—business use	94	137	90
Own a digital camera	107	45	71
Greeting card	103	85	81
Instant breakfast	97	121	98
Barbeque and seasoning sauces	101	103	86
Ready-to-drink iced cappuccino	96	115	133
Cat treat	109	45	57
Charcoal	94	149	105
Attend movies/last 6 months	101	93	101
Went camping/past 12 months	112	19	83
Own a full-size van	112	9	79
Own a camera	107	45	71

*These are index numbers. 100 = average for U.S. population.
Source: Mediamark Research, Inc. Doublebase 2005 Report. All rights reserved. Reprinted by permission.

place a great deal of trust in African American centric media (i.e., black magazines, black TV news, black-owned local newspapers, and black radio news) as a source of information about companies and their products.[38] Approximately $400 million of the $1.7 billion spent annually on ads targeted to African Americans is spent on magazine advertising, which includes such publications as *Black Enterprise, Ebony, Essence, Jet, The Source*, and *Vibe*.[39] Many marketers supplement their general advertising with advertisements in magazines, newspapers, and other media directed specifically to African Americans (see Figure 13.3). For example, Pepsi has a promotion that they run in February, which is Black History Month. In conjunction with a Web site featuring black history and art, students are asked to "write your own history." Ten $10,000 college scholarships are awarded as first prize. New fragrances are being offered to the African American woman—"Goddess" from Coty with Kimora Lee Simmons as spokesperson and P. Diddy's "Carol's Daughter" from Estée Lauder, also backed by celebrities like Jada Pinkett Smith. And entrepreneurs Russell Simmons and Keven Liles have started a company called Def Jam Mobile. The company will deliver ring tones, news alerts, and other content to subscribers (the ring tone market is expected to reach $1 billion by 2007). And let's not forget that Hallmark Cards has a division called "Mahogany," which creates and sells cards targeted to the African American audience (see Figure 13.4).[40]

Major advertisers targeting the African American market have increasingly used the specialized services of African American advertising agencies. These specialized agencies generally provide marketers wanting to target African Americans with the distinctive advantage of access to a staff of African American marketing professionals who thoroughly know the values and customs of this market and its specific subsegments.

FIGURE 13.3

Source: © Wisconsin Department of Tourism. Used with permission. All rights reserved

All that... and then some.

Immerse yourself in family fun & culture in Wisconsin.

If you're looking for a fantastic family getaway, it's right next door - in Wisconsin. We've got the most amazing indoor water parks, ethnic festivals, and art and cultural exhibits – including America's *only* Black Holocaust Museum.

For free getaway information, call 1 800-432-TRIP or visit travelwisconsin.com

WISCONSIN
travelwisconsin.com

Ad Targeting African-American Consumer (Backup)

Asian american consumers

The **Asian American** population is approximately 14 million in size and is the fastest-growing American minority (on a percentage basis). While Asians and Pacific Islanders made up 3.9 percent of the U.S. population in 2000, this group is expected to account for 8.9 percent of America's population in 2050.[41] According to the 2000 Census, six different ethnicities make up about 88 percent of the Asian American population: Chinese (2.4 million), Filipinos (1.9 million), Indian (1.7 million), Vietnamese (1.12 million), Korean (1.1 million), and Japanese (797,000).[42] Asian Americans are today the most diverse ethnic group in the United States, and includes the influences of 15 different cultures and a wide range of languages.[43]

Asian Americans are largely family oriented, highly industrious, and strongly driven to achieve a middle-class lifestyle. They are an attractive market for increasing numbers

FIGURE 13.4

Source: Courtesy of Hallmark
Cards, Inc.

**Mahogany, A Division of
Hallmark Cards, Inc. "I'm
really lucky you were thrown
in with my family package!
Happy Birthday"**

of marketers. Indeed, in 2001, 40 percent of all Asian and Pacific Islander families had incomes of at least $75,000, compared with 35 percent of non-Hispanic white families, and an average household income for this group, at $55,026, is 28 percent more than the U.S. average. With respect to occupations, a higher proportion of Asians and Pacific Islanders (than non-Hispanic whites) were concentrated in managerial and professional jobs. Still further, educational attainment is an important goal for this segment of the population. For the Asian and Pacific Islander population age 25 and older, 51 percent of

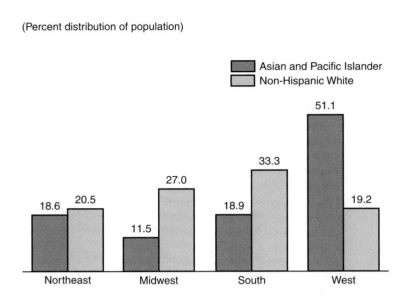

(Percent distribution of population)

Asian and Pacific Islander
Non-Hispanic White

51.1

33.3

27.0

20.5

18.6   11.5   18.9   19.2

Northeast   Midwest   South   West

FIGURE 13.5

Region of Residence for Selected Subcultural Groups

Source: U.S. Census Bureau, Annual Demographic Supplement to the March 2002 Current Population Survey, as contained in "The Asian and Pacific Islander Population of the United States: March 2002," *U.S. Census Bureau,* accessed at www.census.gov/prod/2003pubs/p20-540.pdf, 2.

the men (compared to 32 percent for non-Hispanic white men) and 44 percent of the women (compared to 27 percent for non-Hispanic white women) have earned a Bachelor's Degree or more.[44]

Where are the asian americans?

Asian Americans are largely urban people concentrated in neighborhoods situated in and around a small number of large American cities (95 percent live in metropolitan areas). Nearly half of all Asian Americans live in Los Angeles, San Francisco, and New York, and at present, more than 10 percent of California's population is Asian American. The stereotype that most Chinese live in "Chinatown" is incorrect. Most Chinese, as well as most other Asian Americans, do not live in downtown urban areas; they live in the suburbs.[45] Figure 13.5 presents a comparison of region of residence for Asian and Pacific Islanders versus non-Hispanic whites. It is of interest to note that while close to 20 percent of non-Hispanic whites live in the West, slightly more than half of Asians and Pacific Islanders do.

Understanding the asian american consumer

U.S. Census Bureau data reveal that more Asian Americans, on a per capita basis, own their own businesses than non–Asian American minorities. Those who do not own their own businesses are largely in professional, technical, or managerial occupations. Additionally, many Asian Americans are young and live a good part of their lives in multi-income households. Asian Americans also tend to be more computer literate than the general population. English-speaking Asian Americans are more likely than other Americans to get their news and information online. Asian Americans who go online also tend to be young. Still further, Asian American households are more likely than Hispanic and African American households to have Internet access.[46] Two general-interest Internet sites, **www.Click2Asia.com** and **www.AsianAvenue.com**, have helped create cyberspace communities for Asian Americans.[47] Still further, Asian Americans are much more likely to purchase online than other segments of the U.S. population.

Asian americans as consumers

During the decade of the 1990s, the buying power of Asian Americans increased about 125 percent, to over $250 billion, and is expected to reach about $530 billion by 2009.[48]

As consumers, Asian Americans value quality (associated quality with well-known upscale brands). This population segment tends to be loyal customers, frequently more male oriented when it comes to consumption decisions, and attracted to retailers that make it known that they welcome Asian American patronage.

It is important to remember that Asian Americans are really drawn from diverse cultural backgrounds. Therefore, although Asian Americans have many similarities, marketers should avoid treating Asian Americans as a single market because they are far from being so homogeneous. For example, Vietnamese Americans are more likely to follow the traditional model, wherein the man makes the decision for large purchases; however, Chinese American husbands and wives are more likely to share in the decision-making process.[49] Vietnamese Americans also frown on credit, because in their culture owing money is viewed negatively. In contrast, Korean Americans and Chinese Americans, many of whom have been in the United States for years, accept credit as the American way.[50] A recent article, though, does mention several Asian American youth trends, including the belief among females that the way to stay slim is through self-discipline, and not through fad diets, the desire to be the first to own high-tech gadgets, the addition of Canton Pop artists to MP3 playlists, and a more open-minded attitude toward interracial coupling.[51]

The use of Asian American models in advertising is effective in reaching this market segment. Research reveals that responses to an ad for stereo speakers featuring an Asian model were significantly more positive than responses to the same ad using a Caucasian model.[52] Additionally, the percentage of Asian Americans who prefer advertisements that are not in the English language varies among different Asian American groups. For instance, according to Table 13.11, 93 percent of Vietnamese consumers prefer ad messages in the Vietnamese language, whereas only 42 percent of Japanese Americans prefer ad messages in Japanese. Aware of the increased importance of the Asian American market, Proctor & Gamble Company has named its first Asian American advertising agency, and Wal-Mart has just begun running TV commercials in Mandarin, Cantonese, and Vietnamese, as well as Filipino print ads.[53]

age subcultures

It's not difficult to understand why each major age subgrouping of the population might be thought of as a separate subculture. After all, don't you listen to different music than your parents and grandparents, dress differently, read different magazines, and enjoy different TV shows? Clearly, important shifts occur in an individual's demand for specific types of products and services as he or she goes from being a dependent child to a retired senior citizen. In this chapter, we will limit our examination of **age subcultures** to four

TABLE 13.11	**Language Preference of Specific Asian American Groups**	
ASIAN AMERICAN GROUP	**% WHO PREFER NATIVE LANGUAGE**	**% SPEAKING NATIVE LANGUAGE AT HOME**
Vietnamese	93	71
Chinese	83	66
Korean	81	66
Filipino	66	56
Asian Indian	55	59
Japanese	42	29

Source: **www.ewowfacts.com/pdfs/chapters/61.pdf** (page 609); and *Orienting the U.S. Food and Beverage Market: Strategies Targeting Asian Americans to 2010* (Alexandria, VA: Promar International), June 2000, 87.

age groups, moving from youngest to oldest: **Generation Y**, **Generation X**, **baby boomers**, and **seniors**. These four age segments have been singled out because their distinctive lifestyles qualify them for consideration as subcultural groups.

The generation Y market

This age cohort (a cohort is a group of individuals born over a relatively short and continuous period of time) includes the approximately 71 million Americans born between the years 1977 and 1994 (i.e., the children of baby boomers). Members of Generation Y (also known as "echo boomers" and the "millennium generation") can be divided into three subsegments: Gen Y adults (age 19–28), Gen Y teens (age 13–18), and Gen Y kids, or "tweens" (age 8–12).[54] Keep in mind that while "tweens" are too young to have been born between 1977 and 1994, they nevertheless are still considered to be part of the Gen Y market.

Appealing to generation Y

The teen segment of Generation Y directly spend over $150 billion annually and furthermore influence the purchases of their parents for a substantial amount of other goods and services. They have grown up in a media-saturated environment and tend to be aware of "marketing hype." For example, they would tend to immediately understand that when a shopping center locates popular teen stores at opposite ends of the mall they are being encouraged "to walk the mall."

This age cohort has shifted some of its TV viewing time to the Internet and, when compared with their parents, they are less likely to read newspapers and often do not trust the stores that their parents shop in.[55] Smart retailers have found it profitable to develop Web sites specifically targeted to the interests of the Gen Y consumer. For example, Limited Too (**www.limitedtoo.com**), Rave Girl (**www.goravegirl.com**), and Abercrombie & Fitch (**www.abercrombiekids.com**) have all developed sites targeted to the tween market, despite the fact that a person is supposed to be at least 18 years old to place an order. Still further, about half of all 9- to 17-year-olds are asked by their parents to go online to research products or services.

Tweens

In the United States, the 29 million members of the "tween" market (generally considered to consist of 8- to 14-year-olds) spend an average of $1,294 each, for a total of $38 billion. And their parents will spend almost $126 billion more on them. Still further, in households that include a tween, food purchases account for almost 50 percent of total household spending.[56] Table 13.12 provides some additional information about the tween market. Teenagers also visit shopping malls more frequently than any other age group, spending an average of $46.80 per mall visit.[57]

Gen Y adults are the largest users of cell phone text messaging. A recent study found that 63 percent of Gen Y adults use text messaging, compared with only 31 percent of Gen Xers, 18 percent of cell phone users in their 40s, and 13 percent of those 50-year-olds. In today's cell phone market, 76 percent of 15- to 19-year-olds and 90 percent of consumers in their early 20s regularly use their cell phones for text messaging, ringtones, and games.[58]

Twixters

Spanning the Gen Y and Gen X markets is a group of 21- to 29-year-olds who continue to live with their parents. Many of them are out of college and have decent jobs and incomes—but they are not moving out to get married, nor are they leaving their parents' home. Over half of Twixters graduated college more than $10,000 in debt (some taking 6 years to do so). They tend to have trust in their parents and in established institutions, and often do not marry before they reach their 30th birthday. While these individuals cannot afford to purchase "anything that could be considered an asset," they do purchase gadgets and clothes.[59]

TABLE 13.12	Selected Profile of the "Tween" Market

- Consists of 8- to 14-year-olds
- Spend and influence $1.18 trillion in purchases worldwide
- They know brand images better than an advertising expert
- Tweens in the U.S., U.K., and Australia average seeing 20,000 to 40,000 commercials a year
- Tweens affect their parents' brand choices
  - They may influence up to 80 percent of family brand choices
  - They may have a substantial influence on the final decision in over 60 percent of choices
- They no longer expect to be informed by traditional media (e.g., TV, radio)
- The concept of individual brand loyalty may no longer exist—it is a group decision (i.e., the tween and his/her peers)
- Up to 25 percent of all tweens communicate every week with tweens in other countries
- Almost half of all tweens consider the use of grammatically correct language to be outdated, and prefer TweenSpeak, which combines words, icons, illustrations, and phrases
- Globally, 24 percent of tweens use the Internet as their primary communication tool
- 21 percent of tweens claim that the Internet is the easiest way to find new friends

Source: Adapted from Martin Lindstrom, "Branding Is No Longer Child's Play!," *Journal of Consumer Marketing* 21, no. 3 (2004): 175–182.

The generation X market

This age grouping—often referred to as *Xers*, *busters*, or *slackers*—consists of the almost 50 million individuals born between about 1965 and 1979 (different experts quote different starting and ending years). As consumers, these 25- to 40-year-olds represented $1.4 trillion in spending power in 2004.[60] They do not like labels, are cynical, and do not want to be singled out and marketed to.

Also, unlike their parents, who are frequently baby boomers, they are in no rush to marry, start a family, or work excessive hours to earn high salaries. For Generation X consumers, job satisfaction is typically more important than salary. It has been said, for example, that "Baby Boomers live to work, Gen Xers work to live!" Xers reject the values of older coworkers who may neglect their families while striving to secure higher salaries and career advancement, and many have observed their parents getting laid off after many years of loyalty to an employer. They, therefore, are not particularly interested in long-term employment with a single company but instead prefer to work for a company that can offer some worklife flexibility and can bring some fun aspects into the environment. Gen Xers understand the necessity of money but do not view salary as a sufficient reason for staying with a company—the quality of the work itself and the relationships built on the job are much more important. For Generation X, it is more important to enjoy life and to have a lifestyle that provides freedom and flexibility.

Some additional facts about Generation X are:

- 62 percent are married
- 29.7 million are parents
- 51 percent of children under 18 living at home are in households headed by an Xer
- 31 percent of Gen Xers have earned a college degree

- 81 percent of Xers are employed full-time or part-time
- 37 percent of Gen Xers' mothers worked outside the home when they (as kids) were growing up[61]

Appealing to generation X

Members of Generation X often pride themselves on their sophistication. Although they are not necessarily materialistic, they do purchase good brand names (such as Sony) but not necessarily designer labels. They want to be recognized by marketers as a group in their own right and not as mini–baby boomers. Therefore, advertisements targeted to this audience must focus on their style in music, fashions, and language. One key for marketers appears to be sincerity. Xers are not against advertising but only opposed to insincerity.

Baby boomer media does not work with Generation X members. For example, while 65 percent of 50- to 64-year-olds, and 55 percent of 30- to 49-year-olds read a newspaper regularly, only 39 percent of adults under 30 (the younger Xers) regularly read a newspaper.[62] Xers are the MTV generation, and whereas the three major U.S. TV networks attract an average of only 18 percent of the 18- to 29-year-old group, the Fox network claims that 38 percent of its viewers are in this age group. Still further, Xers use the Internet more than any other age cohort. For example, 60 percent of Xers have tried online banking, while only 38 percent of Generation Y has tried online banking.[63]

Hotel chains are also making changes in their offerings in order to better attract the Gen X traveler, the fastest-growing group of hotel patrons. Marriott, for example, is remodeling rooms to include flat-panel LCD TVs, high-speed Internet access, ergonomic desk chairs, and high thread-count sheets.[64] Additionally, Gen Xers are generally dissatisfied with most current shopping malls—they want to do more than just shop. Xers want to be able to eat a proper sitdown meal at the mall, rather than something quick at the food court. They also want to be able to get a cup of coffee while doing work on their laptop, and perhaps also see a movie.[65]

The baby boomer market

Marketers have found baby boomers a particularly desirable target audience because (1) they are the single largest distinctive age category alive today; (2) they frequently make important consumer purchase decisions; and (3) they contain small subsegments of trendsetting consumers (sometimes known as yuppies, or young upwardly mobile professionals) who have influence on the consumer tastes of other age segments of society.

Who are the baby boomers?

The term *baby boomers* refers to the age segment of the population that was born between 1946 and 1964. Thus, baby boomers are in the broad age category that extends from about 40 to 60. These 78 million or so baby boomers represent more than 40 percent of the adult population. The magnitude of this statistic alone would make them a much sought-after market segment. However, they also are valued because they comprise about 50 percent of all those in professional and managerial occupations and more than one-half of those with at least a college degree.

Although each year more baby boomers turn 50 years of age, they do not necessarily like the idea. Increases in health club memberships and a boom in the sales of vitamin and health supplements are evidence that these consumers are trying hard to look and feel "young"—they do not want to age gracefully but will fight and kick and pay whatever is necessary to look young. In advertisements they want to be portrayed as they see themselves—lively and attractive.[66] Most important to marketers, who understand them, they have money and they want to spend it on what they feel advances the quality of their lives.

Consumer characteristics of baby boomers

Baby boomers tend to be motivated consumers. They enjoy buying for themselves, for their homes or apartments, and for others—they are consumption oriented. As baby boomers age, the nature of the products and services they most need or desire changes. For example, because of the aging of this market segment, sales of "relaxed fit" jeans, and "lineless" bifocal glasses are up substantially, as is the sales of walking shoes. Men's and women's pants with elastic waistbands are also enjoying strong sales. Moreover, bank marketers and other financial institutions are also paying more attention to assisting boomers who are starting to think about retirement. Even St. Joseph's Aspirin has switched its target from babies to boomers, and Disney has ads to entice baby boomers to vacation at their theme parks without their kids.

Yuppies are by far the most sought-after subgroup of baby boomers. Although constituting only 5 percent of the population, they generally are well off financially, well educated, and in enviable professional or managerial careers. They often are associated with status brand names, such as BMWs or Volvo station wagons, Rolex watches, cable TV, and Cuisinart food processors. The Gap, for example, is opening a new chain of stores called Forth & Towne, aimed at women age 35 and older. These women were GAP shoppers for many years, but today they primarily shop department stores, because the specialty stores generally target younger audiences.[67]

Today, though, as many yuppies are maturing, they are shifting their attention away from expensive status-type possessions to travel, physical fitness, planning for second careers, or some other form of new life directions. Indeed, there has been a move away from wanting possessions, to wanting experiences—"boomers today are more interested in doing things than having things."[68]

Recent articles dealing with the baby boom generation have noted that some members of this group are planning to keep working, either full-time or part-time beyond age 65 (which, for the oldest boomers, is just a few years away). While some need to do this for the money, most just want to stay active, and/or are even planning, upon retirement, to start new careers. The majority of this group will not need to work in order to support themselves—by 2020, when the youngest baby boomers turn 55, this age cohort will own $20 trillion in assets.[69]

To sum up, Gen Yers, Gen Xers, and baby boomers differ in their purchasing behavior, attitudes toward brands, and behavior toward ads. Table 13.13 captures some of the differences among these three age cohorts.

TABLE 13.13	Comparison of Selected Age Cohorts Across Marketing-Related Issues		
THEMES	**GENERATION Y**	**GENERATION X**	**BOOMERS**
Purchasing behavior	Savvy, pragmatic	Materialistic	Narcissistic
Coming of age technology	Computer in every home	Microwave in every home	TV in every home
Price–quality attitude	Value oriented: weighing price–quality relationships	Price oriented: concerned about the cost of individual items	Conspicuous consumption: buying for indulgence
Attitude toward brands	Brand embracing	Against branding	Brand loyal
Behavior toward ads	Rebel against hype	Rebel against hype	Respond to image-building type

Source: Stephanie M. Noble and Charles H. Noble, "Getting to Know Y: The Consumption Behaviors of a New Cohort," *AMA Winter Educators' Conference* 11 (Chicago: American Marketing Association, 2000), *Marketing Theory,* Conference Proceedings, 294.

Older consumers

America is aging. A portion of the baby boomers are about to turn 60, and there are plenty of preboomers—those 60 to 65 years old. According to the U.S. Census Bureau (in 2004), there were more than 36 million people in this country who are 65 years of age or older (12 percent of the population). Projecting ahead to the year 2050, it is anticipated that there will be more than 86 million Americans (21 percent of the total population) who will be 65 years of age or older.[70] Still further, from the start to the end of the twentieth century, life expectancy in the United States rose from about 47 years to 77 years, and whereas a 65-year-old in 1900 could expect, on average, to live about 12 more years, a 65-year-old in 2000 can expect about 18 more years of life.[71]

It should also be kept in mind that "later adulthood" (i.e., those who are 50 years of age or older) is the longest adult life stage for most consumers (i.e., often 29 or more years in duration). This is in contrast to "early adulthood" (i.e., those who are 18 to 34 years of age), a stage lasting 16 years, and "middle adulthood" (i.e., those who are 35 to 49 years of age), a stage lasting 14 years. Remember that people over age 50 comprise about one-third of the adult U.S. market.

Although some people think of older consumers as consisting of people without substantial financial resources, in generally poor health, and with plenty of free time on their hands, the fact is that more than 30 percent of men and more than 20 percent of women aged 65 to 69 are employed, as are 19 percent of men and 12 percent of women aged 70 to 74. Additionally, millions of seniors are involved in the daily care of a grandchild, and many do volunteer work. The annual discretionary income of this group amounts to 50 percent of the discretionary income of the United States, and these older consumers are major purchasers of luxury products such as cars, alcohol, vacations, and financial products. Americans over 65 now control about 70 percent of the nation's wealth.

Defining "older" in older consumer

Driving the growth of the elderly population are three factors: the declining birthrate, the aging of the huge baby boomer segment, and improved medical diagnoses and treatment. In the United States, "old age" is officially assumed to begin with a person's 65th birthday (or when the individual qualifies for full Social Security and Medicare). However, people over age 60 tend to view themselves as being 15 years younger than their chronological age.

It is generally accepted that people's perceptions of their ages are more important in determining behavior than their chronological ages (or the number of years lived). In fact, people may at the same time have a number of different perceived or **cognitive ages**. Specifically, elderly consumers perceive themselves to be younger than their chronological ages on four perceived age dimensions: *feel age* (how old they feel); *look age* (how old they look); *do age* (how involved they are in activities favored by members of a specific age group); and *interest age* (how similar their interests are to those of members of a specific age group).[72] The results support other research that indicates that elderly consumers are more likely to consider themselves younger (to have a younger cognitive age) than their chronological age.

For marketers, these findings underscore the importance of looking beyond chronological age to perceived or cognitive age when appealing to mature consumers and to the possibility that cognitive age might be used to segment the mature market. The "New-Age Elderly," when compared to the "Traditional Elderly," are more adventurous, more likely to perceive themselves to be better off financially, and more receptive to marketing information.[73]

Segmenting the elderly market

The elderly are by no means a homogeneous subcultural group. There are those who, as a matter of choice, do not have color TVs or Touch-Tone telephone service, whereas others have the latest desktop computers and spend their time surfing the Internet (cyberseniors will be discussed later in this section).

One consumer gerontologist has suggested that the elderly are more diverse in interests, opinions, and actions than other segments of the adult population.[74] Although this view runs counter to the popular myth that the elderly are uniform in terms of attitudes and lifestyles, both gerontologists and market researchers have repeatedly demonstrated that age is not necessarily a major factor in determining how older consumers respond to marketing activities.

With an increased appreciation that the elderly constitute a diverse age segment, more attention is now being given to identifying ways to segment the elderly into meaningful groupings. One relatively simple segmentation scheme partitions the elderly into three chronological age categories: the *young-old* (65 to 74 years of age); the *old* (those 75 to 84); and the *old-old* (those 85 years of age and older). This market segmentation approach provides useful consumer-relevant insights.

The elderly can also be segmented in terms of motivations and *quality-of-life orientation*. Table 13.14 presents a side-by-side comparison of new-age elderly consumers and the more traditional older consumers. The increased presence of the new-age elderly suggests that marketers need to respond to the value orientations of older consumers whose lifestyles remain relatively ageless. Clearly, the new-age elderly are individuals who feel, think, and do according to a cognitive age that is younger than their chronological age. All this suggests the declining importance of chronological age, and increasing importance of perceived or cognitive age as an indicator of the "aging experience" and age-related quality of life.

Cyberseniors

Although some people might think of older Americans as individuals who still use rotary phones and are generally resistant to change, this stereotype is far from the truth. Few older consumers are fearful of new technology, and there are more Internet users over the age of 50 than under the age of 20. Research studies have found that those over 55 are more likely than the average adult to use the Internet to purchase books, stocks, and computer equipment—92 percent of surfing seniors have shopped online and 78 percent have purchased online.[75] In fact, older Internet users are the fastest-growing demographic group with respect to the U.S. Internet market, and it has been forecast that 48 percent of all seniors will be online by the end of 2005. Additionally, a recent study found that 46 percent of cyberseniors use the Internet more than 10 hours weekly.[76]

What's the attraction for seniors to go online? Certainly, the Internet is a great way to communicate with friends and family members living in other states, including grandchildren in college. But the Web is also a place to find information (e.g., stock prices, health and medication-related information), entertainment, and a sense of community. There also appears to be a relationship between the amount of time an older adult spends on the Internet and his or her level of out-of-home mobility (using the Internet may serve as a substitute for going out of the house). Having a computer and modem "empowers" older consumers—it allows them to regain some of the control that was lost due to the physical and/or social deterioration in their lives. For example, a consumer can pay bills, shop, and e-mail friends. This may be part of the reason why the American Association of Retired Persons (AARP) claims that 2 million of its members are computer users.[77] Figure 13.6 presents the ways in which seniors use the Internet.

Marketing to the older consumer

Older consumers are open to be marketed to, but only for the "right" kinds of products and services and using the "right" advertising presentation. For example, older models tend to be underrepresented in advertisements or are often shown as being infirm or feeble. Part of the problem, according to some writers on the subject, is that the advertising professionals who create the ads are often in their 20s and 30s and have little understanding or empathy for older consumers. Seniors often want to be identified not for what they did in the past but by what they would like to accomplish in the future. Retirement or moving to a sunbelt community is viewed as the opening of a new chapter

TABLE 13.14	Comparison of New-Age and Traditional Elderly

NEW-AGE ELDERLY	TRADITIONAL/STEREOTYPICAL ELDERLY
• *Perceive themselves to be different in outlook from other people their age*	• *Perceive all older people to be about the same in outlook*
• *Age is seen as a state of mind*	• *See age as more of a physical state*
• *See themselves as younger than their chronological age*	• *See themselves at or near their chronological age*
• *Feel younger, think younger, and "do" younger*	• *Tend to feel, think, and do things that they feel match their chronological age*
• *Have a genuinely youthful outlook*	• *Feel that one should act one's age*
• *Feel there is a considerable adventure to living*	• *Feel life should be dependable and routine*
• *Feel more in control of their own lives*	• *Normal sense of being in control of their own lives*
• *Have greater self-confidence when it comes to making consumer decisions*	• *Normal range of self-confidence when it comes to making consumer decisions*
• *Less concerned that they will make a mistake when buying something*	• *Some concern that they will make a mistake when buying something*
• *Especially knowledgeable and alert consumers*	• *Low-to-average consumer capabilities*
• *Selectively innovative*	• *Not innovative*
• *Seek new experiences and personal challenges*	• *Seek stability and a secure routine*
• *Less interested in accumulating possessions*	• *Normal range of interest in accumulating possessions*
• *Higher measured life satisfaction*	• *Lower measured life satisfaction*
• *Less likely to want to live their lives over differently*	• *Have some regrets as to how they lived their lives*
• *Perceive themselves to be healthier*	• *Perceive themselves to be of normal health for their age*
• *Feel financially more secure*	• *Somewhat concerned about financial security*

Source: Reprinted by permission from "The Value Orientation of New-Age Elderly: The Coming of an Ageless Market" by Leon G. Schiffman and Elaine Sherman in *Journal of Business Research* 22 (April 1991): 187–194. Copyright 1991 by Elsevier Science Publishing Co., Inc.

in life and not a quiet withdrawal from life. In the same vein, the increase in the number of older adults taking vacation cruises and joining health clubs signifies a strong commitment to remaining "functionally young."

For some products and services, seniors do exhibit different shopping habits than younger consumers. For example, when shopping for a car, older consumers consider fewer brands, fewer models, and fewer dealers. They also are more likely to choose a long-established brand of automobile.[78] Older shoppers tend to be more store-loyal than younger age groups, especially with respect to supermarkets. Still further, the importance of factors like store location (e.g., distance from home) are often a function of the health status of the senior.[79]

FIGURE 13.6

How Seniors Use the Internet

Source: Jacqueline K. Eastman and Rajesh Iyer, "The Elderly's Uses and Attitudes towards the Internet," *Journal of Consumer Marketing* 21, no. 3 (2004):214.

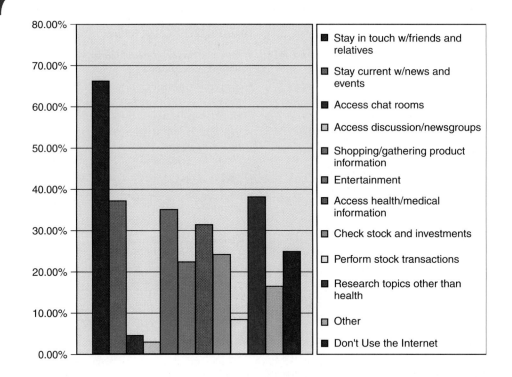

sex as a subculture

Because **sex roles** have an important cultural component, it is quite fitting to examine **gender** as a subcultural category.

Sex roles and consumer behavior

All societies tend to assign certain traits and roles to males and others to females. In American society, for instance, aggressiveness and competitiveness often were considered traditional *masculine traits*; neatness, tactfulness, gentleness, and talkativeness were considered traditional *feminine traits*. In terms of role differences, women have historically been cast as homemakers with responsibility for child care and men as the providers or breadwinners. Because such traits and roles are no longer relevant for many individuals, marketers are increasingly appealing to consumers' broader vision of gender-related role options. However, many studies are still suggesting that even with the large number of middle-class women in the workplace, men are not doing more in terms of housework (e.g., cleaning, cooking, laundry).[80]

A recent study also found that men and women exhibit different reactions to identical print advertisements. Women show superior affect and purchase intention toward ads that are verbal, harmonious, complex, and category-oriented. In contrast, men exhibit superior affect and purchase intention toward ads that are comparative, simple, and attribute-oriented. Consequently, it may be best, where feasible, to advertise differently to men and women.[81]

Consumer products and sex roles

Within every society, it is quite common to find products that are either exclusively or strongly associated with the members of one sex. In the United States, for example, shaving equipment, cigars, pants, ties, and work clothing were historically male products; bracelets, hair spray, hair dryers, and sweet-smelling colognes generally were considered feminine products. For most of these products, the **sex role** link has either diminished or disappeared; for others, the prohibition still lingers. Specifically, although women have historically been the major market for vitamins, men are increasingly being targeted for vitamins exclusively formulated for men. Furthermore, in the past few years men have exhibited more of an interest in personal health and wellness, closing the gap with women with regard to these areas of personal concern.[82]

The appeal of the Internet seems to differ somewhat for men and women. For instance, women go online to seek out reference materials, online books, medical information, cooking ideas, government information, and chat sites. In contrast, men tend to focus on exploring, discovery, identifying free software, and investments. This seems to provide further support for the notion that men are "hunters," whereas women are "nurturers."[83] Still further, although men and women are equally likely to browse commercial sites, women are less likely to purchase online (32% for men versus 19% for women). Evidence suggests that the lower incidence of women purchasing online is due to their heightened concerns about online security and privacy.[84]

Women as depicted in media and advertising

Many women feel that the media and advertising create an expectation of beauty that most women can never achieve. Consequently, they want the definition of "beauty" to change. Dove has an advertising campaign that is challenging the traditional sense of beauty and has been well received by women. "Real" women are portrayed in the company's ads—with gray hair, winkles, and flawed skin—i.e., real people! Importantly, the campaign lets women know that beauty comes in many sizes, shapes, and ages.[85] Supporting Dove's realistic approach, a recent study found that 65 percent of women 35 to 40 years of age felt that most advertisements aimed at them were patronizing, and 50 percent also found the ads to be "old-fashioned."[86]

The working woman

Marketers are keenly interested in the **working woman**, especially the married working woman. They recognize that married women who work outside of the home are a large and growing market segment, one whose needs differ from those of women who do not work outside the home (frequently self-labeled "stay-at-home moms"). It is the size of the working woman market that makes it so attractive. Approximately 60 percent of American women 16 years of age and older are in the labor force, which represents a market of over 65 million individuals. Whereas more than half of all women with children under the age of 1 are working (55 percent), almost 78 percent of women with children ages 6 to 17 are employed.[87]

Because 40 percent of all business travelers today are women, hotels have begun to realize that it pays to provide the services women want, such as healthy foods, gyms, and spas and wellness centers. Female business travelers are also concerned about hotel security and frequently use room service because they do not want to go to the hotel bar or restaurant. The Hilton in Paris, for example, discreetly hands key cards to female patrons, offers valet parking, and allows women to receive guests in an executive lounge located on the hotel's business floor.[88]

Segmenting the working woman market

To provide a richer framework for segmentation, marketers have developed categories that differentiate the motivations of working and nonworking women. For instance, a number of studies have divided the female population into four segments: *stay-at-home* housewives; *plan-to-work* housewives; *just-a-job* working women; and *career-oriented* working women.[89] The distinction between "just-a-job" and "career-oriented" working women is particularly meaningful. "Just-a-job" working women seem to be motivated to work primarily by a sense that the family requires the additional income, whereas

FIGURE 13.7

Consumer Electronics Products Women Are Most Interested in Buying

Source: Beth Snyder Bulik, "Electronics Retailers too Women," *Advertising Age*, November 15, 2004, 16.

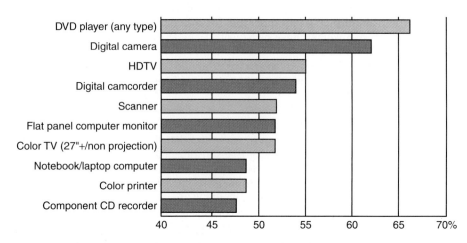

*Percentage of non-owners expecting to purchase product sometime in the future
(*Source:* CEA, CE Ownership and Market Potential–March 2003)

"career-oriented" working women, who tend to be in a managerial or professional position, are driven more by a need to achieve and succeed in their chosen careers. Today, though, with more and more female college graduates in the workforce, the percentage of career-oriented working women is on the rise. As evidence of this fact, 25 percent of all working women bring home a paycheck that is larger than their husband's (10 years ago it was only 17 percent).[90]

Working women spend less time shopping than nonworking women. They accomplish this "time economy" by shopping less often and by being brand and store loyal. Not surprisingly, working women also are likely to shop during evening hours and on weekends, as well as to buy through direct-mail catalogs.

Businesses that advertise to women should also be aware that magazines are now delivering a larger women's audience than television shows. Whereas early 1980s' TV shows had higher ratings than popular magazines, today the top 25 women's magazines have larger audiences than the top 25 television shows targeted to females.[91]

Every year, more and more products and retailers target to women. Recent examples include Beringer's introduction of White Lie Early Season Chardonnay ("This wine speaks to us in our language") and Godiva Chocolate's notion that their product is something that a woman deserves to buy for herself (rather than as a gift for someone else). Best Buy, and other similar electronics stores, are trying harder than ever to make women feel comfortable shopping in their outlets, since women spend $55 billion annually on consumer electronics. A recent study by the Consumer Electronics Association found that 46 percent of women claim that they have the most influence in their households with respect to consumer electronics purchases.[92] Figure 13.7 shows the consumer electronics products that women are most interested in buying.

subcultural interaction

All consumers are simultaneously members of more than one subcultural segment (e.g., a consumer may be a young, Hispanic, Catholic homemaker living in the Midwest). The reality of **subcultural interaction** suggest that marketers should strive to understand how multiple *subcultural* memberships *interact* to influence target consumers' relevant consumption behavior. Promotional strategy should not be limited to target a single subcultural membership.

SUMMARY

Subcultural analysis enables marketers to segment their markets to meet the specific needs, motivations, perceptions, and attitudes shared by members of a specific subcultural group. A subculture is a distinct cultural group that exists as an identifiable segment within a larger, more complex society. Its members possess beliefs, values, and customs that set them apart from other members of the same society; at the same time, they hold to the dominant beliefs of the overall society. Major subcultural categories in this country include nationality, religion, geographic location, race, age, and sex. Each of these can be broken down into smaller segments that can be reached through special copy appeals and selective media choices. In some cases (such as the elderly consumer), product characteristics can be tailored to the specialized needs of the market segment. Because all consumers simultaneously are members of several subcultural groups, the marketer must determine for the product category how specific subcultural memberships interact to influence the consumer's purchase decisions.

DISCUSSION QUESTIONS

1. Why is subcultural analysis especially significant in a country such as the United States?

2. Discuss the importance of subcultural segmentation to marketers of food products. Identify a food product for which the marketing mix should be regionalized. Explain why and how the marketing mix should be varied across geographic areas of the United States.

3. How can marketers of the following products use the material presented in this chapter to develop promotional campaigns designed to increase market share among African American, Hispanic, and Asian American consumers? The products are (a) compact disk players, (b) ready-to-eat cereals, and (c) designer jeans.

4. Asian Americans are a small proportion of the total U.S. population. Why are they an important market segment? How can a marketer of personal computers effectively target Asian Americans?

5. Sony is introducing a new 27-inch TV with a picture-in-picture feature. How should the company position and advertise the product to (a) Generation X consumers and (b) affluent baby boomers?

6. In view of the anticipated growth of the over-50 market, a leading cosmetics company is reevaluating the marketing strategy for its best-selling moisturizing face cream for women. Should the company market the product to younger (under-50) as well as older women? Would it be wiser to develop a new brand and formula for consumers over 50 rather than target both age groups with one product? Explain your answer.

7. Marketers realize that people of the same age often exhibit very different lifestyles. Using the evidence presented in this chapter, discuss how developers of retirement housing can use older Americans' lifestyles to more effectively segment their markets.

8. a. How should marketers promote products and services to working women? What appeals should they use? Explain.

   b. As the owner of a Saturn automobile dealership, what kind of marketing strategies would you use to target working women?

EXERCISES

1. Using one of the subculture categories listed in Table 13.1, identify a group that can be regarded as a subculture within your university or college.

   a. Describe the norms, values, and behaviors of the subculture's members.

   b. Interview five members of that subculture regarding attitudes toward the use of credit cards.

   c. What are the implications of your findings for marketing credit cards to the group you selected?

2. Interview one baby boomer and one Generation X consumer regarding the purchase of a car. Prepare a report on the differences in attitudes between the two individuals. Do your findings support the text's discussion of the differences between boomers and busters? Explain.

3. Many of your perceptions regarding price versus value are likely to be different from those of your parents or grandparents. Researchers attribute such differences to cohort effects, which are based on the premise that consumption patterns are determined early in life. Therefore, individuals who experienced different economic, political, and cultural environments during their youth are likely to be different types of consumers as adults. Describe instances in which your parents or grandparents disagreed with or criticized purchases you had made. Describe the cohort effects that explain each party's position during these disagreements.

4. Find two good and two bad examples of advertising directed toward elderly consumers. To what degree are these ads stereotypical? Do they depict the concept of perceived age? How could these ads be improved by applying some of this chapter's guidelines for advertising to elderly consumers?

KEY TERMS

- **african american consumers**
- **age subcultures**
- **asian american consumers**
- **baby boomers**
- **cognitive ages**
- **gender subcultures**
- **generation X consumers**
- **generation Y**
- **hispanic american subculture**
- **nationality subcultures**
- **racial subcultures**
- **regional subcultures**
- **religious subcultures**
- **seniors**
- **sex roles**
- **subcultural interaction**
- **subculture**

NOTES

1. U.S. Census Bureau, accessed at **www.census.gov**

2. Pui-Wing Tam, "Ethnic Media Muy Popular in California," *Wall Street Journal*, April 23, 2002, B1.

3. Eric Schmitt, "New Census Shows Hispanics Are Even with Blacks in U.S.," *New York Times*, March 8, 2001, A1, A21.

4. Matthew Monks, "Report Shows Nearly Half of Queens in Foreign Born," *Jackson Heights Times*, January 27, 2005, accessed at **http://gothamgazette.com/community/21/news/1184**

5. "Largest Minority Group: Hispanics," *The New York Times*, January 22, 2003, A17; and "Hispanic Fact Pack, 2004 Edition," *A Supplement to Advertising Age Magazine*.

6. Deborah L. Vence, "Pick up the Pieces: Companies Target Lifestyle Segments of Hispanics," *Marketing News*, March 15, 2005, 13–15.

7. U.S. Census Bureau, "Statistical Abstract of the United States 2004–2005," Table No. 16, accessed at **www.census.gov**.

8. U.S. Census Bureau, Statistical Abstract of the United States: 2004–2005, Table No. 56, accessed at **www.census.gov**; and "White U.S. Households Contract, Homes Expand," *AmeriStat*, March 2003, 1.

9. Jeanie Casison, "Snapshot of America," *Incentive*, October 2001, 33–36; Lynn Petrak, "Cultured Products," *Dairy Field*, April 2001, 34–38; and John Robinson, Bart Landry, and Ronica Rooks, "Time and the Melting Pot," *American Demographics*, June 1998, 18–24.

10. Laurel Wentz, "Multicultural? No, Mainstream," *Advertising Age*, May 2, 2005, 3 & 57.

11. "The Hispanic Population: Census 2000 Brief," *U.S. Department of Commerce*, accesses at **www.census.gov**; and "2003 American Community Survey Data Profile Highlights," *U.S. Census Bureau—American FactFinder*, accessed at: **http://factfinder.census.gov**.

12. Ibid.; and Brad Edmondson, "Hispanic Americans in 2001," *American Demographics*, January 1997, 17.

13. Soyeon Shim and Kenneth C. Gehrt, "Native American and Hispanic Adolescent Consumers: Examination of Shopping Orientation, Socialization Factors and Social Structure Variables," in *1995 AMA Educators' Proceedings*, ed. Barbara B. Stern and George M. Zinkan (Chicago: American Marketing Association, 1995), 297–298.

14. Op. cit., "Hispanic Fact Book, 2004 Edition," 35.

15. Catharine P. Taylor, "Barbie Latina Says 'Hola' to Net," *Advertising Age*, October 1, 2001, 54.

16. Rohit Deshpandè, Wayne D. Hoyer, and Naveen Donthu, "The Intensity of Ethnic Affiliation: A Study of the Sociology of Hispanic Consumption," *Journal of Consumer Research* 13 (September 1986): 214–220; and Cynthia Webster, "The Role of Hispanic Ethnic Identification on Reference Group Influence," in *Advances in Consumer Research* 21, ed. Chris T. Allen and Deborah Roedder John (Provo, UT: Association for Consumer Research, 1994), 458–463.

17. "Toyota Corolla: Conill, Los Angeles," *Advertising Age*, April 18, 2005, 38.

18. Laurel Wentz, "J&J Takes Hispanic Outreach Effort on the Road," *Advertising Age*, March 21, 2005, 31.

19. Marcia Mogelonsky, "First Language Comes First," *American Demographics*, October 1995, 21.

20. Abbey Klassen, "Discovery, Nickelodeon Offer more than Soap Operas to Hispanic Viewers," *Advertising Age*, April 11, 2005, 85.

21. Kate Fitzgerald, "Beer, Auto, Retail Energizing Radio Airwaves," *Advertising Age*, January 31, 2005, S-6.

22. Michael Fielding, "The Halo: Christian Consumers Are a Bloc That Matters to All Marketers," *Marketing News*, February 1, 2005, 18 & 20.

23. Kevin Michael Grace, "Is This Kosher," *Report Newsmagazine*, 27, 1, May 8, 2000, 37; Laura Bird, "Major Brands Look for the Kosher Label," *Adweek's Marketing Week*, April 1, 1991, 18–19; and Judith Waldrop, "Everything's Kosher," *American Demographics*, March 1991, 4.

24. Victoria Rivkin, "Godly Gains," *Crain's New York Business*, October 13, 2003, 21 & 27.

25. Heidi J. Shrager, "Closed-Circle Commerce," *Wall Street Journal*, November 19, 2001, B1 & B11.

26. Florence Fabricant, "The Geography of Taste," *New York Times Magazine*, March 10, 1996, 40–41.

27. Marcia Mogelonsky, "America's Hottest Market," *American Demographics*, January 1996, 20–31, 55.

28. U.S. Census Bureau, "Table 3: Annual Estimates of the Population by Sex, Race, Hispanic or Latino Origin for the United States: April 1, 2000 to July 1, 2004," accessed at **www.census.gov**

29. "African American Market Profile," *Magazine Publishers of America*, accessed at **www.magazine.org/marketprofiles**.

30. Mike Beirne, "Has This Group Been Left Behind?," *Brandweek*, March 14, 2005, 33–35.

31. "Understanding Nuances of Language and Culture Is Key in Marketing to Minority Women," *Marketing to Women* 13, no. 2 (February 2000): S1.

32. Youn-Kyung Kim and Seunghae Han, "Perceived Images of Retail Stores and Brands: Comparison Among Three Ethnic Consumer Groups," *Journal of Family and Consumer Sciences* 92, no. 3 (2000): 58–61; and Christy Fisher, "Black, Hip, and Primed (to Shop)," *American Demographics*, September 1996, 52–58.

33. Gerda Gallop-Goodman, "Check This Out," *American Demographics*, 23, no. 5, May 2001, 14–17.

34. Op. cit., "African American Market Profile," 8.

35. Kari Van Hoof, "Surveys Point to Group Differences," *Brandweek*, March 7, 1994, 32–33.

36. Osei Appiah, "Ethnic Identification on Adolescents' Evaluations of Advertisements," *Journal of Advertising Research* 41, no. 5 (September/October 2001): 7–22.

37. Bush, Smith, and Martin, "The Influence of Consumer Socialization Variables," 13–24; and Hillary Chura, "Offerings Hope to Extend the 'Oprah effect'," *Advertising Age*, March 7, 2005, S12.

38. "Understanding Nuances of Language and Culture Are Key in Marketing to Minority Women," S3.

39. Louise Witt, "Color Code Red: African American Magazines Have Loyal Readers, so Why Are They still Having a Hard Time Attracting Advertisers?," *American Demographics*, February 2004, 23–25.

40. Stephanie Thompson, "Coty, Estée Lauder See Opportunity in Hip-hop," *Advertising Age*, May 23, 2005, 9; Jason Ankeny, "Young, Mobile, Def," *American Demographics*, November 2004, 23–25; "Pepsi Connects with Black History," *American Demographics*, November 2004, 33.

41. Op. cit., U.S. Census Bureau, "Table 3: Annual Estimates of the Population by Sex, Race, Hispanic or Latino Origin for the United States: April 1, 2000 to July 1, 2004," accessed at **www.census.gov**.

42. Ibid., 36; and U.S. Census Bureau, Projections Table NP-T5-B; and see **www.ewowfacts.com/pdfs/ chapters/61.pdf**.

43. "Asian-American Market Profile," *Magazine Publishers of America*, accessed at **www.magazine.org/marketprofiles**, 4.

44. "The Asian and Pacific Islander Population in the United States: March 2002," *U.S. Census Bureau*, accessed at **www.census.gov/prod/2003pubs/p20-540.pdf**.

45. **www.ewowfacts.com/pdfs/chapters/61.pdf**.

46. John Fetto, "Cyber Tigers," *American Demographics*, 24, 3, March 2002, 9–10; and Sheila Thorne, "Reaching the Minority Majority," *Pharmaceutical Executive*, 21, 4, April 2001, 156–158.

47. "Orienting the U.S. Food and Beverage Market: Strategies Targeting Asian Americans to 2010," Promar International, Alexandria, VA, June 2000.

48. Op. cit., "Asian-American Market Profile," 4.

49. John Steere, "How Asian-Americans Make Purchase Decisions," *Marketing News*, March 13, 1995, 9.

50. Simpson, "The Future Cardholder," 36–42.

51. "Asian Youth Trends," *American Demographics*, October 2004, 14.

52. Judy Cohen, "White Consumer Response to Asian Models in Advertising," *Journal of Consumer Marketing* (Spring 1992): 17–27.

53. Laurel Wentz, "AZN TV Makes It Easier to Reach Asians," *Advertising Age*, April 18, 2005, 38.

54. Stephanie M. Noble and Charles H. Noble, "Getting to Know Y: The Consumption Behaviors of a New Cohort," in *2000 AMA Winter Educators' Conference*, 11, ed. John P. Workman and William D. Perreault (Chicago: American Marketing Association, 2000), 293–303; and Pamela Paul, "Getting Inside Gen Y," *American Demographics* 23, 9, September 2001, 42–49.

55. Joyce M. Wolburg and James Pokrywczynski, "A Psychographic Analysis of Generation Y College Students,"

Journal of Advertising Research 41, no. 5 (September/October 2001): 33–52.

56. David G. Kennedy, "Coming of Age in Consumerdom," *American Demographics*, April 2004, 14.

57. "Teen Market Profile," *Magazine Publishers of America*, accessed at **www.magazine.org/marketprofiles**.

58. Rob McGann, "Generation Y Embraces SMS," *ClickZ Stats*, accessed at **www.clickz.com/stats/sectors/wireless/article.php/3489776**; and Jyoti Thottam, "How Kids Set the (Ring) Tone," *Time*, April 4, 2005, 40–42 & 45.

59. Clark Crowdus, "Pay Your Respects: Twixters more like Parents Than You'd Think," *Marketing News*, March 15, 2005, 22 & 25.

60. Scott Schroder and Warren Zeller, "Gent to Know Gen X—and Its Segments," *Multichannel News*, March 21, 2005, 55; and Tabitha Armstrong, "GenX Family Values," *The Lane Report*, January 1, 2005, 41.

61. "The Scoop on Gen X," *Work & Family Life* 19 (January 2005): 1.

62. Paula M. Poindexter and Dominic L. Lasorsa, "Generation X: Is Its Meaning Understood?" *Newspaper Research Journal* 20, no. 4 (Fall 1999): 28–36.

63. Rob McGann, "Only Banking Increased 47 Percent Since 2002," *ClickZ Stats*, accessed at **clickz.com/stats/sectors/finance/article.php.3481976**.

64. "Marriott Revamp Targets Gen Xers," *Hotels*, 39, May 2005, 14; and Ed Watkins, "Meet Your New Guest: Generation X," *Lodging Hospitality*, 61, March 15, 2005, 2.

65. James Morrow, "X-It Plans," *American Demographics*, May 2004, 35–38.

66. "Boomer Facts," *American Demographics*, January 1996, 14. Also see Diane Crispell, "U.S. Population Forecasts Decline for 2000, but Rise Slightly for 2050," *Wall Street Journal*, March 25, 1996, B3. "Advertising to 50s and over," *Brand Strategy (London)*, April 5, 2005, 57.

67. Pia Sarkar, "Gap Introduces New Brand for Women 35 and Older/Forth & Towne Stores to Open in Chicago, New York This Fall," *San Francisco Chronicle*, April 22, 2005, C1.

68. Paula Andruss, "The Golden Age," *Marketing News*, April 1, 2005, 21 & 26.

69. Susan Konig, "The Boomers and Their Pots of Gold: They'll Have $20 Trillion by 2020, and Wirehouse Brokers Want to Help Them Manage It," *On Wall Street*, May 1, 2005, 1; and "Help Wanted," *U.S. News & World Report*, June 13, 2005, 44.

70. "No. 14, Resident Population by Race, Hispanic Origin, and Age: 2000 and 2003," *U.S. Census Bureau, Statistical Abstract of the United States: 2004–2005*, 15; and "Facts for Features: Older Americans Month Celebrated in May," *U.S. Census Bureau*, April 25, 2005, accessed at **www.census.gov/press-release/www/releases/archives/facts_for_features_special_editions/004210.html**.

71. Christine L. Himes, "Elderly Americans," *Population Bulletin* 56, no. 4 (December 2001): 3–40; and "Profiles of General Demographic Characteristics 2000," U.S. Department of Commerce, May 2001, accessed via **www.census.gov/prod/cen2000/dp1/2kh00.pdf**.

72. Benny Barak and Leon G. Schiffman, "Cognitive Age: A Nonchronological Age Variable," in *Advances in Consumer Research*, 8, ed. Kent B. Monroe (Ann Arbor, MI: Association for Consumer Research, 1981), 602–606; Elaine Sherman, Leon G. Schiffman, and William R. Dillon, "Age/Gender Segments and Quality of Life Differences," in *1988 Winter Educators' Conference*, ed. Stanley Shapiro and A. H. Walle (Chicago: American Marketing Association, 1988), 319–320; Stuart Van Auken and Thomas E. Barry, "An Assessment of the Trait Validity of Cognitive Age," *Journal of Consumer Psychology* (1995): 107–132; Robert E. Wilkes, "A Structural Modeling Approach to the Measurement and Meaning of Cognitive Age," *Journal of Consumer Research*, (September 1992): 292–301; and Chad Rubel, "Mature Market Often Misunderstood," *Marketing News*, August 28, 1995, 28–29.

73. Elaine Sherman, Leon G. Schiffman, and Anil Mathur, "The Influence of Gender on the New-Age Elderly's Consumption Orientation," *Psychology & Marketing* 18, no. 10 (October 2001): 1073–1089.

74. Elaine Sherman, quoted in David B. Wolfe, "The Ageless Market," *American Demographics*, July 1987, 26–28, 55–56.

75. Isabelle Szmigin and Marylyn Carrigan, "Leisure and Tourism Services and the Older Innovator," *The Service Industries Journal (London)* 21, no. 3 (July 2001): 113–129; and Polyak, "The Center of Attention," 32.

76. Jacqueline K. Eastman and Rajesh Iyer, "The Elderly's Uses and Attitudes towards the Internet," *Journal of Consumer Marketing* 21, no. 3 (2004): 208–220.

77. Charles A. McMellon and Leon G. Schiffman, "Cybersenior Empowerment: How Some Older Individuals Are Taking Control of Their Lives," *The Journal of Applied Gerontology* 21, no. 2 (June 2002): 157–175; and Charles A. McMellon and Leon G. Schiffman, "Cybersenior Mobility: Why Some Older Consumers May Be Adopting the Internet," *Advances in Consumer Research* 27 (2000): 138–144.

78. Raphaëlle Lambert-Pandraud, Gilles Laurent, and Eric Lapersoone, "Repeat Purchasing of New Automobiles by Older Consumers: Empirical Evidence and Interpretations," *Journal of Marketing* 69 (April 2005): 97–113.

79. George Moschis, Carolyn Curasi, and Danny Bellenger, "Patronage Motives of Mature Consumers in the Selection of Food and Grocery Stores," *Journal of Consumer Marketing* 21, no. 2 (2004): 112–133.

80. James W. Gentry, Suraj Commuri, and Sunkyu Jun, "Review of Literature on Gender in the Family," *Academy of Marketing Science Review (Vancouver)*, 2003, 1.

81. Sanjay Putrevu, "Communicating with the Sexes," *Journal of Advertising* 33 (Fall 204): 51–62.

82. "Dudes: Do I Look Fat in This Survey?," *Brandweek*, April 18, 2005, 20.

83. Scott M. Smith and David B. Whitlark, "Men and Women Online: What Makes Them Click?" *Marketing Research* 13, no. 2 (Summer 2001): 20–25.

84. Kara A. Arnold and Lyle R. Wetsch, "Sex Differences and Information Processing; Implications for Marketing on the Internet," in *2001 AMA Winter Educators' Conference* 12, ed. Ram Krishnan and Madhu Viswanathan (Chicago: American Marketing Association 2001), 357–365.

85. Silvia Lagnado, "Getting Real about Beauty," *Advertising Age*, December 6, 2004, 20.

86. Kelley Skoloda, "Reaching Out to Today's 'Multiminding' Woman," *Brandweek*, April 25, 2005, 28–29.

87. Rifka Rosenwein, "The Baby Sabbatical," *American Demographics*, February 2002, 36–40.

88. Anjuman Ali, "Women Travelers: Marooned No More," *Wall Street Journal Europe*, July 6–7, 2001, 29.

89. Thomas Barry, Mary Gilly, and Lindley Doran, "Advertising to Women with Different Career Orientations," *Journal of Advertising Research* 25 (April–May 1985): 26–35.

90. Alice Z. Cuneo, "Advertisers Target Women, but Market Remains Elusive," *Advertising Age*, November 10, 1997, 1, 24–26.

91. Alison Stein Wellner, "The Female Persuasion," *American Demographics*, 24, 2, February 2002, 24–29.

92. Kenneth Hein, "Beringer Fabricates New Ladies Wine," *Brandweek*, April 4, 2005, 15; Stephanie Thompson, "Lenart Turns Godiva toward Stylish, Self-Indulgent Brand," *Advertising Age*, November 15, 2004, 46; and Beth Snyder Bulik, "Electronics Retailers Too Women," *Advertising Age*, November 15, 2004, 16.

chapterfourteen

> ## Cross-Cultural Consumer Behavior: An International Perspective

In our examination of psychological, social, and cultural factors, we have consistently pointed out how various segments of the American consuming public differ. If so much diversity exists among segments of a single society, then even more diversity is likely to exist among the members of two or more societies. To succeed, international marketers must understand the nature and extent of differences between the consumers of different societies—"cross-cultural" differences—so that they can develop effective targeted marketing strategies to use in each foreign market of interest.

In this chapter, we broaden our scope of analysis and consider the marketing implications of cultural differences and similarities that exist between the people of two or more nations. We also compare the views that pin a global marketing perspective—one that stresses the *similarities* of consumers worldwide—against a localized marketing strategy that stresses the *diversity* of consumers in different nations and their specific cultural orientations. Our own view is that marketers must be aware of and sensitive to cross-cultural similarities and differences that can provide expanded sales and profit opportunities. Multinational marketers must be ready to tailor their marketing mixes to the specific customs of each nation that they want to target.

Relax
in the only business class bed to Australia.

The award-winning Qantas Skybed is the only business class bed flying between the
U.S. and Australia. With numerous daily flights from Los Angeles, and our new non-stop
service from San Francisco commencing March 2006, Qantas offers the most relaxing
journey across the Pacific. You'll also earn mileage in your choice of frequent flyer program
from our partners Alaska Airlines, American Airlines, Continental Airlines and US Airways.

qantas.com/us

QANTAS

Available on all B747-400 3-class aircraft to Sydney and Melbourne.

the imperative to be multinational

Today, almost all major corporations are actively marketing their products beyond their original homeland borders. In fact, the issue is generally not *whether* to market a brand in other countries but rather *how* to do it (as the same product with the same "global" advertising campaign, or "tailored" products and localized ads for each country). Because of this emphasis on operating as a multinational entity, the vocabulary of marketing now includes terms such as *glocal*, which refers to companies that are both "global" and "local"; that is, they include in their marketing efforts a blend of standardized and local elements in order to secure the benefits of each strategy.

This challenge has been given special meaning by the efforts of the **European Union** (EU) to form a single market. Although the movement of goods and services among its 25 members (with the potential of becoming 27 members in 2007) has been eased, it is unclear whether this diverse market will really be transformed into a single market of almost 460 million homogeneous "Euroconsumers" with the same or very similar wants and needs.[1] Many people hope that the recent introduction of the euro as a common EU currency will help shape Europe into a huge, powerful, unified market. Furthermore, the rapid acceptance of capitalism by many Eastern European countries also presents a major opportunity and challenge to marketers. Firms such as Coca-Cola, General Motors, Nabisco, P&G, and R.J. Reynolds have been investing extensive sums on product development and marketing to satisfy the needs of Eastern European consumer markets.

The **North American Free Trade Agreement** (NAFTA), which currently consists of the United States, Canada, and Mexico, provides free-market access to more than 430 million consumers. Since its inception, for example, the markets in Canada and Mexico for packaged software from U.S. firms has grown to three times its pre-NAFTA market size.[2] The emerging Association of Southeast Asian Nations (ASEAN), consisting of Indonesia, Singapore, Thailand, the Philippines, Malaysia, Brunei, and Vietnam, is another important economic alliance that offers marketers new global markets. The members of this group have formed the ASEAN Free Trade Area (AFTA) to promote regional trade.

Many firms are developing strategies to take advantage of these and other emerging economic opportunities. A substantial number of firms are now jockeying for market share in foreign markets. For instance, Starbucks has opened a store within the Forbidden City in Beijing, China, and MTV Networks has formed a partnership with @JapanMedia to establish a new 24-hour Japanese language music TV channel.[3]

Firms are selling their products worldwide for a variety of reasons. First, with the buildup of "multinational fever" and the general attractiveness of multinational markets, products or services originating in one country are increasingly being sought out by consumers in other parts of the world. Second, many firms have learned that overseas markets represent the single most important opportunity for their future growth when their home markets reach maturity. This realization is propelling them to expand their horizons and seek consumers scattered all over the world. Moreover, consumers all over the world are increasingly eager to try "foreign" products that are popular in different and far-off places. Consider the following story:

There was this Englishman who worked in the London office of a multinational corporation based in the United States. He drove home one evening in his Japanese car. His wife, who worked in a firm which imported German kitchen equipment, was already home. Her small Italian car was often quicker through the traffic. After a meal which included New Zealand lamb, California carrots, Mexican honey, French cheese and Spanish wine, they settled down to watch a program on their television set, which has been made in Finland. The program was a retrospective celebration of the war to recapture the Falkland Islands. As they watched it they felt warmly patriotic, and very proud to be British.[4]

TABLE 14.1	The World's Most Valuable Brands	
RANK	**BRAND**	**2004 BRAND VALUE ($BILLIONS)**
1	Coca-Cola	67.4
2	Microsoft	61.4
3	IBM	53.8
4	GE	44.1
5	Intel	33.5
6	Disney	27.1
7	McDonald's	25.0
8	Nokia	24.0
9	Toyota	22.7
10	Marlboro	22.1

Note: Only includes brands that obtain at least one-third of their earnings outside of their home country.

Source: Diane Brady, Robert D. Hof, Andy Reinhardt, Moon Ihlwan, Stanley Holmes, and Kerry Capell, "The Top 100 Brands," *Business Week*, August 2, 2004, 68.

According to *Business Week*, Coca-Cola is the most valuable brand in the world, with a brand value of about $65 billion. Table 14.1 presents a list of the world's 10 most valuable brands.

Acquiring exposure to other cultures

As more and more consumers come in contact with the material goods and lifestyles of people living in other parts of the world, they have the opportunity to adopt these different products and practices. How consumers in one culture secure exposure to the goods of other people living in other cultures is an important part of consumer behavior. It impacts the well-being of consumers worldwide and of marketers trying to gain acceptance for their products in countries that are often quite different from their home country. After all, by the time you read this, there may be five models of automobiles available for you to purchase that were made in China, thanks to a deal between Chery Automobiles of China and Malcom Bricklin, chairman of Visionary Vehicles.[5]

Consider Mexico, America's neighbor to the South. While the Mexican culture shares many similarities with those of Central and South American nations, consumers in Mexico differ when it comes to attitude—they have an affinity for American values. Mexican consumers use brands to display status, making conspicuous consumption a part of life, even for the poor. For example, a working class household might keep a large American refrigerator in the living room, instead of the kitchen, because it is viewed as a sign of financial success. Still further, the largest market for Martell cognac outside of France is Mexico, because the product allows the affluent to display their success and wealth.[6]

A portion of consumers' exposure to different cultures tends to come about through consumers' own initiatives—their travel, their living and working in foreign countries, or even their immigration to a different country. Additionally, consumers obtain a "taste" of different cultures from contact with foreign movies, theater, art and artifacts, and most certainly, from exposure to unfamiliar and different products. This second major category of cultural exposure is often fostered by marketers seeking to expand their markets by bringing new products, services, practices, ideas, and experiences to potential consumers residing in a different country and possessing a different cultural view. Within this context, international marketing provides a form of "culture transfer."

Country-of-origin effects

When consumers are making purchase decisions, they may take into consideration the countries of origin (COO) of their choices. Researchers have shown that consumers use their knowledge of where products are made in the evaluation of their purchase options.[7] Such a country-of-origin effect seems to come about because consumers are often aware that a particular firm or brand name is associated with a particular country. For example, a Volkswagen's "Fahrvergnügen" campaign touted German engineering, and Land-Rover's advertising conveys a sophisticated British image. In contrast, Jaguar does not tend to play on its British heritage when marketing its cars in the United States. And then there's Chevrolet, the General Motors division responsible for over half of GM's vehicle sales. Over the years, Chevrolet has used slogans such as "See the U.S.A. in your Chevrolet," and it is currently using the theme "An American Revolution" to introduce 10 new cars and trucks.[8]

In general, many consumers associate France with wine, fashion clothing, and perfume and other beauty products; Italy with pasta, designer clothing, furniture, shoes, and sports cars; Japan with cameras and consumer electronics; and Germany with cars, tools, and machinery. Moreover, consumers tend to have an established *attitude* or even a preference when it comes to a particular product being made in a particular country. This attitude might be positive, negative, or neutral, depending on perceptions or experience. For instance, a consumer in one country might positively value a particular product made in another country (e.g., affluent American consumers may feel that an English Thomas Pink dress shirt or a Bosch dishwasher from Germany are worthwhile investments). In contrast, another consumer might be negatively influenced when he learns that a television set he is considering is made in a country that he does not associate with fine electronics (e.g., a TV made in Costa Rica). Such country-of-origin effects influence how consumers rate quality and which brands they will ultimately select. Recent research suggests, though, that when consumer motivation is high and when a specific model of a product is being evaluated (as opposed to a range of products manufactured in a particular country), then consumers are *less* likely to base judgments on country-of-origin information.[9] However, when consumers are less familiar with foreign products, COO becomes an important extrinsic cue.[10]

Refining the country-of-origin concept, a study that contrasted U.S. and Mexican consumers decomposed country-of-origin into three separate entities: country of design (COD), country of assembly (COA), and country of parts (COP). Of the three, country of parts (COP) had the strongest influence on product evaluations.[11] The study also found that COD was a more important cue in the United States than in Mexico, and that younger Mexicans exhibited a stronger COO effect than older Mexicans.

Beyond perceptions of a product's attributes based on its country of manufacture, research evidence exists that suggests that some consumers may refrain from purchasing products from particular countries due to animosity. A study of this issue found that *high-animosity consumers* in the People's Republic of China owned fewer Japanese products than *low-animosity consumers* (during World War II, Japan occupied parts of China). Although some Chinese consumers might consider Sony to be a high-end, high-quality brand (or perceptions of the product itself might be very positive), they might nevertheless refuse to bring a product manufactured in Japan into the home. Similarly, some Jewish consumers avoid purchasing German-made products due to the Holocaust, and some New Zealand and Australian consumers boycott French products due to France's nuclear tests in the South Pacific.[12]

What is national identity?

One way to explain why a consumer prefers buying products made in one country and does not wish to buy products made in another, or why consumers in different countries exhibit different behaviors, is the existence of a "national identity." As presented in Figure 14.1, national identity consists of four dimensions (for each dimension a sample item from a scale to measure it is included, the entire measure is composed of 17 items):

FIGURE 14.1

**Dimensions of
National Identity**

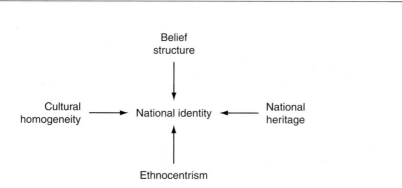

belief structure (e.g., "A true American would never reject their religious belief"), *cultural homogeneity* (e.g., "People frequently engage in activities that identify them as American"), *national heritage* (e.g., "Important people from the country's past are admired by people today"), and *consumer ethnocentrism* (e.g., "Only those products that are unavailable in the USA should be imported"). Using the national identity scale, research has studied consumers in South Korea, Taiwan, Thailand, and Singapore.[13] The research, for example, revealed that Thailand had the strongest national identity and Singapore the weakest. Generally, countries with a weak sense of national identity, coupled with low ethnocentric tendencies, are suitable for use as places to launch new products, because foreign firms are not viewed as threats.

cross-cultural consumer analysis

To determine whether and how to enter a foreign market, marketers need to conduct some form of **cross-cultural consumer analysis**. Within the scope of this discussion, cross-cultural consumer analysis is defined as the effort to determine to what extent the consumers of two or more nations are similar or different. Such analyses can provide marketers with an understanding of the psychological, social, and cultural characteristics of the foreign consumers they wish to target, so that they can design effective marketing strategies for the specific national markets involved.

In a broader context, cross-cultural consumer analysis might also include a comparison of subcultural groups (see Chapter 13) within a single country (such as English and French Canadians, Cuban Americans and Mexican Americans in the United States, or Protestants and Catholics in Northern Ireland). For our purposes, however, we will limit our discussion of cross-cultural consumer analysis to comparisons of consumers of *different* countries.

Similarities and differences among people

A major objective of cross-cultural consumer analysis is to determine how consumers in two or more societies are similar and how they are different. For instance, Table 14.2 presents at least a partial depiction of the differences between Chinese and American cultural traits. Such an understanding of the similarities and differences that exist between nations is critical to the multinational marketer who must devise appropriate strategies to reach consumers in specific foreign markets. The greater the similarity between nations, the more feasible it is to use relatively similar marketing strategies in each nation. On the other hand, if the cultural beliefs, values, and customs of specific target countries are found to differ widely, then a highly *individualized* marketing strategy is indicated for each country. To illustrate, in addition to IKEA furniture company's generic global Web site that uses English, the firm also offers 14 localized Web sites

TABLE 14.2	A Comparison of Chinese and American Cultures

CHINESE CULTURAL TRAITS	AMERICAN CULTURAL TRAITS
• Centered on a set of relationships defined by Confucian doctrine	• Centered on the individual
• Submissive to authority	• Greater emphasis on self-reliance
• Ancestor worship	• Resents class-based distinctions
• Passive acceptance of fate by seeking harmony with nature	• Active mastery in the person–nature relationship
• Emphasizes inner experiences of meaning and feeling	• Concerned with external experiences and the world of things
• A closed worldview, prizing stability and harmony	• An open view of the world, emphasizing change and movement
• Culture rests on kinship ties and tradition with a historical orientation	• Places primary faith in rationalism and is oriented toward the future
• Places weight on vertical interpersonal relationships	• Places weight on horizontal dimensions of interpersonal relationship
• Values a person's duties to family, clan, and state	• Values the individual personality

Source: Adapted from Carolyn A. Lin, "Cultural Values Reflected in Chinese and American Television Advertising," *Journal of Advertising* 30, no. 4 (Winter 2001): 83–94.

(in selected languages) and 30 minisites (in more languages) that only provide contact information. And whereas the IKEA Italian Web site shows a group of people frolicking on their IKEA furniture (nudity is acceptable and commonplace in Italian advertising), the Saudi Arabian Web site uses extremely conservative photographs (**www.ikea.com**).[14] As another example, while 88 percent of adults in both France and Germany drink mineral water, French consumption is strongly associated with concern over the quality of tap water, while German consumption is closely linked to vegetarians.[15]

A firm's success in marketing a product or service in a number of foreign countries is likely to be influenced by how similar the beliefs, values, and customs are that govern the use of the product in the various countries. For example, the worldwide TV commercials of major international airlines (American Airlines, Continental Airlines, Air France, Lufthansa, Swissair, United Airlines, and British Airways) tend to depict the luxury and pampering offered to their business-class and first-class international travelers. The reason for their general cross-cultural appeal is that these commercials speak to the same types of individuals worldwide—upscale international business travelers—who share much in common (Figure 14.2). In contrast, knowing that "typical" American advertising would not work in China, Nike hired Chinese-speaking art directors and copywriters to develop specific commercials that would appeal to the Chinese consumer within the boundaries of the Chinese culture. The resulting advertising campaign appealed to national pride in China.[16] Yet another example of cultural differences necessitating a change in marketing would be the efforts of Western banks to attract Muslim customers. The shari'ah (the sacred law of Islam based on what is written in the Koran) forbids Muslims from charging interest, and prohibits such Western-type financial transactions such as speculation, selling short, and conventional debt financing. Consequently, Western banks in the United Kingdom that want to appeal to that country's two million Muslim residents must develop a new range of products for this group of target consumers.[17]

FIGURE 14.2

Source: © Qantas Airways.
Used with permission.

Relax
in the only business class bed to Australia.

The award-winning Qantas Skybed is the only business class bed flying between the U.S. and Australia. With numerous daily flights from Los Angeles, and our new non-stop service from San Francisco commencing March 2006, Qantas offers the most relaxing journey across the Pacific. You'll also earn mileage in your choice of frequent flyer program from our partners Alaska Airlines, American Airlines, Continental Airlines and US Airways.
qantas.com/us   **QANTAS**

Available on all B747-400 3-class aircraft to Sydney and Melbourne.

The International Business Traveler Seeks to Be Pampered with Services

Further supporting the importance of cultural differences or orientation, consider that Southeast Asia is frequently the largest market for prestige and luxury brands from the West, and that luxury brand companies such as Louis Vuitton, Rolex, Gucci, and Prada are looking to markets such as Hanoi and Guangzhou when they are thinking of expanding their market reach. Indeed, in fine-tuning their marketing, these luxury-brand marketers need to be especially responsive to cultural differences that compel luxury purchases in the Asian and Western markets. To this end, research suggests that while Western consumers tend to "use" a prestige item to enhance their sense of individualism or serve as a source of personal pleasure, for Southeast Asian consumers the same prestige item might serve to further bond the individual with others and to provide visible evidence of the person's value to others.[18] Still further, within the scope of a visible luxury product, a woman in Hong Kong might carry a Fendi handbag (a visible and conspicuous item), but is not likely to be receptive to luxury lingerie because it is not an item that "shows" in public.[19]

The growing global middle class

The growing middle class in developing countries is a phenomenon that is very attractive to global marketers who are often eager to identify new customers for their products. The news media has given considerable coverage to the idea that the rapidly expanding middle class in countries of Asia, South America, and Eastern Europe is based on the reality that, although per capita income may be low, there is nevertheless considerable buying power in a country such as China, where $1,500 of income is largely discretionary income. This means that a Chinese family with $1,500 is middle class and is a target customer for TVs, VCRs, and computers. Indeed, this same general pattern of the growing middle class has also been observed in many parts of South America, Asia, and Eastern Europe.[20] In many parts of the world, an income equivalent to $5,000 is considered the point at which a person becomes "middle class," and it has been estimated that somewhat more than one billion people in the world's developing countries meet this income standard.[21] It is important to note though, that consumers in less-developed nations often cannot afford to pay as much for a product as consumers in the more advanced economies do. As an example, Nestlé has introduced low-price ice cream in China—the product sells for 12 cents.[22] Table 14.3 lists the size of the emerging middle class in 12 different countries. The results reveal that more than 90 percent of the population of South Korea can be considered middle class, whereas less than 5 percent of the populations of Nigeria and Pakistan can be similarly categorized.

The rather rapid expansion of middle-class consumers, over the past 50 years, have attracted the attention of many well-established marketing powerhouses, who were already finding their home markets to be rather mature and reaching what was felt to be a saturation point in terms of sales opportunities. While in 1960 two-thirds of the world's

TABLE 14.3	Size of the Emerging Middle Class in Selected Countries	
	PERCENT OF THE POPULATION	**NUMBER OF PEOPLE (MILLIONS)**
Brazil	35	57.9
China	23	290.4
India	9	91.4
Indonesia	10	21.0
Korea, Republic of	93	44.0
Malaysia	46	10.7
Mexico	46	45.1
Nigeria	<5	<6.3
Pakistan	<5	<6.9
Peru	27	6.9
Philippines	25	18.9
Russian Federation	45	65.5

Source: Benjamin Senauer and Linda Goetz, "The Growing Middle Class in Developing Countries and the Market for High-Value Food Products," *Prepared for the Workshop on Global Markets for High-Value Food, Economic Research Service, USDA*, Washington D.C., February 14, 2003, 13, accessed at **www.farmfoundation.org/documents/ben-sanauerpaper2—10—3-13-03_000.pdf**

TABLE 14.4	Measured Global Progress 1950–2050		
	1950	**2000**	**2050**
Global Output, Per Capita ($)	586	6,666	15,155
Global Financial Market Capitalization, Per Capita ($)	158	13,333	75,000
Percent of Global GDP			
Emerging Markets	5	50	55
Industrial Countries	95	75	45
Life Expectancy (years)			
Emerging Markets	41	64	76
Industrial Countries	65	77	82
Daily Caloric Intake			
Emerging Markets	1,200	2,600	3,000
Industrial Countries	2,200	3,100	3,200
Infant Mortality (per 1000)			
Emerging Markets	140	65	10
Industrial Countries	30	8	4
Literacy Rate (per 100)			
Emerging Markets	33	64	90
Industrial Countries	95	98	99

Sources: Bloomberg, World Bank, United Nations, and author's estimates. Output and financial market capitalization figures are inflation-adjusted. Peter Marber, "Globalization and Its Contents," *World Policy Journal* (Winter 2004/05): 30.

middle class lived in industrialized nations, by the year 2000, some 83 percent of middle-class citizens were living in developing countries. These changes strongly suggest that more people are now living longer, healthier, and better lives—literacy rates in developing countries have risen dramatically in the past 50 years, and today two-thirds, rather than only one-third of the people living in these nations are literate.[23] Table 14.4 captures the global progress over the past 50 years and projects it to year 2050. Note how in 1950 the caloric intake in emerging markets was only 55 percent of industrial countries, while today it is more than 80 percent.

Although a growing middle class provides a market opportunity for products like Big Macs and fries, it should always be remembered that the same product may have different meanings in different countries. For example, whereas a U.S. consumer wants his or her "fast food" to be fast, a Korean consumer is more likely to view a meal as a social or family-related experience. Consequently, convenient store hours may be valued more by a Korean consumer than shorter service time.[24] In China, despite a traditional emphasis on "fresh" (just picked or killed) food, the emerging middle class, with rising incomes and rising demands on their time, are often willing to spend money to save time, in the form of alternatives to home-cooked meals.[25]

Regulations in different countries may preclude the use of some of the marketing practices that a firm employs in the United States. For example, German advertising rules do not allow an ad to compare one brand to another, nor do they permit Lands' End to offer a "lifetime guarantee." And whereas consumers in the United States like to buy with charge cards, the French prefer an invoice and the Germans prefer COD.[26]

Many transnational corporations (a company that had direct foreign investments and owns or controls activities in more than one nation) think in terms of regions as markets, or even the entire world as their market. For example, Nestlé, a giant Swiss firm, generates only 2 percent of its sales in Switzerland, and bases only 4 percent of its workers there. Whenever possible, transnational firms try to avoid having products identified with a particular country, rather they seek to make their product feel "local and natural" to their target customers. Of course, there are exceptions to such strategy. In particular, we might speculate that people throughout the world might generally be expected to prefer a precision Swiss wristwatch, to a wristwatch that is made in their own country. Also fashion clothing items, made in France or Italy, are also likely to be perceived to be more desirable than locally made clothing.

The bottom line, though, is that more consumer goods are sold each year because of the growth of the world's middle-class population, and a marketer would do well to focus more on the emerging middle class in other nations than on people who cannot afford to buy its products in its home market. As a recent article concluded, "Coke is the global soft drink, Macs the global fast-food, and CNN the global television. These are the commodities of a new global middle-class."[27]

The global teenage market

As part of growth of the world middle class, there has been a parallel growth in an affluent global teenage and young adult markets. To be expected, these youthful markets have attracted the attention of marketers. Within reason, these teenagers (and their somewhat older brothers and sisters—"the young adult segment") appear to have quite similar interests, desires, and consumption behavior no matter where they live. Therefore, in response to this perspective, consumer researchers have explored the makeup, composition, and behavior of this segment(s). One particular study considered the fashion consciousness of teenagers in the United States, Japan, and China.[28] The research revealed that American and Japanese teens were highly similar, differing only in that the Japanese teens were more likely to choose style over comfort (most likely because of the importance, in the Japanese Confucian society, of meeting the expectations of group members). In contrast, Chinese teens were less fashion conscious than both the American and Japanese teens, which supports the idea that differences exist between highly developed and less high-developed nations with respect to teen fashion consciousness. Table 14.5 presents the four-item scale employed in the study to measure fashion consciousness; each item was measured using a 7-point Likert-type scale (1="strongly disagree" and 7="strongly agree") with the mean score for each question shown.

TABLE 14.5	Fashion Consciousness Scale Results for Chinese, Japanese, and U.S. Teenagers			
ITEM	**CHINA (μ)**	**JAPAN (μ)**	**USA (μ)**	**GRAND (μ)**
1. I usually have one or more outfits that are of the very latest style	3.06	4.23	4.53	4.17
2. When I must choose between the two, I usually dress for style, not comfort	2.49	4.26	3.57	3.57
3. An important part of my life and activities involves dressing stylishly	2.24	3.72	3.34	3.26
4. Fashionable, attractive styling is very important to me	2.60	3.96	3.77	3.62

Source: R. Stephen Parker, Charles M. Hermans, and Allen D. Schaefer, "Fashion Consciousness of Chinese, Japanese and American Teenagers," *Journal of Fashion Marketing and Management* 8, no. 2 (2004): 181.

Acculturation is a needed marketing viewpoint

Too many marketers contemplating international expansion make the strategic error of believing that if its product is liked by local or domestic consumers, then everyone will like it. This biased viewpoint increases the likelihood of marketing failures abroad. It reflects a lack of appreciation of the unique psychological, social, cultural, and environmental characteristics of distinctly different cultures. To overcome such a narrow and culturally myopic view, marketers must also go through an *acculturation process*. They must learn everything that is relevant about the usage or potential usage of their products and product categories in the foreign countries in which they plan to operate. Take the Chinese culture, for example. For Western marketers to succeed in China, it is important for them to take into consideration *guo qing* (pronounced "gwor ching"), which means "to consider the special situation or character of China."[29] An example of *guo qing* for Western marketers is the Chinese policy of limiting families to one child. An appreciation of this policy means that foreign businesses will understand that Chinese families are open to particularly high-quality baby products for their single child (or "the little emperor").[30] One result of this one-child policy is that in the large cities in China, children are given more than $3 billion a year by their parents to spend as they wish and influence approximately 68 percent of their parents' spending. These Chinese children are also less culture bound than their parents and are, therefore, more open to Western ideas and products.[31]

In a sense, cross-cultural **acculturation** is a dual process for marketers. First, marketers must thoroughly orient themselves to the values, beliefs, and customs of the new society to appropriately position and market their products (being sensitive to and consistent with traditional or prevailing attitudes and values). Second, to gain acceptance for a culturally new product in a foreign society, they must develop a strategy that encourages members of that society to modify or even break with their own traditions (to change their attitudes and possibly alter their behavior). To illustrate the point, a social marketing effort designed to encourage consumers in developing nations to secure polio vaccinations for their children would require a two-step acculturation process. First, the marketer must obtain an in-depth picture of a society's present attitudes and customs with regard to preventive medicine and related concepts. Then the marketer must devise promotional strategies that will convince the members of a target market to have their children vaccinated, even if doing so requires a change in current attitudes.

Distinctive characteristics of cross-cultural analysis

It is often difficult for a company planning to do business in foreign countries to undertake **cross-cultural consumer research**. For instance, it is difficult in the Islamic countries of the Middle East to conduct Western-style market research. In Saudi Arabia, for instance, it is illegal to stop people on the streets, and focus groups are impractical because most gatherings of four or more people (with the exception of family and religious gatherings) are outlawed.[32] American firms desiring to do business in Russia have found a limited amount of information regarding consumer and market statistics. Similarly, marketing research information on China is generally inadequate, and surveys that ask personal questions arouse suspicion. So marketers have tried other ways to elicit the data they need. For example, Grey Advertising has given cameras to Chinese children so they can take pictures of what they like and do not like, rather than ask them to explain it to a stranger. Moreover, AC Nielsen conducts focus groups in pubs and children's playrooms rather than in conference rooms; and Leo Burnett has sent researchers to China to simply "hang out" with consumers.[33]

Applying research techniques

Although the same basic research techniques used to study domestic consumers are useful in studying consumers in foreign lands (see Chapter 2), in cross-cultural analysis an

TABLE 14.6	Basic Research Issues in Cross-Cultural Analysis
FACTORS	**EXAMPLES**
Differences in language and meaning	Words or concepts (e.g., "personal checking account") may not mean the same in two different countries.
Differences in market segmentation opportunities	The income, social class, age, and sex of target customers may differ dramatically between two different countries.
Differences in consumption patterns	Two countries may differ substantially in the level of consumption or use of products or services (e.g., mail catalogs).
Differences in the perceived benefits of products and services	Two nations may use or consume the same product (e.g., yogurt) in very different ways.
Differences in the criteria for evaluating products and services	The benefits sought from a service (e.g., bank cards) may differ from country to country.
Differences in economic and social conditions and family structure	The "style" of family decision making may vary significantly from country to country.
Differences in marketing research and conditions	The types and quality of retail outlets and direct-mail lists may vary greatly among countries.
Differences in marketing research possibilities	The availability of professional consumer researchers may vary considerably from country to country.

additional burden exists because language and word usage often differ from nation to nation. Another issue in international marketing research concerns scales of measurement. In the United States, a 5- or 7-point scale may be adequate, but in other countries a 10- or even 20-point scale may be needed. Still further, research facilities, such as telephone interviewing services, may or may not be available in particular countries or areas of the world.

To avoid such research measurement problems, consumer researchers must familiarize themselves with the availability of research services in the countries they are evaluating as potential markets and must learn how to design marketing research studies that will yield useful data. Researchers must also keep in mind that cultural differences may make "standard" research methodologies inappropriate. Table 14.6 identifies basic issues that multinational marketers must consider when planning cross-cultural consumer research.

alternative multinational strategies: global versus local

Some marketers have argued that world markets are becoming more and more similar and that standardized marketing strategies are, therefore, becoming more feasible. For example, Exxon Mobil has launched a $150 million marketing campaign to promote its brands (Exxon, Esso, Mobil, and General), and the firm wants all the ads to carry the same look and feel, regardless of which one of the 100 countries in the world the ad will appear.[34] In contrast, other marketers feel that differences between consumers of various nations are far too great to permit a standardized marketing strategy. In a practical sense, a basic challenge for many executives contemplating multinational marketing is to decide whether to use *shared needs and values* as a segmentation strategy (i.e., to appeal to consumers in different countries in terms of their "common" needs, values, and goals) or to use *national borders* as a segmentation strategy (i.e., to use relatively different, "local," or specific marketing strategies for members of distinctive cultures or countries).

Favoring a world brand

An increasing number of firms have created **world brand** products that are manufactured, packaged, and positioned in exactly the same way regardless of the country in which they are sold. It is quite natural for a "world class" upscale brand of wristwatches such as Patek Philippe to create a global or uniform advertising campaign to reach its sophisticated worldwide target market (see Figure 14.3). Although the advertising copy is in specific target languages, one might speculate that many of Patek Philippe's affluent target customers do read and write English. Nevertheless, to maximize their "comfort zone," it is appropriate to speak to them in their native languages.

Marketers of products with a wide or almost mass-market appeal have also embraced a world branding strategy. For instance, multinational companies, such as General Motors, Gillette, Estée Lauder, Unilever, and Fiat, have each moved from a local strategy of nation-by-nation advertising to a global advertising strategy.

Still other marketers selectively use a world branding strategy. For example, you might think that Procter & Gamble (P&G), which markets hundreds of brands worldwide, is a company with an abundance of world brands. Recently, though, it was revealed that of its 16 largest brands, only three are truly global brands—Always/Whisper, Pringles, and Pantene. Some of P&G's other brands, such as Pampers, Tide/Ariel, Safeguard, and Oil of Olay, are just starting to establish common positioning in the world market.[35]

Are global brands different?

According to a 12 nation consumer research project, global brands are viewed differently than local brands, and consumers, worldwide, associate global brands with three characteristics: *quality signal*, *global myth*, and *social responsibility*. First, consumers believe that the more people who purchase a brand, the higher the brand's quality (which often results in a global brand being able to command a premium price). Still further, consumers worldwide believe that global brands develop new products and breakthrough technologies at a faster pace than local brands. The second characteristic, global myth, refers to the fact that consumers view global brands as a kind of "cultural ideals," and their purchase and use makes the consumer feel like a citizen of the world, and gives them an identity (i.e., "*Local brands show what we are; global brands show what we want to be*"). Finally, global companies are held to a higher level of corporate social responsibility than local brands, and are expected to respond to social problems associated with what they sell. For the 12 nations studied in this research, the importance of these three dimensions was consistent, and accounted for 64 percent of the variation in the overall brand preferences (quality signal accounts for 44 percent of the explanation, global myth accounts for 12 percent of the explanation, and social responsibility accounts for 8 percent of the explanation).[36]

Additionally, while there was not much variation across the 12 nations studied, there were intracountry differences, which resulted in the conclusion that there were four major segments in each country with respect to how its citizens view global brands. *Global Citizens* (55 percent of the total respondents) use a company's global success as an indication of product quality and innovativeness, and are also concerned that the firm acts in a socially responsible manner. *Global Dreamers* (23 percent of the total

FIGURE 14.3 *Source:* © Patek Philippe Geneva. Used with permission. All rights reserved.

Leading Wristwatch Manufacturer Using a Global Advertising Strategy

respondents) view global brands as quality products, and are not particularly concerned about the social responsible issue. *Antiglobals* (13 percent of the total respondents) feel that global brands are higher quality than local brands, but they dislike brands that preach U.S. values and do not trust global companies to act responsibly. Generally, they try to avoid purchasing global brands. Lastly, *Global Agnostics* (8%) evaluate global brands in the same way they evaluate local brands.[37]

Multinational reactions to brand extensions

Just because a brand may be global in character does not mean that consumers around the world will necessarily respond similarly to a brand extension. A recent study examined reactions to brand extensions among Western culture (U.S.) and Eastern culture (India) consumers, hypothesizing that the Eastern holistic way of thinking (which focuses on the relationships between objects), rather than the Western analytic style of thinking (which focuses on the attributes or parts of objects and on category-based induction) would affect the manner in which consumers judge the "fit" of a brand extension. Indeed, the research results confirmed this hypothesis—low-fit extensions (McDonald's chocolate bar and Coke popcorn) received more positive evaluations from the Eastern culture subjects, while moderate-fit extensions (Kodak greeting cards and Mercedes Benz watches) garnered equal responses from both cultural groups. For the Eastern culture participants, liking Coke products, and the fact that Coke and popcorn were complementary products, in that they can be consumed together, was enough to make the brand extension acceptable. The American subjects, in contrast, saw little product class similarity between Coke and popcorn.[38]

Adaptive global marketing

In contrast to the marketing communication strategy that stresses a common message, some firms embrace a strategy that adapts their advertising messages to the specific values of particular cultures. McDonald's is an example of a firm that tries to localize its advertising and other marketing communications to consumers in each of the cross-cultural markets in which it operates, making it a "glocal" company. For example, the Ronald McDonald that we all know has been renamed Donald McDonald in Japan, because the Japanese language does not contain the "R" sound. Additionally, the McDonald's menu in Japan has been localized to include corn soup and green tea milkshakes.[39] And in Sweden McDonald's developed a new package using woodcut illustrations and a softer design to appeal to the interest the consumers of that nation have in food value and the outdoors.[40]

Like McDonald's, Levi's and Reebok also tend to follow multilocal strategies that calculate cultural differences in creating brand images for their products. For instance, Levi's tends to position its jeans to American consumers, stressing a social-group image, whereas it uses a much more individualistic, sexual image when communicating with European consumers.[41] Still further, Yahoo!, one of the most successful Web sites on the Internet, modifies both its content and communications for each of its 23 country-specific Web sites. Moreover, in a number of Coke's 140-plus markets, what we know as Diet Coke is called Coca-Cola Light, because the word *diet* has an undesirable connotation or no relevance.[42] Similarly, Coke's best-selling beverage in Japan is not Coke Classic—it's Georgia Coffee—packaged in a can and available in more than 10 versions (e.g., black, black with sugar, with milk and sugar, and so on). Other marketers, too, feel that the world brand concept may be going too far. Specifically, when it comes to the marketing of Tiger Woods, one of the premier golfers of our time. In the United States, he is seen as an example of African American success, in Asia he is a sports star with Asian heritage, and in Europe he is seen as a great young athlete who regularly beats older golfers.[43]

When it comes to the design of e-commerce Web sites, a five-nation research study suggests that consumers react best when content is adapted to their local needs.

While in the past some companies felt that local adaptation involved no more than simply translating Web pages into the local language, it is now felt that special attention must also be paid to a number of other factors, including local time and date formats, units of measurement, addresses and telephone numbers, layout and orientation of Web pages, icons, symbols, color, and aesthetics.[44] Still further, one study of American and German Internet users reveals that German users were more likely to withhold or alter personal information on the Internet than American users. Analysis suggests that the German personality has a large private space and a small public space, which translates into a great sense of personal privacy; whereas the opposite is true of the American personality.[45]

Combining global and local marketing strategies

Some firms follow a mixed or combination strategy. For instance, Unilever, Playtex, and Black & Decker have augmented their global strategies with local executions. In taking such an adaptive approach, global advertisers with a knowledge of cross-cultural differences can tailor their supplemental messages more effectively to suit individual local markets. For example, a study has indicated that while U.S. consumers focus more on the product-related claims made in advertisements, Taiwanese consumers focus more on the appropriateness of the ad, such as its aesthetic qualities.[46] There is also some evidence to suggest that Spanish ads may contain a larger proportion of affiliation appeals than U.S. ads do because of Spain's cultural inclination toward femininity in its societal norms (U.S. societal norms tend to reflect masculinity).[47] Because concepts and words often do not easily translate and many regions of the country have their own language, advertisements in China are likely to be more effective if they rely heavily on symbols rather than text.[48] A recent study dealing with visual standardization in print ads concluded that "the standardized approach to global advertising may be able to convey a degree of uniformity in meaning when relying on visually explicit messages. . . . This suggests that there is an ability to create a general consensus of meaning across various cultures by using strong visual images whose fundamental message is highly apparent."[49] It is also important to note that consumers in different countries of the world have vastly different amounts of exposure to advertisements. For instance, the daily amount of advertising aimed at Japanese consumers, at almost $6 a day, is 14 times the amount aimed at the average Laotian consumer over the course of an entire year.[50]

A recent study of foreign advertisers in China found that 11 percent employed a standardized (or global) strategy, 12 percent used a localized strategy, and the remaining 77 percent favored a combination strategy. Of the seven advertising components that were studied, localizing language to blend with the local culture was considered to be the most important, followed by the need to localize product attributes, models, colors of ads, humor, scenic background, and music.[51] Additionally, it has been reported that many of the Western companies that have not been successful in China have acted as if what had worked well in other parts of the world would also prove successful in China. This is a too common mistake.

Perhaps the latest creative hotbed for advertising is Thailand, a nation that generally requires a different advertising focus than most other countries. While over 90 percent of the population is literate, Thais tend not to read as a leisure activity. Consequently, advertisements are designed to visually catch the attention of consumers, and are typically original, humorous, and often slapstick. An example is an ad in which Coke is paired with kung fu, which is not how Coke would be advertised in other markets.[52]

Frameworks for assessing multinational strategies

Multinational marketers face the challenge of creating marketing and advertising programs capable of communicating effectively with a diversity of target markets. To assist in this imposing task, various frameworks have been developed to determine the degree

TABLE 14.7	A Product Recognition Continuum for Multinational Marketing
FACTORS	**EXAMPLES**
Stage One	Local consumers have heard or read of a brand marketed elsewhere but cannot get it at home; a brand is "alien" and unavailable but may be desirable [e.g., Rover (English autos), Havana cigars (made in Cuba), or medicine not approved by the FDA but sold in Europe].
Stage Two	Local consumers view a brand made elsewhere as "foreign," made in a particular country but locally available (e.g., Saab autos, French wine). The fact that the brand is foreign makes a difference in the consumer's mind, sometimes favorable, sometimes not.
Stage Three	Local consumers accord imported brand "national status"; that is, its national origin is known but does not affect their choice (e.g., Molson beer in the United States, Ford autos in southern Europe).
Stage Four	Brand owned by a foreign company is made (wholly or partly) domestically and has come to be perceived by locals as a local brand; its foreign origins may be remembered but the brand has been "adopted" ("naturalized"). Examples are Sony in the United States, Coca-Cola in Europe and Japan.
Stage Five	Brand has lost national identity and consumers everywhere see it as "borderless" or global; not only can people not identify where it comes from but they never ask this question. Examples include the Associated Press and CNN news services, Nescafé, Bayer aspirin.

Source: Adapted from George V. Priovolos, "How to Turn National European Brands into Pan-European Brands." Working paper. Hagan School of Business, Iona College, New Rochelle, NY.

to which marketing and advertising efforts should be either globalized or localized, or mixed or combined.

To enable international marketers to assess the positions their products enjoy in specific foreign markets, Table 14.7 presents a five-stage continuum that ranges from mere awareness of a foreign brand in a local market area to complete global identification of the brand; that is, the brand is accepted "as is" in almost every market, and consumers do not think about its country of origin—"it belongs."

Table 14.8 presents a framework that focuses on four marketing strategies available to a firm contemplating doing business on a global basis. A firm might decide either to standardize or localize its product and either standardize or localize its communications program (thus forming a two-by-two matrix). The four possibilities that this decision framework considers range from a company incorporating a **global strategy** (or standardizing both product and communications program) to developing a completely **local strategy** (or customizing both the product and communications program) for each unique market. In the middle there are two *mixed strategies.* All four cells may represent growth opportunities for the firm. To determine which cell represents the firm's best strategy, the marketer must conduct cross-cultural consumer analysis to obtain consumer reactions to alternative product and promotional

TABLE 14.8	A Framework for Alternative Global Marketing Strategies	
PRODUCT STRATEGY	**COMMUNICATION STRATEGY**	
	Standardized Communications	**Localized Communications**
Standardized Product	**Global Strategy:** Uniform Product/ Uniform Message	**Mixed Strategy:** Uniform Product/ Customized Message
Localized Product	**Mixed Strategy:** Customized Product/ Uniform Message	**Local Strategy:** Customized Product/ Customized Message

executions. To illustrate the strategic importance of product uniformity, Frito-Lay, the U.S. snack-food giant, has been standardizing quality and reducing the many local brand names of potato chip companies that it owns throughout the world. This effort is moving the company along a common global visual appearance that features the Lay's logo as a global brand. Its efforts are driven by research that reveals that potato chips are a snack food that has widespread appeal throughout much of the world.[53]

Another orientation for assessing whether to use a global versus local marketing strategy concentrates on a high-tech to high-touch continuum. **Product standardization** appears to be most successful for high-involvement products that approach either end of the high-tech/high-touch continuum. In other words, products that are at either extreme are more suitable for positioning as global brands. In contrast, low-involvement products in the midrange of the high-tech/high-touch continuum are more suitably marketed as local brands, using market-by-market executions.[54] To illustrate, on a worldwide basis, consumers interested in high-involvement, high-tech products share a common language (such as "bytes" and "microprocessors"), whereas advertisements for high-involvement, high-touch products tend to use more emotional appeals and to emphasize visual images. In either case, according to this perspective (high-involvement products that are either high-tech or high-touch), such products are candidates for global promotional communications.

Some researchers have written that globalization (or standardization) and localization should be viewed as two ends of a continuum and that often the key to success is to "be global but to act local." It is also generally an error to assume that demographic segments in other nations would want to be or act like Americans. When looking for success in a foreign market, it has been suggested that a company should remember the following 3 P's—place, people, and product. Table 14.9 presents the specific elements of these 3 P's and cites the appropriate marketing strategy when using a standardization approach and when using a localization approach.[55]

When marketing high-tech products abroad, it is important to note that many industrialized nations lag behind the United States in computer usage. For example, although more than 90 percent of U.S. white-collar workers use a PC, only 55 percent of Western European white-collar workers do so. Often the goal in many European firms is to rise to a high enough position in the company so you do not have to use a PC (i.e., not using a PC as a status symbol).[56] Moreover, approximately 68 percent of all existing Web pages are in English, 6 percent are in Japanese, 6 percent are in German, and 4 percent are in Chinese (these are the top four languages on the Internet).[57]

Perhaps because of the dominance of English-language pages on the Internet, specific non–English-speaking European nations appear to be out to distinguish themselves and their cultures by designing Web sites that in some way or other

TABLE 14.9	Degree of Fit Between Marketing Strategies and the 3 P's		
		MARKETING STRATEGIES	
THE 3 P'S	**SPECIFIC ELEMENTS**	**STANDARDIZATION**	**LOCALIZATION**
Place	Economy	Prosperous	Struggling
	Partners	Few	Plentiful
	Competition	Low	Intense
People	Tastes	Little preference	High preference
	Sophistication	High	Low
	Segments	Few	Many
	Classification	Industrial/consumer durables	Consumer nondurables
Products	Technology	High	Low
	Culture bound	Low	High
	Reputation	Sterling	Poor or unknown
	Product perception	High	Low

Source: Sangeeta Ramarapu, John E. Timmerman, and Narender Ramarapu, "Choosing Between Globalization and Localization as a Strategic Thrust for Your International Marketing Effort," *Journal of Marketing Theory and Practice* 7, no. 2 (Spring 1999): 101. Reprinted by permission.

reflect their countries and specific cultures. So German Web sites might employ bright colors and a geometrical layout to give it a "German feel"; a French Web site might have a black background; a Dutch Web site might offer video downloads; and a Scandinavian Web site might provide a variety of images of nature.[58] Indeed, a recent study of global American brands examined how these brands standardize their Web sites in Europe (U.K., France, Germany, and Spain). The study found that while manufacturers' Web sites did have a minimal level of uniformity with respect to color, logo, and layout, the textual information and visual images were dissimilar from one market to the next. Still further, as with traditional advertising media, standardization for durable goods was higher than for nondurables.[59] In yet another study, researchers examined the domestic and Chinese Web sites of U.S.-based multinational companies. Findings show that the Internet is not a culturally neutral medium, but is full of cultural markers that allow country-specific Web sites to possess a feel and a look that is unique to the local culture. For example, while Web sites intended for the U.S. consumer often contained patriotic phrases and references to September 11th, Chinese Web sites were loaded with Chinese cultural symbols (e.g., the Great Wall of China, Chinese festivals). The managerial implication of the research is that consumers relate best to Web sites that have a local feel because it reduces the anxiety associated with the Internet (it is a relatively new medium) and makes navigation easier.[60]

cross-cultural psychographic segmentation

The paradox in cross-cultural consumer research is that although worldwide consumers may be similar in many ways (e.g., the increased number of women who work outside of the home), any differences in attitudes or behavior can be crucial in determining satisfaction and may provide an opportunity for segmenting consumers in terms of cultural differences. For example, although more than 50 percent of Japanese and American women work outside of the home (which enhances the need for many convenience and time-saving products), Japanese women have been slower to embrace the liberated attitudes of their counterpart working women in the United States.[61] Seen in this light, the determination of whether or not to market a time-saving cleaning device as a world brand is a critical strategic decision. Some firms might attempt to establish a global branding strategy, whereas others would design an individual or local marketing strategy—one that treats Japanese and American working women differently. One marketing authority aptly summed up the issues years ago by stating: "The only ultimate truth possible is that humans are both deeply the same and obviously different. . . ."[62]

This book endorses the same thesis. Earlier chapters have described the underlying similarities that exist between people and the external influences that serve to differentiate them into distinct market segments. If we believe in tailoring marketing strategies to

TABLE 14.10	Six Global Consumer Market Segments	
SEGMENT NAME	**GLOBAL SIZE**	**DESCRIPTION**
Strivers	23%	Value wealth, status, ambition, and power, and products like cellular telephones and computers. They consider material things extremely important.
Devouts	22%	Have more traditional values, like faith, duty, obedience, and respect for elders. Least involved with the media and least likely to want Western brands. Concentrated in the Mideast, Africa, and Asia.
Altruists	18%	Very outer focused—interested in social issues and causes. Generally well educated, older (median age 44), and more female than the norm. Found in Russia and Latin America.
Intimates	15%	These are "people people," and focus on relationships close to home, such as spouses, significant others, family, and friends. Often found in England, Hungary, the Netherlands, and the United States. Very heavy users of media—gives them something to talk about to others.
Fun Seekers	12%	The youngest group. They value excitement, adventure, pleasure, and looking good, and spend time at bars, clubs, and restaurants. The group loves electronic media and is more global in its lifestyle, especially in music.
Creatives	10%	Dedicated to technology, knowledge, and learning, and are the highest consumers of media, especially books, magazines, and newspapers. Members of this group are global trendsetters in owning and using a PC and in surfing the Web.

Source: Stuart Elliott, "Research Finds Consumers Worldwide Belong to Six Basic Groups That Cross National Lines," *New York Times,* June 25, 1998, D8. Copyright © 1998 The New York Times. Reprinted by permission.

specific segments of the American market, it follows then that we also believe in tailoring marketing strategies to the needs—psychological, social, cultural, and functional—of specific foreign segments.

Global psychographic research often reveals cultural differences of great importance to marketers. For example, Roper Starch Worldwide, a major multinational marketing research company, interviewed 35,000 consumers in 35 countries in order to identify shared values, irrespective of national borders. The research sought to uncover the bedrock values in peoples' lives in order to understand the motivations that drive both attitudes and behavior. After completing the interviews in North and South America, Asia, and Europe, six global value groups were uncovered: *Strivers, Devouts, Altruists, Intimates, Fun Seekers*, and *Creatives*.[63] Table 14.10 presents a brief description of each of these six global market segments.

SUMMARY

With so much diversity present among the members of just one nation (as in the United States), it is easy to appreciate that numerous larger differences may exist between citizens of different nations having different cultures, values, beliefs, and languages. If international marketers are to satisfy the needs of consumers in potentially very distinct markets effectively, they must understand the relevant similarities and differences that exist between the peoples of the countries they decide to target.

When consumers make purchase decisions, they seem to take into consideration the countries of origin of the brands that they are assessing. Consumers frequently have specific attitudes or even preferences for products made in particular countries. These country-of-origin effects influence how consumers rate quality and, sometimes, which brands they will ultimately select.

As increasing numbers of consumers from all over the world come in contact with the material goods and lifestyle of people living in other countries and as the number of middle-class consumers grows in developing countries, marketers are eager to locate these new customers and to offer them their products. The rapidly expanding middle classes in countries of Asia, South America, and Eastern Europe possess relatively substantial buying power

because their incomes are largely discretionary (necessities like housing and medical care are often provided by the state for little or no cost).

For some international marketers, acculturation is a dual process: First, marketers must learn everything that is relevant to the product and product category in the society in which they plan to market, and then they must persuade the members of that society to break with their traditional ways of doing things to adopt the new product. The more similar a foreign target market is to a marketer's home market, the easier is the process of acculturation. Conversely, the more different a foreign target market, the more difficult the process of acculturation.

Some of the problems involved in cross-cultural analysis include differences in language, consumption patterns, needs, product usage, economic and social conditions, marketing conditions, and market research opportunities. There is an urgent need for more systematic and conceptual cross-cultural analyses of the psychological, social, and cultural characteristics concerning the consumption habits of foreign consumers. Such analyses would identify increased marketing opportunities that would benefit both international marketers and their targeted consumers.

DISCUSSION QUESTIONS

1. Will the elimination of trade barriers among the countries of the European Union change consumer behavior in these countries? How can U.S. companies take advantage of the economic opportunities emerging in Europe?

2. With all the problems facing companies that go global, why are so many companies choosing to expand internationally? What are the advantages of expanding beyond the domestic market?

3. Are the cultures of the world becoming more similar or more different? Discuss.

4. What is cross-cultural consumer analysis? How can a multinational company use cross-cultural research to design each factor in its marketing mix? Illustrate your answer with examples.

5. What are the advantages and disadvantages of global promotional strategies?

6. Should Head & Shoulders shampoo be sold worldwide with the same formulation? In the same package? With the same advertising theme? Explain your answers.

7. a. If you wanted to name a new product that would be acceptable to consumers throughout the world, what cultural factors would you consider?

   b. What factors might inhibit an attempt by Apple to position a new laptop computer as a world brand?

8. An American company is introducing a line of canned soups in Poland. (a) How should the company use cross-cultural research? (b) Should the company use the same marketing mix it uses in the United States to target Polish consumers? (c) Which, if any, marketing mix components should be designed specifically for marketing canned soups in Poland? Explain your answers.

9. Mercedes-Benz, a German car manufacturer, is using cross-cultural psychographic segmentation to develop marketing campaigns for a new two-seater sports car directed at consumers in different countries. How should the company market the car in the United States? How should it market the car in Japan?

10. What advice would you give to an American retailer who wants to sell women's clothing in Japan?

11. Select two of the marketing mistakes discussed in the text. Discuss how these mistakes could have been avoided if the companies involved had adequately researched some of the issues listed in Table 14.6.

EXERCISES

1. Have you ever traveled outside the United States? If so, please identify some of the differences in values, behavior, and consumption patterns you noted between people in a country you visited and Americans.

2. Interview a student from another culture about his or her use of (a) credit cards, (b) fast-food restaurants, (c) shampoo, and (d) sneakers. Compare your consumption behavior to that of the person you interviewed and discuss any similarities and differences you found.

3. Much has been written about the problems at Euro Disney, the Walt Disney Company's theme park and resort complex, which opened in France in April 1992. These difficulties were largely attributed to Disney's lack of understanding of European (particularly French) culture and the company's failure to modify its American theme-park concept to fit the preferences and customs of European visitors. Discuss how the Walt Disney Company could have used input from cross-cultural analysis in better designing and operating Euro Disney, using a computerized literature search about Euro Disney from your school's library.

4. Select one of the following countries: Mexico, Brazil, Germany, Italy, Israel, Kuwait, Japan, or Australia. Assume that a significant number of people in the country you chose would like to visit the United States and have the financial means to do so. Now, imagine you are a consultant for your state's tourism agency and that you have been charged with developing a promotional strategy to attract tourists from the country you chose. Conduct a computerized literature search of the databases in your school's library and select and read several articles about the lifestyles, customs, and consumption behavior of people in the country you chose. Prepare an analysis of the articles and, on the basis of what you read, develop a promotional strategy designed to persuade tourists from that country to visit your state.

KEY TERMS

- **acculturation**
- **cross-cultural consumer analysis**
- **cross-cultural consumer research**
- **cross-cultural psychographic segmentation**
- **global strategy versus local strategy**
- **multinational strategies**
- **product standardization**
- **world brand**

NOTES

1. "European Union," *Wikipedia Free Encyclopedia,* accessed at **http://en.wikipedia.org/wiki/European_Union**

2. Mauricio Hurtado and Edgar Ahrens, "International Tax Review, Regional Guides: North America," accessed at **www.internationaltaxreview.com**; and "NAFTA 10 Years Later: Information and Communication Technologies," *U.S. Department of Commerce, International Trade Administration,* accessed at **www.ita.doc.gov/td/industry/ otea/nafta/ict.pdf#search=nafta%20market%20size**

3. Larry Roellig, "Designing Global Brands: Critical Lessons," *Design Management Journal* 12, no. 4 (Fall 2001): 40–45; and "MTV: Music Television and H&Q Asia Pacific's @ Japan Media Group to Launch New 24-Hour Channel in Japan," *PR Newswire,* August 29, 2000, 1.

4. Michael Silk and David L. Andrews, "Beyond a Boundary? Sport, Transnational Advertising, and the Reimagining of National Culture," *Journal of Sport and Social Issues* 25, no. 2 (May 2001): 180–201.

5. Jean Halliday, "Champion of the Yugo to Import Chinese Cars," *Advertising Age,* March 7, 2005, 12.

6. "Marketing to Mexican Consumers," *Brand Strategy (London),* March 4, 2005, 43.

7. Sharyne Merritt and Vernon Staubb, "A Cross-Cultural Exploration of Country-of-Origin Preference," in *1995 AMA Winter Educators' Proceedings,* ed. David W. Stewart and Naufel J. Vilcassim (Chicago: American Marketing Association, 1995), 380; Jill Gabrielle Klein, Richard Ettenson, and Marlene D. Morris, "The Animosity Model of Foreign Product Purchase: An Empirical Test in the People's Republic of China," *Journal of Marketing* 62 (January 1998): 89–100; and Gillian Sullivan Mort, Hume Winzar, and C. Min Han, "Country Image Effects in International Services: A Conceptual Model and Cross-National Empirical Test," in *2001 AMA Educators' Proceedings* 12, ed. Greg W. Marshall and Stephen J. Grove (Chicago: American Marketing Association, 2001), 43–44.

8. Lillie Guyer, "Heritage Tough Sell in Global Arena," *Advertising Age,* April 11, 2005, S-12 & S-13.

9. Zeynep Gurhan-Canli and Durairaj Maheswaran, "Determinants of Country-of-Origin Evaluations," *Journal of Consumer Research* 27 (June 2000): 96–108.

10. Gary S. Insch and J. Brad McBride, "The Impact of Country-of-Origin Cues on Consumer Perceptions of Product Quality: A Binational Test of the Decomposed Country-of-Origin Construct," *Journal of Business Research* 57 (2004): 256–265.

11. Ibid.

12. Klein, Ettenson, and Morris, "The Animosity Model," 89–100.

13. Ian Phau and Kor-Weai Chan, "Targeting East Asian Markets: A Comparative Study on National Identity," *Journal of Targeting, Measurement and Analysis for Marketing* 12 (December 2003): 157–172.

14. Olin Lagon, "Culturally Correct Site Design," *Web Techniques* 5, no. 9 (September 2000): 49–51.

15. "Market Focus: Bottled Mineral Water," *Brand Strategy (London),* February 11, 2004, 42.

16. Robert G. Tian and Charles Emery, "Cross-Cultural Issues in Internet Marketing," *Journal of American Academy of Business* 1, no. 2 (March 2002): 217–224; and Keith E. Thompson and Julia Engelken, "Mapping the Values Driving Organic Food Choice," *European Journal of Marketing* 38, no. 8 (2004): 995–1012.

17. Michael Fielding, "Accrued Interest: Western-Style Banks Tailer Approach to Draw Muslims," *Marketing News,* May 15, 2005, 41–44.

18. Nancy Y. Wong and Aaron C. Ahuvia, "Personal Taste and Family Face: Luxury Consumption in Confucian and Western Societies," *Psychology and Marketing* 15, no. 5 (August 1998): 423–441. Also see Sarah Ellison, "Sex-Themed Ads Often Don't Travel Well," *Wall Street Journal,* March 31, 2000, 87.

19. Kitty Go, "Lessons in How to Love Lingerie: The Opening of Hong Kong's Largest Luxury Lingerie Store Heralds the Beginning of a Process to Educate Women on the Benefits of Wearing Their Wealth Close to the Skin," *Financial Times (London),* May 28, 2005, 9.

20. Chip Walker, "The Global Middle Class," *American Demographics,* September 1995, 40–46; Paula Kephart, "How Big Is the Mexican Market?" *American Demographics,* October 1995, 17–18; and Rahul Jacob, "The Big Rise," *Fortune,* May 30, 1994, 74–90.

21. Rainer Hengst, "Plotting Your Global Strategy," *Direct Marketing,* August 2000, 55.

22. Benjamin Senauer and Linda Goetz, "The Growing Middle Class in Developing Countries and the Market for High-Value Food Products," *Prepared for the Workshop on Global Markets for High-Value Food, Economic Research Service, USDA,* Washington D.C., February 14, 2003, accessed at **www.farmfoundation.org/documents/ben-sanauerpaper 2−10−3-13-03_000.pdf**

23. Peter Marber, "Globalization and Its Contents," *World Policy Journal* (Winter 2004/05): 29–37.

24. Mookyu Lee and Francis M. Ulgado, "Consumer Evaluations of Fast-Food Services: A Cross-National Comparison," *The Journal of Services Marketing* 11, no. 1 (1997): 39–52.

25. Ann Veeck and Alvin C. Burns, "Changing Tastes: The Adoption of New Food Choices in Post-Reform China," *Journal of Business Research,* 58 (2005): 644–652.

26. Hengst, "Plotting Your Global Strategy," 52–57.

27. Keith Suter, "Transnational Corporations: Knitting the World Together," *Social Alternatives* 23, no. 4 (Fourth Quarter 2004): 42–45.

28. R. Stephen Parker, Charles M. Hermans, and Allen D. Schaefer, "Fashion Consciousness of Chinese, Japanese and American Teenagers," *Journal of Fashion Marketing and Management* 8, no. 2 (2004): 176–186.

29. Rick Yan, "To Reach China's Consumers, Adapt to Guo Qing," *Harvard Business Review,* September–October 1994, 66–67.

30. Kathy Chen, "Chinese Babies Are Coveted Consumers," *Wall Street Journal,* May 15, 1998, B1; and Fara Warner, "Western Markets Send Researchers to China to Plumb Consumers' Minds," *Wall Street Journal,* March 28, 1997, B5.

31. Mindy F. Ji and James U. McNeal, "How Chinese Childen's Commercials Differ from Those of the United States: A Content Analysis," *Journal of Advertising* 30, no. 3 (Fall 2001): 78–92.

32. Tara Parker-Pope, "Nonalcoholic Beer Hits the Spot in Mideast," *Wall Street Journal,* December 6, 1995, B1.

33. Warner, "Western Markets Send Researchers," B5.

34. Vanessa O'Connell, "Exxon 'Centralizes' New Global Campaign," *Wall Street Journal,* July 11, 2001, B6.

35. Robert L. Wehling, "Even at P&G, Only 3 Brands Make Truly Global Grade So Far," *Advertising Age International,* January 1998, 8.

36. Douglas B. Holt, John A. Quelch, and Earl L. Taylor, "How Global Brands Compete," *Harvard Business Review,* September 2004, 68–75.

37. Ibid.

38. Alokparna Basu Monga and Debroah Roedder John, "Consumer Response to Brand Extensions: Does Culture Matter?," *Advances in Consumer Research* 31 (2004): 216–222.

39. Friedman, "Big Mac II," A27; and Drew Martin and Paul Herbig, "Marketing Implications of Japan's Social-Cultural Underpinnings," *Journal of Brand Management* 9, no. 3 (January 2002): 171–179.

40. Pamela Buxton, "Helping Brands Take on the World," *Marketing (London),* May 13, 1999, 32.

41. Martin S. Roth, "The Effects of Culture and Socioeconomics on the Performance of Global Brand Image Strategies," *Journal of Marketing Research* 32 (1995): 163–175.

42. Roellig, "Designing Global Brands," 43.

43. Sicco Van Gelder, "Global Brand Strategy," *Journal of Brand Management* 12 (September 2004): 39–48.

44. Nitish Singh, Olivier Furrer, and Massimiliano Ostinelli, "To Localize or to Standardize on the Web: Empirical Evidence from Italy, India, Netherlands, Spain, and Switzerland," *Multinational Business Review* 12 (Spring 2004): 69–87.

45. Desmond Lam and Dick Mizerski, "Cross-Cultural Differences on the Internet: The Case of Internet Privacy," *American Marketing Association Conference Proceedings,* 14, 2003, 257–258.

46. Sharon Shavitt, Michelle R. Nelson, and Rose Mei Len Yuan, "Exploring Cross-Cultural Differences in Cognitive Responding to Ads," in *Advances in Consumer Research,* 24, ed. Merrie Brucks and Deborah J. MacInnis (Provo, UT: Association for Consumer Research, 1997), 245–250.

47. Michael A. Callow, Dawn B. Lerman, and Mayo de Juan Vigaray, "Motivational Appeals in Advertising: A Comparative Content Analysis of United States and Spanish Advertising," in *Proceedings of the Sixth Symposium on Cross-Cultural Consumer and Business Studies,* ed. Scott M. Smith (Honolulu, HI: Association of Consumer Research and the Society for Consumer Psychology, 1997), 392–396.

48. Dean Foster, "Playing with China Dollars," *Brandweek,* November 10, 1997, 20–23.

49. Michael Callow and Leon G. Schiffman, "Sociocultural Meanings in Visually Standardized Print Ads," *European Journal of Marketing,* 38, no. 9/10 (2004): 1113–1128.

50. Kip D. Cassino, "A World of Advertising," *American Demographics,* November 1997, 60.

51. Jiafei Yin, "International Advertising Strategies in China: A Worldwide Survey of Foreign Advertisers," *Journal of Advertising Research* 39, no. 6 (November/December 1999): 25–35.

52. Normandy Madden, "Looking for the Next Brazil? Try Thailand," *Advertising Age,* April 11, 2005, 22.

53. Robert Frank, "Potato Chips to Go Global—or So Pepsi Bets," *Wall Street Journal,* November 30, 1995, B1.

54. Teresa Domzal and Lynette Unger, "Emerging Positioning Strategies in Global Marketing," *Journal of Consumer Marketing* 4 (Fall 1987): 27–29.

55. Sangeeta Ramarapu, John E. Timmerman, and Narender Ramarapu, "Choosing Between Globalization and Localization as a Strategic Thrust for Your International Marketing Effort," *Journal of Marketing Theory and Practice* 7, no. 2 (Spring 1999): 97–105.

56. David Kirkpatrick, "Europe's Technology Gap Is Getting Scary," *Fortune,* March 17, 1997, 26–27.

57. Tian and Emory, "Cross-Cultural Issues in Internet Marketing," 217–224.

58. Ben Vickers, "In Internet Age, Europe Looks to Define Its Many Cultures Against U.S. Online," *Wall Street Journal,* April 2, 2001, B9F.

59. Shintaro Okazaki, "Searching the Web for Global Brands: How American Brands Standardize Their Web Sites in Europe," *European Journal of Marketing* 39, no. 1/2 (2005): 87–109.

60. Nitish Singh, Hongxin Zhao, and Xiaorui Hu, "Cultural Adaptation on the Web: A Study of American Companies' Domestic and Chinese Websites," *Journal of Global Information Management* 11 (July–September 2003): 63–80.

61. Jack Russel, "Working Women Give Japan Culture Shock," *Advertising Age,* January 16, 1995, 1–24.

62. Sidney J. Levy, "Myth and Meaning in Marketing," in *1974 Combined Proceedings,* ed. Ronald C. Curhan (Chicago: American Marketing Association, 1975), 555–556.

63. Stuart Elliott, "Research Finds Consumers Worldwide Belong to Six Basic Groups That Cross National Lines," *New York Times,* June 25, 1998, D8.

PART 4 EXPLORES THE VARIOUS ASPECTS OF CONSUMER DECISION MAKING

Chapter 15 begins with a discussion of personal influence, opinion leadership, and the diffusion of innovations. Chapter 16 examines in detail a simple model of consumer decision making that ties together the psychological, social, and cultural concepts examined throughout the book. The book concludes with a discussion of various related aspects of consumption behavior (such as gift giving) and explores the outcomes of relationship marketing from the consumer's perspective.

chapter**fifteen**

Consumer Influence and the Diffusion of Innovations

This chapter deals with two interrelated issues of considerable importance to consumers and marketers alike—the informal influence that others have on consumers' behavior and the dynamic processes that impact consumers' acceptance of new products and services.

In the first part of this chapter we will examine the nature and dynamics of the influence that friends, neighbors, and acquaintances have on our consumer-related decisions. This influence is often called *word-of-mouth communications* or the *opinion leadership process* (the two terms will be used interchangeably here). We will also consider the personality and motivations of those who influence (opinion leaders) and those who are influenced (opinion receivers). We will end the first part of this chapter with an exploration of how marketers are enhancing their consumer strategies by harnessing the power of natural word-of-mouth in the form of stimulated or market manipulated word-of-mouth. These contrived marketing efforts, unlike "naturally occurring" word-of-mouth or opinion leadership, largely consists of either paid actors or largely unpaid volunteer agents who are engaged by marketers to create

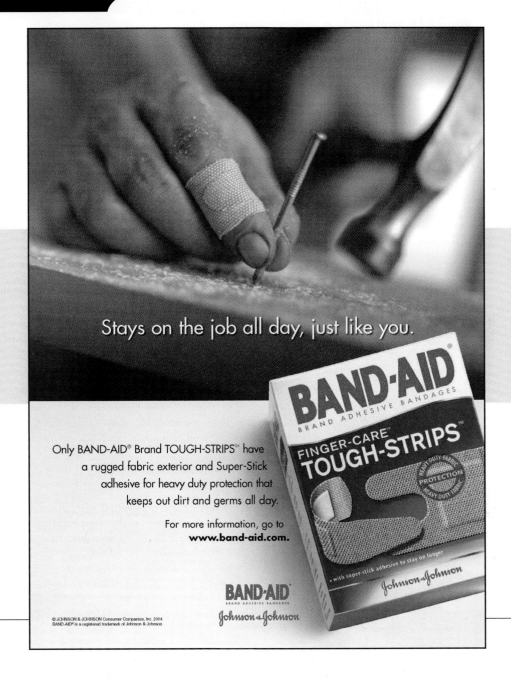

Stays on the job all day, just like you.

BAND·AID®
BRAND ADHESIVE BANDAGES
FINGER-CARE™
TOUGH-STRIPS™
PROTECTION
HEAVY DUTY FABRIC
• with super-stick adhesive to stay on longer
Johnson & Johnson

Only BAND-AID® Brand TOUGH-STRIPS™ have
a rugged fabric exterior and Super-Stick
adhesive for heavy duty protection that
keeps out dirt and germs all day.

For more information, go to
www.band-aid.com.

BAND·AID®
BRAND ADHESIVE BANDAGES

© JOHNSON & JOHNSON Consumer Companies, Inc. 2004
BAND-AID® is a registered trademark of Johnson & Johnson
Johnson & Johnson

buzz and sales for new products that they often freely elect to talk up. In the second part of this chapter, we will explore factors that encourage and discourage acceptance (or rejection) of new products and services. For consumers, new products and services may represent increased opportunities to satisfy personal, social, and environmental needs and add to their quality of life. For the marketer, new products and services provide an important mechanism for keeping the firm competitive and profitable.

what is opinion leadership?

The power and importance of personal influence are captured in the following comment by an ad agency executive: "Perhaps the most important thing for marketers to understand about word-of-mouth is its huge potential economic impact."[1] This decade-old comment is more true today than ever before!

Opinion leadership (or word-of-mouth communications) is the process by which one person (the opinion leader) informally influences the actions or attitudes of others, who may be opinion seekers or opinion recipients. The key characteristic of the influence is that it is interpersonal and informal and takes place between two or more people, *none of whom represents a commercial selling source that would gain directly from the sale of something.* Word-of-mouth implies personal, or face-to-face, communication, although it may also take place in a telephone conversation or within the context of e-mail or a chat group on the Internet. This communication process is likely, at times, to also be reinforced by nonverbal observations of the appearance and behavior of others.

One of the parties in a word-of-mouth encounter usually offers advice or information about a product or service, such as which of several brands is best or how a particular product may be used. This person, the **opinion leader**, may become an **opinion receiver** when another product or service is brought up as part of the overall discussion.

Individuals who actively seek information and advice about products sometimes are called **opinion seekers**. For purposes of simplicity, the terms *opinion receiver* and *opinion recipient* will be used interchangeably in the following discussion to identify both those who actively seek product information from others and those who receive unsolicited information. Simple examples of opinion leadership at work include the following:

1. *A family decides that they need a new gas barbeque for their backyard, and they ask a few of their neighbors which brand they should purchase.*
2. *A person shows his cousin photographs of his recent vacation in Costa Rica, and the cousin suggests that using a different film might produce better pictures of the rain forest.*
3. *During a coffee break, a coworker talks about the new TV series she saw last night and recommends seeing it.*

Most studies of opinion leadership are concerned with the measurement of the behavioral impact that opinion leaders have on the consumption habits of others. Available research, for example, suggests that "influentials" or opinion leaders are almost four times more likely than others to be asked about political and government issues, as well as how to handle teens; three times more likely to be asked about computers or investments; and twice as likely to be asked about health issues and restaurants.[2] There is also research to suggest that when an information seeker feels that he or she knows little about a particular product or service, a "strong-tie source" will be sought (such as a friend or family member), but when the consumer has some prior knowledge of the subject area, then a "weak-tie source" is acceptable (acquaintances or strangers).[3]

Word-of-mouth in today's *always in contact* world

Over the past decade, with the proliferation of cell phone usage and e-mail (and the invention of combination devices like BlackBerry and Web-capable cell phones), many people find themselves, by choice, to be "always" available to friends, family, and business associates. Although Americans have been somewhat slower than consumers in other countries to embrace the notion of receiving e-mail via their cellular telephones, this may be due, in part, to the great number of PCs in use in the United States. Table 15.1 shows, whereas almost 68 percent of Americans are Internet users, the second-place nation in terms of the number of Internet users, China, has only 7.3 percent of its citizens on the Web. In contrast, there are presently about 310 million cellular telephone users in China, which adds up to about 25 percent of its population.[4]

TABLE 15.1	**Top 15 Countries in Terms of the Number of Internet Users in 2005**	
COUNTRY	**NUMBER OF INTERNET USERS (IN MILLIONS)**	**INTERNET PENETRATION**
United States	200.9	67.8
China	94.0	7.3
Japan	67.7	52.8
Germany	46.3	56.0
India	39.2	3.6
United Kingdom	35.2	58.7
South Korea	31.6	63.3
Italy	28.6	48.8
France	24.8	41.2
Russia	22.3	15.5
Canada	20.5	63.8
Brazil	17.9	9.9
Indonesia	15.3	7.0
Spain	14.6	1.4
Australia	13.6	66.4

Source: **http://www.internetworldstats.com/top20.htm**, accessed May 27, 2005.

Along with the explosion of Web-capable cellular telephones is the creation of the "thumb generation," which is known in Japan as *oya yubi sedai*. Young people in Japan learn to send e-mail messages from the cell phones by using their thumbs, and some Japanese TV stations have even held thumbing speed contests. This is just a natural extension of the thumb usage learned from using handheld computer games.[5]

Just how important is word-of-mouth?

A recent study in the United Kingdom asked consumers which information sources would make them "more comfortable" with a company. The answer at the top of the list was "friend's recommendation" (the response of 71 percent of respondents), whereas "past experience" was the response of 63 percent of respondents. Only 15 percent of the consumers mentioned "advertising."[6] Additionally, it has been reported that over 40 percent of U.S. consumers will actively seek the advice of family and friends when in the market for a doctor, lawyer, or automobile mechanic, and the importance of word-of-mouth is even greater with respect to the diffusion of new products.[7]

dynamics of the opinion leadership process

The opinion leadership process is a very dynamic and powerful consumer force. As informal communication sources, opinion leaders are remarkably effective at influencing consumers in their product-related decisions. Some of the reasons for the effectiveness of opinion leaders are discussed next.

Credibility

Opinion leaders are highly credible sources of information because they usually are perceived as objective concerning the product or service information or advice they dispense.

Their intentions are perceived as being in the best interests of the opinion recipients because they receive no compensation for the advice and apparently have no "ax to grind." Because opinion leaders often base their product comments on firsthand experience, their advice reduces for opinion receivers the perceived risk or anxiety inherent in buying new products. The average person is exposed to anywhere from 200 to 1,000 sales communications a day, but he or she is thousands of times more likely to act on the basis of a friend's or colleague's recommendation. Whereas the advertiser has a vested interest in the message being advertised, the opinion leader offers advice that does not have a commercial motive.

Positive and negative product information

Information provided by marketers is invariably favorable to the product and/or brand. Thus, the very fact that opinion leaders provide both favorable and unfavorable information adds to their credibility. An example of an unfavorable or negative product comment is, "The problem with those inexpensive kitchen knives is that they soon go from being sharp to being dull." Compared with positive or even neutral comments, negative comments are relatively uncommon. For this reason, consumers are especially likely to note such information and to avoid products or brands that receive negative evaluations. Over the years, motion pictures have failed due to negative "buzz" about the film, and negative word-of-mouth about new food products have retarded sales or caused the early death of a product. Consumers, it turns out, are generally much more likely to share a negative experience than a positive one.

Information and advice

Opinion leaders are the source of both information and advice. They may simply talk about their *experience* with a product, relate what they know about a product, or, more aggressively, *advise* others to buy or to avoid a specific product. The kinds of product or service information that opinion leaders are likely to transmit during a conversation include the following:

1. Which of several brands is best: *"In my opinion, when you consider picture quality versus price, Sony offers the best value in small digital cameras."*
2. How to best use a specific product: *"I find that my walls look best when I paint with a roller rather than a pad."*
3. Where to shop: *"When Brooks Brothers has a sale, the values are terrific."*
4. Who provides the best service: *"Over the past few years, I've had my car serviced and repaired at Tom's Garage, and I think its service can't be beat."*

Many of the messages being sent and received these days deal with movies, restaurants, shopping, computer games, and other areas of interest to young adults—word-of-mouth communication in the form of telephone or e-mail. Figure 15.1 presents the results of a survey estimating the percentage of Americans that acted on a referral from an opinion leader for selected important product and service categories during the past year.

Opinion leadership is category specific

Opinion leadership tends to be *category specific;* that is, opinion leaders often "specialize" in certain product categories about which they offer information and advice. When other product categories are discussed, however, they are just as likely to reverse their roles and become opinion receivers. A person who is considered particularly knowledgeable about home electronics may be an opinion leader in terms of this subject, yet when it comes to purchasing a new washing machine, the same person may seek advice from someone else—perhaps even from someone who has sought his advice on home electronics.

Opinion leadership is a two-way street

As the preceding example suggests, consumers who are opinion leaders in one product-related situation may become opinion receivers in another situation, even for the same product. Consider the following example. Rob, a new father contemplating the purchase

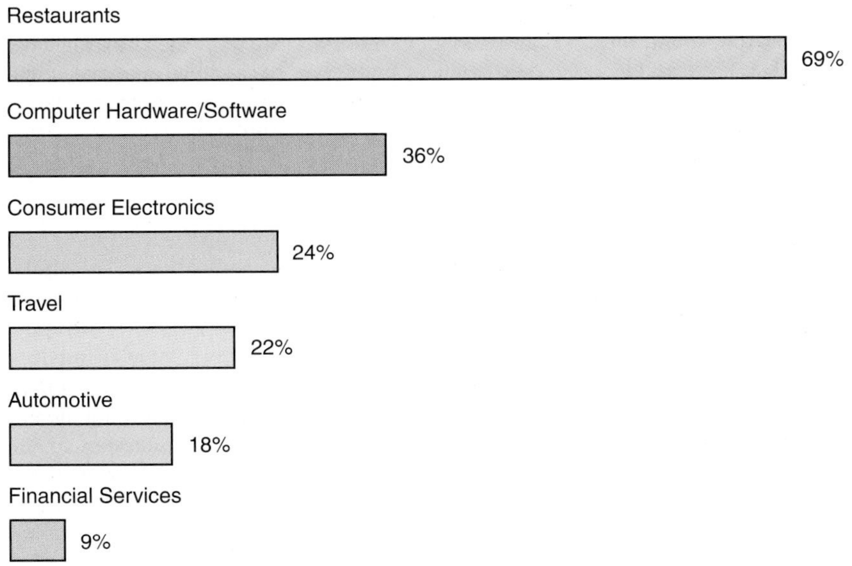

FIGURE 15.1

**Word-of-Mouth
in Action**

Source: Business Week (based on
an online survey of 1,000 adults,
February 2002, Goodmind LLC),
May 6, 2002, 10.

Restaurants

69%

Computer Hardware/Software

36%

Consumer Electronics

24%

Travel

22%

Automotive

18%

Financial Services

9%

of a baby car seat, may seek information and advice from other people to reduce his indecision about which brand to select. Once the car seat has been bought, however, he may experience postpurchase dissonance (see Chapter 8) and have a compelling need to talk favorably about the purchase to other people to confirm the correctness of his own choice. In the first instance, he is an opinion receiver (seeker); in the second, he assumes the role of opinion leader.

An opinion leader may also be influenced by an opinion receiver as the result of a product-related conversation. For example, a person may tell a friend about a favorite hotel getaway in Lake Como, Italy, and, in response to comments from the opinion receiver, come to realize that the hotel is too small, too isolated, and offers vacationers fewer amenities than other hotels.

the motivation behind opinion leadership

To understand the phenomenon of opinion leadership, it is useful to examine the motivation of those who provide and those who receive product-related information.

The needs of opinion leaders

What motivates a person to talk about a product or service? Motivation theory suggests that people may provide information or advice to others to satisfy some basic need of their own (see Chapter 4). However, opinion leaders may be unaware of their own underlying motives. As suggested earlier, opinion leaders may simply be trying to reduce their own postpurchase dissonance by confirming their own buying decisions. For instance, if Bradley subscribes to a satellite TV service and then is uncertain that he made the right choice, he may try to reassure himself by "talking up" the service's advantages to others. In this way, he relieves his own psychological discomfort. Furthermore, when he can influence a friend or neighbor to also get satellite TV, he confirms his own good judgment in selecting the service first. Thus, the opinion leader's true motivation may really be self-confirmation or self-involvement. Furthermore, the information or advice that an opinion leader dispenses may provide all types of tangential personal benefits: It may confer attention, imply some type of status, grant superiority, demonstrate awareness and expertise, and give the feeling of possessing inside information and the satisfaction of "converting" less adventurous souls.

In addition to *self*-involvement, the opinion leader may also be motivated by *product* involvement, *social* involvement, and *message* involvement. Opinion leaders who are motivated by product involvement may find themselves so pleased or so disappointed with a product that they simply must tell others about it. Those who are motivated by social involvement need to share product-related experiences. In this type of situation, opinion leaders use their product-related conversations as expressions of friendship, neighborliness, and love.

The needs of opinion receivers

Opinion receivers satisfy a variety of needs by engaging in product-related conversations. First, they obtain new-product or new-usage information. Second, they reduce their perceived risk by receiving firsthand knowledge from a user about a specific product or brand. Third, they reduce the search time entailed in the identification of a needed product or service. Moreover, opinion receivers can be certain of receiving the approval of the opinion leader if they follow that person's product endorsement or advice and purchase the product. For all of these reasons, people often look to friends, neighbors, and other acquaintances for product information. Indeed, research examining the importance of four specific information sources on a hypothetical $100 purchase of consumer services revealed that *advice from others* was more important than the combined impact of sales representatives, advertising and promotion, and other sources.[8] Table 15.2 compares the motivations of opinion receivers with those of opinion leaders.

Purchase pals

Researchers have also examined the influence of "purchase pals" as information sources who actually accompany consumers on shopping trips. Although purchase pals were used only 9 percent of the time for grocery items, they were used 25 percent of the time for purchases of electronic equipment (e.g., computers, VCRs, TV sets).[9] Interestingly,

TABLE 15.2	A Comparison of the Motivations of Opinion Leaders and Opinion Receivers
OPINION LEADERS	**OPINION RECEIVERS**
Self-Improvement Motivations	
• *Reduce postpurchase uncertainty or dissonance*	• *Reduce the risk of making a purchase commitment*
• *Gain attention or status*	• *Reduce search time (e.g., avoid the necessity of shopping around)*
• *Assert superiority and expertise*	
• *Feel like an adventurer*	
• *Experience the power of "converting" others*	
Product-Involvement Motivations	
• *Express satisfaction or dissatisfaction with a product or service*	• *Learn how to use or consume a product*
	• *Learn what products are new in the marketplace*
Social-Involvement Motivations	
• *Express neighborliness and friendship by discussing products or services that may be useful to others*	• *Buy products that have the approval of others, thereby ensuring acceptance*
Message-Involvement Motivations	
• *Express one's reaction to a stimulating advertisement by telling others about it*	

male purchase pals are more likely to be used as sources of product category expertise, product information, and retail store and price information. Female purchase pals are more often used for moral support and to increase confidence in the buyer's decisions. Similarly, it seems that when a weak tie exists between the purchase pal and the shopper (e.g., neighbor, classmate, or work colleague), the purchase pal's main contribution tends to be functional—the source's specific product experiences and general marketplace knowledge are being relied on. In contrast, when strong ties exist (such as mother, son, husband, or wife), what is relied on is the purchase pal's familiarity and understanding of the buyer's individual characteristics and needs (or tastes and preferences).

Surrogate buyers versus opinion leaders

Although the traditional model of new product adoption shows opinion leaders influencing the purchase of many new products and services, there are instances in which surrogate buyers replace opinion leaders in this role. For example, working women are increasingly turning to wardrobe consultants for help in purchasing business attire, most new drugs start out requiring a doctor's prescription, and many service providers make decisions for their clients (e.g., your service station decides which brand of disk brake pads to install on your car). Consequently, in an increasing number of decision situations, it is a surrogate buyer who primarily influences the purchase. Table 15.3 presents the key differences between opinion leaders and surrogate buyers.

| **TABLE 15.3** | **Key Differences Between Opinion Leaders and Surrogate Buyers** |

OPINION LEADER	SURROGATE BUYER
1. Informal relationship with end users	1. Formal relationship; occupation-related status
2. Information exchange occurs in the context of a casual interaction	2. Information exchange in the form formal instructions/advice
3. Homophilous (to a certain extent) to end users	3. Heterophilous to end users (that in fact is the source of power)
4. Does not get paid for advice	4. Usually hired, therefore gets paid
5. Usually socially more active than end users	5. Not necessarily socially more active than end users
6. Accountability limited regarding the outcome of advice	6. High level of accountability
7. As accountability limited, rigor in search and screening of alternatives low	7. Search and screening of alternatives more rigorous
8. Likely to have (although not always) used the product personally	8. May not have used the product for personal consumption
9. More than one can be consulted before making a final decision	9. Second opinion taken on rare occasions
10. Same person can be an opinion leader for a variety of related product categories	10. Usually specializes for a specific product/service category

Source: Praveen Aggarwal and Taihoon Cha, "Surrogate Buyers and the New Product Adoption Process: A Conceptualization and Managerial Framework," *Journal of Consumer Marketing* 14, no. 5 (1997): 394. Reprinted by permission.

measurement of opinion leadership

Consumer researchers are interested in identifying and measuring the impact of the opinion leadership process on consumption behavior. In measuring opinion leadership, the researcher has a choice of four basic measurement techniques: (1) the *self-designating method,* (2) the *sociometric method,* (3) the *key informant method,* and (4) the *objective method.*

In the *self-designating method*, respondents are asked to evaluate the extent to which they have provided others with information about a product category or specific brand or have otherwise influenced the purchase decisions of others. Figure 15.2 shows two types of self-designating question formats that can be used to determine a consumer's opinion leadership activity. The first consists of a single question, whereas the second consists of a series of questions. The use of multiple questions enables the researcher to determine a respondent's opinion leadership more reliably because the statements are interrelated. The self-designating technique is used more often than other methods for measuring opinion leadership because consumer researchers find it easy to include in market research questionnaires. Because this method relies on the respondent's self-evaluation, however, it may be open to bias should respondents perceive "opinion leadership" (even though the term is not used) to be a desirable characteristic and, thus, overestimate their own roles as opinion leaders.

The *sociometric method* measures the person-to-person informal communication of consumers concerning products or product categories. In this method, respondents are asked to identify (a) the specific individuals (if any) to whom they provided advice or information about the product or brand under study and (b) the specific individuals (if any) who provided them with advice or information about the product or brand under study. In the first instance, if respondents identify one or more individuals to whom they have provided some form of product information, they are tentatively classified as opinion leaders. In the second instance, respondents are asked to identify the individuals (if any) who provided them with information about a product under investigation. Individuals designated by the primary respondent are tentatively classified as opinion leaders. In both cases, the researcher attempts to validate the determination by asking the individuals named whether they did, in fact, either provide or receive the relevant product information.

Opinion leadership can also be measured through the use of a *key informant*, a person who is keenly aware of or knowledgeable about the nature of social communications among members of a specific group. The key informant is asked to identify those individuals in the group who are most likely to be opinion leaders. However, the key informant does not have to be a member of the group under study. For example, a professor may serve as the key informant for a college class, identifying those students who are most likely to be opinion

Self-Designating Questions for Measuring Opinion Leadership

FIGURE 15.2

SINGLE-QUESTION APPROACH:

1. In the last six months have you been asked your advice or opinion about *HDTV?**

Yes _____   **No** _____

MULTIPLE-QUESTION APPROACH:

(Measured on a 5-point bipolar "Agree/Disagree" scale)

1. Friends and neighbors frequently ask my advice about *HDTV*.
2. I sometimes influence the types of *HDTV* friends buy.
3. My friends come to me more often than I go to them about *HDTV*.
4. I feel that I am generally regarded by my friends as a good source of advice about *HDTV*.
5. I can think of at least three people whom I have spoken to about *HDTV* in the past six months.

*Researchers can insert their own relevant product-service or product-service category.

leaders with regard to a particular issue. This research method is relatively inexpensive because it requires that only one individual or at most several individuals be intensively interviewed, whereas the self-designating and sociometric methods require that a consumer sample or entire community be interviewed. However, the key informant method is generally not used by marketers because of the difficulties inherent in identifying an individual who can objectively identify opinion leaders in a relevant consumer group.

Finally, the *objective method* of determining opinion leadership is much like a "controlled experiment"—it involves placing new products or new-product information with selected individuals and then tracing the resulting "web" of interpersonal communication concerning the relevant product(s). In a practical sense, a new restaurant in a downtown business district might apply this approach to speed up the creation of a core customer base by sending out invitations to young, influential business executives to dine with their friends at a reduced introductory price any time during the first month of the restaurant's operations. If the restaurant's food and drink are judged to be superior, the restaurant is likely to enjoy the benefits of enhanced positive word-of-mouth generated by the systematic encouragement of the young clientele to "try it out" and who "talk it up" to their friends after experiencing the new restaurant.

Table 15.4 presents an overview of each of the four methods of measuring opinion leadership, together with advantages and limitations.

TABLE 15.4	Methods of Measuring Opinion Leadership: Advantages and Limitations			
OPINION LEADERSHIP MEASUREMENT METHOD	**DESCRIPTION OF METHOD**	**SAMPLE QUESTIONS ASKED**	**ADVANTAGES**	**LIMITATIONS**
Self-Designating Method	Each respondent is asked a series of questions to determine the degree to which he or she perceives himself or herself to be an opinion leader.	"Do you influence other people in their selection of products?"	Measures the individual's own perceptions of his or her opinion leadership.	Depends on the objectivity with which respondents can identify and report their personal influence.
Sociometric Method	Members of a social system are asked to identify to whom they give advice and to whom they go for advice and information about a product category.	"Whom do you ask?" "Who asks you for information about that product category?"	Sociometric questions have the greatest degree of validity and are easy to administer.	It is very costly and analysis often is very complex. Requires a large number of respondents. Not suitable for sample design where only a portion of the social system is interviewed.
Key Informant Method	Carefully selected key informants in a social system are asked to designate opinion leaders.	"Who are the most influential people in the group?"	Relatively inexpensive and less time consuming than the sociometric method.	Informants who are not thoroughly familiar with the social system are likely to provide invalid information.
Objective Method	Artificially places individuals in a position to act as opinion leaders and measures results of their efforts.	"Have you tried the product?"	Measures individual's ability to influence others under controlled circumstances.	Requires the establishment of an experimental design and the tracking of the resulting impact on the participants.

Source: Adapted with the permission of The Free Press, a division of Simon & Schuster, from *Diffusion of Innovations*. Fourth Edition by Everett M. Rogers. Copyright © 1995 by Everett M. Rogers. Copyright © 1962, 1971, 1983 by the Free Press.

a profile of the opinion leader

Just who are opinion leaders? Can they be recognized by any distinctive characteristics? Can they be reached through specific media? Marketers have long sought answers to these questions, for if they are able to identify the relevant opinion leaders for their products, they can design marketing messages that encourage them to communicate with and influence the consumption behavior of others. For this reason, consumer researchers have attempted to develop a realistic profile of the opinion leader. This has not been easy to do. As was pointed out earlier, opinion leadership tends to be category specific; that is, an individual who is an opinion *leader* in one product category may be an opinion *receiver* in another product category. Thus, the generalized profile of opinion leaders is likely to be influenced by the context of specific product categories.

Although it is difficult to construct a generalized profile of the opinion leader without considering a particular category of interest (or a specific product or service category), Table 15.5 does present a summary of the generalized characteristics that appear to hold true regardless of product category. The evidence indicates that opinion leaders across all product categories generally exhibit a variety of defining characteristics. First, they reveal a keen sense of knowledge and interest in the particular product or service area, and they are likely to be consumer innovators. They also demonstrate a greater willingness to talk about the product, service, or topic; they are more self-confident; and they are more outgoing and gregarious ("more sociable"). Furthermore, within the context of a specific subject area, opinion leaders receive more information via nonpersonal sources and are considered to have expertise in their area of influence. They also usually belong to the same socioeconomic and age groups as their opinion receivers.

When it comes to their mass-media exposure or habits, opinion leaders are likely to read special-interest publications devoted to the specific topic or product category in which they "specialize."[10] For example, an automobile opinion leader might read publications such as *Car and Driver, Motor Trend*, and *Automobile*. These special-interest magazines serve not only to inform automotive-oriented consumers about new cars, tires, audio systems, and accessories that may be of personal interest, but also provide them with the specialized knowledge that enables them to make recommendations to relatives, friends, and neighbors. Thus, the opinion leader tends to have greater exposure to media specifically relevant to his or her area of interest than the nonleader. Summing up it for us, a recent study found that opinion leaders "gain influence through their informational advantages relative to others in the same environment."[11]

TABLE 15.5	Profile of Opinion Leaders
GENERALIZED ATTRIBUTES ACROSS PRODUCT CATEGORIES	**CATEGORY-SPECIFIC ATTRIBUTES**
Innovativeness	Interest
Willingness to talk	Knowledge
Self-confidence	Special-interest media exposure
Gregariousness	Same age
Cognitive differentiation	Same social status
	Social exposure outside group

frequency and overlap of opinion leadership

Opinion leadership is not a rare phenomenon. Often more than one-third of the people studied in a consumer research project are classified as opinion leaders with respect to some self-selected product category. The frequency of consumer opinion leadership suggests that people are sufficiently interested in at least one product or product category to talk about it and give advice concerning it to others.

This leads to the interesting question: Do opinion leaders in one product category tend to be opinion leaders in other product categories? The answer to this question comes from an area of research aptly referred to as *opinion leadership overlap*. Accordingly, opinion leadership tends to overlap across certain combinations of interest areas. Overlap is likely to be highest among product categories that involve similar interests (such as televisions and VCRs, high-fashion clothing and cosmetics, household cleansers and detergents, expensive wristwatches and writing instruments, hunting gear, and fishing tackle). Thus, opinion leaders in one product area often are opinion leaders in related areas in which they are also interested.

Market mavens

Research suggests the existence of a special category of consumer influencer, the **market maven**. These consumers possess a wide range of information about many different types of products, retail outlets, and other dimensions of markets. They both initiate discussions with other consumers and respond to requests for market information. Market mavens like to shop, and they also like to share their shopping expertise with others. However, although they appear to fit the profile of opinion leaders in that they have high levels of brand awareness and tend to try more brands, unlike opinion leaders their influence extends beyond the realm of high-involvement products. For example, market mavens may help diffuse information on such low-involvement products as razor blades and laundry detergent.[12] Furthermore, market mavens appear to be motivated by a sense of obligation to share information, a desire to help others, and the feeling of pleasure that comes with telling others about products.[13]

While both innovators and market mavens spend more time shopping than other consumers, innovators tend to be price insensitive. Market mavens are not primarily concerned with price, but are nevertheless more value conscious than other shoppers and are heavy users of coupons.[14] Table 15.6 compares consumer innovators to market mavens, including breadth of knowledge and reaction to promotions. The table, for example, reveals that while the opinion leader's knowledge extends only to a specific product category, market mavens possess a wide range of market information. Table 15.7 presents a Market Maven Scale that uses a 7-point Agree/Disagree response format to identify market mavens.

It would be wrong to discuss market mavens without specifically citing the role played by teenagers. Seventy percent of teens use the Internet regularly, and they know how to search for and find information both for themselves and as information requests from others. Research has found that in families where both parents and teenagers are heavy Internet users, both the teens and their parents recognize the teens' expertise and value the child's contribution to family decision-making.[15]

Just as the examination of the relationship between being an opinion leader and being an innovator led to the recognition of the existence of the market maven, research on the market maven has uncovered yet another category of consumers, the *social hub*. These are individuals who direct social traffic—they have relationships with many people, they frequently bring these people together, and they do so for personal pleasure (rather than for some tangible reward). It is possible that social hubs may prove to be an excellent way to predict the number of people that are told about a consumption experience.[16]

TABLE 15.6	Consumer Innovativeness and Market Mavenism Compared	
CONSTRUCT OF INTEREST	**INNOVATIVENESS**	**MARKET MAVENISM**
Information and Knowledge	Knowledgeable about specific product categories	Wide variety of market information; information seekers
Opinion Leadership	Act as opinion leaders for new products	Act as opinion leaders for many aspects of the marketplace
Search Behavior	Exposed to a variety of information sources	Exposed to a variety of information sources
Involvement	Involved in the marketplace; especially new products	Involved in many aspects of the marketplace
Promotion	Interested in information heavy or centrally processed communications	Heavy users of coupons, shopping lists, grocery budgets, and ads
Brand Awareness	Aware of new brands in specific product fields	Aware of new brands in many fields
Assertiveness	No reason to expect an assertive style of shopping and buying.	More assertive than other consumers
Value conscious	More interested in newness than price; not bargain conscious	More value conscious than other consumers; seek bargain prices
Fashion Consciousness	Fashion innovators are fashion conscious	Market Mavens are not fashion conscious

Source: Ronald E. Goldsmith, Leisa R. Flynn, and Elizabeth B. Goldsmith, "Innovation Consumers and Market Mavens," *Journal of Marketing Theory and Practice* 11 (Fall 2003): 56.

TABLE 15.7	Market Maven Scale (Six-point Agree/Disagree Response Format)

1. I like introducing new brands and products to my friends.
2. I like helping people by providing them with information about many kinds of products.
3. People ask me for information about products, places to shop, or sales.
4. If someone asked where to get the best buy on several products, I could tell him or her where to shop.
5. My friends think of me as a good source of information when it comes to new products or sales.
6. Think about a person who has information about a variety of products and likes to share this information with others. This person knows about new products, sales, stores, and so on, but does not necessarily feel he or she is an expert on one particular product. How well would you say that this description fits you?

Source: Ronald E. Goldsmith, Leisa R. Flynn, and Elizabeth B. Goldsmith, "Innovation Consumers and Market Mavens," *Journal of Marketing Theory and Practice* 11 (Fall 2003): 58.

the situational environment of opinion leadership

Product-related discussions between two people do not take place in a vacuum. Two people are not likely to meet and spontaneously break into a discussion in which product-related information is sought or offered. Rather, product discussions generally occur within relevant situational contexts, such as when a specific product or a similar product is used or served or as an outgrowth of a more general discussion that touches on the product category. For example, while drinking coffee, one person might tell the other person about a preferred brand of coffee.

Moreover, it is not surprising that opinion leaders and opinion receivers often are friends, neighbors, or work associates, for existing friendships provide numerous opportunities for conversation concerning product-related topics. Close physical proximity is likely to increase the occurrences of product-related conversations. A local health club or community center, for example, or even the local supermarket, provides opportunities for neighbors to meet and engage in informal communications about products or services. In a similar fashion, the rapid growth in the use of the Internet is also creating a type of close "electronic proximity" or "communities"—one in which people of like minds, attitudes, concerns, backgrounds, and experiences are coming together in "chat sessions" to explore their common interests. Within this context, the Internet is a fertile environment for word-of-mouth communications of the kind that consumer marketers are interested in impacting.

the interpersonal flow of communication

A classic study of voting behavior concluded that ideas often flow from mass media (e.g., newspapers, magazines radio, TV) to opinion leaders and from them to the general public.[17] This so-called **two-step flow of communication theory** portrays opinion leaders as direct receivers of information from impersonal mass-media sources, who in turn, transmit (and interpret) this information to the masses. This theory views the opinion leader as an intermediary between the impersonal mass media and the majority of society. Figure 15.3 presents a model of the two-step flow of communication theory. Information is depicted as flowing in a single direction (or one way) from the mass media to opinion leaders (Step 1) and then from the opinion leaders (who interpret, legitimize, and transmit the information) to friends, neighbors, and acquaintances, who constitute the "masses" (Step 2).

Multistep flow of communication theory

A more comprehensive model of the interpersonal flow of communication depicts the transmission of information from the media as a multistep flow. The revised model takes into account the fact that information and influence often are two-way processes in which opinion leaders both influence and are influenced by opinion receivers. Figure 15.4 presents a model of the **multistep flow of communication theory**. Steps 1a and 1b depict the flow of information from the mass media simultaneously to opinion leaders, opinion receivers/seekers, and information receivers (who neither influence nor are influenced by

Two-Step Flow of Communication Theory

FIGURE 15.3

FIGURE 15.4

Multistep Flow of Communication Theory

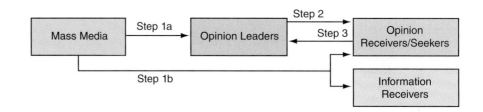

others). Step 2 shows the transmission of information and influence from opinion leaders to opinion receivers/seekers. Step 3 reflects the transfer of information and influence from opinion receivers to opinion leaders.

Advertising designed to stimulate/simulate word-of-mouth

In a world before the Internet, Weblogs, and viral or buzz marketing, firms' advertising and promotional programs largely relied on *stimulating or persuading consumers* to "tell your friends how much you like our product." This is one way in which marketers encourage consumer discussions of their products or services. For instance, Daffy's, an off-price retailer operating in several northeastern states (**www.daffys.com**), used an outdoor poster (at bus shelters and subway stations) to boldly state that "Friends don't let friends pay retail." Here the implication is that you should share your knowledge and experience with others. The objective of a promotional strategy of stimulation is to run advertisements or a direct-marketing program that is sufficiently interesting and informative to provoke consumers into discussing the benefits of the product with others.

In a classic study, a group of socially influential high school students (class presidents and sports captains) were asked to become members of a panel that would rate newly released musical recordings. As part of their responsibilities, panel participants were encouraged to discuss their record choices with friends. Preliminary examination suggested that these influentials would not qualify as opinion leaders for musical recordings because of their relatively meager ownership of the product category.[18] However, some of the records the group evaluated made the Top 10 charts in the cities in which the members of the group lived; these same recordings did not make the Top 10 charts in any other city. This study suggests that product-specific opinion leaders can be created by taking socially involved or influential people and deliberately increasing their enthusiasm for a product category.

A more recent research effort explored the notion of increasing enthusiasm for a product category. Over a 12-week period of time, half the participants were assigned to look at corporate Web sites (i.e., marketer-generated information sources), and half were asked to look at online discussions (e.g., chat rooms, forums). Consumers who got their information from online discussions reported greater interest in the product category. It is felt that chat rooms and other forums provide consumers with personal experiences and may offer greater credibility, trustworthiness, relevance, and empathy than marketer-generated Internet Web sites.[19]

Another related form of advertising message (much less common than ads designed to stimulate word-of-mouth) are ads designed to *simulate word-of-mouth* was from time-to-time used by a small number of marketing firms to supplement their regular advertising image or brand advertising. Ads designed to *simulate word-of-mouth* portrayed people in the act of informal communication.

Word-of-mouth may be uncontrollable

Although most marketing managers believe that word-of-mouth communication is extremely effective, one problem that they sometimes overlook is the fact that informal communication is difficult to control. Negative comments, frequently in the form of rumors that are untrue, can sweep through the marketplace to the detriment of a product.

Some common rumor themes that have plagued marketers in recent years and unfavorably influenced sales include the following: (1) The product was produced under unsanitary conditions, (2) the product contained an unwholesome or culturally unacceptable ingredient, (3) the product functioned as an undesirable depressant or stimulant, (4) the product included a cancer-causing element or agent, and (5) the firm was owned or influenced by an unfriendly or misguided foreign country, governmental agency, or religious cult.

A particularly challenging form of "negative" word-of-mouth can be generated today over the Internet, when a dissatisfied consumer decides to post his or her story on a bulletin board for all to see. Consider, for example, the Apple iPod. When two brothers in New York City found that a failed battery could not be easily or inexpensively replaced (Apple was charging $200 to replace the battery), they went online (**www.ipodsdirtysecret.com**). Consumers critical of Starbucks can vent their anger at **www.ihatestarbucks.com**, and people who dislike Microsoft can always log onto **www.watchingmicrosoft.com**. As one advertising industry executive has commented, "One determined detractor can do as much damage as 100,000 positive mentions can do good."[20]

marketers seek to take control of the opinion leadership process

Marketers have long been aware of the power that opinion leadership exerts on consumers' preferences and actual purchase behavior. For this reason marketers are increasingly designing products with characteristics or design factors that make them easy to talk about and whip up interest about. They are also looking at ways to more directly intervene and take control of the word-of-mouth process. This effort to control the flow of word-of-mouth about a product is not new. However, what is new is the degree of interest and available technologies that makes it easier to accomplish (e.g., consumers' buddy lists).

Marketers are now moving beyond primarily employing advertising to stimulate or simulate word-of-mouth, to an environment where they are seeking to manage (i.e., to create and control) word-of-mouth. In this section we will consider marketers' efforts to create products with greater word-of-mouth potential, and to harness the power of mouth by either hiring paid actors to go out and create product buzz; or securing the involvement of largely unpaid consumer volunteers, who act as buzz agents to drum up awareness, interest, and intention to purchase the clients' new products. As part of this discussion we will consider viral marketing and Weblogs.

Creating products with built-in buzz potential

New-product designers take advantage of the effectiveness of word-of-mouth communication by deliberately designing products to have word-of-mouth potential. A new product should give customers something to talk about ("buzz potential"). Examples of products and services that have had such word-of-mouth appeal include iPods, cell phones with digital cameras, and a host of other sought after technologies and luxury brands. Such high-demand products have attained market share advantages because consumers are willing to "sell" them to each other by means of word-of-mouth. Motion pictures also appear to be one form of entertainment in which word-of-mouth operates with some degree of regularity and a large degree of impact. It is very common to be involved directly or overhear people discussing which movies they liked and which movies they advise others to skip. Proof of the power of word-of-mouth are those cases in which critics hate a movie and the viewing public like it and tell their friends.

For instances in which informal word-of-mouth does not spontaneously emerge from the uniqueness of the product or its marketing strategy, some marketers have deliberately attempted to stimulate or to simulate opinion leadership.

Strategy designed to simulate buzz

The nature and scope of the Internet has inspired marketers to expand opportunities to take control of the process of word-of-mouth. For instance, they are increasingly hiring buzz marketing agencies that maintain large armies of largely volunteer consumer buzz agents who seem to greatly enjoy telling other consumers (often friends and family, and people on their buddy list) about a product that they have been exposed to and feel that they would like to talk about. An example of such a consulting agency is Bzzagent (see **www.bzzagent.com**). They assist their clients in creating word-of-mouth or buzz marketing campaigns. For instance, for chicken sausage producers and a publisher of mass-appeal books, Bzzagent agent assisted these clients to use their largely volunary bzzagents to talk about these products and to dramatically enhance their market success.[21]

Similarly, P&G has created a company known as Tremor (see the Web site at **www.tremor.com**) that specializes in the teen market and the market of their mothers. In contrast to Bzzagent, which does not screen their agents to ascertain that they would be good at stimulating interest, Tremor actually provides a series of screening tests and only selects those who meet their standards in terms of being likely to be an effective word-of-mouth communicator.

Some marketers prefer to hire actors to go out and simulate for a product. For instance, a campaign for Hennessy Cognac used paid actors to visit Manhattan bars and nightclubs and order Cognac martinis made with Hennessy. Although they were instructed to act as if they were ordering a new fad drink, in reality they were attempting to create a new fad drink.[22] The objective of a promotional strategy of stimulation is to run advertisements or a direct-marketing program that is sufficiently interesting and informative to provoke consumers into discussing the benefits of the product with others.

There has also been a tremendous growth in product placements over the past few years. For instance, reality shows like *The Apprentice* and *Survivor* have shown just how valuable product placements can be, and the amount spent on product placements reached a record $4.25 billion in 2005, a 23 percent increase over the prior year.[23]

Viral marketing

Also known as "buzz marketing," "wildfire marketing," "avalanche marketing," or any one of a dozen other names, *viral marketing* "describes any strategy that encourages individuals to pass on a marketing message to others, creating the potential for exponential growth in the message's exposure and influence."[24] Viral marketing is the marriage of e-mail and word-of-mouth. It is also named "viral" because it allows a message to spread like a virus. Consider HotMail, the first free Web e-mail service. By giving away free e-mail addresses and services, and by attaching a tag to the bottom of every message that reads "Get your private, free e-mail at **http://www.hotmail.com**," every time a HotMail user sent an e-mail, there was a good chance that the receiver of the e-mail would consider signing up for a free HotMail account. And with the expectation of more than 150 million Instant Messenger (IM) users, companies like ActiveBuddy create custom software applications to connect IM users to information that they want, while "mimicking, in a crude way, the banter of a fellow IM user at the other end of the data link."[25] Table 15.8 presents the demographic characteristics of adult Instant Messenger users.

Consider some other recent examples of viral marketing in action. M80 Interactive Marketing (a viral marketing firm) has its employees surf the Web to locate enthusiastic music fans who can be used to generate "buzz" about Britney Spears, one of the firm's clients. These fans may be asked, for example, to swamp MTV's request line demanding the star's latest hit. Beanie Babies, the VW Beetle, the movie *The Blair Witch Project,* and ICQ (an Internet chat service) were also able to generate word-of-mouth hype that

TABLE 15.8	A Profile of Adult Instant Messaging (IM) Users

Who uses instant messaging

The IM population is dominated by young adults and suburbanites. High percentages of minorities and those living in households with modest incomes also trade instant messages. The percentages in the right column do not at times add up to 100 because of rounding

	The percent of internet users in each group who are IM users (e.g. 42% of online men are IM users)	The proportion of the IM population each group makes up (e.g. 50% of all IM-ers are men)
Men	42%	50%
Women	42	50
Race/ethnicity		
Whites	41%	73%
Blacks	44	8
Hispanics	52	9
Other	40	10
Age		
Gen Y (ages 18–27)	62%	31%
Gen X (ages 28–39)	37	28
Trailing Boomers (ages 40–49)	33	20
Leading Boomers (ages 50–58)	29	12
Matures (ages 59–68)	25	7
After Work (age 69+)	29	3
Household income		
Less than $30,000	53%	31%
$30,000–$50,000	42	24
$50,000–$75,000	36	19
$75,000+	39	27
Educational attainment		
Did not graduate from HS	49%	8%
High school grad	44	31
Some college	48	32
College degree+	34	29
Community type		
Urban	45%	30%
Suburban	42	49
Rural	40	21
Type of internet connection at home		
Broadband	46%	41%
Dialup	39	59

Source: Eulynn Shiu and Amada Lenhart, "How Americans Use Instant Messaging," *Pew Internet & American Life Project*, September 1, 2004, accessed at **www.Pewinternet.org**.

resulted in explosive consumer demand. Volkswagen even sold 2,000 Reflex Yellow and Vapor Blue Beetles online, and *only* online. Vespa, the Italian motor scooter manufacturer, has its in-house agency hire models to hang out on scooters outside trendy nightclubs and cafes in Los Angeles.[26] Procter & Gamble is using viral marketing in a big way. The company has developed kiosks for shopping malls that present and sell new P&G products—all in the hope that shoppers will tell their friends what they have seen. And if shoppers purchase a product at the kiosk, they are invited to join an "Innovator's Club" that offers discounts, a Web site, and puts the shopper into the P&G database for future new product introductions.[27]

There appears to be two principal types of "buzz." *Uncodified buzz* occurs when an innovator encounters a new product, movie, etc., that he or she likes and passes on the information. While the level of trust and credibility that a consumer gives such communication, because it comes from a friend, is very high, this type of buzz is not something that is controllable by the firm, and could be either positive or negative. In contrast, *codified buzz* is something that is "incubated, fostered, and underwritten by the firm," and may take the form of trial versions, testimonials, observable usage, endorsements, gift certificates, hosted chat rooms, and so on. The firm should understand that the observability and the trialability of the viral marketing program for the new product (these two concepts will be fully discussed later in this chapter) are critical elements. For example, a money-back guarantee makes trialability a win-win undertaking for the consumers because it reduces the risk perceived with regard to making a purchase.[28]

One way in which the "buzz" can spread quickly is through the forwarding of e-mails. It is estimated that 90 percent of Internet users use e-mail, and about 50 percent of them use it daily. The term *Viral Maven* has been coined to refer to an individual who receives and sends pass-along e-mail frequently, as opposed to *Infrequent Senders*. One Viral Maven, for example, forwarded an e-mail about the band Nsync to 500 of her friends because it contained video messages from band members that were not available anywhere else.[29] Table 15.9 presents the motives for sending pass-along e-mail. Note how four of the six top-rated reasons deal with enjoyment and/or entertainment, and the other two concern social motivations. Recently, Nescafé Café con Leche (Nestle Argentina) recruited 50 of the drink's target consumers who were "big" e-mail forwarders and asked them to forward a spot for the product to at least 15 people each. In the month after the product's introduction, the spot and link were forwarded 100,000 times, and 15 to 20 percent of visitors to the site answered a four-question survey.[30]

To learn more about viral and buzz marketing check out the Web site of the Viral and Buzz Marketing Association, a group of marketing practitioners who desire to advance the art and science of word-of-mouth and to benefit and protect interests of consumers (**www.vbma.net**).

Weblogs as word-of-mouth

One of the newest mediums for disseminating word-of-mouth is the blog (short for Weblog), with over five million of these Web journals appearing on the Internet over the past few years. Recently, *Fortune Magazine* named the blog the number one tech trend, and estimated that 23,000 new Weblogs are created daily—both by consumers and by companies. Consider the power and impact of blogs on a company's products. Specifically, when a person posted information on a group discussion site that U-shaped Kryptonite bicycle locks could be picked with a Bic ballpoint pen, within a few days a number of blogs had videos demonstrating how this could be done. Four days after the original posting, Kryptonite issued a statement promising that their new line of bicycle locks would be tougher. But bloggers kept up the pressure, and shortly thereafter *The New York Times* and The Associated Press published articles about the problem. Over a ten-day period (see Figure 15.5) about 1.8 million people read postings about Kryptonite, and the company announced that it would offer free exchange for any affected lock. And anyone can create a blog. For example, you can just go to Google's Blogger.com or Spaces.MSN.com and create an account. If you're interested if anyone is reading your blog, you can register with a service like Feedburner to see how many hits you're getting.[31]

TABLE 15.9	Motives for Sending Pass-Along E-mail

Item

Because it's fun

Because I enjoy it

Because it's entertaining

To help others

To have a good time

To let others know I care about their feelings

To thank them

To get away from what I'm doing

Because it peps me up

To show others encouragement

Because it allows me to unwind

Because it's exciting

Because it relaxes me

Because it's stimulating

To get something I don't have

To get away from pressures

Because it's a pleasant rest

Because I'm concerned about them

Because it makes me feel less tense

To put off something I should be doing

Because I have nothing better to do

Because it's reassuring to know someone's there

Because I want someone to do something for me

Because it's thrilling

To tell others what to do

Because I just need to talk

Because I need someone to talk to

Because it makes me feel less lonely

Source: Joseph E. Phelps, Regina Lewis, Lynne Mobilio, David Perry, and Niranjan Raman, "Viral Marketing or Electronic Word-of-Mouth Advertising: Examining Consumer Responses and Motivations to Pass Along Email," *Journal of Advertising Research*, December 2004, 343.

Participants were asked to indicate the importance of 28 reasons for communicating with others via pass-along e-mail. Listed in descending order of importance.

diffusion of innovations

The second part of this chapter examines a major issue in marketing and consumer behavior—the acceptance of new products and services. The framework for exploring consumer acceptance of new products is drawn from the area of research known as the **diffusion of innovations**. Consumer researchers who specialize in the diffusion of innovations are primarily interested in understanding two closely related processes: the **diffusion process** and the **adoption process**. In the broadest sense, diffusion is a macro process concerned with the spread of a new product (an innovation) from its source to the consuming public. In contrast, adoption is a micro process that focuses on the stages through which an individual consumer passes when deciding to accept or reject a new

FIGURE 15.5

Kryptonite's Blogstorm How Ten Days of Internet Chatter Crippled a Company's Reputation

Source: David Kirkpatrick and Daniel Roth, "Why There's No Escaping the BLOG," *Fortune*, January 10, 2005, 48.

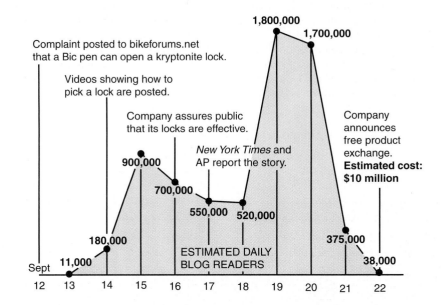

product. In addition to an examination of these two interrelated processes, we present a profile of **consumer innovators**, those who are the first to purchase a new product. The ability of marketers to identify and reach this important group of consumers plays a major role in the success or failure of new-product introductions.

And why are new-product introductions so important? Consider General Motors' OnStar system, which is in widespread use today. When it was first introduced, it was a dealer-installed option that required consumers to obtain their own cellular accounts. When dealers informed GM that this procedure was overly cumbersome and was limiting sales, General Motors made a deal with a cellular telephone company, which allowed OnStar to be packaged as a factory-installed fully functioning communications device. GM was also told by consumers that they did not need the detailed diagnostic engine reports that the system was providing—they only needed to know the difference between a problem that required immediate emergency attention and one that could wait for a routine service appointment.[32] These changes to the original GM version of OnStar undoubtedly increased its popularity with GM vehicle purchasers.

the diffusion process

The diffusion process is concerned with how innovations spread, that is, how they are assimilated within a market. More precisely, diffusion is the process by which the acceptance of an innovation (a new product, new service, new idea, or new practice) is spread by communication (mass media, salespeople, or informal conversations) to members of a social system (a target market) over a period of time. This definition includes the four basic elements of the diffusion process: (1) the innovation, (2) the channels of communication, (3) the social system, and (4) time.

The innovation

No universally accepted definition of the terms product **innovation** or *new product* exists. Instead, various approaches have been taken to define a new product or a new service; these can be classified as *firm-, product-, market-,* and *consumer-oriented definitions of innovations*.

Firm-oriented definitions

A *firm-oriented* approach treats the newness of a product from the perspective of the company producing or marketing it. When the product is "new" to the company, it is considered new. This definition ignores whether or not the product is actually new to the marketplace (i.e., to competitors or consumers). Consistent with this view, copies or modifications of a competitor's product would qualify as new. Although this definition has considerable merit when the objective is to examine the impact that a "new" product has on the firm, it is not very useful when the goal is to understand consumer acceptance of a new product.

Product-oriented definitions

In contrast to firm-oriented definitions, a *product-oriented* approach focuses on the features inherent in the product itself and on the effects these features are likely to have on consumers' established usage patterns. One product-oriented framework considers the extent to which a new product is likely to disrupt established behavior patterns. It defines the following three types of product innovations:[33]

1. *A* **continuous innovation** *has the least disruptive influence on established patterns. It involves the introduction of a modified product rather than a totally new product. Examples include the redesigned BMW 3-Series, the latest version of Microsoft Windows, reduced-fat Vienna Finger cookies, Hershey dark chocolate Kisses, American Express Travel Checque Card, and Band-Aid Tough Strips (see Figure 15.6).*

2. *A* **dynamically continuous innovation** *is somewhat more disruptive than a continuous innovation but still does not alter established behavior patterns. It may involve the creation of a new product or the modification of an existing product. Examples include digital cameras, digital video recorders, MP3 players, tablet PCs, USB flash drives, and disposable diapers.*

3. *A* **discontinuous innovation** *requires consumers to adopt new behavior patterns. Examples include airplanes, radios, TVs, automobiles, fax machines, PCs, videocassette recorders, medical self-test kits, and the Internet.*

Figure 15.7 shows how the telephone, a discontinuous innovation of major magnitude, has produced a variety of both dynamically continuous and continuous innovations and has even stimulated the development of other discontinuous innovations.

Market-oriented definitions

A *market-oriented* approach judges the newness of a product in terms of how much exposure consumers have to the new product. Two market-oriented definitions of product innovation have been used extensively in consumer studies:

1. *A product is considered new if it has been purchased by a relatively small (fixed) percentage of the potential market.*

2. *A product is considered new if it has been on the market for a relatively short (specified) period of time.*

Both of these market-oriented definitions are basically subjective because they leave the researcher with the task of establishing the degree of sales penetration within the market that qualifies the product as an "innovation" (such as the first 5 percent of the potential market to use the new product) or how long the product can be on the market and still be considered "new" (i.e., the first three months that the product is available).

Consumer-oriented definitions

Although each of the three approaches described have been useful to consumer researchers in their study of the diffusion of innovations, some researchers have favored a *consumer-oriented* approach in defining an innovation.[34] In this context, a "new" product is any product that a potential consumer judges to be new. In other words, newness is based on the consumer's perception of the product rather than on physical features or market

FIGURE 15.6

Source: © Johnson & Johnson.
Used with permission.

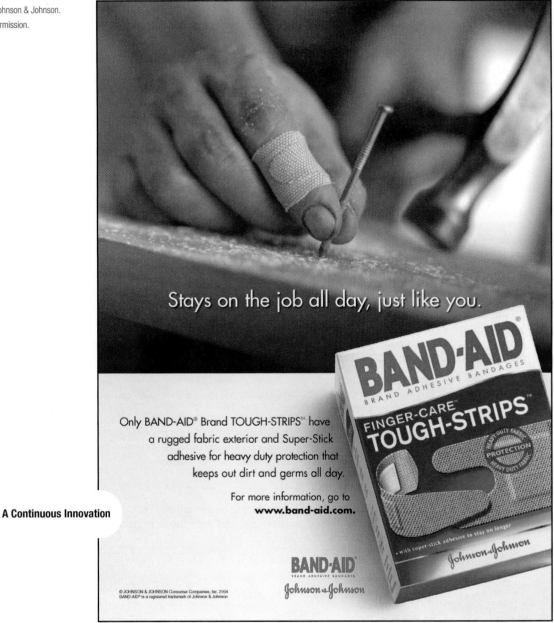

A Continuous Innovation

realities. Although the consumer-oriented approach has been endorsed by some advertising and marketing practitioners, it has received little systematic research attention.

Additionally, it should be pointed out that although this portion of the chapter deals primarily with what might be described as "purchase" innovativeness (or time of adoption), a second type of innovativeness, "use innovativeness," has been the subject of some thought and research. A consumer is being *use innovative* when he or she uses a previously adopted product in a novel or unusual way. In one study that dealt with the adoption of VCRs and PCs, early adopters showed significantly higher use innovativeness than those who adopted somewhat later along the cycle of acceptance of the innovation.[35]

FIGURE 15.7

The Telephone Has Led to Related Innovations

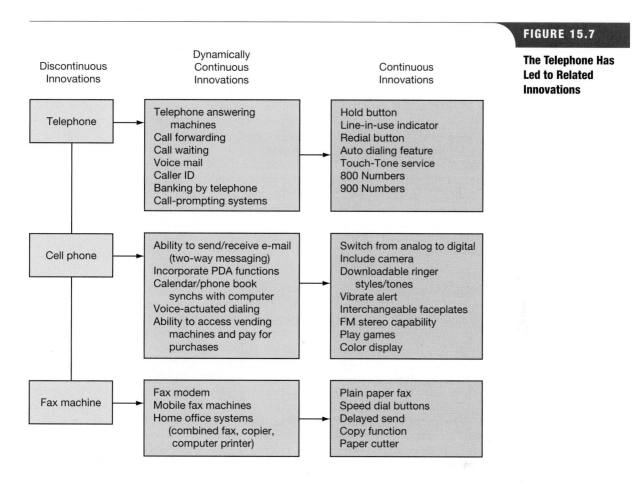

Product characteristics that influence diffusion

All products that are new do not have equal potential for consumer acceptance. Some products seem to catch on almost overnight (cordless telephones), whereas others take a very long time to gain acceptance or never seem to achieve widespread consumer acceptance (trash compactors).

The uncertainties of product marketing would be reduced if marketers could anticipate how consumers will react to their products. For example, if a marketer knew that a product contained inherent features that were likely to inhibit its acceptance, the marketer could develop a promotional strategy that would compensate for these features or decide not to market the product at all. Pickups trucks are now being designed for the female driver, and manufacturers are careful to design door handles that do not break nails. Ford even offers adjustable gas and brake pedals.[36]

Although there are no precise formulas by which marketers can evaluate a new product's likely acceptance, diffusion researchers have identified five product characteristics that seem to influence consumer acceptance of new products: (1) relative advantage, (2) compatibility, (3) complexity, (4) trialability, and (5) observability.[37] Based on available research, it has been estimated that these five product characteristics account for much of the dynamic nature of the rate or speed of adoption.[38]

Relative Advantage   The degree to which potential customers perceive a new product as superior to existing substitutes is its *relative advantage*. For example, although many people carry beepers so that their business offices or families can contact them, a cellular telephone enables users to be in nearly instant communication with the world and allows users to both receive and place calls. The fax machine is another example of an innovation that offers users a significant relative advantage in terms of their ability to communicate. A document can be transmitted in as little as 15 to 18 seconds at perhaps one-tenth the cost of an overnight express service, which will not deliver the document until the following day.

Compatibility   The degree to which potential consumers feel a new product is consistent with their present needs, values, and practices is a measure of its *compatibility*. For instance, an advantage of 3M's Scotch™ Pop-up Tape Strips is that they are easier to use than roll-tape for certain tasks (such as wrapping gifts), yet they represent no new learning for the user. Similarly, in the realm of shaving products, it is not too difficult to imagine that a few years ago when Gillette introduced the MACH3 razor, some men made the transition from inexpensive disposable razors and other men shifted from competitive nondisposable razors (including Gillette's own Sensor razors). This new product is fully compatible with the established wet-shaving rituals of many men. However, it is difficult to imagine male shavers shifting to a new depilatory cream designed to remove facial hair. Although potentially simpler to use, a cream would be basically *incompatible* with most men's current values regarding daily shaving practices.

Complexity   *Complexity*, the degree to which a new product is difficult to understand or use, affects product acceptance. Clearly, the easier it is to understand and use a product, the more likely it is to be accepted. For example, the acceptance of such convenience foods as frozen french fries, instant puddings, and microwave dinners is generally due to their ease of preparation and use. Interestingly, although VCRs can be found in most American homes, millions of adults still need help from their children in programming the machine to record a particular television program. The introduction, awhile ago, of VCR Plus+ and TV have helped a little to reduce the ongoing challenge to easily use a VCR to record a TV program.

The issue of complexity is especially important when attempting to gain market acceptance for high-tech consumer products. Four predominant types of "technological fear" act as barriers to new product acceptance: (1) fear of technical complexity, (2) fear of rapid obsolescence, (3) fear of social rejection, and (4) fear of physical harm. Of the four, *technological complexity* was the most widespread concern of consumer innovators.[39]

Trialability   *Trialability* refers to the degree to which a new product is capable of being tried on a limited basis. The greater the opportunity to try a new product, the easier it is for consumers to evaluate it and ultimately adopt it. In general, frequently purchased household products tend to have qualities that make trial relatively easy, such as the ability to purchase a small or "trial" size. Because a computer program cannot be packaged in a smaller size, many computer software companies offer free working models of their latest software to encourage computer users to try the program and subsequently buy the program.

Aware of the importance of trial, marketers of new supermarket products commonly use substantial cents-off coupons or free samples to provide consumers with direct product experience. On the other hand, durable items, such as refrigerators or ovens, are difficult to try without making a major commitment. This may explain why publications such as *Consumer Reports* are so widely consulted for their ratings of infrequently purchased durable goods.

Observability   *Observability* (or communicability) is the ease with which a product's benefits or attributes can be observed, imagined, or described to potential consumers. Products that have a high degree of social visibility, such as fashion items, are more easily diffused than products that are used in private, such as a new type of deodorant. Similarly, a tangible product is promoted more easily than an intangible product (such as a service).

It is also important to recognize that a particular innovation may diffuse differently throughout different cultures. For example, although shelf-stable milk (milk that does not require refrigeration) has been successfully sold for years in Europe, Americans thus far have resisted the aseptic milk package. Table 15.10 summarizes the product characteristics that influence diffusion.

TABLE 15.10	Product Characteristics That Influence Diffusion	
CHARACTERISTICS	**DEFINITION**	**EXAMPLES**
Relative Advantage	The degree to which potential customers perceive a new product as superior to existing substitutes	HDTV over standard TV, MP3 player over a traditional CD player
Compatibility	The degree to which potential consumers feel a new product is consistent with their present needs, values, and practices	Gillette MACH3 Turbo over disposable razors, digital alarm clocks over analog alarm clocks
Complexity	The degree to which a new product is difficult to understand or use	Products low in complexity include hot and cold cereals, disposable razors, and soap
Trialability	The degree to which a new product is capable of being tried on a limited basis	Trial-size jars and bottles of new products, free trials of software, free samples, cents-off coupons
Observability	The degree to which a product's benefits or attributes can be observed, imagined, or described to potential customers	Clothing, such as Ralph Lauren jeans, sneakers, laptops, messenger bags

Resistance to innovation

What makes some new products almost instant successes, while others must struggle to achieve consumer acceptance? To help answer such a question, marketers look at the product characteristics of an innovation. Such characteristics offer clues to help determine the extent of consumer resistance, which increases when perceived relative advantage, perceived compatibility, trialability, and communicability are low, and perceived complexity is high. The term *innovation overload* is used to describe the situation in which the increase in information and options available to the consumer is so great that it seriously impairs decision making. As a result, the consumer finds it difficult to make comparisons among the available choices. In a world in which consumers often find themselves with too little time and too much stress, increased complexity of products wastes time and may reduce or eliminate acceptance of the product.

The channels of communication

How quickly an innovation spreads through a market depends to a great extent on communications between the marketer and consumers, as well as communication among consumers (word-of-mouth communication). Of central concern is the uncovering of the relative influence of impersonal sources (advertising and editorial matter) and interpersonal sources (salespeople and informal opinion leaders). Over the past decade or so, we have also seen the rapid increase of the Internet as a major consumer-related source of information. The Internet is particularly interesting since it can on the one hand be seen as an interpersonal source of information (e.g., with its Internet ads, e-commerce Web sites that function like a direct-mail category, and the introduction and growth of Webpods). In contrast, the Internet can concurrently be seen as a highly personal and interpersonal source of information. In this second context, the Internet consumers have an incredible number of company- and noncompany-sponsored forums and discussion groups to chat away with people who have expertise and experience that is vital to making an informed decision.

Still further, in recent years, a variety of new channels of communication have been developed to inform consumers of innovative products and services. Consider the growth of interactive marketing messages, in which the consumer becomes an important part of the communication rather than just a "passive" message recipient. For example, for the past several years, an increasing number of companies, such as the Ford Motor Company, General Motors, and other major automobile manufactures, have used CD-ROMs to promote their products.

As of this writing, perhaps the newest and rapidly growing medium for word-of-mouth is the podcast, which some consumers are seeking out as alternatives to TV, radio, and print. It has been estimated that there are now thousands of podcasts available on the Internet, which the consumer can download as an audio file (e.g., computer, MP3 player). For example, the *Harvard Business Review* is available in audio format as a podcast.[40]

The social system

The diffusion of a new product usually takes place in a social setting frequently referred to as a *social system.* In the context of consumer behavior, the terms *market segment* and target market may be more relevant than the term *social system* used in diffusion research. A social system is a physical, social, or cultural environment to which people belong and within which they function. For example, for a new hybrid-seed corn, the social system might consist of all farmers in a number of local communities. For a new drug, the social system might consist of all physicians within a specific medical specialty (e.g., all neurologists). For a new special diet product, the social system might include all residents of a geriatric community. As these examples indicate, the social system serves as the *boundary* within which the diffusion of a new product is examined.

The orientation of a social system, with its own special values or norms, is likely to influence the acceptance or rejection of new products. When a social system is modern in orientation, the acceptance of innovations is likely to be high. In contrast, when a social system is traditional in orientation, innovations that are perceived as radical or as infringements on established customs are likely to be avoided. According to one authority, the following characteristics typify a *modern social system:* [41]

- *A positive attitude toward change*
- *An advanced technology and skilled labor force*
- *A general respect for education and science*
- *An emphasis on rational and ordered social relationships rather than on emotional ones*
- *An outreach perspective, in which members of the system frequently interact with outsiders, thus facilitating the entrance of new ideas into the social system*
- *A system in which members can readily see themselves in quite different roles*

Furthermore, a social system (either modern or traditional) may be national in scope and may influence members of an entire society or may exist at the local level and influence only those who live in a specific community. The key point to remember is that a social system's orientation is the climate in which marketers must operate to gain acceptance for their new products. For example, in recent years, the United States has experienced a decline in the demand for beef, from just under 80 pounds per person in 1970 to a little over 60 pounds per person in the first few years of this century.[42] The growing interest in health and fitness throughout the nation has created a climate in which beef is considered too high in fat and in caloric content. At the same time, the consumption of chicken and fish has increased because these foods satisfy the prevailing nutritional values of a great number of consumers.

Time

Time is the backbone of the diffusion process. It pervades the study of diffusion in three distinct but interrelated ways: (1) the *amount of purchase time,* (2) the identification of *adopter categories,* and (3) the *rate of adoption.*

Purchase time

Purchase time refers to the amount of time that elapses between consumers' initial awareness of a new product or service and the point at which they purchase or reject it. Table 15.11 illustrates the scope of purchase time by tracking a hypothetical professor's purchase of a new PC for his home.

Table 15.11 illustrates not only the length and complexity of consumer decision making but also how different information sources become important at successive steps

TABLE 15.11	Time Line for Selecting a Computer
WEEK	**PRECIPITATING SITUATIONS/FACTORS**
0	Richard is a college professor, who, in addition to teaching, is also a marketing researcher. He uses his home computer to create PowerPoint presentations for use in class, to tabulate and analyze marketing research survey data, to create marketing research reports, to search the Internet for information, and to communicate (via e-mail) with both students, clients, and friends. His current computer is almost 5 years old, and at times can be a bit slow, especially compared to the new, state-of-the-art computer that was recently installed in his college office.
	DECISION PROCESS BEGINS
1–2	Richard visits a number of computer stores and talks to salespeople about the pros and cons of various computer brands and models. He also visits several dozen Web sites where he reads both the specifications of different computers and a number of computer model reviews.
3–7	The transmission in the family's 5-year-old SUV breaks and has to be replaced. Because of the expense involved, Richard puts the notion of buying a new computer on "hold" for a while.
	INTEREST IS RETRIGGERED
8	As July is drawing to a close and with the start of the new fall semester only a month away, Richard again starts thinking about buying a new computer, in order to have it set up in his home, with his software installed, before the beginning of the new semester.
	CONSUMER ACQUIRES A MENTOR (OPINION LEADER)
9	Richard asks one of his colleagues at the college, a fellow teacher who knows a great deal about computers, to serve as his mentor (opinion leader) with respect to PCs, and he agrees.
	FEATURES AND BRAND OPTIONS ARE REVIEWED
10–11	With the advice of the mentor, Richard narrows down his choice to one Sony Vaio model, one Hewlett Packard model, and one Dell model. While he knows that he wants a 19-inch LCD display, he is unsure about how much memory he really needs, and whether a DVD burner is really necessary.
12–13	Richard revisits several computer stores to look at the Sony and HP models of interest, and spends time on the Dell Web site reading about the numerous ways that this brand of PC can be configured.
14	After his mentor tells him to check the **www.gotapex.com** Web site daily, he discovers one morning that the site is offering a Dell coupon worth $400. So the Dell PC that he was considering, which was going to cost $1,200, now will cost only $800.
	ORDERING THE COMPUTER
	Richard calls his mentor and tells him about the coupon, and his mentor replies "It's a great deal— take it!" So Richard accesses the Dell Web site, orders the computer (which includes free shipping), and five days later, via UPS delivery, the computer arrives at his front door. He unpacks it, follows the color-coded directions for setting it up, and turns it on. Everything works perfectly, and he spends the next day installing his software, his files, and his broadband Internet connection. By the time the new semester begins, Richard has a computer that is up-and-running and is several times faster than his old one.

in the process. Purchase time is an important concept because the average time a consumer takes to adopt a new product is sometimes a useful predictor of the overall length of time it will take for the new product to achieve widespread adoption. For example, when the individual purchase time is short, a marketer can expect that the overall rate of diffusion will be faster than when the individual purchase time is long.

Adopter categories

The concept of **adopter categories** involves a classification scheme that indicates where a consumer stands in relation to other consumers in terms of time (or when the consumer adopts a new product). Five adopter categories are frequently cited in the diffusion literature: *innovators, early adopters, early majority, late majority,* and *laggards.* Table 15.12 describes each of these adopter categories and estimates their relative proportions within the total population that eventually adopts the new product. It should also be mentioned that the person first to buy an innovation is often an individual who serves as a bridge to other networks, an opinion broker between groups, rather than within groups.[43]

TABLE 15.12	**Adopter Categories**	
ADOPTER CATEGORY	**DESCRIPTION**	**RELATIVE PERCENTAGE WITHIN THE POPULATION THAT EVENTUALLY ADOPTS**
Innovators	*Venturesome*—very eager to try new ideas; acceptable if risk is daring; more cosmopolite social relationships; communicate with other innovators	2.5%
Early Adopters	*Respect*—more integrated into the local social system; the persons to check with before adopting a new idea; category contains greatest number of opinion leaders; are role models	13.5
Early Majority	*Deliberate*—adopt new ideas just prior to the average time; seldom hold leadership positions; deliberate for some time before adopting	34.0
Late Majority	*Skeptical*—adopt new ideas just after the average time; adopting may be both an economic necessity and a reaction to peer pressures; innovations approached cautiously	34.0
Laggards	*Traditional*—the last people to adopt an innovation; most "localite" in outlook; oriented to the past; suspicious of the new	16.0
		100.0%

Source: Adapted/Reprinted with the permission of The Free Press, a division of Simon & Schuster, from *Diffusion of Innovations,* 3rd edition, by Everett M. Rogers. Copyright © 1995 by Everett M. Rogers. Copyright © 1962, 1971, 1983 by The Free Press.

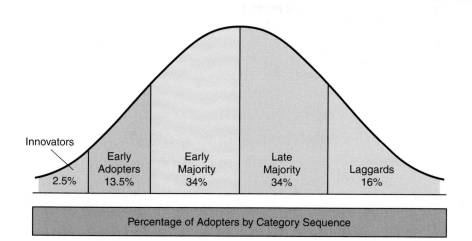

FIGURE 15.8

The Sequence and Proportion of Adopter Categories Among the Population That Eventually Adopts

Source: Adapted/Reprinted with the permission of The Free Press, a division of Simon & Schuster, from *Diffusion of Innovations,* 3rd edition, by Everett M. Rogers. Copyright © 1995 by Everett M. Rogers. Copyright © 1962, 1971, 1983 by The Free Press.

As Figure 15.8 indicates, the adopter categories are generally depicted as taking on the characteristics of a normal distribution (a bell-shaped curve) that describes the total population that ultimately adopts a product. Some argue that the bell curve is an erroneous depiction because it may lead to the inaccurate conclusion that 100 percent of the members of the social system under study (the target market) eventually will accept the product innovation. This assumption is not in keeping with marketers' experiences, because very few, if any, products fit the precise needs of all potential consumers. For example, all renters/purchasers of movies who have in the past rented video cassettes could theoretically be expected to use (or try) DVDs. In fact, it is unrealistic for the movie rental/sales industry to expect all prerecorded movie renters/purchasers to switch to DVD. For this reason, it is appropriate to add an additional category, that of *nonadopters.* The "nonadopter" category is in accord with marketplace reality—that *not* all potential consumers adopt a particular product or service innovation. For example, 28 percent of U.S. adults do not own a cell phone.[44]

Instead of the classic five-category adopter scheme, many consumer researchers have used other classification schemes, most of which consist of two or three categories that compare *innovators* or *early triers* with *later triers* or nontriers. As we will see, this focus on the innovator or early trier has produced several important generalizations that have practical significance for marketers planning the introduction of new products.

Rate of adoption

The rate of adoption is concerned with how long it takes a new product or service to be adopted by members of a social system, that is, how quickly it takes a new product to be accepted by those who will ultimately adopt it. The general view is that the rate of adoption for new products is getting faster or shorter. Fashion adoption is a form of diffusion, one in which the rate of adoption is important. Cyclical fashion trends or "fads" are extremely "fast," whereas "fashion classics" may have extremely slow or "long" cycles.

In general, the diffusion of products worldwide is becoming a more rapid phenomenon. For example, it took black-and-white TVs about 12 years longer to reach the same level of penetration in Europe and Japan as in the United States. For color TVs, the lag time dropped to about five years for Japan and several more years for Europe. In contrast, for VCRs there was only a three- or four-year spread, with the United States (with its emphasis on cable TV) lagging behind Europe and Japan. Finally, for compact disk players, penetration levels in all three countries were about even after only three years.[45] Table 15.13 presents the time required for a sample of electronic products to penetrate 10 percent of the mass market in the United Kingdom.

TABLE 15.13	Time Required for Electronic Products to Penetrate 10 Percent of the Mass Market in the United Kingdom

PRODUCT	NUMBER OF YEARS
Pager	41
Telephone	38
Cable television	25
Fax machine	22
VCR	9
Cellular phone	9
Personal computer	7
CD-ROM*	6
Wireless data service*	6
Screen-phone*	6
Interactive television*	3

*Predicted.
Source: Eric Chi-Chung Shiu and John A. Dawson, "Cross-National Consumer Segmentation of Internet Shopping for Britain and Taiwan," *The Service Industries Journal (London),* 22, January 2002, 163. Reprinted by permission.

The objective in marketing new products is usually to gain wide acceptance of the product as quickly as possible. Marketers desire a rapid rate of product adoption to penetrate the market and quickly establish market leadership (obtain the largest share of the market) before competition takes hold. A *penetration policy* is usually accompanied by a relatively low introductory price designed to discourage competition from entering the market. Rapid product adoption also demonstrates to marketing intermediaries (wholesalers and retailers) that the product is worthy of their full and continued support.

Under certain circumstances, marketers might prefer to avoid a rapid rate of adoption for a new product. For example, marketers who wish to use a pricing strategy that will enable them to recoup their development costs quickly might follow a *skimming policy:* They first make the product available at a very high price to consumers who are willing to pay top dollar and then gradually lower the price in a stepwise fashion to attract additional market segments at each price reduction plateau. For example, when 17-inch computer monitors (not flat-screen LCD panels) were first introduced, they sold for more than $700. Today they can be purchased for $100 or less.

In addition to how long it takes from introduction to the point of adoption (or when the purchase actually occurs), it is useful to track the extent of adoption (the diffusion rate). For instance, a particular corporation might not upgrade its employees' computer systems to the Windows XP environment until after many other companies in the area have already begun to do so. However, once it decides to upgrade, it might install Windows XP software in a relatively short period of time on all of its employees' PCs. Thus, although the company was relatively "late" with respect to *time* of adoption, its *extent* of adoption was very high.

Although sales graphs depicting the adoption categories (again, see Figure 15.8) are typically thought of as having a normal distribution in which sales continue to increase prior to reaching a peak (at the top of the curve), some research evidence indicates that a third to a half of such sales curves, at least in the consumer electronics industry, involve an initial peak, a trough, and then another sales increase. Such a "saddle" in the sales curve has been attributed to the early market adopters and the main market adopters being two separate markets.[46] Figure 15.9 presents two examples of sales curves with saddles—PCs and VCR decks with stereo.

FIGURE 15.9

**"Sales Saddle"
Differentiates Early
Market Adopters
from the Main
Market Adopters**

Source: Jacob Goldenberg,
Barak Libai, and Eitan Muller,
"Riding the Saddle: How Cross-
Market Communications Can
Create a Major Slump in Sales,"
Journal of Marketing 66
(April 2002): 5.

A: Saddle in PCs

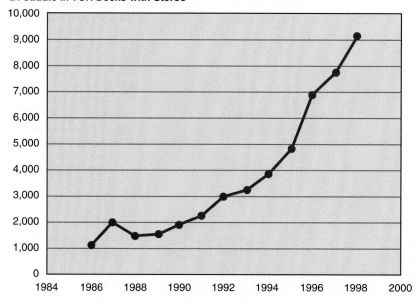

B: Saddle in VCR Decks with Stereo

the adoption process

The second major process in the diffusion of innovations is *adoption*. The focus of this process is the stages through which an individual consumer passes while arriving at a decision to try or not to try, or to continue using or to discontinue using a new product. (The *adoption process* should not be confused with *adopter categories.*)

Stages in the adoption process

It is often assumed that the consumer moves through five stages in arriving at a decision to purchase or reject a new product: (1) awareness, (2) interest, (3) evaluation, (4) trial, and (5) adoption (or rejection). The assumption underlying the adoption process is that consumers engage in extensive information search (see Chapter 7), whereas consumer involvement theory suggests that for some products, a limited information search is more likely (for low-involvement products). The five **stages in the adoption process** are described in Table 15.14.

TABLE 15.14	**The Stages in the Adoption Process**	

NAME OF STAGE	WHAT HAPPENS DURING THIS STAGE	EXAMPLE
Awareness	Consumer is first exposed to the product innovation.	Eric sees an ad for a 23-inch thin LCD HDTV in a magazine he is reading.
Interest	Consumer is interested in the product and searches for additional information.	Eric reads about the HDTV set on the manufacturer's Web site and then goes to an electronics store near his apartment and has a salesperson show him the unit.
Evaluation	Consumer decides whether or not to believe that this product or service will satisfy the need—a kind of "mental trial."	After talking to a knowledgeable friend, Eric decides that this TV will fit nicely on top of the chest in his bedroom. He also calls his cable company and finds out that he can exchange his "standard" TV cable box for an HDTV cable box at no cost and no additional monthly fee.
Trial	Consumer uses the product on a limited basis.	Since an HDTV set cannot be "tried" like a small tube of toothpaste, Eric buys the TV at his local electronics store on his way home from work. The store offers a 14-day (from the date of purchase) full refund policy.
Adoption (Rejection)	If trial is favorable, consumer decides to use the product on a full rather than a limited basis—if unfavorable, the consumer decides to reject it.	Eric loves his new HDTV set and expects many years of service from it.

Although the traditional adoption process model is insightful in its simplicity, it does not adequately reflect the full complexity of the consumer adoption process. For one, it does not adequately acknowledge that there is quite often a need or problem-recognition stage that consumers face before acquiring an awareness of potential options or solutions (a need recognition preceding the awareness stage). Moreover, the adoption process does not adequately provide for the possibility of evaluation and rejection of a new product or service after each stage, especially after trial (i.e., a consumer may reject the product after trial or never use the product on a continuous basis). Finally, it does not explicitly include postadoption or postpurchase evaluation, which can lead to a strengthened commitment or to a decision to discontinue use. Figure 15.10 presents an enhanced representation of the adoption process model, one that includes the additional dimensions or actions described here.

The adoption of some products and services may have minimal consequences, whereas the adoption of other innovations may lead to major behavioral and lifestyle changes. Examples of innovations with such major impact on society include the automobile, the telephone, the electric refrigerator, the television, the airplane, the personal computer, and the Internet.

FIGURE 15.10

**An Enhanced
Adoption Process
Model**

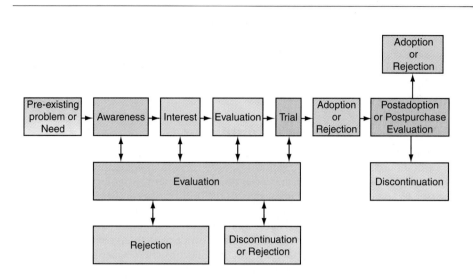

The adoption process and information sources

The adoption process provides a framework for determining which types of information sources consumers find most important at specific decision stages. For example, early purchasers of USB storage devices or keys (often used to back up or store computer files) might first become aware of the products via mass-media sources (e.g., *PC Magazine* or Internet sites like **www.news.com**). Then these early or innovative consumers' final pretrial information might be an outcome of informal discussions with personal sources (e.g., other innovators at a technology forum or chat room). The key point is that impersonal mass-media sources tend to be most valuable for creating initial product awareness; as the purchase decision progresses, however, the relative importance of these sources declines while the relative importance of interpersonal sources (friends, salespeople, and others) increases. Figure 15.11 depicts this relationship.

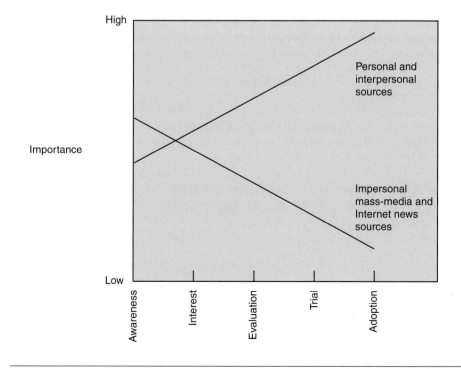

**The Relative
Importance of
Different Types of
Information Sources
in the Adoption
Process**

FIGURE 15.11

a profile of the consumer innovator

Who is the consumer innovator? What characteristics set the innovator apart from later adopters and from those who never purchase? How can the marketer reach and influence the innovator? These are key questions for the marketing practitioner about to introduce a new product or service.

Defining the consumer innovator

Consumer innovators can be defined as the relatively small group of consumers who are the earliest purchasers of a new product. The problem with this definition, however, concerns the concept of *earliest,* which is, after all, a relative term. Sociologists have treated this issue by sometimes defining innovators as the first 2.5 percent of the social system to adopt an innovation. In many marketing diffusion studies, however, the definition of the consumer innovator has been derived from the status of the new product under investigation. For example, if researchers define a new product as an innovation for the first three months of its availability, then they define the consumers who purchase it during this period as "innovators." Other researchers have defined innovators in terms of their *innovativeness,* that is, their purchase of some minimum number of new products from a selected group of new products. For instance, in the adoption of new fashion items, innovators can be defined as those consumers who purchase more than one fashion product from a group of 10 new fashion products. Noninnovators would be defined as those who purchase none or only one of the new fashion products. In other instances, researchers have defined innovators as those falling within an arbitrary proportion of the total market (e.g., the first 10 percent of the population in a specified geographic area to buy the new product).

Interest in the product category

Not surprisingly, consumer innovators are much more interested than either later adopters or nonadopters in the product categories that they are among the first to purchase. If what is known from diffusion theory holds true in the future, the earliest purchasers of small electric automobiles are likely to have substantially greater interest in automobiles (they will enjoy looking at automotive magazines and will be interested in the performance and functioning of automobiles) than those who purchased conventional small cars during the same period or those who purchased small electric cars during a later period. Also, early adopters of products containing a nonfat synthetic cooking oil (i.e., olestra) were found to have a high interest in such a product because of health and diet concerns.

Consumer innovators are more likely than noninnovators to seek information concerning their specific interests from a variety of informal and mass-media sources. They are more likely to give greater deliberation to the purchase of new products or services in their areas of interest than noninnovators.

The innovator is an opinion leader

When discussing the characteristics of the opinion leader earlier in this chapter, we indicated a strong tendency for consumer opinion leaders to be innovators. In the present context, an impressive amount of research on the diffusion of innovations has found that consumer innovators provide other consumers with information and advice about new products and that those who receive such advice frequently follow it. Thus, in the role of opinion leader, the consumer innovator often influences the acceptance or rejection of new products.

When innovators are enthusiastic about a new product and encourage others to try it, the product is likely to receive broader and quicker acceptance. When consumer innovators are dissatisfied with a new product and discourage others from trying it, its acceptance will be severely limited, and it may die a quick death. For products that do not generate much excitement (either positive or negative), consumer innovators may not be sufficiently motivated to provide advice. In such cases, the marketer must rely almost entirely on mass media and personal selling to influence future purchasers; the absence of informal influence is also likely to result in a somewhat slower rate of acceptance (or rejection) of the new product. Because motivated consumer innovators can influence the rate of acceptance or rejection of a new product, they influence its eventual success or failure.

Personality traits

In Chapter 5, we examined the personality traits that distinguish the consumer innovator from the noninnovator. In this section, we will briefly highlight what researchers have learned about the personality of the consumer innovator.

First, consumer innovators generally are *less dogmatic* than noninnovators. They tend to approach new or unfamiliar products with considerable openness and little anxiety. In contrast, noninnovators seem to find new products threatening to the point where they prefer to delay purchase until the product's success has been clearly established.

Consistent with their open-mindedness, it appears that innovative behavior is an expression of an individual's *need for uniqueness.*[47] Some researchers have found that a tension exists in decision making between two opposing objectives—conformity and distinction. The need for uniqueness allows an individual to distinguish himself by purchasing a rare item, which is a socially acceptable behavior. Consequently, those new products, both branded and unbranded, that represent a greater change in a person's consumption habits were viewed as superior when it came to satisfying the need for uniqueness. Therefore, to gain more rapid acceptance of a new product, marketers might consider appealing to a consumer's need for uniqueness.

Still further, consumer innovators also differ from noninnovators in terms of *social character.* Consumer innovators are *inner-directed;* that is, they rely on their own values or standards when making a decision about a new product. In contrast, noninnovators are *other-directed,* relying on others for guidance on how to respond to a new product rather than trusting their own personal values or standards. Thus, the initial purchasers of a new line of automobiles might be inner-directed, whereas the later purchasers of the same automobile might be other-directed. This suggests that as acceptance of a product progresses from early to later adopters, a gradual shift occurs in the personality type of adopters from inner-directedness to other-directedness.

There also appears to be a link between *optimum stimulation level* and consumer innovativeness. Specifically, individuals who seek a lifestyle rich with novel, complex, and unusual experiences (high optimum stimulation levels) are more willing to risk trying new products, to be innovative, to seek purchase-related information, and to accept new retail facilities.

Researchers have isolated a link between *variety seeking* and purchase behavior that provides insights into consumer innovators. Variety-seeking consumers tend to be brand switchers and purchasers of innovative products and services. They also possess the following innovator-related personality traits: They are open-minded (or low in dogmatism), extroverts, liberal, low in authoritarianism, able to deal with complex or ambiguous stimuli, and creative.[48]

To sum up, consumer innovators seem to be more receptive to the unfamiliar and the unique; they are more willing to rely on their own values or standards than on the judgment of others. They also are willing to run the risk of a poor product choice to increase their exposure to new products that will be satisfying. For the marketer, the personality traits that distinguish innovators from noninnovators suggest the need for separate promotional campaigns for innovators and for later adopters.

Perceived risk and venturesomeness

Perceived risk, which is discussed in detail in Chapter 6, is another measure of a consumer's likelihood to try new brands or products. Perceived risk is the degree of uncertainty or fear about the consequences of a purchase that a consumer feels when considering the purchase of a new product. For example, consumers experience uncertainty when they are concerned that a new product will not work properly or as well as other alternatives. Research on perceived risk and the trial of new products overwhelmingly indicates that consumer innovators are low-risk perceivers; that is, they experience little fear of trying new products or services. Consumers who perceive little or no risk in the purchase of a new product are much more likely to make innovative purchases than consumers who perceive a great deal of risk. In other words, high-risk perception limits innovativeness.

Venturesomeness is a broad-based measure of a consumer's willingness to accept the risk of purchasing new products. Measures of venturesomeness have been used to evaluate a person's general values or attitudes toward trying new products. A typical measurement scale might include such items as:

- *I prefer to (try a shampoo when it first comes out) (wait and learn how good it is before trying it).*
- *When I am shopping and see a brand of coffee I know about but have never tried, I am (very anxious or willing to try it), (hesitant about trying it), (very unwilling to try it).*
- *I like to be among the first people to buy and use new products that are on the market (measured on a five-point "agreement" scale).*

Research that has examined venturesomeness has generally found that consumers who indicate a willingness to try new products tend to be consumer innovators (as measured by their actual purchase of new products). On the other hand, consumers who express a reluctance to try new products are, in fact, less likely to purchase new products. Therefore, venturesomeness seems to be an effective barometer of actual innovative behavior.

Purchase and consumption characteristics

Consumer innovators possess purchase and usage traits that set them apart from noninnovators. For example, consumer innovators are *less* brand loyal; that is, they are more apt to switch brands. This is not surprising, for brand loyalty would seriously impede a consumer's willingness to try new products.

Consumer innovators are more likely to be *deal prone* (to take advantage of special promotional offers such as free samples and cents-off coupons). They are also likely to be *heavy users* of the product category in which they innovate. Specifically, they purchase larger quantities and consume more of the product than noninnovators. Finally, for products like VCRs, PCs, microwave ovens, 35-mm cameras, and food processors, usage variety is likely to be a relevant dimension of new-product diffusion. An understanding of how consumers might be "usage innovators"—that is, finding or "inventing" new uses for an innovation—might create entirely new market opportunities for marketers' products. Still further, a recent study of Indian consumers' attitudes toward the purchase of new food products found that "intention to buy" was an accurate predictor of behavior for highly innovative consumers, but failed to predict purchase behavior for less innovative Indian consumers.[49] This suggests that more innovative consumers are more likely to act on their reported intentions to purchase than less innovative consumers with the same intention of purchase.

To sum up, a positive relationship exists between innovative behavior and heavy usage. Consumer innovators are not only an important market segment from the standpoint of being the first to use a new product, but they also represent a substantial market in terms of product volume. However, their propensity to switch brands or to use products in different or unique ways and their positive response to promotional deals also suggest that innovators will continue to use a specific brand only as long as they do not perceive that a new and potentially better alternative is available.

Media habits

Comparisons of the media habits of innovators and noninnovators across such widely diverse areas of consumption as fashion clothing and new automotive services suggest that innovators have somewhat greater total exposure to magazines than noninnovators, particularly to special-interest magazines devoted to the product category in which they innovate. For example, fashion innovators are more likely to read magazines such as *Gentlemen's Quarterly* and *Vogue* than noninnovators; financial services innovators have greater exposure to such special-interest magazines as *Money* and *Financial World*.

Consumer innovators are also less likely to watch television than noninnovators. This view is consistently supported by research that over the past decade or so has compared the magazine and TV exposure levels of consumer innovators. The evidence indicates that consumer innovators have higher-than-average magazine exposure and lower-than-average TV exposure. It will be interesting, though, to observe over the next few years what the impact of the convergence of computers and television will be. Studies concerning the relationship between innovative behavior and exposure to other mass media, such as radio and newspapers, have been too few, and the results have been too varied to draw any useful conclusions.

Social characteristics

Consumer innovators are more socially accepted and socially involved than noninnovators. For example, innovators are more socially integrated into the community, better accepted by others, and more socially involved; that is, they belong to more social groups and organizations than noninnovators. This greater social acceptance and involvement of consumer innovators may help explain why they function as effective opinion leaders.

Demographic characteristics

It is reasonable to assume that the age of the consumer innovator is related to the specific product category in which he or she innovates; however, research suggests that consumer innovators tend to be younger than either late adopters or noninnovators. This is no doubt because many of the products selected for research attention (such as fashion, convenience grocery products, or new automobiles) are particularly attractive to younger consumers.

Consumer innovators have more formal education, have higher personal or family incomes, and are more likely to have higher occupational status (to be professionals or hold managerial positions) than late adopters or noninnovators. In other words, innovators tend to be more upscale than other consumer segments and can, therefore, better afford to make a mistake should the innovative new product or service being purchased prove to be unacceptable.

Table 15.15 summarizes the major differences between consumer innovators and late adopters or noninnovators. The table includes the major distinctions examined in our current presentation of the *consumer innovator profile*.

Are there generalized consumer innovators?

Do consumer innovators in one product category tend to be consumer innovators in other product categories? The answer to this strategically important question is a guarded "no." The overlap of innovativeness across product categories, like opinion leadership, seems to be limited to product categories that are closely related to the same basic interest area. Consumers who are innovators of one new food product or one new appliance are more likely to be innovators of other new products in the same general product category. In other words, although no single or generalized consumer-innovativeness trait seems to operate *across* broadly different product categories, evidence suggests that consumers who innovate *within* a specific product category will innovate again within the same product category. For example, up to the point of "innovator burnout" (i.e., "what I have is good enough"), a person who was an innovator in buying an early 2 megapixel digital camera in the 1990s was most likely again to be an innovator in buying a 3 megapixel digital camera, a 5 megapixel digital camera, and a 7 megapixel digital camera, and is likely again to be an innovator when it comes to the next generation of digital cameras. For the marketer, such a pattern suggests that it is generally a good marketing strategy to target a new product to consumers who were the first to try other products in the same basic product category.

TABLE 15.15	Comparative Profiles of the Consumer Innovator and the Noninnovator or Late Adopter

CHARACTERISTIC	INNOVATOR	NONINNOVATOR (OR LATE ADOPTER)
Product Interest	More	Less
Opinion Leadership	More	Less
Personality		
Dogmatism	Open-minded	Closed-minded
Need for uniqueness	Higher	Lower
Social character	Inner-directed	Other-directed
Optimum stimulation level	Higher	Lower
Variety seeking	Higher	Lower
Perceived risk	Less	More
Venturesomeness	More	Less
Purchase and Consumption Traits		
Brand loyalty	Less	More
Deal proneness	More	Less
Usage	More	Less
Media Habits		
Total magazine exposure	More	Less
Special-interest magazines	More	Less
Television	Less	More
Social Characteristics		
Social integration	More	Less
Social striving (e.g., social, physical, and occupational mobility)	More	Less
Group memberships	More	Less
Demographic Characteristics		
Age	Younger	Older
Income	Higher	Lower
Education	More	Less
Occupational status	Higher	Lower

Technology and innovators

In the realm of high-tech innovations, there is evidence suggesting that there is a generalized "high-tech" innovator—known as a "change leader."[50] Such individuals tend to embrace and popularize many of the innovations that are ultimately accepted by the mainstream population, such as computers, cellular telephones, and fax machines. They tend to have a wide range of personal and professional contacts representing different occupational and social groups; most often these contacts tend to be "weak ties" or acquaintances. Change leaders also appear to fall into one of two distinct groups: a *younger group* that can be characterized as being stimulation seeking, sociable, and having high levels of fashion awareness or a *middle-aged group* that is highly self-confident and has very high information-seeking needs.

Similar to change leaders, "technophiles" are individuals who purchase technologically advanced products soon after their market debut. Such individuals tend to be technically curious people. Also, another group responding to technology are adults who are categorized as "techthusiasts"—people who are most likely to purchase or subscribe to emerging products and services that are technologically oriented. These consumers are typically younger, better educated, and more affluent.[51]

Advancing our understanding of the relationship between technology and consumer innovation has been explored within the context of the technology acceptance model (TAM). Within the domain of work perceived usefulness or utilitarian aspect of a technology has been revealed to be most important; however, within consumer context of consumers' response to a new handheld Internet device, the most powerful determinant of attitudes toward usage was the "fun" of using the device—a hedonic aspect. The implication for marketers is clear—a consumer may purchase a new bit of technology more for the fun they can have with the device than for the ability it gives them to accomplish particular functions.[52]

Research conducted with over 500 adult Internet users found that purchasing online was positive related to technology-related innovativeness. Still further, the gathering of store or product information online was positively related to the number of years online and the weekly number of hours spent online.[53] Still further, when exploring the adoption of mobile gaming (games delivered via cell phone), a market that is expected to grow worldwide from $950 million in 2001 to $17.5 billion in 2006, researchers discovered important additions to the traditional list of product characteristics that influence the rate of adoption (e.g., relative advantage, complexity). What they perceived as risk were navigation (maneuvering ergonomics associated with the mobile device), critical mass (the more people that have adopted the innovation, the more attractive it is to others), and payment options (because of the expense of the mobile device, trialability is not an option). Perceived risk was found to play the most important role in the adoption process, followed by complexity and compatibility.[54]

SUMMARY

Opinion leadership is the process by which one person (the opinion leader) informally influences the actions or attitudes of others, who may be opinion seekers or merely opinion recipients. Opinion receivers perceive the opinion leader as a highly credible, objective source of product information who can help reduce their search time and perceived risk. Opinion leaders, in turn, are motivated to give information or advice to others, in part because doing so enhances their own status and self-image and because such advice tends to reduce any postpurchase dissonance that they may have. Other motives include product involvement, "other" involvement, and message involvement.

Market researchers identify opinion leaders by such methods as self-designation, key informants, the sociometric method, and the objective method. Studies of opinion leadership indicate that this phenomenon tends to be product specific; that is, individuals "specialize" in a product or product category in which they are highly interested. An opinion leader for one product category may be an opinion receiver for another.

Generally, opinion leaders are gregarious, self-confident, innovative people who like to talk. Additionally, they may feel

differentiated from others and choose to act differently (or public individuation). They acquire information about their areas of interest through avid readership of special-interest magazines and by means of new-product trials. Their interests often overlap adjacent product areas; thus, their opinion leadership may extend into related areas. The market maven is an intense case of such a person. These consumers possess a wide range of information about many different types of products, retail outlets, and other dimensions of markets. They both initiate discussions with other consumers and respond to requests for market information over a wide range of products and services. Market mavens are also distinguishable from other opinion leaders, because their influence stems not so much from product experience but from a more general knowledge or market expertise that leads them to an early awareness of a wide array of new products and services.

The opinion leadership process usually takes place among friends, neighbors, and work associates who have frequent physical proximity and, thus, have ample opportunity to hold informal product-related conversations. These conversations usually occur naturally in the context of the product-category usage.

The two-step flow of communication theory highlights the role of interpersonal influence in the transmission of information from the mass media to the population at large. This theory provides the foundation for a revised multistep flow of communication model, which takes into account the fact that information and influence often are two-way processes and that opinion leaders both influence and are influenced by opinion receivers.

Marketers recognize the strategic value of segmenting their audiences into opinion leaders and opinion receivers for their product categories. When marketers can direct their promotional efforts to the more influential segments of their markets, these individuals will transmit this information to those who seek product advice. Marketers try to both simulate and stimulate opinion leadership. They have also found that they can create opinion leaders for their products by taking socially involved or influential people and deliberately increasing their enthusiasm for a product category.

The diffusion process and the adoption process are two closely related concepts concerned with the acceptance of new products by consumers. The diffusion process is a macro process that focuses on the spread of an innovation (a new product, service, or idea) from its source to the consuming public. The adoption process is a micro process that examines the stages through which an individual consumer passes when making a decision to accept or reject a new product.

The definition of the term *innovation* can be firm oriented (new to the firm), product oriented (a continuous innovation, a dynamically continuous innovation, or a discontinuous innovation), market oriented (how long the product has been on the market or an arbitrary percentage of the potential target market that has purchased it), or consumer oriented (new to the consumer). Market-oriented definitions of innovation are most useful to consumer researchers in the study of the diffusion and adoption of new products.

Five product characteristics influence the consumer's acceptance of a new product: relative advantage, compatibility, complexity, trialability, and observability (or communicability).

Diffusion researchers are concerned with two aspects of communication—the channels through which word of a new product is spread to the consuming public and the types of messages that influence the adoption or rejection of new products. Diffusion is always examined in the context of a specific social system, such as a target market, a community, a region, or even a nation.

Time is an integral consideration in the diffusion process. Researchers are concerned with the amount of purchase time required for an individual consumer to adopt or reject a new product, with the rate of adoption, and with the identification of sequential adopters. The five adopter categories are innovators, early adopters, early majority, late majority, and laggards.

Marketing strategists try to control the rate of adoption through their new-product pricing policies. Marketers who wish to penetrate the market to achieve market leadership try to acquire wide adoption as quickly as possible by using low prices. Those who wish to recoup their developmental costs quickly use a skimming pricing policy but lengthen the adoption process.

The traditional adoption process model describes five stages through which an individual consumer passes to arrive at the decision to adopt or reject a new product: awareness, interest, evaluation, trial, and adoption. To make it more realistic, an enhanced model is suggested as one that considers the possibility of a preexisting need or problem, the likelihood that some form of evaluation might occur through the entire process, and that even after adoption there will be postadoption or purchase evaluation that might either strengthen the commitment or alternatively lead to discontinuation.

New-product marketers are vitally concerned with identifying the consumer innovator so that they may direct their promotional campaigns to the people who are most likely to try new products, adopt them, and influence others. Consumer research has identified a number of consumer-related characteristics, including product interest, opinion leadership, personality factors, purchase and consumption traits, media habits, social characteristics, and demographic variables that distinguish consumer innovators from later adopters. These serve as useful variables in the segmentation of markets for new-product introductions.

DISCUSSION QUESTIONS

1. a. Why is an opinion leader a more credible source of product information than an advertisement for the same product?

   b. Are there any circumstances in which information from advertisements is likely to be more influential than word-of-mouth?

2. Why would a consumer who has just purchased an expensive fax machine for home use attempt to influence the purchase behavior of others?

3. A company that owns and operates health clubs across the country is opening a health club in your town. The company has retained you as its marketing research consultant and has asked you to identify opinion leaders for its service. Which of the following identification methods would you recommend: the self-designating method, the sociometric method, the key informant method, or the objective method? Explain your selection. In your answer, be sure to discuss the advantages and

disadvantages of the four techniques as they relate to the marketing situation just described.

4. Do you have any "market mavens" among your friends? Describe their personality traits and behaviors. Describe a situation in which a market maven has given you advice regarding a product or service and discuss what you believe was his or her motivation for doing so.

5. Describe how a manufacturer might use knowledge of the following product characteristics to speed up the acceptance of pocket-sized cellular telephones:
   a. Relative advantage
   b. Compatibility
   c. Complexity
   d. Trialability
   e. Observability

6. Toshiba has introduced an ultra-slim laptop computer that weighs about two pounds, has a color screen, and has a powerful processor into which a full-size desktop screen and keyboard can be easily plugged. How can the company use the diffusion-of-innovations framework to develop promotional, pricing, and distribution strategies targeted to the following adopter categories?
   a. Innovators
   b. Early adopters

   c. Early majority
   d. Late majority
   e. Laggards

7. Is the curve that describes the sequence and proportion of adopter categories among the population (Figure 15.9) similar in shape to the product life cycle curve? Explain your answer. How would you use both curves to develop a marketing strategy?

8. Sony is introducing a 27-inch TV with a built-in VCR, a picture-in-picture feature, and a feature that allows the viewer to simultaneously view frozen frames of the last signals received from 12 channels.
   a. What recommendations would you make to Sony regarding the initial target market for the new TV model?
   b. How would you identify the innovators for this product?
   c. Select three characteristics of consumer innovators (as summarized in Table 15.15). Explain how Sony might use each of these characteristics to influence the adoption process and speed up the diffusion of the new product.
   d. Should Sony follow a penetration or a skimming policy in introducing the product? Why?

EXERCISES

1. Describe two situations in which you served as an opinion leader and two situations in which you sought consumption-related advice or information from an opinion leader. Indicate your relationship to the persons with whom you interacted. Are the circumstances during which you engaged in word-of-mouth communications consistent with those in the text's material? Explain.

2. a. Find ads that simulate and ads that stimulate opinion leadership and present them in class.
   b. Can you think of negative rumors that you have heard recently about a company or a product? If so, present them in class.

3. Identify a product, service, or style that recently was adopted by you or some of your friends. Identify what

type of innovation it is and describe its diffusion process up to this point in time. What are the characteristics of people who adopted it first? What types of people did not adopt it? What features of the product, service, or style are likely to determine its eventual success or failure?

4. With the advancement of digital technology, some companies plan to introduce interactive TV systems that will allow viewers to select films from video libraries and view them on demand. Among people you know, identify two who are likely to be the innovators for such a new service and construct consumer profiles using the characteristics of consumer innovators discussed in the text.

KEY TERMS

- **adopter categories**
- **adoption process**
- **consumer innovators**

- **continuous innovation**
- **diffusion of innovations**
- **diffusion process**

- **discontinuous innovation**
- **dynamically continuous innovation**
- **innovation**

- market maven
- multistep flow of communication theory
- opinion leader

- opinion leadership
- opinion receiver
- opinion seekers

- stages in the adoption process
- two-step flow of communication theory

NOTES

1. Chip Walker, "Word-of-Mouth," *American Demographics,* July 1995, 40.

2. Ibid., 42.

3. Dale F. Duhan, Scott D. Johnson, James B. Wilcox, and Gilbert D. Harrell, "Influences on Consumer Use of Word-of-Mouth Recommendation Sources," *Journal of the Academy of Marketing Science* 25, no. 4 (1997): 283–295.

4. Marc Perton, "Worldwide Cellphone Usage Doubles," Engadget, December 14, 2004, accessed at **www.engadget.com/entry/1234000943023492**

5. James Brooke, "Youth Let Their Thumbs Do the Talking in Japan," *New York Times,* April 30, 2002, A14.

6. David Fletcher, "Advertising through Word-of-Mouth," *Brand Strategy (London)*, June 2004, 38.

7. John E. Hogan, Katherine N. Lemon, and Barak Libai, "Quantifying the Ripple: Word-of-Mouth and Advertising Effectiveness," *Journal of Advertising Research* (September 2004): 271–280.

8. Pamala L. Alreck and Robert B. Settle, "The Importance of Word-of-Mouth Communications to Service Buyers," in *1995 AMA Winter Educators' Proceedings,* ed. David W. Stewart and Naufel J. Vilcassim (Chicago: American Marketing Association, 1995), 188–193.

9. Cathy L. Hartman and Pamela L. Kiecker, "Marketplace Influencers at the Point of Purchase: The Role of Purchase Pals in Consumer Decision Making," in *1991 AMA Educators' Proceedings,* ed. Mary C. Gilly and F. Robert Dwyer, et al. (Chicago: American Marketing Association, 1991), 461–467.

10. Matthew Creamer, "Study: Go Traditional to Influence Influencers," *Advertising Age,* March 7, 2005, 8.

11. Christine H. Roch, "The Dual Roots of Opinion Leadership," *The Journal of Politics* 67, no. 1 (February 2005): 110.

12. Michael T. Elliott and Anne E. Warfield, "Do Market Mavens Categorize Brands Differently?" in *Advances in Consumer Research,* 20, ed. Leigh McAlister and Michael L. Rothschild (Provo, UT: Association for Consumer Research 1993), 202–208; and Frank Alpert, "Consumer Market Beliefs and Their Managerial Implications: An Empirical Examination," *Journal of Consumer Marketing* 10, no. 2 (1993): 56–70.

13. Gianfranco Walse, Kevin P. Gwinner, and Scott R. Swanson, "What Makes Mavens Tick? Exploring the Motives of Market Mavens' Initiation of Information Diffusion," *The Journal of Consumer Marketing* 21, no. 2 (2004): 109–122.

14. Ronald E. Goldsmith, Leisa R. Flynn, and Elizabeth B. Goldsmith, "Innovation Consumers and Market Mavens," *Journal of Marketing Theory and Practice* 11 (Fall 2003): 54–65.

15. Michael A. Belch, Kathleen A. Krentler, and Laura A. Willis-Flurry, "Teen Internet Mavens: Influence in Family Decision Making," *Journal of Business Research* 58 (May 2005): 569–575.

16. Andrea C. Wojnicki, "Social Hubs: A Valuable Segmentation Construct in the Word-of-Mouth Consumer Network," *Advances in Consumer Research* 31 (2004): 521–522.

17. Paul F. Lazarsfeld, Bernard Berelson, and Hazel Gaudet, *The People's Choice,* 2d ed. (New York: Columbia University Press, 1948), 151.

18. Joseph R. Mancuso, "Why Not Create Opinion Leaders for New Product Introduction?" *Journal of Marketing* 33 (July 1969): 20–25.

19. Barbara Bickart and Robert M. Schindler, "Internet Forums as Influential Sources of Consumer Information," *Journal of Interactive Marketing* 15, no. 3 (Summer 2001): 31–39.

20. Nat Ives, "Marketing's Flop Side: The 'Determined Detractor'," *New York Times*, December 27, 2004, C1 & C7.

21. Rob Walker, "The Hidden (in Plain Sight) Persuaders," *New York Times Magazine*, December 30, 2004, 9–12.

22. "In the News: Ploys," *New York Times Magazine,* February 13, 1994, 19.

23. Marc Graser, "Product-Placement Spending Poised to Hit $4.25 Billion in '05," *Advertising Age*, April 4, 2005, 16.

24. Ralph F. Wilson, "The Six Simple Principles of Viral Marketing," *Web Marketing Today,* 70, February 1, 2000, accessed at **www.wilsonweb.com/wmt5/viral-principles.htm**; and **searchcrm.techtarget.com/sDefinition/0,sid11_ gci213514,00.html**.

25. Marc Weingarten, "The Medium Is the Instant Message," *Business 2.0,* February 2002, 98–99.

26. "Virtual Viral Marketing Virus," *Wired,* November 2000, 116; Renée Dye, "How to Create Explosive Self-Generating Demand," *Advertising Age,* November 8, 1999, S20; Thomas E. Weber, "The Web's Newest Ploy May Not Make You a Very Popular Friend," *Wall Street Journal,* September 13, 1999, B1; Beth Snyder Bulik, "Upping the Cool Quotient," *Business 2.0,*

August 22, 2000, 94–96; and John Gaffney, "The Cool Kids Are Doing It. Should You?" *Business 2.0,* November 2001, 140–141.

27. Jack Neff, "P&G Goes Viral with Test of Innovation Locations," *Advertising Age,* September 4, 2000, 4.

28. Greg Metz Thomas, Jr., "Building the buzz in hive mind," *Journal of Consumer Behaviour* 4 (October 2004): 64–72.

29. Joseph E. Phelps, Regina Lewis, Lynne Mobilio, David Perry, and Niranjan Raman, "Viral Marketing or Electronic Word-of-Mounth Advertising: Examining Consumer Responses and Motivations to Pass Along Email," *Journal of Advertising Research* (December 2004): 333–348.

30. Charles Newbery, "Nescafé Builds Buzz via Viral e-mail Effort," *Advertising Age,* May 2, 2005, 24.

31. David Kirkpatrick and Daniel Roth, "Why There's No Escaping the BLOG," *Fortune,* January 10, 2005, 44–50.

32. Lauren Keller Johnson, "Harnessing the Power of the Customer," Harvard Business Review, March 2004, 3.

33. Thomas S. Robertson, "The Process of Innovation and the Diffusion of Innovation," *Journal of Marketing* 31 (January 1967): 14–19.

34. Everett M. Rogers, *Diffusion of Innovations,* 4th ed. (New York: Free Press, 1995); and Hubert Gatignon and Thomas S. Robertson, "Innovative Decision Processes," in *Handbook of Consumer Behavior,* ed. Thomas S. Robertson and Harold H. Kassarjian (Upper Saddle River, NJ: Prentice Hall, 1991), 316–348.

35. S. Ram and Hyung-Shik Jung, "Innovativeness in Product Usage: A Comparison of Early Adopters and Early Majority," *Psychology and Marketing* 11 (January–February 1994): 57–67; A. R. Petrosky, "Gender and Use Innovation: An Inquiry into the Socialization of Innovative Behavior," in *1995 AMA Educators' Proceedings,* ed. Barbara B. Stern and George M. Zinkan (Chicago: American Marketing Association, 1995), 299–307; Kyungae Park and Carl L. Dyer, "Consumer Use Innovative Behavior: An Approach Toward Its Causes," in *Advances in Consumer Research* 22, ed. Frank R. Kardes and Mita Sujan (Provo, UT: Association for Consumer Research 1995), 566–572.

36. Earle Eldridge, "Pickups Get Women's Touch," *USA Today,* June 13, 2001, 1B, 2B.

37. Rogers, *Diffusion of Innovations,* 15–16.

38. Hsiang Chen and Kevin Crowston, "Comparative Diffusion of the Telephone and the World Wide Web: An Analysis of Rates of Adoption," in Suave Lobodzinski and Ivan Tomek (eds.), *Proceedings of WebNet '97—World Conference of the WWW, Internet and Intranet,* Toronto, Canada, 110–115.

39. Susan H. Higgins and William L. Shanklin, "Seeding Mass Market Acceptance for High Technology Consumer Products," *Journal of Consumer Marketing* 9 (Winter 1992): 5–14.

40. Albert Maruggi, "Podcasting Offers a Sound Technique," *Brandweek,* May 2, 2005, 21.

41. Everett M. Rogers and F. Floyd Shoemaker, *Communication of Innovations,* 2nd ed. (New York: Free Press, 1971), 32–33; see

also Elizabeth C. Hirschman, "Consumer Modernity, Cognitive Complexity, Creativity and Innovativeness," in *Marketing in the 80's: Changes and Challenges,* ed. Richard P. Bagozzi et al. (Chicago: American Marketing Association, 1980), 135–139.

42. "BSE Economics: What's at Stake in Wisconsin?," Wisconsin Department of Agriculture, Trade & Consumer Protection, January 8, 2004, 1, accessed at **www.datcp.state.wi.us/ah/ agriculture/animals /disease/bse/pdf/economic_ impacts_BSE.pdf**

43. Thomas W. Valente and Rebecca L. Davis, "Accelerating the Diffusion of Innovations Using Opinion Leaders," *Annals of the American Academy of Political and Social Sciences,* 566, November 1999, 55–67; and Ronald S. Burt, "The Social Capital of Opinion Leaders," *Annals of the American Academy of Political and Social Sciences,* 566, November 1999, 37–54.

44. Bradley Johnson, "Marketers Who Ignore the Tech-Shy Disconnect Huge Potential for Profits," *Advertising Age,* March 7, 2005, 26.

45. Kenichi Ohmae, "Managing in a Borderless World," *Harvard Business Review,* May–June 1989, 152–161.

46. Jacob Goldenberg, Barak Libai, and Eitan Muller, "Riding the Saddle: How Cross-Market Communications Can Create a Major Slump in Sales," *Journal of Marketing* 66, no. 2 (April 2002): 1–16.

47. David J. Burns and Robert F. Krampf, "A Semiotic Perspective on Innovative Behavior," in *Developments in Marketing Science,* ed. Robert L. King (Richmond, VA: Academy of Marketing Science, 1991), 32–35.

48. Wayne D. Hoyer and Nancy M. Ridgway, "Variety Seeking as an Explanation for Exploratory Purchase Behavior: A Theoretical Model," in *Advances in Consumer Research* 11, ed. Thomas C. Kinnear (Provo, UT: Association for Consumer Research, 1984), 114–119.

49. HoJung Choo and Jae-Eun Chung, "Antecedents to New Food Product Purchasing Behavior among Innovator Groups in India," *European Journal of Marketing* 38, no. 5/6 (2004): 608–625.

50. Bruce MacEvoy, "Change Leaders and the New Media," *American Demographics,* January 1994, 42–48.

51. Susan Mitchell, "Technophiles and Technophobes," *American Demographics,* February 1994, 36–42.

52. Cordon C. Bruner II and Anand Kumar, "Explaining Consumer Acceptance of Handheld Internet Devices," *Journal of Business Research* 58 (2005): 553–558.

53. Mary Long, Leon Schiffman, and Elaine Sherman, "Exploring the Dynamics of Online Retail-Related Activities," in *Retailing 2003: Strategic Planning in Uncertain Times,* Proceedings of the Seventh Triennial National Retailing Conference, Academy of Marketing Sciences, Columbus, Ohio, November 2003.

54. Mirella Kleijnen, Ko de Ruyter, and Martin Wetzels, "Consumer Adoption of Wireless Services: Discovering the Rules While Playing the Game," *Journal of Interactive Marketing* 18 (Spring 2004): 51–61.

chaptersixteen

> ## Consumer Decision Making and Beyond

This chapter draws together many of the psychological, social, and cultural concepts developed throughout the book into an overview framework for understanding how consumers make decisions. Unlike the second part of Chapter 15, which examined the dynamics of *new*-product adoption, this chapter takes a broader perspective and examines **consumer decision making** in the context of all types of *consumption choices*, ranging from the consumption of new products to the use of old and established products. It also considers consumers' decisions not as the end point but rather as the beginning point of a **consumption process**.

Reduces those unsightly lines.

The Hertz #1 Club.® Spend less time at the rental counter. Less time returning your car. Don't thank France or some pricey rejuvenative spa for the latest innovation in line reduction. Thank us. Because The Hertz #1 Club offers a special #1 Club Express® counter to reduce your waiting time and speed you on your way. Your profile and car preference are already on file. So all you do is sign and go. And when you want to make your flight fast, Hertz Instant Return is our fastest way to return your car. Go straight from your car to the plane. It's just one of the many ways The Hertz #1 Club can get your vacation off to a great start. Membership is free. Just go to **hertz.com/join** to sign up. After all, who wouldn't be happier with fewer lines? That's renting wisely.

Rent Wisely.™

Hertz rents Fords and other fine cars. ® Reg. U.S. Pat. Off. © 2005 Hertz System, Inc.
FOR YOUR INFORMATION: Advance reservations are required. Standard rental conditions and return restrictions must be met. Restrictions apply. #1 Club Express available at over 50 locations in the U.S. and Canada. Minimum rental age is 25 (exceptions apply).

what is a decision?

Every day, each of us makes numerous decisions concerning every aspect of our daily lives. However, we generally make these decisions without stopping to think about how we make them and what is involved in the particular decision-making process itself. In the most general terms, a decision is the selection of an option from two or more alternative choices. In other words, for a person to make a decision, a choice of alternatives must be available. When a person has a choice between making a purchase and not making a purchase, a choice between brand X and brand Y, or a choice of spending time doing A or B, that person is in a position to make a decision. On the other hand, if the consumer has no alternatives from which to choose and is literally *forced* to make a particular purchase or take a particular action (e.g., use a prescribed medication), then this single "no-choice" instance does not constitute a decision; such a no-choice decision is commonly referred to as a "Hobson's choice."

In actuality, no-choice purchase or consumption situations are fairly rare. You may recall from our discussion of core American cultural values (Chapter 12) that for consumers, *freedom* is often expressed in terms of a wide range of product choices. Thus, if there is almost always a choice, then there is almost always an opportunity for consumers to make decisions. Moreover, experimental research reveals that providing consumers with a choice when there was originally none can be a very good business strategy, one that can substantially increase sales.[1] For instance, when a direct-mail electrical appliance catalog displayed two coffeemakers instead of just one (the original coffeemaker at $149 and a "new" only slightly larger one at $229), the addition of the second *comparison* coffeemaker seemed to stimulate consumer evaluation that significantly increased the sales of the original coffeemaker.

Table 16.1 summarizes various types of consumption and purchase-related decisions. Although not exhaustive, this list does serve to demonstrate that the scope of consumer decision making is far broader than the mere selection of one brand from a number of brands.

levels of consumer decision making

Not all consumer decision-making situations receive (or require) the same degree of information research. If all purchase decisions required extensive effort, then consumer decision making would be an exhausting process that left little time for anything else. On the other hand, if all purchases were routine, then they would tend to be monotonous and would provide little pleasure or novelty. On a continuum of effort ranging from very high to very low, we can distinguish three specific levels of consumer decision making: **extensive problem solving**, **limited problem solving**, and **routinized response behavior**.

Extensive problem solving

When consumers have no established criteria for evaluating a product category or specific brands in that category or have not narrowed the number of brands they will consider to a small, manageable subset, their decision-making efforts can be classified as *extensive problem solving*. At this level, the consumer needs a great deal of information to establish a set of criteria on which to judge specific brands and a correspondingly large amount of information concerning each of the brands to be considered.

Limited problem solving

At this level of problem solving, consumers already have established the basic criteria for evaluating the product category and the various brands in the category. However, they have not fully established preferences concerning a select group of brands.

TABLE 16.1	Types of Purchase or Consumption Decisions

DECISION CATEGORY	ALTERNATIVE A	ALTERNATIVE B
Basic Purchase or Consumption Decision Brand Purchase or Consumption Decision	To purchase or consume a product (or service)	Not to purchase or consume a product (or service)
	To purchase or consume a specific brand	To purchase or consume another brand
	To purchase or consume one's usual brand	To purchase or consume another established brand (possibly with special features)
	To purchase or consume a basic model	To purchase or consume a luxury or status model
	To purchase or consume a new brand	To purchase or consume one's usual brand or some other established brand
	To purchase or consume a standard quantity	To purchase or consume more or less than a standard quantity
	To purchase or consume an on-sale brand	To purchase or consume a nonsale brand
	To purchase or consume a national brand	To purchase or consume a store brand
Channel Purchase Decisions	To purchase from a specific type of store (e.g., a department store)	To purchase from some other type of store (e.g., a discount store)
	To purchase from one's usual store	To purchase from some other store
	To purchase in-home (by phone or catalog or Internet)	To purchase in-store merchandise
	To purchase from a local store	To purchase from a store requiring some travel (outshopping)
Payment Purchase Decisions	To pay for the purchase with cash	To pay for the purchase with a credit card
	To pay the bill in full when it arrives	To pay for the purchase in installments

Their search for additional information is more like "fine-tuning"; they must gather additional brand information to discriminate among the various brands.

Routinized response behavior

At this level, consumers have experience with the product category and a well-established set of criteria with which to evaluate the brands they are considering. In some situations, they may search for a small amount of additional information; in others, they simply review what they already know.

Just how extensive a consumer's problem-solving task is depends on how well established his or her criteria for selection are, how much information he or she has about each brand being considered, and how narrow the set of brands is from which the choice will be made. Clearly, extensive problem solving implies that the consumer must seek more information to make a choice, whereas routinized response behavior implies little need for additional information.

All decisions in our lives cannot be complex and require extensive research and consideration—we just cannot exert the level of effort required. Some decisions have to be "easy ones."

models of consumers: four views of consumer decision making

Before presenting an overview model of how consumers make decisions, we will consider several schools of thought that depict consumer decision making in distinctly different ways. The term *models of consumers* refers to a general view or perspective as to how (and why) individuals behave as they do. Specifically, we will examine models of consumers in terms of the following four views: (1) an *economic view*, (2) a *passive view*, (3) a *cognitive view*, and (4) an *emotional view*.

An economic view

In the field of theoretical economics, which portrays a world of perfect competition, the consumer has often been characterized as making rational decisions. This model, called the *economic man* theory, has been criticized by consumer researchers for a number of reasons. To behave rationally in the economic sense, a consumer would have to (1) be aware of all available product alternatives, (2) be capable of correctly ranking each alternative in terms of its benefits and disadvantages, and (3) be able to identify the one best alternative. Realistically, however, consumers rarely have all of the information or sufficiently accurate information or even an adequate degree of involvement or motivation to make the so-called "perfect" decision.

It has been argued that the classical economic model of an all-rational consumer is unrealistic for the following reasons: (a) People are limited by their existing skills, habits, and reflexes; (b) people are limited by their existing values and goals; and (c) people are limited by the extent of their knowledge.[2] Consumers operate in an imperfect world in which they do not maximize their decisions in terms of economic considerations, such as price–quantity relationships, marginal utility, or indifference curves. Indeed, the consumer generally is unwilling to engage in extensive decision-making activities and will settle, instead, for a "satisfactory" decision, one that is "good enough."[3] For this reason, the economic model is often rejected as too idealistic and simplistic. As an example, recent research has found that consumers' primary motivation for price haggling, which was long thought to be the desire to obtain a better price (i.e., better dollar value for the purchase), may instead be related to the need for achievement, affiliation, and dominance.[4]

A passive view

Quite opposite to the rational economic view of consumers is the *passive* view that depicts the consumer as basically submissive to the self-serving interests and promotional efforts of marketers. In the passive view, consumers are perceived as impulsive and irrational purchasers, ready to yield to the aims and into the arms of marketers. At least to some degree, the passive model of the consumer was subscribed to by the hard-driving super-salespeople of old, who were trained to regard the consumer as an object to be manipulated.

The principal limitation of the passive model is that it fails to recognize that the consumer plays an equal, if not dominant, role in many buying situations—sometimes by seeking information about product alternatives and selecting the product that appears to offer the greatest satisfaction and at other times by impulsively selecting a product that satisfies the mood or emotion of the moment. All that we have studied about motivation (see Chapter 4), selective perception (Chapter 6), learning (Chapter 7), attitudes (Chapter 8), communication (Chapter 9), and opinion leadership (Chapter 15) serves to support the proposition that consumers are rarely objects of manipulation. Therefore, this simple and single-minded view should also be rejected as unrealistic.

A cognitive view

The third model portrays the consumer as a *thinking problem solver*. Within this framework, consumers frequently are pictured as either receptive to or actively searching for products and services that fulfill their needs and enrich their lives. The cognitive model focuses on the processes by which consumers seek and evaluate information about selected brands and retail outlets.

Within the context of the cognitive model, consumers are viewed as information processors. Information processing leads to the formation of preferences and, ultimately, to purchase intentions. The cognitive view also recognizes that the consumer is unlikely to even attempt to obtain all available information about every choice. Instead, consumers are likely to cease their information-seeking efforts when they perceive that they have sufficient information about some of the alternatives to make a "satisfactory" decision. As this information-processing viewpoint suggests, consumers often develop shortcut decision rules (called **heuristics**) to facilitate the decision-making process. They also use decision rules to cope with exposure to too much information (i.e., **information overload**).

The cognitive, or problem-solving, view describes a consumer who falls somewhere between the extremes of the economic and passive views, who does not (or cannot) have total knowledge about available product alternatives and, therefore, cannot make *perfect* decisions, but who nonetheless actively seeks information and attempts to make *satisfactory* decisions.

Consistent with the problem-solving view is the notion that a great deal of consumer behavior is goal directed. For example, a consumer might purchase a computer in order to manage finances or look for a laundry detergent that will be gentle on fabrics. Goal setting is especially important when it comes to the adoption of new products because the greater the degree of "newness," the more difficult it would be for the consumer to evaluate the product and relate it to his or her need (because of a lack of experience with the product). Figure 16.1 diagrams goal setting and goal pursuit in consumer behavior.

An emotional view

Although long aware of the *emotional* or *impulsive* model of consumer decision making, marketers frequently prefer to think of consumers in terms of either economic or passive models. In reality, however, each of us is likely to associate deep feelings or emotions,

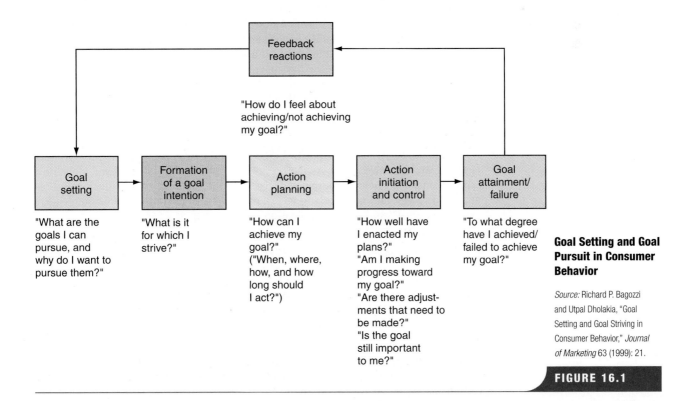

Goal Setting and Goal Pursuit in Consumer Behavior

Source: Richard P. Bagozzi and Utpal Dholakia, "Goal Setting and Goal Striving in Consumer Behavior," *Journal of Marketing* 63 (1999): 21.

FIGURE 16.1

such as joy, fear, love, hope, sexuality, fantasy, and even a little "magic," with certain purchases or possessions. These feelings or emotions are likely to be highly involving. For instance, a person who misplaces a favorite fountain pen might go to great lengths to look for it, despite the fact that he or she has six others at hand.

Possessions also may serve to preserve a sense of the past and act as familiar transitional objects when one is confronted with an uncertain future. For example, members of the armed forces invariably carry photographs of "the girl (or guy) back home," their families, and their lives in earlier times. These memorabilia frequently serve as hopeful reminders that normal activities will someday resume.

If we were to reflect on the nature of our recent purchases, we might be surprised to realize just how impulsive some of them were. Rather than carefully searching, deliberating, and evaluating alternatives before buying, we are just as likely to have made many of these purchases on impulse, on a whim, or because we were emotionally driven.

When a consumer makes what is basically an emotional purchase decision, less emphasis is placed on the search for prepurchase information. Instead, more emphasis is placed on current mood and feelings ("Go for it!"). This is not to say that emotional decisions are not rational. As Chapter 4 pointed out, buying products that afford emotional satisfaction is a perfectly rational consumer decision. Some emotional decisions are expressions that "you deserve it" or "treat yourself." For instance, many consumers buy designer-label clothing, not because they look any better in it, but because status labels make them feel better. This is a rational decision. Of course, if a man with a wife and three children purchases a two-seater Porsche 911 Carrera (**www.porsche.com**) for himself, the neighbors might wonder about his level of rationality (although some might think it was deviously high). No such question would arise if the same man selected a box of Godiva chocolate (**www.godiva.com**), instead of a Whitman Sampler (**www.whitmans.com**), although in both instances, each might be an impulsive, emotional purchase decision.

Consumers' **moods** are also important to decision making. Mood can be defined as a "feeling state" or state of mind.[5] Unlike an emotion, which is a response to a particular environment, a mood is more typically an unfocused, preexisting state—already present at the time a consumer "experiences" an advertisement, a retail environment, a brand, or a product. Compared to emotions, moods are generally lower in intensity and longer lasting and are not as directly coupled with action tendencies and explicit actions as emotions.

Mood appears to be important to consumer decision making, because it impacts on *when* consumers shop, *where* they shop, and *whether* they shop alone or with others. It also is likely to influence *how* the consumer responds to actual shopping environments (i.e., at point of purchase). Some retailers attempt to create a mood for shoppers, even though shoppers enter the store with a preexisting mood. Research suggests that a store's image or atmosphere can affect shoppers' moods; in turn, shoppers' moods can influence how long they stay in the store, as well as other behavior that retailers wish to encourage.[6]

In general, individuals in a positive mood recall more information about a product than those in a negative mood. As the results of one study suggest, however, inducing a positive mood at the point-of-purchase decision (as through background music, point-of-purchase displays, etc.) is unlikely to have a meaningful impact on specific brand choice unless a previously stored brand evaluation already exists.[7]

a model of consumer decision making

This section presents an overview model of consumer decision making (briefly introduced in Chapter 1) that reflects the *cognitive* (or *problem-solving*) consumer and, to some degree, the *emotional consumer*. The model is designed to tie together many of the ideas on consumer decision making and consumption behavior discussed throughout the book. It does not presume to provide an exhaustive picture of the complexities of consumer decision making. Rather, it is designed to synthesize and coordinate relevant concepts into a significant whole. The model, presented in Figure 16.2, has three major components: input, process, and output.

FIGURE 16.2

**A Simple Model of
Consumer Decision
Making**

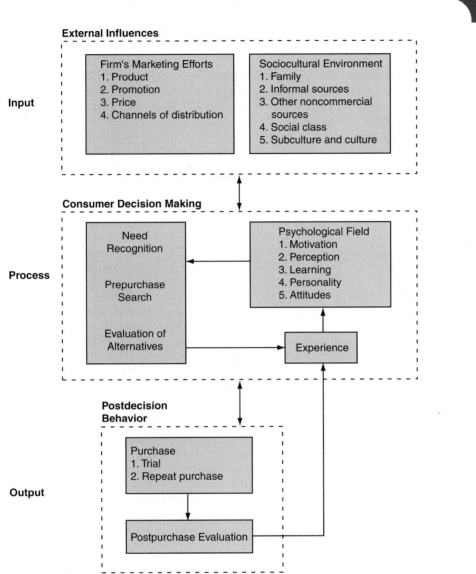

Input

The *input* component of our consumer decision-making model draws on external influences that serve as sources of information about a particular product and influence a consumer's product-related values, attitudes, and behavior. Chief among these input factors are the *marketing mix activities* of organizations that attempt to communicate the benefits of their products and services to potential consumers and the nonmarketing *sociocultural influences*, which, when internalized, affect the consumer's purchase decisions.

Marketing inputs

The firm's marketing activities are a direct attempt to reach, inform, and persuade consumers to buy and use its products. These inputs to the consumer's decision-making process take the form of specific marketing mix strategies that consist of the product itself (including its package, size, and guarantees); mass-media advertising, direct marketing, personal selling, and other promotional efforts; pricing policy; and the selection of distribution channels to move the product from the manufacturer to the consumer.

Ultimately, the impact of a firm's marketing efforts in large measure is governed by the consumer's perception of these efforts. Thus, marketers do well to remain diligently alert to consumer perceptions by sponsoring consumer research, rather than to rely on the *intended* impact of their marketing messages.

Sociocultural inputs

The second type of input, the *sociocultural environment*, also exerts a major influence on the consumer. Sociocultural inputs (examined in Part III) consist of a wide range of noncommercial influences. For example, the comments of a friend, an editorial in the newspaper, usage by a family member, an article in *Consumer Reports*, or the views of experienced consumers participating in a special-interest discussion group on the Internet are all noncommercial sources of information. The influences of social class, culture, and subculture, although less tangible, are important input factors that are internalized and affect how consumers evaluate and ultimately adopt (or reject) products. The unwritten codes of conduct communicated by culture subtly indicate which consumption behavior should be considered "right" or "wrong" at a particular point in time. For example, Japanese mothers maintain much more control over their children's consumption than American mothers, because in the United States children are socialized to be individualistic (*to stand out*), whereas in Japan children are socialized to be integrated with others (*to stand in*).

The cumulative impact of each firm's marketing efforts; the influence of family, friends, and neighbors; and society's existing code of behavior are all inputs that are likely to affect what consumers purchase and how they use what they buy. Because these influences may be directed to the individual or actively sought by the individual, a two-headed arrow is used to link the *input* and *process* segments of the model (Figure 16.2).

Process

The *process* component of the model is concerned with how consumers make decisions. To understand this process, we must consider the influence of the psychological concepts examined in Part II. The *psychological field* represents the internal influences (motivation, perception, learning, personality, and attitudes) that affect consumers' decision-making processes (what they need or want, their awareness of various product choices, their information-gathering activities, and their evaluation of alternatives). As pictured in the *process* component of the overview decision model (Figure 16.2), the act of making a consumer decision consists of three stages: (1) **need recognition**, (2) **prepurchase search**, and (3) **evaluation of alternatives**.

Need recognition

The *recognition of a need* is likely to occur when a consumer is faced with a "problem." For example, consider the case of Eric, a 25-year-old college graduate working for an equity research firm in New York. He is totally computer literate, having had computers in the classroom since elementary school, and, like others his age, knows a great deal about other high-tech gadgets, such as MP3 players, HDTV, and cell phones. In fact, he recently purchased a thin 23-inch LCD HDTV for his bedroom, and exchanged his digital cable box, with a digital video recorder, for its HDTV equivalent. Eric frequently visits Web sites to find out about new state-of-the-art digital and electronic equipment, knows which Web sites offer reviews and comparisons of high-tech gear, and knows a number of Web sites where highly specialized e-tailers are offering state-of-the-art equipment. In the messenger bag, which he carries almost everywhere, is his Dell MP3 player (with hard drive), a USB flash drive, and, sometimes, his personal laptop computer. Interestingly, while in college he scheduled his life using his PDA, he no longer bothers to carry it around.

Eric often gets together with his friends for birthday parties, holiday parties, or just plain "let's meet at a restaurant for the evening," and he also likes to travel during his three weeks of annual vacation time. He has been taking photos for the past six or seven years with a small, 35mm zoom lens film camera that was a gift from his parents. Since he is part of the "digital age," he would like to replace his film camera with an even smaller digital camera that, for the sake of convenience, can fit easily into his pants or jacket pocket.

Among consumers, there seem to be two different need or problem recognition styles. Some consumers are *actual state* types, who perceive that they have a problem when a product fails to perform satisfactorily (as a cordless telephone that develops constant static). In contrast, other consumers are *desired state* types, for whom the desire for something new may trigger the decision process.[8] Since Eric's current camera can do the job, he appears to be a desired state consumer.

Prepurchase search

Prepurchase search begins when a consumer perceives a need that might be satisfied by the purchase and consumption of a product. The recollection of past experiences (drawn from storage in long-term memory) might provide the consumer with adequate information to make the present choice. On the other hand, when the consumer has had no prior experience, he or she may have to engage in an extensive search of the outside environment for useful information on which to base a choice.

The consumer usually searches his or her memory (the *psychological field* depicted in the model) before seeking external sources of information regarding a given consumption-related need. Past experience is considered an internal source of information. The greater the relevant past experience, the less external information the consumer is likely to need to reach a decision. Many consumer decisions are based on a combination of past experience (internal sources) and marketing and noncommercial information (external sources). The degree of perceived risk can also influence this stage of the decision process (see Chapter 6). In high-risk situations, consumers are likely to engage in complex and extensive information search and evaluation; in low-risk situations, they are likely to use very simple or limited search and evaluation tactics.

The act of shopping is an important form of external information. According to a recent consumer study, there is a big difference between men and women in terms of their response to shopping. Whereas most men do not like to shop, most women claim to like the experience of shopping; and although the majority of women found shopping to be relaxing and enjoyable, the majority of men did not feel that way.[9]

An examination of the external search effort associated with the purchase of different product categories (TVs, VCRs, or personal computers) found that, as the amount of total search effort increased, consumer attitudes toward shopping became more positive, and more time was made available for shopping. Not surprisingly, the external search effort was greatest for consumers who had the least amount of product category knowledge.[10] It follows that the less consumers know about a product category and the more important the purchase is to them, the more time they will make available and the more extensive their prepurchase search activity is likely to be. Conversely, research studies have indicated that consumers high in subjective knowledge (a self-assessment of how much they know about the product category) rely more on their own evaluations than on dealer recommendations.

It is also important to point out that the Internet has had a great impact on prepurchase search. Rather than visiting a store to find out about a product or calling the manufacturer and asking for a brochure, manufacturers' Web sites can provide consumers with much of the information they need about the products and services they are considering. For example, many automobile Web sites provide product specifications, sticker prices and dealer cost information, reviews, and even comparisons with competing vehicles. Audi's Web site (**www.audiusa.com**), for example, lets you "build" your own car, and see how it would look, for example, in different colors. Some auto company Web sites will even list a particular auto dealer's new and used car inventory. And then there are Web sites such as The Fox Company (**www.thefoxcompany.net**) that allow women to customize any number of cosmetic and beauty care products, and My Tailor (**www.mytailor.com**) that lets men design their own clothing, such as dress shirts.

With respect to surfing the Internet for information, consider one consumer's comments drawn from a recent research study: "I like to use the Web because it's so easy to find information, and it's really easy to use. The information is at my finger-tips and

I don't have to search books in libraries."[11] However, a Roper Starch Survey found that an average user searching the Internet gets frustrated in about 12 minutes, on average, and new research findings suggest that although the Internet may reduce physical effort, "the cognitive challenge of interacting with computers and online information limits consumer information search in the Web-based marketspace."[12]

How much information a consumer will gather also depends on various situational factors. Getting back to Eric, while he works long hours in Manhattan, he is willing to spend time researching his desired purchase. He starts by sitting at his office desk with his office computer connected to the firm's network broadband connection. He visits the Web sites of digital camera manufacturers such as Nikon (**www.nikonusa.com**), Canon (**www.canonusa.com**), Sony (**www.sony.com**), Pentax (**www.pentaximaging.com**), and Hewlett Packard (**www.hp.com**), as well as e-tailer Web sites like Amazon (**www.amazon.com**) and Newegg (**www.newegg.com**), to see which brands and models of digital cameras are small and lightweight. Still further, he visits the Web sites of two major New York City camera stores—B&H (**www.bhphotovideo.com**) and Adorama (**www.adorama.com**). He finds several small lightweight digital cameras that seem like possibilities.

Eric also talks to some of his friends and coworkers who are even more into digital cameras than he is. One suggests that he try to find product reviews of any camera that he considers to be a possibility on such Web sites as as CNET (**www.cnet.com**), Digital Photograph Review (**www.dpreview.com**), Digital Camera Resource (**www.dcresource.com**), and Steve's Digicams (**www.steves-digicams.com**).

As Table 16.2 indicates, a number of factors are likely to increase consumers' prepurchase search. For some products and services, the consumer may have ongoing experience on which to draw (such as a skier purchasing a "better" pair of skis), or the purchase may essentially be discretionary in nature (rather than a necessity), so there is no rush to make a decision. In the case of Eric, our equity researcher, while there is no particular need to rush into the purchase of the digital camera, he would like to have it in a month, when he is planning to take a week's vacation.

Let's consider several of the prepurchase search alternatives open to a digital camera buyer. At the most fundamental level, search alternatives can be classified as either personal or impersonal. *Personal* search alternatives include more than a consumer's past experience with the product or service. They also include asking for information and advice from friends, relatives, coworkers, and sales representatives. For instance, Eric spoke with a few friends and coworkers and asked them what they know about digital cameras. Eric also investigated whether photography magazines, such as *Popular Photography*, or computer magazines, such as *Computer Shopper*, might have rated the various brands or models of digital cameras. Table 16.3 presents some of the sources of information that Eric might use as part of his prepurchase search. Any or all of these sources might be used as part of a consumer's search process.

Evaluation of alternatives

When evaluating potential alternatives, consumers tend to use two types of information: (1) a "list" of brands (or models) from which they plan to make their selection (the evoked set) and (2) the criteria they will use to evaluate each brand (or model). Making a selection from a *sample* of all possible brands (or models) is a human characteristic that helps simplify the decision-making process.

Evoked Set   Within the context of consumer decision making, the **evoked set** refers to the specific brands (or models) a consumer considers in making a purchase within a particular product category. (The evoked set is also called the *consideration set*.) A consumer's evoked set is distinguished from his or her **inept set**, which consists of brands (or models) the consumer excludes from purchase consideration because they are felt to be unacceptable (or they are seen as "inferior"), and from the **inert set**, which consists of brands (or models) the consumer is indifferent toward because they are perceived as not having any particular advantages. Regardless of the total number of brands (or models) in a

TABLE 16.2	Factors That Are Likely to Increase Prepurchase Search

Product Factors

Long interpurchase time (a long-lasting or infrequently used product)

Frequent changes in product styling

Frequent price changes

Volume purchasing (large number of units)

High price

Many alternative brands

Much variation in features

Situational Factors

EXPERIENCE

First-time purchase

No past experience because the product is new

Unsatisfactory past experience within the product category

SOCIAL ACCEPTABILITY

The purchase is for a gift

The product is socially visible

VALUE-RELATED CONSIDERATIONS

Purchase is discretionary rather than necessary

All alternatives have both desirable and undesirable consequences

Family members disagree on product requirements or evaluation of alternatives

Product usage deviates from important reference groups

The purchase involves ecological considerations

Many sources of conflicting information

Product Factors

DEMOGRAPHIC CHARACTERISTICS OF CONSUMER

Well educated

High income

White-collar occupation

Under 35 years of age

PERSONALITY

Low dogmatic

Low-risk perceiver (broad categorizer)

Other personal factors such as high product involvement and enjoyment of shopping and search

product category, a consumer's evoked set tends to be quite small on average, often consisting of only three to five brands (or models).

The evoked set consists of the small number of brands the consumer is familiar with, remembers, and finds acceptable. Figure 16.3 depicts the evoked set as a subset of all available brands in a product category. As the figure indicates, it is essential that a product be part of a consumer's evoked set if it is to be considered at all. The five terminal positions in the model that do not end in purchase would appear to have perceptual problems. For example, (1) brands (or models) may be *unknown* because of the consumer's selective

TABLE 16.3	Alternative Prepurchase Information Sources for an Ultralight Laptop
PERSONAL	**IMPERSONAL**
Friends	Newspaper articles
Neighbors	Magazine articles
Relatives	*Consumer Reports*
Coworkers	Direct-mail brochures
Computer salespeople	Information from product advertisements
	Internal Web sites

exposure to advertising media and selective perception of advertising stimuli; (2) brands (or models) may be *unacceptable* because of poor qualities or attributes or inappropriate positioning in either advertising or product characteristics; (3) brands (or models) may be perceived as not having any special benefits and are regarded *indifferently* by the consumer; (4) brands (or models) may be *overlooked* because they have not been clearly positioned or sharply targeted at the consumer market segment under study; and (5) brands (or models) may not be selected because they are perceived by consumers as *unable to satisfy* perceived needs as fully as the brand that is chosen.

In each of these instances, the implication for marketers is that promotional techniques should be designed to impart a more favorable, perhaps more relevant, product image to the target consumer. This may also require a change in product features or attributes (more or better features). An alternative strategy is to invite consumers in a particular target segment to consider a specific offering and possibly put it in their evoked set.

Research also suggests that the use of white space and choice of typeface in advertisements may influence the consumer's image of the product. For example, quality, prestige, trust, attitude toward the brand, and purchase intention have been shown to be positively conveyed by white space, and typefaces that were perceived as being attractive, warm, and liked when they were simple, more natural, and include a typefont with serifs.[13]

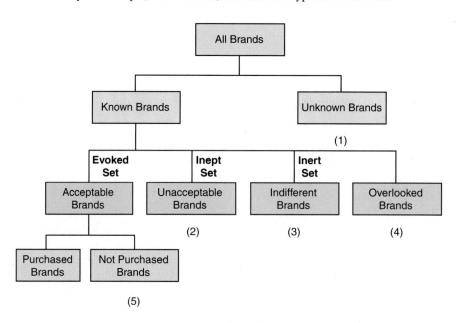

The Evoked Set as a Subset of All Brands in a Product Class

FIGURE 16.3

It has also been suggested that consumers may not, all at once, reduce down the number of possible choices into their evoked set, but instead may make several decisions within a single decision process. These screening decisions, or decision waves, are used to eliminate unsuitable alternatives before gathering information or comparing options, and help reduce decision complexity to a more manageable level.[14]

Criteria Used for Evaluating Brands   The criteria consumers use to evaluate the alternative products that constitute their evoked sets usually are expressed in terms of important product attributes. Examples of product attributes that consumers have used as criteria in evaluating nine product categories are listed in Table 16.4.

When a company knows that consumers will be evaluating alternatives, it sometimes advertises in a way that recommends the criteria that consumers should use in assessing product or service options.

We have probably all had the experience of comparing or evaluating different brands or models of a product and finding the one that just feels, looks, and/or performs "right." Interestingly, research shows that when consumers discuss such "right products," there is little or no mention of price; brand names are not often uppermost in consumers' minds; items often reflect personality characteristics or childhood experiences; and it is often "love at first sight." In one study, the products claimed to "just feel right" included Big Bertha golf clubs, old leather briefcases, Post-it notes, and the Honda Accord.[15] And, a product's country of origin can also play a role in how a consumer evaluates a brand (see Chapter 14).

Research has explored the role of brand credibility (which consists of trustworthiness and expertise) on brand choice, and has found that brand credibility improves the chances that a brand will be included in the consideration set. Three factors that impact

TABLE 16.4	**Possible Product Attributes Used as Purchase Criteria for Nine Product Categories**

PERSONAL COMPUTERS	**CD PLAYERS**	**WRISTWATCHES**
Processing speed	Mega bass	Watchband
Price	Electronic shock protection	Alarm feature
Type of display	Length of play on batteries	Price
Hard-disk size	Random play feature	Water resistant
Amount of memory	Water resistant	Quartz movement
Laptop or desktop		Size of dial
VCRS	**COLOR TVS**	**FROZEN DINNERS**
Ease of programming	Picture quality	Taste
Number of heads	Length of warranty	Type of main course
Number of tape speeds	Cable ready	Type of side dishes
Slow-motion feature	Price	Price
Automatic tracking	Size of screen	Preparation requirements
35MM CAMERAS	**FOUNTAIN PENS**	**COLOR INKJET PRINTERS**
Autofocus	Balance	Output speed
Built-in flash	Price	Number of ink colors
Automatic film loading	Gold nib	Resolution (DPI)
Lens type	Smoothness	Length of warranty
Size and weight	Ink reserve	USB capability

a brand's credibility are: the perceived quality of the brand, the perceived risk associated with the brand, and the information costs saved with that brand (due to the time and effort saved by not having to shop around).[16] Still further, the study indicates that trustworthiness is more important than expertise when it comes to making a choice.

Let's return for a moment to Eric and his search for a small, lightweight digital camera. As part of his search process, he has acquired information about a number of relevant issues (or attributes) that could influence his final choice. For example, Eric has learned that the overall size of a digital camera is very much a function of the features that it contains, such as whether or not the camera has a viewfinder, how powerful its flash is, whether it offers manual control of functions such as shutter speed and aperture, and the size of its camera back LCD screen. Still further, Eric realizes that the higher the megapixel count of the pictures the camera takes, the higher the camera's price is going to be (i.e., a 5 megapixel digital camera can typically take photos that can be enlarged to 8 × 10 inches and still be sharp, while a 3 megapixel camera's photos may not appear sharp when enlarged bigger than 5 × 7 inches). He reasoned that for the types of photos that he takes (he gets 4 × 6-inch prints and on rare occasions makes a 5 × 7-inch enlargement), 5 megapixels is plenty.

As part of his search process, Eric has also acquired information about other relevant issues (or attributes) that could influence his final choice (see Table 16.5). For example, he has learned that some digital camera zoom lenses have less of a zoom range than others, and that all LCD screens are not equally sharp because some have only half or two-thirds the number of pixels of others (the greater the number of pixels, the sharper the image on the camera-back LCD screen).

On the basis of his information search, Eric realizes that he is going to have to make a decision regarding what he really wants from this new digital camera. Does he want just a digital version of his current 35mm point-and-shoot camera, or is he willing to sacrifice some features for a camera that is substantially smaller and lighter? He comes to realize that he always has his current camera set to "auto" when he takes pictures, and

TABLE 16.5	Comparison of Selected Characteristics of Digital Cameras		
FEATURE	**NIKON**	**CANON**	**PENTAX**
Megapixels	5.1	5.0	5.0
Weight (ozs.)	4.2	4.6	3.7
Dimensions	3.5×2.3×0.8	3.4×2×0.8	3.3×2×0.8
Lens focal length (35mm equivalent)	35–105	35–105	36–107
Viewfinder	No	Yes	Yes
LCD screen size	2.5 inches	2 inches	1.8 inches
LCD resolution	110,000 pixels	118,000 pixels	85,000 pixels
Media	SD card	SD card	SD card
Manual control	Program auto	Program & exposure compensation	Program & exposure compensation
Battery/Charger	Proprietary battery, camera charges on proprietary cradle	Proprietary battery, small plug-in charger	Proprietary battery, camera charges on proprietary cradle
Price	$340	$345	$330

Source: Information from B&H catalog (Summer 2005) and manufacturers' Web sites.

that the only features he really wants, in addition to small size, is autofocus (which all the digital cameras he's investigated have) and a zoom lens. Thus, Eric realizes that he is willing to give up some functionality (such as manual control of shutter speed) in exchange for reduced size and weight.

Consumer Decision Rules   Consumer decision rules, often referred to as *heuristics, decision strategies*, and *information-processing strategies*, are procedures used by consumers to facilitate brand (or other consumption-related) choices. These rules reduce the burden of making complex decisions by providing guidelines or routines that make the process less taxing.

Consumer decision rules have been broadly classified into two major categories: **compensatory** and **noncompensatory decision rules**. In following a compensatory decision rule, a consumer evaluates brand or model options in terms of each relevant attribute and computes a weighted or summated score for each brand. The computed score reflects the brand's relative merit as a potential purchase choice. The assumption is that the consumer will select the brand that scores highest among the alternatives evaluated. Referring to Table 16.6, it is clear that when using a compensatory decision rule, the Canon digital camera scores highest.

A unique feature of a compensatory decision rule is that it allows a positive evaluation of a brand on one attribute to balance out a negative evaluation on some other attribute. For example, a positive assessment of the energy savings made possible by a particular brand or type of lightbulb may offset an unacceptable assessment in terms of the bulb's diminished light output.

In contrast, noncompensatory decision rules do not allow consumers to balance positive evaluations of a brand on one attribute against a negative evaluation on some other attribute. For instance, in the case of an energy-saving lightbulb, the product's negative (unacceptable) rating on its light output would not be offset by a positive evaluation of its energy savings. Instead, this particular lightbulb would be disqualified from further consideration. If Eric's choice of a digital camera was based on the desire to have a built-in viewfinder, rather than just an LCD screen on the camera's back (refer again to Table 16.5), a noncompensatory decision rule would have eliminated the Nikon.

Three noncompensatory rules are considered briefly here: the *conjunctive* rule, the *disjunctive* rule, and the *lexicographic* rule.

In following a **conjunctive decision rule**, the consumer establishes a separate, minimally acceptable level as a cutoff point for each attribute. If any particular brand or

TABLE 16.6	Hypothetical Ratings for Digital Cameras		
FEATURE	**NIKON**	**CANON**	**PENTAX**
MegaPixels	9	9	9
Weight	7	6	8
Dimensions	6	8	8
Lens focal length	9	9	9
Viewfinder	4	8	8
LCD screen size	9	8	6
LCD resolution	8	9	5
Media	9	9	9
Manual Control	5	9	9
Battery/Charger	5	9	5
Price	8	8	8
Total	79	92	84

model falls below the cutoff point on any one attribute, the option is eliminated from further consideration. Because the conjunctive rule can result in several acceptable alternatives, it becomes necessary in such cases for the consumer to apply an additional decision rule to arrive at a final selection, for example, to accept the first satisfactory brand. The conjunctive rule is particularly useful in quickly reducing the number of alternatives to be considered. The consumer can then apply another more refined decision rule to arrive at a final choice.

The **disjunctive rule** is the "mirror image" of the conjunctive rule. In applying this decision rule, the consumer establishes a separate, minimally acceptable cutoff level for each attribute (which may be higher than the one normally established for a conjunctive rule). In this case, if an option meets or exceeds the cutoff established for any one attribute, it is accepted. Here again, a number of brands (or models) might exceed the cutoff point, producing a situation in which another decision rule is required. When this occurs, the consumer may accept the first satisfactory alternative as the final choice or apply another decision rule that is perhaps more suitable.

In following a **lexicographic decision rule**, the consumer first ranks the attributes in terms of perceived relevance or importance. The consumer then compares the various alternatives in terms of the single attribute that is considered most important. If one option scores sufficiently high on this top-ranked attribute (regardless of the score on any of the other attributes), it is selected and the process ends. When there are two or more surviving alternatives, the process is repeated with the second highest-ranked attribute (and so on), until reaching the point that one of the options is selected because it exceeds the others on a particular attribute.

With the lexicographic rule, the highest-ranked attribute (the one applied first) may reveal something about the individual's basic consumer (or shopping) orientation. For instance, a "buy the best" rule might indicate that the consumer is *quality oriented*; a "buy the most prestigious brand" rule might indicate that the consumer is *status oriented*; a "buy the least expensive" rule might reveal that the consumer is *economy minded*.

A variety of decision rules appear quite commonplace. According to a consumer survey, 9 out of 10 shoppers who go to the store for frequently purchased items possess a specific shopping strategy for saving money. The consumer segment and the specific shopping rules that these segments employ are:[17]

1. *Practical loyalists—those who look for ways to save on the brands and products they would buy anyway.*

2. *Bottom-line price shoppers—those who buy the lowest-priced item with little or no regard for brand.*

3. *Opportunistic switchers—those who use coupons or sales to decide among brands and products that fall within their evoked set.*

4. *Deal hunters—those who look for the best bargain and are not brand loyal.*

We have considered only the most basic of an almost infinite number of consumer decision rules. Most of the decision rules described here can be combined to form new variations, such as conjunctive-compensatory, conjunctive-disjunctive, and disjunctive-conjunctive rules. It is likely that for many purchase decisions, consumers maintain in long-term memory overall evaluations of the brands in their evoked sets. This would make assessment by individual attributes unnecessary. Instead, the consumer would simply select the brand with the highest perceived overall rating. This type of synthesized decision rule is known as the **affect referral decision rule** and may represent the simplest of all rules.

Table 16.7 summarizes the essence of many of the decision rules considered in this chapter in terms of the kind of mental statements that Eric might make in selecting a digital camera.

How Do Functionally Illiterate Consumers Decide?

The National Adult Literacy Survey found that a bit more than 20 percent of American consumers did not possess the

TABLE 16.7	Hypothetical Use of Popular Decision Rules in Making a Decision to Purchase a Digital Camera
DECISION RULE	**MENTAL STATEMENT**
Compensatory rule	"I selected the digital camera that came out best when I balanced the good ratings against the bad ratings."
Conjunctive rule	"I selected the digital camera that had no bad features."
Disjunctive rule	"I picked the digital camera that excelled in at least one attribute."
Lexicographic rule	"I looked at the feature that was most important to me and chose the camera that ranked highest on that attribute."
Affect referral rule	"I bought the brand with the highest overall rating."

rudimentary skills in language and arithmetic needed for the typical retail environment, and that perhaps as much as half of all U.S. consumers lack the skills needed to master specific aspects of shopping, such as sales agreements and credit applications. Furthermore, despite the fact that functionally illiterate consumers have only 40 percent as much purchasing power as their literate counterparts, they may spend as much as $380 billion annually.[18]

Research has found that functionally illiterate consumers do make decisions differently, in terms of cognitive predilections, decision rules and trade-offs, and coping behaviors (see Figure 16.4). For example, they use concrete reasoning and noncompensatory decision rules, meaning that they base the purchase decision on a single piece of information, without regard to other product attributes (e.g., "I just look at the tag and see what's cheapest. I don't look by their sizes"). Such consumers, if confronted with two boxes of a product at the same price, would tend to purchase the one in the physically larger box, even if the label on the smaller sized package indicated a higher weight or greater volume. And through what might be referred to as "sight reading," they recognize brand logos the same way they might recognize people in a photograph. In fact, functionally illiterate consumers treat all words and numbers as pictorial elements. They also become anxious when shopping in a new store (they prefer to shop in the same store, especially if they have

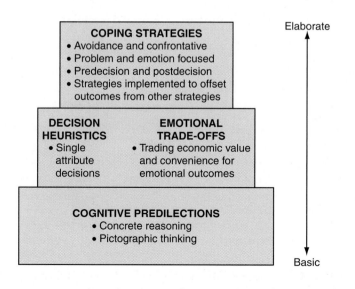

The Decision Process for Functionally Illiterate Consumers

Source: Madhubalan Viswanathan, José Antonio Rosa, and James Edwin Harris, "Decision Making and Coping of Functionally Illiterate Consumers and Some Implications for Marketing Management," *Journal of Marketing* 69 (January 2005): 19.

FIGURE 16.4

established a rapport with a friendly and helpful employee), and often give all their money to the cashier expecting him/her to return the proper change.[19] Table 16.8 presents the coping strategies used by functionally illiterate consumers. Note how such consumers avoid purchasing unknown brands and try to carry limited amounts of cash to the store.

Going Online to Secure Assistance in Decision Making   For the past several years researchers have been examining how the Internet has impacted the way consumers make decisions. It is often hypothesized that because consumers have limited information-processing capacity, they must develop a choice strategy based on both individual factors

TABLE 16.8	Coping Strategies of Functionally Illiterate Consumers
COPING STRATEGIES	**CLASSIFICATIONS**
AVOIDANCE	
Shop at the same store: avoids stress of unfamiliar environment	Problem focused: shops effectively Predecision: habitual choice about store helps with choices about products
Shop at smaller stores: avoids cognitive demands from product variety	Emotion focused: reduces stress Predecision: requires advance planning
Single-attribute decisions: avoids stressful and complex product comparisons	Problem focused: makes decisions manageable Emotion focused: preserves image of competence Predecision: requires advance planning
Avoid percentage- and fraction-off discounted items: avoids difficult numerical tasks	Emotion focused: reduces stress Problem focused: less chance of mistakes Predecision: implements habitually
Buy only known brands (loyalty): avoids risks from unknown brands	Problem focused: facilitates shopping Predecision: implements habitually
Rationalize outcomes to shift responsibility: avoids responsibility for outcomes	Emotion focused: protects self esteem Postdecision: implements after outcome is clear
Carry limited amounts of cash: avoids risks of overspending and being cheated	Problem focused: controls transactions Predecision: requires advance planning
Buy small amounts more often: avoids risk of large scale cheating	Problem focused: controls transactions Predecision: requires advance planning
Pretend disability: avoids revealing deficiencies and embarrassment	Problem focused: obtains assistance Emotion focused: preserves public image Predecision: requires advance planning
Pretend to evaluate products and prices: avoids revealing deficiencies indirectly	Emotion focused: preserves public image Predecision: requires advance planning
CONFRONTATIVE	
Shop with family members and friends: enables others to know deficiencies	Problem focused: helps shop on a budget Predecision: involves advance planning
Establish relationships with store personnel: enables others to know deficiencies	Emotion focused: avoids embarrassment and stress Predecision: Involves advance planning

(Continued)

TABLE 16.8	Continued
Seek help in the store: enables others to know deficiencies	Problem focused: facilitates final decision Predecision: leads to a purchase decision
Give all money in pockets to cashier: admits deficiencies, plays on honesty standards	Problem focused: avoids not being able to count Predecision: implements habitually
Buy one item at a time: addresses the problem of loss of control when turning over cash	Problem focused: controls pace of transactions and flow of funds Predecision: requires advance planning
Confront store personnel and demand different treatment: focuses on responses and behaviors of others	Emotion focused: seeks to minimize or eliminate embarrassment and to preserve or restore public image Postdecision: implements in response to others
Plan expenditures with assistance from others: enables others to know deficiencies	Problem focused: facilitates a budget Predecision: involves advance planning

Source: Madhubalan Viswanathan, José Antonio Rosa, and James Edwin Harris, "Decision Making and Coping of Functionally Illiterate Consumers and Some Implications for Marketing Management," *Journal of Marketing* 69 (January 2005): 25.

(e.g., knowledge, personality traits, demographics) and contextual factors (characteristics of the decision tasks). The three major contextual factors that have been researched are *task complexity* (number of alternatives and amount of information available for each alternative), *information organization* (presentation, format, and content), and *time constraint* (more or less time to decide).[20] Table 16.9 compares these contextual factors for both the electronic and traditional environments.

A reason to go online is that a number of Web sites allow a consumer to build his or her own anything. For example, you can order M&Ms imprinted with your own message at **www.shop.mms.com/custom**, or order personalized shower gels and hand soaps at **www.samsoap.com**. About 75 percent of Mini Cooper purchasers pour through 70 options to design their vehicles online.[21]

Lifestyles as a Consumer Decision Strategy   An individual's or family's decisions to be committed to a particular lifestyle (e.g., devoted followers of a particular religion) impacts on a wide range of specific everyday consumer behavior. For instance, the Trends Research Institute has identified "voluntary simplicity" as one of the top 10 lifestyle trends.[22] Researchers there estimate that 15 percent of all "boomers" seek a simpler lifestyle with reduced emphasis on ownership and possessions. Voluntary simplifiers are making do with less clothing and fewer credit cards (with no outstanding balances) and moving to smaller, yet still adequate, homes or apartments in less populated communities. Most importantly, it is not that these consumers can no longer afford their affluence or "lifestyle of abundance"; rather, they are seeking new, "reduced," less extravagant lifestyles. As part of this new lifestyle commitment, some individuals are seeking less stressful and lower-salary careers or jobs. In a telephone survey, for example, 33 percent of those contacted claimed that they would be willing to take a 20 percent pay cut in return for working fewer hours.[23] Time pressure may also play a role in the consumer's decision process, as research has positively associated this factor with both sale proneness (i.e., respond positively to cents-off coupons or special offers) and display proneness (e.g., respond positively to in-store displays offering a special price).[24]

As another lifestyle issue, consider the humongous success of the Apple iPod. Especially among teenagers and young adults, the iPod is overwhelmingly the portable music player of choice. While some might argue that the introduction of the iPod Shuffle

TABLE 16.9	Comparison of Electronic and Traditional Information Environment

		ELECTRONIC ENVIRONMENT **CONSUMERS USE BOTH "HEADS" AND COMPUTERS TO MAKE DECISIONS. THE TOTAL CAPACITY IS EXTENDED.**	**TRADITIONAL ENVIRONMENT** **CONSUMERS USE "HEADS" TO MAKE DECISIONS. THEIR COGNITIVE CAPACITY IS FIXED.**
ASSUMPTION			
Contextual Factors	Task Complexity	More alternatives and more information for each alternative are available.	Information is scattered and information search is costly.
	Information Organization	Information is more accessible. Information presentation format is flexible. It can be reorganized and controlled by consumers. Product utilities can be calculated by computers without consumers' direct examination of the attributes.	Information presentation format and organization are fixed. They can only be "edited" by consumers manually (e.g., using pencil and paper).
	Time Constraint	Time is saved by using computers to execute the decision rules; extra time is needed to learn how to use the application.	Complex choice strategies require more time to formulate and execute.

Source: Lan Xia, "Consumer Choice Strategies and Choice Confidence in the Electronic Environment," *American Marketing Association Conference Proceedings,* American Marketing Association, 10, 1999, 272.

(starting at $99) cheapens the product's image, it could also be a way for Apple to offer a product that allows more modest income parents to placate their teenagers. One industry analyst has commented that "The cachet is not in the price, it's in the brand. iPod is an affordable luxury item, and they're simply bringing it to another level of buyers. People who want an iPod will forgo buying an MP3 player at all saying 'If I buy, I will buy an iPod.' "[25]

Incomplete Information and Noncomparable Alternatives   In many choice situations, consumers face incomplete information on which to base decisions and must use alternative strategies to cope with the missing elements. Missing information may result from advertisements or packaging that mentions only certain attributes, the consumer's own imperfect memory of attributes for nonpresent alternatives, or because some attributes are experiential and can only be evaluated after product use. There are at least four alternative strategies that consumers can adopt for coping with missing information:[26]

1. *Consumers may delay the decision until missing information is obtained.*
2. *Consumers may ignore missing information and decide to continue with the current decision rule (e.g., compensatory or noncompensatory), using the available attribute information.*

3. *Consumers may change the customarily used decision strategy to one that better accommodates missing information.*

4. *Consumers may infer ("construct") the missing information.*

In discussing consumer decision rules, we have assumed that a choice is made from among the brands (or models) evaluated. Of course, a consumer also may conclude that none of the alternatives offers sufficient benefits to warrant purchase. If this were to occur with a necessity, such as a home water heater, the consumer would probably either lower his or her expectations and settle for the best of the available alternatives or seek information about additional brands, hoping to find one that more closely meets predetermined criteria. On the other hand, if the purchase is more discretionary (a second or third NFL team jersey), the consumer probably would postpone the purchase. In this case, information gained from the search up to that point would be transferred to long-term storage (in the psychological field) and retrieved and reintroduced as input if and when the consumer regains interest in making such a purchase.

In Apply Decision Rules   It should be noted that, in applying decision rules, consumers may at times attempt to compare dissimilar (noncomparable) alternatives. For example, a consumer may be undecided about whether to buy a new computer system or a new set of golf clubs, because the individual can afford one or the other but not both. Another example: A consumer may try to decide between buying a new overcoat or a new raincoat. When there is great dissimilarity in the alternative ways of allocating available funds, consumers abstract the products to a level in which comparisons are possible. In the foregoing examples, a consumer might weigh the alternatives (golf clubs versus PC or overcoat versus raincoat) in terms of which alternative would offer more pleasure or which, if either, is more of a "necessity."

A Series of Decisions   Although we have discussed the purchase decision as if it were a single decision, in reality, a purchase can involve a number of decisions. For example, when purchasing an automobile, consumers are involved in multiple decisions such as choosing the make or country of origin of the car (foreign versus domestic), the dealer, the financing, and particular options. In the case of a replacement automobile, these decisions must be preceded by a decision as to whether or not to trade in one's current car.

Decision Rules and Marketing Strategy   An understanding of which decision rules consumers apply in selecting a particular product or service is useful to marketers concerned with formulating a promotional program. A marketer familiar with the prevailing decision rule can prepare a promotional message in a format that would facilitate consumer information processing. The promotional message might even suggest how potential consumers should make a decision. For instance, a direct-mail piece for a desktop computer might tell potential consumers "what to look for in a new PC." This mail piece might specifically ask consumers to consider the attributes of hard disk size, amount of memory, processor speed, monitor size and maximum resolution, video card memory, and CD burner speed.

Output

The output portion of the consumer decision-making model concerns two closely associated kinds of postdecision activity: **purchase behavior** and **postpurchase evaluation**. The objective of both activities is to increase the consumer's satisfaction with his or her purchase.

Purchase behavior

Consumers make three types of purchases: *trial purchases, repeat purchases*, and *long-term commitment purchases*. When a consumer purchases a product (or brand) for the first time and buys a smaller quantity than usual, this purchase would be considered a trial. Thus, a trial is the exploratory phase of purchase behavior in which consumers attempt to evaluate a product through direct use. For instance, when consumers purchase a new brand of laundry detergent about which they may be uncertain, they are likely to purchase smaller trial quantities than if it were a familiar brand. Consumers can also be encouraged to try a new product through such promotional tactics as free samples, coupons, and/or sale prices.

When a new brand in an established product category (toothpaste, chewing gum, or cola) is found by trial to be more satisfactory or better than other brands, consumers are likely to repeat the purchase. Repeat purchase behavior is closely related to the concept of *brand loyalty*, which most firms try to encourage because it contributes to greater stability in the marketplace (see Chapter 7). Unlike trial, in which the consumer uses the product on a small scale and without any commitment, a repeat purchase usually signifies that the product meets with the consumer's approval and that he or she is willing to use it again and in larger quantities.

Trial, of course, is not always feasible. For example, with most durable goods (refrigerators, washing machines, or electric ranges), a consumer usually moves directly from evaluation to a long-term commitment (through purchase) without the opportunity for an actual trial. While purchasers of the new Volkswagen Beetle were awaiting delivery of their just-purchased cars, they were kept "warm" by being sent a mailing that included a psychographic tool called "Total Visual Imagery" that was personalized to the point that it showed them the precise model and color they had ordered.[27]

Consider Eric and his decision concerning the selection of a digital camera. Since he lives and works in Manhattan, it was easy for him to visit several of the large camera stores. His first stop was Adorama, where all three of the cameras he was considering were on display. He was able to hold each one, play with all of the camera controls, and, since the store keeps batteries in its demo models, Eric was able to take pictures with each one. The salesperson was neutral in his opinion, feeling that all three cameras were essentially equivalent, and all took excellent pictures. A few days later, Eric stopped at B&H on his way home from the office. Again, he was able to handle all three cameras and take pictures with them. It seemed to him that the Canon felt better in his hands than the other two, and the controls seemed to fall right where he placed his fingers when holding the camera (a positive). Also, the Canon had an optical finder, which was the way Eric was used to taking pictures.

Next, Eric again went to the Internet. He had been told by a coworker that there were many digital camera discussion groups on the Internet, and that many of them were camera-model specific. So he spent one evening in his apartment reading owner/user comments on the forums of Digital Photography Review and Digital Camera Resource. He learned what some owners liked and disliked about each of the three cameras that he was considering. He also learned that the capacity of the memory cards packaged with each camera were too small to be of any use, and that along with purchasing a memory card with greater capacity he should also purchase a spare battery for whichever camera he bought. He also posted a message on the dpreview.com forum, asking which of the three cameras might be best for him, and within a day he had received five responses. The general sense was that all three cameras were excellent, but that the Canon, with its new, improved Digic II image processor, might be the best of the three because it would have the least amount of shutter lag (the hesitation of the camera between the time the shutter release is pressed and the camera actually takes the picture).

Eric is now convinced that the Canon is the digital camera he should purchase. It has a viewfinder, which is a feature that he likes and is used to, it is small and light in weight, and he considers its appearance to be very stylish. Also, he feels that he will have no difficulty carrying the camera by slipping it into his pants or jacket pocket. So he checks the prices for this camera both at the New York City retailers that he visited, and at several e-tailers. He finds that the lowest price for the camera is at Amazon.com, which includes free shipping, and he orders it. He had been told by friends that he can use any brand of SD memory card in the camera, and that rather than pay a lot of money for the genuine Canon battery (in order to have a spare), he should go online where he should be able to find a spare battery at less than half the cost of the genuine one. Eric goes to several e-tailer Web sites, and is able to find a 512MB SD card for $25 (after rebate), and a spare battery for $13—he orders both. Within the next week, UPS delivers his new Canon digital camera, as well as his SD memory card and spare battery.

Postpurchase evaluation

As consumers use a product, particularly during a trial purchase, they evaluate its performance in light of their own expectations. There are three possible outcomes of these evaluations: (1) actual performance matches expectations, leading to a neutral feeling; (2) performance exceeds expectations, causing what is known as *positive disconfirmation of expectations* (which leads to satisfaction); and (3) performance is below expectations, causing *negative disconfirmation of expectations* and dissatisfaction. For each of these three outcomes, consumers' expectations and satisfaction are closely linked; that is, consumers tend to judge their experience against their expectations when performing a postpurchase evaluation.

An important component of postpurchase evaluation is the reduction of any uncertainty or doubt that the consumer might have had about the selection. As part of their postpurchase analyses, consumers try to reassure themselves that their choice was a wise one; that is, they attempt to reduce *postpurchase cognitive dissonance.* As Chapter 8 indicated, they do this by adopting one of the following strategies: They may rationalize the decision as being wise; they may seek advertisements that support their choice and avoid those of competitive brands; they may attempt to persuade friends or neighbors to buy the same brand (and, thus, confirm their own choice); or they may turn to other satisfied owners for reassurance.

The degree of postpurchase analysis that consumers undertake depends on the importance of the product decision and the experience acquired in using the product. When the product lives up to expectations, they probably will buy it again. When the product's performance is disappointing or does not meet expectations, however, they will search for more suitable alternatives. Thus, the consumer's postpurchase evaluation "feeds back" as *experience* to the consumer's psychological field and serves to influence future related decisions. Although it would be logical to assume that customer satisfaction is related to customer retention (i.e., if a consumer is satisfied with his Nautica jacket, he will buy other Nautica products), a recent study found no direct relationship between satisfaction and retention. The findings show that customer retention may be more a matter of the brand's reputation—especially for products consumers find difficult to evaluate.[28]

What was Eric's postpurchase evaluation of his new digital camera? He absolutely loves it! First of all, because it is so small in size, he can carry it in his pants pocket anywhere he goes, and therefore is always ready to take pictures, which is something he very much enjoys doing. His 256MB secure digital card allows him to take about 200 photos before filling up, even using the camera's "best picture" setting. After coming back from a friend's party, where he took about 25 pictures, he quickly transferred the photos from his camera to his laptop (using the software and cord supplied with the camera), easily cropped a few of the photos and eliminated "red eye" in others, and then uploaded the 15 photos he really liked to the CVS Drugstore Web site. The next day, after work, he stopped by his local CVS store (located less than a block from his apartment) and picked up 4 × 6-inch reprints of his digital photos. He was absolutely thrilled with how sharp and colorful his pictures were, and couldn't wait to share these photos with his friends.

consumer gifting behavior

In terms of both dollars spent each year and how they make givers and receivers feel, gifts are a particularly interesting part of consumer behavior. Products and services chosen as gifts represent more than ordinary "everyday" purchases. Because of their symbolic meaning, they are associated with such important events as Mother's Day, births and birthdays, engagements, weddings, graduations, and many other accomplishments and milestones.

Gifting behavior can be thought of as the *gift exchange* that takes place between a giver and a recipient. The definition is broad in nature and embraces gifts given voluntarily ("Just

TABLE 16.10	Five Giver-Receiver Gifting Subdivisions		
		RECEIVERS "OTHER"	
GIVERS	**INDIVIDUAL**	**GROUP**	**SELF***
Individual	Interpersonal gifting	Intercategory gifting	Intrapersonal gifting
Group	Intercategory gifting	Intergroup gifting	Intragroup gifting

*This "SELF" is either singular self ("me") or plural ("us").

Source: Based on Deborah Y. Cohn and Leon G. Schiffman, "Gifting: A Taxonomy of Private Realm Giver and Recipient Relationships," Working Paper, City University of New York, Baruch College, 1996, 2–7.

to let you know I'm thinking of you"), as well as gifts that are an obligation ("I had to get him a gift").[29] It includes gifts given to (and received from) others and gifts to oneself, or **self-gifts**. Indeed, although 96 percent of Americans purchased at least one "gift" last year, the majority of products that we refer to as "gifts" are self-purchased (i.e., they are self-gifts).[30] Furthermore, gift purchases represent 10 percent of all retail purchases in North America, and over $100 billion is spent annually on gifts in the United States.[31]

Still further, gifting is an act of symbolic communication, with explicit and implicit meanings ranging from congratulations, love, and regret to obligation and dominance. The nature of the relationship between gift giver and gift receiver is an important consideration in choosing a gift. Indeed, gifting often impacts the relationship between the giver and the recipient.[32] Table 16.10 presents an enumeration of the relationships between various combinations of gift givers and gift receivers in the consumer gifting process. The model reveals the following five gifting subdivisions: (1) intergroup gifting, (2) intercategory gifting, (3) intragroup gifting, (4) interpersonal gifting, and (5) intrapersonal gifting.

Intergroup gifting behavior occurs whenever one group exchanges gifts with another group (such as one family and another). You will recall from Chapter 10 that the process and outcome of family decision making is different from individual decision making. Similarly, gifts given to families will be different than those given to individual family members. For example, a "common" wedding gift for a bride *and* a groom may include products for setting up a household rather than a gift that would personally be used by either the bride or the groom. When it comes to *intercategory gifting*, either an individual is giving a gift to a group (a single friend is giving a couple an anniversary gift) or a group is giving an individual a gift (friends chip in and give another friend a joint birthday gift). The gift selection strategies "buy for joint recipients" or "buy with someone" (creating intercategory gifting) are especially useful when it comes to a difficult recipient situation (when "nothing seems to satisfy her"). These strategies can also be applied to reduce some of the time pressure associated with shopping for the great number of gifts exchanged during the American Christmas season gift-giving ritual. For example, a consumer may choose to purchase five intercategory gifts for five aunt and uncle pairs (intercategory gifting), instead of buying 10 personal gifts for five aunts and five uncles (interpersonal gifting). In this way, less time, money, and effort may be expended.

An *intragroup gift* can be characterized by the sentiment "we gave this to ourselves"; that is, a group gives a gift to itself or its members. For example, a dual-income couple may find that their demanding work schedules limit leisure time spent together as husband and wife. Therefore, an anniversary gift ("to us") of a cruise to Bermuda would be an example of an intragroup gift. It would also remedy the couple's problem of not spending enough time together. In contrast, *interpersonal gifting* occurs between just two individuals, a gift giver and gift receiver. By their very nature, interpersonal gifts are "intimate" because they provide an opportunity for a gift giver to reveal what he or she thinks of the gift receiver. Successful gifts are those that communicate that the giver knows and understands the receiver and their relationship. For example, a pair of cufflinks given to a friend in just the right shape and size can be viewed as "she really knows me." In contrast, a toaster oven given as a Valentine's Day gift, when the recipient is expecting a more "intimate" gift, can mean the deterioration of a relationship. Still further, researchers who have explored the gender of gift givers and their feelings about same-sex gifting (female to female or male to male) and opposite-sex gifting (male to female or female to male) have found that both male and female gift givers feel more comfortable in giving gifts to the same sex; however, they also reported that they felt more intense feeling with respect to gifts given to members of the opposite sex.[33] Additionally, although females get more pleasure than males from giving gifts and generally play the dominant role in gift exchanges, both sexes are strongly motivated by feelings of obligation. Still further, everyone knows that selecting and giving a gift can be the cause of "gifting anxiety" (which is related to social anxiety) on the part of the givers, the recipients, and the gifting situations themselves. Knowledge of such gender differences are useful for marketers to know because it implies that additional support might be appreciated at the point of purchase (while in a store) when a consumer is considering a gift for an opposite-sex recipient.

A recent study of gifts purchased online found that the variety-seeking trait (see Chapter 5) extends to gifting, as subjects with this trait considered a wider range of product categories when buying gifts for others.[34] Table 16.11 presents a picture of the dynamics of the gift continuum in Hong Kong. Note how a number of issues associated with the gift, such as risk, emotional expectations, and the "why," vary across the four categories of gifts. For example, a gift given to a "romantic other" involves a high emotional expectation, but one given to a friend has a low emotional expectation.[35]

One study examined mothers giving gifts to their children (*interpersonal gifting*) across three different cultures: (1) Anglo-Celtic (mothers born in Australia), (2) Sino-Vietnamese

TABLE 16.11	The Dynamics of a Gift Continuum in Hong Kong			
WHO	**ROMANTIC OTHER**	**CLOSE FRIENDS**	**JUST FRIENDS**	**HI/BYE FRIENDS**
Chinese Terminology	*Sui Iáih maht*	*Yihhei*	*Renqing*	*Guanxi*
When (examples)	(1) Birthday Gift	(1) Birthday Gift	(1) Birthday Gift	(1) Birthday Gift
	(2) Special Occasions (e.g., Valentine's Day)	(2) Special Occasions (e.g., leaving on a trip)	(2) Maintenance Gift (e.g., souvenir from a trip)	
	(3) Spontaneous (e.g., small gifts)	(3) Spontaneous (e.g., special awards)		
	(4) Formal/Ceremonial (e.g., Mid-Autumn Festival)	(4) Formal/Ceremonial (e.g., New Year)		
Type of Gift	Expressive	Expressive	Expressive/Instrumental	Instrumental
Emotional Expectations	High	High	Medium	Low
Selection Criteria	Inexpensive (early) Expensive (later) No Gift (family)	Mostly Expensive	Somewhat Expensive	Inexpensive
Effort in Selection	Match Needs (e.g., jewelry)	Match Needs (e.g., desired clothing)	Typical Gift (e.g., having meal)	Typical Gift (e.g., birthday card)
Token Gift (Interim)	Often	Often	Occasionally	Occasionally
Why	Win Hearts	Care	Care/Build Network	Build Network
Face	Social (early) Moral (later)	Moral	Mostly Social	Social
Risks	Guilt/Shame	Guilt/Shame	Loss of Face	Loss of Face

Source: Annamma Joy, "Gift Giving in Hong Kong and the Continuum of Social Ties," *Journal of Consumer Research* 28 (September 2001): 244. Reprinted by permission of the publisher.

(mothers born in Vietnam), and (3) Israeli (mothers born in Israel).[36] Whereas in all three of these cultures the mother plays a central role in family gift giving, Table 16.12 presents the major differences among these groups. For instance, when it comes to gift giving, Anglo-Celtic mothers were found to be motivated to select status or prestige gifts, whereas Sino-Vietnamese mothers were likely to pick practical gifts, and Israeli mothers tended to select gifts that they felt would be important to the recipient. Examine the table for other differences.

Intrapersonal gifting, or a self-gift (also called "monadic giving"), occurs when the giver and the receiver are the same individual. To some extent a self-gift is a "state of mind." If a consumer sees a purchase as the "buying of something I need," then it is simply a purchase.

TABLE 16.12	Major Differences between Gift-Giving Behavior of Anglo-Celtic, Sino-Vietnamese, and Israeli Mothers		
GIFT-GIVING ELEMENTS	**ANGLO-CELTIC MOTHERS**	**SINO-VIETNAMESE MOTHERS**	**ISRAELI MOTHERS**
1. Motivation			
Justification	Short-term goals	Long-term goals	Long-term/ short-term goals
Significance	Prestige gifts Birthday gifts	Practical gifts Lucky money	Importance to recipient
Timing	Special occasions (e.g., birthdays, Christmas)	Chinese New Year and academic reward	Birthdays and general needs
2. Selection			
Involvement	High priority Social and psychological risks	Low priority Financial risks	Low priority
Family Influences	Children	Mother	Mother dominant with younger children and influenced by older children
Promotional Influences	Status symbols	Sale items	Sale items
Gift Attributes	Quality	Price	Price
	Money unsuitable	Money suitable	Money suitable
3. Presentation			
Presentation Messages	Immediate self-gratification	Delayed self-gratification	Immediate self-gratification
Allocation Messages	Multiple gifts	Single gifts	Single gifts
	Mothers favored	Eldest child favored	
Understanding of Messages	Always	Not always	Never
4. Reaction			
Achievement	Often	Most of the time	Never
Feedback	More expressive	Less expressive	Least expressive
Usage	Often private	Often shared	Never shared

Source: Constance Hill and Celia T. Romm, "The Role of Mothers as Gift Givers: A Comparison Across Three Cultures," in *Advances in Consumer Research*, 23, ed. Kim P. Corfman and John G. Lynch, Jr. (Provo, UT: Association for Consumer Research, 1996), 26. Reprinted by permission.

TABLE 16.13	Reported Circumstances and Motivations for Self-Gift Behavior

CIRCUMSTANCES	MOTIVATIONS
Personal accomplishment	To reward oneself
Feeling down	To be nice to oneself
Holiday	To cheer oneself up
Feeling stressed	To fulfill a need
Have some extra money	To celebrate
Need	To relieve stress
Had not bought for self in a while	To maintain a good feeling
Attainment of a desired goal	To provide an incentive toward a goal
Others	Others

Source: David Glen Mick and Mitchelle DeMoss, "To Me from Me: A Descriptive Phenomenology of Self-Gifts," in *Advances in Consumer Research*, 23. Marvin E. Goldberg, Gerald Gorn, and Richard W. Pollay, ed. (Provo, UT: Association for Consumer Research, 1990), 677–682. Reprinted by permission.

On the other hand, if the same consumer sees the same purchase as a "self-gift," then it is something special, with special meaning. Consumers may treat themselves to self-gifts that are products (clothing, compact disks, or jewelry), services (hair styling, restaurant meals, spa membership), or experiences (socializing with friends). For example, while purchasing holiday gifts for others, some consumers find themselves in stores that they might not otherwise visit or find themselves looking at merchandise (such as a scarf) that they want but would not ordinarily buy. Such intrapersonal gifts have their own special range of meaning and context. Table 16.13 illustrates specific circumstances and motivations that might lead a consumer to engage in self-gift behavior.

Finally, Table 16.14 summarizes the five gifting behavior subdivisions explored earlier.

TABLE 16.14	Gifting Relationship Categories: Definitions and Examples

GIFTING RELATIONSHIP	DEFINITION	EXAMPLE
Intergroup	A group giving a gift to another group	A Christmas gift from one family to another family
Intercategory	An individual giving a gift to a group or a group giving a gift to an individual	A group of friends chips in to buy a new mother a baby gift
Intragroup	A group giving a gift to itself or its members	A family buys a VCR for itself as a Christmas gift
Interpersonal	An individual giving a gift to another individual	Valentine's Day chocolates presented from a boyfriend to a girlfriend
Intrapersonal	Self-gift	A woman buys herself jewelry to cheer herself up

Source: Adapted from Deborah Y. Cohn and Leon G. Schiffman, "Gifting: A Taxonomy of Private Realm Giver and Recipient Relationships," Working Paper, City University of New York, Baruch College, 1996, 2.

beyond the decision: consuming and possessing

Historically, the emphasis in consumer behavior studies has been on product, service, and brand choice decisions. As shown throughout this book, however, there are many more facets to consumer behavior. The experience of using products and services, as well as the sense of pleasure derived from *possessing, collecting,* or *consuming* "things" and "experiences" (mechanical watches, old fountain pens, or a baseball card collection) contributes to consumer satisfaction and overall quality of life. These consumption outcomes or experiences, in turn, affect consumers' future decision processes.

Thus, given the importance of possessions and experiences, a broader perspective of consumer behavior might view consumer choices as the beginning of a **consumption process**, not merely the end of a consumer decision-making effort. In this context, the choice or purchase decision is an *input* into a process of consumption. The input stage includes the establishment of a *consumption set* (an assortment or portfolio of products and their attributes) and a *consuming style* (the "rules" by which the individual or household fulfills consumption requirements). The *process* stage of a simple model of consumption might include (from the consumer's perspective) the *using, possessing* (or having), *collecting,* and *disposing* of things and experiences. The output stage of this process would include changes in a wide range of feelings, moods, attitudes, and behavior, as well as reinforcement (positive or negative) of a particular lifestyle (e.g., a devotion to physical fitness), enhancement of a sense of self, and the level of consumer satisfaction and quality of life.[37] Figure 16.5 presents a simple *model of consumption* that reflects the ideas discussed here and throughout the book.

Products have special meanings and memories

Consuming is a diverse and complex concept. It includes the simple utility derived from the continued use of a superior toothpaste, the stress reduction of an island

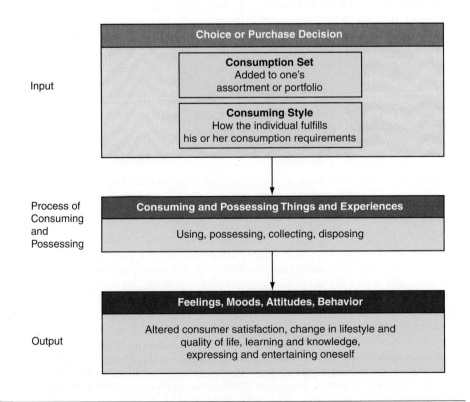

A Simple Model of Consumption

FIGURE 16.5

holiday, the stored memories of a DVD reflecting one's childhood, the "sacred" meaning or "magic" of a grandparent's wristwatch, the symbol of membership gained from wearing a school tie, the pleasure and sense of accomplishment that comes from building a model airplane, and the fun and even financial rewards that come from collecting almost anything (even jokers from decks of cards). In fact, one man's hobby of collecting old earthenware drain tiles has become the Mike Weaver Drain Tile Museum.[38] There are special possessions that consumers resist replacing, even with an exact replica, because the replica cannot possibly hold the same meaning as the original. Such possessions are often tied, in the consumer's mind, to a specific physical time or person.

Consider the male love affair with cars, which can manifest itself in many ways. Clearly, some men identify themselves with the automobiles that they own—it becomes an extension of the self, and some men personalize their vehicles in order to bond more fully with them (e.g., special paint color, custom wheels). Some individuals even take on the characteristics of their vehicles, with a powerful engine giving the owner a sense of greater power, and high performance handling providing the man with the notion that he is similarly capable of high performance. Some even feel that the "right" car will make them irresistible to women. Cars can also sometimes serve as children, lovers, and friends (e.g., "It's kind of like my baby—I wouldn't sell the car to just anyone—they must take care of the car or it would be like child abuse"), and some men attribute certain personality characteristics to their vehicles, call it a "she."[39] In a similar vein, a recent study of male motorcycle owners found that the type of "love" these bikers expressed toward their motorcycles was similar to interpersonal love—it is passionate, possessive, and selfless in nature.

Some possessions serve to assist consumers in their effort to create "personal meaning" and to maintain a sense of the past. To this end, it has been suggested that nostalgia permits people to maintain their identity after some major change in their life. This nostalgia can be based on family and friends; on objects such as toys, books, jewelry, and cars; or on special events, such as graduations, weddings, and holidays.[40] Providing the triple benefits of a sense of nostalgia, the fun of collecting, and the attraction of a potential return on investment, there is a strong interest in collecting Barbie® dolls. It is estimated that there are currently more than 100,000 Barbie doll collectors, who are dedicated to hunting down rare and valuable Barbie dolls to add to their collections.

And it appears that you're never too young to start collecting, as evidenced by the following story about a child who started collecting at the age of 2:

> *Cars have always interested Kevin LaLuzerne, a fifth-grader at Oakhurst Elementary in Largo. He has boxes and boxes of Hot Wheels, Micro Machines and other cars—more than 600! He started collecting them when he was just 2, and he still enjoys seeing all of the different cars and trucks he has collected over the years. He even has a "Weinermobile," the Oscar Meyer hot dog car. Kevin's newest addition to his collection is a limited-edition Chevron car that has a cartoon mouth, eyes and ears.*[41]

There is even a Web site devoted to kids who collect, which includes "An A to Z Guide to What Kids Can Collect" (**www.countrycollector.com/kids.html**).

At the other end of the age continuum, older consumers are often faced with the issue of how they should dispose of such special possessions. Indeed, in the past several years, a number of researchers have examined this subject area. Sometimes it is some precipitating event, such as the death of a spouse, illness, or moving out of one's home (to a nursing home or retirement community), that gets the consumer thinking about the disposition of his or her possessions. Often the older person wants to pass a family legacy on to a child, ensure a good home for a cherished collection, and/or influence the lives of others. The aim is not to "sell" the items, because they could do that themselves.

relationship marketing

Many firms have established **relationship marketing** programs (sometimes called *loyalty programs*) to foster usage loyalty and a commitment to their company's products and services. Relationship marketing is exceedingly logical when we realize credit card research has shown that "75 percent of college students keep their first card for 15 years, and 60 percent keep that card for life."[42] This kind of loyalty is enhanced by relationship marketing, which at its heart is all about building *trust* (between the firm and its customers) and keeping *promises* ("making promises," "enabling promises," and "keeping promises" on the part of the firm and, possibly, on the part of the customer).[43]

Indeed, it is the aim of relationship marketing to create strong, lasting relationships with a core group of customers. The emphasis is on developing long-term bonds with customers by making them feel good about how the company interacts (or does business) with them and by giving them some kind of personal connection to the business (see Figure 16.6). A review of the composition of 66 consumer relationship marketing programs revealed three elements shared by more than 50 percent of the programs. They are (1) fostering ongoing communication with customers (73 percent of the programs); (2) furnishing loyalty by building in extras like upgrades and other perks (68 percent of the programs); and (3) stimulating a sense of belonging by providing a "club membership" format (50 percent of the programs).[44] A real relationship marketing program is more than the use of database marketing tactics to better target customers—the consumer must feel that he or she has received something for being a participant in the relationship. In a positive vein, businesses have been finding that the Internet is an inexpensive, efficient, and more productive way to extend customer services. This has resulted in "permission marketing." It is the "art of asking consumers if they would like to receive a targeted e-mail ad, promotion, or message *before* it appears in their in-box." The opposite tact, sending a consumer spam and offering the option to "Click here to opt out," annoys consumers and is not permission marketing.[45]

Although direct marketing, sales promotion, and general advertising may be used as part of a relationship marketing strategy, relationship marketing stresses long-term commitment to the individual customer. Advances in technology (such as UPC scanning equipment, and relational databases) have provided techniques that make tracking customers simpler, thus influencing the trend toward relationship marketing. Indeed, Wal-Mart's database is second in size only to the database of the U.S. government.[46] Still further, a recent study suggests that relationship marketing programs are more likely to succeed if the product or service is one that buyers consider to be high involvement due to its association with financial, social, or physical risk.[47]

Relationship marketing programs have been used in a wide variety of product and service categories. Many companies call their relationship programs a club, and some even charge a fee to join. Membership in a club may serve as a means to convey to customers the notions of permanence and exclusivity inherent in a committed relationship. Additionally, those firms that charge a fee (such as the American Express Platinum card) increase customers' investment in the relationship that may, in turn, lead to greater commitment to the relationship and increased usage loyalty.

Airlines and major hotel chains, in particular, use relationship marketing techniques by awarding points to frequent customers that can be used to obtain additional goods or services from the company. This kind of point system may act as an exit barrier because starting a new relationship would mean giving up the potential future value of the points and starting from ground zero with a new service provider. That is why, for example, Hilton considers the 6.5 million members of the Hilton HHonors loyalty program the most important customers the company has.[48]

Moreover, companies have recently been broadening the scope of such relationship programs. For example, Table 16.15 lists the many products and services offered to

FIGURE 16.6

Source: © 2005 Hertz System, Inc. Hertz is a registered service mark and trademark of Hertz System, Inc.

Reduces those unsightly lines.

The Hertz #1 Club.® **Spend less time at the rental counter. Less time returning your car.** Don't thank France or some pricey rejuvenative spa for the latest innovation in line reduction. Thank us. Because The Hertz #1 Club offers a special #1 Club Express® counter to reduce your waiting time and speed you on your way. Your profile and car preference are already on file. So all you do is sign and go. And when you want to make your flight fast, Hertz Instant Return is our fastest way to return your car. Go straight from your car to the plane. It's just one of the many ways The Hertz #1 Club can get your vacation off to a great start. Membership is free. Just go to **hertz.com/join** to sign up. After all, who wouldn't be happier with fewer lines? That's renting wisely.

Hertz
Rent Wisely.™

Hertz rents Fords and other fine cars. ® Reg. U.S. Pat. Off. © 2005 Hertz System, Inc.
FOR YOUR INFORMATION: Advance reservations are required. Standard rental conditions and return restrictions must be met. Restrictions apply. #1 Club Express available at over 50 locations in the U.S. and Canada. Minimum rental age is 25 (exceptions apply).

Hertz Ad Points Out Benefits of Its Relationship Program

participants in the American Airlines AAdvantage Mileage Program. Still further, research has found that airline frequent flyer programs contribute in a positive way to the frequent business traveler's lifestyle and to his/her quality of life, perhaps by compensating for some of the negative aspects of frequent business travel. In addition, happy frequent business travelers perceived themselves to be more loyal to a particular airline than their less happy counterparts.[49]

Ultimately, it is to a firm's advantage to develop long-term relationships with existing customers because it is easier and less expensive to make an additional sale to an existing customer than to make a new sale to a new consumer.[50] Figure 16.7 portrays some of the characteristics of the relationship between the firm and the customer within the spirit of relationship marketing.

TABLE 16.15	A Broad-Based Relationship Program

AIRLINES

Canadian Airlines International
Cathay Pacific Airlines
Hawaiian Airlines
Qantas Airways
Keno Air
Singapore Airlines
TWA
US Airways

HOTELS

Conrad Hotels
Forte Hotels
Forum Hotels
Hilton Hotels & Resorts
Hilton International Hotels
Holiday Inns
Inter-Continental Hotels
ITT Sheraton Hotels, Inns, Resorts, and All-Suites
Marriott Hotels, Resorts, and Suites
Vista Hotels
Wyndham Hotels & Resorts

CAR RENTAL

Avis Rent A Car
Hertz

OTHER

Citibank AAdvantage Visa or MasterCard application
MCI Long-Distance
American AAdvantage Money Market Fund
The American Traveler Catalog

Why is relationship marketing so important? Research indicates that consumers today are less loyal than in the past, due to six major forces: (1) the abundance of choice, (2) availability of information, (3) entitlement (consumers repeatedly ask "What have you done for me lately?"), (4) commoditization (most products/services appear to be similar—nothing stands out), (5) insecurity (consumer financial problems reduce loyalty), and (6) time scarcity (not enough time to be loyal). These six forces result in consumer defections, complaints, cynicism, reduced affiliation, greater price sensitivity, and litigiousness.[51]

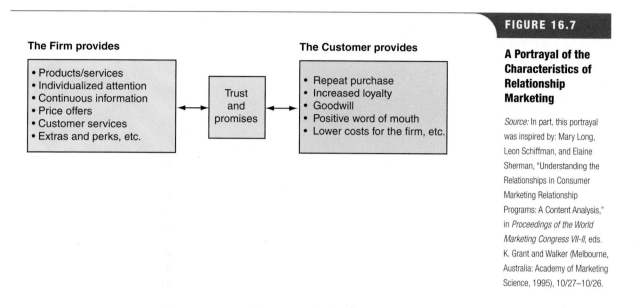

FIGURE 16.7

A Portrayal of the Characteristics of Relationship Marketing

Source: In part, this portrayal was inspired by: Mary Long, Leon Schiffman, and Elaine Sherman, "Understanding the Relationships in Consumer Marketing Relationship Programs: A Content Analysis," in *Proceedings of the World Marketing Congress VII-II,* eds. K. Grant and Walker (Melbourne, Australia: Academy of Marketing Science, 1995), 10/27–10/26.

SUMMARY

The consumer's decision to purchase or not to purchase a product or service is an important moment for most marketers. It can signify whether a marketing strategy has been wise, insightful, and effective, or whether it was poorly planned and missed the mark. Thus, marketers are particularly interested in the consumer's decision-making process. For a consumer to make a decision, more than one alternative must be available. (The decision not to buy is also an alternative.)

Theories of consumer decision making vary, depending on the researcher's assumptions about the nature of humankind. The various models of consumers (economic view, passive view, cognitive view, and emotional view) depict consumers and their decision-making processes in distinctly different ways.

An overview consumer decision-making model ties together the psychological, social, and cultural concepts examined in Parts II and III into an easily understood framework. This decision model has three sets of variables: input variables, process variables, and output variables.

Input variables that affect the decision-making process include commercial marketing efforts, as well as noncommercial influences from the consumer's sociocultural environment. The decision process variables are influenced by the consumer's psychological field, including the evoked set (or the brands in a particular product category considered in making a purchase choice). Taken as a whole, the psychological field influences the consumer's recognition of a need, prepurchase search for information, and evaluation of alternatives.

The output phase of the model includes the actual purchase (either trial or repeat purchase) and postpurchase evaluation. Both prepurchase and postpurchase evaluation feeds back in the form of experience into the consumer's psychological field and serves to influence future decision processing.

The process of gift exchange is an important part of consumer behavior. Various gift-giving and gift-receiving relationships are captured by the following five specific categories in the gifting classification scheme: (1) intergroup gifting (a group gives a gift to another group); (2) intercategory gifting (an individual gives a gift to a group or a group gives a gift to an individual); (3) intragroup gifting (a group gives a gift to itself or its members); (4) interpersonal gifting (an individual gives a gift to another individual); and (5) intrapersonal gifting (a self-gift).

Consumer behavior is not just making a purchase decision or the act of purchasing; it also includes the full range of experiences associated with using or consuming products and services. It also includes the sense of pleasure and satisfaction derived from possessing or collecting "things." The outputs of consumption are changes in feelings, moods, or attitudes; reinforcement of lifestyles; an enhanced sense of self; satisfaction of a consumer-related need; belonging to groups; and expressing and entertaining oneself.

Among other things, consuming includes the simple utility of using a superior product, the stress reduction of a vacation, the sense of having a "sacred" possession, and the pleasures of a hobby or a collection. Some possessions serve to assist consumers in their effort to create personal meaning and to maintain a sense of the past.

Relationship marketing impacts consumers' decisions and their consumption satisfaction. Firms establish relationship marketing programs (sometimes called loyalty programs) to foster usage loyalty and a commitment to their products and services. At its heart, relationship marketing is all about building trust (between the firm and its customers), and keeping promises made to consumers. Therefore, the emphasis in relationship marketing is almost always on developing long-term bonds with customers by making them feel special and by providing them with personalized services.

DISCUSSION QUESTIONS

1. Compare and contrast the economic, passive, cognitive, and emotional models of consumer decision making.

2. What kinds of marketing and sociocultural inputs would influence the purchase of (a) a TV with a built-in VCR, (b) a concentrated liquid laundry detergent, and (c) fat-free ice cream? Explain your answers.

3. Define extensive problem solving, limited problem solving, and routinized response behavior. What are the differences among the three decision-making approaches? What type of decision process would you expect most consumers to follow in their first purchase of a new product or brand in each of the following areas: (a) chewing gum, (b) sugar, (c) men's aftershave lotion, (d) carpeting, (e) paper towels, (f) a cellular telephone, and (g) a luxury car? Explain your answers.

4. a. Identify three different products that you believe require a reasonably intensive prepurchase search by a consumer. Then, using Table 16.2 as a guide, identify the specific characteristics of these products that make an intensive prepurchase search likely.

   b. For each of the products that you listed, identify the perceived risks that a consumer is likely to experience before a purchase. Discuss how the marketers of these products can reduce these perceived risks.

5. Let's assume that this coming summer you are planning to spend a month touring Europe and are, therefore, in need of a good 35mm camera. (a) Develop a list of product attributes that you will use as the purchase criteria in evaluating various 35mm cameras. (b) Distinguish the differences that would occur in your decision process if you were to use compensatory versus noncompensatory decision rules.

6. How can a marketer of very light, very powerful laptop computers use its knowledge of customers' expectations in designing a marketing strategy?

7. How do consumers reduce postpurchase dissonance? How can marketers provide positive reinforcement to consumers after the purchase to reduce their dissonance?

8. The Gillette Company, which produces the highly successful Sensor shaving blade, has recently introduced a clear gel antiperspirant and deodorant for men. Identify the perceived risks associated with the purchase of this new product and outline a strategy designed to reduce these perceived risks during the product's introduction.

9. Albert Einstein once wrote that "the whole of science is nothing more than a refinement of everyday thinking." Do you think that this quote applies to the development of the consumer decision-making model presented in Figure 16.2?

EXERCISES

1. Find two print advertisements, one that illustrates the cognitive model of consumer decision making and one that illustrates the emotional model. Explain your choices. In your view, why did the marketers choose the approaches depicted in the advertisements?

2. Describe the need recognition process that took place before you purchased your last can of soft drink. How did it differ from the process that preceded the purchase of a new pair of sneakers? What role, if any, did advertising play in your need recognition?

3. List the colleges that you considered when choosing which college or university to attend and the criteria that you used to evaluate them. Describe how you acquired information on the different colleges along the different attributes that were important to you and how you made your decision. Be sure to specify whether you used compensatory or noncompensatory decision rules.

4. Select one of the following product categories: (a) compact disk players, (b) fast-food restaurants, or (c) shampoo, and: (1) write down the brands that constitute your evoked set, (2) identify brands that are not part of your evoked set, and (3) discuss how the brands included in your evoked set differ from those that are not included in terms of important attributes.

5. Select a newspaper or magazine advertisement that attempts (a) to provide the consumer with a decision strategy to follow in making a purchase decision or (b) to reduce the perceived risk(s) associated with a purchase. Evaluate the effectiveness of the ad you selected.

KEY TERMS

- **affect referral decision rule**
- **compensatory decision rules**
- **conjunctive decision rule**
- **consumer decision making**
- **consumption process**
- **disjunctive rule**
- **evaluation of alternatives**
- **evoked set**
- **extensive problem solving**

- **gifting behavior**
- **heuristics**
- **inept set**
- **inert set**
- **information overload**
- **lexicographic decision rule**
- **limited problem solving**
- **moods**
- **need recognition**

- **noncompensatory decision rules**
- **postpurchase evaluation**
- **prepurchase search**
- **purchase behavior**
- **relationship marketing**
- **routinized response behavior**
- **self-gifts**

NOTES

1. Itamar Simonson, "Shoppers' Easily Influenced Choices," *New York Times*, November 6, 1994, 11.

2. Herbert A. Simon, *Administrative Behavior*, 2nd ed. (New York: Free Press, 1965), 40.

3. James G. March and Herbert A. Simon, *Organizations* (New York: Wiley, 1958), 140–241.

4. Michael A. Jones, Philip J. Trocchia, and David L. Mothersbaugh, "Noneconomic Motivations for Price Haggling: An Exploratory Study," in *Advances in Consumer Research* 24, ed. Merrie Brucks and Deborah J. MacInnis (Provo, UT: Association for Consumer Research, 1997), 388–391.

5. Meryl Paula Gardner, "Mood States and Consumer Behavior: A Critical Review," *Journal of Consumer Research* 12 (December 1985): 281–300; and Robert A. Peterson and Matthew Sauber, "A Mood Scale for Survey Research," in *1983 AMA Educators' Proceedings*, ed. Patrick E. Murphy, et al. (Chicago: American Marketing Association, 1983), 409–414.

6. Ruth Belk Smith and Elaine Sherman, "Effects of Store Image and Mood on Consumer Behavior: A Theoretical and Empirical Analysis," in *Advances in Consumer Research* 20, ed. Leigh McAlister and Michael L. Rothschild (Provo, UT: Association for Consumer Research, 1993), 631.

7. Knowles, Grove, and Burroughs, "An Experimental Examination."

8. Gordon C. Bruner, II, "The Effect of Problem-Recognition Style on Information Seeking," *Journal of the Academy of Marketing Science* 15 (Winter 1987): 33–41.

9. Matthew Klein, "He Shops, She Shops," *American Demographics,* March 1998, 34–35.

10. Sharon E. Beatty and Scott M. Smith, "External Search Effort: An Investigation Across Several Product Categories," *Journal of Consumer Research* 14 (June 1987): 83–95.

11. Niranjan V. Raman, "A Qualitative Investigation of Web-Browsing Behavior," in *Advances in Consumer Research*, ed. Brucks and MacInnis (Provo, UT: Association for Consumer Research, 1997), 511–516.

12. Kuan-Pin Chiang, Ruby Roy Dholakia, and Stu Westin, "Needle in the Cyberstack: Consumer Search for Information in the Web-based Marketspace," *Advances in Consumer Research* 31, 2004, 88–89.

13. John W. Pracejus, G. Douglas Olsen, and Thomas C. O'Guinn, "Nothing Is Something: The Production and Reception of Advertising Meaning Through the Use of White Space," *Advances in Consumer Research* 30, ed. Punam Anand Keller and Dennis W. Rook (Valdosta, GA: Association for Consumer Research, 2003), 174; and Pamela Henderson, Joan Giese, and Joseph A. Cote, "Typeface Design and Meaning: The Three Faces of Typefaces," *Advances in Consumer Research* 30 (2003), 175.

14. Ashley Lye, Wei Shao, and Sharyn Rundle-Thiele, "Decision Waves: Consumer Decisions in Today's Complex World," *European Journal of Marketing* 39, no. 1/2 (2005): 216–230.

15. Jeffrey F. Durgee, "Why Some Products 'Just Feel Right,' or, the Phenomenology of Product Rightness," in *Advances in Consumer Research* 22, ed. Frank R. Kardes and Mita Sujan (Provo, UT: Association for Consumer Research, 1995), 650–652.

16. Tulin Erdem and Joffre Swait, "Brand Credibility, Brand Consideration, and Choice," *Journal of Consumer Research* 31 (June 2004): 191–198

17. Laurie Peterson, "The Strategic Shopper," *Adweek's Marketing Week*, March 30, 1992, 18–20.

18. Madhubalan Viswanathan, José Antonio Rosa, and James Edwin Harris, "Decision Making and Coping of Functionally

Illiterate Consumers and Some Implications for Marketing Management," *Journal of Marketing* 69 (January 2005): 15–31.

19. Ibid.

20. Lan Xia, "Consumer Choice Strategies and Choice Confidence in the Electronic Environment," in *1999 AMA Educators Proceedings* 10, ed. Stephen P. Brown and D. Sudharshan (Chicago: American Marketing Association, 1999), 270–277.

21. Laura Daily, "If You Can Dream It, They Can Make It," *American Way*, April 1, 2005, 30.

22. Carey Goldberg, "Choosing the Joys of a Simplified Life," *New York Times*, September 21, 1995, C1, C9.

23. Ibid.

24. Nancy Spears, "The Time Pressured Consumer and Deal Proneness: Theoretical Framework and Empirical Evidence," in *2000 AMA Winter Educators' Conference*, 11, ed. John P. Workman and William D. Perreault (Chicago: American Marketing Association, 2000), 35–40.

25. Beth Snyder Bulik, "Apple Puts iPod Halo to Test with Shuffle and Mini," *Advertising Age*, January 17, 2005, 33 & 28; and Walter S. Mossberg, "The Newest iPod mini Rival: iRiver's $280 H10," *The Wall Street Journal*, February 23, 2005, D4.

26. Sarah Fisher Gardial and David W. Schumann, "In Search of the Elusive Consumer Inference," in *Advances in Consumer Research*, ed. Goldberg, Gorn, and Pollay (Provo, UT: Association for Consumer Research, 1990), 283–287; see also Burke.

27. Emily Booth, "Getting Inside a Shopper's Mind," *Marketing (U.K.)*, June 3, 1999, 33.

28. Kare Sandvik, Kjell Gronhaug, and Frank Lindberg, "Routes to Customer Retention: The Importance of Customer Satisfaction, Performance Quality, Brand Reputation and Customer Knowledge," in *AMA Winter Conference*, ed. Debbie Thorne LeClair and Michael Hartline (Chicago: American Marketing Association, 1997), 211–217.

29. Russell W. Belk and Gregory S. Coon, "Gift Giving as Agapic Love: An Alternative to the Exchange Paradigm Based on Dating Experiences," *Journal of Consumer Research* 20 (December 1993): 393–417.

30. "More Consumers Buy Gifts for Themselves Than to Give as Gifts; 'Gift Market' Is a Misnomer, Since Most Consumers Buy Gift Products for Personal Consumption," *Business Wire*, April 17, 2000, 1.

31. Michel Laroche, Gad Saad, Elizabeth Browne, Mark Cleveland, and Chankon Kim, "Determinants of In-Store Information Search Strategies Pertaining to a Christmas Gift Purchase," *Revue Canadienne des Sciences de l'Administration* 17, no. 1 (March 2000): 1–19.

32. Julie A. Ruth, Cele C. Otnes, and Frédéric F. Brunel, "Gift Receipt and the Reformulation of Interpersonal Relationships," *Journal of Consumer Research* 25 (March 1999): 385–402.

33. Stephen J. Gould and Claudia E. Weil, "Gift-Giving and Gender Self-Concepts," *Gender Role* 24 (1991): 617–637.

34. Tilottama G. Chowdhury, S. Ratneshwar, and Kalpesh K. Desai, "Do Unto Others As You Would Do Unto Yourself: Variety-Seeking Motives in Gift Giving," *Advances in Consumer Research* 31, ed. Barbara E. Kahn and Mary Frances Luce (Valdosta, GA: Association for Consumer Research, 2004), 22–23.

35. Annamma Joy, "Gift Giving in Hong Kong and the Continuum of Social Ties," *Journal of Consumer Research* 28, no. 2 (September 2001): 239–256.

36. Constance Hill and Celia T. Romm, "The Role of Mothers as Gift Givers: A Comparison Across Three Cultures," in *Advances in Consumer Research* 23, ed. Kim P. Corfman and John G. Lynch, Jr. (Provo, UT: Association for Consumer Research, 1996), 21–27.

37. Kathleen M. Rassuli and Gilbert D. Harrell, "A New Perspective on Choice," in *Advances in Consumer Research*, ed. Goldberg, Gorn, and Pollay, 737–744.

38. James M. Perry, "Mike Weaver Proves That Everything Can Be a Collection," *Wall Street Journal*, August 16, 1995, 1.

39. Russell W. Belk, "Men and Their Machines," *Advances in Consumer Research* 31, 2004, 273–278.

40. Stacey Menzel Baker and Patricia F. Kennedy, "Death by Nostalgia: A Diagnosis of Context-Specific Cases," in *Advances in Consumer Research* 21, ed. Chris T. Allen and Deborah Roedder John (Provo, UT: Association for Consumer Research, 1994), 169–174.

41. Andy Wright, "Oh, the Stuff We Collect Series: XPRESS," *The St. Petersburg Times*, August 30, 1999, 3D.

42. Robert Bryce, "Here's a Course in Personal Finance 101, the Hard Way," *New York Times*, April 30, 1995, F11.

43. Susan M. Lloyd, "Toward Understanding Relationship Marketing from the Consumer's Perspective: What Relationships Are and Why Consumers Choose to Enter Them," in *2000 AMA Educators' Proceedings* 11, ed. Gregory T. Gundlach and Patrick E. Murphy (Chicago: American Marketing Association, 2000), 12–20; Leonard L. Berry, "Relationship Marketing of Services—Growing Interest, Emerging Perspectives," *Journal of the Academy of Marketing Science* 23 (Fall 1995): 236–245; and Mary Jo Bitner, "Building Service Relationships: It's All About Promises," *Journal of the Academy of Marketing Science* 23 (Fall 1995): 246–251.

44. Mary Long, Leon Schiffman, and Elaine Sherman, "Understanding the Relationships in Consumer Marketing Relationship Programs: A Content Analysis," in *Proceedings of the World Marketing Congress VII-II*, ed. K. Grant and

Walker (Melbourne, Australia: Academy of Marketing Science, 1995), 10/27–10/32.

45. Lauren Barack, "Pretty, Pretty, Please," *Business 2.0,* April 2000, 176–180.

46. Emily Nelson, "Why Wal-Mart Sings, 'Yes, We Have Bananas,' " *Wall Street Journal,* October 6, 1998, B1, B4.

47. Mary Ellen Gordon and Kim McKeage, "Relationship Marketing Effectiveness: Differences between Women in New Zealand and the United States," in *1997 AMA Educators' Proceedings,* ed. William M. Pride and G. Tomas M. Hult (Chicago: American Marketing Association, 1997), 117–122.

48. Mike Beirne, "Burke Customizing Hilton HHonors," *Brandweek,* October 11, 2004, 17.

49. Mary M. Long, Sylvia D. Clark, Leon G. Schiffman, and Charles McMellon, "In the Air Again: Frequent Flyer Relationship Programs and Business Travelers' Quality of Life," *International Journal of Tourism Research* 5 (2003): 421–432.

50. Jagdish N. Sheth and Atul Parvatiyar, "Relationship Marketing in Consumer Marketing: Antecedents and Consequences," *Journal of the Academy of Marketing Science* 23 (Fall 1995): 255–271.

51. Steve Schriver, "Customer Loyalty: Going, Going. . . ," *American Demographics,* September 1997, 20–23.

Consumer Behavior: Its Origins and Strategic Applications

Case One: Digitization = Customization

The marketing concept states that companies must focus on consumer needs and develop products and services that meet these needs. Market segmentation and targeting—the strategic approaches that originate in the marketing concept— enable marketers to subdivide large markets into distinct consumer segments with relatively homogeneous needs, and to select one or more of these groups as the target market(s) for the companies' offerings.

Broadly speaking, the premise of the marketing concept is the delivery of products geared to individual's needs, a strategy seemingly congruent with such promotional slogans as "Have It Your Way" and "You're the Boss." In reality, however, the products offered by companies that moved from mass production (i.e., a single version of the product for all consumers) to market-focused strategies are not truly personalized products. Marketing-oriented companies offer consumers numerous versions and models of their products, each designed to meet the needs of a distinct, but still rather large, group of individual consumers.

Now, for the first time ever, digital technologies enable marketers to truly customize many products to the specific and individual needs of customers. For example:

1. *Dell Computer Corporation offers built-to-order computer systems at* **www.dell.com** *where consumers can design their own notebook or desktop PCs.*
2. *At* **www.acumins.com***, customers fill out The Vitamin Advisor—an extensive questionnaire regarding one's health, diet, and daily habits. Based on an analysis of their answers to the survey, customers can purchase packages of vitamins and supplements customized specifically for them.*
3. *At* **www.nikeid.com** *buyers can choose among many models of sneakers in different price ranges, customize their chosen shoes from among several colors and features, have a personal ID applied to each shoe, pay for the product, and have it shipped directly to them.*

Questions

1. Will the marketing concept (as discussed in Chapter 1) become an obsolete concept as more and more companies adopt the kind of customization strategies illustrated in this case? Explain your answer.

2. Select a product or industry (other than the ones featured here) for which, in your view, product customization is impractical and where traditional market segmentation and targeting are more applicable. Explain your answer.

Case Two: Whole Foods Market versus FreshDirect.com

Whole Foods Market is a supermarket chain with less than two-hundred stores selling healthy, gourmet products such as organic vegetables, free-range poultry, foods without artificial ingredients or hydrogenated fats, and many environment-friendly products such as nonpolluting detergents and chlorine-free diapers. The company began in the 1970s as a natural-food store that catered to hippies. Through the purchase of small health-food stores in major cities, the company gained more exposure and access to distribution channels for natural foods. During the late 1980s and the 1990s, the company's growth was fueled by the upsurge in Americans' desire for healthy living and their interest in gourmet cooking. Whole Foods does very little advertising but receives constant free media exposure because it is often mentioned in popular TV series, praised by celebrities on talk shows, and featured in newspapers and magazines as a business success story. The company educates consumers about foods, provides recipes, and even arranges trips where customers meet with local fishermen. Its supermarket cashiers and stock personnel receive education about foods and earn above-average wages. Whole Foods' prices are significantly higher than products in traditional supermarkets because the keys to its profitability are higher-profit margins for products that traditionally yield slim margins, and much larger per-square-foot sales than those of conventional supermarkets. But, as the company's CEO pointed out, Americans spend far less of their income on food than other nations and that's why most of it doesn't taste very good; if they want to eat higher-quality foods, they have to pay for them. In 2005, Whole Foods stated its plans to double the number of its stores by 2015.

FreshDirect.com is an online grocer operating in New York City since 2002 that delivers both fresh and processed foods and other perishable and nonperishable groceries, ordered by customers online via user-friendly shopping list software. The fresh foods are prepared and the orders are assembled in a single facility, and the company uses computers and sophisticated, highly automated assembly and delivery tools. The orders are delivered to thousands of customers during specified "time windows," which are very difficult to keep because of New York's heavy and unpredictable traffic patterns. Learning from the mistakes of long-gone online grocers, the company offers a limited selection of products, but its meat and seafood orders are freshly prepared. FreshDirect has plans to expand even before becoming profitable. The keys to the company's success are increasing the number of its subscribers and ensuring that customers order consistently, reducing its operating costs through more powerful technology and automation, and maintaining the accuracy of the orders and the delivery periods. Generally, customers have been satisfied with the quality of the products, although occasionally, the quality of the meats, seafood, and fresh produce fell below the expectations of some customers. Unlike Whole Foods, FreshDirect does not specialize in organic foods but carries a line of such items and its prices are comparable and sometimes lower than those in conventional supermarkets.

Questions

1. "Although very different, Whole Foods and FreshDirect are both successful because they understand consumer behavior and effectively cater to customers' needs." Discuss this statement.

2. How do the emergence and operations of each company illustrate applications of the marketing concept?

3. Please identify, describe, and compare the challenges that each company faces as it tries to expand.

Sources: Mary Raitt Jordan, "Whole Foods Plans Bigger, More Stores across Country," *Gourmet News*, July 2005, 18–20; Renuka Rayasam, "Whole Foods Shuns Ads, Sells Lifestyle; Spending Sparingly on Marketing, Grocer Thrives by Creating a Shopping Experience," *Austin American Statesman*, July 10, 2005, J1; Daniel McGinn, "The Green Machine," *Newsweek*, March 21, 2005, E8–12; Jon Springer, "New FreshDirect Chair Says IPO A 'Possibility'," *Supermarket News*, June 6, 2005, 1; Carol S. Marganti, "Swim Different," *Food Logistics*, May 15, 2005, 20–27; Jane Black, "Online at the Grocer's," *New York Magazine Online*, October 14, 2002; Larry Dignan, "FreshDirect: Ready to Deliver," *Baseline*, February 2004; *Business Week Online*, "Joe Fedele, FreshDirect," September 29, 2003.

Consumer Research

Case One: Using Secondary Data in Targeting Consumers

The importance and strategic value of secondary data are discussed in the text. Today, thanks to technology, high-quality secondary marketing data are readily available to marketing students and educators. For example, Mediamark Research Inc. is a well-known provider of specialized, syndicated secondary data describing the audiences of selected media. The company also provides online access to some of its data through its MRI + service.

In this hands-on case, we would like you to use some of Mediamark's secondary data. First, in order to use the data, you must register (for free) with Mediamark at **www.mriplus.com**.

After you register and your user status is activated, sign in and go to "Create Reports." Then, under "Pocketpieces," select "MRI—Magazine Pocketpiece." Check all of the data categories in the "Select Data to Display" window. Then select up to five magazines that you read or are familiar with and generate Pocketpiece Reports for them. You can then download these reports as Excel files.

Then obtain recent copies of the magazines for which you selected the MRI reports and make a list of all the products and brands featured in full-page ads in these publications. You now have the two sets of data needed to complete this case study.

Questions

1. In general, are the products prominently advertised in each magazine consistent or inconsistent with the magazine's MRI audience profile? Explain your answers.

2. Rather than relying on MRI's data, should the marketers of the products you selected collect their own data about the audiences of magazines in which they want to advertise their offerings? Why or why not? In your answer, be sure to describe the advantages and limitations of relying on secondary research data in making strategic marketing decisions.

Case Two: Wal-Mart Knows Its Customers

Wal-Mart is the world's largest retailer. In the United States, the company has 3,600 stores visited by approximately 100 million customers each week. Wal-Mart's "every-day low prices" have, in effect, "raised" the incomes of many Americans by providing more purchase power. The key to Wal-Mart's financial profitability is offering a large assortment of products under one roof, high turnover, and low inventory. In order to ensure that it always has the products that consumers want at a particular place and time, Wal-Mart monitors the behavior of its customers obsessively. Each sale is tracked as it occurs and the information from the bar code is used to identify trends and consumption patterns across regions and seasons. On average, there are 120,000 items in a Wal-Mart store. When the company monitors, say, clothing, it tracks what colors, sizes, and designs are selling. This information is immediately fed into the supply chain where those products that are in demand are quickly produced and delivered to the stores. The company also uses this information to satisfy needs that emerge suddenly. For example, during the very active 2004 hurricane season, Wal-Mart discovered that the sales of PopTarts and beer greatly increased before a predicted hurricane. Then, when a hurricane was forecast for a particular area, these and other products that consumers stocked up on before previous hurricanes were quickly shipped to the area to ensure that no Wal-Mart store ran out of these products. When a store is reaching the end of its inventory of a popular product, an order is generated and transmitted to the warehouse and the product is shipped to the store shortly thereafter. The use of information technology to monitor customers' purchases continuously also gives the company great leverage with its suppliers. Because Wal-Mart knows exactly what is being sold, when and where, it knows what to order and producers of these products compete for these large orders. Subsequently, the company dictates to producers what it will pay for these products and, in effect, lowers the profit margins of the producers while increasing its own. In its quest for more cheaply produced products that will sell at low prices but in large quantities in the United States, many of Wal-Mart's products are now produced in China. A significant portion of America's trade deficit with China is due to Wal-Mart's operations.

Questions

1. How can Wal-Mart benefit from combining the data it collects with information about its customers' characteristics (gathered from customers' credit cards and drivers' licenses, and through cashing their paychecks at Wal-Mart)? What are some of the privacy issues involved in combining the two sets of data?

2. Like many other consumers, Wal-Mart shoppers knowingly or unknowingly provide the retailer with extensive personal information. Do you believe that most consumers would knowingly sacrifice their privacy for shopping convenience and lower prices? Explain your answer.

3. What are some of the negative implications, if any, for the larger society when a huge company, such as Wal-Mart, amasses extremely large quantities of data about their customers' consumption behavior?

Sources: *Frontline*, PBS, "Is Wal-Mart Good for America?" Broadcast on November 16, 2004; Constance L. Hays, "What Wal-Mart Knows about Customers' Habits," **www.nytimes.com**, November 14, 2004.

Market Segmentation

Case One: Watching M&M's Grow

I n the early '90s M&M added peanut butter and almond varieties, blue was introduced in '95 and green in '97, Crispy M&M's made their debut in 1999, and Minis Mega Tubes in 2000. Now there are Mega M&M's. Not only are they physically bigger—55 percent larger in size—but they also come in more sophisticated colors that are designed to appeal to adults. Red will be replaced with maroon, the blue will now be a blue/gray, and turquoise will replace green. Advertising for this new M&M's variety retains the humorous flavor of other current M&M's ads, but with more of an adult edge.

Not all M&M's products have succeeded. For example, as of this writing, you would probably have a difficult time finding Crispy M&M's in your local supermarket, drug store, or mass merchandiser. And Minis only account for about $24 million of the brand's more than $500 million in annual sales.

Questions

1. Do you think that it was a good segmentation strategy for M&M's to develop a new version targeting adults?

2. Would M&M's be better off pursuing a mass-marketing approach?

Source: Stephanie Thompson, "M&M's Gain Weight, Get New Dye Job," *Advertising Age* (June 6, 2005): 8.

Case Two: Growing the Airwalk Market

Airwalk sells shoes and clothing to skateboard enthusiasts, which could be construed as a niche market. The company's newest advertising campaign, though, targets both extreme and mainstream consumers, is hoped that its message will communicate "cool" to both groups. Indeed, the company's aim is "to be the coolest brand that talks to the mainstream consumer," while also attracting the skateboard enthusiast. It is believed that while many people have never stepped onto a skateboard, they want the independence and the rebellious spirit that is provided by action sports. As the creative director for the campaign has commented, "We want to position this brand as the primary brand that attracts these people to get into that world."

The images presented in the advertisements feature the boarding lifestyle, rather than skateboard action shots, and will appear in music and action sports publications. The only copy in these ads will be "**www.airwalk.com**." So while the advertisements might appear to have a narrow focus, in reality, the company is aiming at a broad market.

Question

1. To which VALS segment (or segments) do you feel this Airwalk advertising campaign will especially appeal?

Source: Sandra O'Loughlin, "Airwalk Grabs a 'Cool' Ride," *Brandweek*, May 2, 2005, 14.

Consumer Motivation

Case One: The Product Collection at New Product Works

The essence of the marketing concept is understanding consumer needs and developing products that meet these needs effectively. And yet, every year, scores of new products are withdrawn from the market soon after their introduction; many other products also "fail" when their sales fall short of providing the revenues needed both to cover their development costs and to generate profits. Clearly, understanding consumer needs is a complex issue.

Most of the new products introduced, including failed products, fall within the product categories sold in supermarkets—such as food, beverage, household maintenance, personal care, baby care, and other categories. In an effort to pinpoint causes of product failures in these areas, an organization named New Product Works maintains a vast collection of food, beverage, household, and personal care products that were introduced and subsequently withdrawn from the marketplace (see **www. newproductworks.com**).

The objective of New Product Works is to provide marketplace-based advice to companies developing new products. The organization's product collection also provides insights into how misunderstanding consumer needs can lead to the development and introduction of costly but unsuccessful products.

Questions

1. Visit the online product collection at New Product Works. Go to the "Poll: Hits or Misses?" link. Rate three of the new products featured on this link, compare your ratings to those of previous respondents, and explain your ratings in the context of consumer needs and motivations.

2. Now go to the "Hits & Misses" section (located within the "Poll" section). Scroll down to "Favorite Failures." Select three of the products featured there and explain why they failed in the context of consumer needs and motivations.

Case Two: Need-Focused Definition of Business

As illustrated in Table 4.1, successful companies define their missions and business domains in terms of the needs that they satisfy rather than the products that they create. Doing so enables such companies to be in the forefront of searching for new products and solutions that satisfy consumers' needs more effectively than older products.

Here are several additional companies whose philosophies illustrate need-focused definitions of business:

1. *Merck—at* **www.merck.com** *go to "About Merck" and then "Mission Statement."*
2. *Montblanc—at* **www.monblanc.com** *go to "Sitemap" and then "Philosophy."*
3. *Johnson & Johnson—at* **www.jnj.com** *go to "Our Company," and then "Our Credo."*

Questions

1. Go to the sites listed above and prepare a short summary of each company's vision and definition of its business.

2. Based on their Web sites, list the major product lines of each of the three companies. Then describe how each company's products stem from its definition of the business in which it operates.

Personality and Consumer Behavior

Case One: Hello Starbucks!

Walk several blocks in almost any city in America and you'll pass at least one Starbucks, if not more. And the same is true for most cities outside of the United States. The Starbucks empire has grown to 6,000 U.S. outlets and about 2,500 international locations.

For some consumers, Starbucks is an obsession, and they just can't begin their day without their cup of Starbucks coffee! In addition, while years ago people used to hang out at the corner candy store, today many people spend considerable time at their local Starbucks. They drink coffee, tea, and/or other specialty beverages, they bring their laptop and wirelessly connect to the Internet, they meet friends to chat, or they meet business associates to make deals. Is there anyone in America, at least old enough to be in kindergarten, who doesn't know what Starbucks is?

Questions

Since everybody knows Starbucks, answer the following questions (if you need any help with your answers, you might want to access **www.starbucks.com**):

1. If Starbucks was a person, describe the person in terms of demographics, personality, and lifestyle characteristics.

2. If Starbucks was an animal, which animal would it be, and why?

3. If Starbucks was a color, which color would it be, and why?

4. If Starbucks was a celebrity (e.g., a sports figure, a movie or TV star), which celebrity would it be, and why? And why was your choice male or female?

Source: Data on store numbers obtained from **www.starbucks.com**

Case Two: It's a Whirlpool, from Schorndorf

Go to any store selling top-of-the-line appliances and you'll see a number of brands that are imported from Germany, such as Miele and Bosch-Siemens. But neither of these companies is the leading exporter of German-made washing machines to the United States. That accomplishment belongs to Whirlpool. While Whirlpool's top-loading washers are made in Clyde, Ohio, the front-loaders are made in Germany, where Whirlpool had been manufacturing front-loaders for the European market before the design caught on in America (the design has been popular in Europe for many years because it uses less water and less electricity). Since Whirlpool began importing the washing machines to the United States, it has sold almost two million of them, at about $1,200 each.

While labor costs at its U.S. plants, including benefits, run $23 an hour, Whirlpool's labor costs in Germany are $32 an hour. So the front-loaders are not being manufactured in Germany because of lower labor costs. Whirlpool already had a trained labor force and a factory in Germany when it made the decision to market front-loading washing machines in the United States. To understand the even bigger picture, more than 40 percent of U.S. imports come from the overseas subsidiaries of U.S. companies.

Questions

1. Considering discussion of consumer ethnocentrism in Chapter 5, how do you think most consumers would react if they knew that the Whirlpool front-loading washing machine that they were considering was made in Germany?

2. Do you feel that there is really any difference, in a consumer's mind, between a Whirlpool washing machine and a Bosch washing machine, if it is known that they both were manufactured in Germany?

Source: Louis Uchitelle, "Globalization: It's Not Just Wages," *The New York Times*, June 17, 2005, C1–C4.

Consumer Perception

Case One: "The Two Billion Dollar Man"

Mr. Sidney Frank, 85, has been in the spirits business most of his adult life, and understands the importance of marketing, branding, and packaging in creating a mystique around products that are very similar to others. In 1997, Mr. Frank decided to start importing vodka made in France, since many vodkas from European countries had taken significant market share from Russia—the largest exporter of vodka at one time. Mr. Frank decided to call the new product Grey Goose—a name that he had used years earlier for an inexpensive German wine that flopped. Grey Goose vodka was made of water from French springs filtered through limestone, and came in elegant-looking, narrow frosted-glass bottles that were packaged in wooden boxes, like expensive French wines. It was positioned as a premium vodka and cost way more than other vodkas. So, naturally, consumers assumed that it was the best, and the product was an instant hit.

Although Grey Goose still has only a small niche and market share in the vodka market, in 2004 Bacardi, one of the world's largest producers of spirits, bought the Grey Goose brand from Mr. Frank for $2.3 billion. So, seven years after he had made up a new brand of vodka from thin air, Mr. Frank became "The Two Billion Dollar Man."

Questions

1. List and describe three aspects of consumer perception that are illustrated by the success of Grey Goose Vodka.

2. Think of another beverage and develop a concept for a premium brand in that product category, including the product, its name, packaging, advertising theme, and price. Explain the rationale for your product category selection and the design of your concept for the new brand.

Sources: Frank J. Prial, "The Seller of the Goose That Laid a Golden Egg," **www.nytimes.com**, January 1, 2005; Steven Stevenson, "The Cocktail Creationist," *NY Magazine Online,* January 10, 2005.

Case Two: A Movie or One LONG Commercial?

As new technology enables consumers to skip more and more commercials, marketers are increasingly turning to *product placements* (also termed "branded entertainment"). These terms and their ethical implications are discussed in the chapter. While we are very much used to seeing products and brands prominently featured within the storylines of movies and TV programs, critics complain that some movies are more focused on the products placed within them than on the storyline. In Disney's movie, *Herbie: Fully Loaded,* the main character says she will kill for Tropicana orange juice, and is always wearing her Goodyear cap. The cable network ESPN (owned by Disney) is part of the story line. Reporters criticized the movie for featuring an unreasonably large number of brands, while some maintained that a promotion was included in virtually every frame. The movie's creators claimed that since the movie's storyline is centered around a journalist-turned-Nascar-driver, and since Nascar has commercial ties to many products, placing many products in the film was needed to maintain the movie's authenticity and were also needed to obtain Nascar's support for the film, which could not have been done without it.

Questions

1. Have you noticed an increase in product placements in movies and TV programs? Explain your answer.

2. What are the ethical implications of product placements in the context of consumer perception?

3. Good product placements are "seamlessly" integrated into a movie's or TV program's storyline. List and describe one movie or TV program that you recall seeing in which there was a good fit between the product placed and the storyline, and one example in which the fit was not so good.

Source: Ross Johnson, "Product Placement for the Whole Family," *The New York Times,* July 6, 2005, E5.

Consumer Learning

Case One: The Dental Care Aisle of Confusion

Stimulus generalization is one of the outcomes of consumer learning. It enables marketers to extend the number of product versions and to introduce new forms of products under existing brand names that are strongly recognized and favored by consumers. However, such extensions, designed to provide more choice to consumers, sometimes result in consumer confusion and frustration. For example, in stores' toothcare aisles, consumers must choose among scores of toothpastes providing different benefits (e.g., tartar control, special benefits for sensitive teeth, control of gum disease) that are offered in different forms (e.g., paste, gel, in combination with mouthwash) and in almost any conceivable flavor, and packaged in several different ways. In addition to toothpastes that offer bright smiles and perfectly white teeth, there are many whitening products in the forms of strips, gels, and liquids (each with its own method of application). There are also many versions of manual toothbrushes in different sizes, designs, and bristle strengths. There are electric toothbrushes and teeth-cleaning "systems." And, there are now many versions of dental floss. In addition, consumers can now engage in "on-the-go oral care" by using Brush Ups—a disposable combination of toothpaste and toothbrush head that fit on one's finger (the finger is the "handle" for the provided head).

Almost all of the toothpastes and related products are offered by either Crest or Colgate—two highly successful brands that have been competing with one another for decades. Facing saturated markets and competition, the two brands recognized the strategic value of stimulus generalization. Using the consumers' strong and favorable associations with the terms Crest and Colgate, the two brands have been trying to get consumers to use more toothpaste and households to buy more than a single version of the product by offering them a seemingly endless array of ways to care for their teeth. However, the result is often consumer confusion and frustration. First, consumers must decide which toothpaste is right for them. Then, they must find it in shelves crowded with many versions, and doing so takes time. Since stores cannot carry all of the versions all the time, they often alternate the toothpaste items carried and, at times, consumers may be unable to purchase their preferred versions of toothpaste in the stores where they regularly shop. There is also the anxiety that one is missing out on something by being brand-loyal to a particular brand or flavor while all the new and "exciting" toothpastes are coming out. Regarding the instantly popular teeth whiteners, some point out that toothpastes are already designed to keep teeth both white and clean and that extensive use of whiteners, induced by the quest for a perfect smile, may damage the enamel of teeth and dental crowns. So, it seems that stimulus generalization may lead marketers down a path that results in consumer confusion.

Questions

1. Do the strategic benefits of stimulus generalization outweigh its possible disadvantages in strategic marketing? Explain your answer.

2. How can the marketers of Crest and Colgate decrease consumer confusion regarding toothpastes and related oral hygiene products?

3. Discuss the issue of the vast array of oral hygiene products with a few of your peers and find out how many have experienced "consumer confusion" or were unable to find easily their preferred products. On the basis of these talks, discuss how you, as the marketer, would promote brand extensions while minimizing consumer confusion.

Source: Stacey Schiff, "One Nation with Niches for All," *The New York Times,* June 11, 2005, A13; Alana Tugend, "Smile, You're in the Dental Care Aisle," *The New York Times,* August 6, 2005.

Case Two: Does Observational Learning Cause Obesity?

For years, Americans believed that children learn and often imitate what they see on TV and expressed concern regarding the negative impact of TV on children's behavior. Increases in violent crime have been partially attributed to the once-widespread depiction of sex and violence on TV; as a result, TV programmers have curtailed showing such behaviors. The characters featured on TV no longer smoke or drink alcohol because these products are not advertised on TV, mostly because of their potential, negative impact on children. In sitcoms and dramas, the "good guys" always win at the end and characters always end up doing "the right thing," even in storylines where opposite actions or outcomes appear to be more likely, in order to convey the "right values" to young viewers. Now, many attribute the growing rates of obesity and associated illnesses among children and teenagers to the overconsumption of high-calories and high-fat foods that critics complain are the results of the heavy promotion of foods to children. Indeed, advertisers spend about $10 billion a year and most of the items advertised are high in fat and sugar but low in nutrition. In fact, several countries have already either banned or restricted the advertising of foods to children. Influential consumer advocacy groups have called for restricting the advertising of "junk foods" on TV, in movie placements, and in schools, and it appears likely that a bill giving the Federal Trade Commission more effective power to regulate advertising to children will be introduced in Congress. In addition, several individuals have sued food companies for causing their obesity or obesity-related health problems.

Recognizing these concerns and facing legal restrictions on their advertising to children, some fast-food companies eliminated the "super-size" servings from their menus, started offering and advertising more vegetable and fruit products, and began stressing the importance of physical activity in their commercials. The marketers of major brands of soft drinks voluntarily stopped marketing full-calorie carbonated drinks in elementary schools and are developing healthier soft drinks. Food and restaurant companies are also pursuing legislation that will prevent consumers from suing them on the grounds that long-term consumption of their foods resulted in health problems. It is obvious that marketing foods to children has many negative results, and that societal concerns will result in changes, voluntary or mandated, in the ways food companies target the young.

Questions

1. Do you believe that the government, rather than parents only, should regulate the consumption behavior of children? Why or why not? Please list all the examples you can think of where laws and regulations affect what children can or cannot consume, or how they must use certain products.

2. Some maintain that it is strictly up to parents to determine what their children eat and to educate them about food products, and that food marketers should not be blamed for child obesity. They feel that advertising food to children is a First Amendment right. Others say that parents cannot effectively compete with the heavy advertising of foods to children and the widespread presence of "junk foods," and that children are likely to pick up bad eating habits regardless of what parents might try to teach them. Therefore, the advertising of foods to children must be regulated. Which position do you agree with and why?

3. Some schools now forbid parents to include such items as cookies or soft drinks in their children's lunch boxes. Thinking back to the time when you were in primary school and middle school, do you wish that such school regulations would have been in place? Explain your answer.

Sources: Marian Burros, "It'd Be Easier if SpongeBob Were Hawking Brocolli," **www.nytimes.com**, January 12, 2005; Melanie Warner, "You Want Any Fruit With That Big Mac?" **www.nytimes.com**, February 20, 2005; Nat Ives, "McDonald's Says It's Time to Exercise," **www.nytimes.com**, March 9, 2005; Melanie Warner, "Guidelines Are Urged in Food Ads for Children," **www.nytimes.com**, March 17, 2005; Melanie Warner, "The Food Industry Empire Strikes Back," **www.nytimes.com**, July 7, 2005; Bloomberg News, "Soda Makers Widen a Ban on School Sales," **www.nutimes.com**, August 18, 2005.

Consumer Attitude Formation and Change

Case One: The Not-So-Extreme Sport

It wasn't that long ago that skateboarding was considered to be an extreme sport—some have even called it the "ultimate outlaw road sport." To quote a line from Sony's new film that deals with southern California skateboarders in the mid-1970s, "Everywhere we go, man, people hate us." In its early days, skateboarding was banned by many communities and embraced by participants for its "go-to-hell attitude."

But times have changed, and skateboarding, once a sport for bad boys, is the new Little League. In fact, today it's about as counterculture as yoga. Parents have embraced the sport for their children, and there are now rules about safety. Some parents have even taken up skateboarding as a way to bond with their children. Skateboarding has recently been characterized as being "more fun and better organized than Little League," and there are now about 2,000 skateboarding parks located throughout the United States, with about 1,000 more in the development stage. Even some churches are backing the sport by building skate parks, and, yes, June 21 has been established as National Skateboard Day.

Today's skateboarders are typically polite and friendly, and are willing to skateboard where helmets are required, rather than on the street (which can result in a fine). For some teens, "it's a fashion thing," even if they don't skateboard. Last year, $4.4 billion was spent on "soft goods" related to skateboarding, such as T-shirts, shorts, and sunglasses, while actual skateboarding equipment, such as boards and helmets, had sales of $809 million.

Question

1. On the basis of the Theory of Reasoned Action presented in Chapter 8, how would you explain the 180-degree shift in attitudes about skateboarding that has occurred over the past 30 years?

Source: Damien Cave, "Dogtown, U.S.A.," *The New York Times,* June 12, 2005, Section 9, 1–6.

Case Two: Rebates with Attitude

To attract potential consumers into automobile showrooms, GM, Chrysler, and Ford have each used buyers rebates and other promotions estimated to be about $4,000 per vehicle. In contrast, rebates and promotions from European auto brands are averaging about $2,300, and Asian brands are offering about $1,700 per vehicle. Compared to a year ago, this represents an increase of 8.9 percent for domestic and Asian brands, and a decrease of 15 percent for European brands.

A component of the current promotions employed by the three major domestic car companies is a one-price approach. GM started the ball rolling with their "GM Employee Discount for Everyone" promotion, and Ford followed with its "Ford Family Plan," and Chrysler followed with its "Employee Pricing Plus." Rather than haggling with the car dealer over price, the consumer is expected to walk into the dealership and accept the price that employees of the car manufacturer would pay if they were purchasing the vehicle.

Questions

1. Since these rebates and other promotional programs are expensive for the manufacturers, how could they develop an exit strategy within the framework of the attitude-toward-the-ad model presented in the chapter?

2. In terms of consumers' attitudes, should automobiles be sold using a one-price approach? Why or why not?

Source: Bradley Johnson, " 'Discount' Ploy Could Bite Detroit," *Advertising Age,* July 11, 2005, 1–33.

Communication and Consumer Behavior

Case One: The Impact of Blogs

WebLogs or blogs are consumer-controlled electronic postings on the Internet where consumers describe their experiences and express their opinions, including criticisms and reviews of products, service providers, films, TV shows, travel, and virtually any topic one can think of. In many cases, marketers can now gather consumer feedback more accurately and quickly than ever before and respond to it. For example, traditionally, TV shows have exemplified impersonal, mass, commercially driven programming. Much like a book or a movie, such programming arose without significant input from the audience—the receivers of the communication. Only after a one-way electronic dissemination did others analyze, critique, rate, and review the programming. Generally, Nielsen ratings have been used to gauge the "success" of TV programs and determine the advertising rates for various broadcasts. Until the arrival of the Internet, the unidirectional nature of television remained pretty much unchanged. Viewers may have "talked back" to their television sets, but the producers never heard them. Now they do, and they listen with increased attentiveness.

Internet Web sites such as **Televisionwithoutpity.com** ("TWoP") closely track, discuss, summarize, grade, criticize, and occasionally compliment approximately 35 television shows weekly. Though such discussions may have taken place informally, TWoP offers a centralized location that vast numbers of people can virtually visit immediately after or even during a broadcast to discuss their views about a particular show. Because the viewers who post their comments about such shows represent a much larger number of viewers, the producers of such shows in turn care about these viewers' comments and they now monitor them to get a sense of what the viewers are thinking. Because television production generally occurs several weeks prior to a broadcast, television producers can and have changed yet-to-be-broadcast programming to address concerns expressed by viewers' TWoP postings. Not only can programmers now receive an enormous amount of feedback but also much of this feedback is almost instantaneous. There are a number of instances where storylines of TV programs were adjusted in a way that reflected the criticisms and opinions of viewers.

Questions

1. In terms of source credibility, how would you assess the effectiveness of reviews of a TV program posted on TWoP versus a review of the same program in a magazine or a newspaper?

2. After examining several blogs on TWoP, give five examples that provide useful information to the respective marketers who may want to adjust their programs. Explain why.

3. Please identify and describe the disadvantages of blogs from the marketers' perspective.

Case Two: Is Targeting the "Right" Audience Always Right?

In marketing most consumer products, the audiences targeted by marketers' persuasive communications are the consumers or potential buyers of these products. In some cases, like prescription drugs, the targeted audience used to be the doctors who prescribe these medications, not the patients who are the final consumers of these products. But in 1997, the Food and Drug Administration allowed the pharmaceutical industry to advertise directly to consumers, an action that provided these marketers with an additional audience to target. Since then, consumers have been bombarded with ads for such disorders as erectile dysfunction, depression, and high cholesterol, stating that "if you have such and such symptoms then this drug is for you." Of course, all ads included the standard disclaimer that "this is a prescription medication and the final decision whether it is right for you is up to your doctor." Print ads listed the risks associated with using the medications, usually in the bottom of the ads and in much smaller print than the advertising copy itself. TV ads generally portrayed healthy and active individuals who have either taken the drug or were the kind of person who, in spite of appearing healthy, may have a health problem, such as high cholesterol. Typically, in these ads, the list of risks are cited at the end of the commercial by a soothing voice calmly listing the sometimes fatal results that the medication may cause. The initial introduction of a medication in TV ads is usually followed by 15-second reminder ads portraying the product and reminding consumers that it is still around.

Until 1997, pharmaceutical companies spent relatively little money on marketing prescription medications since the audiences for such promotions were primarily doctors and other healthcare providers who were exposed to ads promoting prescription drugs in professional magazines and conferences. But, since 1997, pharmaceutical firms have drastically increased their advertising spending, and—like any marketer facing a competitive marketplace with many similar products—used highly skilled advertising agencies to position and advertise their products. Since people are generally concerned with their physical well-being, consumers responded to the ads. Many consumers self-diagnosed themselves according to the "instructions" in the ads and then flocked to their doctors to ask for the advertised medications by name. In numerous cases, people consumed medications they did not truly need or used prescription drugs for problems that could have been treated with over-the-counter medications. The direct-to-consumer advertising also increased the rate of new drug introductions and, in some cases, like Vioxx—a once-popular painkiller—sometimes fatal side effects were discovered only after the medication had been on the market for years. In other cases, the FDA discovered unsubstantiated advertising claims where the risks of using the drugs were minimized or not clearly stated. It has become rapidly clear that marketing drugs directly to consumers is not in the consumers' best interests and it appeared imminent that the government was going to step in and regulate such advertising. To fend off such action, an industry group representing most pharmaceutical companies announced self-regulatory guidelines for future direct-to-consumer ads of prescription medications.

Questions

1. "The key to effective communications is reaching an audience with the right persuasive message. Direct-to-consumer advertising of prescription drugs has been

effective because the marketers of these products understood that people are concerned about their health, and so designed messages that addressed these concerns effectively and persuaded consumers to seek the applicable products." Please evaluate this statement in the context of this case.

2. The self-regulatory guidelines mentioned above include: (1) the elimination of 15-second reminder ads that do not have enough time to both promote a drug and list its risks; (2) submit all ads to an FDA review before they are used; and (3) after introducing a new drug, take the time to educate the doctors about it before launching a consumer campaign. Do you believe that these measures will resolve the problems of marketing medications directly to consumers? Why or why not?

3. Do you believe that the government should regulate the marketing of prescription drugs to consumers? Explain your answer.

Sources: Barry Meier and Stephanie Saul, "Marketing of Vioxx: How Merck Played Game of Catch-Up," **www.nytimes.com**, February 11, 2005; Amy Barrett, "A New Rx for Drug Pitches," **www.businesswek.com**, June 16, 2005; Stephanie Saul, "A.M.A. to Study Effect of Marketing Drugs to Consumers," **www.nytimes.com**, June 22, 2005; Stephanie Saul, "Drug Makers to Police Consumer Campaigns," **www.nytimes.com**, August 3, 2005.

Reference Groups and Family Influences

Case One: Keeping Up with the Joneses

Finland, like the United States, is a wealthy country. Its economy is open—providing consumers a wide variety of choices when it comes to consumer products. What sets Finland apart, though, is that the country keeps very detailed records about its citizens—including everything from the ages, sex, and incomes of people living in the same household, the amount they spend annually on commuting, and vehicle purchases.

Consider this: Researchers have determined that when a Finnish household buys a new car, the odds that one of that household's nearest 10 neighbors will purchase the same brand vehicle during the next week and a half increases by 86 percent!

Question

1. What factors contained in Chapter 10 might be used to explain this phenomenon?

Source: David Leonhardt, "See the New Car in the Jones's Driveway? You May Soon Be Driving One Just Like It," *The New York Times,* June 13, 2005, C5.

Case Two: Here's the DVD, Now Please Pass the Popcorn

Movie theater attendance has been down for three of the past five years (in number of attendees), and the film studios are wondering whether it reflects a rash of bad movies or if it's something more significant. There's no doubt that more and more people are choosing to stay at home, and the Hollywood studios today make more on DVD sales and licensed products than they do on movie theater showings. Not only are digital video recorders (e.g., TiVo) and video-on-demand movies keeping people at home, but high-definition TV and multichannel sound systems bring a movie-theater-quality visual and audio experience into a consumer's home.

Some U.S. consumers feel that there are very few movies that are worth going to a theater to see, and believe that quality has declined over the past few years. Additionally, some of the time that a person used to spend at the movie theater is today taken up by playing video games. Indeed, for some consumers, playing video games has replaced going with friends to a movie theater. And having a large-screen HDTV set at home with a multichannel sound system means no driving or parking hassles at the theater, and no lines to wait on. And you can pause the movie for a bathroom break or to deal with a crying child.

Over the past five years, movie theater box office receipts rose 8.3 percent. In contrast, video games were up 20.3 percent, and time spent watching cable and satellite TV were up 31.3 percent. Also, time spent on the Internet rose 76.6 percent.

Question

1. Within the context of the consumer socialization of children, adult consumer socialization, and intergenerational socialization (all discussed in Chapter 10), how do you suppose that the increased at-home viewing of movies on DVD will impact the typical American family?

Source: Laura M. Holson, "With Popcorn, DVDs and TiVo, Moviegoers Are Staying Home," *The New York Times,* May 27, 2005, A1 & C3.

Social Class and Consumer Behavior

Case One: Will the Real Costco Shopper Please Stand Up!

Costco Wholesale, the warehouse membership outlet, is the fifth largest retailer in the United States. Founded in Seattle in 1983, and merged with Price Club in 1993, the company now runs 457 stores. While most of its locations are in the United States, the company operates outlets in Canada, the United Kingdom, Taiwan, South Korea, and Japan. Its two largest competitors are Sam's Club (owned by Wal-Mart) and BJ's Wholesale Club (started by Zayre's).

Because it is a membership club, the 44.6 million Costco consumers each pay $45 a year, and small businesses pay $100 annually. Each location stocks approximately 4,000 types of items, but only a few brands or versions of each. For example, Costco may stock only four brands of toothpaste, while a typical Wal-Mart may carry 60 brands and sizes of toothpaste, and over 100,000 different types of items.

Costco attempts to keep prices low, to make it impossible for another retailer to offer the same merchandise for less. Their cardinal rule is that no branded item can be marked up more than 14 percent, and no private-label item by more than 15 percent. As a comparison, supermarkets often use a 25 percent markup, and department stores typically mark up merchandise by 50 percent or more.

Question

1. From what you already know about Costco (if you are already a Costco customer), and/or from what you can glean from the company's Web site (**www.costco.com**), what social classes in America would you consider to be Costco customers?

Source: Steven Greenhouse, "How Costco Became the Anti-Wal-Mart," *The New York Times,* July 17, 2005, Section 3, 1 & 8.

Case Two: $30,000 for a Hyundai— Are You Kidding?

For the 2006 model year, Hyundai introduced its Azera sedan, complete with luxury goodies and a 10-year warranty, and aimed squarely at Toyota Avalon and Nissan Maxima drivers. While many of its dealers were asking for a pickup truck, Hyundai's Korean executives wanted the cachet of offering consumers an upscale car. The Azera is part of Hyundai's plan to sell one million vehicles in the United States by 2010.

And the Azera comes with a lot of upscale features, including eight air bags, five-speed automatic transmission, a V6 265 horsepower engine, stability control, premium sound system, rain-sensing wipers, and telescoping steering wheel. That's a lot of car for the money.

Will the Azera appeal to American consumers? Buyers have thus far resisted spending over $70,000 for the Volkswagen Phaeton, and it could be argued that VW has the advantage, in the consumers' mind, of "German engineering." When Hyundai first started selling cars in the United States about twenty years ago, they were best known for "rattletrap econoboxes." But since then they have offered larger, better-made cars, as well as minivans and SUVs, while keeping their value image.

Hyundai feels that the Azera may be sold via reverse chic—like very wealthy people who shop at Costco. These consumers will tell their friends about the great deal their cars were, and will value the "bargain" they got.

Questions

1. If you were a member of the Hyundai Azera marketing team, to which social class (or classes) would you market the car?

2. Do you think the Azera will succeed in the American marketplace?

Source: Kathleen Kerwin, "Hyundai Takes a Hard Curve into Swank," *Business Week,* July 18, 2005, 42.

The Influence of Culture on Consumer Behavior

Case One: Gum for Adults

American's favorite snack is chewing gum, with chocolate second, and fresh fruit third. Indeed, in the $3.3 billion gum business, the emphasis has recently been on developing new gums for adults. At a recent industry trade show, 86 new gums were introduced.

While bubble gum has been in a slump since the late 1980s and early 1990s, sales of regular chewing gum are strong, with about two-thirds of Americans using the product. The use of bolder flavors in all types of food is on the increase, and this is true for gum, although some analysts wonder just how much hotter and icier consumers can go. There are also functional gums being sold—some gums provide as much caffeine as a cup of coffee, and a new "diet" gum contains herbs that are supposed to increase the user's metabolism. Gum manufacturers also know that gum chewers are fickle, with 60 percent changing flavors and/or brands on a regular basis.

Why are adults chewing so much gum? Probably the desire for fresher breath is and always has been the number one reason. But for people who have quit smoking, or are trying to quit, gum allows them to put something in their mouths other than cigarettes. Also, many people today are trying to lose or to maintain their weight, and a piece of gum is certainly lower in calories than a chocolate bar or cookies.

Even classic flavors of gum, like Wrigley Doublemint and spearmint, have seen sales increases. Some immigrant groups view these well-known American gums as a way to assimilate.

Question

1. Is there any relationship between adult gum chewing and the core American values presented in Chapter 12?

Source: Kim Severson, "Adults Now Grab for Gum, Elbowing the Children Aside," *The New York Times,* June 19, 2005, 22.

Case Two: Privacy: A New Facet of American Culture?

For many of us, the Internet is a wonderful tool. It makes it possible to e-mail our friends and family, helps us bank and pay our bills, compare different brands that we might consider purchasing, and find the best price for a desired item. But how much of this "wonderfulness" are we willing to exchange for our personal data?

Marketers want to know who we are, and where we go on the Internet. So, for example, they've been installing cookies on our computers for years. That's why once we've visited a Web site, the next time we want to click on it its listing is a different color. And if you increase the security level of your computer so that your PC will not accept cookies, then chances are that a Web site you want to visit won't let you on.

Google has been particularly criticized by those with security concerns because of how it operates its G-mail system. G-mail automatically delivers ads to the user, based on e-mail content. Many users are not happy that Google is monitoring their e-mail in order to send them ads, even if, based on e-mail content, the ads are relevant.

In today's world of identify theft and computer viruses, consumers are resisting swapping personal information for increased value, whether it is taking place online or offline. Jupiter Research has found that 58 percent of Internet users say that they have deleted cookies, with as many as 39 percent claiming to do so monthly. And 28 percent of Internet users are selectively rejecting third-party cookies, like those placed by online ad networks. In January 2003, only 3 percent did so.

Question

1. Is personal privacy a new U.S. cultural value?

Source: Jack Neff, "Are We Too Targeted?," *Advertising Age's Point Magazine*, June 2005, 8–11.

Subcultures and Consumer Behavior

Case One: Kraft Woos Asian Americans

According to Vincent Tam, director of client services at Admerasia, a New York based ad agency, "food companies have been slow to target Asian Americans . . . they find it daunting and complex that there are so many Asian groups. But as diverse as we are, we have shared values."

Tam's firm recently won Kraft's Asian business, and is in the process of developing in-language print ads aimed at immigrant Chinese-speaking moms that will appear in Chinese newspapers in Los Angeles and New York. These ads will feature such Kraft products as Oreos, Ritz, Kraft Barbecue Sauce, Capri Sun, and Philly Cream Cheese, and will do so in "culturally relevant settings." Interestingly, the focus of the campaign is not to get Chinese-speaking moms to use these products in their own Chinese cooking, but to teach them how to use Kraft products for Western-style meals. As an example, a common condition among Asians is lactose intolerance, and Tam's research has found that Chinese-speaking immigrant moms feed their lactose-intolerant children cheese, because of the calcium that cheese provides.

The president of the Asian American Advertising Federation, Bill Imada, feels that "Kraft's entry will make a big difference to those food marketers who are on the fence." This could result in significantly more advertising money being channeled to the Asian American market.

Question

1. Considering the text discussion of Asian American consumers (and a targeted search of this subcultural market on the Internet), why is this demographic segment particularly ripe for increased attention?

Source: Sonia Reyes, "Kraft Initiative Woos Asian American Moms," *Brandweek,* July 25, 2005, 10.

Case Two: Sorry, You're Too Old (or Young) to Buy This Car!

Automobile manufacturers have been creating cars targeted to specific age groups. For example, the Toyota Matrix, the three versions of the Toyota Scion, and the Honda Element were all designed and targeted to 20-somethings. But targeting a vehicle to a specific age group, and getting that age group to purchase the car, is not the same thing.

Consider the Toyota Matrix, a vehicle whose expected drivers were supposed to have a median age of 28.8. In reality, the median age of Matrix drivers is 42.7, almost 50 percent older. Honda anticipated that its Element drivers would average 28.6 years of age, but, instead, they are 44.7 years old, on average. Honda has commented that they designed the Element for 18- to 25-year-old males, with a square design, resembling a big box—a rolling dorm room with enough space for all of the driver's "stuff." Instead, though, the Element is being purchased by older hobbyists, families, and businesses, who appreciate the vehicle's utility and the fact that it can be hosed out (it has a rubber floor).

Traditional U.S. auto companies are not immune from this problem. The Dodge Neon was expected to appeal to young drivers with an average age of 22.7, but the real average age of Neon drivers is almost 40. Pontiac expected that Vibe owners would average 30 years of age, but they really average almost 50.

In the past, Toyota had tried selling Echos and Matrixes to young people, and the result of this failure was the establishment of the Scion—a separate brand that employs unconventional methods to reach its market (e.g., parking a custom version near a hip night spot, so the "right" people discover it on their own). The company feels that one of the reasons why its Echo did not appeal to 20-somethings is because it was a Toyota, and this is the reason why the Scion division was created.

Question

1. Considering the discussion of age in Chapter 13, how do you explain why vehicles often targeted to 20-something drivers are being purchased by drivers who are considerably older?

Source: George P. Blumberg, "The Car Is for Kids, But Gramps Is Driving," *The New York Times,* July 3, 2005, Section 12, 1 & 4.

Cross-Cultural Consumer Behavior: An International Perspective

Case One: Cat Food Strategy

A product that has been a success in one country may not easily find success in another. For example, consider Iams, a premium brand of dog and cat food sold in the United States. This dry pet food (kibbles) is very high in animal protein content, which is similar to what dogs and cats would eat in the wild. In the United States, the brand has a reputation for being driven by product innovation.

But the European market for pet foods is different. Iams first introduced their cat food in Europe, and the reception was decidedly cool. In northwest Europe, the cat food market is dominated by wet food (cans), and in the south there is a reliance on home-made pet food, such as paste, rice, and table scraps. Additionally, while Iams kibble is oval-shaped and a dull uniform brown color, European kibble tends to be multicolored, and sometimes elaborately shaped. Furthermore, although Iams believes that cats do not need variety in their diets, Europeans tend to believe that a variety of foods is best for their pets.

So what did Iams do? The company first introduced a "wet" canned version of its kibbles, but its high price limited its sales. And its kibbles were not selling well because European cat owners disliked the package's stark design. Clearly, it was time for Iams to change tactics.

The company felt that the best way to stop competing with existing brands of cat food and to get its health claims across to European cat owners was to distribute its brand only through pet stores and veterinarians. Iams also enlisted the help of other influentials, such as breeders. Endorsement of these knowledgeable individuals persuaded many pet owners to select the Iams brand for their pet, and, despite its high price, to stick with the brand for the pet's entire life.

Questions

1. What was Iams initial mistake?

2. What lessons can be learned from the Iams experience?

Source: Sicco Van Gelder, "Global Brand Strategy," *Brand Management,* 12, September 2004, 39–48.

Case Two: Would Mickey Mouse Eat Shark's Fin Soup?

Controversy started brewing at Hong Kong Disneyland even before the park opened in the fall of 2005. At Disney theme parks around the world, weddings and wedding receptions are a profitable business. Disney is planning to offer shark's fin soup as an option on wedding reception menus at Hong Kong Disneyland.

Clearly, Disney wants to show its appreciation for Chinese traditions, and claims that it is doing nothing more than following local standards—the dish is considered an essential part of a Chinese wedding banquet, and can be priced at up to $150 at the best restaurants. However, environmental groups from all over the world are up in arms over the prospect of Disney serving this soup, which points out a difference between Chinese and Western traditions.

Although shark's fin soup has been a Chinese favorite for 200 years, some environmental groups are concerned that China's increasing wealth has led to a greater appetite for rare species. For example, Hong Kong authorities recently stopped a shipment of 1,800 freeze-dried penguins that were being smuggled into mainland China. Some animal advocates are afraid that down the road entire species could be threatened.

Question

1. As a member of the top management team at the Walt Disney Company, do you keep or delete shark's fin soup from the wedding banquet menu at Hong Kong Disneyland?

Source: Keith Bradsher, "Chinese Delicacy Has Disney in Turbulent Waters," *The New York Times,* June 17, 2005, C1 & C7.

Consumer Influence and the Diffusion of Innovations

Give the Kid a Cell Phone

Cellular telephone providers are now realizing that they've made a mistake. For years, they assumed that many teens and college students could not afford to subscribe to postpaid cellular services, and so they pushed prepaid cellular to this group. Wrong!

The major cellular telephone companies have finally come to understand that members of the younger generation possess three characteristics that marketers want: (1) they have disposable income, (2) they have grown up with technology, and (3) they view the cellular phone as their No. 1 possession. Still further, young adults (age 18 to 34) are two or three times more likely to also use services such as e-mail, news and text alerts, all of which produce additional revenue for the cellular phone company. Just think of all the photographs that teens take with their cellular phones, and all of the ring tones that they pay to download.

Questions

1. Considering the teenage and college student market segments, what other features can cellular telephone companies offer these groups over the next five to ten years?

2. What role will innovators and opinion leaders play in this era of new cell phone enhancements?

Sources: Alice Z. Cuneo, "Wireless Services Get Wakeup Call from Youth," *Advertising Age*, June 6, 2005, 16; and Ian Rowley, "$5,000? Sure, Put It on My Cell Phone," *Business Week*, June 6, 2005, 56.

Case Two: We Have a Relationship—We Blog!

As a way to enhance relationships with customers, e-tailers are beginning to test Web logs (blogs). Online merchants feel that their blogs will give their e-stores more of a personality, and will get customers to return to their Web sites even when they are not in the mood to shop.

For example, eHobbies is a small company with 25 employees. On its new blog it posts photographs of employees and photos taken at trade shows. The firm believes that its blog helps "humanize" the company by showing that it is "a company of hobbyists," who in many ways are just like their customers.

But there can be problems with a company having a blog. One difficulty is how do you keep the customer from straying from the store Web site (where he or she can purchase merchandise) to the blog, and then not returning to the store's site? After all, most blogs contain links to other articles on the Web. Another issue is that some customers might not like the language used on the blog or might not appreciate a scorching review or comment.

Perhaps the most controversial company with a blog is GoDaddy.com, a firm offering Internet domains and hosting services. On its blog, the company's owner, Bob Parsons, offers his thoughts on a lot of different topics, and often his comments are highly opinionated. While this is enough for some individuals who visit this blog to never return, Mr. Parsons feels that his blog lets his company become more to consumers than just "some name with a URL on the Internet," and also lets people "understand why we do things the way we do them."

Question

1. How do you think blogs fit into the diffusion process that you read about in Chapter 15?

Source: Bob Tedeschi, "Yes, You Sell Sweaters, but Should You Really Blog About It?," *The New York Times,* July 4, 2005, C6.

Consumer Decision Making and Beyond

Caes One: Deciding on Satellite Radio

It seems that since the birth of satellite radio there have been two competing stations—XM and Sirius. While one has a contract with Howard Stern, the other carries major league baseball games—and they both offer 24/7 commercial-free listening, as well as programming that does include commercials (e.g., the weather and traffic channel).

Marketers believe that there are several reasons why satellite radio will become an important advertising medium. One reason is cost—a 30-second spot on XM may cost as little as $25 (or, depending on audience size, may cost much, much more). Also, satellite radio allows an advertiser like Subaru to run different spots targeted to different areas of the country. For example, an ad run in the Northeast in January would play up the car's full-time four-wheel drive system that is great in snow, while a spot aired in the south would have a different theme. Also, the large number of channels offered by each satellite radio company means that they can air programs targeted to specific audiences. As an example, Sirius' programs include OutQ radio, a station providing news, information, and entertainment for the gay and lesbian community. If advertisers want to target this audience, they now have a new medium, and individuals listening to this station also appreciate that the medium exists.

Questions

1. If you were purchasing a new vehicle and satellite radio was a low-cost option, what factors might you consider when making your decision?

2. What might your prepurchase search activity include?

Source: Deborah L. Vence, "Channel Advertising Efforts: Satellite Radio Offers Marketers New Options," *Marketing News,* April 15, 2005, 11–12.

Case Two: Women Want More Horses

A recent article in the *New York Times* presented a story about two Connecticut women, both in their early 50s, both mothers, both now single (one widowed and one divorced), and both wanting to celebrate their lives by pleasing themselves. So what did they do? They both bought new Mercedes automobiles.

Indeed, over the past few years, there has been a growth in the sales of fun or extravagant cars to middle-aged women, and a movement by these women away from minivans and SUVs. Car dealers have reported that women are walking into their dealerships and are exhibiting much more interest in horsepower than in trunk space. While there is no particular brand of vehicle that is preferred, middle-age women have been buying a lot of convertibles and other "nonfamily" type cars. If the woman drove a convertible when she was young and single, and enjoyed the experience, then she wants a convertible now. If she considered pickup trucks to be "tough and sexy" when she was a young woman, then it's a pickup truck she now wants to be driving.

While some might call this a midlife crisis—after all, quite a few men want a Corvette for their 50th birthday—others call it an "unrealistic desire," with the buyer wanting to go back to the person she remembers being before becoming a Mom and needing a minivan. And these women are walking into car dealerships very knowledgeable, often thanks to the information acquired over the Internet.

Question

1. How can the concept of self-gifting be used to explain the increased interest of women in purchasing nonfamily type vehicles?

Source: Alex Williams, "What Women Want: More Horses," *The New York Times,* June 12, 2005, Section 9, 1 & 7.

Glossary

Absolute Threshold. The lowest level at which an individual can experience a sensation.

Acculturation. The learning of a new or "foreign" culture.

Acquired Needs. Needs that are learned in response to one's culture or environment (such as the need for esteem, prestige, affection, or power). Also known as *psychogenic* or *secondary needs*.

Acquisition-Transaction Utility. This theory suggests that there are two types of utilities that are associated with consumer purchases: acquisition utility, which represents the consumer's perceived economic gain or loss associated with a purchase, and transaction utility, which concerns the perceived pleasure or displeasure associated with the financial aspect of the purchase.

Actual Self-Image. The image that an individual has of himself or herself as a certain kind of person, with certain characteristic traits, habits, possessions, relationships, and behavior.

Adopter Categories. A sequence of categories that describes how early (or late) a consumer adopts a new product in relation to other adopters. The five typical adopter categories are innovators, early adopters, early majority, late majority, and laggards.

Adoption Process. The stages through which an individual consumer passes in arriving at a decision to try (or not to try), to continue using (or discontinue using) a new product. The five stages of the traditional adoption process are awareness, interest, evaluation, trial, and adoption.

Advertising Resonance. Wordplay, often used to create a double meaning, used in combination with a relevant picture.

Advertising Wearout. Overexposure to repetitive advertising that causes individuals to become satiated and their attention and retention to decline.

Affect Referral Decision Rule. A simplified decision rule by which consumers make a product choice on the basis of their previously established overall ratings of the brands considered, rather than on specific attributes.

Affluent Market. Upscale market segment that consists of households with incomes that are higher than average (e.g., income over $75,000).

African American Consumers. Constituting more than 39 million Americans or 13 percent of the U.S. population.

Age Subcultures. Age subgroupings of the population.

AIOs. Psychographic variables that focus on activities, interests, and opinions. Also referred to as lifestyle.

Approach Object. A positive goal toward which behavior is directed.

Asian American Consumers. The fastest-growing American minority with a population of about 14 million in size made up of Chinese, Filipinos, Indian, Vietnamese, Korean, and Japanese.

Attitude. A learned predisposition to behave in a consistently favorable or unfavorable manner with respect to a given object.

Attitude Scales. Research measurement instrument used to capture evaluative data.

Attitude-Toward-Behavior Model. A model that proposes that a consumer's attitude toward a specific behavior is a function of how strongly he or she believes that the action will lead to a specific outcome (either favorable or unfavorable).

Attitude-Toward-Object Model. A model that proposes that a consumer's attitude toward a product or brand is a function of the presence of certain attributes and the consumer's evaluation of those attributes.

Attitude-Toward-the-Ad Model. A model that proposes that a consumer forms various feelings (affects) and judgments (cognitions) as the result of exposure to an advertisement, which, in turn, affect the consumer's *attitude toward the ad* and *beliefs and attitudes toward the brand*.

Attitudinal Measures. Measures concerned with consumers' overall feelings (i.e., evaluation) about the product and the brand and their purchase intentions.

Attribution Theory. A theory concerned with how people assign causality to events, and form or alter their attitudes after assessing their own or other people's behavior.

Attributions Towards Others. When consumers feel that another person is responsible for either positive or negative product performance.

Attributions Towards Things. Consumers judge a product's performance and attribute its success or failure to the product itself.

Audience Profile. Psychographic/demographic profile of the audience of a specific medium.

Autonomic (Unilateral) Decision. A purchase decision in which either the husband or the wife makes the final decision.

Avoidance Object. A negative goal from which behavior is directed away.

Baby Boomers. Individuals born between 1946 and 1964 (approximately 40% of the adult population).

Behavioral Learning Theories. Theories based on the premise that learning takes place as the result of observable responses to external stimuli. Also known as *stimulus response theory*.

Behavioral Measures. Measures based on observable responses to promotional stimuli.

Benefit Segmentation. Segmentation based on the kinds of benefits consumers seek in a product.

Brand Equity. The value inherent in a well-known brand name.

Brand Loyalty. Consumers' consistent preference and/or purchase of the same brand in a specific product or service category.

Brand Personification. Specific "personality-type" traits or characteristics ascribed by consumers to different brands.

Broad versus Narrow Categorizers. Broad categorizers are uninvolved consumers who are likely to be receptive to a greater number of advertising messages regarding a product category and will consider more brands. Narrow categorizers are highly involved consumers that find fewer brands acceptable.

Celebrity Credibility. The audience's perception of the endorser's expertise and trustworthiness.

Central and Peripheral Routes to Persuasion. A promotional theory that proposes that highly involved consumers are best reached through ads that focus on the specific attributes of the product (the central route) while uninvolved consumers can be attracted through peripheral advertising cues such as the model or the setting (the peripheral route).

Chapin's Social Status Scale. A social class rating scheme that focuses on the presence or absence of certain items of furniture and accessories in the home.

Class Consciousness. A feeling of social-group membership that reflects an individual's sense of belonging or identification with others.

Classical Conditioning. (See Conditioned Learning.)

Closure. A principle of Gestalt psychology that stresses the individual's need for completion. This need is reflected in the individual's subconscious reorganization and perception of incomplete stimuli as complete or whole pictures.

Co-Branding. When two brand names are featured on a single product.

Cognitive Age. An individual's perceived age (usually 10 to 15 years younger than his or her chronological age).

Cognitive Associative Learning. The learning of associations among events through classical conditioning that allows the organism to anticipate and represent its environment.

Cognitive Dissonance. The discomfort or dissonance that consumers experience as a result of conflicting information. (See Balance Theory.)

Cognitive Learning Theory. A theory of learning based on mental information processing, often in response to problem solving.

Cognitive Personality. *Need for cognition* and *visualizers versus verbalizers* are two cognitive personality traits that influence consumer behavior.

Communication. The transmission of a message from a sender to a receiver by means of a signal of some sort sent through a communications channel (e.g., medium) of some sort.

Comparative Advertising. Advertising that explicitly names or otherwise identifies one or more competitors of the advertised brand for the purpose of claiming superiority, either on an overall basis or on selected product attributes.

Comparative Reference Group. A group whose norms serve as a benchmark for highly specific or narrowly defined types of behavior. (See also Normative Reference Group.)

Compensatory Decision Rule. A type of decision rule in which a consumer evaluates each brand in terms of each relevant attribute and then selects the brand with the highest weighted score.

Composite-Variable Index. An index that combines a number of socioeconomic variables (such as education, income, occupation) to form one overall measure of social class standing. (See also Single-Variable Index.)

Comprehension. A function of the message characteristics, the consumer's opportunity and ability to process the information, and the consumer's motivation to do so (e.g., level of involvement).

Compulsive Consumption. When buying becomes an addiction; consumers who are compulsive buyers are in some respects "out of control," and their actions may have damaging consequences to them and to those around them.

Concentrated Marketing. Targeting a product or service to a single market segment with a unique marketing mix (price, product, promotion, method of distribution).

Conditioned Learning. According to Pavlovian theory, conditioned learning results when a stimulus paired with another stimulus that elicits a known response serves to produce the same response by itself.

Conditioned Stimuli. When consumers associate new products bearing a well-known symbol or brand name with the original product in the belief that it embodies the same attributes as the name it is associated with.

Conjunctive Decision Rule. A noncompensatory decision rule in which consumers establish a minimally acceptable cutoff point for each attribute evaluated. Brands that fall below the cutoff point on any one attribute are eliminated from further consideration.

Consumer Action Group. Groups that are dedicated to providing consumers with assistance in making the "right" purchase decisions and in avoiding "poor" decisions; sometimes based on political activism such as avoiding products manufactured in "sweat shops" and other unhealthy worker environments. Also called consumer activists and consumer advocates.

Consumer Behavior. The behavior that consumers display in searching for, purchasing, using, evaluating, and disposing of products, services, and ideas.

Consumer Conformity. The willingness of consumers to adopt the norms, attitudes, and behavior of reference groups.

Consumer Decision Making. The process of making purchase decisions based on cognitive and emotional influences such as impulse, family, friends, advertisers, role models, moods, and situations that influence a purchase.

Consumer Decision Rules. Procedures adopted by consumers to reduce the complexity of making product and brand decisions.

Consumer Ethnocentrism. A consumer's predisposition to accept or reject foreign-made products.

Consumer Fieldwork. Observational research by anthropologists of the behaviors of a small sample of people from a particular society.

Consumer Imagery. Products and brands have symbolic value for individuals, who evaluate them on the basis of their consistency with their personal pictures of themselves.

Consumer Innovativeness. The degree to which consumers are receptive to new products, new services, or new practices.

Consumer Innovators. Those who are among the first to purchase a new product.

Consumer Materialism. A personality-like trait of individuals who regard possessions as particularly essential to their identities and lives.

Consumer Profile. Psychographic/demographic profile of actual or proposed consumers for a specific product or service.

Consumer Research. Methodology used to study and interpret consumer behavior.

Consumer Socialization. The process, started in childhood, by which an individual learns the skills and attitudes relevant to consumer purchase behavior.

Consumption Process. A process consisting of three stages: the *input stage* establishes the consumption set and consuming style; the *process* of consuming and possessing, which includes using, possessing, collecting, and disposing of things; and the *output stage*, which includes changes in feelings, moods, attitudes, and behavior toward the product or service based on personal experience.

Content Analysis. A method for systematically analyzing the content of verbal and/or pictorial communication. The method is frequently used to determine prevailing social values of a society in a particular era under study.

Continuous Innovation. A new product entry that is an improved or modified version of an existing product rather than a totally new product. A continuous innovation has the least disruptive influence on established consumption patterns.

Copy Pretest. Testing an advertisement before it is run to determine which, if any, elements of the advertising message should be revised before major media expenses are incurred.

Copy Posttest. Testing an ad after it is run. A posttest is used to evaluate the effectiveness of an ad that has already appeared and to see which elements, if any, should be revised to improve the impact of future advertisements.

Core Values. Criteria that both affects and reflects the character of American society.

Countersegmentation Strategy. A strategy in which a company combines two or more segments into a single segment to be targeted with an individually tailored product or promotion campaign.

Cross-Cultural Consumer Analysis. Research to determine the extent to which consumers of two or more nations are similar in relation to specific consumption behavior.

Cross-Cultural Consumer Research. Research methods designed to find the similarities and differences among consumers in a marketer's domestic market and those it wants to target in a foreign country.

Cross-Cultural Psychographic Segmentation. Tailoring marketing strategies to the needs (psychological, social, cultural, and functional) of specific foreign segments.

Cues. Stimuli that give direction to consumer motives (i.e., that suggest a specific way to satisfy a salient motive).

Culture. The sum total of learned beliefs, values, and customs that serve to regulate the consumer behavior of members of a particular society.

Customer Lifetime Value. Profiles based on the collection and analysis of internal secondary data.

Customer Retention. Providing value to customers continuously so they will stay with the company rather than switch to a competitor.

Customer Satisfaction. An individual's perception of the performance of the product or service in relation to his or her expectations.

Customer Satisfaction Measurement. Quantitative and qualitative measures that gauge the level of customer satisfaction and its determinants.

Customer Value. The ratio between the customer's perceived benefits and the resources used to obtain those benefits.

Defense Mechanisms. Methods by which people mentally redefine frustrating situations to protect their self-images and their self-esteem.

Defensive Attribution. A theory that suggests consumers are likely to accept credit for successful outcomes (internal attribution) and to blame other persons or products for failure (external attribution).

Demographic Characteristics. Objective characteristics of a population (such as age, sex, marital status, income, occupation, and education) which are often used as the basis for segmenting markets.

Demographic Segmentation. The division of a total market into smaller subgroups on the basis of such objective characteristics as age, sex, marital status, income, occupation, or education.

Depth Interview. A lengthy and relatively unstructured interview designed to uncover a consumer's underlying attitudes and/or motivations.

Differential Threshold. The minimal difference that can be detected between two stimuli. Also known as the *j.n.d. (just noticeable difference)*. See also Weber's Law.

Differentiated Marketing. Targeting a product or service to two or more segments, using a specifically tailored product, promotional appeal, price, and/or method of distribution for each.

Diffusion of Innovations. The framework for exploring the spread of consumer acceptance of new products throughout the social system.

Diffusion Process. The process by which the acceptance of an innovation is spread by communication to members of a social system over a period of time.

Direct Mail. Advertising that is sent directly to the mailing address of a targeted consumer.

Direct Marketing. A marketing technique that uses various media (e.g., mail, print, broadcast, Internet, telephone) to solicit a direct response from a consumer. Also known as database marketing.

Discontinuous Innovation. A dramatically new product entry that requires the establishment of new consumption practices.

Disjunctive Rule. A noncompensatory decision rule in which consumers establish a minimally acceptable cutoff point for each relevant product attribute; any brand meeting or surpassing the cutoff point for any one attribute is considered an acceptable choice.

Distributed Learning. Learning spaced over a period of time to increase consumer retention. (See also Massed Learning.)

Dogmatism. A personality trait that reflects the degree of rigidity a person displays toward the unfamiliar and toward information that is contrary to his or her own established beliefs.

Downward Mobility. Consumers who have a lower social class level than their parents in terms of the jobs they hold, their residences, level of disposable income, and savings.

Dynamically Continuous Innovation. A new product entry that is sufficiently innovative to have some disruptive effects on established consumption practices.

Ego-Defensive Function. A component of the functional approach to attitude-change that suggests that consumers want to protect their self-concepts from inner feelings of doubt.

Elaboration Likelihood Model (ELM). A theory that suggests that a person's level of involvement during message processing is a critical factor in determining which route to persuasion is likely to be effective. (See also Central and Peripheral Routes to Persuasion.)

Emotional Motives. The selection of goals according to personal or subjective criteria (e.g., the desire for individuality, pride, fear, affection, status).

Encoding. The process by which individuals select and assign a word or visual image to represent a perceived object or idea.

Enculturation. The learning of the culture of one's own society.

Endorsements. When celebrities or the so-called man-in-the-street—who may or may not be users of a particular product or service—lend their names to advertisements for such products or services for a fee.

Evaluation of Alternatives. A stage in the consumer *decision-making process* in which the consumer appraises the benefits to be derived from each of the product alternatives being considered.

Evoked Set. The specific brands a consumer considers in making a purchase choice in a particular product category.

Expectations. What people expect to see based on familiarity or previous experience.

Expected Self. How individuals expect to see themselves at some specified future time.

Exploratory Study. A small scale study that identifies critical issues to include in a large-scale research study.

Extended Family. A household consisting of a husband, wife, offspring, and at least one other blood relative.

Extended Self. When a consumer uses self-altering products or services to conform to or take on the appearance of a particular type of person (e.g., a biker, a physician, a lawyer, a college professor).

Extensive Problem Solving. Decision making efforts by consumers who have no established criteria for evaluating a product category or specific brands in that category, or have not narrowed the number of brands to a manageable subset.

External Attribution. A theory that suggests that consumers are likely to credit their successes to outside sources (e.g., their graduate degrees or other persons).

Extrinsic Cues. Cues external to the product (e.g., price, store image, or brand image) that serve to influence the consumer's perception of a product's quality.

Family. Two or more persons related by blood, marriage, or adoption who reside together.

Family Branding. The practice of marketing several company products under the same brand name.

Family Life Cycle. Classification of families into significant stages. The five traditional *FLC* stages are Bachelorhood, Honeymooners, Parenthood, Postparenthood, and Dissolution.

Feedback. Communication—either verbal or nonverbal (body language)—that is communicated back to the sender of a message by the receiver.

Field Observation. An anthropological measurement technique that focuses on observing behavior within a natural environment (often without the subjects' awareness).

Figure and Ground. A Gestalt principle of perceptual organization that focuses on contrast. *Figure* is usually perceived clearly because [in contrast to (back) *ground*] it appears to be well defined, solid, and in the forefront, while the *ground* is usually perceived as indefinite, hazy, and continuous. Music can be figure or (back) ground.

Focus Group. A qualitative research method in which about eight to ten persons participate in an unstructured group interview focused on a product or service concept.

Foot-in-the-Door Technique. A theory of attitude change that suggests individuals form attitudes that are consistent with their own prior behavior.

Formal Communications Sources. A source that speaks on behalf of an organization—either a for-profit (commercial) or a not-for-profit organization.

Freudian Theory. A theory of personality and motivation developed by the psychoanalyst Sigmund Freud. (See Psychoanalytic Theory.)

Functional Approach. An attitude-change theory that classifies attitudes in terms of four functions: *utilitarian*, *ego-defensive*, *value-expressive*, and *knowledge* functions.

Gender Subcultures. Sex roles are an important cultural component and require products that are either exclusively or strongly associated with the members of one sex.

Generation X. Born between 1965 and 1979, this is a post baby-boomer segment (also referred to as *Xers* or *busters*).

Generation Y. The approximately 71 million Americans who were born between the years 1977 and 1994 (i.e., the children of baby boomers). Members of Generation Y (also known as "echo boomers" and the "millennium generation") can be divided into three subsegments: Gen Y adults (age 19–28), Gen Y teens (age 13–18), and Gen Y kids, or "tweens."

Generic Goals. The general classes or categories of goals that individuals select to fulfill their needs. (See also Product-Specific Goals.)

Geodemographic Clusters. A composite segmentation strategy that uses both geographic variables (zip codes, neighborhoods, or blocks) and demographic variables (e.g., income, occupation, value of residence) to identify target markets.

Geographic Segmentation. The division of a total potential market into smaller subgroups on the basis of geographic variables (e.g., region, state, city, or zip code).

Gestalt. A German term meaning "pattern" or "configuration" that has come to represent various principles of perceptual organization.

Gifting Behavior. The process of gift exchange that takes place between a giver and a recipient.

Global Strategy. Standardizing both product and communications programs when conducting business on a global basis.

Group. Two or more individuals who interact to accomplish either individual or mutual goals.

Grouping. A Gestalt theory of perceptual organization that proposes that individuals tend to group stimuli automatically so that they form a unified picture or impression. The perception of stimuli as groups or chunks of information, rather than as discrete bits of information, facilitates their memory and recall.

Hemispheral Lateralization. Learning theory in which the basic premise is that the right and left hemispheres of the brain "specialize" in the kinds of information that they process. Also called split brain theory.

Heuristics. (See Consumer Decision Rules.)

Hispanic American Subculture. The largest American minority group, representing about 14 percent of the U.S. population. The three largest groups are Mexican Americans, Puerto Ricans, and Cubans.

Hybrid Segmentation. The use of several segmentation variables to more accurately define or "fine-tune" consumer segments.

Ideal Self-Image. How individuals would *like* to perceive themselves (as opposed to Actual Self-Image—the way they *do* perceive themselves).

Ideal Social Self-Image. How consumers would like others to see them.

Imagery. The ability to form mental images.

Impersonal Communication. Communication directed to a large and diffuse audience, with no direct communication between source and receiver. Also known as *mass communication*.

Index of Status Characteristics (ISC). A composite measure of social class that combines occupation, source of income (not amount), house type, and dwelling area into a single weighted index of social class standing. Also known as *Warner's ISC*.

Indirect Reference Groups. Individuals or groups with whom a person identifies but does not have direct face-to-face contact, such as movie stars, sports heroes, political leaders, or TV personalities.

Inept Set. Brands that a consumer excludes from purchase consideration.

Inert Set. Brands that a consumer is indifferent towards because they are perceived as having no particular advantage.

Informal Group. A group of people who see each other frequently on an informal basis, such as weekly poker players or social acquaintances.

Information Overload. A situation in which the consumer is presented with too much product- or brand-related information.

Information Processing. A cognitive theory of human learning patterned after computer information processing that focuses on how information is stored in human memory and how it is retrieved.

Innate Needs. Physiological needs for food, water, air, clothing, shelter, and sex. Also known as *biogenic* or *primary needs*.

Inner-Directedness. Consumers who tend to rely on their own "inner" values or standards when evaluating new products and who are likely to be consumer innovators.

Innovation. A totally new product, new service, new idea, or new practice.

Institutional Advertising. Advertising designed to promote a favorable company image rather than specific products.

Instrumental Conditioning. A behavioral theory of learning based on a trial-and-error process, with habits formed as the result of positive experiences (reinforcement) resulting from specific behaviors. (See also Conditioned Learning.)

Intention-to-Buy Scales. A method of assessing the likelihood of a consumer purchasing a product or behaving in a certain way.

Interference Effects. The greater the number of competitive ads in a product category, the lower the recall of brand claims in a specific ad.

Internal Attributions. Consumers attribute their success in using a product or source to their own skill.

Interpersonal Communication. Communication that occurs directly between two or more people by mail, by telephone, by e-mail, or in person.

Interpretivism. A postmodernist approach to the study of consumer behavior that focuses on the act of consuming rather than on the act of buying.

Intrinsic Cues. Physical characteristics of the product (such as size, color, flavor, or aroma) that serve to influence the consumer's perceptions of product quality.

Involvement Theory. A theory of consumer learning postulating that consumers engage in a range of information processing activity, from extensive to limited problem solving, depending on the relevance of the purchase.

Joint Decisions. Family purchase decisions in which the husband and wife are equally influential. Also known as *syncratic decisions*.

Just Noticeable Difference (j.n.d.). The minimal difference that can be detected between two stimuli. (See also Differential Threshold and Weber's Law.)

Knowledge Function. A component of the functional approach to attitude-change theory that suggests that consumers have a strong need to know and understand the people and products with which they come into contact.

Learning. The process by which individuals acquire the knowledge and experience they apply to future purchase and consumption behavior.

Level of Aspiration. New and higher goals that individuals set for themselves.

Lexicographic Decision Rule. A noncompensatory decision rule in which consumers first rank product attributes in terms of their importance, then compare brands in terms of the attribute considered most important. If one brand scores higher than the other brands, it is selected; if not, the process is continued with the second ranked attribute, and so on.

Licensing. The use by manufacturers and retailers of well-known brands, celebrity or designer names (for a fee) to acquire instant recognition and status for their products.

Limited Problem Solving. A limited search by a consumer for a product that will satisfy his or her basic criteria from among a selected group of brands.

Local Strategy. Customizing both product and communications programs by area or country when conducting business on a global basis.

Long-Term Store. In information-processing theory, the stage of real memory where information is organized, reorganized, and retained for relatively extended periods of time.

Market Mavens. Individuals whose influence stems from a general knowledge and market expertise that lead to an early awareness of new products and services.

Market Segmentation. The process of dividing a potential market into distinct subsets of consumers and selecting one or more segments as a target market to be reached with a distinct marketing mix.

Marketing Concept. A consumer-oriented philosophy that suggests that satisfaction of consumer needs provides the focus for product development and marketing strategy to enable the firm to meet its own organizational goals.

Marketing Ethics. Designing, packaging, pricing, advertising, and distributing products in such a way that negative consequences to consumers, employees, and society in general are avoided.

Marketing Mix. The unique configuration of the four basic marketing variables (product, promotion, price, and channels of distribution) that a marketing organization controls.

Maslow's Need Hierarchy. A theory of motivation that postulates that individuals strive to satisfy their needs according to a basic hierarchical structure, starting with physiological needs, then moving to safety needs, social needs, egoistic needs, and finally self-actualization needs.

Mass Marketing. Offering the same product and marketing mix to all consumers.

Massed Learning. Compressing the learning schedule into a short time span to accelerate consumer learning. (See also Distributed Learning.)

Megabrands. Well-known brand names.

Message Framing. Positively framed messages (those that specify benefits to be *gained* by using a product) are more persuasive than negatively framed messages (those that specify benefits *lost* by not using a product).

Micromarketing. Highly regionalized marketing strategies that use advertising and promotional campaigns specifically geared to local market needs and conditions.

Modeling. (See Observational Learning.)

Mood. An individual's subjectively perceived "feeling state."

Motivation. The driving force within individuals that impels them to action.

Motivational Research. Qualitative research designed to uncover consumers' subconscious or hidden motivations. The basic premise of motivational research is that consumers are not always aware of, or may not wish to reveal, the basic reasons underlying their actions.

Multiattribute Attitude Models. Attitude models that examine the composition of consumer attitudes in terms of selected product attributes or beliefs.

Multinational Strategies. Decisions that marketers make on how to reach all potential consumers of their products in countries throughout the world.

Multiple Self or Selves. Consumers have different images of themselves in response to different situations and are quite likely to act differently with different people and in different situations.

Multistep Flow of Communication Theory. A revision of the traditional two-step theory that shows multiple communication flows: from the mass media simultaneously to opinion leaders, opinion receivers, and information receivers (who neither influence nor are influenced by others); from opinion leaders to opinion receivers; and from opinion receivers to opinion leaders.

National Subcultures. Nationality subcultures in a larger society in which members often retain a sense of identification and pride in the language and customs of their ancestors.

Need for Cognition. The personality trait that measures a person's craving for or enjoyment of thinking.

Need Recognition. The realization by the consumer that there is a difference between "what is" and "what should (or can) be."

Negative Motivation. A driving force away from some object or condition.

Negative Reinforcement. An unpleasant or negative outcome that serves to encourage a specific behavior. (Not to be confused with punishment, which discourages repetition of a specific behavior.)

Neo-Freudian Personality Theory. A school of psychology that stresses the fundamental role of social relationships in the formation and development of personality.

Neo-Pavlovian Conditioning. The creation of a strong association between the conditioned stimulus (CS) and the unconditioned stimulus (US) requiring (1) forward conditioning; (2) repeated pairings of the CS and the US; (3) a CS and US that logically belong together; (4) a CS that is novel and unfamiliar; and (5) a US that is biologically or symbolically salient.

Noncompensatory Decision Rule. A type of consumer decision rule by which positive evaluation of a brand attribute does not compensate for (i.e., is not balanced against) a negative evaluation of the same brand on some other attribute.

Nonprobability Sample. Findings are representative of the population.

Normative Reference Group. A group that influences the general values or behavior of an individual. (See Comparative Reference Group.)

Nuclear Family. A household consisting of a husband and wife and at least one offspring.

Objective Price Claims. Specific phrases that are used to promote a single discount level for a product line, an entire department, or sometimes an entire store.

Objectives. The goals for a research study that will help determine the type and level of information that is needed.

Observational Learning. A process by which individuals observe the behavior of others, remember it, and imitate it. Also known as *modeling*.

Observational Research. A form of consumer research that relies on observation of consumers in the process of buying and using products.

One-Sided Versus Two-Sided Messages. A one-sided message tells only the benefits of a product or service; a two-sided message also includes some negatives, thereby enhancing the credibility of the marketer.

Opinion Leader. A person who informally gives product information and advice to others.

Opinion Leadership. The process by which one person (the *opinion leader*) informally influences the consumption actions or attitudes of others, who may be *opinion seekers* or *opinion recipients*.

Opinion Receiver (Recipient). An individual who either actively seeks product information from others or receives unsolicited information.

Opinion Seeker. Individuals who actively seek information and advice about products from others.

Optimum Stimulation Level (OSL). A personality trait that measures the level or amount of novelty or complexity that individuals seek in their personal experiences. High OSL consumers tend to accept risky and novel products more readily than low OSL consumers.

Organizational Consumer. A business, government agency, or other institution (profit or nonprofit) that buys the goods, services, and/or equipment necessary for the organization to function.

Other-Directedness. Consumers who tend to look to others for direction and for approval.

"Ought-To" Self. Consists of traits or characteristics that an individual believes it is his or her duty or obligation to possess.

Participant Observers. Researchers who participate in the environment that they are studying without notifying those who are being observed.

Passive Learning. Without active involvement, individuals process and store right-brain (nonverbal, pictorial) information.

Perceived Price. How a consumer perceives a price—as high, as low, or as fair.

Perceived Quality. Consumers often judge the quality of a product or service on the basis of a variety of informational cues that they associate with the product; some of these cues are intrinsic to the product or service; others are extrinsic, such as price, store image, service environment, brand image, and promotional messages.

Perceived Risk. The degree of uncertainty perceived by the consumer as to the consequences (outcome) of a specific purchase decision.

Perception. The process by which an individual selects, organizes, and interprets stimuli into a meaningful and coherent picture of the world.

Perceptual Blocking. The subconscious "screening out" of stimuli that are threatening or inconsistent with one's needs, values, beliefs, or attitudes.

Perceptual Distortion. The influences on an individual that separate that person's perception of a stimulus from reality.

Perceptual Mapping. A research technique that enables marketers to plot graphically consumers' perceptions concerning product attributes of specific brands.

Personal Consumer. The individual who buys goods and services for his or her own use, for household use, for the use of a family member, or for a friend. (Also referred to as the *Ultimate Consumer* or *End User*.)

Personality. The inner psychological characteristics that both determine and reflect how a person responds to his or her environment.

Positioning. Establishing a specific image for a brand in relation to competing brands. (See also Product Positioning.)

Positive Motivation. A driving force toward some object or condition.

Positive Reinforcement. A favorable outcome to a specific behavior that strengthens the likelihood that the behavior will be repeated.

Positivism. A consumer behavior research approach that regards the consumer behavior discipline as an applied marketing science. Its main focus is on consumer decision making.

Postpurchase Evaluation. An assessment of a product based on actual trial after purchase.

Prepotent Need. An overriding need, from among several needs, that serves to initiate goal-directed behavior.

Prepurchase Search. A stage in the consumer decision-making process in which the consumer perceives a need and actively seeks out information concerning products that will help satisfy that need.

Price-Quality Relationship. The perception of price as an indicator of product quality (e.g., the higher the price, the higher the perceived quality of the product).

Primary Needs. (See Innate Needs.)

Primary Research. Original research undertaken by individual researchers or organizations to meet specific objectives. Collected information is called *primary data*.

PRIZM (Potential Rating Index by Zip Market). A composite index of geographic and socioeconomic factors expressed in residential zip-code neighborhoods from which geodemographic consumer segments are formed.

Probability Sample. Findings are projectable to the total population.

Product Benefits. Benefits featured in a product's positioning reflect attributes that are important to and congruent with the perceptions of the targeted consumer segment.

Product Conspicuousness. The degree to which a product stands out and is noticed.

Product Line Extension. A marketing strategy of adding related products to an already established brand (based on the Stimulus Generalization Theory).

Product Positioning. A marketing strategy designed to project a specific image for a product.

Product-Specific Goals. The specifically branded or labeled products that consumers select to fulfill their needs. (See also Generic Goals.)

Product Standardization. An orientation for assessing whether to use a global versus local marketing strategy concentrating on a high-tech to high-touch continuum.

Psychoanalytic Theory. A theory of motivation and personality that postulates that unconscious needs and drives, particularly sexual and other biological drives, are the basis of human motivation and personality.

Psychographic Inventory. A series of written statements designed to capture relevant aspects of a consumer's personality, buying motives, interests, attitudes, beliefs, and values.

Psychographic Segmentation. Identifying segments of consumers based on their responses to statements about their activities, interests, and opinions.

Psychological Noise. A barrier to message reception (i.e., competing advertising messages or distracting thoughts).

Psychological Reactance. When people become motivationally aroused by a threat to or elimination of a behavioral freedom.

Psychological Segmentation. The division of a total potential market into smaller subgroups on the basis of intrinsic characteristics of the individual, such as personality, buying motives, lifestyle, attitudes, or interests.

Publicity. When commercial or noncommercial messages appear in space or time that is not paid for and usually reserved for editorial messages.

Purchase Behavior. Behavior that involves two types of purchases: *trial purchases* (the exploratory phase in which consumers evaluate a product through direct use) and *repeat purchases*, which usually signify that the product meets with the consumer's approval and that the consumer is willing to use it again.

Qualitative Research. Research methods (e.g., interviews, focus groups, metaphor analysis, collage research, projective techniques) that are primarily used to obtain new ideas for promotional campaigns and products.

Quantitative Research. Research methods (e.g., experiments, survey techniques, observations) that enable researchers to understand the effects of various promotional inputs on the consumer, thus enabling marketers to predict consumer behavior

Racial Subcultures. The major racial subcultures in the United States are Caucasian, Hispanic, African American, Asian American, and American Indian.

Rational Motives. Motives or goals based on economic or objective criteria, such as price, size, weight, or miles-per-gallon.

Receivers. The recipients of a message.

Recognition and Recall Tests. Tests conducted to determine whether consumers remember seeing an ad, the extent to which they have read it or seen it and can recall its content, their resulting attitudes toward the product and the brand, and their purchase intentions.

Reference Group. A person or group that serves as a point of comparison (or reference) for an individual in the formation of either general or specific values, attitudes, or behavior.

Reference Prices. External or internal prices that a consumer uses as a basis for comparison in judging another price.

Regional Subcultures. Groups who identify with the regional or geographical areas in which they live.

Rehearsal. The silent, mental repetition of material.

Reinforcement. A positive or negative outcome that influences the likelihood that a specific behavior will be repeated in the future in response to a particular cue or stimulus.

Relationship Marketing. Marketing aimed at creating strong, lasting relationships with a core group of customers by making them feel good about the company and by giving them some kind of personal connection to the business.

Reliability. The degree to which a measurement instrument is consistent in what it measures.

Religious Subcultures. Groups classified by religious affiliation that may be targeted by marketers because of purchase decisions that are influenced by their religious identity.

Repetition. A basic concept that increases the strength of the association between a conditioned stimulus and an unconditioned stimulus and slows the process of forgetting.

Repositioning. Changing the way a product is perceived by consumers in relation to other brands or product uses.

Response. How individuals react to a drive or cue.

Retention. The ability to retain information in the memory.

Retrieval. The stage of information processing in which individuals recover information from long-term storage.

Ritual. A type of symbolic activity consisting of a series of steps (multiple behaviors) occurring in a fixed sequence and repeated over time.

Rokeach Value Survey. A self-administered inventory consisting of eighteen "terminal" values (i.e., personal goals) and eighteen "instrumental" values (i.e., ways of reaching personal goals).

Role. A pattern of behavior expected of an individual in a specific social position, such as mother, daughter, teacher, lawyer. One person may have a number of different roles, each of which is relevant in the context of specific social situations.

Routinized Response Behavior. A habitual purchase response based on predetermined criteria.

Secondary Data. Data that has been collected for reasons other than the specific research project at hand.

Secondary Needs. (See Acquired Needs.)

Secondary Research. Research conducted for reasons other than the specific problem under study. Resulting data are called *secondary data*.

Self-Gifts. Gifts to oneself.

Self-Perception Theory. A theory that suggests that consumers develop attitudes by reflecting on their own behavior.

Seniors. Individuals 65 years of age and older.

Sensation. The immediate and direct response of the sensory organs to simple stimuli (e.g., taste, color, smell, brightness, loudness, feel).

Sensation Seeking. A trait characterized by the need for varied, novel, and complex sensations and experience, and the willingness to take physical and social risks for the sake of such experience.

Sensory Adaptation. "Getting used to" certain sensations; becoming accommodated to a certain level of stimulation.

Sensory Receptors. The human organs (eyes, ears, nose, mouth, skin) that receive sensory inputs.

Sensory Store. The place in which all sensory inputs are housed very briefly before passing into the short-term store.

Shaping. Reinforcement performed before the desired consumer behavior actually takes place.

Shopping Group. Two or more people who shop together.

Short-Term Store. The stage of real memory in which information received from the sensory store for processing is retained briefly before passing into the long-term store or forgotten.

Single-Parent Family. Households consisting of only one parent and at least one child.

Single-Variable Index. The use of a single socioeconomic variable (such as income) to estimate an individual's relative social class. (See also Composite-Variable Index.)

Sleeper Effect. The tendency for persuasive communications to lose the impact of source credibility over time (i.e., the influence of a message from a high credibility source tends to *decrease* over time; the influence of a message from a low credibility source tends to *increase* over time).

Social Class. The division of members of a society into a hierarchy of distinct status classes, so that members of each class have either higher or lower status than members of other classes.

Social Marketing Concept. Satisfying the needs and wants of target markets in ways that preserve and enhance the well-being of customers and society as a whole.

Social Self-Image. How consumers feel others see them.

Social Status. The amount of status members of one social class have in comparison with members of other social classes.

Socialization of Family Members. A process that includes imparting to children and other family members the basic values and modes of behavior consistent with the culture.

Societal Marketing Concept. A revision of the traditional marketing concept that suggests that marketers adhere to principles of social responsibility in the marketing of their goods and services; that is, they must endeavor to satisfy the needs and wants of their target markets in ways that preserve and enhance the well-being of consumers and society as a whole.

Sociocultural Variables. Sociological and anthropological variables that provide further bases for market segmentation.

Socioeconomic Status Scores (SES). A multivariable social class measure used by the United States Bureau of the Census that combines occupational status, family income, and educational attainment into a single measure of social class standing.

Source. The initiator of a message.

Source Credibility. The perceived honesty and objectivity of the source of the communication.

Spokesperson. A celebrity or company executive who represents a product, brand, or company over an extended period of time, often in print, on television, and in personal appearances.

Stages in the Adoption Process. (See Adoption Process.)

Stimulus Discrimination. The ability to select a specific stimulus from among similar stimuli because of perceived differences.

Stimulus Generalization. The inability to perceive differences between slightly dissimilar stimuli.

Stimulus Response Theories. The premise that observable responses to specific external stimuli signal that learning has taken place.

Subcultural Interaction. Because consumers are simultaneously members of several subcultural groups, marketers must determine how consumer's specific subcultural memberships interact to influence the consumer's purchase decisions.

Subculture. A distinct cultural group that exists as an identifiable segment within a larger, more complex society.

Subliminal Perception. Perception of stimuli received *below* the level of conscious awareness.

Substitute Goal. A goal that replaces an individual's primary goal when that goal cannot be achieved.

Symbol. Anything that stands for something else.

Symbolic Group. A group with which an individual identifies by adopting its values, attitudes, or behavior despite the unlikelihood of future membership.

Targeting. The selection of a distinct market segment at which to direct a marketing strategy.

Tensile Price Claims. Specific phrases that are used to promote a *range* of price discounts for a product line, an entire department, or sometimes an entire store.

Testimonial. A promotional technique in which a celebrity that has used a product or service speaks highly of its benefits in order to influence consumers to buy.

Theory of Reasoned Action. A comprehensive theory of the interrelationship among attitudes, intentions, and behavior.

Theory of Trying-to-Consume. Recasts the theory-of-reasoned-action model by replacing actual *behavior* with *trying to behave* (i.e., consume) as the variable to be explained and/or predicted.

Traditional Family Life Cycle. A progression of stages through which many families pass.

Trait Theory. A theory of personality that focuses on the measurement of specific psychological characteristics.

Tricomponent Attitude Model. An attitude model consisting of three parts: a cognitive (knowledge) component, an affective (feeling) component, and a conative (doing) component.

Two-Step Flow of Communication Theory. A communications model that portrays opinion leaders as direct receivers of information from mass-media sources who, in turn, interpret and transmit this information to the general public.

Upward Mobility. Movement upward in social-class standing from the social-class position into which the consumer was born.

Usage-Situation Segmentation. Segmentation that is based on the idea that the occasion or situation often determines what consumers will purchase or consume (i.e., certain products for certain situations, special usage occasions).

Use-Related Segmentation. Popular and effective form of segmentation that categorizes consumers in terms of product, service, or brand–usage characteristics, such as usage rate, awareness status, and degree of brand loyalty.

Utilitarian Function. A component of the functional approach to attitude-change theory that suggests consumers hold certain attitudes partly because of the brand's utility.

Validity. The degree to which a measurement instrument accurately measures what it is designed to measure.

VALS. (See Values and Lifestyle System.)

Value-Expressive Function. A component of the functional approach to attitude-change theory that suggests that attitudes express consumers' general values, lifestyles, and outlook.

Values and Lifestyle System. A research service that tracks marketing-relevant shifts in the beliefs, values, and lifestyles of psychological segments of the American population

Variety-Novelty Seeking. A personality trait similar to *OSL*, which measures a consumer's degree of variety seeking.

Verbalizers. Consumers who prefer verbal or written information and products, such as membership in book clubs or audiotape clubs. (See also Visualizers.)

Virtual Personality or Self. A notion that provides an individual with the opportunity to "try on" different personalities or different identities, such as creating a fictitious personality in an online chat room.

Visualizers. Consumers who prefer visual information and products that stress the visual, such as membership in a DVD club. (See also Verbalizers.)

Weber's Law. A theory concerning the perceived differentiation between similar stimuli of varying intensities; that is, the stronger the initial stimulus, the greater the additional intensity needed for the second stimulus to be perceived as different. (See also Just Noticeable Difference.)

Word-of-Mouth Communication. Informal conversations between friends concerning products or services.

World Brands. Products that are manufactured, packaged, and positioned the same way regardless of the country in which they are sold.

Company Index

Name Index

Subject Index